Remedies

Third Edition

Remedies

Third Edition

Richard L. Hasen
Chancellor's Professor of Law and Political Science
University of California, Irvine School of Law

Wolters Kluwer
Law & Business

To contact Customer Service, e-mail customer.service@wolterskluwer.com, call 1-800-234-1660, fax 1-800-901-9075, or mail correspondence to:

> Wolters Kluwer Law & Business
> Attn: Order Department
> PO Box 990
> Frederick, MD 21705

Printed in the United States of America.

1 2 3 4 5 6 7 8 9 0

ISBN 978-1-4548-1550-1

Library of Congress Cataloging-in-Publication Data

Hasen, Richard L.
  Remedies / Richard L. Hasen, Chancellor's Professor of Law and Political Science, University of California Irvine School of Law. — Third edition.
    pages cm
  Includes bibliographical references and index.
  ISBN 978-1-4548-1550-1
  1. Remedies (Law) — United States — Outlines, syllabi, etc. I. Title.

  KF9010.H37 2013
  347.73'77 — dc23

                                            2012038856

SUSTAINABLE FORESTRY INITIATIVE

Certified Sourcing
www.sfiprogram.org
SFI-01234

SFI label applies to the text stock

About Wolters Kluwer Law & Business

Wolters Kluwer Law & Business is a leading global provider of intelligent information and digital solutions for legal and business professionals in key specialty areas, and respected educational resources for professors and law students. Wolters Kluwer Law & Business connects legal and business professionals as well as those in the education market with timely, specialized authoritative content and information-enabled solutions to support success through productivity, accuracy and mobility.

Serving customers worldwide, Wolters Kluwer Law & Business products include those under the Aspen Publishers, CCH, Kluwer Law International, Loislaw, Best Case, ftwilliam.com and MediRegs family of products.

CCH products have been a trusted resource since 1913, and are highly regarded resources for legal, securities, antitrust and trade regulation, government contracting, banking, pension, payroll, employment and labor, and healthcare reimbursement and compliance professionals.

Aspen Publishers products provide essential information to attorneys, business professionals and law students. Written by preeminent authorities, the product line offers analytical and practical information in a range of specialty practice areas from securities law and intellectual property to mergers and acquisitions and pension/benefits. Aspen's trusted legal education resources provide professors and students with high-quality, up-to-date and effective resources for successful instruction and study in all areas of the law.

Kluwer Law International products provide the global business community with reliable international legal information in English. Legal practitioners, corporate counsel and business executives around the world rely on Kluwer Law journals, looseleafs, books, and electronic products for comprehensive information in many areas of international legal practice.

Loislaw is a comprehensive online legal research product providing legal content to law firm practitioners of various specializations. Loislaw provides attorneys with the ability to quickly and efficiently find the necessary legal information they need, when and where they need it, by facilitating access to primary law as well as state-specific law, records, forms and treatises.

Best Case Solutions is the leading bankruptcy software product to the bankruptcy industry. It provides software and workflow tools to flawlessly streamline petition preparation and the electronic filing process, while timely incorporating ever-changing court requirements.

ftwilliam.com offers employee benefits professionals the highest quality plan documents (retirement, welfare and non-qualified) and government forms (5500/PBGC, 1099 and IRS) software at highly competitive prices.

MediRegs products provide integrated health care compliance content and software solutions for professionals in healthcare, higher education and life sciences, including professionals in accounting, law and consulting.

Wolters Kluwer Law & Business, a division of Wolters Kluwer, is headquartered in New York. Wolters Kluwer is a market-leading global information services company focused on professionals.

To Deborah, Shana, and Jared
With love, for a bright future

Summary of Contents

PART I. COMPENSATORY DAMAGES

PART II. EQUITABLE REMEDIES

PART III. RESTITUTION

PART IV. OTHER IMPORTANT REMEDIES CONCEPTS

Contents

Chapter 4 Contract Damages 61

Chapter 5 The Unusual: Expectancy Damages in Tort and Reliance Damages in Contract 99

Chapter 6 Ensuring the Rightful Position: A Look at Certainty, Mitigation, Offsetting Benefits, and the Collateral Source Rule 117

PART II. EQUITABLE REMEDIES

PART III. RESTITUTION

PART IV. OTHER IMPORTANT REMEDIES CONCEPTS

Acknowledgments
for Third Edition

For this Third Edition, I want to express my appreciation for the research assistance of Denny Chan and Jim Buatti, and the administrative assistance of Sara Galloway. Thanks also to UC Irvine Law School and our dean, Erwin Chemerinsky, who have supported me in all of my teaching and scholarly endeavors. Finally, thanks to Kenny Chumbley for his excellent and cheerful production work.

This Third Edition is current through the end of the Supreme Court's 2011 term (ending June 2012) and includes important new cases decided since the Second Edition.

I continue to receive insightful questions and comments from book users. If you have questions or suggestions, please send an email to rhasen@law.uci.edu, and I will use those comments to improve the next edition.

Once again, I am grateful to the American Law Institute for granting permission to quote from two of its publications:

For Restatement material: Copyright © 2013 by The American Law Institute. Reprinted with permission. All rights reserved.

For UCC material: Copyright © by the American Law Institute and the National Conference of Commissioners on Uniform State Laws. Reproduced with the permission of the Permanent Editorial Board for the Uniform Commercial Code. All rights reserved.

Irvine
November 2012

Acknowledgments
for Second Edition

For this Second Edition, I want to express my appreciation for the library assistance of Lisa Schultz, the research assistance of Rachael Ettinger, and the administrative assistance of Carla Heidlberg. Thanks also to Loyola Law School and our dean, Victor Gold. Loyola has provided me with exemplary support for scholarship, teaching and writing.

The Second Edition of this book addresses some recent Supreme Court decisions concerning injunctions, punitive damages, and other remedial areas. The Court's rulings have added new twists and turns in Remedies to be mastered by student and practitioner alike.

If nothing else, I know this edition is an improvement on the last edition because I have benefited from insightful questions and comments from First Edition book users. If you have questions or suggestions, please send an email to rick.hasen@lls.edu.

Once again, I am grateful to the American Law Institute for granting permission to quote from two of its publications:

For Restatement material: Copyright 1977, 1981, and 2000-2009 by the American Law Institute. Reprinted with permission. All rights reserved.

For UCC material: Copyright by the American Law Institute and the National Conference of Commissioners on Uniform State Laws. Reproduced with the permission of the Permanent Editorial Board for the Uniform Commercial Code. All rights reserved.

Los Angeles
December 2009

Acknowledgments for First Edition

This book owes an intellectual debt to two exemplary scholars and teachers. In 1997, Laurie Levenson, then Loyola Law School's associate dean, agreed to let me come as a visitor to teach Remedies, a course I had never taught before. I was anxious to get back to L.A., and I was willing to come even if it meant teaching a course I did not especially want to teach. Now, having taught the course numerous times, it has become one of my favorites to teach, pulling together interesting tidbits from all parts of the first-year curriculum, and allowing me to move back and forth between theory and practice with seasoned law students.

The other scholar to whom I owe a debt is Doug Laycock, whose Remedies casebook is a tremendous teaching tool and a wonderful resource. That casebook (and its Teacher's Manual) was my bible in 1997, and it has guided me in understanding Remedies both in and out of the classroom. Doug also has been consistently responsive to e-mail questions I have peppered him with over the years. Anyone familiar with Laycock's book will see the influence his view of Remedies has had on mine.

I also owe a debt to my Remedies students, beginning with my 1997 guinea pigs. I was assigned the 8:10-10:10 p.m. slot, twice a week, for the course. I expected a group of tired, graduating students with little interest in the course. To my pleasant surprise, the students were intellectually engaged, serious, and blessed with an understanding of the real world that only evening students have. For my Remedies students through the years, the course is really a nice capstone, bridging the law school and real worlds. I have learned a great deal from my students.

This book is much stronger because of the excellent research assistance of Vince Shang and Christina Wang, with additional assistance from Danielle De Smeth, Tony Sain, and Joel Yanovich, and the terrific library assistance of Lisa Schultz and the Loyola Law School library staff. Lynn Churchill and Barbara Roth at Aspen have provided constant encouragement and sage advice. Betty Kinuthia, Valda Hahn, and the Loyola faculty support staff provided wonderful administrative support. A slew of anonymous reviewers provided important suggestions and corrections to the manuscript. All remaining errors are mine alone.

None of my work would be possible without the love and encouragement of my wife, Lori Klein, who supports me in all that I do. This book is

Acknowledgments for First Edition

dedicated to our three most successful joint ventures: Deborah, Shana, and Jared.

I am grateful to the American Law Institute for granting permission to quote from two of its publications:

For Restatement material: Copyright 1977, 1981, and 2000-2006 by the American Law Institute. Reprinted with permission. All rights reserved.

For UCC material: Copyright by the American Law Institute and the National Conference of Commissioners on Uniform State Laws. Reproduced with the permission of the Permanent Editorial Board for the Uniform Commercial Code. All rights reserved.

Los Angeles
March 2007

How to Use This Book

No matter how your professor starts this course, you should begin with Chapter 1. It sets forth some basic terminology and ideas that are used throughout the book, including the important "rightful position" standard. After Chapter 1, you can begin at the beginning of Part I (on damages), Part II (on injunctions and other equitable remedies), Part III (on restitution), or Part IV (presenting the remedies topics of punitive damages, declaratory judgments, ancillary (or helping) remedies, and remedial defenses). Within each Part (except for Part IV), I expect that you will begin with the first chapter in each Part, which defines basic concepts and sets the stage for what comes next.

You should save the last chapter, Chapter 19, for the end of the course. It is to help you with issue spotting and choosing remedies skills that you cannot test until you master the material in the first eighteen chapters.

For the most part, this book follows standard Bluebook citation format. However, I usually avoid putting in pin cites in an effort not to clutter up the text, and I don't always note when I've deleted internal citations or footnotes. Before quoting any material in this book, be sure to check the original source. There are two sources that I cite so often that I just use a short form. I cite DAN B. DOBBS, LAW OF REMEDIES: DAMAGES, EQUITY, RESTITUTION (1993) simply as DOBBS §. I cite DOUGLAS LAYCOCK, MODERN AMERICAN REMEDIES: CASES AND MATERIALS (4th ed. 2010) simply as LAYCOCK.

Remedies

Third Edition

CHAPTER 1

Read This Chapter First: Why Remedies? What Remedies?

1.1 WHY SHOULD A LAW STUDENT CARE ABOUT REMEDIES?

Students may have many reasons to take a course in Remedies. In places such as California, for example, Remedies is heavily tested on the bar exam, and many students feel obligated to take a "bar course." Even in states that do not test Remedies independently on the bar, it is a good bar preparation course because much material from the first year of law school — particularly from Constitutional Law, Contracts, Property, and Torts — gets covered, albeit from a different angle. Other students may take Remedies because they like the instructor teaching it, or because it fits into their schedule. I have run into very few students (though there are some) who take Remedies out of an intrinsic interest in the subject.

Fortunately, however, many students complete a course in Remedies with their (admittedly low) expectations exceeded — there are some intellectually interesting issues related to Remedies, many of which are covered in this book. Consider these examples:

- Jane steals Bill's idea for a new invention and makes millions of dollars selling it. Should a court award Bill a sum of money equal to his loss (perhaps the amount of money he would have charged Jane to use his intellectual property), or to Jane's gain (some or all of her profits from the invention)? In some cases, there can be huge differences between these two figures.

- Gary makes repeated defamatory statements about Roxanne, injuring Roxanne's business reputation. May a court order Gary to shut up about Roxanne, or does such an order run afoul of the First Amendment?
- Phillip fraudulently induces Hector to enter into a contract. Can Hector have the court rewrite the contract more to his liking, or must the contract be cancelled, with Hector entitled to nothing more than a return of his consideration?
- Tomorrow Acme Wrecking Company is going to bulldoze what the Main Street Preservation Society believes is a building of historical importance protected by state law. How should a court decide, in the face of much ignorance on the merits of the Society's case because there is no time to get up to speed, whether to issue an order temporarily preventing the demolition?
- From 1850 to 1950, the State of Pacifica discriminated against African-Americans in educational and housing opportunities. Since 1950, there has been no official state discrimination, but African-American residents of Pacifica still lag behind in education, and much of the state's housing market remains unintegrated. What remedies, if any, can — or should — a judge order against Pacifica today to assist Pacifica's current African-American residents, many of whom were born after the period of official state discrimination?
- Sarah and Larry rob a bank together, agreeing to split the loot equally. Sarah doesn't give Larry his half. Should courts allow Larry's suit against Sarah to go forward, or should the suit be barred because of Larry's bad conduct?

If the intellectual feast in store to answer these questions does not convince you that Remedies is a course well worth your attention, there is an even more compelling reason for a student to take a course in Remedies: your future clients want you to do so.

1.2 WHY SHOULD A LAWYER CARE ABOUT REMEDIES?

Ask a practicing lawyer what clients care about the most, and the answer typically is "the bottom line." The client's attitude is often: Don't talk to me about abstractions — problems of proximate cause, supplemental jurisdiction, or the Statute of Frauds. Tell me what I have to lose or gain in this case. How likely is it that I'll prevail? If I prevail, how much will I get? Or if I lose, how much will it cost me?

In that sense, clients care about remedies mostly because remedies translate abstract legal rules into concrete consequences. Suppose that even if Bill has a good case for prevailing on the merits against Jane for her misappropriation of Bill's invention, it may not be worth bringing suit if Bill could only get money equal to his loss. On the other hand, if Bill has a chance of capturing Jane's "ill gotten gains" (through the law of restitution), it may make economic sense for Bill to sue. Indeed, if Jane has a good chance of losing her profits to Bill, she might be more likely to settle her case than if all that is at stake is paying Bill's losses. A good lawyer has to think not only about substantive law — the legal basis for Bill's claim that Jane has wronged him — but also about the range of available remedies. Similarly, just as it is not always obvious what substantive law addresses a particular legal dispute, there is often much up in the air about available remedies. Part of a lawyer's job, whether as a litigator or as a transactional lawyer, is to figure out the range of applicable remedies in a given case.

Example 1

Abbott and Costello are entering into a contract for the sale of widgets. You represent Abbott, the seller. What remedies issues might you wish to address in the contract?

Explanation

Good transactional lawyers will consider many remedies issues that could arise should something go sour between the parties to the contract. Here are a few remedies issues for Abbott's lawyer to consider:

- Should the contract contain a provision allowing the winning party to obtain attorney's fees in the event of a dispute under the contract? Would it be permissible to draft a provision allowing only Abbott to get attorney's fees in the event that such a dispute arises and Abbott wins?
- Should the contract specify the amount of damages in the event of a breach? If so, how can the clause be written so that it is an enforceable "liquidated damages provision" rather than an unenforceable contractual penalty?
- Should the contract exclude certain remedies, such as consequential damages?
- Which state's law should apply to contractual disputes? (Chapter 4 explains that for some contracts governed by the Uniform Commercial Code, the choice of state's law may not matter because the law is the same for all states.) Might there be some state whose remedies law is more advantageous to Abbott?

1.3 REMEDIES AS THE LAWYER'S TOOLBOX

Some have compared remedies to the "lawyer's toolbox." Just as a carpenter carries around a number of tools and decides on the right tool to use for a particular project, a good lawyer does the same (whereas a bad lawyer can commit malpractice by failing to use the right tool for the job). If the legal rules allow for the recovery of either Bill's losses or Jane's gains, and Jane's gains are substantially larger than Bill's losses, Bill's lawyer must be in a position to go for the more lucrative recovery, and that requires knowing when restitution might be the better tool than damages. Jane's lawyer, too, must keep an eye not only on the choices of remedies that Bill's lawyer might pull out of the toolbox, but also on Jane's own possible remedial defenses. For example, if Bill waited a long time to sue, Jane's lawyer should consider if the action could be barred by the defense of "laches," a doctrine which bars some suits because of unreasonable delay.

The toolbox analogy doesn't exactly hit the nail on the head (sorry — you can expect bad puns like this throughout the book), because it suggests that the choice of remedies is rather mechanical: everyone knows, for example, that one uses a hammer and not a screwdriver to put a nail through a piece of wood. There is a lot more creativity, however, involved in choosing an appropriate remedy than in choosing whether to use a hammer or screwdriver. Good lawyers can come up with creative arguments for or against the use of particular remedies in particular cases, just as good lawyers may make creative arguments for creative application of the underlying substantive law. But there are some constraints on creativity.

One particular constraint involves plaintiff's *choice of remedies*. Bill at some point will be forced to choose between recovering his losses or Jane's gains. We usually don't let him get both — and courts sometimes are reluctant to allow plaintiffs to change their minds after electing to seek a particular remedy. In addition, certain remedies might violate a constitutional right, such as the right to a jury trial, or the remedy might be precluded by statute or be limited for reasons of public policy (think of Larry's suit to get his share of the bank robbery loot from Sarah). One of the most important rules in choosing a remedy, as we will see, says that court orders (often an injunction) are commonly unavailable when a damages remedy would be "adequate" in redressing plaintiff's concerns.

Even within classes of remedies, however, there is room for lawyerly creativity. If Bill is only entitled to his losses, how do we measure his losses? If he is entitled to Jane's gains, how do we measure Jane's gains? As we shall see, sometimes damages are awarded for losses we expect a plaintiff to incur in the future, which creates its own complications.

Example 2

Mary causes a serious automobile accident, permanently disabling Fred, a 50-year-old white male. Fred will need round-the-clock nursing assistance. This year, his nursing care cost $100,000 per year. How much should a court award for nursing care Fred could need 10 years from now?

Explanation

There may be considerable uncertainty over how much medical care Fred will need in 10 years — or whether Fred even will be alive then. But even if we overcome these problems about Fred's condition, the jury will have to consider issues related to the costs of goods and services in the future (a topic explored in Chapter 2.5.2). In cases where enough money is at stake, lawyers will need to bring in experts, including economists, to make predictions about the future economy. These experts will have their depositions taken and, in cases that go to trial, they will be subject to examination and cross-examination on their economic assumptions driving the "bottom line." That means that good lawyers will have to understand rudimentary economic principles applicable to these kinds of problems. I know that many of you chose law school because you hate the sight of blood — thereby precluding medical school — and because you hate math — thereby precluding business school. Unfortunately, however, for the innumerate, good lawyers need to understand some mathematical content beyond that which is necessary to bill clients in six-minute increments. Also, I hope the amount of blood you see in your job is minimal.

So suppose that the jury believes that Fred will need exactly the same medical care in 10 years that he needs today, and today it costs $100,000 to provide this care. Economists will have to make assumptions about medical technology and the costs of medical goods and services to predict how much the care will cost in 10 years. Economists will have to make further predictions about how much money we would need to give Fred today to invest so that it will yield the right amount of money for Fred to pay his bills 10 years from now. This is the issue of *present value*, discussed in Chapter 2.5.2.

1.4 THE CATEGORIES OF REMEDIES

Remedies teachers usually divide the major remedial tools into three categories:

- Damages — an amount of money awarded to a wronged party from the party who committed the wrong to *compensate* for that wrong.

- Injunction — a court order to a defendant to do or not to do something in relation to the plaintiff. Sometimes this category is referred to as "Equity," because injunctions were the most important of a class of remedies once issued by courts of equity (as opposed to courts of law).
- Restitution — money awarded to a wronged party from the party that committed the wrong, measured by the gain to the party that committed the wrong, and not by the loss to the wronged party.

These tools do not form the complete universe of remedies, but they serve as useful organizing principles for much of the material in the course, and they are covered in the first three parts of this book. The final part of this book covers other important remedies, including punitive damages, declaratory judgments, and ancillary (helping) remedies (including attorney's fees). It also considers remedial defenses.

Thinking about the "Why" in Remedies.   In some Remedies courses, it is all trees and no forest. The course moves from remedial tool to remedial tool, much like the carpenter who teaches the trade tool by tool. "This is a screwdriver. You use the screwdriver by turning it clockwise in the following situations . . ." Other Remedies courses are more theoretical, looking for connections among remedies and differences in form and function. These courses also focus more on the "why" of remedies: what purpose do particular remedies serve, and how can one with a particular theoretical orientation (say, to maximize economic efficiency) choose the right remedies?

I have written this book to help students whose instructors focus only on trees, only on the forest, or on a mixture of forest and trees. All students need to understand how remedial tools work. For some students, those remedies are all they will need to understand. Other students will need to understand the more theoretical questions, which are explored in the appropriate chapters. While students who have "tree" professors might be tempted to skip the more theoretical part of the reading, I hope that these students keep reading — not only because this material is interesting, but also because developing a deeper understanding of remedies will help these students think creatively as lawyers.

The most important concept in the Remedies course is the "rightful position" standard, a term coined by Professor Douglas Laycock. It serves as a benchmark for judging various remedies. The rightful position standard says to choose the remedy that puts the plaintiff back (or keeps the plaintiff) in the position that she would have been in but for the defendant's wrong. Embedded within this definition are assumptions about the ability of courts to identify plaintiff's position before and after the wrong, as well as about remedies that restore plaintiff to (or keep plaintiff in) the rightful position. But there are also broad philosophical issues behind the rightful position standard. What social purpose is served by the rightful position standard? Under what circumstances would it be better (from whatever normative point of view) to give plaintiff more or less than the rightful position? Some remedies, at least in theory, try to tailor themselves to the rightful position standard while others do not.

One argument in favor of the rightful position standard comes from the law and economics school, where at least some scholars, such as Judge Richard Posner of the Seventh Circuit, have argued for legal rules—like the rightful position standard—which seek to maximize overall social wealth (and not worry about distribution of that wealth—who wins and who loses under different legal rules). This efficiency standard is sometimes referred to as "Kaldor-Hicks efficiency," after two economists who had discussed the concept. Further, the theory of "efficient breach" (discussed in Chapter 4.2) provides that courts award damages for breach of contract that are measured by what the non-breaching party would have stood to achieve had the contract not been breached, placing the non-breaching party in the position she would have been in but for the contract breach. These damages therefore are tied to the rightful position. Posner likes this remedy not because it helps plaintiffs (remember, economists don't care about distribution), or because it is morally right, but because he believes it best promotes economic efficiency.

Other jurisprudential theories also have much to say in favor of the rightful position standard. Philosophers going back to Aristotle have advocated forcing defendant to restore what had been taken from plaintiff as a matter of justice. Indeed, Aristotle's restoration principle ties justice to the rightful position standard.

The law often deviates from this rightful position standard, however. Suppose Alice steals $100 from Bob's wallet, runs to the casino, gambles, and walks away from the table with $1,000. If a court awards Bob a sum of money equal to Alice's gains rather than his losses, it has chosen a (restitutionary) award not tied to the rightful position. Consider Figure 1.1, measuring Bob's financial situation.

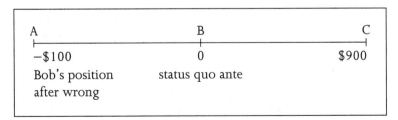

Figure 1.1

Handwritten margin note: Posner argues for economicly efficient B

We might think of Bob at Point B, the status quo ante, or 0, before he ever meets Alice. When Alice steals his money, we can think of him as moving to Point A, −$100, his position after the wrong. A damages remedy tied to the rightful position standard says that giving Bob $100 will move him back to the status quo ante (Point B) and restore him to the rightful position. (Of course, this is an oversimplification because it ignores Bob's costs of finding an attorney, the lost value of money over time, and other factors that we will consider in due course. But for now let us say that $100 perfectly moves Bob back to 0.)

If we give Bob a choice, however, between damages and a restitutionary remedy that gives him Alice's gain of $1,000, we can see why Bob would choose restitution. That remedy moves him from −$100, Point A, to Point C, or $900. (Why does it not move Bob to $1,000? Although Bob would receive $1,000 from Jane, he is already out $100 from the initial theft, so he now has in his wallet only $900 more than he had in the past.)

Sometimes the law allows for the recovery of gains, and when it does so, it deviates from the rightful position. In our case, the rightful position is Point B, but restitution leaves Bob at Point C, better than his position before the wrong. Why might the law decide to give Bob what appears to be a windfall? Should it have something to do with the wrongfulness of Alice's conduct? To test your thinking about this question, consider whether we should still give Bob the choice of damages or restitution if Alice took the $100 honestly believing it was her money.

These are issues we will take up in later chapters. The point now is that the rightful position standard serves as a useful benchmark in evaluating the choice of remedies. We can use it when considering how to use remedies to reach (or at least approximate) the rightful position standard, and also when it is appropriate to allow litigants to deviate from the rightful position.

With this introduction, you are ready to move forward. How you should proceed depends upon how your instructor has organized the course. You can begin at the beginning of Part I (on damages), Part II (on injunctions and other equitable remedies), Part III (on restitution), or Part IV (presenting the remedies topics of punitive damages, declaratory judgments, ancillary (or helping) remedies, and remedial defenses). Within each part (except for Part IV), I expect that you will begin with the opening chapter, which defines basic concepts and sets the stage for what comes next.

You should save the last chapter, Chapter 19, for the end of the course. It is provided to help you with issue spotting and skills in choosing remedies that you cannot test until you master the material in the first 18 chapters.

Example 3

Frank punches Javier in the nose, breaking Javier's nose and causing him to miss work for a week. What is Javier's rightful position, and how would a court go about putting Javier back in the rightful position?

Explanation

Even this simple example of a punch in the nose shows the gap between the theory of the rightful position and its implementation. In theory, we want to move Javier from Point A in Figure 1.1, his position after the punch in the nose, back to B, the status quo ante. But how do we do so? Certainly, Javier will have some losses that will be easy to quantify. For example, we can look at his doctor's bills to know how much Javier has paid out of his pocket for medical care, and we can look at a recent pay stub to see how much money Javier would have earned had he not needed to miss work for a week of recuperation. But other costs will be harder to measure, the most important of which are his pain and suffering. We do not know exactly how to quantify in dollars this kind of emotional distress damage, and it may be that there is no amount of money that Javier would have willingly exchanged for the punch in the nose. So the law sometimes engages in a fiction that money can in fact put the plaintiff back to the position he would have been in but for the wrong.

Example 4

Same facts as in Example 3. A jury awards Javier damages for his hospital bills and lost work, and an additional $5,000 in punitive damages (damages which are intended to punish and deter Frank and people like Frank). Do the punitive damages restore Javier to the rightful position?

Explanation

If compensatory damages were perfect at putting plaintiff in the rightful position, punitive damages would put plaintiff in a better position than would apply had there been no wrong. In terms of Figure 1.1, the compensatory damages would move Javier from A (below 0) to B (0, or the status quo ante). The punitive damages would then move Javier beyond C, to +$5,000, or $5,000 better than where Javier would have been had Frank never punched him. This potential "windfall" to plaintiff troubles some opponents of large punitive damages awards.

The analysis in the last paragraph assumed that compensatory damages were perfect at compensating Javier. But the explanation to Example 3 tells us that the compensatory damages might undercompensate Javier by underestimating his emotional distress damages. Javier also might be undercompensated because Javier will likely incur some attorney's fees (because this is a torts case, Javier will likely give up a percentage of his recovery from Frank to his lawyer under a contingency fee arrangement). Punitive damages, therefore, might be justified as making it more likely that plaintiff in fact is put back in the rightful position. There are other justifications for punitive damages as well, as we shall see in Chapter 15.

PART I

Compensatory Damages

CHAPTER 2

Introduction to Damages: Show Me the Money

Damages = substitutionary relief

2.1 COMPENSATORY DAMAGES AS SUBSTITUTIONARY RELIEF

One of the most common remedies given by courts to a complaining plaintiff is an award of compensatory damages. We refer to the award of damages as *substitutionary relief* because money substitutes for the thing that has been lost or damaged.

Why would a plaintiff want substitutionary relief? Sometimes, substitutionary relief is all that is available because it is not physically possible to restore to the plaintiff that which defendant has lost or destroyed. When Alex burns down Barbara's house while carelessly playing with matches, there is no way for Barbara to get her house back. The same principle applies when Carly breaks Dan's arm while rollerblading. Money substitutes for that which plaintiff would really want: the house as it stood before the fire or the unbroken arm.

Sometimes, it is possible to give plaintiff back the very thing that was taken, or prevent threatened harm to the plaintiff from occurring. We call such a remedy *specific relief*. When specific relief is available, a plaintiff may not want damages. For example, if Erica steals Franny's bike, Franny may want to bring an action to have the bike returned, at least if the bike is undamaged. Such an action may be in the form of replevin, discussed in Chapters 7 and 13. As we shall see, we don't give Erica the option of keeping the bike and paying Franny damages if Franny wants her bike back.

In addition to the bike, Franny may want damages to compensate for any losses she suffered by being deprived of the use of the bike between the time of Erica's theft and the time of its return.

The fact that damages are substitutionary raises a whole host of measurement problems. When Erica returns the bike undamaged, we don't have to worry about how to value it. That is an advantage for the courts in granting specific relief. But even in cases of specific relief, some amount of substitutionary relief will also be necessary. In Franny's case, a court may have to come up with a measure for the value of the loss of use of the bike during the period it was in Erica's possession. How is the court to do so?

e.g. paying for substitute transportation!

Valuation problems pervade awards of compensatory damages. When Alex burns the house down, valuation problems immediately emerge: How much would it cost Barbara to rebuild the house? What about money to replace the lost contents of the house? Suppose Barbara has an old but reliable refrigerator in her kitchen. Does she get the market value of that fridge (very low) or the cost of a new replacement (much higher)? Suppose the fire destroyed some sentimental one-of-a-kind photographs. How should those be valued?

The measurement problems are even more profound when it comes to personal injury. Consider Dan's broken arm. Some of the costs associated with the break will be easy to measure; think, for example, of the bill from the emergency room. But what about damages for the loss of use of the arm for a specified period? And what of emotional distress/pain and suffering? Should such damages be compensable, and if so, how should they be measured?

Even more easily measured costs such as hospital bills can create valuation problems. Suppose Dan is reimbursed by his health insurer for the hospital bill. Can he recover again from Carly? Or suppose Dan doesn't get a damage award from Carly until two years after the accident. Is he entitled to interest on his money?

We will consider all of these questions in this chapter or in later chapters, but the point now is that substitutionary relief creates valuation problems for the courts, problems that don't exist with specific relief.

Example 1

Gary owns a 1966 Thunderbird convertible in excellent condition. He received the car as a gift from his mother, who was the car's original owner. The original purchase price of the car in 1966 was $3,000. Its current market value as a collectible is $30,000, and Gary recently turned down an offer to sell his car for $50,000 to a collector. Heidi, who works for Acme Construction Company, accidentally flattens Gary's car with a steamroller that she was driving down Gary's street as part of a paving project. Gary is devastated by the loss of his car, and he sues Heidi and Acme for negligence. Will Gary ask for specific or substitutionary relief? If Gary asks for substitutionary relief, how do you think his loss should be measured in monetary terms?

Explanation

The first question is a no-brainer: Gary will want substitutionary relief because specific relief (such as the return of the car in its original condition) is not available. Returning a flattened car to him is of no use; he will want a sum of money to compensate him for his loss. The money *substitutes* for the car and therefore damages are a kind of substitutionary relief. The harder question is: how to value the loss? Before you continue with the rest of the chapter (and the other chapters on damages) to see how the law answers this question, ask yourself the normative question of what *should* be the proper measure. Is the original purchase price relevant? The fact that Gary received the car as a gift? The current market price? What about the emotional loss he may feel from the loss of a car he loved that came from his mother? Whatever answers you give to these questions, ask yourself another question: if Gary receives the sum that you think is the right one, does that sum truly "substitute" for the destroyed car? And reconsider your answer after you have completed the material in this chapter.

2.2 COMPENSATORY DAMAGES AND THE RIGHTFUL POSITION STANDARD   *baseline Damages.*

We have discussed how compensatory damages are substitutionary, but we have thus far ignored the "compensatory" label. The label is significant in that it gives a possible *baseline* for a court to determine the amount of damages. Such damages should *compensate*: "make satisfactory payment or reparation to; recompense or reimburse." AMERICAN HERITAGE DICTIONARY OF THE ENGLISH LANGUAGE 376 (4th ed. 2000). Under this definition, and according to most courts, compensatory damages are oriented toward plaintiffs' losses (unlike restitution, which, as we shall see, is oriented toward defendants' gains), and they require a payment that is "satisfactory" to repair the loss suffered by the plaintiff. In this way, they are different from (at least the conventional understanding of) other kinds of damages we will discuss later: nominal damages, which serve a declaratory function, and punitive damages, which serve punishment and deterrence functions.

2. Introduction to Damages: Show Me the Money

The idea that damages should serve a compensatory function traces far back in history. Aristotle, for example, wrote of the need for "corrective justice" in his *Nicomachean Ethics*, Book V. As Professor Weinrib explains,

> Corrective justice . . . features the maintenance and restoration of the notional equality with which the parties enter the transaction. This equality consists in persons' having what lawfully belongs to them. Injustice occurs when, relative to this baseline, one party realizes a gain and the other a corresponding loss. The law corrects this injustice when it re-establishes the initial equality by depriving one party of the gain and restoring it to the other party. Aristotle likens the parties' initial positions to two equal lines. The injustice upsets that equality by adding to one line a segment detached from the other. The correction removes that segment from the lengthened line and returns it to the shortened one. The result is a restoration of the original equality of the two lines.[1]

In this way, the corrective justice understanding of damages lines up with the rightful position standard, discussed in Chapter 1: ideally, awarding a plaintiff compensatory damages puts the plaintiff back in the position she would have been in but for the defendant's wrong.

To see how compensatory damages can serve to restore the plaintiff to the rightful position, consider again Alex's burning down Barbara's house. Let's make two unrealistic assumptions: first, we can perfectly compute the value of the loss to Barbara (we will set it at $100,000); and second, Alex, after burning down the house, instantaneously makes a payment of compensatory damages to Barbara (thereby eliminating questions about the relationship of time and money discussed in section 2.5.1 below).

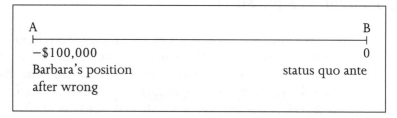

Figure 2.1

The money line in Figure 2.1 measures Barbara's position before and after Alex's wrong. Before the wrong, Barbara was at Point B, or at zero in relation to Alex. After the wrong, Barbara is at −$100,000. If Alex pays Barbara $100,000 instantaneously, she can use it to "buy" her way back to B,

---

1. Ernest J. Weinrib, *Corrective Justice in a Nutshell*, 52 U. Toronto L.J. 349, 349 (2002) (footnote omitted). Aristotle writes of a situation where plaintiff's loss equals defendant's gain, which, as we shall see in the chapter on restitution, is not always the case.

the status quo ante. In that way, compensatory damages return the plaintiff to the rightful position. (Mathematically, the court awards Barbara (B − A), or (0 − (−100,000)), or $100,000 [remember, convert the two minus signs into a plus].)

The money line also nicely illustrates how valuation problems can threaten the rightful position. Imagine that Barbara really suffers $100,000 in losses (putting her at Point A), but the court underestimates her damages at $80,000. In that case, as Figure 2.2 shows, Barbara is not returned to the rightful position. Instead, she is brought to place B−, which is at −$20,000. The damages award does not put her in the place she was at before the wrong. She will need another $20,000 to restore her house to its previous state.

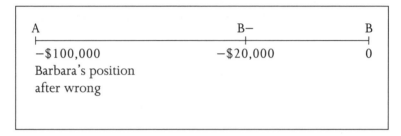

Figure 2.2

Valuation problems don't necessarily work against plaintiffs. So again imagine that Barbara really suffers $100,000 in losses (putting her at Point A), but this time the court *overestimates* her damages at $150,000. In that case, as Figure 2.3 shows, Barbara is brought to a position better than the rightful position. She will be at position B+, which is at +$50,000. (Do you see why? The first $100,000 of damages moves Barbara from A back to B, and then the next $50,000 moves her into positive territory on the money line to $50,000.) In this scenario, Barbara is actually better off than she was before Alex burned her house down. Even after paying to get her house back into the same shape it was in before the loss, she has an extra $50,000 in her bank account.

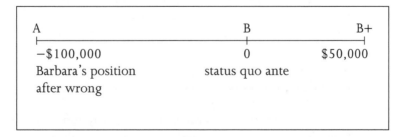

Figure 2.3

Figures 2.2 and 2.3 show that in order for compensatory damages to successfully meet the rightful position standard, courts will need to value accurately the position that plaintiffs would be in but for the wrong.

In the typical torts case, such as Barbara v. Alex, the rightful position means accurately measuring the plaintiff's losses, which will necessarily be somewhere in the region less than B, or 0. In typical contracts cases, however, the rightful position means accurately considering the gains that plaintiff failed to realize because of a defendant's breach of contract. So imagine that Irina was going to buy a valuable painting from Juan at a cost of $25,000. The market price of the painting is $35,000. They had a valid binding contract and Irina paid in advance. Juan decided not to sell to Irina after he realized he could make more money selling to someone else. He sells the painting to another buyer for $35,000.

Consider in Figure 2.4 how we might represent the rightful position:

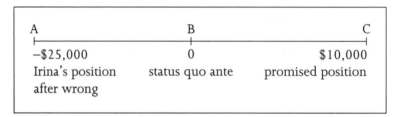

Figure 2.4

Before Irina entered into any contract with Juan, she was at position B, the status quo ante (or zero). When Irina paid Juan in advance and received nothing, she landed at position A, −$25,000. At first blush, it might appear that giving Irina $25,000 would put her back in the rightful position by restoring her to the status quo ante position. But remember that the rightful position is the position that the plaintiff would have been in but for the defendant's wrong. In this case, had Juan not breached the contract, Irina would have spent $25,000 for an item that she could then turn around and sell for $35,000, yielding a profit of $10,000 (putting aside the costs of entering into the two transactions and other complexities that we will discuss later) and placing her in position C, +$10,000. To place her into the position she would have been in without Juan's breach (think of a list of her assets with a net balance increase of $10,000), Juan is going to have to pay her $35,000: the first $25,000 takes her back to 0, and the next $10,000 puts her above the status quo ante, the position she would have been in but for the breach (a court would compute these damages as C − A, or 10,000 − (−25,000), or $35,000).

Later chapters will consider how and why tort and contract damages typically differ in this way, with tort damages usually geared toward restoring the status quo and contract damages usually geared toward giving the

[handwritten margin note, left-top:] K cases — gains that π would have realized as well!

[handwritten margin note, left-bottom:] pays her the mkt value, that's what she would Have realized

torts: status quo
K: benefit of the bargain. — *Both =*
still
compensatory!

2. Introduction to Damages: Show Me the Money

plaintiff the benefit of the bargain. Chapter 5 considers some exceptions to this rule, especially for fraud cases in tort. For now, keep your eye on the general point: if we value gains and losses correctly, compensatory damages can put the plaintiff into the rightful position.

One final point on the rightful position standard and compensatory damages: while corrective justice adherents such as Aristotle focus on the rightful position as a means of *compensating plaintiffs*, some adherents of the economic analysis of law focus as well on how compensatory damages affect the incentives of defendants.[2]

Consider, for example, the incentives facing Juan, who is wondering whether he should breach the painting contract with Irina. Suppose Juan has another willing buyer who will pay $35,000 for the painting. Would Juan — assuming he cares only about the immediate bottom line and not about any moral obligation to keep a contract or about his long-term reputation — decide to breach? He likely would not decide to do so if he is going to have to pay that $35,000 over to Irina as compensatory damages (though he would if the measure of damages was the undercompensatory $25,000 measure).[3] Think also of Carly, who was not careful and collided into Dan in a rollerblading accident, breaking Dan's arm. The possibility that Carly will have to pay damages if she rollerblades carelessly and injures someone will motivate Carly to take the right amount of care. In this way, damages serve to influence the behavior of defendants. (In the economic model, the possibility of recovering damages also influences the behavior of plaintiffs. Think of the extra precautions Dan might choose to take if he knew that Carly or others could injure him and not have to pay anything.)

Accurate valuation is important for the economic view of compensatory damages as well. Recall the example (illustrated in Figure 2.2) wherein Barbara really suffers $100,000 in losses (putting her at Point A), but the court underestimates her damages at $80,000. For purposes of the economic analysis, if courts consistently underestimate losses or, equivalently, if too many plaintiffs who should win their lawsuits end up losing their lawsuits, then damages might not create sufficient incentives for defendants not to wrong plaintiffs. Indeed, for this reason, some

---

2. Economists care about this question because they want courts to choose legal rules that promote "Kaldor-Hicks efficiency," or maximizing overall social wealth for society. Creating the right incentives for defendants and plaintiffs is part of a court's task in promoting efficiency. For an introduction to the concept of Kaldor-Hicks efficiency and economic analysis in general, see RICHARD A. POSNER, ECONOMIC ANALYSIS OF LAW 10-16 (7th ed. 2007).

3. He also would choose to sell to a new buyer if he found a buyer willing to pay $40,000. Remember, the market price is $35,000, which forms the basis for Irina's compensatory damages. In the case of a new buyer willing to pay over the market price, Juan could pay Irina the $35,000 and still end up with a $5,000 profit. Economists call this idea "efficient breach," and it is one to which we shall return in Chapter 4.2.

economists say that the possibility of a plaintiff's recovery of additional punitive damages might be necessary to provide the "efficient" amount of deterrence.

To sum up to this point: compensatory damages aim to put the plaintiff in the rightful position: the position the plaintiff would have been in but for the wrong. There are both philosophical reasons and economic arguments in favor of utilizing compensatory damages to bring plaintiff to the rightful position, and both views depend on courts being able to accurately value plaintiff's losses. It is to this valuation process that we turn next.

Example 2

One day after Laurent bought a new chocolate Labrador retriever puppy from a breeder for $1,000, Kira stole it. The market price for similar puppies is $2,000. Kira sold the puppy to Mary, who has left the country with it. Laurent sues Kira. Would compensatory damages put Laurent in the rightful position? If so, how much should the compensatory damages be?

Explanation

Laurent might have become emotionally attached to his new puppy (though he's only had it for one day), and it may be hard to value any emotional loss. However, dogs are not one-of-a-kind items, and presumably Laurent could use compensatory damages to buy a replacement dog. There should be some amount of money that puts him in the position where he was before the wrong, possibly setting aside the emotional distress. As for the *amount* of damages, absent evidence that Laurent could buy another dog for half the market price, it is going to take $2,000 — and not merely $1,000 — to put him into the position he was in before the wrong: owning a new puppy.

Example 3

Nina enters into a binding contract with Olivia for the sale of a rare coin. Nina agreed to pay $1,000 for the coin. The market price for this type of coin in the same condition is $700. Olivia breaches the contract because she has misplaced the coin. Nina has paid nothing in advance. Would compensatory damages put Nina in the rightful position? Is so, how much should the compensatory damages be?

Explanation

This looks like a lucky break for Nina. Had Olivia held up her end of the contract, Nina would have purchased an item worth $700 for $1,000. On an imaginary ledger of Nina's net worth, we would say after the purchase her net worth would have declined by $300. Thus, because this is a losing contract, compensatory damages are not going to be helpful in putting Nina in the rightful position. As we will see in Chapter 11.4, in the case of losing contracts, plaintiffs sometimes seek the remedy of restitution rather than compensatory damages because there are no damages.

2.3 VALUING COMPENSATORY DAMAGES

2.3.1 Damages in a Well-Functioning Market

Let's return to Barbara and her home (burned down by Alex) to begin our exploration of valuation for purposes of compensatory damages. Consider first the structure of the home itself, rather than its contents. How should the home be valued? Initially, we have to choose between an objective measure of damages (such as market value) and a subjective measure of damages (such as the value that Barbara would place on her home).

For example, suppose that a competent builder would charge $50,000 to rebuild a home for Barbara of the same general size and quality as the one that burned down. This market value is an objective measure; though the parties can disagree about how much competent builders charge to build such a home, the court can resolve this dispute through the taking of evidence from experts in the construction market in Barbara's area, and using data about the type of home Barbara had before the fire. Alternatively, we might ask how much Barbara personally valued her home. Suppose that this was her childhood home, and that it had great sentimental value to her. Indeed, imagine that Barbara had recently turned down an offer for the purchase of her home and land for $400,000 — many times the fair market value of the land and home — because she loved it so much. In other words, a person's subjective valuation does not necessarily line up with objective market value.

Generally speaking, when there is a well-functioning market (meaning that there are many buyers and sellers), courts use an objective market measure for calculating a plaintiff's compensatory damages. "Determinations based on value are pervasive in damage measures. Familiar damage measures include the value of the property taken or destroyed, the difference between the value of property before damage and the value after damage, and the difference between the contract price and the market value of property promised but not delivered." LAYCOCK

p. 22. In Barbara's case, the portion of damages for the loss of her home is going to be measured by the objective market cost to replace the damaged home, and not by Barbara's subjective value.

Objective market measures of value will be undercompensatory when plaintiffs subjectively value items more than the market does.

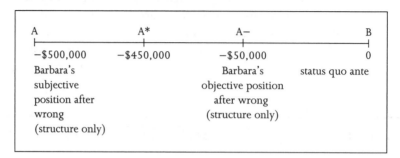

Figure 2.5

Imagine that Barbara would not have moved from her house unless someone paid her $500,000 (plus more money for the land, but we'll ignore that complication). Figure 2.5 shows how the use of objective market value will undercompensate her in this instance. If Barbara is truly at position A (−$500,000) after the fire, it will take a $500,000 damages award to move her back to B, the status quo ante. But the law, using market valuation, treats her loss as being at A−, giving her compensation of only $50,000. In fact, the $50,000 award moves Barbara from position A to position A*, at −$450,000. It is grossly undercompensatory.

If that's the case, it seems unfair to Barbara to use objective market valuation. But courts have gravitated to it in part because objective measures are much easier to administer. When a market is functioning well, it is easy to get figures for repair or replacement costs. Subjective measures exist only inside the head of the plaintiff and thus are harder to identify accurately. There is also the risk that plaintiffs will exaggerate subjective values after a loss. Thus, even if Barbara hated her house and valued it at less than the $50,000 cost of rebuilding, if the law allowed her to receive compensatory damages based on subjective valuation, she may be tempted (but for fear of committing perjury) to state her subjective value as $500,000.

One way that the law can allow subjective valuation in through the back door is to allow emotional distress damages as an element of damages in appropriate cases. Thus, a court in Barbara's negligence case against Alex might allow her to recover the $50,000 cost to repair the home plus some additional amount of damages to compensate for emotional distress. We return in Chapter 3.2 to a consideration of when emotional distress damages may be available as an element of damages.

Even with market-based valuation, issues of subjectivity can surface in cases involving damage to property that do not diminish the overall market value of the property. Consider these examples:

- Percy cuts down a tree on Quentin's land in order to use the lumber. The tree provided Quentin with shade near his home. The cost to replace the tree is $1,000, but the market value of the land without the tree is unchanged. (*See* DOBBS at § 3.3(6), p. 310.)
- Ralph cuts down a tree from a forest of trees on Samir's land in order to use the lumber. Samir did not even notice that the tree was gone until Ralph told him about it. The cost to replace the tree is $1,000, but the market value of the land without the tree is unchanged.
- Tomas signs a contract with Ursula, a building contractor, to construct a building. The contract provides that Ursula will install plumbing using Alpha brand copper pipe. Ursula inadvertently uses Beta brand copper pipe instead, which is of identical quality to Alpha pipe. The error is discovered as the house is completed. The cost to replace the pipes in the building is $20,000, but the value of the home with Beta brand rather than Alpha brand remains unchanged. *See* Jacob & Youngs, Inc. v. Kent, 129 N.E. 889, 891 (N.Y. 1921).

Repair or Replacement Cost

In each of these examples, the costs to repair or replace are high, but the overall impact on market value of the loss is low. Plaintiffs have at times successfully argued for the repair or replace measure when they can show subjective value in the item that was lost or damaged, or at least when they can show they intended to actually make the repair or replacement. *See, e.g.*, McKinney v. Christiana Cmty. Builders, 280 Cal. Rptr. 242, 246 (1991) (unpublished opn.); DOBBS, *supra*. For example, Quentin may really want his shade tree replaced, and arguably the court should allow him to recover damages to do so. But one suspects that someone like Tomas might sue, claiming repair costs, and never make the repair, hoping to gain a windfall from the minor error of a contractor or the inadvertent tort of a defendant.

In cases where plaintiff cannot show any subjective reason to prefer the replacement cost, as in Samir's case against Ralph, it is tempting to say that there should be no damages. But an economist might bristle at the suggestion, because it would create no deterrence for Ralph, who would pay no damages for the theft. Samir might then be forced to take expensive measures to prevent theft from people such as Ralph.

In response to these concerns, some courts will allow the more generous cost of repair measure when a defendant engages in a willful breach of contract. *See, e.g.*, Groves v. John Wunder Co., 286 N.W. 235, 236 (Minn. 1939). The same principle should apply to intentional torts as

restitution
↓
unfair/unjust
enrichment

well, such as those committed by Percy and Ralph (but not the inadvertent breach by Ursula). The law also offers Quentin and Samir an alternative remedy, restitution (see Part III), which would allow them to recover the value of the *gain* to defendant, rather than damages tied to plaintiff's losses.

/

When measuring market value, courts usually measure damages *at the time of the loss.* In cases involving items that fluctuate in value, however, such as stocks or crops, courts sometimes show greater flexibility. As to stocks, courts are split on approaches, with many states "resolv[ing] doubts against defendant by awarding the highest value between the time of the wrong and the time of trial, the time of filing suit, or some similar date." *See* LAYCOCK p. 34. Similar kinds of issues arise when there is damage to a farmer's crops before those crops have matured. Assuming that a farmer may prove damages with reasonable certainty (see Chapter 6.1), a court might allow damages measured from the time the immature crops would have been harvested rather than at the time of the loss.

measure
@
the time of
the
loss!
—

Example 4

Reconsider the fact pattern in Example 1: Heidi flattens Gary's 1966 Thunderbird convertible with a steamroller. The original purchase price of the car in 1966 was $3,000. Its current retail value as a collectible is $30,000. Gary recently turned down an offer to sell the car for $50,000. Putting aside possible emotional distress damages, how does the law measure Gary's loss of the car?

Explanation

A court will likely award Gary $30,000, putting aside any emotional distress damages and assuming that the car has no scrap value that Gary can recover. The $3,000 original purchase price might ordinarily be evidence of a car's current market value; cars tend to lose value with age. But this is a collectible car, and it has gained value over time. We generally measure market value *at the time of the loss,* and therefore the $30,000 figure is appropriate. It appears that Gary valued the car at more than its market value; that is at least implicit in his failure to sell the car for above-market value. But courts generally will not allow Gary to recover this subjective measure of damages. Does the law's answer jibe with your own values as expressed in your answer to Example 1?

Example 5

Victor, while jogging carelessly, entered Wanda's garden and stepped on Wanda's prized tulips, which she had grown herself. The cost of tulip seeds is $50. The cost to buy fully grown replacement tulips is $500. Wanda had planned to cut these tulips and enter them in a flower contest, where the first prize was $1,000. She cannot enter purchased tulips into the contest. The value of Wanda's home is the same with and without the tulips. To what amount in compensatory damages is Wanda entitled?

Explanation

A court is likely to award Wanda $500 for the tulips. Although it is true that the market value of her home has not decreased because of the loss of the tulips, the evidence shows that Wanda was growing these tulips for fun and potential profit; they were not like Samir's unnoticed lost tree in the earlier example. The fact that Victor acted negligently rather than deliberately, however, is an argument in favor of no damages (that is, damages as measured by the loss in value of the house). It seems least likely that Wanda will receive $1,000, or the amount she could have won if she could have entered her tulips in a flower contest. As we will see in Chapter 6.1, damages must be proven with reasonable certainty, and it is too speculative to say whether Wanda would have won the contest with her tulips. And again, we are ignoring the possibility that Wanda will ask for an additional amount of damages for her emotional distress.

Victor might try to argue he is liable to pay for only the cost of replacement seeds. But that appears undercompensatory, because it accounts neither for the value of whatever work Wanda put in to grow her tulips nor for the risk that the tulip seeds would not grow. It also does not follow the principle that we generally measure value at the time of the loss.

Example 6

Xavier puts in a "buy" order to his stockbroker Yolanda for 100 shares of Futurco stock, at $5.00 per share. Xavier sends $500 electronically to Yolanda. Yolanda bought the stock for Xavier (at a total cost of $500), but negligently sold it the same day (for the same $500 price). She failed to inform Xavier, putting the $500 into a general account for clients. One month later, Futurco stock is trading at $20.00 per share and Xavier puts in a "sell" order. Yolanda then tells Xavier of her error. Xavier sues, and at the time of trial Futurco stock is trading at $15.00 per share. To how much is Xavier entitled in damages?

Explanation

This problem raises an issue about property whose value fluctuates over time. If we measure the value at the time of the loss (which presumably occurred the same day as the purchase and sale of the stock), Xavier would be entitled only to $500. But we could choose a more generous measure, such as the highest value before Xavier discovered the loss (yielding damages of $2,000 (100 shares at the $20/share price)) or at the time of trial (yielding damages of $1,500 (100 shares at the $15/share price)). The rule to be applied will depend upon the jurisdiction.

2.3.2 Damages Without a Well-Functioning Market

When markets work well, the dispute is primarily an *evidentiary* one: what is the going price for mature tulips, or rebuilding a home, or emergency room visits? The parties may have pitched battles over this evidentiary question in particular cases, but the court's mission is clear: to figure out the market value to repair or replace the item damaged or lost. But not every loss has a potential repair or replacement value in a well-functioning market. For some losses, there is no market at all—most important, there is no good market for losses caused by emotional distress (or pain and suffering). We cannot refer to a market in pain to compute damages for Dan's broken arm. The next chapter will consider how courts value such losses (termed *non-economic* losses or *special* damages by some courts, as compared to *economic* losses or *general* damages for losses that have a readier market measure).

Here we consider economic losses that occur in less than perfectly functioning markets. A good example is Barbara's refrigerator, destroyed in the fire set by Alex. Suppose Barbara bought the fridge five years ago for $600. A comparable fridge today costs $800. But if Barbara had tried to sell her five-year-old fridge just before it was destroyed, she would have been lucky to get $100 for it. Unfortunately for Barbara, the law generally uses market value at the time of loss, so she stands to get only $100 for the lost fridge.

Some courts will be more generous and allow a higher value based on replacement cost less depreciation for household goods and apparel. *See, e.g., Lane v. Oil Delivery Co.*, 524 A.2d 405 (N.J. Super. 1987). But that more generous rule typically is not applied to other consumer goods, including cars.

Why is the fridge's value so low? Part of the reason is that there is not a robust market for certain used goods, and even where there is a market, prices tend to be depressed. Economist George Akerlof described a "lemon" effect that makes the market for such goods—he used the example of cars—poorly functioning. George Akerlof, *The Market for Lemons*, 84 Q.J.

ECON. 488 (1970). It is difficult to judge the quality of these goods, and uncertainty about whether the good is of high quality or is a poor-quality "lemon" pervades the market. Buyers offer lower prices for these goods to take into account the uncertainty, and the lower price means that fewer sellers with the high-quality goods would choose to sell. In this way, higher-quality goods are driven from the market, leaving an abundance of "lemons."

Thus, when Barbara gets the $100 in damages for her fridge, she is taking a chance if she goes out to actually buy a used fridge at this price — it might be a lemon. If Barbara is lucky, she has purchased homeowners' insurance that provides for the cost of *replacing* lost items with new items of similar quality.[4] If she doesn't have insurance, she might look for another source of money to buy a new, comparable refrigerator. For these reasons, the $100 damage award likely will be undercompensatory.

Another circumstance in which markets don't function well is when there are few buyers or sellers. Consider a collection of family home movies, also destroyed in Barbara's fire. Before the fire, virtually no one would have been interested in buying those goods, but for Barbara they were very valuable. The movies are irreplaceable, and their only market value is sentimental value. In such cases, courts will sometimes allow recovery for their value — again, these are sometimes allowed not for the economic value of the destroyed goods, but as part of the noneconomic emotional distress damages. *See Williford v. Emerton*, 935 So. 2d 1150 (Ala. 2004).

sentimental value.

Example 7

Zane owned an acre of land with his home in a rural part of the state. Alice bought land adjacent to Zane's land, with the intention of building a ranch to raise emus. Alice brought in a bulldozer to clear the part of her land with a dense collection of trees. Her workers accidentally cleared some of the dense trees growing on Zane's land as well. Zane sued Alice for trespass and sought damages. The uncontroverted evidence showed that the inadvertent clearing of Zane's land increased the market value of his land by $15,000. At trial, Zane testified as follows: "Well, I bought this land to build a retirement home on and I am 57 and my wife is 56, and she's not well, so she wants to get out in the country, too. And we bought that for that reason and now we are afraid to go out of our house. And the reason we're afraid is because of the exotic animals that will be put next to us. We hoped the trees would serve as a buffer." The jury awarded Zane $20,000. Can the award stand?

---

4. We put off until Chapter 6.4 the question whether Barbara would be allowed to keep both her insurance proceeds *and* damages from Alex.

Explanation

There is no dispute that the market value of Zane's land has not decreased; it has increased. The only way that Zane can recover damages is if the court allows for the award of the subjective value of the land. Many courts would not allow Zane to recover such damages, but some would allow it when actual damages do not compensate the plaintiff for the loss. (These facts come from *Porras v. Craig*, 675 S.W.2d 503 (Tex. 1984).)

2.4 NOMINAL DAMAGES

Suppose in Example 7 Zane did not claim any losses based upon his loss of his privacy. Instead, he is annoyed that Alice has sent her workers on his land — even though the workers' clearing of his land has increased its value. Is there any incentive for Zane to still sue for damages?

The answer may be "yes." In cases such as trespass, where there is no actual damage, a plaintiff might sue to obtain nominal damages, or a trivial sum of damages (such as $1) awarded by a court in lieu of actual damages. At first blush, it might appear irrational for Zane to sue for $1 in damages. Attorney's fees are likely to cost many times more than that expected recovery (and are usually not recoverable by the winning party (see Chapter 17.3)). But the $1 damage award can serve an important "declaratory" function: telling the world where the property line is between Zane and Alice, and declaring that it is a trespass for Alice to enter Zane's land.[5] (This can be especially useful if Zane and Alice have a bona fide dispute over where their property line is.) Eventually, if Alice continues to trespass on Zane's land, Zane might go back to the court and point to the nominal damages award and Alice's continuing conduct as a reason to get an injunction ordering Alice to stay off Zane's land.

In addition, an award of nominal damages might serve as a predicate to allow the jury to award punitive damages (Chapter 15.1). Many states require an award of compensatory damages before a jury can award additional punitive damages, and sometimes an award of nominal damages is enough to allow for the punitive award. *See* Richard C. Tinney, *Sufficiency of Showing of Actual Damages to Support Award of Punitive Damages — Modern Cases*, 40 A.L.R. 4th 11 §§ 6-9 (1985 & 2005 Supp.) (collecting cases on both sides of

---

5. See Chapter 16 for a discussion of declaratory judgments, the quintessential declaratory remedy.

issue). But *see* N.J. STAT. ANN. 2A:15-5.13(c) (nominal damages cannot support the award of punitive damages).

Finally, an award of nominal damages can serve as a predicate to allow the jury to award attorney's fees in cases litigated under statutes that provide for the award of attorney's fees. But when the jury awards only nominal damages (and no other relief, such as a declaration or injunction), the amount of attorney's fees allowed might be very small, as we shall see in Chapter 17.3.

Example 8

While Barry was sleeping in the grass on the quad, Charlene—who had never met Barry before but liked how he looked—came over and kissed him on the lips. Barry slept through the whole thing, but later heard about what happened from some friends. Barry wants to sue for the tort of battery, but tells you that he suffered no significant emotional distress. Would you advise Barry to sue for nominal damages?

Explanation

It depends upon what Barry would like to accomplish. If Barry wants to "send a message" to Charlene (or others like her), he might want to sue, assuming, as is likely, that he can make out the technical elements of battery. *See* RESTATEMENT (SECOND) OF TORTS § 18 (1965). Even without emotional distress damage, he should be able to obtain nominal damages. (He also might be able to recover damages for dignitary harm, discussed in the next chapter.) Because Barry would have to pay attorney's fees, it may cost him much more to sue than what he would recover in nominal damages. So he would have to feel pretty strongly about sending a message—unless the jurisdiction allows for the award of punitive damages to accompany nominal damages, and Barry hopes to recover a large amount in punitive damages.

2.5 TIME AND THE VALUE OF MONEY

2.5.1 Prejudgment and Postjudgment Interest

Recall Barbara, whose house Alex accidentally burned down. We said that if it would cost $100,000 for Barbara to rebuild the house, and if Alex paid Barbara the cost of the losses instantly, an award of $100,000 would restore

Barbara to the rightful position. But payments do not come instantly in most cases. Alex may dispute liability or the amount of damages (or, worse for Barbara, Alex may not have enough money to pay for the damage he has caused).

Suppose that it takes one year from the time that Alex burns down the house until the time of judgment. Awarding Barbara $100,000 one year after the accident will not put her in the rightful position. To see why, imagine that the day after the fire, Barbara secured a loan to rebuild the property. The lender charged 10% interest per year (compounded annually, an assumption we'll continue to make throughout this chapter to keep things simple). She rebuilds the house as the lawsuit goes forward. One year after the fire, her loss is $110,000, no longer the $100,000 loss represented in Figure 2.1. See Figure 2.6.

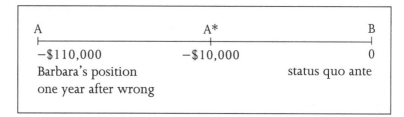

Figure 2.6

The jury measures the loss at the time of the wrong, or $100,000. But awarding Barbara $100,000 a year after the wrong does not restore her to the rightful position. Instead, it brings her only to A*, −$10,000. For this reason, courts sometimes allow the award of prejudgment interest, measured from the time of the wrong until the time of judgment. This award helps put plaintiff in the rightful position.

The availability of prejudgment interest depends upon the jurisdiction and sometimes on the type of case. Traditionally, prejudgment interest was unavailable when damages were not "liquidated" or "ascertainable." In practice, this meant that prejudgment interest was not available for personal injury actions. Some states have abandoned this rule and now allow for prejudgment interest even in personal injury cases.

When prejudgment interest is available, the rate of interest varies by jurisdiction. For example, Rhode Island sets the amount of prejudgment interest by statute at 12% per year. R.I. GEN. LAWS § 9-21-10 (1997). Other jurisdictions index the amount to some other measure. Iowa, for example, sets prejudgment interest "at a rate equal to the treasury constant maturity index published by the federal reserve in the H15 report settled immediately prior to the date of the judgment plus two percent." IOWA CODE § 668.13 (1999).

In federal courts, prejudgment interest is routinely available, but there is no set rate of prejudgment interest. Accordingly, there is much room for creative arguments about which measure best puts the plaintiff back in the rightful position. *See* Michael S. Knoll & Jeffrey M. Colon, *The Calculation of Prejudgment Interest* (May 31, 2005), http://ssrn.com/abstract=732765.

There is much at stake in these federal cases. As Professors Knoll and Colon note: "When the injury occurred long before the judgment, prejudgment interest can greatly exceed the original judgment. . . . In 1992, the Seventh Circuit awarded plaintiffs $65 million in damages and $148 million in prejudgment interest in a suit arising out of the grounding of the supertanker, *Amoco Cadiz*, off the coast of Brittany on March 16, 1978." Because of the flexibility of the federal standard, the court's decision could be worth millions. The authors note that a 1% increase in the interest rate in the *Amoco Cadiz* case would have increased the award by $20 million, and that if the court had compounded interest quarterly rather than annually, the plaintiffs could have received an extra $11 million.

Postjudgment interest — for the period between the time of judgment and the time that the judgment debtor pays (or "satisfies") the judgment — is also necessary to put plaintiff in the rightful position. So suppose that a court awards Barbara $110,000 for the fire damages, with $10,000 of that money representing the prejudgment interest. Alex decides to appeal, and it is yet another year before Alex, upon losing the appeal, pays Barbara the damages. Barbara, who has borrowed money from the bank to pay for her repairs, is still accruing interest on her loan, so the award of $110,000 will not put her in the rightful position. Assuming she had to pay for another year of interest at $10,000, compounded annually (on her principal and interest), her total loan will now cost $121,000 to repay (in the second year, interest accrues at 10% on the $110,000 loan balance).

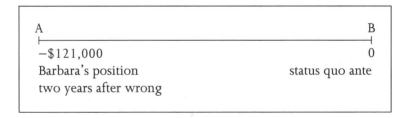

Figure 2.7

In the federal courts, postjudgment interest is awarded at the set rate of the 52-week Treasury bill, and many states set the rate by statute as well. At least some states allow postjudgment interest on the total amount of damages, including prejudgment interest. *See Quality Engineered Installation, Inc. v. Higley South, Inc.*, 670 So. 2d 929, 931 (Fla. 1996).

Example 9

Enid alleges that Deirdre breached a contract to pay Enid $100,000 for a computer system that Deirdre has used in her business. The dispute takes place in Rhode Island and the issue is litigated in Rhode Island's court. If Deirdre is found liable for breach of contract, the court will order her to pay Enid $100,000 plus prejudgment interest. The current rate of interest that individuals can get on their money in a safe investment is 5%. Which party to the litigation will want to bring this case to trial quickly? How might that result differ if individuals can get 20% on their money in a safe investment?

Explanation

There may be reasons of liquidity (the fact that Enid needs the $100,000 now) that could lead Enid to push the case to trial as quickly as possible regardless of the interest rate. But putting aside such a concern, you can see that the rate of prejudgment interest can affect the parties' incentives to litigate quickly or slowly. When normal interest rates are low, defendants like Deirdre may want the case to be decided quickly, so that, if found liable, Deirdre won't have to pay a very high rate of interest. For Enid in such circumstances, prejudgment interest may look like a good "investment." Think of this: If Enid gets her $100,000 today from Deirdre and invests it in the bank at 5% (annual interest), after a year she will have $105,000. But if the case drags on for another year, Deirdre will owe her $112,000, because of Rhode Island's statutory 12% rate of prejudgment interest.

The incentives are reversed if general interest rates are high. If Enid can get 20% on her money, she'd rather have Deirdre pay now. Deirdre, on the other hand, would rather invest the $100,000 now in an investment yielding 20%, eventually paying off Enid under the statutory 12% rate and pocketing the difference.

2.5.2 Present Value

Prejudgment and postjudgment interest facilitate compensation for plaintiffs for harm that has already occurred. But sometimes a plaintiff receives compensation for injuries the jury believes plaintiff will sustain in the future because of the defendant's past conduct. Consider Frank, who caused serious injuries to Greta when he negligently ran her over with his Hummer. Suppose Greta, a 30-year-old woman who was healthy before the accident, is now paralyzed from the waist down. She can no longer work as a letter carrier, and she will need special medical care for the rest of her life.

By the time Greta's case against Frank goes to trial, Greta will have already incurred medical expenses and loss of wages from the time of the

Future injuries?

accident until the time of trial. The jury can decide the appropriate amount for these damages that have already occurred. Depending upon the state law, Greta may be entitled to prejudgment interest on at least some of these damages, and she should be able to obtain postjudgment interest as well for amounts reduced to judgment. Putting aside additional emotional distress damages, would compensation for these past losses put Greta in the rightful position?

No. Even if Frank compensates Greta for the harm that has already occurred as a result of Frank's actions, Greta still faces future medical expenses and loss of wages. Five years from now, Greta might still need weekly visits from a nurse and other medical care. She may also never be able to return to work. (If Greta could perhaps take a different job, a court might reduce her damages for failure to mitigate if she does not do so. See Chapter 6.2.)

These future damages present special valuation problems. Imagine that this year, Greta's medical bills as a result of the accident are $20,000, and the salary she would have earned (but for the injury) as a letter carrier is $35,000. The experts agree that she will suffer similar damages five years from now. Because we require the plaintiff to sue for all of her damages in a single trial (rather than come back to court periodically for an assessment of recent additional damages), a court will have to figure out how much to compensate Greta now for her future medical expenses and lost wages.

This is indeed a difficult undertaking that involves a host of educated guesses about the future. Will Greta need the same amount of medical care five years from now? How much will such medical care cost in five years? How much would Greta have earned five years from now had she not been injured? Would she have received promotions by then?

These problems are compounded by the uncertain time frame for damages for serious injuries. Damages will have to be awarded to compensate Greta for the rest of her life in this single trial. Consider these questions: When would Greta have stopped working? How much longer will she live and need medical care? Even after the jury makes determinations of these amounts (in high-value cases, likely based upon the testimony of dueling experts), there is another complication: the time value of money.

Suppose the jury determines that five years from now, Greta will need the same level of medical care, which today costs $20,000, and that she would have been promoted two grades at the postal service, to a position where the current salary is $40,000. These figures do not take into account the issue of inflation. Over time, prices rise. But predicting how much prices will rise is not easy. Indeed, knowing something about the general rate of inflation is not enough: the cost of medical care has in recent years exceeded the general inflation rate. Wages, too, might increase faster or slower than the general rate of inflation. It might be that postal workers' salaries in general have kept up with the general rate of inflation. And postal workers' salaries are easier to predict than salaries of those who have a more uncertain career path, such as that of a first-year associate at a large law firm. Can you predict with any certainty how much you will be earning ten years from now?

Imagine that the jury determines that the medical care today costing Greta $20,000 would cost $25,000 in five years, and that the salary for a postal worker who is two grades above Greta will be $45,000 five years from now. Five years from now, therefore, the jury's best guess is that Greta would need $70,000 for medical expenses and lost wages.[6]

But if the jury awards Greta $70,000 to compensate for expected losses five years from now, Greta would be *overcompensated* because she will have the use of that money five years early. If Greta received the $70,000 today, she could invest it for the next five years. At the end of five years, if she invested that $70,000 at 5% per year compounded annually, she would have over $89,000.

So we need a more sophisticated way to deal with this problem, one that takes into account two *countervailing tendencies*. On the one hand, the cost of things like medical care and wages will go up over time. On the other hand, Greta will have the money from the judgment before she needs it, and because she can invest the money, she will need less money now.

If these figures were exactly offsetting, we could ignore both the effects of medical and wage inflation and the benefits of getting the money early. And some courts have said it is permissible to do just that. *See Jones & Laughlin Steel Corp. v. Pfeifer*, 462 U.S. 523 (1983) (rejecting this "total offset" method as *mandatory* in the federal courts but noting that parties could stipulate to this method of computing damages). This means, to use the example above, that a jury might simply award Greta $20,000 per year for each year she is expected to need medical care, and $35,000 to replace her salary for each year she would have worked but for the accident. She can then take that money and invest it with the expectation that the principal from the judgment plus the interest income would give her just the right amount at the time she should need the funds.

But plaintiffs and defendants, at least in cases with large stakes, might battle over future cost and wage increases. They too might disagree over the proper rate of interest that Greta would be able to get for safe investments. Calculating *present value* allows jurors (or, more realistically, the expert witnesses upon whose testimony the jurors will rely) to consider these two countervailing forces at once.

To use a simple example, take Greta's medical care one year from now, which in today's dollars will cost $20,000. Suppose the evidence shows that medical care is expected to rise by 3% in the next year, and that Greta could invest her money in a safe investment for a year earning 4.5% interest. Rather than increase the $20,000 by 3% (to account for increased cost)

---

6. Here, as elsewhere in this book, we are ignoring the issue of how taxation affects these calculations.

and then decrease it by the 4.5% interest rate (to account for the amount Greta may earn on her money), we can simply "discount" the $20,000 by the difference in interest rates, or 1.5% (4.5% − 3%). Using a present value table or a present value calculator (easy to find on the Internet with a Google search), the value of that amount is $19,704.[7] The calculation must be done for each year of medical expenses and each year of wages.

This example shows how complicated the computation of future damages can be. We have dealt with only one year out of many years of Greta's expected future medical expenses. Small changes in assumptions can make a big difference over time. It is no wonder that in such cases, plaintiffs and defendants are going to bring in economic experts to present competing models of future damages. In a case with serious personal injuries, tens of thousands of dollars can be at stake depending upon the discount rate used.

Example 10

You are Frank's lawyer. Do you want an economic expert who predicts that medical inflation and wage inflation will be high, or one who predicts it will be low? Do you want an expert who predicts a high rate of return on safe investments, or one who predicts a low rate? Is it ethical to shop for an expert on the basis of the expert's expected opinions?

Explanation

Generally speaking, it is better for defendants when the expert predicts that medical care inflation and wage inflation will be low, and that the general rate of return on investments will be high (plaintiffs will want the opposite assumptions to be made). Consider Greta's costs in ten years. A prediction that medical inflation and wage inflation will be low means that Greta won't need much more money ten years from now than she does today to make up for what she's lost. And the more money she can earn on her investments, the less principal she'll need today to yield the right amount tomorrow.

Ethically, one should not choose an expert who is going to commit perjury or sell her testimony to the highest bidder. But it is common practice to look at an expert's track record before retaining that expert and using that expert in a case. The most credible experts are those who sometimes testify for plaintiffs and sometimes testify for defendants.

---

7. For those using a present value table, one would look under the column for the 1.5% discount rate at period 1. The rate there is 0.98522157, which, when multiplied by $20,000, yields $19,704.

Example 11

A jury awards Greta a sum of damages based upon the assumption that she will be able to earn 5% per year on her investments. Five years after judgment, Frank discovers that Greta invested her money in the stock market and earned an average of 18% on her money in the first five years. Can Frank go back to court and ask for a refund?

Explanation

No. The same is true if Greta was unable to earn as much on her money as the jury assumed, or if medical costs increased at a much faster rate than the jury predicted. Whatever damages are awarded at trial is usually the last word.

One way to deal with this uncertainty is to have defendants make periodic payments to plaintiffs every few years that are adjusted for inflation. Sometimes cases are settled to provide for such payments, with the defendant paying a lump sum to an insurer, who bears risks such as a change in the rate of inflation. Some states require the use of periodic payments in certain kinds of cases, such as medical malpractice cases.

Tort Damages

CHAPTER 3

3.1 INTRODUCTION TO TORT DAMAGES

This chapter considers special issues that arise in the context of tort damages, beginning with the general measure of tort damages. When we speak of the rightful position in torts cases, we are almost always comparing the position of plaintiff before the wrong committed by the defendant (the "status quo ante," which we set at 0) and the position of plaintiff after the wrong.[1] See Figure 3.1.

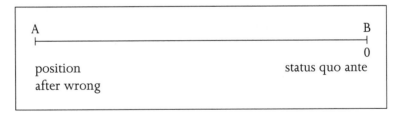

Figure 3.1

To use the final example of the last chapter, Greta was at B, or 0, before Frank ran her over. The accident moved her to some point below zero, at A. Tort damages are measured as $(B - A)$, and at least theoretically, the award

---

1. The notable exception is for fraud damages, discussed in Chapter 5. In addition, in certain torts cases, one may choose not to seek tort damages but instead to sue in restitution. Part III of this book explores such restitutionary remedies.

37

of damages equal to (B — A) should put Greta in the position she would have been in but for the wrong.

Greta's example presents many complications, especially because of the difficulty of measuring her damages for pain and suffering. Before we consider her case further, let's return to a simpler example from the last chapter, the case of Alex burning down Barbara's house:

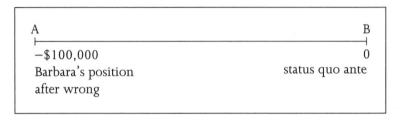

Figure 3.2

Mathematically, the court awards Barbara (B — A), or (0 — (—100,000)), or $100,000 (remember, convert the two minus signs into a plus sign). See Figure 3.2. Though the parties may vigorously dispute the correct value of A, the parties usually do not dispute that the court should award damages meant to put plaintiff in the position she would have been in but for the wrong, the goal of the (B — A) formula.

The use of this (B — A) formula for tort damages (which some call "reliance damages" for reasons that will become clear in the next chapter, dealing with contract damages) nicely illustrates cases where only nominal damages may be available. Recall Charlene, who committed a battery by kissing Barry in the quad while he was sleeping. Barry suffered no measurable damages (the facts told us he suffered no emotional distress), so in that case A = 0, and therefore (B — A) equals zero. Because Barry suffered no damages, he will lose his case for failure to prove damages, unless the court allows him to recover nominal damages.

As we have already seen in earlier chapters, the idea that tort damages restore the plaintiff to the position she would have been in but for defendant's wrong can sometimes be little more than a fiction. The use of market valuation rather than subjective valuation, the inability of some plaintiffs to obtain prejudgment interest, and the lack of recovery (in most cases) of plaintiff's attorney's fees are all reasons we have already considered why a plaintiff's tort damages may be undercompensatory, thus putting plaintiff in a worse position than she would have been in had the defendant not injured her.

In tort damages, by far the largest gap in restoring plaintiff to the rightful position arises in serious personal injury cases such as Greta's. While in theory Barbara may be indifferent between her house being burned down by Alex and a sum of money compensating her for the loss of the house in the fire, it is hard to imagine that Greta, or anyone else, would agree to be permanently paralyzed or disabled in exchange for any sum of money, even if she were to be perfectly compensated for her medical expenses and future lost wages. Furthermore, if we are going to use money to compensate Greta for the emotional distress she has suffered, what is the proper measure of such damages? It is to this issue that we turn in the next section.

Example 1

Hillary steals Ira's digital camera and throws it into the river, destroying it. Ira bought the camera for $300 one year ago. Today a camera with similar features is worth $200. The market value of Ira's camera at the time Hillary stole it was $75. Ira sues Hillary in tort. What is the value of B in Figure 3.1? What is the value of A? How much are Ira's total damages in his tort suit against Hillary?

Explanation

The value of B is the easy part of this question. It is always zero. From the preceding chapter, we know that courts typically use market value at the time of the loss to measure plaintiff's losses. This means that A would be $75. But Ira might be able to argue for the higher replacement cost measure of $200 less depreciation (the camera is a year old, and thus worth less than a new camera). Recall that some courts allow for the higher measure of damages based upon replacement costs for certain household and consumer goods. (Alternatively, Ira might argue for the higher measure of damages based upon Hillary's bad conduct.) The total compensatory damages would therefore likely be either $75 or some amount near $200, plus (potentially, depending on the jurisdiction) prejudgment interest and likely postjudgment interest. There are no future expected losses, so there is no need to reduce any amounts to present value. This may also be a case where additional punitive damages are available (see Chapter 15).

3.2 PAIN AND SUFFERING, EMOTIONAL DISTRESS, AND OTHER "NONECONOMIC" DAMAGES

Courts and lawyers use different terminology to describe types of compensatory damages; "general," "special," "actual," "pecuniary," and "consequential" are some of the common names.[2] The labels are sometimes

---

2. For discussion of terminology, see DOBBS § 3.3; LAYCOCK pp. 56-58. See also *Federal Aviation Administration v. Cooper*, 132 S. Ct. 1441 (2012), on the varied meanings of "actual damages" and "general damages."

inconsistent and contradictory; to the extent possible, this book avoids such terminology and focuses instead on the principles that courts employ, regardless of the labels courts use.

Here, however, it is important to introduce a relatively new and increasingly important damages term in tort cases: noneconomic damages. *Noneconomic damages* include damages plaintiffs may claim for items with no functioning economic market, such as pain, suffering, and emotional distress. Such damage claims are distinct from *economic damages*, which are damages for which there *is* an economic market, such as the lost wages, property damages, and medical expenses we considered in the last chapter. Of course, even though noneconomic damages involve losses for which there is no functioning market, the losses they compensate for still have great value to people; most people who suffer serious pain because of a defendant's tort likely would not have accepted the pain for any amount of money offered by the defendant before the tort.

The economic/noneconomic distinction is important, because in recent years some states have enacted statutes[3] that have limited the amount or availability of noneconomic damages as part of the "tort reform" movement in an effort to limit the ability of plaintiffs to recover large damages awards. In California, for example, plaintiffs who are injured by a health care provider may recover no more than $250,000 in noneconomic damages. *See* CAL. CIV. CODE § 3333.2 (West 1997). The limit does not apply to other negligence suits.

Caps on noneconomic damages have been such a popular element of defendant-oriented tort reform in recent years because jurors sometimes award high noneconomic damages because there is no functioning market to serve as a baseline for jury determinations. The insurance industry in particular has claimed that caps on noneconomic damages are necessary to keep liability insurance rates — particularly medical malpractice insurance rates — in a reasonable range, pointing to a few cases of very high awards for noneconomic damages. On the other hand, plaintiffs' lawyers have argued that such caps are unnecessary, that the insurance "crisis" is a fiction, and that these limits tend to penalize the most severely injured people by undercompensating them. The empirical debate is rich, and is beyond what we can cover here.

In places where caps do not operate, and even in places where they do (for amounts below the cap), the question is how juries are to determine the value of noneconomic damages.[4] The problem begins with the lack of a

---

3. Much of tort law is judicially created common law. Legislatures can modify or reverse particular aspects of the common law by passing a statute.

4. For a useful contemporary debate over this question and related questions, see Symposium, *Who Feels Their Pain? The Challenge of Noneconomic Damages in Civil Litigation*, 55 DEPAUL L. REV. 249 (2006). Perhaps the title of Professor Abel's article sums up of the frustrations some scholars have shown with the award of noneconomic damages: Richard Abel, *General Damages Are Incoherent, Incalculable, Incommensurable, and Inegalitarian (but Otherwise a Great Idea)*, 55 DEPAUL L. REV. 253 (2006).

working market. As in the case with subjective valuation, as discussed in Chapter 2, there is no objective baseline for jurors to use in picking a number to compensate for the pain and suffering that someone like Greta suffers as a result of the accident. Some economists want to look for market proxies such as the amount of insurance an individual would choose to buy covering her own health, but these measures generally are not introduced as evidence, and even among scholars debate rages over whether this insurance theory is appropriate for measuring noneconomic damages. For a critical analysis, see Ellen Smith Pryor, *The Tort Law Debate, Efficiency and the Kingdom of the Ill: A Critical Critique of the Insurance Theory of Compensation*, 79 VA. L. REV. 91 (1993).

An experiment I like to run in my Torts and Remedies classes is to give a variety of fact patterns such as Greta's that involve both more and less severe personal injury cases in which plaintiffs suffer noneconomic damages. I ask the students to independently write down how much they, as jurors, would award in such cases for the noneconomic portion of the damages, and I then poll the class. The range of responses is astounding, with responses usually ranging anywhere from zero to millions of dollars.

How much would you award Greta? How did you decide on that number? What other information would you want to know before deciding on an amount?

As one of the party's lawyers, think about how you might argue on Greta's or Frank's behalf for the right amount of damages for Greta's pain and suffering. If you were Greta's lawyer, you might try to ask for a certain amount per day (the "per diem" argument), which, when carried out over a long period of time, can yield a significant amount of damages. Suppose you ask for $10 per hour, 16 hours a day, 7 days a week, 52 weeks per year, for 40 years. That amounts to over $2.3 million.[5] Some courts allow such per diem arguments, but others do not. *See Botta v. Brunner*, 138 A.2d 713 (N.J. 1958) (partially overruled by statute). What could you, as Frank's lawyer, say in response to a per diem argument if plaintiff is allowed to make the argument?

Lack of adequate market valuation for noneconomic damages leads to other, bigger problems. We all recognize that in serious cases of noneconomic damages, any award of damages is likely to be undercompensatory because there is no amount of money that, say, a healthy 30-year-old woman would trade for a lifetime of paralysis and pain. On the other hand, courts (and society) won't tolerate infinitely large damage awards, while in cases of less severe noneconomic damages, some courts are suspicious that plaintiffs may overstate the extent of their noneconomic damages to reap a windfall from the defendant. Finally, the lack of any established

---

5. Should the amount of noneconomic damages be reduced to present value? Michigan by statute requires that damages be so reduced. *See* MICH. COMP. LAWS ANN. § 600.6306(1)(e).

market means that juries are likely to reach highly divergent decisions on the appropriate amount of noneconomic damages.

How do courts deal with these conflicting forces and the non-uniformity in those situations where the legislature has not imposed a cap or other limit on the amount of noneconomic damages?

Courts sometimes will lower the amount of such damages on a motion from the defendant on grounds that the amount of the award is so high as to "shock the conscience" (or some similar verbal formulation). The "shock the conscience" standard allows for more open-ended judicial review of verdicts; sometimes to achieve a level of uniformity across cases, judges will compare verdicts in similar cases and make adjustments to outlier verdicts.

Procedurally, the judge who wishes to lower the amount of damages awarded by a jury uses the device of *remittitur*, which gives the plaintiff the option of either taking the lower amount chosen by the judge or having a new trial on the issue of damages. In some jurisdictions, a judge may use the device of *additur*, which gives the defendant the option of taking a *higher* amount of damages chosen by the judge or a new trial on the issue of damages. But the *additur* procedure in some states, and on the federal level, has been held to violate the right to a jury trial and is therefore unavailable. (In a jurisdiction barring *additur*, a trial judge believing the amount of damages is too low can only order a new trial.)

In addition, courts traditionally have put limits on plaintiffs' ability to recover damages for emotional distress that is unaccompanied by any physical injury to plaintiffs — in part out of the fear that plaintiffs could feign or exaggerate their emotional distress injuries. Some jurisdictions have relaxed the requirement of a "physical impact" to one requiring plaintiffs to be in the "zone of physical danger" (e.g., plaintiff suffers emotional distress when nearly hit by an automobile). Going further, in some jurisdictions, one can recover emotional distress damages for witnessing injury to another (e.g., witness sees victim run over by a car driven by defendant). But the courts often impose additional requirements on witness recoveries, such as a requirement that the witness suffer *severe* emotional distress and that the victim and witness be relatives (or that the witness manifest some physical symptom from witnessing the injury). *See Dillon v. Legg,* 441 P.2d 912 (Cal. 1968); RESTATEMENT (SECOND) OF TORTS § 46; RESTATEMENT (THIRD) OF TORTS: LIABILITY FOR PHYSICAL AND EMOTIONAL HARM § 45. Depending upon the jurisdiction, these requirements are not always hard-and-fast rules; some courts will allow recovery in cases not meeting the usual limits and even in cases absent physical harm where emotional distress damages are *particularly foreseeable*, such as in the case of mishandling of human remains. *Christensen v. Superior Court,* 820 P.2d 181 (Cal. 1991).

Finally, courts sometimes allow plaintiffs to recover for "dignitary" losses. A dignitary harm awards damages for an affront to the person, such as the offensive battery Charlene committed when she kissed Barry as he slept. As Dobbs explains: "in a great many of the cases, the only harm is the affront to the plaintiff's dignity as a human being, the damage to his self-image, and the resulting mental distress." DOBBS § 7.1(1). Even without proof of emotional distress, courts sometimes allow the recovery of substantial damages "merely upon showing that the tort was committed at all." Id.

Example 2

While undergoing a Caesarean section at the hospital, Emma suffered oxygen deprivation as a result of the negligence of Doctor G. The oxygen deprivation resulted in severe brain damage and left Emma in a permanent comatose condition. Can Emma recover noneconomic damages? If so, how much should she collect?

Explanation

The facts of this example are based on *McDougald v. Garber*, 536 N.E.2d 372 (N.Y. 1989). The problem is this: Suppose plaintiff is too injured to experience pain and suffering. Should compensation still be available? Plaintiff's lawyers argued that even if plaintiff could not experience emotional distress, loss of enjoyment of life was an objective loss (like the loss of a leg) that should be compensated for, even if plaintiff is not aware of the loss. Many courts accept such arguments (sometimes under the label "hedonic damages"), but a majority of the *McDougald* court rejected the argument. The majority noted the paradox under its rule that the greater the degree of brain injury inflicted by the negligent defendant, the smaller the award of damages. But the court said that this argument "has nothing to do with meaningful compensation for the victim" and is instead rooted in a temptation "to punish the defendant in proportion to the harm inflicted." The court did hold, however, that if there was evidence of *any* cognitive awareness on the part of the plaintiff, the plaintiff could recover damages for pain and suffering in an amount set by the jury.

As to the amount (assuming plaintiff has some cognitive awareness of pain), this is going to be a very difficult decision for the jury, with a very sympathetic and innocent plaintiff who suffered a terrible loss. It will be a delicate job on the part of defense lawyers to argue against a large damages award. Note that in California, the most that Emma could recover in noneconomic damages is $250,000. But if another plaintiff suffered an identical injury as the result of Doctor G.'s negligent driving, there would be no limit on the amount of noneconomic damages.

Example 3

Charlie donated blood at the local blood bank. Dave, the technician drawing the blood, accidentally drew Charlie's blood with a used needle. "Whoops," Dave said, explaining to Charlie that he should get tested for HIV (the virus which causes the disease AIDS) in six months because there was a small risk Charlie had been exposed to HIV by the used needle, and it took that long for HIV to show up in blood tests. Charlie suffered severe emotional distress for the next six months and saw a therapist regularly. Fortunately for Charlie, his blood test six months later was negative for any signs of HIV. Can Charlie recover damages? If so, for what?

Explanation

Charlie will have a strong argument for the costs of medical monitoring (including his HIV tests) to make sure that he does not have the potentially deadly disease. But those costs will be relatively low. Charlie will want to recover potentially larger damages for his emotional distress, which looks real and severe. On policy grounds, however, some courts have held that defendants cannot be liable for emotional distress damages for fear of getting a disease, unless the plaintiff can prove that she is more likely than not to actually get the disease. *Potter v. Firestone Tire & Rubber*, 863 P.2d 795 (Cal. 1993). The courts are apparently concerned about a flood of suits arising from fear-of-cancer claims and similar claims related to toxic waste dumps.

Charlie could not meet the *Potter* standard with his negative HIV test result, and it looks like the damage rule, if applied in Charlie's jurisdiction, will ensure that Charlie's recovery will not restore him to the rightful position. Moreover, if Dave's conduct was only negligent, Charlie will not be able to recover punitive damages either (see Chapter 15).

Example 4

Jeff Spicoli was a student at Ridgemont High School. The school's principal saw Spicoli smoking what the principal believed, by shape and smell, to be a marijuana cigarette. Without recovering the cigarette or giving Spicoli a chance to explain himself, the principal suspended Spicoli for 20 days. Applicable constitutional precedent gives someone in Spicoli's position the right to a hearing before suspension. Spicoli suffered no emotional distress, and he did not contend he was innocent of the principal's allegations. He sued for the dignitary harm of losing his due process right to a hearing. Can Spicoli recover damages?

Explanation

This claim is somewhat distinct from the earlier claims in that here the intangible loss is not emotional distress but rather a dignitary harm — in this case, harm that occurs when a government body violated Spicoli's constitutional rights. In *Carey v. Piphus*, 435 U.S. 247 (1978), the Supreme Court held that proof of a constitutional violation entitled the student, Piphus, to nominal damages, but that he could not recover additional damages unless he could prove them (for example, prove that he suffered emotional distress). Piphus had argued the jury should be able to simply award him "presumed" damages (see section 3.4), but the Court rejected the argument.

This ruling is significant. True, there will be many cases where the government's unconstitutional conduct can cause emotional distress (or even physical harm). But in those cases where emotional distress is absent, the *Piphus* ruling may well be limiting the deterrent value of bringing such lawsuits, especially because a later Supreme Court case has suggested that in cases where the court awards only nominal damages, a reasonable attorney's fee (available by statute in federal civil rights cases) could be no fee at all. *Farrar v. Hobby*, 506 U.S. 103 (1992). Nonetheless, an award of nominal damages could keep the door open for punitive damages in an appropriate case.

3.3 SPECIAL RULES FOR WRONGFUL DEATH, SURVIVOR, AND LOSS OF CONSORTIUM ACTIONS

3.3.1 Wrongful Death

The ultimate mismatch between the rightful position standard and applicable damages rules occurs when the defendant's injury results in death. The mismatch occurs in two ways. First, there is no amount of money that most of us would ever exchange for our own lives; therefore any amount of money for wrongful death is going to be undercompensatory (especially considering that the person who has died as the result of the defendant's actions will not receive any of the money). Second, by an accident of history, wrongful death damages are statutorily limited to be less generous than the typical tort measures available to plaintiffs in cases that do not result in death. The upshot of this mismatch is that defendants often pay more damages when they seriously injure someone than when death results (hence the apocryphal morbid statement of the defense attorney, "Fortunately for my client, the plaintiff died").

I start with the history, because — as with much of the material that we will see in this book — the dead hand of history drives many of the current remedies rules that seem counterintuitive or outdated. Briefly,[6] in 1808 a judge in England rejected the husband's claim for damages when the defendant's wrongful conduct caused the death of the husband's wife, holding that the common law did not allow for such damages. *Baker v. Bolton*, (1808) 170 Eng. Rep. 1033 (K.B.). The English Parliament overruled *Baker* in 1846, but the statute doing so set forth limits on who could recover and the kind of damages allowed. The parliamentary decision precluded any further evolution of the common law, which meant that the extent of plaintiffs' recovery in the case of wrongful death depended upon how the legislative body defined the scope of recovery.

Baker was accepted as precedent in many parts of the United States. Even today, in many states the ability of a person to recover damages for the wrongful death of a family member depends upon, and is limited by, the state's wrongful death statute. Here is a portion of Kansas's wrongful death statute:

> (a) In any wrongful death action, the court or jury may award such damages as are found to be fair and just under all the facts and circumstances, but the damages, other than pecuniary loss sustained by an heir at law, cannot exceed in the aggregate the sum of $250,000 and costs.

KAN. STAT. ANN. § 60-1903(a) (2005). Note the key limiting feature here: heirs can recover for financial losses, but spouses face a cap of $250,000 on "non-pecuniary" damages, a term which the Kansas courts read as equivalent to noneconomic damages. *See Howell v. Calvert*, 1 P.3d 310, 316 (Kan. 2000). Children, as we shall see, cannot recover noneconomic damages for loss of a parent.

Kansas's wrongful death statute is generous compared to New Jersey's statute:

> In every action brought under the provisions of this chapter the jury may give such damages as they shall deem fair and just with reference to the pecuniary injuries resulting from such death, together with the hospital, medical and funeral expenses incurred for the deceased, to the persons entitled to any intestate personal property of the decedent. . . .

N.J. STAT. ANN. § 2A:31-5 (2007). Note how the statute limits recovery for wrongful death only to pecuniary losses. The New Jersey Supreme Court defined pecuniary losses under this statute to include "the contributions, reduced to monetary terms, which the decedent might reasonably have been

---

6. For a very readable summary of the development of the law of wrongful death and related areas, *see* RICHARD A. EPSTEIN, CASES AND MATERIALS IN TORTS 901-909 (9th ed. 2008).

expected to make to his or her survivors," as well as "the hospital, medical and funeral expenses incurred for the deceased." *Smith v. Whitaker*, 734 A.2d 243, 248 (N.J. 1999). Moreover, punitive damages are not available under New Jersey's wrongful death statute. *Id.*

Example 5

Eric, driving home drunk from a party, runs over Ferdinand and his 8-year-old daughter Gina, killing them both. Ferdinand and Gina are survived by Henrietta (Ferdinand's wife and Gina's mother) and Isaac (Ferdinand's son and Gina's brother). Ferdinand worked as a school teacher, earning $60,000 per year. He was 40 years old. Henrietta and Isaac sue Eric for wrongful death, and both are emotionally devastated. Who can sue successfully? Explain.

Explanation

There is no way to confidently answer this question without knowing the state where the accident occurred and its applicable wrongful death statute. So let's consider things under the Kansas and New Jersey statutes I have provided. In Kansas, the "heirs at law" are able to recover, so you would need to consult Kansas law over who constitutes an heir. Assuming that Henrietta is an heir, she will be able to recover pecuniary damages (which will include funeral expenses for both her husband and child) and the present value of the expected support that Ferdinand would have provided to her had he not been killed by Eric. Recall from the last chapter that the jury, in computing this amount, would need to make predictions about the likely job and salary prospects for Ferdinand had he continued to work. The jury would likely start with the $60,000 per year salary and then, relying upon experts, would make certain assumptions about what Ferdinand would have earned for the rest of his working career. The total amount of the award would then be reduced to present value.

Note that because Henrietta cannot prove with any reasonable certainty that she would have been financially supported at any time in her life by Gina had Gina not died, there would be no recovery for pecuniary damages for the death of Gina aside from funeral expenses. Henrietta would also be able to recover up to $250,000 each for non-pecuniary damages for emotional distress.

If Isaac does not count as an heir under Kansas law, he would not be able to recover anything (nor would any other relatives or close friends of Ferdinand or Gina who do not count as heirs). If he is an heir, as we'll see below in the discussion of loss of consortium claims, he can recover emotional distress damages for the death of a parent.

Things would be much the same for the surviving family members under New Jersey law, except that neither Henrietta nor Isaac could recover non-pecuniary damages in a cause of action for wrongful death. But, as we shall see, that does not exhaust the possible causes of action.

3.3.2 Survival of Personal Injury Actions

While Kansas may seem more generous than New Jersey when it comes to compensation for surviving family members of a tort victim, that's only because we have focused only on one possible cause of action, that for wrongful death. But there are other ways survivors may recover damages. Some states, like New Jersey for example, have reversed a common law rule that a personal injury action dies with the person. Consequently, surviving family members can recover damages for any pain and suffering that the tort victim suffered before his death. In New Jersey, even if a tort victim is killed instantly (and therefore suffered no pain before his death), the surviving family members can recover nominal damages for pain and suffering. Then, using those nominal damages as a hook, the surviving family members may recover punitive damages if the defendant's conduct was sufficiently bad. *Whitaker*, 734 A.2d at 253.

In Kansas, in contrast, there must be evidence of *conscious* pain and suffering before death in order for such damages to be recoverable in a survival action. *St. Clair v. Denny*, 781 P.2d 1043, 1049 (Kan. 1989). If there is such evidence, punitive damages may be awarded with the amount being based on the survival action only. *See Lake v. Res-Care Kansas, Inc.*, No. 98-1019-JTR, 2002 WL 32356436 (Kan. Feb. 4, 2002). This last limitation is significant because, as we shall see in Chapter 15.3, the amount of punitive damages generally must be within a single-digit ratio (that is, less than ten times) of the amount of compensatory damages. The Kansas rule would use the survival action damages as the baseline for judging the propriety of the ratio of punitive damages, which means that the punitive damage award would be much lower than an award that is pegged to damages that are recoverable in the wrongful death action as well.

Example 6

Henrietta and Isaac (from Example 5) are New Jersey residents. Their lawyer, Jamie, brings suit against Eric for wrongful death on the day before the statute of limitations runs on their claims. Jamie does not bring a survivor action, even though the evidence shows that before his death Ferdinand was in tremendous pain for a few hours after Eric ran him over. Eric, it turns out, is very wealthy. The jury awards wrongful death damages of $1 million, based upon the financial support that Ferdinand would have supplied to his surviving family members. May Henrietta and Isaac recover any other sums? From whom?

Explanation

They should sue Jamie! Jamie has committed legal malpractice by failing to bring a survivor action. Not only would this have allowed Henrietta to recover for Ferdinand's conscious pain and suffering (which the jury could have valued highly), it would have given the jury a hook for the award of punitive damages against Eric, who engaged in bad conduct by driving drunk and causing the accident. As we will see in Chapter 15.3, the fact that Eric is wealthy may not be a constitutionally permissible reason to increase the amount of punitive damages, but it does suggest that Eric should be able to pay the damages. Because the statute of limitations has run, the chance to bring suit against Eric has passed. This leaves a possible action against Jamie for failing to bring suit.

The broader lesson here is that lawyers bringing suit need to consider which causes of action allow for the remedies that are most advantageous for their clients. To the uninitiated looking at Henrietta and Isaac's case, it might appear that simply suing for "wrongful death" would be good enough. But, especially in this area of the law, where the dead hand of history controls so much, it is important to carefully research the right causes of action that allow for the most generous remedies for the clients.

3.3.3 Loss of Consortium Claims

One final claim that may be brought in connection with the death (or in some cases, the serious injury) of a close relative is an action for "loss of consortium." Such claims compensate the surviving family member for the emotional distress that results from the death or injury of a loved one. In England, such claims are barred. *See* EPSTEIN, *supra*, at 907. In the United States, the rules on loss of consortium differ from state to state. Earlier cases tended to show a distinct gender bias, limiting recovery to husbands and fathers and disallowing recovery by wives, mothers, and children. Now, the gender bias has disappeared.

Sometimes, a surviving spouse need not bring loss of consortium as a separate claim. Rather, the emotional distress damages (called non-pecuniary damages in this context) may be available in a statutory wrongful death action. Separate loss of consortium claims in those jurisdictions, however, might be needed in cases where a spouse is seriously injured but not killed.

In Kansas, a spouse may recover emotional distress damages (with a $250,000 cap) resulting from the injury or death of a spouse, whereas children (minor or adult) may not recover for the emotional loss resulting from injury to a parent. *Natalini v. Little*, 92 P.3d 567, 570 (Kan. 2004). Thus, children can recover loss of consortium damages for the death of a parent, but not for a parent's serious injury. (What is the logic behind that result?) *See Klaus v. Fox Valley Sys., Inc.*, 912 P.2d 703 (Kan. 1996).

In New Jersey, spouses may recover uncapped damages for loss of consortium, whereas children may not. *Russell v. Salem Transp. Co.*, 295 A.2d 862 (N.J. 1972). Moreover, parents may not recover for loss of consortium related to the death or injury of their children. *See Tynan v. Curzi*, 753 A.2d 187 (N.J. Ct. App. Div. 2000).

Although the law is in flux, today only a minority of states recognize a parent's right to recover for loss of consortium upon the death or injury of the parent's child, Todd R. Smyth, Annotation, *Parent's Right to Recover for Loss of Consortium in Connection with Injury to Child*, 54 A.L.R. 4th 112 (1987 & Supp. 2005), or the right of a child to recover for loss of consortium upon the death or injury of the child's parent. *ATLA's Litigating Tort Cases*, § 25:16.

Example 7

Jane and Kate are two women who live together as a married couple. The state they are living in does not recognize gay marriage. Jane is seriously injured in an automobile accident. May Kate recover for loss of consortium from the defendant, who caused the accident?

Explanation

The overwhelming weight of authority denies unmarried cohabitants the possibility of recovering damages for loss of consortium. Although a California court of appeal had at one point recognized the right of unmarried cohabitants to recover, the California Supreme Court rejected that precedent. *Elden v. Sheldon*, 758 P.2d 582, 589-590 (Cal. 1988).

Why do the courts tend to be unwilling to extend loss of consortium claims? The *Elden* court explained why the cause of action must be "narrowly circumscribed": "We advanced as reasons for this policy the intangible nature of the loss, the difficulty of measuring damages, and the possibility of an unreasonable increase in the number of persons who would be entitled to sue for the loss of a loved one." Convincing?

Beyond fact patterns that involve non-married cohabitants, in the process of drawing lines there are always going to be examples of cases with unfair results. As explained earlier, Kansas allows children whose parents are killed by the tortious conduct of defendant to recover emotional distress damages. The state, however, allows no emotional distress damages for children whose parents are permanently disabled (even to the point of not being able to function at all as parents). In many cases, courts uphold distinctions that appear arbitrary, and they leave it to legislatures to pass statutes in this area to create more uniform rules of liability.

3.4 PRESUMED DAMAGES (DEFAMATION)

Defamation is a tort defined as "the act of harming the reputation of another by making a false statement to a third person." BLACK'S LAW DICTIONARY 448 (8th ed. 2004). Oral defamation is slander; written defamation is libel. *Id.* A plaintiff who is defamed may suffer a variety of damages, including business losses (due to a damaged reputation) and emotional distress.

As we will see in Chapter 6.1, plaintiffs ordinarily must prove that their damages are *reasonably certain* in order to be able to recover them. What is unusual about defamation is that the common law allowed plaintiffs who sued for defamation to recover damages *even if they could not prove with reasonable certainty that they suffered such damages.*[7] These "presumed damages" can be significant in particular cases. Alternatively, a plaintiff could seek proven actual damages, sometimes referred to as "special damages" in this context.

Why relax the certainty requirement in certain defamation actions? Epstein explains that the exception has often been justified "to avoid the administrative and evidentiary problems that arise in seeking to prove special damages. The key premise is that a rough estimate is a better first approximation of the true state of affairs than the alternative presumption, which denies recovery altogether." EPSTEIN, *supra*, at 1063. It is not clear, however, that problems of proof in defamation actions are significantly different from problems of proof in other areas so as to justify the special rule of presumed damages in defamation cases.

Although defamation is a common law tort, the Supreme Court has ruled that the First Amendment places certain limits on the tort because the threat of liability could inhibit speech that is protected by the First Amendment. This is not surprising, given the numerous defamation cases that are brought against the news media, which often raises freedom of speech and freedom of press exemptions as defenses.

The first Supreme Court case limiting the tort of defamation on First Amendment grounds held that public figures could not recover damages for defamation without proof that the defendant made a false statement with "actual malice," which means proof that the defendant made the statement either with knowledge of its falsity or with reckless disregard of the truth. *New York Times Co. v. Sullivan*, 376 U.S. 254 (1964).

---

7. To be more precise, presumed damages were available only for cases of libel and for cases of "slander per se," involving: "(1) serious criminal offense or one of moral turpitude, (2) a 'loathsome' and communicable disease, (3) any matter incompatible with business, trade, profession, or office, and sometimes, (4) serious sexual misconduct." DAN B. DOBBS, THE LAW OF TORTS § 408 (2000). Any other slander would constitute "slander per quod," where proof of actual damages is necessary. In the nineteenth century some courts started allowing claims for "libel per quod," requiring proof of actual damages. *Id.*, § 409. The debate over the appropriateness of presumed damages in the defamation context continues today.

These First Amendment concerns in defamation cases have come to limit certain defamation *remedies* as well. In *Gertz v. Robert Welch, Inc.*, 418 U.S. 323 (1974), the Supreme Court held that the First Amendment sometimes precluded the award of presumed damages, such as in cases where a private person sues for defamation involving a matter of public concern.[8] The Court explained the clash between defamation law and the First Amendment as follows:

> The common law of defamation is an oddity of tort law, for it allows recovery of purportedly compensatory damages without evidence of actual loss. Under the traditional rules pertaining to actions for libel, the existence of injury is presumed from the fact of publication. Juries may award substantial sums as compensation for supposed damage to reputation without any proof that such harm actually occurred. The largely uncontrolled discretion of juries to award damages where there is no loss unnecessarily compounds the potential of any system of liability for defamatory falsehood to inhibit the vigorous exercise of First Amendment freedoms. Additionally, the doctrine of presumed damages invites juries to punish unpopular opinion rather than to compensate individuals for injury sustained by the publication of a false fact. More to the point, the States have no substantial interest in securing for plaintiffs such as this petitioner gratuitous awards of money damages far in excess of any actual injury.

Id. at 350.

The Supreme Court then limited *Gertz* in *Dun & Bradstreet, Inc. v. Greenmoss Builders, Inc.*, 472 U.S. 749 (1985). There the Court upheld an award of $50,000 in presumed damages (and an additional $300,000 in punitive damages), and held that the First Amendment did not limit the award of presumed damages in defamation cases related to speech that "do not involve matters of public concern." 472 U.S. 749, 763 (1985).

Example 8

Helen Willing, who is mentally unstable, is protesting for several hours each day against her former attorneys, wearing a sign reading "Law-Firm of Quinn-Mazzocone Stole Money from me and sold me out to the insurance company." The statement is a false one and it constitutes defamation under state law. As the lawyer representing the law firm, are you better off trying to prove the firm's damages or simply seeking to get the jury to award presumed damages (if available in the jurisdiction)? Would an award of presumed damages against Willing violate the First Amendment?

---

8. The Supreme Court also limited the ability of plaintiffs to recover punitive damages in defamation cases involving issues of public concern.

Explanation

Assuming presumed damages are available (this may constitute slander per se, because it involves the plaintiff's profession), it is risky to rely solely on presumed damages because the jury will still have to be convinced that there is some damage. The more proof you can provide, the better. The problem for the law firm here is that it does not know who is going to see the sign or how the defamatory statement is going to affect the law firm's reputation. It may be possible to find potential clients who were deterred by the sign (or actual clients who fired the firm), but it seems unlikely you could find much proof that Helen Willing's tactics deterred clients from employing the firm. If you were a potential client on your way to the offices of Quinn-Mazzocone, wouldn't you think twice before going up the elevator to hire the firm?

In appropriate cases, it makes sense to provide proof of the emotional distress that the defamatory statement caused a plaintiff. In a business or legal context, however, it may be more difficult to obtain significant damages for emotional distress; lawyers might not make the most sympathetic plaintiffs, and emotional distress may not be available in a business dispute. A problem arises with non-sympathetic plaintiffs when serious emotional distress (which could be proven through direct testimony) and losses to reputation (which are difficult to prove) are both considerations. For example, suppose Willing falsely accused her lawyer of sexually harassing her and of embezzling money from her. That sort of claim could lead to serious emotional distress and difficult-to-measure reputational loss. Given the difficulty of measuring emotional loss, does it make sense that the plaintiff would have to prove his emotional distress with reasonable certainty but not his reputational loss?

Because of the difficulty of proving reputational loss in defamation cases, it might make more sense to get an injunction preventing the defendant from making defamatory statements in the future (this is especially true if the defendant would not be able to pay for the damage she may cause). Unfortunately for plaintiffs in this position, however, the First Amendment might bar that alternative remedy as well as a prior restraint on speech, a point we shall return to in Chapter 7.5. *See Willing v. Mazzocone*, 393 A.2d 1155 (Pa. 1978).

The First Amendment may limit the ability of the lawyers to get presumed damages in this case as well. It depends upon what the Supreme Court in *Dun & Bradstreet* considers to be speech that does "not involve matters of public concern." Is it of public concern whether a lawyer stole money from a client? Arguably, the answer is yes, but in the *Dun & Bradstreet* case itself, the Justices disagreed on whether a false statement in a credit report sent privately to five recipients was a statement of no public concern.

The bottom line in a case such as Willing's is that First Amendment concerns may limit the ability of defamed plaintiffs to get a remedy that will truly compensate them for losses attributable to the defamatory statement.

3.5 OTHER LIMITS ON TORT DAMAGES: PROXIMATE CAUSE AND THE ECONOMIC HARM RULE

Many first-year law students start their torts courses with *Vosburg v. Putney,* 50 N.W. 403 (Wis. 1891), a case in which an 11-year-old kicked a 14-year-old in the shin. Unfortunately for both plaintiff and defendant, plaintiff had a preexisting infection, and the kick led to a nasty bone infection which resulted in the permanent loss of the use of plaintiff's leg. Although *Vosburg* is an important case on the tort question of the intent necessary to commit the intentional tort of battery,[9] for our purposes *Vosburg* is most noteworthy for its damages rule: you take the plaintiff as you find him.

Also known as the thin-skulled or egg-shell plaintiff rule (think Humpty Dumpty falling off the wall), the principle is one where, when it comes to tort damages, a plaintiff can recover all of his damages, even if the *extent* of his harm was unforeseeable. As we shall see, this rule contrasts markedly with damages in contract law, where the foreseeability of the extent of the harm is usually a requirement for the recovery of damages.

The defendant in *Vosburg* certainly never intended to permanently disable the plaintiff, yet once the defendant tortiously injured the plaintiff, he became liable for the full extent of damages. Damages are likely to be substantial to compensate a child who will face pain, suffering, and disability for the rest of his life. The harshness of the thin-skulled plaintiff rule for defendants likely put pressure on tort law to limit damages in other ways, and it is to those other ways that we now turn.

First, we have already seen in section 3.2 that courts (and sometimes legislatures) have limited *the noneconomic damages* that some plaintiffs receive. Though in recent decades it certainly has become easier for plaintiffs to recover for such injuries, courts continue to impose — and even create — new limits on the ability of plaintiffs to recover for certain emotional distress and pain and suffering damages.

Proximate cause also functions like a limitation on damages even though it is, strictly speaking, part of plaintiff's prima facie case that she must prove in tort law. As anyone who has sat through a Torts class knows, the rules of proximate cause are confusing, contradictory, and complex. What is important for our purposes, however, is not to master the intricacies of the distinction between the directness test of the *Polemis* case[10] and the "foreseeability of type of harm" test in *Wagon Mound* (No. 1).[11] Rather, it is

---

9. The court held that intent to harm the plaintiff was not required for proof of battery, just an unconsented intentional touching.
10. In *re Polemis & Furness, Withy & Co.,* 3 K.B. 560 (1921).
11. *Overseas Tankship (U.K.) Ltd. v. Morts Dock & Eng'g Co.,* [1961] A.C. 388 (P.C. 1961) (appeal taken from Austl.). The new Restatement (Third) Torts: General Principles § 29 may well add some much needed clarity to this area of the law by abandoning the Second Restatement's

to note that proximate cause holds certain acts as too "remote" or not a "substantial factor" in causing plaintiff's harm to act as a rule that limits damages, and one that does so on policy grounds. Recall Justice Andrews' famous words in his dissent in *Palsgraf v. Long Island R.R.*, 162 N.E. 99 (N.Y. 1928) (Andrews, J., dissenting):

> A cause but not the proximate cause. What we do mean by the word "proximate" is, that because of convenience, of public policy, of a rough sense of justice, the law arbitrarily declines to trace a series of events beyond a certain point. This is not logic. It is practical politics.

Indeed, Justice Andrews used this political explanation to justify a (now discredited) proximate cause rule for New York, which stated that if a defendant negligently started a fire and burned down a row of houses, the defendant would be liable to pay damages only for the first house burned. The destruction of the following houses, by contrast, was not "proximately caused" by the defendant's negligent conduct. *Id.*, discussing the rule in *Ryan v. New York Cent. R.R. Co.*, 35 N.Y. 210 (1866).

The policy behind the "one-house rule" of *Ryan* was a fear of "crushing liability": "To hold that the owner must not only meet his own loss by fire, but that he must guarantee the security of his neighbors on both sides, and to an unlimited extent, would be to create a liability which would be the destruction of all civilized society." *Id.* The court in *Ryan* thus placed the fear of crushing liability over the rights of the plaintiff to recovery. The court neither recognized bankruptcy law as a natural stopping point for the payment of damages, nor considered the inconsistency of this approach with the rationale behind the rule of *Vosburg* (which held defendants responsible for the full extent of damages caused to the plaintiff); rather, the *Vosburg* court held that between two parties, one of whom tortiously caused damage and the other of whom is innocent, it is fairer to put the burden of damages on the party who tortiously caused the damage.

Ryan is no longer good law even in New York, but the concern about crushing liability in tort law remains. In this regard, imagine that you are driving on one of the massive freeways that make Los Angeles famous, and because you are trying to text-message your friend while driving, you get into a fender-bender. You hit the car in front of you and get bashed from behind, and the three-car pileup you have created leads to a massive traffic jam. You cause literally hundreds of people behind you to be late for work, and they want to come after you because your negligence has led to their lost wages. (Indeed, in one of the cars behind you is a partner at the law firm

---

"substantial factor" test and replacing it with a rule that limits an actor's liability to harms "that result from the risks that made the actor's conduct tortious." This "harm within the risk" approach is roughly equivalent to the "foreseeability of type of harm" test adopted in the *Wagon Mound II* case.

where you worked as a summer associate, and you have caused her to miss a meeting that she would bill at $650 per hour.)

With this hypothetical, you may have gained a little more sympathy for the *Ryan* defendant who burned down the row of houses. Imagine if you could be liable for all the damages of everyone who was stuck in that traffic jam. It is no exaggeration to say that you might need to declare bankruptcy. Indeed, if it were the rule that those involved in an automobile accident would be liable to everyone who suffered economic harm as a result of the accident, the cost of obtaining automobile liability insurance might be prohibitive.

Fortunately for defendants who cause freeway accidents that tie up traffic, there is the *economic harm rule*. The rule provides that a plaintiff cannot recover for lost wages or other financial kinds of injury caused by a defendant's tortious conduct in the absence of physical impact resulting in personal injury or property damage.[12]

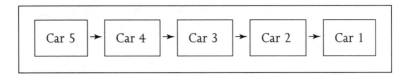

Figure 3.3 The Economic Harm Rule in Motion

To understand the application of this rule, reconsider the hypothetical using the diagram in Figure 3.3. You are the driver of Car 2. You rear-end Car 1 and then Car 3 crashes into you. Everyone agrees the accident is solely your fault. Cars 4 and 5 (not to mention cars 400 and 500) are then stuck for hours behind you on the freeway, but they were able to stop in time and were not involved in the collision. The driver of Car 3 and Car 4 work in the same office, and they are each paid $100 per hour for accounting services.

Under the economic harm rule, the drivers of Cars 1 and 3 can recover the full extent of the damages that you caused, from personal injury (whiplash anyone?) to property damage (dented bumper?) to lost wages on account of the accident. These lost wages are economic harm, but they can be *parasitic to* (that is, latch onto) the property damage and personal injury inflicted by the defendant. In contrast, the drivers of Cars 4 and 5 (and down the line), suffering neither property damage nor personal injury, cannot recover for their economic harm.

---

12. The American Law Institute is in the midst of a project to codify and clarify the economic harm rule as part of the Restatement (Third) of Torts: Liability for Economic Harm. Note that I am using the term "economic" in this case differently than the way I used it to contrast economic and noneconomic damages for purposes of limiting emotional distress and pain and suffering damage. Property damage does not count as "economic harm" for purposes of the economic harm rule, but it does count as economic damages under the rules differentiating between economic and noneconomic harm.

Note how this rule treats two similarly situated plaintiffs very differently. The drivers of Cars 3 and 4 both miss work because of your negligent driving. They work in the same place and get paid the same wages. But the driver of Car 3 gets to recover her economic losses because she was "lucky" enough to suffer personal injury or property damage from you as well.

What explains the economic harm rule? Again, the concern is crushing liability. The practical political concerns mentioned by Justice Andrews in his *Palsgraf* dissent animate the idea that sometimes the rightful position principle and the idea of full compensation for plaintiffs must give way for other social goods.

The economic harm rule is subject to an important exception: it does not apply when the only kind of harm a defendant can inflict upon the plaintiff is economic harm. Thus, if you go to your accountant and your accountant commits malpractice, causing you to pay a substantial tax penalty, the accountant cannot defend herself in a malpractice suit by claiming that you are only seeking compensation for economic harm. In this case, the only way that your accountant (as your accountant) can harm you is through this kind of economic harm, and if we applied the rule, accountants would virtually never be liable for accountant malpractice.

Example 9

Allied Chemical tortiously dumped a dangerous chemical into Chesapeake Bay, an area renowned for its commercial and sport fishing. The chemical caused a great deal of damage to the fish and wildlife, and as a result fishermen could not catch fish, owners of bait and tackle shops and restaurateurs lost business, and employees of the shops and restaurants were laid off. They all sue Allied. Must Allied pay for all the losses it caused?

Explanation

Although precisely how a court would sort through claims is open to question, it seems unlikely that all of the people who suffered losses as a result of Allied's tortious chemical pollution would be able to collect damages. Some of the plaintiffs, such as the employees of the restaurants, would likely lose under the economic harm rule. Can you see why? They suffered no physical impact resulting in property damage or personal injury.

Other plaintiffs might lose on proximate cause grounds, on duty grounds (courts since *Palsgraf* have held that only *foreseeable plaintiffs* may recover in negligence actions), or, if they seek emotional distress damages, because of limits on those kinds of recovery.

In the actual case upon which this hypothetical is based, *Pruitt v. Allied Chem. Corp.*, 523 F. Supp. 975 (E.D. Va. 1981), Allied conceded that commercial fishermen who depended upon the sea could recover for their lost profits even though they suffered neither personal injury nor property damage (they did not own the fish in the sea). The court held that certain other classes of plaintiffs could recover (including the shop and marina owners) but that those who purchased and marketed seafood from commercial fishermen could not recover. Echoing Justice Andrews in *Palsgraf*, the court stated, "The Court thus finds itself with a perceived need to limit liability, without any articulable reason for excluding any particular set of plaintiffs."

If Allied had not conceded that it was liable to the commercial fishermen, the court could have held that Allied could escape liability to all plaintiffs under the economic harm rule. However, the court seemed concerned that strict application of the economic harm rule could create insufficient deterrence for potential defendants similarly situated to Allied. On the other hand, allowing everyone who suffered some indirect harm from Allied's spill to recover damages could indeed lead to the bankruptcy of Allied, and the inability of other companies similar to Allied to obtain reasonably priced insurance. It is these concerns of "practical politics" that sometimes lead courts to draw somewhat arbitrary lines in these cases.

Example 10

The negligence of the captains of two ships, the Shiras and the Tewksbury, led to a collision between them on the Buffalo River in January. After the ships collided, they drifted, with one of them barely nicking another ship, the Farr. The two damaged ships crashed into a bridge over the river, forming a dam that stopped all river traffic for the winter. Grain being hauled on the Farr spoiled and could not be unloaded, leading to a $1 million loss. Grain on another ship, the Gilles, also was lost, leading to $500,000 in spoiled cargo. The owners of both the Farr and the Gilles sue the owners of the Shiras and the Tewksbury for the value of their lost cargo. Should the court allow them to recover? Explain.

Explanation

These are the facts of a famous economic harm case, the *Kinsman II, Petitions of the Kinsman Transit Co.*, 388 F.2d 321 (2d Cir. 1968). The court there denied recovery under the economic harm rule, but it noted that the case related to the Farr was "more troublesome of the two because the Farr was struck by either the Shiras or the Tewksbury and where there is physical damage to a vessel the owner can recover for the loss of use until repairs are completed . . . . But apparently [the owners of the Farr have] not sought recovery for physical damage to the Farr." *Id.* at n.7. The footnote hints at a possible claim of legal malpractice against the lawyer for the owners of the Farr: had the lawyer sued for the relatively minor physical damage caused in the collision, it is likely that the much more substantial economic harm could have been recovered as parasitic to this property damage. For the owner of the Gilles, however, it does not appear that good lawyering could get around application of the economic harm rule. Again, the lesson is that understanding the details of the damages rules is crucial to maximizing your client's recovery or defense.

Example 11

Larry pulled into an office parking lot to visit his financial advisor, Moe. Unfortunately, as Larry was coming in, Moe negligently backed out of his parking space, crashing into Larry. Larry suffered back injuries, damage to his car, and lost wages for one month. Another of Moe's client's, Curly, who was also trying to exit the lot, was stuck behind the collision and could not exit the parking lot. Because of the collision, he missed two hours of work at his software firm, losing $200 in salary. Who can recover from Moe? In what amounts?

Explanation

Larry will be able to recover damages for his personal injury (including his pain and suffering damages, subject to state law rules), property damage, and lost wages. These lost wages are economic harm, but they are parasitic to the personal injury and property damage caused by physical impact.

As a review, make sure you understand how the court is going to value the back injury (past medical expenses plus future medical expenses, reduced to present value, plus noneconomic damages as allowed in the jurisdiction), the damage to the car (cost of repair or decline in market value; see Chapter 2), plus the lost wages and interest.

Curly does not get to recover for his lost wages, because he suffered no physical impact leading to personal injury or property damage. His case falls squarely into the economic harm rule exception. Curly could *not* successfully argue that the exception to the economic harm rule should apply in this case, even though he suffered economic harm caused by his financial advisor, Moe. In this case, Moe caused economic harm to Curly not *as his financial advisor* but *as a driver*. It is a mere coincidence here that Moe is Curly's financial advisor, and Moe could have just as easily caused personal injury or property damage to Curly through Moe's negligent driving.

Contract Damages

4

4.1 INTRODUCTION TO CONTRACT DAMAGES: EXPECTANCY VERSUS RELIANCE

This chapter considers special issues that arise in the context of contract damages, beginning with the general measure of contract damages. As with tort damages, contract damages are concerned with restoring plaintiff to the *rightful position*, but as we shall see, courts usually measure the rightful position differently in torts and contracts cases.

Recall that when we speak of the rightful position in torts cases, we are almost always comparing the position of plaintiff before the wrong committed by the defendant (the "status quo ante," or Point B, which we set at 0) and the position of plaintiff after the wrong, Point A. See Figure 4.1.

Figure 4.1

4. Contract Damages

When it comes to damages in contracts, however, we are almost always comparing the position *that the plaintiff would have been in but for the wrong* ("breach") *committed by the defendant* and the position of the plaintiff after the wrong. Consider Figure 4.2.

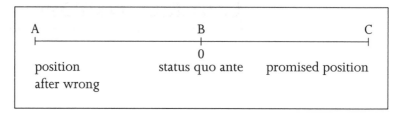

Figure 4.2

While the tort damage measure is typically (B − A), the contract damage measure is typically (C − A), or the *expectancy damages* (the difference between what was promised and what was received).

Why the difference? Consider this hypothetical. You own a window washing business. You sign a contract with Gary's World of Glass to wash the 200 windows on the outside of Gary's showroom. Gary agrees to pay you $3,000 upon completion of the work. You pay your crew to wash the windows and buy some window washing supplies. The total cost to you is $1,000. Your crew does a perfect job, but Gary refuses to pay, and you sue him for damages.

If we just used the regular tort measure of damages, your damages would be $1,000. You began at B, or 0, in relation to Gary. At the end of the transaction, you were out of pocket $1,000. Thus, A was −$1,000. It would take $1,000 to move you back to position B, making your damages under the tort measure $1,000.

In contract law, we would call those (B − A) damages your "reliance" damages. *In reliance on the contract with Gary*, you expended $1,000. In rare circumstances, as we will see in Chapter 5.3, courts will award plaintiffs in contracts suits only their reliance damages. But if you received merely reliance damages in this case, you likely would not feel as though you were put in the rightful position. Why not?

Imagine that Gary had not breached the contract. In that case, your account ledger would include costs of $1,000 (to perform the window washing contract) and a payment of $3,000 from Gary's business. Thus, focusing only on this transaction, your business's net balance would have been up by $2,000 — the profit you *expected* to make from the deal with Gary's World of Glass.

Contract law is about enforcing promises, and so the measure of damages *aims to put you in the same position as if the breaching party had performed the contract* (or what we might call the "rightful position" in contracts cases).

This expectancy damages measure requires comparing your position after the wrong to the *promised position* — *the position you would have been in but for the defendant's breach.*

In the case with Gary, the promised position (position C in Figure 4.2) is $2,000. This represents the profit that you would have earned had Gary not breached the contract. Your total damages would be (C − A), or ($2,000 − (−$1,000)), or $3,000.

This makes sense if the law is aiming at the rightful position standard. If you received damages of $3,000 after you had spent $1,000 having Gary's windows washed, you would have a net profit of $2,000, or the same amount as if there had been no breach (putting aside issues of attorney's fees, court costs, and the time value of money, discussed in Chapter 2).

Although in this example the amount of damages is equal to the contract price, it is not always the case that expectancy damages equal the contract price. For example, as we'll see below and in Chapter 6.2, if Gary had breached the contract *before* you had performed, you would have been treated as though you had made reasonable efforts to find alternative work during that time. If you had failed to *mitigate* your damages when you had the opportunity to do so, your damages would have been below your contract price. We will see many other situations (including Examples 1 and 2) in which expectancy damages do not equal the contract price.

Supporters of expectancy damages have offered both moral and economic justifications for the practice. As a matter of morality, if people fail to keep the promises they *should* keep, then the law should require them to pay *as though* they kept their promises.[1] In contrast, "[c]ompensation based on the reliance interest would assume that it is equally acceptable to perform or withdraw the promise, and that the promisee's only right is not to be made worse off than if the promise had never been made." Laycock p. 44.

There are efficiency arguments in favor of the expectancy measure as well. Without expectancy damages, people would have less reason to count on others to keep their promises, and therefore they would not be able to plan as efficiently for the future. Imagine in your window washing business that you did not know if your suppliers were going to show up with supplies as promised, or if your landlord was going to keep to his promises regarding maintenance of your leased space. Your employees might be wary of working for you if there were no laws backing up your promise to pay them wages for work completed. Future promises also have current value when they are backed up by expectancy damages.

---

1. One of the leading moral arguments for contract law is found in Charles Fried, Contract as Promise (1981).

Although the principle of expectancy damages is well ensconced in American law, it does have some academic critics. These critics argue that promisors should have the freedom to change their minds, or that promisees suffer little when a promise is broken, and therefore promisees should be able to recover no more than their reliance damages.[2] But this is by far a minority position among those who study American contract law.

Courts often give non-breaching parties the choice between reliance damages and expectation damages. This is useful for plaintiffs, especially in cases where expectation damages are hard to prove. They also could be useful in losing contracts. There is, however, some authority stating that expectation damages should serve as a cap on the amount of damages one can recover. *See* Richard L. Lord, 24 Williston on Contracts § 64:2 (4th ed. 2006) ("Expectation damages usually set the upper limit of recovery because they are designed to give the plaintiff exactly what was bargained for, and no more or less."). In losing contracts, as we will see in Chapter 11.4, restitution may turn out to be the best remedy for plaintiffs.

Example I

Assume the same facts as in the original window washing example above except that Gary paid you half the money in advance. Upon completion of the contract, Gary refuses to pay the remaining balance. Putting aside attorney's fees, court costs, and the time value of money, what are your damages?

Explanation

This is a contract case, so we want to use our $(C - A)$ expectancy damages measure rather than our $(B - A)$ reliance damages measure. Thus, we need to compute the values of C and A. The value of C is the same as in the original hypothetical. You, as the owner of the window washing company, expected a profit of $2,000 on this transaction. The value of A — the position you are in after Gary's breach — is a bit more complicated. It is sometimes useful to imagine a checkbook with money going in and out. In this variation on the window washing hypothetical, you have costs of $1,000 and a payment from Gary of $1,500. This means that your position after the wrong is $500.

This is significant, and worth a pause. In all the examples we have seen up to this point, the plaintiff's position after the wrong, A, has been *below* B, the status quo of 0. In this case, A is above B. See Figure 4.3. Using the $(C - A)$ formula, your damages would be $2,000 - $500, or $1,500.

---

2. One of the leading academic arguments against the expectancy measure of contract damages is found in P.S. Atiyah, The Rise and Fall of Freedom of Contract (1979).

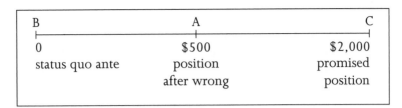

Figure 4.3

Example 2

Assume the same facts as in the original window washing example above except that Gary breached the contract before you performed, so you incurred no costs. (To eliminate problems related to mitigation, assume that Gary did so just before you were supposed to perform, so there was no other work you could get for the appropriate time.) Gary paid you nothing in advance. Putting aside attorney's fees, court costs, and the time value of money, what are your damages?

Explanation

Because this is a contracts case, we want to use our expectancy measure of damages, $(C - A)$. In this case, A is 0 because you have incurred no reliance costs: you have not paid for any workers to do the work, nor have you paid for any supplies. C remains at $2,000. Remember, C is *not* the contract price; it is the expected profit you stood to make had Gary kept his promise. Thus, your damages are $(C - A)$, or $2,000.

Again, this makes sense. At the end of the day, had you performed the contract, you would have received $3,000 in payment and spent $1,000 to fulfill your end of the deal, leaving you with a profit of $2,000. The expectancy measure leaves you in exactly the same place as if there had been performance.

Example 3

If courts enforced only reliance damages and not expectancy damages, what would your damages be under the original hypothetical where you spent $1,000 to perform and Gary failed to pay you after you performed the contract? What would the reliance damages be in Example 2? What would they be in Example 1, and how does your answer in terms of Example 1 make any sense?

Explanation

Recall that reliance damages measure your damages using the $(B - A)$ formula, where B is always the status quo ante, or 0. In the original example, A was $-\$1,000$, because you had spent $\$1,000$ on labor and supplies. Your reliance damages would be $(B - A)$, or $0 - (-\$1,000)$, or $\$1,000$ (compare this to the $\$3,000$ in expectancy damages from the original example).

In Example 2, $(B - A) = 0$. You had no reliance costs, and you therefore would recover nothing. (This compares to a recovery of $\$2,000$ in expectancy damages.)

In Example 1, recall that you had received a $\$1,500$ deposit, and that we computed the value of A as $\$500$. Using the formula $(B - A)$, the result would be something that looks like negative damages, $-\$500$! (This compares to a recovery of $\$1,500$ in expectancy damages.) When your damages total a negative number, it means that you are not entitled to damages.

When you think about it, this measure makes sense. Your reliance costs were $\$1,000$, yet you received $\$1,500$ as a deposit from Gary. So Gary's deposit more than covered your reliance losses. Indeed, if reliance were the proper measure of damages, Gary would likely be able to recover $\$500$ from you through an action in restitution, covered in Part III of this book.

These three examples should have shown you how much less generous the reliance measure of damages is compared to the expectancy measure. Think about how Gary — or others in situations similar to Gary's — might be more willing to breach the contract if the usual measure of damages is reliance damages because the cost of breaching is lower.

Similarly, think about your own willingness to enter into contracts if the measure of damages was only the reliance measure. You might be less willing to enter into contracts because you will have to reduce (or "discount") the upside potential of the surplus you make from a contract by the chances that the other party is going to breach the contract. Also, though you may want to ask for payment in advance because of the chance the other party might breach, the other party knows you might breach as well, and therefore, that other party may also be less willing to make payments in advance.

Example 4

Assume the same facts as in the original window washing example above except that Gary breached the contract after you had already spent $\$1,000$ on the project. To complete the project, you would have had to spend an additional $\$2,500$. What are your expectancy damages? What are your reliance damages?

Explanation

As soon as you start looking at the numbers, you will realize that this is a losing contract. Had Gary not breached the contract when he did, you would have spent $3,500 on a contract that would have yielded only a $3,000 payment. Thus, your expected position (had there been no breach) would have been a loss of $500, so your promised position in the expectancy formula is at −$500. Your position after the wrong is at −$1,000, or the amount you had spent in reliance on Gary's agreement to pay you.

Expectancy damages = (C − A) = −$500 − (−$1,000) = $500 Reliance damages = (B − A) = 0 − (−$1,000) = $1,000.

By now you should be able to see that expectancy damages put you in the same position that you would have been in had the contract been performed. Recall that if Gary had paid and you had performed, your bottom line would have been −$500 for this transaction. Similarly, if you had spent $1,000 in reliance costs and received $500 in damages, your bottom line upon recovering expectancy damages is −$500.

Because this is a losing contract, reliance damages look like a better deal for you than expectancy damages. There is, however, some authority stating that expectation damages should serve as a cap on the amount of damages one can recover. See Chapter 11.4. Under this rule, your reliance damages would be capped at the $500 expectancy damages measure.

There is another possible way for you to recover, however. If you have given Gary a benefit by washing some of his windows, you might be able to recover in restitution. Indeed, as we will see in Chapter 11.4, non-breaching parties to losing contracts often choose restitution as a way of maximizing their recovery.

4.2 THE THEORY OF EFFICIENT BREACH

We have seen that both the moral theorists (who view contracts as binding obligations) and the economic theorists (who want the courts or legislatures to choose efficient legal rules) tend to favor the use of expectancy damages in contract disputes. But they take very different views on the propriety of certain breaches of contract.

Going back to our window washing example, assume that you, rather than Gary of Gary's World of Glass, decided to breach the $3,000 window washing contract. You did so because you have only one crew and you received a call from Wanda's World of Windows to wash the windows of their showroom on the same day, but Wanda was willing to pay you $6,000. It would cost you the same $1,000 to do the work for Wanda as it would cost for Gary.

Both the moral theorists and economic theorists agree that if you break the contract, you should have to pay expectancy damages. The difference is that the moral theorists would tell you not to break the contract because when you made the contract you undertook a moral obligation to fulfill it. The economist, on the other hand, would tell you to break the contract if it is efficient to do so.

To explain this efficiency point, let's suppose that you gave Gary a good price on the window washing contract. When you breached the contract, Gary went out and hired a replacement window washing company to do the job at the prevailing market rate of $3,500. (How do we know the going market rate? Look back at the discussion in Chapter 2 on market valuations.)

Gary's expectation damages are $500. Do you see why? He was prom-ised window washing services worth $3,500 for $3,000. Thus, his prom-ised position (C) was $500, and he received nothing from you (though he had no reliance costs). His position after the wrong (A) is zero. Putting aside search costs to find a replacement window washing company, his damages are $500 − 0, or $500. This puts Gary in the same position he would have been in had the contract been performed. He spent $3,500 to have his windows washed. Now his windows are washed, and after receiving the $500 in damages from you, his total cost is $3,000, exactly the position he would have been in but for your breach.

But now think about your ledger. Had you kept your end of the bargain with Gary, you would have made a profit of $2,000 (remember, you had $1,000 in expenses on a $3,000 contract). If you break the contract and wash Wanda's windows, your total profit will be $4,500, which is $2,500 better than if you had kept your promise. Why $4,500? Again, you have $1,000 in expenses, but this time you are working on a $6,000 contract. That gives you $5,000 profit. You then have to pay damages of $500 to Gary, which leaves you with an overall balance of $4,500.

You can now see why an economist would think that breach makes sense in this case. It is efficient. Note that Gary is no worse off (putting aside the aggravation that comes from the lawsuit), and you are much better off.[3] In the meantime, your services have gone to the highest-valued user, or Wanda in this case. An economist would call this an *efficient breach* and would encourage you to do it. (The moralist, as we have said, would discourage the breach because it requires you to break your word.)

Not all breaches are efficient — but when the market works well with enough competition we won't see many inefficient breaches. In our latest window washing hypothetical, imagine that everything is the same except

---

3. Under the Kaldor-Hicks notion of efficiency (see Chapter 2), it is not required that Gary not be made worse off — it is only required that the gains to the winners exceed the losses to the losers. The fact that no party is made worse off means the transaction is also "Pareto efficient."

that you break the contract with Gary to do the job for Wanda at a cost of $3,100. When you break the contract, Gary is entitled to $500 for the breach. You take in $3,100 from Wanda, pay $1,000 in expenses, and then pay $500 to Gary, leaving you with $1,600. Remember, if you did not breach, you would have ended up with an overall profit $2,000.

Thus, if you understand these numbers, you would never choose to breach the contract with Gary *unless the additional amount you could make under the new contract exceeds the amount of damages you will need to pay to the non-breaching party.* In this case, Wanda would have to be offering more than $500 above Gary's contract price (and in the real world, probably considerably more than that if you care about your reputation) for it to be worthwhile for you to breach the contract.

Example 5

Use the same facts as in the original example in this section: you have a binding contract with Gary, and Wanda offers you $6,000 to do the same work for her instead of Gary. Gary, however, is one of your best repeat customers. Is it efficient for you to breach the contract with Gary? Even if it is efficient, what reasons would you have *not* to breach the contract with him?

Explanation

At first glance it appears efficient to breach the contract because the economic gains to the winners exceed any losses to the losers (and indeed, if damages are perfectly compensatory, Gary is made no worse off and you are made better off). But there are two reasons why you might choose not to breach the contract with Gary despite the efficiency of doing so. First, knowing Gary as you do, you might feel a moral obligation not to breach the contract. But even if you lack these moral scruples, it may not be in your economic interest to do so. Looking solely at the single transaction, it appears to make economic sense for you to breach. But if you have a long-term relationship with Gary, breaching now might harm your reputation with Gary as someone who keeps promises. Without that reputation, Gary might look to other businesses than yours next time he needs window washing services. In other words, the economic theory posits that Gary is indifferent between your performance and substitute performance from another vendor so long as you pay damages to compensate him for the lost value of the contract. But in the real world, Gary would probably be far from indifferent, particularly if he knows that you breached the contract to take a better deal. The human factor in breaching a contract is relevant, whether one cares about the morality of breaking a contract or only about pure economic gain. If the reputational costs of breaching exceed the benefits of breaching, it would be inefficient to breach.

4.3 CONSEQUENTIAL DAMAGES

Recall the defendant in *Vosburg v. Putney* (the "thin-skulled plaintiff" case in Chapter 3.5) who was unlucky enough to kick another child who had a preexisting medical condition. The kick, which should have led to a small bruise and no lawsuit, led instead to the plaintiff's loss of use of that leg and the defendant's facing a huge damage judgment.

The tort rule is that a defendant is liable to the plaintiff for all damages proximately caused by defendant's conduct, whether or not those damages are foreseeable.[4] If this rule applied in contracts as well, it potentially could greatly increase the cost of contracting.

To understand why, consider the seminal English case of *Hadley v. Baxendale* [1854] 9 Exch. 341, which you probably encountered in your Contracts class. The plaintiff operated a mill. The crankshaft at the mill broke, shutting down the mill. The plaintiff contracted with the defendant to bring the crankshaft to the engineers for repair. The defendant was late in delivering the crankshaft, breaching the contract. The mill was closed for a few extra days because of the late delivery, and the mill lost profits. Plaintiff tried to recover the lost profits caused by the defendant's breach. Just like the defendant in *Vosburg*, who was unlucky enough to kick the leg of the fragile plaintiff, the defendant in *Hadley* was unlucky enough to breach a contract with an economically fragile plaintiff.

The *Hadley* court, however, chose a different path from the one used by the *Vosburg* court. It set forth the following rule:

> Where two parties have made a contract which one of them has broken, the damages which the other party ought to receive in respect of such breach of contract should be such as may fairly and reasonably be considered either arising naturally, i.e., according to the usual course of things, from such breach of contract itself, or such as may reasonably be supposed to have been in the contemplation of both parties, at the time they made the contract, as the probable result of the breach of it.

The court then held that the plaintiff could not recover lost profits because they were not sufficiently foreseeable:

> Here it is true that the shaft was actually sent back to serve as a model for a new one, and that the want of a new one was the only cause of the stoppage of the mill, and that the loss of profits really arose from not sending down the new shaft in proper time, and that this arose from the delay in delivering the broken

---

4. This is something of an oversimplification, of course. As we saw in the last chapter, sometimes proximate cause, the economic harm rule, or some other tort limitation allows defendants to escape liability for some damage that they cause.

one to serve as a model. But, it is obvious that, in the great multitude of cases millers sending off broken shafts to third parties by a carrier under ordinary circumstances, such consequences would not, in all probability, have occurred; and these special circumstances were here never communicated by the plaintiffs to the defendants.[5]

The "rule" of Hadley thus divides the world of contract damages into those that are "natural," for which the plaintiff may recover, and those that are "consequential," for which plaintiff may recover only if the damages are sufficiently "foreseeable."

The dividing line between these "natural" damages (more commonly referred to as "general" damages) and consequential damages may at times not be crystal clear. Professor Dobbs provides a good first cut at the distinction: "General damages measure the losses in the very thing to which the plaintiff is entitled. . . . Consequential damages measure something else; not the very thing the plaintiff was entitled to but income it can produce or losses it can avoid." DOBBS § 3.3(4).[6]

For example, if you break the contract with Gary to wash his windows, the loss of value on the contract constitutes his general damages. In the example above, those general damages are $500, or the difference between the price you were offering to do the job for ($3,000) and the going market rate for the transaction ($3,500). There are likely no consequential damages in this example. But suppose that Gary cannot get the replacement window washers to do the job for three days. In the interim, Gary loses sales from three customers, who come to his showroom and decide not to purchase windows because they are turned off by the dirty windows in Gary's store. These lost sales would be consequential damages — damages which Gary would not be able to recover from you unless they were foreseeable at the time of contracting, that is, unless you knew (or reasonably should have known) at the time of contracting that Gary would suffer these losses because of your breach.[7] If you knew about these potential losses at the time of contracting, you might have decided to charge Gary a higher

---

5. This portion of the opinion seems to contradict the beginning of the case, which reports, "The plaintiffs' servant told the [defendant's] clerk that the mill was stopped, and that the shaft must be sent immediately. . . . " Hadley v. Baxendale, [1854] 9 Exch. 341. See also Donald C. Langevoort, Agency Law Inside the Corporation: Problems of Candor and Knowledge, 71 U. CINN. L. REV. 1187, 1188 n.9 (2003) ("Hadley v. Baxendale is confusing on its facts because of an inconsistency as to whether the railroad 'knew' of the factory's special needs. Its agent was apparently told, but it was unclear at that time whether that was sufficient notice to the principal.").

6. Section 4.5 below discusses the Uniform Commercial Code's definition of consequential damages.

7. Even if the consequential damages in this circumstance were sufficiently foreseeable, Gary might have a problem proving the damages with reasonable certainty, a requirement we discuss in Chapter 6.1. Note also that special damages have to be specifically stated in a complaint in federal court. See FED. R. CIV. P. 9(g).

premium to compensate for the increased risk you faced for breaching the contract.

Hadley sets forth *a default rule* that breaching parties are not liable for special losses plaintiff may suffer by virtue of the breach absent evidence the defendant knew (or perhaps should have known) of the danger of plaintiff suffering these special losses. This is a default rule because it is the rule that is in place unless the parties *bargain around it*. (The next section of this chapter discusses liquidated damages and other ways that parties may bargain around contractual remedies.) The default rule on consequential damages may lower the cost of contracting by picking the rule that most contracting parties would likely agree to if they actually bargained over it. Indeed, it has become common for parties to put a "no consequential damages" clause in their standard form contracts just to be sure that there won't be a claim later that the defendant actually knew of the special losses plaintiff would suffer in the event of defendant's breach. Here is language from a FedEx shipping contract:

> WE WILL NOT BE LIABLE FOR ANY DAMAGES, WHETHER DIRECT, INCIDENTAL, SPECIAL OR CONSEQUENTIAL, IN EXCESS OF THE DECLARED VALUE [OF A SHIPMENT] . . . WHETHER OR NOT WE KNEW OR SHOULD HAVE KNOWN THAT SUCH DAMAGES MIGHT BE INCURRED, INCLUDING, BUT NOT LIMITED TO LOSS OF INCOME OR PROFITS.

If "no consequential damages" is the default rule for contracts claims, why is it not also the default rule for torts claims? The reason is that most torts do not involve a voluntary transaction entered into by two willing parties (think of the plaintiff in *Vosburg* who received the kick in the leg). In the world of torts, the costs of bargaining — what economists call transaction costs — are exceptionally high, so the parties will not bargain around any default rules. Thus, the choice of default rules matters a great deal in torts (much more than in contracts). The law chooses a rule allowing consequential damages in torts (the thin-skulled plaintiff rule) that arguably most of us would choose if transaction costs for torts were not so high.

The rule regarding consequential damages in contracts is subject to an important exception. Let's return for a moment to our original window washing hypothetical where Gary breaches his promise to pay you $3,000 after you wash the windows perfectly.

We're going to add a few more facts to this fact pattern. Suppose that before you entered into the contract, you said to Gary: "It's a good thing for me that we've signed this contract. If I don't get this payment from you right after my crew washes your windows, I won't have enough money to pay my business rent and I'll be kicked out of my office." After Gary failed to pay for your services as promised, you are evicted from your office, thereby losing a great deal of other business.

In addition to suing Gary for general damages under the contract for the contract price that he owes you (the difference between what was promised and received, here $3,000), you may also consider suing him for the lost profits that resulted, arguing that they were consequential damages caused by Gary's nonpayment. It would be hard for Gary to claim that these damages were unforeseeable because *you specifically told him about the losses you would incur* if he failed to pay the contract on time. Thus, it looks like Gary could be on the hook to you for a lot more than the $3,000 contract price.

Fortunately for Gary (but unfortunately for you), the rule regarding consequential damages in contracts is subject to an important exception: when the only breach of contract is the nonpayment of money, the non-breaching party may not be able to recover for consequential damages. Instead, the non-breaching party may recover only the general damages (the unpaid money) plus interest at the prevailing legal rate of interest. *See Meinrath v. Singer Co.*, 87 F.R.D. 422 (S.D.N.Y. 1980).

The exception for nonpayment of money is itself subject to some exceptions, the most important being a suit by an insured against an insurer for a bad faith refusal to pay policy benefits. "The insured has no claim merely for failure to pay or delay in payment. But if the insurer refuses or delays in bad faith, knowing that it is liable, plaintiff can sue not only for interest, but also for consequential damages, emotional distress, and punitive damages." *See* LAYCOCK p. 62. The law treats these cases as torts, and not merely as breaches of contract, allowing for the recovery of consequential damages.

Do these distinctions make sense? If the true test for consequential damages in contracts cases is foreseeability, why shouldn't Gary have to pay you for those additional damages that were clearly foreseeable at the time of contracting — especially when you may well have to pay him for consequential damages you cause if you breach the contract? Perhaps the concern is that there would end up being many more disputes over what was "foreseeable" in cases involving the nonpayment of money than in other cases. Should a concern over the administrability of the rule allow the courts to treat you and Gary differently?

Perhaps the easiest way to deal with cases involving the nonpayment of money is to assume that non-breaching parties who are not paid will simply go out and borrow money from someone else to cover their expenses until the breaching party pays damages. One problem with this theory is that some of these non-breaching parties, who may be in dire financial straits, won't be able to borrow money or will have to borrow money at rates of interest higher than the prevailing rate (because they are bad credit risks). Note that non-breaching parties who must pay the higher rate of interest often cannot recover it. *See id.*

Finally, why the exception to the exception in the bad faith insurance cases? This distinction may be easier to understand if one views insurance contracts as special: plaintiffs arguably are especially vulnerable, or plaintiffs are "buying peace of mind" rather than simply entering into business arrangements. Still, there's no denying that the rule, exception, and exception to the exception in the case of consequential damages will end up treating similarly situated non-breaching parties differently.

Example 6

Helena was moving to Chicago from Nashville. While in Chicago, she signed a contract with Ivan to rent an apartment at the rate of $1,500 per month for a year, beginning immediately. She told Ivan she would return to Nashville and transport her household items immediately. Helena returned to Nashville, packed up her things, and had a moving truck transport her stuff from Nashville to Chicago for $4,000. When Helena arrived in Chicago, she found that Ivan had rented the apartment to someone else for $2,200 per month for a year. Helena checked into a hotel for a week, at a rate of $125 per night. She put her stuff in storage for $300. After diligently searching for another apartment, she found one comparable to the one she had agreed to rent from Ivan for $2,000 a month. She signed a year lease at the new apartment. She sued Ivan for breach of contract. The court agreed that Ivan breached the contract and owed Helena damages. How much is Helena entitled to receive in damages? Explain.

Explanation

You can see here that there are going to be both general damages (for the loss of the apartment) and a host of consequential damages attributable to the breach. We begin with the general damages in an effort to figure out the promised position (C) of Helena.

Helena had a contract to rent an apartment for $1,500 per month that arguably had a market rate of $2,000 per month. (The $2,200 contract price for the apartment is some contrary evidence of the market rate, but it may be that the new renters are paying over the contract price. The facts tell you that $2,000 is the market rate for this type of apartment.) Helena thus was expecting $500 per month in gains ($2,000 market rate −$1,500 contract rate) for 12 months, or $6,000. Those are her general damages.

The next question is whether Helena may be able to recover *consequential damages*. Because this is a contracts case rather than a torts case, Helena may recover only consequential damages that were *reasonably foreseeable* to the contracting parties at the time of contract formation. Helena told Ivan that she was moving her stuff from Nashville, with the expectation that she could have moved in immediately. Arguably the jury will find that the additional damages that Helena suffered because of Ivan's breach were reasonably foreseeable to the parties.

In thinking about consequential damages, we are asking how Helena has been made worse off *because of the breach*. The best way to approach a problem like this is to look at all the potential damages items and ask separately whether each one is recoverable:

   a. *$4,000 in moving expenses*. These are *not* recoverable. Helena would have paid this same amount whether or not Ivan breached, as it is the cost of moving from Nashville to Chicago. There's no indication that it cost her more for this transportation because of the breach.
   b. *One week's hotel stay at $125 per night*. These damages likely are recoverable as compensatory damages. Because of Ivan's breach, Helena was out of pocket $875 in hotel bills, money she would not have had to pay but for Ivan's breach.
   c. *$300 in storage expenses*. This item as well appears to be a consequential damages amount that Helena would not have incurred but for the breach. Had Ivan kept his promise, Helena would have moved into the first apartment immediately and avoided this extra expense.

Helena's position after the wrong (A) is −$1,175 ($875 in hotel expenses and $300 in storage costs). Her expectancy damages are (C − A), or $6,000 − (−$1,175), or $7,175.

Example 7

The Oregon Bank promised to loan Doyle and one of his businesses $1 million. At the time of the loan, the bank was aware that Doyle was in a distressed financial condition. The bank knew that at the time Doyle applied for the loan, Doyle had been unable to secure other financing. After the bank agreed to lend the money, bank officers reversed the decision. Doyle was unable to obtain a loan elsewhere, and as a result, he was unable to harvest timber on his property, losing profits of $10,000. Is Doyle entitled to recover for the lost profits?

Explanation

In this case, the lost profits would be a claim for consequential damages. One hurdle the plaintiff would face is that these consequential damages might not have been sufficiently foreseeable by the defendant. While it appears foreseeable that Doyle would have faced a business default if he did not receive the loan, it does not appear that the bank had specific information about this particular loss.

Even putting aside the question of foreseeability, there is the question whether a breach of a contract to lend money falls into the same category as the breach of a contract to *pay* money, for which the only kind of consequential damages available is the payment of interest at the prevailing legal rate. In *Doyle v. Oregon Bank*, 764 P.2d 1379 (Or. Ct. App. 1988), an Oregon appellate court refused to decide whether a plaintiff in Doyle's circumstances could recover damages for defendants' breach of a loan contract. Laycock reports that a majority of courts allow the recovery of consequential damages for breach of a loan agreement, provided the damages are sufficiently foreseeable. So here's another exception to the exception.

4.4 LIQUIDATED DAMAGES AND OTHER CONTRACTUAL LIMITATIONS ON REMEDIES

In the discussion of consequential damages above, I introduced the concept (which you likely already know from your Contracts course) of the *default rule*. This rule governs parties' contracts absent an express agreement otherwise. The excerpted FedEx provision above — which disclaims liability for consequential damages whether or not FedEx knew of a sender's specific needs to have a package delivered by a certain time — is an example of a contractual provision overriding a default rule.

Contractual provisions that alter default contractual remedies are fairly common. In addition to consequential damages disclaimers, contracts often contain attorney's fees provisions (providing that the winner must pay the loser for attorney's fees), and sometimes contracts contain other limitations on remedies besides consequential damages.

As with any provision of a contract, a clause changing the remedies available to the non-breaching party may be challenged in that particular case as unconscionable or as against public policy. You may recall from your Contracts class that parties can raise *procedural* unconscionability claims and, in some cases, *substantive* unconscionability claims. Procedural claims look at *how* the clause was presented to the party. A one-sided remedies provision buried in the fine print of an adhesion contract (a contract offered on a take-it-or-leave-it basis without the opportunity for negotiation, like the FedEx contract) could be struck down on procedural unconscionability grounds. To avoid such claims, contract drafters would do well to make sure that onerous remedies provisions are prominent in a contract and written in easy-to-explain language.

More difficult to make are arguments against limitations on remedies based on substantive unconscionability. These are claims based not upon *how* the parties bargained around a default remedies rule, but on the *fairness* of the bargain. For example, the California Supreme Court struck down, on substantive unconscionability grounds, a provision in an employment agreement that required employees to arbitrate their wrongful termination claims against the employer, but did not require the employer to arbitrate claims it may have had against the employees. *Armendariz v. Found. Health Psychcare Servs., Inc.*, 6 P.3d 669 (Cal. 2000). You can find more on unconscionability in Chapter 18.1.

Sometimes, limitations on the form of contract remedies are set by statute rather than by court decision. For example, Article II of the Uniform Commercial Code, which we will consider in more detail in the next section, provides that limitations on consequential damages for personal injury caused by consumer goods are prima facie unconscionable, while limitations for commercial losses are not. U.C.C. § 2-719(3). To give another example, a California statute states that if a contract provides for only one side to receive attorney's fees if it prevails in a dispute arising from the contract, the contract is to be read so that it applies to *both* parties to the contract. Cal. Civ. Code § 1717 (West 1998).

Among the most important provisions parties use to contract around default remedies provisions are "liquidated damages provisions." These are provisions that, in the event of a breach by one of the parties, actually set the amount (or provide some formula or benchmark for setting the amount) of damages to the exclusion of jury-determined damages under the usual rules.

For example, Dave contracts with the state to build a highway. The contract provides that Dave will be paid $5 million for his work, and that the work is due January 1, 2012. It also provides that for every month Dave is late, he must pay the state $100,000 in damages. Dave is three months late. The state pays him only $4.7 million, deducting $300,000 under the contract's liquidated damages provision. Dave claims that the state suffered damages that were less than this $300,000 amount, and argues that the liquidated damages provision is unenforceable.

Before considering whether courts would hold the clause unenforceable, let's first ask why the state might have wanted this provision. Two reasons to include the clause are to *coerce Dave's performance, and to punish him for late performance.* If Dave knows he faces a sure $100,000 loss for each month that he is late, he's likely to want to do his best to get the contract completed on time.

This "coercion" is not necessarily unfair to Dave. Presumably, Dave and the state entered into this contract freely. Dave probably was able to demand something in exchange for his agreement to the provision. He may have received a promise of more money, which he could have used to pay extra workers to have made sure that the work was completed on time.

Another reason the state may have wanted the liquidated damages provision included in the contract is that computing actual damages in this case is likely to be difficult. *Liquidated damages clauses can remove uncertainty about how jurors are going to value the benefits of a contract.* How much does a state lose when one of its highways does not open on time? It is going to be hard to put a fixed figure on it, especially given the requirement that plaintiffs prove their damages with reasonable certainty (more on that in Chapter 6.1). Neither party can be sure about the extent of liability should Dave be late on the contract.

Given these benefits of liquidated damages provisions, it is puzzling why courts traditionally have been reluctant to enforce them. Courts may have viewed them as an encroachment on the power of the judiciary to set a remedy. The Restatement (Second) of Contracts section 356(1) sets forth the more modern view:

> Damages for breach by either party may be liquidated in the agreement but only at an amount that is reasonable in the light of the anticipated or actual loss caused by the breach and the difficulties of proof of loss. A term fixing unreasonably large liquidated damages is unenforceable on grounds of public policy as a penalty.

Thus, the modern law draws a distinction between enforceable and unenforceable liquidated damages provisions based upon the reasons the parties included the provision in the contract. If the reason is coercion or punishment (which might be evidenced by an "unreasonably large" liquidated damages provision), the clause is impermissible; if the clause is a good faith attempt to set the amount of compensatory damages, it is permissible. Of course, drawing the line between these two reasons is sometimes going to be difficult in practice, meaning that the parties are going to have to litigate over the enforceability of the liquidated damages clause. The irony is that under the Uniform Commercial Code, or U.C.C., the parties are going to have to introduce evidence of actual or anticipated damages, the very thing they were trying to avoid by including the provision in the contract in the first place.

Under this standard, a case like the highway construction case will be an easy one so long as the amount of damages is not extraordinarily large. *See Dave Gustafson & Co. v. State*, 156 N.W.2d 185 (S.D. 1968).

But note the paternalism of the rule: suppose the state agrees to pay Dave a generous amount for the contract in exchange for an exorbitant penalty provision in the contract to ensure Dave completes the work on time. Under the Restatement and *Dave Gustafson & Co.*, this limit is unenforceable, even if both parties went into the contract with their eyes open, and even if they explicitly bargained over the penalty provision in the contract. When a liquidated damages clause is unenforceable, non-breaching parties may recover remedies under default contract law rules.

There is one other important damages limitation issue, one that arises most commonly under Article 2 of the U.C.C.: what happens when a limitation on a remedy "fails in its essential purpose"? We discuss that in the final section of this chapter.

Example 8

Assume the same facts as in our original Dave versus State hypothetical (involving the highway contract) except that the state wants to use a large amount of money to coerce Dave's compliance instead of running afoul of the standards for the enforceability of liquidated damages provisions. The state still wants the highway completed by January 1, 2012. The parties therefore include the following provision in their contract: "Dave shall finish all work by March 1, 2012, at a rate of $3 million. In the event Dave finishes early, he shall receive a bonus of $1 million per month that he completes the job before the deadline, with a maximum bonus of $2 million."

Is this clause enforceable? If so, does it accomplish the same purposes as the original liquidated damages provision?

Explanation

This clause would likely be held enforceable because it gives a *bonus* for early performance rather than a penalty for late performance. The prohibition on penalty clauses does not apply because there is no penalty for late performance. In some ways, the original penalty provision and the bonus provision are equivalent: Dave ends up with $5 million under either provision if he finishes building by January 1, 2012. But in other ways they are not equivalent. Under the original provision, Dave would be in breach of contract on January 2, 2012, but under the bonus provision there would be no breach until *March* 2, 2012. More generally, the bonus provision can provide only a carrot (an incentive) and not a stick (a penalty). If Dave is running *really* late, and doesn't have the highway completed on March 2, 2012, the contract's bonus provision does nothing to motivate him to finish on time. In contrast, the original penalty provision adds damages for each time period that Dave is late.

Example 9

James contracts with Kika, a contractor, to remodel James's kitchen. It is very important to James that the work be completed by June 1, because he is planning on having his boss and the firm's most important client over for a fancy dinner party on June 10. James tells Kika how urgent it is that the work be done on time. James says to Kika: "My job depends on it!" James and Kika draft up a contract for Kika to undertake the remodeling for $20,000, with the following provision: "Time is of the essence with this contract. If this contract is not completed by June 1, Kika will pay damages of $1,000, with the damages to double each day that Kika is late." Kika completes the kitchen on June 15. James, who was unable to have the dinner party at his house because Kika was late on the contract, is fired by his boss for this reason. A court finds that Kika has breached the contract by being late. To what damages is James entitled?

Explanation

The provision in the contract will undoubtedly be struck down as unenforceable because it will be seen as too harsh of a penalty. After 14 days, the penalty of $1,000, doubled every day, would have multiplied to $8,192,000! Obviously, the purpose of the clause was to coerce Kika's timely performance, but once the clause has failed to do so, the courts won't allow such a harsh result.

If the courts strike down the liquidated damages provision as unenforceable, James will be able to recover his regular contract damages. First, consider the promised position, C. The difference between what was promised and what was received was James's being able to get into his kitchen 14 days earlier. This will be hard to value. Perhaps James can point to the extra amounts of money he spent eating at restaurants during that period rather than eating at home.

But James is also going to want to recover for consequential damages (assuming the contract does not have a provision barring such consequential damages in the event the contractual, liquidated damages provision is struck down — a clause always worth considering for addition to a contract if you are drafting one). In this case, James is going to claim that the loss of his job was directly attributable to Kika's breach in being late with the kitchen remodel. Under the rule from *Hadley*, it appears that Kika could be on the hook for these extra damages because James specifically told Kika he could lose his job if his kitchen was not ready in time. Perhaps Kika took this as an exaggeration, or a jury, seeing the potential harshness of making Kika liable for James's loss of a job, may hold that such losses were not sufficiently foreseeable to allow James to recover for these damages.

4.5 CONTRACT DAMAGE ISSUES UNDER ARTICLE 2 OF THE UNIFORM COMMERCIAL CODE

[Note: This section goes into more detail than many instructors do in a Remedies course. You may want to skip it or just read the sections that pertain to issues covered in your course. But even if you are not responsible for these issues in your course, reading about the U.C.C.'s approach should help you understand the general issues in the course, as well as important material that could well be on your state's bar exam.]

Article 2 of the Uniform Commercial Code governs the sale of goods in all states in the United States.[8] It governs every domestic sales contract involving a moveable good, from a stick of bubble gum to a supercomputer. In this, the final section of this chapter, we consider the specific U.C.C. damage rules.

4.5.1 Buyers' Remedies

U.C.C. § 2-711 sets forth the general rule on buyers' remedies. These remedies include the possibility (set forth in § 2-716) that the buyer might obtain an injunction (order of specific performance) from a court requiring the seller to deliver the goods to the plaintiff, but we put off discussion of this equitable remedy until Part II of this book. At this point, we consider only U.C.C. Article 2 damages remedies.

Section 2-711 gives the buyer a choice of two damages remedies when the seller has failed to make delivery, repudiated the contract, or delivered goods that the buyer had rightfully rejected because they did not conform to the contract. Under either measure the buyer is entitled to a refund of any funds paid to the seller in addition to further damages.

(1) Cover. Under § 2-712, a buyer can "cover" by making a good faith purchase of substitute goods without unreasonable delay. If the buyer makes such a good faith purchase, the buyer is entitled to the difference between the cover price and the contract price, together with incidental and consequential damages, less expenses saved as a consequence of seller's breach.

So the § 2-712 formula is:

> Amounts toward the purchase price paid to seller + (cover price − contract price) + incidental and consequential damages − expenses saved

For example, Lisa promises Mona in a valid written contract that she will deliver to Mona a 2003 red Lexus convertible for $25,000. The car is in excellent shape, except that it needs its air conditioning repaired at a cost of $1,000. Mona pays Lisa a $5,000 deposit. The next day, Lisa tells Mona she cannot deliver the car because it was damaged during delivery. Mona searches for a similar used car. She cannot find a 2003 red Lexus convertible in good

---

8. Louisiana has adopted parallel provisions to the U.C.C. in its civil code. *See* Robert K. Rasmussen, *The Uneasy Case Against the Uniform Commercial Code*, 62 LA. L. REV. 1097, 1097 n.1 (2002). Though the U.C.C. Article 2 provisions are mostly uniform across the states, there are variations on interpretations of the Code across states, because some of the provisions are vague. *See id.* at 1105 & n.30.

condition, but she finds a 2004 silver Lexus convertible at a purchase price of $28,000. Lisa spends $50 in gas checking out cars before she purchases the silver Lexus. Assume the court finds that the purchase by Lisa of the silver Lexus convertible constitutes a reasonable "cover." If so, Lisa can recover:

$5,000	(purchase price paid to seller)
+ $3,000	(the difference between the cover price and contract price)
+ $ 50	(the incidental cost of obtaining cover (see below for a definition of incidental damages)
− $ 1000	(the expenses saved: the air conditioning repair no longer necessary)
= $7,050	(Total damages)

The damages measure contained in § 2-712 aims to do just what the $(C − A)$ expectancy damages measure aims to do: to put the non-breaching party in the same position as if the seller had not breached the contract. The primary difference is that rather than using some indirect market measure of the loss (such as testimony from an expert as to the value of a 2003 red Lexus convertible in good condition) in valuing the difference between what was promised and what was received, § 2-712 allows for the purchase of a substitute as a surrogate for determining that market value.

(2) Market Damages. Under § 2-713, the buyer can recover the difference between the market price at the time when the buyer learned of the breach and the contract price, together with incidental and consequential damages less expenses saved. Market price is determined at the place of tender or, in the case of rejection after arrival or revocation of acceptance, at the place of arrival.

So the 2-713 market measure formula is:

> Amounts toward the purchase price paid to seller + (market price at the place of tender − contract price) + incidental and consequential damages − expenses saved

For example, suppose that the Mona-Lisa facts are exactly the same, but that after Lisa breached, Mona decided to buy a brand new red Lexus convertible for $50,000. The court agreed that Lisa breached, but it decided that Mona's purchase did not constitute a good faith substitute purchase qualifying as "cover" under § 2-712, because the new convertible was too different from the used car under the contract.

Without the ability to claim "cover," Mona would likely seek to recover damages under § 2-713. In order to compute damages under this section, we need one more piece of information: the market price of the car at the time of the breach at the place of tender. Let us suppose the market price is $29,000.[9] Using these figures, Mona can recover:

$5,000	(her deposit)
+ $4,000	(the difference between the market price at the time the buyer learned of the breach and the contract price)
+ 0	(there do not appear to be any incidental or consequential damages in this example)
− $1,000	(the expenses saved: the air conditioning repair no longer necessary)
= $8,000	(Total damages)

Note again that this measure aims to give Mona her expectancy. The examples also show that sometimes a non-breaching party's cover might be lower (or higher in other cases) than the market measure of § 2-713.

Remedy for Accepted Goods. In addition to these two measures, under § 2-714, when the buyer has *accepted goods* that don't conform to the contract (how to determine when that's happened is a subject more appropriate for a Contracts than a Remedies course) and the buyer has given notice of the non-conformity, the buyer can obtain damages resulting from the non-conformity "as determined in any manner that is reasonable," in addition to incidental and consequential damages. Moreover, when the buyer can prove a breach of warranty, the buyer can obtain from the seller "the difference at the time and place of acceptance between the value of the goods accepted and the value they would have had if they had been as warranted, unless special circumstances show proximate damages of a different amount."

For example, suppose that in the Mona-Lisa example, Lisa did not tell Mona that the car's air conditioning needed to be repaired. Instead, Lisa promised Mona that the air conditioning (along with the rest of the car) was in perfect working order. Mona took delivery of the car, and at some point under the U.C.C., the law treats Mona as having "accepted" the contract for the sale of the car. Once there has been an acceptance, Mona will be allowed

---

9. This figure supposes that Lisa was selling the car at a price below the market price. Why might Lisa do so? First, she might not know the going market price. Second, she might know the market price but be willing to cut the price in order to make a quick sale (perhaps she needs the money for something else).

to recover damages under § 2-714. Her likely damages will be the $1,000 cost to repair the air conditioning, which seems to be the cheapest way to compensate Mona for "the difference at the time and place of acceptance between the value of the goods accepted and the value they would have had if they had been as warranted."

Incidental and Consequential Damages. For each of the three remedies above, the buyer may recover both *incidental* and *consequential* damages. The U.C.C. defines *incidental damages* as "expenses reasonably incurred in inspection, receipt, transportation and care and custody of goods rightfully rejected, any commercially reasonable charges, expenses or commissions in connection with effecting cover and any other reasonable expenses incident to the delay or other breach." U.C.C. § 2-715(1). It defines *consequential damages* to include "any loss resulting from general or particular requirements and needs of which the seller at the time of contracting had reason to know and which could not reasonably be prevented by cover or otherwise." Consequential damages also include personal injury or property damage that results from any breach of warranty. U.C.C. § 2-715(2).

Significantly, the U.C.C. allows consequential damages to be excluded by contract, in which case they are not recoverable unless the exclusion is unconscionable. U.C.C. § 2-719. As noted above, however, the Code treats exclusion of consequential damages for personal injury as prima facie unconscionable. U.C.C. § 2-719(3).

Example 10

Ned agrees to buy a vintage pinball machine on eBay in excellent condition for $1,500, which includes shipping to his home. The price is to be paid upon delivery. Othello refuses to deliver the pinball machine. Ned finds an identical pinball machine at a local dealer for $1,400 and purchases it, but he pays an additional $50 for delivery. To what damages, if any, is Ned entitled?

Explanation

Ned is entitled to no damages. It appears that Ned has covered by buying the identical item from another dealer. Using the formula from earlier in the chapter, it appears that Ned has no damages:

> Amounts toward the purchase price paid to seller + (cover price − contract price) + incidental and consequential damages − expenses saved

$$0 + (\$1,400 - \$1,500) + \$50 \text{ (delivery charge)} - 0 = -\$50$$

There are no damages.

Example 11

Same facts as in Example 10, but this time, Ned pays $1,500 in advance to Othello. To what damages, if any, is Ned entitled?

Explanation

It appears that Ned would be entitled to $1,500. Othello might argue that if we mechanically used the formula above, Othello would owe damages of only $1,450 ($1,500 − $100 + $50 − 0 = $1,450). However, that would award the benefit of Ned's covering to Othello, the breaching party. In such a case, Ned could simply argue for a refund of the purchase price under § 2-711 and not seek cover. See *Allied Semi-Conductor Int'l, Ltd. v. Pulsar Components Int'l, Inc.*, 907 F. Supp. 618, 632 (E.D.N.Y. 1995) ("[The breaching party] cites no authority for the proposition that a breaching seller is entitled to retain a portion of the purchase price upon a buyer's proper rejection and return of defective goods in the event that the buyer covers its resale contract at a lower price than it paid to the breaching seller. In such a situation the aggrieved buyer sustains no cover damages as a consequence of the seller's breach and the seller's liability is limited to the purchase price paid as a matter of clear statutory mandate.").

Example 12

Same facts as in Example 10, but the fair market price of the pinball machine Othello promised to sell Ned is $1,800. What damages, if any, may Ned recover?

Explanation

This is a fairly unlikely real-world scenario because, in this case, there would be two sellers (Othello and the new seller) willing to sell the vintage pinball machine for significantly less than the market price. In any case, in this circumstance, Ned has a choice. First, because he did cover, he could use the formula of § 2-712, which, as we know from Example 10, yields him no damages.

Alternatively, Ned could use the damages available under § 2-713:

> Amounts toward the purchase price paid to seller + (market price at the place of tender − contract price) + incidental and consequential damages − expenses saved

$$0 + (\$1,800 - \$1,500) + 0 - 0 = \$300$$

Note that we did not add in the $50 delivery charge that Ned sustained in making the substitute purchase. He is entitled to that only if he is claiming cover under § 2-712.

Othello may want to argue that Ned in fact did cover by making his substitute purchase, and therefore damages must be measured under the § 2-712 measure, which is more advantageous to Othello. But the official comment to § 2-712 explains that "cover is not a mandatory remedy for the buyer. The buyer is always free to choose between cover and damages for non-delivery under" § 2-713. U.C.C. § 2-712, official comment b.

Example 13

Pam, a farmer, agrees to buy six cows from Quincy for $700 per head. Quincy promises that these cows are suitable for breeding. Quincy delivers the cows, and Pam pays Quincy $4,200. The next day, Pam has a veterinarian examine the cows, and the veterinarian discovers that each of them is infertile. Pam calls Quincy and revokes her acceptance (which we will assume she is allowed to do under applicable contract law). She tells Quincy to pick the cows up. Quincy comes a week later to pick up the cows. Pam spent $200 caring for the cows during that week. The market value of a fertile cow is $700. The market value of an infertile cow is $300. Pam planned on using the six cows to breed other cows, and she expected to make a profit of $5,000 from selling their offspring. How much may Pam receive in damages? (Assume that under the U.C.C. she has rightfully rejected the cows.)

Explanation

Because Pam has revoked acceptance and there is no indication that she has covered, she is entitled to damages under 2-713. First, she is entitled to the *amounts toward purchase price paid to seller*, or $4,200. She receives nothing for the *difference between the market price and the contract price*, because they are identical. (Quincy was selling the goods at the market price, and Pam presumably can now go out and make a substitute purchase at the market price.) Note that the $300 value of the infertile cow is not relevant to the § 2-713 formula.

Pam can also recover the $200 in incidental damages she incurred for the care of the goods she rightfully rejected. But she *cannot* recover the $5,000 in lost profits as consequential damages, because these damages cannot be considered "to include any loss resulting from general or particular requirements and needs of which the seller at the time of contracting had reason to know *and which could not reasonably be prevented by cover or otherwise.*" This is the mitigation principle built into the Code. Pam cannot sit on her hands after the breach. If she still wanted to raise cows for their offspring, she should have gone out and bought replacement cows to breed. The facts tell us nothing about any *expenses saved*. Pam's total damages: $4,400.

Example 14

Same facts as in the last example, but assume that Pam does not do an inspection, and she does not discover the cows are infertile for six months. She then notifies Quincy of the non-conformity, but he does nothing. Pam has spent $1,000 caring for the cows. She sends the cows to the slaughterhouse and receives $400 per head. How much may Pam receive in damages? (Assume that under the U.C.C. she has accepted the goods and cannot revoke her acceptance.)

Explanation

In this case, because Pam has accepted the goods, she must receive her remedy under U.C.C. § 2-714. Pam may obtain damages resulting from the non-conformity "as determined in any manner that is reasonable" in addition to incidental and consequential damages. Moreover, by proving a breach of warranty, Pam may obtain from the seller "the difference at the time and place of acceptance between the value of the goods accepted and the value they would have had if they had been as warranted, unless special circumstances show proximate damages of a different amount."

In this case, Pam likely would be entitled to $2,400, representing the difference between the value of the six cows as they had been warranted ($700 each) and the value they actually had ($300 each) at the time and place of acceptance. Note that we do not use the value that the animals had six months later ($400), because § 2-714 measures value at the time and place of acceptance.

Pam will also seek to recover the $1,000 that it cost her to care for the animals as incidental damages, and the $5,000 in lost profits as consequential damages. As to the $1,000, because Pam did not "rightfully reject" the goods, these damages likely do not qualify as incidental damages. To recover her lost profits, there will likely be a big question as to whether Pam reasonably could have prevented these damages from accruing. If, for example, she could have discovered the cows' infertility in a timelier manner, these damages would not be recoverable as consequential damages.

Note that if Pam could recover the additional $5,000 as consequential damages, Quincy could require that the jury *deduct expenses saved*. Thus, if it would have cost Pam an additional $800 to care for the cows had they been fertile, this amount would have figured into the actual profits she would have earned.

4.5.2 Sellers' Remedies, Including the "Lost Volume Seller"

Just as Article 2 of the U.C.C. gives buyers a choice of remedies, sellers dealing with breaching buyers have some choices as well. Under U.C.C. § 2-703, sellers facing buyers who wrongfully reject goods, wrongfully revoke acceptance, or fail to pay as promised can cancel the contract, stop delivery of the goods, and then either resell and recover damages (§ 2-706), recover damages for non-acceptance (§ 2-708), or bring an action on the price (§ 2-709). We consider each of these in turn.

Resale (§ 2-706). The first option a non-breaching seller has is to resell the goods to another buyer. When the seller makes a resale "in good faith and in a commercially reasonable manner," "the seller may recover the difference between the resale price and the contract price together with any incidental damages allowed under the provisions of this Article (Section 2-710), but less expenses saved in consequence of the buyer's breach." (You should immediately see the parallel to the buyer's remedy of cover here.)

So the § 2-706 formula is:

(contract price − resale price) + incidental damages − expenses saved

To use a variation on an earlier example, suppose Lisa promises Mona in a valid written contract that she will deliver to Mona a 2003 red Lexus convertible for $25,000. The car is in excellent shape except that it needs its air conditioning repaired at a cost of $1,000. Lisa promises to repair the air conditioning before delivering the car to Mona. Before Lisa has a chance to fix the air conditioning, Mona announces that she is not going to pay the contract price or take delivery of the car. This constitutes a breach of the contract. Lisa puts an ad in the local newspaper at a cost of $25 to sell the car. She gets a few offers, and sells it to the highest bidder, who pays $22,000 and does not require Lisa to repair the air conditioning.

Under U.C.C. § 2-706, Lisa can recover the following:

$3,000	($25,000 − $22,000, the difference between the resale price and contract price)
+ $25	(incidental damages for the advertisement)
− $1,000	(expenses saved: the air conditioning that need not be repaired)
= $2,025	(Total damages)

Note that this is a way of measuring expectancy damages, assuming that the resale price is close to the contract price. Had the contract been fulfilled, Lisa would have sold a car worth $22,000 to Mona for $25,000 and yielded a $3,000 profit. Lisa then would have spent $1,000 on the air conditioning repair, which means that at the end of the day, her balance ledger would have shown a $2,000 gain. With Mona's breach, Lisa takes in $2,025 in damages and pays $25 for the ad, leaving her with that same $2,000 gain.

Damages for Non-Acceptance (§ 2-708). The seller need not make the immediate resale of the goods as contemplated by § 2-706. Instead, the seller can recover under § 2-708(1) "the difference between the market price at the time and place for tender and the unpaid contract price together with any incidental damages provided in this Article (Section 2-710), but less expenses saved in consequence of the buyer's breach." The section also provides an alternative measure of damages in § 2-708(2) that we shall return to shortly.

So the § 2-708(1) formula is:

> (contract price − market price) + incidental damages − expenses saved

Thus, if Mona broke the contract to buy the red Lexus for $25,000, and Lisa did not resell it, Lisa could seek to recover damages under § 2-708(1). Let's suppose that the market value of the car at the time and place of sale (and without the air conditioning repair) was $23,500. Under those circumstances, Lisa could recover under § 2-708:

$1,500	($25,000 − $23,500, the difference between the resale price and contract price)
+ $0	(no incidental damages)
− 1,000	(expenses saved: the air conditioning that need not be repaired)
= $500	(Total damages)

Action on the Price (§ 2-709).   When the buyer fails to pay for goods as they are due, and either the buyer keeps the goods or the goods are lost or damaged after the risk of loss has passed to the buyer, the seller can bring an action to recover the contract price plus incidental damages. The seller can also recover such damages for goods still in the seller's possession if the seller "is unable after reasonable effort to resell them at a reasonable price or the circumstances reasonably indicate that such effort will be unavailing."

Thus, the § 2-709 formula is:

---

contract price + incidental damages

Thus, Lisa and Mona sign a valid contract for delivery of the red Lexus convertible for $25,000, provided Lisa repairs the air conditioning (at a cost of $1,000). Lisa repairs the air conditioning and the car is delivered to Mona. The car is struck by lightning after it is delivered to Mona, and at this time, contract law says that "the risk of loss" has shifted to Mona. If Mona refuses to pay, Lisa may recover $25,000, the contract price. She has no incidental damages.

Incidental Damages (§ 2-710).   Under the three damage formulas for sellers set forth above, the sellers are entitled to incidental damages (though not to consequential damages as buyers are). Section 2-710 defines seller's incidental damages to include "any commercially reasonable charges, expenses or commissions incurred in stopping delivery, in the transportation, care, and custody of goods after the buyer's breach, in connection with return or resale of the goods or otherwise resulting from the breach."

Suppose Lisa and Mona sign a valid contract for delivery of the red Lexus at a price of $25,000. Mona changes her mind after Lisa pays $300 to a delivery service to deliver the car. After the car is returned, Lisa spends $200 selling the car to another buyer. The $300 and $200 expenses are incidental damages that Lisa may recover in a claim for damages under § 2-706.

The Lost Volume Seller. One issue that arises with some frequency (especially on Remedies exams) is the case of the lost volume seller. A leading case here is *Neri v. Retail Marine Corp.*, 285 N.E.2d 311 (N.Y. 1972). In *Neri*, buyer contracted to buy a new boat from a boat seller for $12,587.40. The buyer breached the contract, and the seller incurred $674 in costs for storing the boat until it could be sold to another buyer. The evidence indicated that the seller could have made the sale both to the original buyer and to the new buyer, and therefore the seller lost a profit of $2,579 on the first sale.

In considering the damages that the seller in *Neri* could receive,[10] note that damages under §§ 2-706 and 2-708(1) appear inadequate (damages under § 2-709 would not be available because the buyer neither kept the goods nor were they lost or destroyed after risk of loss had passed to the buyer). Under § 2-706, the difference between the contract price and the resale price is 0, leaving only the incidental damages of $674. But that amount of damages does not appear to put the seller in the rightful position because the seller *could have made both sales at a profit*. In essence, this awards only the seller's reliance damages (B − A, that amount below the status quo ante where the seller was left after the buyer's breach of contract).

Similarly, damages under § 2-708(1) are inadequate, assuming that the contract price for the boat was equal to the market price. Again, the seller would be left with only the $674 in incidental (reliance) damages.

Most courts therefore invoke U.C.C. § 2-708(2), which provides:

> If the measure of damages provided in subsection (1) is inadequate to put the seller in as good a position as performance would have done then the measure of damages is the profit (including reasonable overhead) which the seller would have made from full performance by the buyer, together with any incidental damages provided in this Article (Section 2-710), due allowance for costs reasonably incurred and due credit for payments or proceeds of resale.

So the § 2-708(2) formula is:

> Profit + incidental damages − credit for junk value[11]

Through § 2-708(2), courts have allowed "lost volume sellers," such as the boat seller in *Neri*, to recover their *lost profits plus incidental damages*. In this

---

10. In the actual case, the buyer had given a deposit, which was then credited against the amount of damages the buyer owed the seller. (The buyer had the right to a return of the deposit after deducting damages, under principles of restitution.) But in this example, I ignore this aspect of the *Neri* facts to focus on the lost volume seller issue.

11. The reason I have used the term "credit for junk value" rather than "due credit for proceeds of resale" is that courts, including *Neri*, have read the section's language to apply only to junk value. *See Neri*, 285 N.E.2d at 314 n.2. Otherwise, if we really subtracted credits for resale, this would eliminate any profit and render the section nonsensical in this context.

case, that would be the $2,579 in lost profits plus the $674 in incidental damages, for a total of $3,253 in damages.

This measure puts the boat seller in the rightful position. Had the sale gone through, the boat seller would have realized a profit of $2,579. With the breach, the seller receives $3,253 in damages and, after paying for the costs of holding the boat, ends up with the same $2,579 profit.

Not every seller qualifies as a lost volume seller. According to one test, a non-breaching party claiming to be a lost volume seller "must establish three factors: (1) that it possessed the capacity to make an additional sale, (2) that it would have been profitable for it to make an additional sale, and (3) that it probably would have made an additional sale absent the buyer's breach." *R.E. Davis Chem. Corp. v. Diasonics, Inc.*, 924 F.2d 709, 711 (7th Cir. 1991).

Example 15

Ian contracts to sell Courtney his private jet for $85,000 with delivery on June 1. On June 1, Courtney refuses to accept delivery. Ian immediately resells the jet to another buyer for $86,000. The reasonable market value of the jet is $80,000. What damages, if any, may Ian recover from Courtney?

Explanation

It appears that Ian may not recover any damages from Courtney. Because there has been a resale, § 2-706 applies. Recall that the § 2-706 formula is:

$$\text{(contract price} - \text{resale price)} + \text{incidental damages} - \text{expenses saved}$$

Because the contract price was lower than the resale price and there were no incidental damages, Ian has no damages.

Would Ian have been better off not selling? No. By selling to the new buyer, Ian received a profit of $6,000 (because the new contract price of $86,000 is $6,000 above the market price of $80,000). If Ian had not sold, he would have been able to recover damages under § 2-708(1) of:

$$\text{(contract price} - \text{market price)} + \text{incidental damages} - \text{expenses saved}$$

$$\$85,000 - 80,000 + 0 - 0 = \$5,000$$

Ian would have a $5,000 damages award plus a plane that he can presumably sell for $80,000, the going market rate. When he sells at the market rate, his ledger is up by only the $5,000, rather than the $6,000 that would apply if he had sold to the new buyer.

Notably, Ian cannot claim to be a lost volume seller. Unlike the boat seller in *Neri*, Ian has only one plane to sell.

Example 16

Pam, a farmer, agrees to buy six cows from Quincy for $700 per head. The current market price is $750 per head, but Quincy needs money quickly to pay off his farm debts. Quincy spends $250 transporting the cows to Pam's farm, but Pam breaches the contract, refusing to pay the $4,200 contract price. Quincy takes the cattle back to his farm. Two days later, and before Quincy has found another buyer, there is a scare over "mad cow disease," and the price of cattle plummets. The new market rate for the cows is $200. Rather than sell the cows at that price, Quincy decides to hold on to them. In the meantime, because Pam breached, Quincy does not have the money to make the loan payment for his tractor. The bank repossesses his tractor, and Quincy loses another $10,000 in income because he does not have a tractor to harvest his crops. What damages, if any, can Quincy recover from Pam?

Explanation

Quincy did not make a resale, so he cannot take advantage of § 2-706. It looks like he would have to seek damages under § 2-708(1) of:

> (contract price − market price) + incidental damages − expenses saved

The contract price here is $4,200 (6 cows @ $700/head). The market price is $4,500 (6 cows @$750/head). Note that we use the market value *at the time of sale*, not later (when the market takes a nosedive to $200/head). The incidental damages are $250 (the cost of transporting the cows). There are no expenses saved. Thus:

$$(4200 - 4500) + 250 = -\$50$$

Quincy has no net damages under this formula and can recover nothing. At best, he could argue that § 2-703 allows him to recover his incidental damages of $250.

Quincy cannot recover from Pam any consequential damages that he suffers from not being able to make his tractor loan payment as a result of Pam's breach. Sellers under the U.C.C. do not get to recover consequential damages as buyers do. It thus appears that the U.C.C. follows the general exception for consequential damages that we saw earlier in this chapter (section 4.3); at most, some courts interpret the U.C.C. to allow sellers to receive interest on money unpaid under a contract as a form of "incidental" damages. *Bulk Oil (U.S.A.), Inc. v. Sun Oil Trading Co.*, 697 F.2d 481 (2d Cir. 1983).

Example 17

Same facts as above, except Quincy delivers the cows to Pam. It costs him $250 to deliver the cows. The next day, the government orders Pam to put the cows down to prevent the feared spread of mad cow disease. Pam destroys the cattle and does not pay the $4,200 contract price. Quincy sues for damages. What result? Explain.

Explanation

In this case, Quincy will bring an action on the price under § 2-709. Recall the § 2-709 formula:

> contract price + incidental damages

Quincy can recover the $4,200, assuming substantive contract law says the risk of loss of the goods passed to Pam at the time of delivery. Quincy *cannot* recover the $250 in transportation costs as incidental damages. These are expenses he would have incurred had Pam not breached. If we allowed Quincy to recover those additional damages, the damages measure would have left him better off than if Pam had performed the contract.

4.5.3 U.C.C. Article 2 Limitations on Remedies

As with non-U.C.C. contracts, default rules in contracts governed by Article 2 of the U.C.C. are subject, with some limits, to being overridden by express contractual provisions. Indeed, I have already noted that U.C.C. contracts can exclude consequential damages unless the exclusion is unconscionable. Exclusions for personal injuries resulting from defective products are prima facie unconscionable. *See* U.C.C. § 2-719(3).

In addition, the Article 2 provision on liquidated damages mirrors the rules of the Restatement of Contracts. *See* U.C.C. § 2-718(1) ("Damages for breach by either party may be liquidated in the agreement but only at an amount which is reasonable in the light of the anticipated or actual harm caused by the breach, the difficulties of proof of loss, and the inconvenience or nonfeasibility of otherwise obtaining an adequate remedy. A term fixing unreasonably large liquidated damages is void as a penalty.").

Perhaps the most interesting aspect of Article 2's approach to the parties' ability to change the default remedy rules appears in the official comment to section 2-719:

> Under this section parties are left free to shape their remedies to their particular requirements and reasonable agreements limiting or modifying remedies are to be given effect.
>
> However, it is of the very essence of a sales contract that at least minimum adequate remedies be available. If the parties intend to conclude a contract for sale within this Article they must accept the legal consequence that there be at least a fair quantum of remedy for breach of the obligations or duties outlined in the contract. Thus any clause purporting to modify or limit the remedial provisions of this Article in an unconscionable manner is subject to deletion and in that event the remedies made available by this Article are applicable as if the stricken clause had never existed. Similarly, under subsection (2), where an apparently fair and reasonable clause because of circumstances fails in its purpose or operates to deprive either party of the substantial value of the bargain, it must give way to the general remedy provisions of this Article.

The last reference in this excerpt refers to § 2-719(2), providing that "[w]here circumstances cause an exclusive or limited remedy to fail of its essential purpose, remedy may be had as provided in this Act." In the typical case arising under this clause, a contract provides a strict limitation on remedy in the case of the seller's breach, such as limiting the buyer's remedy to repair or replacement of the product (at the seller's option). When the seller tries repeatedly to repair a faulty machine, the courts may declare that the remedy "has failed of its essential purpose" and resort to other contractual provisions or the default rules under the Act.

An interesting subsidiary question arises when the default rules and other contractual provisions conflict after a repair-or-replace remedy has failed its essential purpose. *Kearney & Trecker Corp. v. Master Engraving Co.*, 527 A.2d 429 (N.J. 1987), is a typical case. Buyer bought a computer-controlled machine tool from seller that repeatedly malfunctioned and could not be repaired. The contract provided *both* that the buyer's remedy was limited to repair or replacement at the seller's option *and* that the seller would under no circumstances be liable for any incidental or consequential damages. At first glance, it might appear that the limitation on incidental or consequential damages was lawyerly overkill given the repair-or-replace limitation, but the clause limiting consequential damages turned out to be quite prudent drafting.

The court ruled that the repair-or-replace remedy failed its essential purpose when the seller could not successfully get the machine to work. The question the court faced then was whether the buyer could recover consequential damages under § 2-714 or whether the limitation on consequential damages clause in the contract remained valid. The New Jersey Supreme Court in *Kearney & Trecker Corp.* noted the conflict among the courts on the issue, and sided with the seller, holding the consequential damage limitation enforceable so long as the clause was not unconscionable. Other courts have held the consequential damages limitation unenforceable, thereby allowing the buyer to recover consequential damages.

Note that the holding of *Kearney & Trecker Corp.* did not deprive the buyer of all remedies. Under § 2-714(2), the buyer can obtain the difference between the value of the machine as warranted and the value of the machine as delivered. Thus, if the seller promised a machine tool that could do x, and such a machine tool has a value of $1 million if working and zero if constantly broken, § 2-714(2) could allow the buyer to recover a significant amount of damages (perhaps $1,000,000 − 0).

Example 18

Rex promises to deliver a fancy CT scanner to Samantha for use in her high-tech medical lab in exchange for a payment of $2 million. They sign a form contract provided by Rex. The contract provides that the only remedy Samantha has in case the machine fails to work as promised is repair or replacement at Rex's option. It further provides that "in the event the repair or replacement remedy is found to fail of its essential purpose, the buyer shall be entitled to liquidated damages of $10,000." Samantha pays in full for the machine, but for six months the machine is broken more than it works. A court determines that Rex's failure to deliver a working machine constitutes a breach of contract. To what damages, if any, is Samantha entitled?

Explanation

Samantha will want to recover damages under § 2-714 for the difference between the value of the CT scanner as warranted (a working scanner) and as delivered (very little), plus any incidental and consequential damages (such as lost business because of the broken scanner). Rex will argue that the remedy is limited to repair and replacement, but a court, following *Kearney & Trecker Corp.*, will likely hold that the repair-or-replace remedy failed in its essential purpose.

Rex would likely then argue that Samantha's damages should be limited under the liquidated damages provision. But under U.C.C. § 2-718, a court could well hold that the liquidated damages provision does not appear to be a reasonable amount in light of actual or anticipated harm (Samantha would be receiving only $10,000 for a nonworking machine that she paid $2 million to buy). Alternatively, a court might declare the liquidated damages provision substantively unconscionable. If that is the case, as in the case in which the court strikes down the liquidated damages provision, Samantha will be able to recover her damages under § 2-714, damages that could be substantial.

The Unusual: Expectancy Damages in Tort and Reliance Damages in Contract

5.1 REVIEW OF THE USUAL TORT AND CONTRACT DAMAGE MEASURES

As we have seen in the last two chapters, the usual measure of tort damages is the reliance measure $(B - A)$, and the usual measure of contract damages is the expectancy measure $(C - A)$. See Figure 5.1.

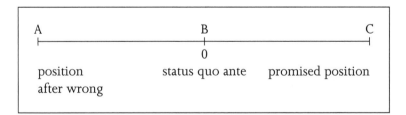

Figure 5.1

In this chapter, we consider the relatively rare situations in which (1) a plaintiff seeks to recover expectancy damages in tort or (2) a non-breaching party is permitted to recover only reliance damages in contract. Before turning to those exceptions, however, here are some brief review examples so that you can consider the usual rules in tort and contract cases.

Example 1

Tina, driving negligently, runs over Ursula's foot. Ursula pays $10,000 in medical bills, misses work for six weeks (she is paid $1,000 per week as a secretary), and still experiences a great deal of pain (the accident itself was excruciating for Ursula). Ursula is an avid tennis player, and the doctors believe she won't be able to play tennis again for at least two years. To what damages is Ursula entitled?

Explanation

This is a standard torts case, so we want to use our (B − A) reliance damages rather than the (C − A) expectancy damages formula. As you should see, we would never consider using expectancy damages here because, between Tina and Ursula, there *is no promised position*. So we are concerned only with figuring out position A, Ursula's position after the wrong. Ursula will be able to recover her reasonable medical expenses ($10,000) and lost wages ($1,000 for six weeks, or $6,000). There do not appear to be any future medical expenses or future lost wages, which saves us from having to worry about reducing future payments to present value. Ursula will also be able to recover something for her pain and suffering/emotional distress, including any emotional distress she is likely to suffer in the future from pain and the inability to play tennis (this amount perhaps should be reduced to present value). As for economic damages, she likely would be able to obtain pre-judgment interest.

Example 2

Vinny promises to sell Walter a painting by Picasso. The painting has a market value of $1 million, but Vinny agrees to accept $900,000 if Walter pays cash. Walter makes a $100,000 down payment, and the parties sign a valid contract requiring Vinny to deliver the picture by the next day. Unfortunately, the painting is destroyed in a fire in Vinny's home. (Assume that substantive contract law says this risk of loss remained on Vinny, and that by failing to deliver the painting Vinny breached his contract with Walter.) Walter is very disappointed. He goes out and purchases a painting by Cezanne for $2 million. To what damages is Walter entitled?

Explanation

Because this is a contracts case, we will use the expectancy measure of damages. But rather than the generic (C − A) formula, we will use the U.C.C. Article 2 damage provisions for buyers. (U.C.C. Article 2 applies because this contract is for the sale of a painting, which qualifies as a good.) Walter is entitled to a refund of his purchase price ($100,000). He would not be successful in arguing that he "covered" (U.C.C. § 2-712) when he purchased the Cezanne — though they are both paintings, the Cezanne and Picasso differ significantly in value, so a court would be unlikely to view the Cezanne painting as a substitute purchase.

Accordingly, Walter will seek damages under the U.C.C. § 2-713 formula:

> Amounts toward the purchase price paid to seller + (market price at the place of tender − contract price) + incidental and consequential damages − expenses saved

	$100,000	(amount toward purchase price)
+	$100,000	($1 million market price at the place of tender − $900,000 contract price)
+	0	(there is no evidence of any incidental or consequential damages)
−	0	(there is no evidence of expenses saved)
=	$200,000	(Total damages)

Note that the C − A formula would yield exactly the same result. (Make sure you understand why by computing the values of C and A.) If Walter is limited to recovering his reliance damages, he will get only his $100,000 deposit back and no compensation for the lost "benefit of the bargain."

5.2 EXPECTANCY DAMAGES IN TORT? THE SPECIAL CASE OF FRAUD

The question of expectancy damages in tort usually does not come up. When Tina hits Ursula with her car, there is no "promised position," making the possibility of locating C in Figure 5.1 an impossibility. Instead, courts award reliance damages to restore Ursula to a point as close as possible to the status quo ante with an award of money.

In tort cases involving fraud, however, there is a promised position. Here is how the Restatement (Second) of Torts § 525 defines the tort of fraudulent misrepresentation:

> One who fraudulently makes a misrepresentation of fact, opinion, intention or law for the purpose of inducing another to act or to refrain from action in reliance upon it, is subject to liability to the other in deceit for pecuniary loss caused to him by his justifiable reliance upon the misrepresentation.

Fraudulent misrepresentations involve false statements, which can be promises just like a contractual promise. Therefore, in fraud cases, there is at least the possibility of a recovery based upon the expectancy measure even though the case is a torts case. To use an example from the last chapter, suppose that Ivan had intentionally lied to Helena, who had come from Nashville to Chicago looking for an apartment to rent. Ivan lied when he told Helena that he had an apartment available to rent for a year at $1,500 a month, in order to obtain the deposit from Helena. Regardless of whether Ivan's conduct counts as a breach of contract, it appears his conduct would satisfy the elements of fraudulent misrepresentation under the Restatement of Torts.

Recall some additional facts about the Helena-Ivan hypothetical. Helena returned to Nashville, packed up her things, and had a moving truck transport her belongings from Nashville to Chicago for $4,000. When Helena arrived in Chicago, she discovered that Ivan had rented the apartment to someone else for $2,200 per month for a year. Helena checked into a hotel for a week at $125 per night. She put her belongings in storage for $300. After diligently searching for another apartment, she found one comparable to the one she had agreed to rent from Ivan for $2,000 a month. She signed a year lease at the new apartment.

If Helena were able to recover only her reliance damages from Ivan, her recovery would be limited to the week's hotel stay ($875) and the storage expenses ($300). These are damages for which she is "out of pocket," a term frequently used in tort fraud cases. Giving her those damages puts her in the same position as if there had been no fraudulent promise. Under the reliance measure, she would not be eligible for the $6,000 annual differential in rent payment between the contract price she was promised and the going market rate.

Some courts have taken the position that when a plaintiff like Helena pleads her cause of action in tort rather than contract, she is limited to these reliance (or out-of-pocket) damages. See Smith v. Bolles, 132 U.S. 125 (1889); LAYCOCK pp. 50-52. In jurisdictions still following this rule, why would anyone ever plead a cause of action in tort rather than allege breach of warranty in contract? There are a number of possible reasons to do so (apart from attorney malpractice!):

- The tort cause of action might allow for punitive damages, which are generally not allowed in contract.
- The tort cause of action might make it easier to recover for certain consequential damages even if not foreseeable by the breaching party at the time of the contracting/misrepresentation.
- The contract cause of action might prove problematic (for example, if there was not a valid contract because the contract was not in writing as required by the statute of frauds).
- The tort cause of action might be subject to a longer statute of limitations than the contract cause of action (though in practice it is often the other way around).

In many jurisdictions today, however, the rule against allowing plaintiffs to recover expectancy damages in tort suits has been relaxed. Courts sometimes refer to such expectancy damages in fraud suits as "benefit of the bargain" damages.

The Restatement (Second) of Torts § 549 provides the following remedies in the case of a fraudulent misrepresentation:

> (1) The recipient of a fraudulent misrepresentation is entitled to recover as damages in an action of deceit against the maker the pecuniary loss to him of which the misrepresentation is a legal cause, including
>> (a) the difference between the value of what he has received in the transaction and its purchase price or other value given for it; and
>> (b) pecuniary loss suffered otherwise as a consequence of the recipient's reliance upon the misrepresentation.
> (2) The recipient of a fraudulent misrepresentation in a business transaction is also entitled to recover additional damages sufficient to give him the benefit of his contract with the maker, if these damages are proved with reasonable certainty.

Thus, under the Restatement and in a majority of states (32, according to the 1977 Reporter's Note to § 549), Helena will likely be able to recover not only her reliance damages, but also the additional $6,000 lost rent expectancy differential under § 549(2), which allows for expectancy damages in fraudulent business transactions when proven with reasonable certainty. Depending on the jurisdiction, Helena might be able to sue for punitive damages as well.

The law regarding when expectancy damages are available in tort suits alleging fraudulent misrepresentation remains unclear, however, in a significant minority of jurisdictions. While some states still generally allow for recovery of reliance damages only (for example, New York — see *Lama Holding Co. v. Smith Barney, Inc.*, 668 N.E.2d 1370, 1373-74 (N.Y. 1996)), others, following the lead of *Selman v. Shirley*, 85 P.2d 384 (Or. 1938), have developed a "flexible" test depending upon the circumstances of each case. See also CHARLES T. MCCORMICK, HANDBOOK ON THE LAW OF DAMAGES § 121 (1935) (suggesting that the trial judge should use discretion in deciding which measure of damages should apply in fraud cases, "in view of the probable moral culpability of the defendant and of the definiteness of the representations and the ascertainability of the represented value"). For a strong critique of the *Selman* "flexible" test, see *Goldstein v. Miles*, 859 A.2d 313 (Md. Ct. Spec. App. 2004). In *Goldstein*, the court held that a plaintiff suing for fraud could not recover expectancy damages absent proof that there was an otherwise *enforceable contract* between the parties.

Note also that the Restatement § 549 standard allows recovery only for "pecuniary loss"; it mentions nothing about whether a plaintiff may recover *emotional distress* damages in a case involving fraudulent misrepresentation, and a fair reading is that it does not. Obviously, it is much more attractive for lawyers to bring suit in tort (rather than contract) for fraudulent misrepresentation if emotional distress damages will be available to plaintiffs in particular cases.

Professor Dobbs has taken the position that because the tort of fraudulent misrepresentation is an economic tort (because it usually leads to the loss of money), emotional distress damages generally should not be available. DOBBS § 9.2(4). He notes that the cases where such emotional distress damages have been allowed have been those where the risk of emotional distress had to be quite foreseeable to the party engaging in the fraudulent activity. These serious cases include:

> (1) [A]dopting a baby suffering from serious diseases and developmental disabilities; (2) allowing the implant of a dangerous mechanical heart valve with a substantial chance of death; (3) having sexual relations while concealing venereal diseases or misrepresenting health; and (4) not viewing a body because maggots had eaten away the face when the funeral home actually wanted to avoid preparing the body.

See *McConkey v. Aon Corp.*, 804 A.2d 572, 593 (N.J. Super. Ct. App. Div. 2002) (summarizing Dobbs). The court in *McConkey* noted that "[n]o judicial consensus exists on the propriety of awarding emotional distress damages in fraud cases." *Id.*

Example 3

Xavier sells an exercise machine, the "Fat-eraser," on television, promising that it is "guaranteed to take inches off your waistline in 30 days." Yoko buys the Fat-eraser for three easy payments of $39.99 and uses it as directed. Yoko uses it for 30 days, but it has no effect on her waistline. Indeed, the product is designed poorly, and Yoko injures her back using it, incurring doctor's bills of $1,000. Xavier sold the Fat-eraser with a contract limiting liability to repair or replacement at the seller's option. A similar exercise machine that would have taken inches off Yoko's waistline in 30 days using a similar effort from Yoko would have cost Yoko $500. What damages may Yoko receive?

Explanation

This is a contract for the sale of goods, governed by Article 2. U.C.C. § 2-721 allows victims of fraudulent misrepresentation to get all remedies available for non-fraudulent breaches. Therefore, even though the contract contains a clause limiting Xavier's liability to repair or replacement, this likely won't limit damages in this case. In the first place, any tort suit for injuries Yoko received from the defective product may be recovered in tort despite the provision. *See* U.C.C. § 2-719(3). Thus, the $1,000 should be recoverable.

Additionally, Xavier has made an express warranty that the product would take inches off a user's waistline in 30 days — which the product failed to do. Yoko will therefore argue that she should be entitled to damages for the difference between the product as warranted ($500) and the value of what she received (arguably 0). Neither repair nor replacement will remedy the product's failing to live up to the warranty; the provision therefore likely failed in its essential purpose.

Yoko might want to sue instead in tort even if she would be limited to her reliance damages and medical expenses. The reliance damages here are $119.97 (the three easy payments of $39.99) plus the $1,000 in medical expenses. But if she is able to sue in tort, she might also be able to get emotional distress/pain and suffering damages along with punitive damages.

Example 4

Phillip works as the manager of insurance services at Ross and Company. He is approached by A & A to leave that position and to come work for A & A as the director of insurance services for a $20,000/year raise. Phillip asks Frank, the CEO of A & A, about whether Frank is contemplating selling A & A in the near future to a larger insurance company. Frank tells Phillip that there are no such plans, but this is a lie. Frank wants Phillip to come in and get the business into shape so that it will be more attractive to a buyer (that is, he wants to fatten up the turkey before Thanksgiving). Phillip takes the job as an at-will employee and, based on Frank's statements, assures all of the employees at the firm that it is not going to be offered for sale. Six months later, Frank tells Phillip that he has sold A & A to a larger insurance company, and that Phillip has one day to move out of his office. Phillip feels sick to his stomach. Phillip, having repeated Frank's lies to so many people, is not able to find a job in the insurance industry. He is now working as a data entry consultant for half of what he was paid at A & A. Assuming Phillip can prove that Frank and A & A committed the tort of fraudulent misrepresentation, to what damages is Phillip entitled?

Explanation

This fact pattern is based on the *McConkey* case cited above. Phillip was hired as an at-will employee (meaning he could be fired any time without the firm incurring liability). Therefore, under substantive contract law, he likely does not have a cause of action for breach of contract. The fraud committed by Frank might allow Phillip to rescind (or cancel) the contract, as we will see in Chapter 14, but that likely is not a helpful remedy here.

Assuming that Phillip can make out the elements for the tort of fraudulent concealment, the courts would differ on whether he could get expectation (or benefit of the bargain) damages. Some courts would hold that because there was no enforceable promise (such as a promise of employment), plaintiff could recover only reliance damages.

Phillip is going to claim the loss of past and future salary, which he suffered from giving up his original job in reliance on Frank's promise that the business would not be sold. The jury would have to determine that loss in salary, which arguably would restore Phillip to the position he would have been in had there been no wrong. It is here that the difference in reliance and expectancy damages might matter.

Suppose Phillip's salary at Ross and Company was $100,000 per year, his salary at A & A was $120,000 per year, and his salary working in data entry is $60,000 per year. In terms of reduced wages, reliance damages would measure how much better off Phillip would have been if he had never taken the A & A job. Thus, for reliance damages, we would be looking at the difference in salaries between a continued career at Ross and Company and Phillip's new career path in data entry. It appears we would not compare the difference between his wages at A & A and those at his data entry job. That comparison appears to be the appropriate measure for expectancy damages: What would his salary path have looked like had he continued to work in the field at his new position at A & A, and how does that position differ from where he ended up in data entry?

If Phillip sues in tort, he would also want to recover emotional distress damages for this fraud, but many courts would deny Phillip damages for this distress. This looks like an economic transaction and not like a contract where fraud or breach would likely give rise to serious emotional distress damages (such as a contract for funeral services).

In the actual *McConkey* case, the court allowed the plaintiff to recover damages for lost past earnings, lost future earnings (which need to be properly discounted to present value), and punitive damages (the court upheld the $5 million punitive damages award). It reversed the jury's award of $2 million in emotional distress damages, finding that even if New Jersey would allow plaintiffs to recover such damages as part of the tort of misrepresentation, there was not enough evidence in this case to sustain them: "There is no evidence that plaintiff's purported suffering was of long duration, or that his daily routine or functions were interrupted."

5.3 RELIANCE DAMAGES IN CONTRACT?

Just as it is unusual to have plaintiffs in torts cases asking for expectancy damages, it is unusual for plaintiffs in contracts cases to receive only reliance damages. Because reliance damages are going to be less than expectancy damages, it won't be the plaintiff who asks for them — except as a fallback when expectancy damages are not available. Rather, the defendant will be the party arguing that plaintiff should recover no more than reliance damages.

There are three situations in which courts may award reliance damages rather than expectancy damages in contract:

- The non-breaching party has a problem with the substantive contract claim, such as a lack of consideration or lack of a writing as required by the statute of frauds.
- There are compelling public policy reasons to limit damages to a lesser amount.
- The non-breaching party has trouble proving expectancy damages with reasonable certainty.

We consider each of these scenarios in turn.

Problems with the Substantive Contract Claim. In the well-known contracts case of *Ricketts v. Scothorn*, 77 N.W. 365 (Neb. 1898), a grandfather saw his granddaughter working in a store. He told her, "None of my grand-children work and you don't have to." He then gave her a promissory note for $2,000 plus 6% annual interest (a substantial sum at the time). He had not paid off that note by the time he died, and the granddaughter brought an action against the grandfather's estate. The estate defended by raising a substantive contracts objection: the promise from the grandfather lacked consideration; it looked like a gift.

The court held that the granddaughter's reliance on the promise from the grandfather created an estoppel that prevented the estate from raising lack of consideration as a defense.

Allowing the granddaughter in *Ricketts* to recover the full $2,000 payment plus interest gave her the expectancy damages in the contract. That is, the court let the granddaughter recover the same damages she would have received had the contract been supported by consideration.

Reliance represents a middle path between non-enforcement of the promise and treating the contract as valid — as the product of a bar-gained-for exchange. For example, suppose that after the granddaughter received the promissory note, she quit working and borrowed $200 from the bank for her living expenses until the grandfather paid (remember that these 1890s dollars went a lot farther!). The $200 would be her reliance damages.

When should a court decide in such circumstances whether to award the usual expectancy damages or the less generous reliance measure? On this question, the Restatement (Second) of Contracts has been influential. Section 90(1) provides:

> A promise which the promisor should reasonably expect to induce action or forbearance on the part of the promisee or a third person and which does induce such action or forbearance is binding if injustice can be avoided only by enforcement of the promise. The remedy granted for breach may be limited as justice requires.

Comment *d* to the section further states:

> A promise binding under this section is a contract, and full-scale enforcement by normal remedies is often appropriate. But the same factors which bear on whether any relief should be granted also bear on the character and extent of the remedy. In particular, relief may sometimes be limited to restitution or to damages or specific relief measured by the extent of the promisee's reliance rather than by the terms of the promise. See §§ 84, 89; compare Restatement, Second, Torts § 549 on damages for fraud. Unless there is unjust enrichment of the promisor, damages should not put the promisee in a better position than performance of the promise would have put him. See §§ 344, 349. In the case of a promise to make a gift it would rarely be proper to award consequential

damages which would place a greater burden on the promisor than performance would have imposed.

The Restatement's approach, therefore, gives discretion to courts to limit a plaintiff's recovery of reliance damages "as justice requires," such as when reliance serves as a substitute for consideration.

The Restatement takes a similar position on the availability of reliance damages when parties to a contract fail to satisfy the statute of frauds. Under § 139, reliance can substitute for a writing to satisfy the statute of frauds, but the courts must limit remedies as justice requires. Although this Restatement section has been influential, not all courts have adopted it or adopted it fully. In Alaska, for example, plaintiffs can recover reliance damages for breach of an employment contract that fails to comply with the statute of frauds, but plaintiffs cannot recover reliance damages for breach of a contract for the sale or lease of real estate that fails to comply with the statute of frauds. *Valdez Fisheries Dev. Ass'n v. Alyeska Pipeline Serv. Co.*, 45 P.3d 657, 669 (Alaska 2002).

Policy Reasons to Limit Damages to Reliance Damages. Sullivan v. O'Connor, 296 N.E.2d 183 (Mass. 1973), is the leading case on the use of reliance damages rather than expectancy damages for reasons of policy in a contracts case. Plaintiff was an entertainer who contracted with defendant, a plastic surgeon, for a nose job. The surgeon promised the plaintiff a more beautiful nose, but plaintiff was left in worse condition than she was in before the operation.[1] She endured pain, suffering, and emotional distress as a result of the operations. She sued the doctor in tort (for malpractice) and for breach of contract — in particular, for breach of the promise of a better nose.[2] The jury found for the doctor on the malpractice claim but for the plaintiff on the breach of contract claim. (These verdicts are not inconsistent; the doctor could have complied with the customary standard of care in performing the surgeries but still have broken his promise to provide a better nose.) Thinking only about the status of plaintiff's nose for a moment

---

1. According to the court, "the plaintiff's nose had been straight, but long and prominent; the defendant undertook by two operations to reduce its prominence and somewhat to shorten it, thus making it more pleasing in relation to the plaintiff's other features. Actually the plaintiff was obliged to undergo three operations, and her appearance was worsened. Her nose now had a concave line to about the midpoint, at which it became bulbous; viewed frontally, the nose from bridge to midpoint was flattened and broadened, and the two sides of the tip had lost symmetry." *Sullivan*, 296 N.E. 2d at 185.

2. Upon reading the facts of this case, you might recall a similar, earlier contracts case, *Hawkins v. McGee*, 146 A. 641 (N.H. 1929). In the so-called "Hairy Hand case," the defendant doctor promised the plaintiff with a deformed hand a perfect hand. In *Hawkins*, the court allowed the plaintiff to recover expectancy damages: the difference between what was promised and what was received.

(and putting aside the emotional distress damages), we can see a nice contrast between the expectation and reliance measures (see Figure 5.2).

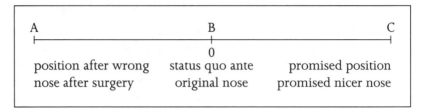

Figure 5.2 Sullivan v. O'Connor

To award plaintiff reliance damages (B − A) is to compensate her enough to bring her from her bad nose after the surgery back to the status quo ante. To award plaintiff expectation damages (C − A) is to award her the difference between what she was promised (the nicer nose) and what she ended up receiving (the worse nose after surgery), putting her in the same position as if the contract had been performed as promised.

The trial judge allowed plaintiff to recover her reliance damages, and both sides objected. The doctor wished to repay only the cost of her original surgery (his gain using a restitution measure) and not any pain and suffering damages. The plaintiff wanted expectation damages, but abandoned that claim on appeal.

The court held that reliance damages were the appropriate measure in this case. Note that this is not a case, like the earlier cases we discussed, where the underlying contract was unenforceable. The parties had a valid contract for surgery. Instead, the court pointed to a *policy reason* for limiting the damages to reliance damages in such cases:

> Considering the uncertainties of medical science and the variations in the physical and psychological conditions of individual patients, doctors can seldom in good faith promise specific results. Therefore it is unlikely that physicians of even average integrity will in fact make such promises. Statements of opinion by the physician with some optimistic coloring are a different thing, and may indeed have therapeutic value. But patients may transform such statements into firm promises in their own minds, especially when they have been disappointed in the event, and testify in that sense to sympathetic juries.

Id. at 186.

Fearing that a meager restitution measure (return of the doctor's fee) would provide not enough deterrence and that the expectation measure could be too harsh and discourage encouraging words from doctors, the court settled on the middle ground of reliance damages.

The court also rejected the defendant's argument that pain and suffering damages should be non-compensable, finding the question turned on the intent of the parties to the particular contract: "Suffering or distress resulting from the breach going beyond that which was envisaged by the treatment as agreed, should be compensable on the same ground as the worsening of the patient's conditions because of the breach." *Id.* at 189.

Let's explore further the choice between expectancy and reliance damages. To make things concrete, albeit a bit artificial, let's assume that had the nose surgery been successful, plaintiff would have had to undergo two operations and the pain of each of these operations would have been worth $10,000. Because the first two surgeries were unsuccessful, however, she had to undergo a third operation. Assume the jury would have valued the pain associated with the third operation at $15,000. The emotional distress resulting from having a worse nose was valued at $50,000. Plaintiff valued the promised nose at $100,000 (less the $20,000 in pain from undergoing the two operations to achieve it, and the $5,000 contract price for the surgeries, for a $75,000 expected gain). How would we compute the damages plaintiff should receive under (a) the expectancy measure and (b) the reliance measure?

Let's begin with the expectancy measure by considering the plaintiff's promised position. Had the surgery been successful, plaintiff would have received the promised nose valued at $100,000 − $20,000 (pain from the first two operations) − $5,000 (contract price) = $75,000. So C = $75,000. The value of A (the position she is in after the wrong) is composed of the following losses

- $20,000 (pain of the first two operations)
- $5,000 (contract price)
- $15,000 (the pain of the third operation)
- $50,000 (the emotional distress from having the worse nose)

for a total position below zero, of −$90,000. Total damages: $75,000 − (−$90,000) = $165,000. See Figure 5.3.

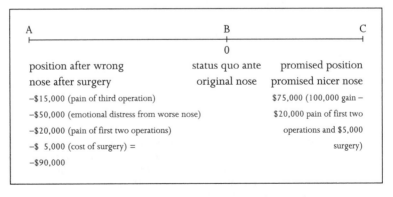

Figure 5.3 *Sullivan*—**Detailed Look at Damages**

Note how this $165,000 damage measure puts the plaintiff in the same position as she would have been in had the doctor performed the contract as promised. If the contract had been performed as promised, plaintiff would have had a gain of $100,000 and "expenses" of $25,000 (the hard cost of the operation and the soft costs of the pain of the first two surgeries). She would have been ahead by $75,000, the value embodied by plaintiff's new and improved nose.

Now consider the $165,000 damage award. Plaintiff uses the first $25,000 to pay herself back for her originally anticipated "expenses," bringing the figure down to $140,000. The next $65,000 compensates the plaintiff for the pain of the third operation and the emotional distress from having the worse nose — both expenses she incurred because of the defendant's breach. This leaves her with $75,000, exactly where she would have been had the defendant kept his promise. The difference is that plaintiff has this $75,000 value in cash, rather than in an improved appearance.

Consider now the alternative reliance measure. Remember, the goal of reliance damages is to put the plaintiff in the position she would have been in had there been no contract. The measure of damages here is (B − A), or 0 − (−$90,000), or $90,000. Had the contract never been entered into, the plaintiff never would have paid the $5,000 fee, suffered the pain from the first two operations ($20,000),[3] suffered the pain from the third operation ($15,000), or suffered the emotional distress from having the worse nose ($50,000). These losses total $90,000. Under the reliance measure, the plaintiff does not receive any damages compensating for the $75,000 promised gain under the contract.

Problems with Certainty. The final type of case in which courts sometimes award a non-breaching party reliance damages rather than expectancy damages occurs when the plaintiff has difficulty proving the value of the expectancy. The court in *Sullivan v. O'Connor* raised this point as a further rationale for awarding only reliance damages, noting: "To attempt, moreover, to put a value on the condition that would or might have resulted, had the treatment succeeded as promised, may sometimes put an exceptional strain on the imagination of the fact finder."

Applied to *Sullivan*, this argument is unconvincing. If the jury already had valued the pain and suffering and emotional distress related to the difference

---

3. As the *Sullivan* court noted: "Indeed it can be argued that the very suffering or distress 'contracted for' — that which would have been incurred if the treatment achieved the promised result — should also be compensable on the [reliance] theory. . . . For that suffering is 'wasted' if the treatment fails. Otherwise stated, compensation for this waste is arguably required in order to complete the restoration of the status quo ante." *Sullivan*, 296 N.E.2d at 189.

between the post-breach nose and the status quo nose, how much harder is it to come up with a value for the promised nose as well? But there are other cases where certainty is a greater problem, and thus the resort to reliance damages over expectancy damages makes more sense.

Consider in this regard the facts of *Copeland v. Baskin Robbins U.S.A.*, 117 Cal. Rptr. 2d 875 (Cal. Ct. App. 2002). Baskin Robbins was looking to sell one of its ice cream plants, and Kevin Copeland was interested in buying it. They entered into negotiations, signing an agreement to negotiate in good faith. Copeland made it clear to Baskin Robbins that a key part of the deal was that Baskin Robbins would purchase a large amount of ice cream manufactured by him at the plant (about 7 million gallons over a three-year period). Eventually, Baskin Robbins would not agree on a side deal for purchasing ice cream from Copeland, and the purchase fell through. As the court put it, "'[m]any millions of dollars' in anticipated profits had melted away like so much banana ripple ice cream on a hot summer day." Realizing that he could not take the risk in buying the plant without the deal to sell the ice cream, Copeland sued for breach of contract.

While the court rejected the idea that a contract to negotiate in good faith was unenforceable (thus, as in *Sullivan*, the parties had a valid binding contract), it held that Copeland could not recover his expectancy damages from breach of such an agreement. "The plaintiff cannot recover for lost expectations (profits) because there is no way of knowing what the ultimate terms of the agreement would have been or even if there would have been an ultimate agreement." *See Copeland*, 117 Cal. Rptr. 2d at 885. Instead, damages "are measured by the injury the plaintiff suffered in relying on the defendant to negotiate in good faith. This measure encompasses the plaintiff's out-of-pocket costs in conducting the negotiations and may or may not include lost opportunity costs." *Id.* In the actual case, plaintiff did not try to prove he had any reliance costs, and therefore the court concluded he could recover nothing.

Example 5

Same facts as in *Ricketts* but assume that after the grandfather makes the promise, the granddaughter goes to the bank and gets a $2,000 loan to buy a house. When the grandfather fails to pay, the bank evicts the granddaughter, and she becomes homeless. Living on the street, she develops a number of diseases and incurs $4,000 in medical bills. To what damages, if any, is the granddaughter entitled to in a jurisdiction that has adopted the Restatement (Second) of Contracts § 90?

Explanation

Recall that under the Restatement (Second) of Contracts § 90, the remedy may be limited as justice requires. In this case, a court could decide that justice requires enforcing the entire contract ("full-scale enforcement by normal remedies is often appropriate," id. cmt. d). The contract here is a promise to pay money, however, and normal expectation damages would limit the recovery to the promised amount of money plus interest at the prevailing rate — $2,000 plus interest in this case.

The granddaughter could argue that she should get her reliance damages — which should include her medical expenses that are a consequence of the grandfather's breach. A court would be quite reluctant to grant such damages for two reasons. First, under Hadley, it does not appear that such damages are a foreseeable consequence of the grandfather's breach. Second, comment d to the Restatement section provides that "[i]n the case of a promise to make a gift it would rarely be proper to award consequential damages which would place a greater burden on the promisor than performance would have imposed."

Example 6

Same facts as in Sullivan v. O'Connor, except assume that before the surgeon promises the plaintiff a beautiful nose, plaintiff tells the surgeon: "I must have a more beautiful nose. I have been promised the lead in a new movie opposite Tom Cruise, contingent on my obtaining plastic surgery to fix my nose's appearance. They are going to pay me $200,000 for the role, and if the movie is successful it will launch my career as a movie star, which could earn me millions of dollars in the future." Unfortunately, after the unsuccessful surgery, plaintiff loses her movie role. How, if at all, does this change the calculation of damages in this case?

Explanation

To the extent that the court is compensating only for reliance damages (for the policy reasons set forth in Sullivan), these additional facts do not affect the amount of damages. We do not treat forgone opportunities as reliance costs; rather, they are part of the expectancy. To put plaintiff back to the status quo ante would require only payments for the pain of the three surgeries, the cost of the surgery, and the emotional distress that comes from having the worse-looking nose.

If plaintiff could recover expectation damages, it is possible that these additional facts could affect the amount of recovery. In essence, the plaintiff would be arguing that her promised position was high because of the promise of the contract. These appear to be consequential damages (coming after the initial breach, which is the failure of the surgery to produce a more beautiful nose). The $200,000 lost salary could be recoverable as consequential damages because the statement by the plaintiff to the surgeon shows that the lost, potential profit was reasonably foreseeable. Some courts have held, however, that when the breach of a contract would cause disproportionate damages given the risks taken, these damages would not be recoverable. *See Postal Instant Press, Inc. v. Sealy*, 51 Cal. Rptr. 2d 365, 373 (Cal. Ct. App. 1996); *see also* RESTATEMENT (SECOND) OF CONTRACTS § 351(3) ("A court may limit damages for foreseeable loss by excluding recovery for loss of profits, by allowing recovery only for loss incurred in reliance, or otherwise if it concludes that in the circumstances justice so requires in order to avoid disproportionate compensation."). The damages related to future career prospects seem too uncertain to be recoverable, for reasons we will consider in the next chapter.

Example 7

Same facts as in the *Copeland* case but assume the following: Baskin Robbins and Copeland sign a valid contract for Copeland to buy the ice cream factory for $2 million. Baskin Robbins promises to buy at least 7 million gallons of ice cream over three years at the price of $1 over Copeland's cost, with "cost" determined by a complex formula in the contract. After Copeland takes possession of the factory, but before he invests anything to gear up the factory, Baskin Robbins announces it will buy no ice cream from him. (This anticipatory repudiation constitutes a breach of contract under substantive contract law.) Over the next three years, Copeland does his best to sell ice cream, and he sells 3 million gallons of ice cream to other sellers, earning a profit of $1 per gallon. To what damages is Copeland entitled?

Explanation

The parties have a valid written contract, and there are no policy reasons for limiting Copeland to recovering only his reliance damages. Accordingly, if he can prove his damages with reasonable certainty, he is going to be able to recover expectancy damages. Also, since this is a contract for the sale of goods, Article 2 of the U.C.C. governs. The buyer has breached, so the seller can resort to his remedies for breach.

One possibility is that Copeland will claim damages under U.C.C. § 2-706, which gives the seller the difference between the contract price and the retail price plus incidental damages less expenses saved. Copeland stood to make $7 million on the contract. After the breach, he sold enough ice cream to make only $3 million on the contract. Copeland is left with $4 million plus any incidental costs associated with making the new $3 million sales, less any expenses he saved from having to produce only 3 million rather than

7 million gallons of ice cream. (Some of these costs are going to be reflected in the "cost" element of the contract price formula, and an economist will have to look carefully to figure out how to measure the costs correctly.)

Alternatively, Copeland might argue that he was a lost volume seller. Specifically, he might try to prove that he had the capacity to produce both the ice cream under the original contract with Baskin Robbins and the new ice cream he sold after Baskin Robbins breached. If he can meet the requirements of a lost volume seller, he would be able to recover his "profit (including reasonable overhead) which the seller would have made from full performance by the buyer, together with any incidental damages" less the junk value of any salvage value of goods rejected by the buyer. U.C.C. § 2-708(2). Copeland would recover $7 million under this measure. There do not appear to be any incidental damages associated with not producing the 7 million gallons (he cannot look at his costs of producing the 3 million other gallons of ice cream), nor is there any salvage value to any goods rejected by the buyer.

Ensuring the Rightful Position: A Look at Certainty, Mitigation, Offsetting Benefits, and the Collateral Source Rule

So far, we have established that damages are meant to put the plaintiff in the rightful position, and much of the discussion in last four chapters dealt with how damage rules are an attempt to do so. In this chapter, we deal with four more issues to round out our discussion of damages and the rightful position standard:

1. How certain does the jury have to be about the amount of damages suffered by plaintiff?
2. What steps must the plaintiff take to minimize loss?
3. How should we treat expenses and losses that plaintiff avoids because of the defendant's wrong?
4. How should we treat collateral sources — that is, insurance and government payments that plaintiff receives on account of injuries caused by the defendant?

6.1 THE CERTAINTY REQUIREMENT

It is often said that the plaintiff must prove damages with "reasonable certainty." This statement needs to be taken with a grain of salt in the context of civil litigation, where the dominant standard is that plaintiff must prove her prima facie case by a preponderance of the evidence — a "more likely than not" standard that is much lower than the "beyond a reasonable doubt" standard applicable in criminal cases. Just as plaintiff has to prove the other elements of the case (for example, that defendant breached either a duty in a negligence case or a contract in a contracts case) under this preponderance standard, plaintiff must prove damages as an essential element of the prima facie case by the same standard.[1]

In a torts case, the amount of proof courts require appears to vary depending upon whether the plaintiff seeks economic or noneconomic damages. For example, to the extent to which a plaintiff seeks damages for lost wages and medical expenses, the court often will insist upon proof of expenses for past loss and expert testimony regarding future costs and valuation based upon evidence of market rates. However, to the extent to which plaintiff seeks recovery for pain and suffering or emotional distress, courts do not require any certainty regarding the amount of damages, but the jury must still be reasonably certain that the plaintiff suffered these kinds of damages if it is to allow recovery of noneconomic damages at all. Rather than limit noneconomic damages on grounds of uncertainty, courts sometimes lower the amount of such damages under a "shock the conscience" standard or other rule that limits the amount of noneconomic damages.

In contracts cases, courts are a bit more demanding in terms of the proof of certainty of damages. Restatement (Second) of Contracts § 352 provides: "Damages are not recoverable for loss beyond an amount that the evidence permits to be established with reasonable certainty." The comments to the section emphasize that a greater degree of certainty is required in contracts cases compared to torts cases.

The certainty principle frequently arises in contracts cases involving a non-breaching party's claim for lost business profits as damages. An illustrative case is RSB Lab. Servs., Inc. v. BSI Corp., 847 A.2d 599 (N.J. Super. Ct. App. Div. 2004). In RSB, plaintiff ran a "bleeding station," an office to which doctors refer patients to have blood or other bodily fluids drawn for analysis in a laboratory. (Patients would probably rather not hear the term doctors use to refer to such a facility!) The business was a successful one, and the plaintiff decided to convert the business into a full-service medical laboratory. Plaintiff secured the necessary license and had a strong potential client base for the full lab from its existing bleeding station business.

Plaintiff contracted with the defendant to buy laboratory equipment, most importantly a refurbished "Hitachi 704" machine used to detect

---

1. We have seen two exceptions to this principle. Chapter 2 first noted that plaintiffs sometimes may recover nominal damages (such as $1) when plaintiff cannot prove that she suffered actual (compensatory) damages. These nominal damages often serve as a "declaration" to the world of the rights of plaintiff and defendant or provide a hook for the award of punitive damages or attorney's fees. Second, Chapter 3 noted that plaintiffs alleging defamation sometimes may be able to recover "presumed damages" when they cannot (or do not wish to) prove actual damages.

chemical imbalances in the blood. Ultimately, the defendant could not get the supplied Hitachi 704 to work properly, thereby breaching the contract. Plaintiff abandoned the plans for the full-service laboratory and sued for breach of contract. The jury agreed that the defendant breached, and the question on appeal concerned the damages.

An accountant testified at trial as an expert witness for plaintiff on the amount of damages. The expert reviewed paperwork from the existing bleeding station business, obtained data about the profitability of competitors, and performed other work to estimate the amount of profits plaintiffs would have made in running a full-service medical laboratory. The jury awarded approximately $255,000 in damages for lost profits, attorney's fees (allowed under the contract), costs, and prejudgment interest.

On appeal, the main issue was whether the full-service laboratory was a continuation of the bleeding station business or a new business. To someone unfamiliar with the legal issues surrounding the certainty principle, that question probably seems a bit bizarre. Why should plaintiff's recovery of damages for lost profits turn on whether the plaintiff's losses came from a new or existing business?

The answer is that New Jersey is among a minority of jurisdictions that has a per se rule that new businesses cannot recover damages for lost profits. These minority jurisdictions view such damages as too speculative, violating the certainty requirement. This is an older view of the certainty requirement that most jurisdictions and the Restatement have rejected.[2] RESTATEMENT (SECOND) OF CONTRACTS § 352. Fortunately for the plaintiff in RSB, the New Jersey appellate court concluded that the full-service laboratory was a continuation of the bleeding station business, and therefore the plaintiff could recover the lost profits. Unfortunately for other plaintiffs in New Jersey, however, the court reaffirmed the so-called "new business rule" in New Jersey, rejecting cases from the Third Circuit, predicting that the New Jersey Supreme Court would overturn the rule. Thus, until the New Jersey Supreme Court rules otherwise, it appears that plaintiffs starting new businesses won't be able to prove their claims for lost profits in courts applying New Jersey law.

In the majority of jurisdictions that have rejected the new business rule, plaintiffs who claim lost profits from new businesses don't get a free ride on

---

2. Similarly, comment 4 to U.C.C. § 2-715 (on incidental and consequential damages) provides: "The burden of proving the extent of loss incurred by way of consequential damage is on the buyer, but the section on liberal administration of remedies rejects any doctrine of certainty which requires almost mathematical precision in the proof of loss. Loss may be determined in any manner which is reasonable under the circumstances." Article 2 applies to the RSB contract because it is a contract for the sale of goods. New Jersey has adopted § 2-715. See N.J. STAT. ANN. § 12A:2-715 (West). But the comments are not part of the statute, and § 2-715 itself does not necessarily preclude New Jersey's new business rule.

proving damages. Defense lawyers can hammer home the certainty requirement to the jury, arguing about all kinds of reasons why the plaintiff's claim for lost profits from a new business is too speculative. Thus, in a majority of jurisdictions, whether a claim is too speculative is decided on a *case-by-case basis by the* jury rather than rejected on a per se basis as in jurisdictions like New Jersey.

Example 1

Yoni owns a business selling the latest trendy fashions. Sometimes he makes great profits, but at other times his business does quite poorly (if he fails to predict the latest fashion trends). Yoni hires Zena, a contractor, to remodel his business. Zena promises to complete construction in three months. Zena is late, however, and it takes her seven months to complete the remodeling work. Zena's failure to finish on time constitutes a breach of contract. May Yoni recover his lost profits? If so, how will he prove them?

Explanation

Yoni has an existing business, so the per se new business rule won't bar his recovery of lost profits even in the minority of jurisdictions (such as New Jersey). Even though the new business rule does not apply, it is uncertain whether Yoni would be able to prove his damages with reasonable certainty. Yoni's past performance is the best predictor of profits. Because he is in a business in which sometimes he makes a profit and sometimes he does not, Zena's lawyer will have an opening to argue to the jury that the award of damages in this case would be too speculative. Yoni's lawyers would have to make some argument as to why his business would have been profitable during the four-month period in which the store remained closed due to Zena's breach.

Example 2

Marcia Miller and her passenger are severely injured when Miller's new car crashes into a wall. According to Miller, the car's accelerator got stuck, thereby causing an unavoidable collision with a retaining wall. The automobile is a total loss. While Miller is recuperating in the hospital, her father, who is an attorney, contacts Malkin, an agent of Allstate, which is her automobile insurer. Miller's father informs Malkin that Marcia wants to retain possession of the automobile in order to have it examined by an expert for defects. Her father is of the opinion that his daughter has a products liability claim against the manufacturer. Malkin tells Miller and her father that Allstate wants temporary possession of the car because they plan to have an expert examine it for defects as they anticipate that the passenger injured in the accident will file a claim against Allstate. Eventually the parties reach an agreement whereby Miller relinquishes possession of the car to Allstate so it may prepare for its defense against the claim by the passenger. In exchange, Allstate promises to preserve the car and to make it available for inspection by Miller's experts. The existence of the oral agreement is not disputed. Before any expert examination is performed, however, Allstate, in breach of the agreement, sells the car to a salvage yard, where it is disassembled and disposed of. Miller sues Allstate, alleging that, as a result of Allstate's breach of the agreement to preserve the wrecked automobile for expert inspection, she is denied the opportunity to maintain a products liability action against the manufacturer. To what damages, if any, is Miller entitled for Allstate's breach of contract?

Explanation

The statement of facts in this example is taken from a Florida appellate court opinion, *Miller v. Allstate Ins. Co.*, 573 So. 2d 24 (Fla. Dist. Ct. App. 1990). This case presents a very difficult question under the certainty principle. It is well established, as the *Miller* court noted, that "although damages usually must be established within a reasonable degree of certainty, . . . when the difficulty in establishing damages is caused by the defendant, he should bear the risk of uncertainty that his own wrong created." *Miller*, 573 So. 2d at 28. So if an arsonist burns down plaintiff's house and destroys all of plaintiff's belongings, the arsonist cannot defend a tort suit on grounds that plaintiff cannot prove the value of his possessions with reasonable certainty.

This case is harder, however, because the destruction of plaintiff's car did not deprive her of her property but only of a *chance* to prove her products liability case against a manufacturer. We don't know whether the destroyed car was defective. In the case of the arsonist, in contrast, there is no question that the fire caused plaintiff's losses; the only question is the *market value* of those losses.

In the *Miller* case, the court allowed plaintiff to recover damages for the loss of the *opportunity* to prove her products liability case. It is not clear, however, exactly how the jury is supposed to value this lost opportunity. To award the full value of a products liability suit that only had a chance of success seems to put the plaintiff in a position better than the rightful position (she was deprived of a *chance*, not of a sure claim).

One possible way to award damages consistent with the rightful position standard would be to assess the damages that plaintiff would have been able to recover in the products liability suit had it been successful, discounted by the probability that plaintiff would have successfully proven her products liability case. For example, if plaintiff could have recovered damages of $100,000 from the products liability suit, and the jury believed she had a 30% chance of winning her products liability suit, her damages would be $100,000 × 0.30, or $30,000. But defendants could reasonably question whether such a standard is consistent with the usual preponderance of the evidence standard applicable in civil cases: looking at the 30% figure, we cannot say she was more likely than not to have sustained these losses. All in all, a very difficult question.

6.2 THE MITIGATION REQUIREMENT

6.2.1 Avoidable Losses: Rules and Economic Rationale

In assessing damages, the law treats plaintiffs as though they took reasonable steps to avoid further loss whether or not they actually did so. This "avoidable consequences" or "mitigation" rule helps defendants minimize the amount of damages they must pay, and when it is misunderstood or misapplied by plaintiffs, it can lead to damages awards that leave plaintiffs in a position below the rightful position.

To take a simple example, suppose Alice negligently knocks Bea over on the street. Bea gets some cuts and scrapes on her right leg. Rather than take care of the cuts and scrapes by applying an antibiotic ointment, Bea does nothing. Bea develops a stubborn infection, and her leg eventually is amputated to prevent the infection from killing her.

At first glance, Bea might look no different from the plaintiff in *Vosburg* (see Chapter 3) who lost a leg as the result of the defendant's kick. There we said the defendant had to pay for all the damages he caused under the "thin-skulled" or "egg shell plaintiff" rule: you take the plaintiff as you find him. Though plaintiff sought medical attention, he still lost the use of his leg. Plaintiff in *Vosburg* recovered damages covering the entire loss he suffered.

In the Alice-Bea hypothetical, however, the additional harm could have been prevented by Bea, but it wasn't. In that situation, a court would say — if Alice's lawyer raised the issue — that Bea could recover only for losses that were *unavoidable*. This failure to mitigate, therefore, could prevent Bea from getting damages to restore her to the rightful position. To give a numerical example, suppose that a jury would value Bea's loss of a leg (and accompanying noneconomic damages) at $500,000. If we consider Bea's position after the wrong, she is at −$500,000. If the jury believes, however, that it is more likely than not that Bea could have avoided the loss of the leg through reasonable mitigation, and that if she had mitigated her injury she would have suffered $1,000 in damages, Bea recovers only the $1,000. This leaves her at −$499,000 (Point A-) — far from B, the status quo ante. See Figure 6.1.

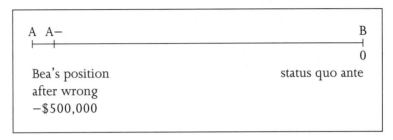

Figure 6.1

Though it is sometimes said that plaintiffs have a "duty to mitigate," this terminology is confusing. Alice cannot be sued by Bea if Bea fails to take reasonable steps to mitigate her injuries. But because the law of damages requires the jury to treat Bea as though she mitigated when the defendant raises the issue, Bea has every incentive to mitigate. (Besides the possibility of tort recovery, Bea has every incentive to take reasonable steps to mitigate because damages cannot adequately substitute for the loss of a leg; thus, we would expect Bea would still take care of the health of her leg.)

We can easily see the potential unfairness to defendants in allowing plaintiffs to "pile on damages" that reasonably could be avoided. But there is an efficiency rationale for the rule as well: so long as plaintiffs understand the rule in advance, it makes plaintiffs no worse off and makes defendants better off.[3] To illustrate it, consider the classic mitigation case, *Rockingham County v. Luten Bridge Co.*, 35 F.2d 301 (4th Cir. 1929). Rockingham County contracted with Luten Bridge Company to build a bridge. After the bridge company had spent about $1,900 on labor and materials, the county said it was breaching the contract. The county no longer wanted the bridge, because it had changed its development plans, and therefore it did not want to pay any more for a "bridge to nowhere."

Even after the county told the bridge company about the breach, however, Luten continued to build the bridge. Luten then sued for $18,000, the amount plaintiff claimed it was due for the work done.

Let's suppose that the total cost of the bridge for the bridge company was $10,000. Had there been no breach, the bridge company stood to make a profit of $8,000 ($18,000 − $10,000), or Luten's promised position.

---

3. Not only is the rule Kaldor-Hicks efficient (see Chapter 2, footnote 2) because the gains to the winners exceed the losses to the losers, but it is also Pareto efficient because no party is made worse off and at least one party is made better off.

Now, suppose we did not have the mitigation rule and the bridge company had completed its work. In assessing the bridge company's total damages, its promised position, C in Figure 6.2, was $8,000, or the profit it was anticipating before the breach. Its position after the wrong, A, was −$10,000, or the amount the company spent building the bridge. Its total damages would be (C − A), or $8,000 − (−$10,000), or $18,000. After paying itself back for its expenses ($10,000), the bridge company's ledger would show a profit of $8,000. The county, on the other hand, is out $18,000 with a bridge to nowhere.

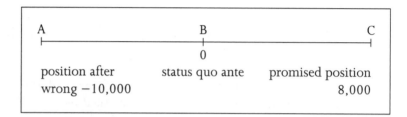

Bridge company profit: **$8,000**
County's cost: **$18,000**

Figure 6.2 Bridge Company Damages Under No Mitigation Rule

Now consider the same county-bridge scenario except that this time, there is a mitigation rule, and the bridge company stops working immediately when it hears of the breach (after it has spent $1,900—its reliance costs). The bridge company then promptly sues for damages.

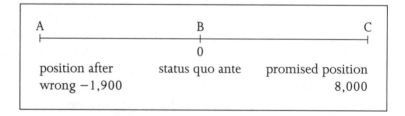

Bridge company profit: **$8,000**
County's cost: **$9,900**

Figure 6.3 Bridge Company Damages Under a Mitigation Rule
Where Bridge Company Mitigates

As in the last example, the bridge company's promised position, C, was $8,000, or the profit it was anticipating before the breach. Its position after the wrong, A, was −$1,900, or the amount the company had spent in building the bridge until it heard about the breach. (See Figure 6.3.)

Its total damages would be (C − A), or $8,000 − (−$1,900), or $9,900. After paying itself back for its expenses, the bridge company's ledger would show a profit of $8,000. The county, on the other hand, is out $9,900, with only a partially built bridge to nowhere.

The example demonstrates the economic efficiency of the mitigation rule. Whether or not there is a mitigation rule, the bridge company ends up with $8,000 in profit. A mitigation rule, however, saves the county $8,100, which represents the cost of completing the bridge to nowhere after the county had told the bridge company of the county's breach. The rule is thus efficient because it leaves a non-breaching party (who understands the rule) in the same position, but also can greatly aid the defendant.

The result in the *Rockingham County* case demonstrates that a plaintiff fails to mitigate at its own peril. Using the numbers set out above, the law allows the bridge company to recover damages *as though it mitigated*, meaning damages of $9,900 rather than the $18,000 contract price. Because the bridge company spent $10,000 finishing the bridge, the company ends up with its ledger at −$100 (it spent $10,000 to build the bridge and received damages of only $9,900) rather than at +$8,000, a costly mistake.

Example 3

Charlie is driving down Main Street very carefully, but he is not wearing a seat belt. Daniella is driving drunk the wrong way down Main Street, and slams head first into Charlie's car. Charlie is paralyzed from the waist down because of the accident, and he won't be able to work again. A jury considering the extent of his damages would value them at $1 million. The experts agree that if Charlie had been wearing a seat belt, he would only have sustained relatively minor injuries, and his damages would not have exceeded $50,000. Should Charlie's failure to wear a seat belt be considered a failure to mitigate? If so, what should Charlie's damages be?

Explanation

The question of how to deal with an injured party's failure to wear a seat belt has been a contentious issue in the states. The failure to wear a seat belt might be relevant to the question of mitigation, the tort affirmative defense of comparative negligence (which in many states would reduce the plaintiff's recovery based upon the jury's determination of the percentage of plaintiff's fault or responsibility in not wearing the seat belt), or neither. See *Derheim v. N. Fiorito Co.*, 492 P.2d 1030 (Wash. 1972). Other courts (and in some cases legislatures via statute) have allowed evidence of plaintiff's failure to wear a seat belt as relevant to the mitigation question. See *Spier v. Barker*, 323 N.E.2d 164 (N.Y. 1974); N.Y. Veh. & Traf. § 1229-c(8).

The *Spier* court noted the chronological oddity, however, of treating the failure to wear a seat belt as a mitigation issue:

> We concede that the opportunity to mitigate damages prior to the occurrence of an accident does not ordinarily arise, and that the chronological distinction, on which the concept of mitigation damages rests, is justified in most cases. However, in our opinion, the seat belt affords the automobile occupant an unusual and ordinarily unavailable means by which he or she may minimize his or her damages *prior* to the accident.

Spier, 323 N.E.2d at 168.

The issue would matter a great deal to Charlie. Under a rule treating the failure to wear a seat belt as a failure to mitigate, if the jury finds that had Charlie mitigated he would have suffered only $50,000 in damages (rather than the $1 million he actually suffered), Charlie's recovery would be $50,000.

6.2.2 Mitigation Under Article 2 of the U.C.C.

Note how the U.C.C. provisions build in mitigation principles. When a seller breaches and a buyer does not cover (we'll be talking about when the buyer *does* cover in the next section, on offsetting benefits), the buyer is entitled to market damages under §2-713 (see Chapter 4.5.1). Recall the formula:

> Amounts toward the purchase price paid to seller + (market price at the place of tender − contract price) + incidental and consequential damages − expenses saved

Recall the hypothetical from Chapter 4 in which Mona agrees to buy an automobile worth $29,000 for $25,000. Putting aside amounts already paid to the seller (Lisa), incidental and consequential damages, and expenses saved, Mona is entitled to $4,000, the difference between the market price at the time of tender and the contract price. This formula *builds in the idea of mitigation.* It treats Mona as if she went out and made the substitute purchase of the automobile for $29,000. By giving her $4,000 in damages (again, ignoring the further complications in the §2-713 formula), she gets the same benefit of the bargain: she gets to have her red Lexus convertible for a total cost of $25,000, $4,000 below the going market price.

The same principle is at work when a buyer breaches a contract governed by Article 2 of the U.C.C. When the buyer breaches and the seller does not resell immediately (we'll be talking about when the seller does resell in the next section, on offsetting benefits), the seller is entitled to damages for non-acceptance under § 2-708(1):[4]

> (contract price − market price) + incidental damages − expenses saved

Again, recall the hypothetical from Chapter 4 where Mona broke the promise to buy the automobile from Lisa. If Mona agreed to buy it for $1,500 above the market price, then Lisa is entitled to that difference (putting aside incidental damages and expenses saved). The formula treats Lisa *as though she resold the car* at the (lower) market price, even if she doesn't sell the automobile. When Lisa doesn't sell and gets damages from Mona, she is left in the same position as if the contract had gone through. She has the value of the automobile plus the $1,500 profit she expected to make on the sale to Mona.

Example 4

Ernesto manufactured a custom piece of glass to be installed in Fred and Gertrude's dream home. Fred and Gertrude promised to pay $10,000 for the glass. Ernesto received a $5,000 deposit. After Ernesto finished manufacturing the glass but before he delivered it, Fred and Gertrude decided to get a divorce, and a court determined they breached the contract by not paying. Ernesto cannot resell the glass to anyone else because it is a custom size and shape. Its value as scrap is $100. How much may Ernesto recover in damages from Fred and Gertrude?

Explanation

This is a contract for the sale of a moveable good governed by Article 2 of the U.C.C. Recall that sellers can bring an "action on the price" under § 2-709 for goods still in his possession if the seller "is unable after reasonable effort to resell them at a reasonable price or the circumstances reasonably indicate that such effort will be unavailing." A custom piece of glass cannot be resold. The § 2-709 formula is:

> contract price + incidental damages

---

4. We are ignoring cases governed by § 2-709, when the goods have been accepted but not paid for. See Example 4 in this chapter, discussing mitigation issues under § 2-709. The next section, on offsetting benefits, discusses lost volume seller issues.

Ernesto has already received $5,000 in payment. He should be able to recover an additional $5,000 toward the contract price, plus any incidental damages he had in having to store the good. Ernesto's recovery should be reduced by $100, the scrap value of the window.

Example 5

Same facts as in Example 4, but Fred and Gertrude don't get a divorce. Instead, Ernesto, who is busy with other jobs, fails to deliver the glass window as promised to Fred and Gertrude's house on July 1. The market price of a replacement window is $10,000, but it will take two weeks to manufacture and deliver. July 1 was the day that Fred and Gertrude had all of their possessions delivered to the house. Because the house was missing the large glass window, thieves were able to enter the house and steal $50,000 worth of Fred and Gertrude's goods. How much may the couple recover from Ernesto?

Explanation

Again, this contract is governed by Article 2 of the U.C.C. Fred and Gertrude did not go out and cover, so they should be able to recover damages under the § 2-713 market measure:

> Amounts toward the purchase price paid to seller + (market price at the place of tender − contract price) + incidental and consequential damages − expenses saved

They certainly can recover the $5,000 purchase price paid to the seller. The difference between the market price and the contract price is 0 (both Ernesto and the market would charge $10,000 for the window). The real battle here is going to be over the consequential damages. Ernesto has two arguments as to why he should not have to pay consequential damages for the stolen property. First, it may not have been reasonably foreseeable that Fred and Gertrude would suffer these losses. Sure, a missing window can be an opportunity for crime. But most people would have taken steps (such as having the area boarded up with plywood) until a replacement window could be made available. Unforeseeable consequential damages are not recoverable. The second point is related to the first: Fred and Gertrude failed to take reasonable steps in mitigation to provide a temporary barrier to prevent entry into their home. They therefore might not be able to recover anything beyond the $5,000 deposit from Ernesto.

If Fred and Gertrude had been smart and had the area boarded up with plywood, the expenses of doing so arguably would count as incidental damages that they could recover under U.C.C. § 2-715(1) as "reasonable expenses incident to the delay or other breach."

6.2.3 What Are "Reasonable" Steps in Mitigation?

While the law treats plaintiffs as though they took reasonable steps to mitigate losses, it is not required that they take unreasonable steps to avoid loss to help the defendant. A good example of this principle is found in *McGinley v. United States*, 329 F. Supp. 62 (E.D. Pa. 1971). There the court held that plaintiff, who had already undergone surgical procedures to alleviate pain from a herniated disc in his back, could collect future lost wages damages for his back injury. The court rejected the defendant's argument that the damages should have been reduced because plaintiff refused to undergo additional surgery to help his back problem, which could have allowed him to work.

The court held that plaintiff need not have mitigated by having further surgery, which had only a 60% to 70% chance of being successful and could in fact have worsened his condition. The court wrote:

> It is, of course, settled law that if injuries may be cured or alleviated by a simple and safe surgical operation, then refusal to submit thereto should be considered in mitigation of damages. . . . This is not true, however, where the operation is a serious one, or one attended by grave risk of death or failure. . . . A plaintiff has a duty to submit to reasonable medical treatment and the test of reasonableness is to be determined by the triers of fact.

Id. at 66 (citations omitted).

Often, steps to mitigate are straightforward. For example, if the lab owner in the *RSB* case easily could have purchased a different "Hitachi 704" machine for use in the lab, the failure to do so would preclude the recovery of any damages (such as lost profits) that could have been avoided by the substitute purchase. In other words, rather than sit around thinking about one's losses caused by a defendant, a plaintiff needs to go out and proactively take reasonable steps to minimize the loss.

One area where the mitigation issue is often litigated concerns claims for lost wages when the plaintiff fails to obtain substitute employment. A notorious case in this regard is *Parker v. Twentieth Century–Fox Film Corp.*, 474 P.2d 689 (Cal. 1970), involving the actress Shirley MacLaine. MacLaine had a contract with 20th Century Fox to star in a movie musical called "Bloomer Girl." Her contract provided for filming in California and for MacLaine's approval of the director. Fox breached the contract. Right after the breach, Fox offered her a part in a Western movie, "Big Country, Big Man," to be filmed in Australia (without MacLaine's choice of director).

When MacLaine sued for breach, Fox argued that MacLaine failed to mitigate her damages because she did not accept the substitute employment. The California Supreme Court rejected the argument, holding that an employee must take alternative employment to mitigate only when the employment is not different or inferior from the promised employment. Here, the court said that the new employment was different: it involved no singing or dancing; it was a Western, not a musical; MacLaine had no choice of director; and it had been filmed in Australia, not California.

The rule in *Parker* is one that primarily protects the social position of a professional. A court is not going to hold that an attorney who has been wrongfully terminated from his job at a law firm has to mitigate damages by taking a job flipping hamburgers at McDonald's, but it might hold that an unskilled garment worker who has been wrongfully terminated from a job in a clothing factory has to take that McDonald's job. In part, this rule might be justified, because it is going to be much harder for the fired attorney to get another attorney's job after working some time at McDonald's than for the garment worker to get a similar job after working some time at McDonald's. Still, there's a certain elitism to the rules regarding mitigation and employment.

Example 6

Hila runs over Ivan with her Hummer, causing serious internal injuries. Because of Ivan's religious convictions, he refuses to have a blood transfusion, and dies. Ivan's family brings a wrongful death case against Hila. The undisputed medical evidence establishes that had Ivan taken the blood transfusion, he would have recovered completely, suffering only $15,000 in damages. Should the court allow Ivan's family to recover no more than the $15,000, on grounds that Ivan failed to mitigate?

Explanation

This hypothetical puts the rule on mitigation directly in conflict with First Amendment principles of religious freedom. Putting aside the religion issue, failure to undergo a life-saving blood transfusion is going to be viewed by most juries as an unreasonable choice, and the jury would likely find that the injured party should have mitigated. But the freedom of religion issue complicates matters a great deal. If a jury would hold that the failure to mitigate was unreasonable, it might be making a decision that the injured party's religious convictions were unreasonable.

Perhaps unsurprisingly, courts have split over how to deal with the mitigation question in these circumstances. *Compare Munn v. Algee*, 924 F.2d 568 (5th Cir. 1991) (religious views irrelevant to mitigation question), with *Rozewicz v. New York City Health and Hosps. Corp.*, 656 N.Y.S.2d 593 (N.Y. Sup. Ct.

1997) (no issue of mitigation and no assumption of risk defense if refusal was based on sincere religious belief), *and Williams v. Bright*, 658 N.Y.S.2d 910 (N.Y. App. Div. 1997) (no mitigation problem if injured party acted as a "reasonable believer"). Consider whether or not Ivan looks like the "thin-skulled" plaintiff we've seen in earlier chapters. Is it true, when you injure someone with these religious convictions, that you "take the plaintiff as you find him"?

6.3 OFFSETTING BENEFITS

Mitigation claims arise when a plaintiff can takes steps to avoid further loss but fails to do so. The issue of *offsetting benefits* arises when a plaintiff actually takes steps to avoid loss. In such a case, those steps taken to avoid loss must be taken into account in computing plaintiff's damages so as to prevent the plaintiff from obtaining a double recovery.

Recall the window washing hypothetical from Chapter 4. You own a window washing business. You sign a contract with Gary's World of Glass to wash the 200 windows on the outside of Gary's showroom. Gary agrees to pay you $3,000 to wash the windows upon completion of the work.

Suppose that two weeks before you are supposed to begin washing Gary's windows, Gary breaches. You then receive a call from John offering you $3,000 to do the same work at his business on the same day. To do either Gary's original job or John's job would cost you $1,000. You do not have multiple crews, and there is no way you would have been able to complete both Gary's job and John's job. You accept the deal with John and then sue Gary for damages.

In this hypothetical, there is no question that although Gary has breached the contract, you will not be entitled to damages. To see why, recall that if Gary had kept his promise, your ledger would have been up $2,000 (the profit on the job: the $3,000 contract price less your $1,000 cost). If you sued Gary for breach of contract, at first glance it would appear that you would be entitled to $2,000: the difference between the promised position (C) of $2,000 and the position after the wrong (A), when you were paid nothing by Gary, or 0.

This analysis is incomplete, however, because it fails to take into account the offsetting benefits issue. Gary's breach *has freed up resources* that you may use for other jobs. When you took the job with John, you used resources you could not have used had Gary kept his promise. So we must take this into account in the calculation. Because the job with John yielded the same $2,000 profit, and because there were no incidental costs (such as searching for a new job) or consequential damages, your damages would be zero.

It might be tempting for you then to say that there's no point in taking that additional job from John, in the hopes that a jury would award you the $2,000 profit from the original job (better to get the $2,000 from not working than from working, perhaps). But that would be a mistake, because, as we just saw in section 6.2, the failure to take reasonable steps in mitigation reduces the plaintiff's recovery. The law is going to treat you as if you took reasonable steps in mitigation whether you did so or not.

Now suppose that John called and offered to hire you for the same $3,000 contract price, but because John has more windows, it is going to cost you $1,300 rather than $1,000 to complete the job. It is reasonable for you to take the job with John, because if you don't, there is a good chance you won't find other work to do that day. In that case, you would be able to recover damages based on the difference between the promised position (C) and the position you ended up in after the wrong (A). See Figure 6.4.

In this case, the promised position (C) is the $2,000 profit you would have made had Gary not breached. The tricky part here is the position after the wrong (A). By taking the substitute job with John, your ledger is up by $1,700 (the difference between the substitute contract price of $3,000 and your $1,300 costs). The total damages are $300 (C − A).

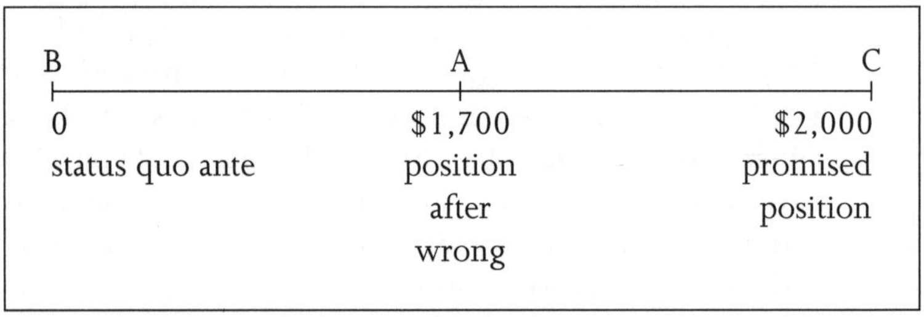

B	A	C
0	$1,700	$2,000
status quo ante	position after wrong	promised position

Figure 6.4 Profits After Offsetting Benefits Taken into Account in Window Washing Hypothetical

You should see how this calculation of damages makes sense. You take on the substitute work, ending up with $1,700 in profits on your ledger. The $300 in damages moves you to $2,000, the position you would have been in but for Gary's breach of contract.

Offsetting benefits arise not only when resources are freed up on account of defendant's wrong. They also occur when there are *expenses saved* on account of the breach. Indeed, we have already seen this principle at work in one of the Lisa-Mona hypotheticals from Chapter 4 under U.C.C. § 2-712.

Lisa promises Mona in a valid written contract that she will deliver to Mona a 2003 red Lexus convertible for $25,000. The car was in excellent shape, except that it needed its air conditioning repaired at a cost of $1,000.

Mona pays Lisa a $5,000 deposit. The next day, Lisa tells Mona she cannot deliver the car, because it was damaged during delivery. Mona searches for a similar used car. She cannot find a 2003 red Lexus convertible in good condition, but she finds a 2004 silver Lexus convertible at a purchase price of $28,000. Lisa spends $50 in gas checking out cars before she purchases the silver Lexus. Assume the court finds that the purchase by Lisa of the silver Lexus convertible constitutes a reasonable cover.

The purchasing of a substitute car takes care of any issues related to mitigation. Here, consider the $1,000 air conditioning repair expense that Lisa was able to avoid in making her substitute purchase. This is an expense saved, and it counts as an offsetting benefit *that must be subtracted from the total recovery under the* § 2-712 *formula.*[5] Lisa can recover:

$5,000	(purchase price paid to seller)
+ $3,000	(the difference between the cover price and contract price)
+ $50	(the incidental cost of obtaining cover (see above for a definition of incidental damages))
− $ 1,000	(the expenses saved: the air conditioning repair no longer necessary)
= $7,050	(Total damages)

U.C.C. seller's remedies also account for mitigation and offsetting benefits issues. U.C.C. § 2-706 provides that when the seller makes a resale "in good faith and in a commercially reasonable manner," "the seller may recover the difference between the resale price and the contract price together with any incidental damages allowed under the provisions of this Article (section 2-710), but less expenses saved in consequence of the buyer's breach."

The one instance where proceeds of resale are not subtracted as an offsetting benefit arises in the case of the lost volume seller, described in more detail in Chapter 4.5.2. Resale proceeds do not count as an offsetting benefit for the lost volume seller, because the whole idea behind the lost volume seller concept is that the seller could make both sales at a profit. To use an example not governed by Article 2 of the U.C.C., if you had enough staff at your window washing business to wash *both* Gary's windows *and* John's windows

---

5. Recall that the § 2-712 formula is:

> Amounts toward the purchase price paid to seller + (cover price − contract price) + incidental and consequential damages − expenses saved

and earn your profits, you might be able to recover the $2,000 profit you expected to make on the contract with Gary. In that circumstance it would not be a double recovery for you to collect both damages from Gary and contract proceeds from John. In contrast, in the original hypothetical, where you could do only one of the two jobs, allowing you to recover both sums would be a double recovery, giving you $2,000 from Gary and $2,000 in profits from the job with John, putting you in a position $2,000 better than you would have been in had there been no breach.

Example 7

Rudolph was a successful ballet dancer until Jesse robbed him one day. In the course of the robbery Jesse shot Rudolph in the leg. Rudolph suffered serious personal injuries and will never be able to dance again. His salary at the Big City Ballet was $100,000 per year, for working 80-hour weeks when the ballet was in season. He likely would have worked for 10 more years as a ballet dancer. His past medical bills for the shooting were $50,000 and he will need physical therapy for the next five years. He has suffered serious emotional distress. While recuperating, Rudolph wrote a novel that has turned out to be a blockbuster, earning him $2 million in royalties. He never would have had the time to write the novel while dancing. He has signed an advance of $3 million for his next novel. A jury finds Jesse liable for the tort of battery. What damages may Rudolph recover from Jesse?

Explanation

Putting aside the offsetting benefits issue for a moment, Rudolph is going to be entitled to his past and expected future wages and medical expenses, discounted to present value. There could be testimony as to what Rudolph's salary would be over his expected 10-year career as a ballet dancer, as well as his future earning potential losses as a result of the shooting. He will also be able to get $50,000 in medical expenses, plus the expected future costs of physical therapy as discounted to present value. He will also be able to recover his emotional distress damages, which could be substantial.

The interesting offsetting benefits issue in this case arises from Rudolph's writing of the novel. It appears that the shooting freed up resources (namely, Rudolph's free time) that allowed for the writing of the novel. Just as you could not wash both Gary's windows and John's windows, Rudolph could not both dance ballet and write the novel. So there is an argument that Rudolph's damages should be reduced by the significant benefits he has received (and will receive, discounted to present value) for his future career as a novelist. Perhaps Rudolph's lawyer can convince a court that these damages should be used to offset only the future lost wages, rather than the entirety of the damages (including medical expenses and emotional distress damages). I am not aware of any cases that have addressed this issue.

6.4 THE COLLATERAL SOURCE RULE

Suppose Ken drove his car down the street, crashing into Lola's fence. The crash causes $1,000 in property damage. Lola makes a claim with her insurance company. The company applies Lola's $250 deductible to her claim, sending her a check for $750 to pay for repairing the fence. Lola then sues Ken for negligence, and the jury agrees that Ken was negligent.

If we apply the principles from the previous section of this chapter, on offsetting benefits, Lola should be entitled to only $250 in damages. She received the $750 check from her insurance company *as a benefit* that she would not have received but for Ken's wrong. In this way, the insurance check is like John's payment for washing your windows, which you received *as a benefit* after Gary breached the window washing contract. Recall that we must deduct those payments from John under offsetting benefit principles.

But we do not treat the two kinds of benefits the same. Under the *collateral source rule, insurance and certain government benefit payments that are wholly independent of the tortfeasor do not get deducted from the plaintiff's award of tort damages.* Lola therefore would get to keep her $750 insurance payment *and* collect $1,000 in damages, bringing her to a *better position* than had Ken not crashed into her fence. As illustrated in Figure 6.5, after the wrong, Lola moves to position A, which is at −$1,000. The award of $1,000 in damages from Ken moves Lola back to 0 (B), the status quo ante. The additional check from Lola's insurance company, however, moves her to a position better than 0, to B+, which is at +$750. Thus, after the accident, recovery of damages, and receipt of money from the collateral source, Lola is in a better position than she would have been in (position B, or 0) had Ken never crashed his car into Lola's fence.

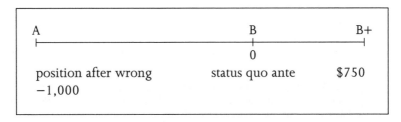

Figure 6.5 Plaintiff's Position Under the Collateral Source Rule

Why does the collateral source rule allow plaintiffs such as Lola to get what looks like a double recovery? The most persuasive answer is that the rule encourages people to purchase insurance. There are going to be a number of cases where an injured person won't have a defendant to sue, or the defendant will have no assets to pay for damages. The collateral source rule encourages potential tort victims to purchase insurance.

There is also a potential fairness argument. If we limited Lola to recovering only $250, it means that Ken, rather than Lola, would get the benefit of the insurance Lola purchased. On the other hand, it is Gary, rather than you, who gets the benefit of the payments you receive from John after Gary breached the contract with you.

The California Supreme Court also has justified the rule "to compensate for the attorney's share" of the damages award that personal injury plaintiffs receive under a contingency fee agreement. See Helfend v. Southern California Rapid Transit Dist., 465 P.2d 61 (Cal. 1970). But the collateral source rule seems to be a blunt tool with which to deal with problems of attorney's fees.

The collateral source rule does not inevitably lead to a double recovery. For example, if Ken ran over Lola rather than Lola's fence, and Lola sought damages for the personal injuries she sustained, she might be able to recover damages for her medical expenses as well as have her medical expenses paid by her private insurer (a collateral source). But her contract with the medical insurance company could contain a subrogation clause, requiring that any payments Lola receives to compensate her for medical expenses must first go to pay back the insurer for its costs in taking care of Lola.[6]

Because plaintiffs may in some cases receive a double recovery, some states have abolished or changed the rule, often by statute (though the restrictions have sometimes been challenged as violating applicable state constitutional provisions; see LAYCOCK p. 101 n.8). In California, for example, Civil Code § 3333.1 abolishes the collateral source rule as to medical malpractice claims against health care providers. That section provides, however, that plaintiff may recover the value of the premium payments paid to become entitled to the insurance benefits.

Notably, when Congress established the fund to compensate victims of the terrorist attacks on September 11, 2001, it expressly provided that the special master administering the fund deduct the amount of compensation "by the amount of the collateral source compensation the claimant has received or is entitled to receive as a result of the terrorist-related air crashes of September 11, 2001." Air Transportation Safety and System Stabilization Act, Pub. L. No. 107-42, § (405)(b)(6). It included among collateral

---

6. This subrogation clause creates some interesting incentives when it comes to settling cases. Plaintiff and defendant might collude to classify very little of a settlement payment as reimbursement for medical expenses, thereby attempting to avoid the subrogation rule. (Defendant might agree to do this in order to pay a lower overall amount to the plaintiff.) Such practices, at the very least, raise serious ethical concerns.

benefits "all collateral sources, including life insurance, pension funds, death benefit programs, and payments by Federal, state, or local governments" related to the September 11 attacks. *Id.*, § 402(4).

In his final report, the special master stated that the issue of collateral source reductions "proved to be one of the fund's most contentious issues," with some opponents "vociferously argu[ing]" that the rule "unfairly penalized families of victims who planned ahead by purchasing life insurance or other means of securing financial security for their families and that collateral sources are typically not offset in wrongful death suits." Final Report of the Special Master of the September 11 Victim Compensation Fund of 2001 at 44 (http://www.usdoj.gov/final_report.pdf). The special master created detailed rules "to reconcile the unequivocal language of the Act on collateral sources with the Fund's purpose of providing financial support to victims' families based upon their individual needs and circumstances." *Id.* If you were in Congress, would you have included a rule on deducting collateral sources? Why, or why not?

Example 8

Miguel is injured in an automobile accident caused by Nancy. He receives $10,000 worth of medical care, paid for by his health insurer. Miguel paid a $500 premium for the medical coverage during the relevant time period. Miguel misses six weeks of work, thereby failing to earn $15,000 in salary. The jury awards plaintiff $25,000 in economic damages and $6,000 in noneconomic damages for his pain and suffering. Should the judge deduct the value of the medical care paid for by the Miguel's insurance company from Miguel's award? If so, how much should the judge deduct?

Explanation

If the jurisdiction applies the collateral source rule, the value of the medical care paid for by the insurer should *not* be deducted; that is the point of the collateral source rule. Miguel therefore can get a double recovery for the medical portion of the cost of his injuries (that is, his medical care has been paid for by his insurer, and he receives additional amounts to compensate him for this medical care from the jury's award of damages paid by Nancy). Miguel won't get the double recovery, however, if the contract with his medical insurer contains a subrogation clause, and the insurer actually goes after Miguel for the payment (not all insurers will do so).

If the jurisdiction has repealed the collateral source rule, then those costs must be deducted from Miguel's recovery, less the payment of premiums. Thus, if the jury awarded $25,000 in economic damages, the judge would have to deduct $9,500 ($10,000 in benefits less the $500 premium) from the award, leaving Miguel with a total of $15,500 in economic damages (the award for noneconomic damages is not affected).

Example 9

Robert is a veteran entitled to free medical care from the Department of Veterans Affairs of the U.S. government. While recovering from surgery at a government-run Veterans Hospital, the staff negligently disconnects the alarm system on the ventilator to which he was attached. While the alarm was disconnected, the tube supplying oxygen to Robert became disengaged. When these disconnections were discovered, approximately eight minutes later, Robert was in complete cardiac arrest. He was not resuscitated for approximately a half hour. The oxygen deprivation left Robert with irreversible brain damage, requiring a ventilator for breathing and a nasogastric tube for nutrition and hydration. He sued the government hospital for negligence and won the suit. Experts project he is going to need $1 million worth of future medical care, which he receives free as a veteran. The court awards Robert $1 million in future medical costs. May Robert receive these damages?

Explanation

The facts of this hypothetical come from *Mozlof v. United States*, 6 F.3d 461 (7th Cir. 1993). If the jurisdiction has repealed the collateral source rule, Robert would not be able to recover that $1 million, because he is going to receive that future medical care for free. The more difficult question occurs in states that continue to apply the collateral source rule. Recall that the rule requires that the collateral sources be wholly independent of the tortfeasor. In this case, the U.S. government Veterans Administration is both paying for the medical care *and* paying the tort damages.

In the actual *Mozlof* case, the court ruled that plaintiff could recover the damages without an offset:

> Just because both recoveries come from the *defendant*, however, does not necessarily mean that they are coming from the same *source*. "The source of the funds may be determined to be collateral or independent, even though the [tortfeasor] supplies such funds. . . . Application of the collateral source rule depends less upon the source of funds than upon the character of the benefits received." Thus, in order to determine whether the collateral source rule is applicable, courts have looked to the nature of the payment and the reason the payment is being made rather than simply looking at whether the defendant is paying twice.

(Citation omitted.)

6. Ensuring the Rightful Position

The court held that as to future medical payments, the collateral source rule would not apply:

> The plaintiff may not be satisfied with the public facilities; he may feel that a particular private physician is superior; in the future because of over-crowded conditions he may not even be able to receive timely care. These are only a few of many considerations with which an individual may be faced in selecting treatment. The plaintiff's past use of the government facilities does not ensure his future use of them. He will now have the funds available to him to enable him to seek private care. He should not be denied this opportunity.

PART II

Equitable Remedies

Injunctions and Other Equitable Remedies: Stop Me Before I Harm (Again)!

7.1 INTRODUCTION: INJUNCTIONS AS SPECIFIC RELIEF

We first saw in Chapter 1 the concept of the "rightful position": the position in which plaintiff would be but for the defendant's wrong. Part I of this book focused on how courts (sometimes unsuccessfully) use compensatory damages to restore plaintiff to the rightful position after the defendant's wrong. In this part, we focus on how *injunctions* — court orders to defendants (or others) to do or not do something — can keep the plaintiff in the rightful position by preventing the plaintiff from being harmed or minimizing the extent of such harm.

Recall one of Chapter 1's early hypotheticals that contrasted damage awards with restitution: Alice steals $100 from Bob's wallet, runs to the casino, gambles, and walks away from the table with $1,000. The court could award Bob compensatory damages of $100, bringing Bob back to the rightful position, or the court could give him a restitutionary award of $1,000, which would force Alice to give up her ill-gotten gains. See 7.1.

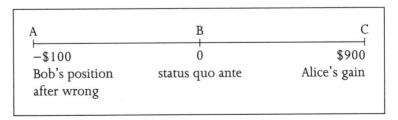

Figure 7.1

In the Alice-Bob example, an injunction is no help. The harm is complete and there is nothing a court order can do (short of ordering Alice to return the money, something we'll consider a little farther down the line).

Suppose, however, that before Alice stole the money, she warned Bob of the theft (far-fetched to be sure, but we'll encounter some real-world examples soon enough). A court order — or injunction — that would have prevented Alice from stealing Bob's money serves to prevent the harm from ever occurring. Thinking about Bob's status in terms of Figure 7.1, *an injunction would have kept Bob in position B*, the status quo ante, obviating the need for him to recover his losses from Alice. In other words, like damages, an injunction can aim at the rightful position. Unlike damages, an injunction can potentially *keep* plaintiff in that position rather than having to restore plaintiff to that position. What's more, when injunctions work, they eliminate the risks that plaintiffs face when seeking damages. Damages, for example, might be too hard to measure, or the defendant may be difficult to find, poor, or judgment-proof. A plaintiff might decide it is simply better to prevent harm, rather than allow the harm and then seek an after-the-fact remedy.

Why would Alice obey a court order? Perhaps she would not, but most litigants do obey court orders, such as injunctions, which can be backed up with the court's *contempt* power (discussed in Chapter 10). Contempt can help motivate reluctant defendants to act when they otherwise would not, or refrain from acting when they otherwise would. (Why not issue a court order *requiring* Alice to pay money in the case of damages? Generally speaking, outside cases involving family law issues — such as child support — a damages judgment is *not* backed up by the court's contempt power. We discuss ways that successful plaintiffs may recover damages in Chapter 17.1.)

Injunctions are a neat tool to have in the lawyer's toolbox. Indeed, you already came across injunctions in your first year of law school in contracts class under the label "specific performance." Consider this example: Oscar contracts with Pnina for Pnina to manufacture a custom-made widget for use in Oscar's broom factory. Without the widget, which takes weeks to manufacture, the factory cannot operate. There are no spare widgets available for sale. About halfway into the job, Pnina announces she is going to breach the contract because a better opportunity has arisen for her (think: "efficient breach" from Chapter 4.2).

Oscar could sue Pnina for damages, but he really wants the widget. You can see that a court order, or injunction, requiring Pnina to deliver the completed widget could be Oscar's best remedy. We call that the remedy of *specific performance*. Specific performance is simply an injunction ordering a breaching party to a contract to perform as promised (the order is sometimes accompanied by a judgment that the breaching party pay damages for the delay in performance).

Note the use of the term "specific." Specific performance and other types of injunctions are forms of *specific relief* that give the plaintiff the very thing he or she lost (or stands to lose). Oscar, for example, gets his promised widget. Specific performance contrasts with damages, which is a kind of *substitutionary relief*: money substitutes for the thing that plaintiff has lost. If Oscar gets only damages (cover damages under U.C.C. § 2-712 or market damages under U.C.C. § 2-713 — see Chapter 4.5), he is not in as good a position as he would be if he gets the widget. With damages, he will have to go out and purchase a *substitute* for the custom-made widget or make a new plan for allocating his resources at the broom factory. Also, with a damages remedy, he bears the risk of the court's errors in valuing the widget.

Over the next four chapters, this book explores injunctions and related remedies, answering the following kinds of questions:

- What does a plaintiff have to show to obtain an injunction?
- What factors should courts consider in choosing between specific relief, such as an injunction, and substitutionary relief, such as damages?
- Can injunctions be used to restructure government institutions such as prisons and school systems?
- How may injunctions be modified?
- To what extent may injunctions bind or burden third parties?
- Under what circumstances may a plaintiff obtain preliminary relief, such as a preliminary injunction, to prevent harm from occurring before a case goes to final judgment?
- What kinds of contempt power do courts have, and under what circumstances may parties ignore injunctions without facing a court finding of contempt?

Example 1

Quincy and Rudolfo are neighbors. As a courtesy, Quincy lets Rudolfo know that he is planning on cutting down a large oak tree near the property line between their two houses to put in a swimming pool. Rudolfo believes the tree is on his side of the property line (meaning Quincy does not have the legal right to cut it down), and Rudolfo does not want it cut down: it provides shade for his backyard, which he enjoys during the summer months. Quincy insists that the tree is on his side of the property line, and that he has the right to cut it down.

Assume that Rudolfo is right: the tree is in fact on his property. Before reading the rest of this chapter and learning the rules related to injunctions, ask yourself the following questions:

a. Should Rudolfo have the choice between damages for the lost tree and an injunction preventing Quincy from cutting it down, or should the law prefer one remedy over the other?
b. Which remedy places a greater burden on the courts?
c. Which remedy is more likely to put (or keep) Rudolfo in the rightful position?

Does your answer to any of these questions change if Rudolfo does not depend on the tree for shade or otherwise care if it is cut down?

Explanation

(a) There is of course no "right answer" to these normative questions. But it is useful to begin this material by testing your own values before learning the rules applicable to injunctive relief. Many students would leave the choice to Rudolfo, and most students in Rudolfo's position would prefer the injunction in part because of the difficulty of replacing a mature tree providing shade in someone's backyard, and in part because of the difficulty of computing damages for the loss of the tree.

(b) Both remedies impose some burdens on the courts. With damages, the court is going to have to compute the amount of damages. With an injunction, the court may need to determine whether Quincy violated the injunction and, for this reason, whether to punish Quincy for contempt. In the abstract, it is difficult to say which is more burdensome.

(c) Injunctive relief is more likely to keep Rudolfo closer to the rightful position for the aforementioned reasons: the difficulty of using money to buy a replacement for what would be lost and the difficulty of measuring the value of the lost tree to Rudolfo.

Notice, however, that the answers to these questions may depend at least in part on the specifics about the losses. Thus, for example, suppose the tree provided no shade or aesthetic value to Rudolfo. If that were the case, the computation of damages might be easier (we would not need to worry about the value of a mature, shady tree on the property), and we might be less interested in backing up a judicial remedy with the contempt power. Giving Rudolfo the right to an injunction can also have important distributional consequences (that is, consequences for how much money Quincy is going to have to transfer to Rudolfo for the removal of the tree). With a damages remedy, the court sets the price for removal. With an injunction,

Rudolfo can hold out for a higher price, especially if Quincy really needs that tree removed in order to put in his swimming pool. This means that Rudolfo may get a windfall for the removal of the tree if the parties must bargain around Rudolfo's right to an injunction. You should be able to see the potential bargaining power that the right to an injunction could give to Rudolfo.

It is not even clear that the parties would reach a bargain in such circumstances. In a situation of "bilateral monopoly," where there is only one buyer and one seller (Rudolfo is the only one selling the right to remove a tree, and Quincy is the only one who wants to buy the right to remove the tree), the parties might not bargain efficiently for the removal of the tree. Rudolfo, for example, might drive too hard a bargain even if it is in both of their interests for the tree to be removed.

If the concepts in the last two paragraphs sound familiar, it is because they are related to the debate in the economic analysis of law over the choice between "property rules" (such as injunctions) and "liability rules" (such as damages) when transaction costs (the costs of bargaining) are high. For the classic articles in this area, see Guido Calabresi & A. Douglas Melamed, *Property Rules, Liability Rules and Inalienability: One View of the Cathedral*, 85 Harv. L. Rev. 1089 (1972); and Ronald H. Coase, *The Problem of Social Cost*, 3 J.L. & Econ. 1 (1960). A wide-ranging and fascinating debate beyond the scope of this book is taking place in the "law and economics" arena over the efficiency of the choice between damages and injunctions. In brief, the conventional economic wisdom appears to be that courts should prefer injunctions when transaction costs (the costs of bargaining) are low and damages when transaction costs are high. When transaction costs are low, the parties will be expected to bargain to an efficient allocation of resources (this market transaction, then, would determine whether the tree should be removed). Injunctions let the market, rather than the courts, set the price for violation of a legal right, and the parties are more likely than the court to set an accurate price. In contrast, when there are high transaction costs (as with the bilateral monopoly situation described between Quincy and Rudolfo), the parties may not bargain to an efficient result. In such circumstances, it is more efficient to allow Quincy to cut the tree and the court to set the efficient price.

The economic analysis suggests that courts should decide on the propriety of injunctions rather than damages based upon the extent of transaction costs in bargaining. Regardless of whether that is a practical endeavor for the courts, it does not appear that courts do so in deciding on the propriety of granting an injunction. Moreover, it does not appear that much bargaining takes place after courts issue injunctions. *See* Ward Farnsworth, *Do Parties to Nuisance Cases Bargain after Judgment? A Glimpse Inside the Cathedral*, 66 U. Chi. L. Rev. 373 (1999).

7.2 REQUIREMENTS FOR INJUNCTIONS, THE ORIGINS OF EQUITABLE RELIEF, AND A NOTE ON REPLEVIN

Regardless of your answers to the questions posed in Example 1, the fact of the matter is that injunctions are not available as a matter of course. As we shall see, in order to obtain an injunction (rather than settling for another remedy, such as compensatory damages), a plaintiff is typically going to have to prove two things (though the standards may be changing, as we shall see in section 7.5 below):

1. *Propensity:* The defendant is likely to engage in the conduct that plaintiff seeks to enjoin; and
2. *Irreparable injury:* A "legal" remedy, such as damages, is not as good a remedy for plaintiff as an injunction.
   Even when plaintiff makes such a finding, however, a court may decline to grant an injunction where
3. Other strong policy reasons exist for denying the injunction.

Article 2 of the U.C.C. (applicable to the sale of moveable goods — see Chapter 4.5) similarly limits the availability of the injunctive remedy of specific performance, though in a more open-ended way than the classic common law formulation above. U.C.C. § 2-716(1) provides that for non-breaching buyers, "Specific performance may be decreed when the goods are unique or in other proper circumstances."[1]

What explains why injunctive relief is not available as a matter of course? The answer is in large part a vestige of a centuries-old turf war among English courts. This is not the place to detail the story,[2] but briefly: Different courts began to emerge in England in the thirteenth century. The Chancery branch of the Court of the Exchequer began as a court designed to handle, among other things, requests to the king for justice or mercy from complainants who claimed they could not get justice in other courts. Eventually, "the Chancellor," or the head of this court branch, was given the power to grant such relief in appropriate cases backed by what we would now call contempt power.

---

1. The comments to the section explain that it is an attempt to "further a more liberal attitude than some courts have shown" in the grant of specific performance. It also notes that "inability to cover is strong evidence of 'other proper circumstances' justifying the remedy of specific performance." In recent years, U.C.C. drafters have considered, but not adopted, a proposal to make specific performance more easily available for non-consumer contracts. As a consumer, wouldn't you want specific performance made available more easily?
2. For details, see F.W. MAITLAND, EQUITY 1-7 (1969).

From this origin sprang the "chancery," or "equity," courts, which granted "equitable relief," including injunctions. The equitable relief issued by the chancery courts encroached on the power of other courts, however, and eventually, the English crown prohibited the equity courts from granting relief unless the complaining party could demonstrate that he had no adequate remedy in the law courts (our "courts of law" that grant remedies such as "legal relief").

One would think this debate would have little relevance to contemporary law, especially given that today, centuries after this turf war, the courts of law and courts of equity have merged into a single court in most places. In California, for example, one can go into a superior court and ask for legal relief such as damages or equitable relief such as injunctions. The same is true of federal district courts, which grant equitable relief such as injunctions all the time.

Nonetheless, in order to get equitable relief even today, a plaintiff must demonstrate that *she has no adequate remedy at law* (otherwise known as the "irreparable injury" rule).[3] Section 7.4 discusses what it means for a legal remedy to be "inadequate," but before we get to that, there are a few other matters to consider.

How does one know, for example, what qualifies as a legal or equitable remedy? The answer largely comes from history. At least for remedies that existed before the merger of the courts, the question is whether the remedy would have been granted by the law courts or the equity courts. Those granted by the law courts are legal remedies and those granted by the equity courts are equitable remedies. *See* DOBBS § 2.1(1) ("Even today, when the two systems of courts are substantially merged, lawyers speak of 'legal' remedies, meaning those traditionally recognized by the old separate law courts, and 'equitable' remedies, meaning those distinctive remedies utilized by the Chancellors.").

A claim for compensatory damages, as mentioned, is a classic legal remedy, and a claim for an injunction is a classic equitable remedy. Other important equitable remedies include rescission and constructive trusts — discussed in Part III. Remedies for breach of trust are equitable as well, and equity courts historically played a key role in the development of the law of trusts.

For remedies that did not exist before the merger of the courts, the question whether to classify a remedy as "legal" or "equitable" is more difficult and has important consequences. For example, plaintiffs seeking equitable relief must satisfy the burden of showing irreparable injury. Also, the Seventh Amendment to the U.S. Constitution grants the right to a jury trial for actions at common law, but not for suits in equity. (Many states have parallel provisions in their constitutions.) The issue of whether a modern statutory

---

3. The notion of having no adequate remedy at law and the irreparable injury rule are just different formulations of the same concept. *See* DOBBS § 2.5(1); LAYCOCK p. 380.

remedy is legal or equitable has vexed the U.S. Supreme Court in several contexts, including decisions on the right to a jury trial. *See, e.g., Chauffeurs, Teamsters, and Helpers Local No. 1391 v. Terry*, 494 U.S. 558 (1990) (applying a two-part test to determine whether plaintiff's action against labor union for alleged breach of duty of fair representation was legal or equitable — and therefore whether plaintiff was entitled to a jury trial); *Mertens v. Hewitt Assocs.*, 508 U.S. 248 (1993) (deciding what "equitable relief" meant in the context of plaintiff's claim for a remedy under a provision of federal ERISA statute); *Dairy Queen v. Wood*, 369 U.S. 469 (1962) (in an action presenting both legal claims and equitable claims, courts should resolve the legal questions first through a jury trial). If you are a plaintiff who wants equitable relief such as an injunction, you likely won't have the right to a jury trial.

Furthermore, there is also a class of equitable defenses that defendants may raise only in connection with plaintiff's request for equitable relief (explored in Chapter 18).

The dead hand of history seems like a pretty weak reason to require plaintiffs to jump through the "irreparable injury" hoop, given that today the same courts can give both legal and equitable relief. Indeed, some have argued that in modern law, the irreparable injury rule is dead — that courts do not take the rule seriously. *See* Douglas Laycock, The Death of the Irreparable Injury Rule (Oxford University Press 1991). As you work through the material, ask yourself what role the irreparable injury rule does, and should, play in the law of remedies.

One possible answer to the continued apparent discrimination against injunctions and equitable relief is that there should be extraordinary reasons to grant specific relief because specific relief is more onerous. Do we really want to *require* Pnina, under the threat of a contempt holding, to supply the custom-made widget for Oscar's broom factory if she does not want to? Maybe the law should instead prefer that Oscar receive money to cover his losses when it is feasible.

We'll explore this explanation further in this chapter, but it is worth noting that some legal relief can be *specific* as opposed to the usual substitutionary remedy of compensatory damages. For example, *replevin* is a legal remedy that allows for specific relief: in some circumstances, a plaintiff can use replevin to recover personal property wrongfully taken by the defendant. (Chapter 13 further explores replevin.) Because replevin is a legal remedy, a plaintiff need not prove irreparable injury to get it.[4] As Laycock argues, any

---

4. For its part, Article 2 of the U.C.C. does not give non-breaching buyers a right to replevin as a matter of course. Under § 2-716(3), "The buyer has a right of replevin for goods identified to the contract if after reasonable effort he is unable to effect cover for such goods or the circumstances reasonably indicate that such effort will be unavailing or if the goods have been shipped under reservation and satisfaction of the security interest in them has been made or tendered." This right does not appear to be broader than the right to specific performance set forth in U.C.C. § 2-716(1).

defense of the irreparable injury rule for equitable relief based upon *specific* relief will have to deal with the availability of replevin (a specific *legal* remedy) as a matter of course in appropriate cases.

Example 2

Susan has stolen your family's prized chalice. Its market value is $10,000, and its sentimental value to you is greater than $10,000. In your suit against Susan for the tort of conversion (the correct tort cause of action to recover damages for Susan's theft), would you prefer damages, an injunction ordering return of the chalice, or replevin? Could you ask the court to give you *both* compensatory damages *and* an injunction?

Explanation

Each of these remedies has costs and benefits. The main cost of a damages remedy is that it is likely to be undercompensatory. As we saw in the chapters on damages, courts usually base their award of compensatory damages on market measures, and a $10,000 market measure is not going to compensate for the full value of the chalice to you. On the other hand, some courts say that in order to recover punitive damages (see Chapter 15) aimed at punishing and deterring bad conduct, a court must first award compensatory damages. Thus, damages might be a good way to get a large recovery. This assumes, of course, that Susan would have the resources to pay (compensatory and possibly punitive) damages. If Susan does not have the resources, a damages award will be worthless.

The main benefit of both injunctive relief and replevin is that each entitles you to *specific* relief: you get back the very item that has been taken from you. You likely won't be able to recover punitive damages. The preference between replevin and an injunction might depend upon whether you know where Susan has put the chalice. If you know the location of the chalice, and it is easily accessible, then replevin may be a better remedy because as a legal remedy, you need not demonstrate irreparable injury. After the court agrees that you are entitled to replevin, you can get an order from the court directing the sheriff to seize the property. (More on ancillary remedies such as seizure can be found in Chapter 17.1.)

Alternatively, if you don't know where the chalice is, then replevin would be of little use to you. In such circumstances, you likely will want an injunction that would order Susan to turn over the chalice or be held in contempt of court. If it turns out that the chalice is not available (perhaps Susan has sold it and it cannot be found), then damages would be best. If and when Susan has assets, they can be seized by the sheriff and sold to pay you back for your losses.

A court will not allow you to recover both damages (for the full amount of the chalice) and an injunction (ordering a return of the chalice). That would allow you a double recovery. To see why, consider Figure 7.2.

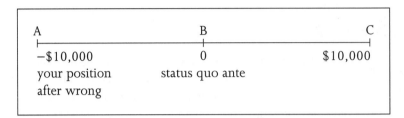

Figure 7.2

Putting aside the sentimental value (and other complications of damages discussed in Part I), your position after the wrong is A, −$10,000. When you receive the chalice back through the injunction, it brings you back to B, the status quo ante (0). If the court also awards damages for the loss, $10,000, it brings you to position C, +$10,000. Thus, you end up in a position *better than* if there had been no theft.

Now you might take the position that this is perfectly appropriate. Susan engaged in theft and should be punished. But that's not supposed to be the purpose of either compensatory damages or injunctions, which are based on the rightful position standard. We could use punitive damages to punish Susan (and sometimes restitution as well, as we will see in Part III). But courts ordinarily will make you *elect a remedy* at some point so as to *preclude double recovery*.

That's not to say that one can never receive damages along with an injunction. In this case, if you obtain an injunction and get the return of the chalice, you are also entitled to damages for the temporary loss of use of the chalice. Thus, if Susan steals the chalice on January 1 and you don't get it back until March 1, you suffered two months without the chalice that you own. That loss may be hard to value, but it is not a double recovery to both give you back the chalice and award you damages for the loss in the interim.

A similar concept applies in the case of specific performance. Suppose Pnina promised to deliver to Oscar the widget that he needs to run his factory by January 1. Pnina breaches, and the court orders specific performance. By the time Pnina finishes making the widget, it is March 1, and the factory has been closed for two months. Courts will often allow a grant of specific performance to be accompanied by *delay damages* — the equivalent of damages for the temporary loss of use in the chalice example to compensate for the delay in promised performance. This does not give a double recovery: had Pnina performed as promised, Oscar would have had the widget on January 1, and he would not have suffered losses in his closed factory from January 1 to March 1. By granting specific performance in a situation where Pnina cannot perform until March 1, the court is not fully restoring Oscar to the rightful position. He is still out the losses for two months. Only the injunction *plus* delay damages will put Oscar into the rightful position.

7.3 THE PROPENSITY REQUIREMENT AND THE SCOPE OF INJUNCTIONS

7.3.1 Propensity, Ripeness, and Mootness

Before turning in depth to the irreparable injury requirement, we first consider the propensity requirement for injunctions along with the proper scope of injunctions (an issue Chapter 8.1 returns to in considering "structural injunctions").

The *propensity* rule requires that plaintiffs demonstrate there is a *realistic threat from the defendant of future harm* (or *future injury from past harm*) before a court will issue an injunction. Demonstrating propensity sometimes is a no-brainer because the defendant has already committed wrongful conduct, and it is a question of preventing future harm. For example, after Pnina announced she was breaching the contract to produce the custom-made widget, there is no question that Oscar is about to suffer harm. The same is true when Quincy announces to Rudolfo that he plans to cut down the tree on their property line. Thus, propensity sometimes is easily found whether the injunction is *reparative* (preventing the future bad effects of past harm, as in the Oscar-Pnina hypothetical) or *preventive* (preventing future harm, as in the Quincy-Rudolfo hypothetical).

But sometimes the matter of propensity is not quite as clear. Suppose Rudolfo and Quincy are neighbors who do not get along. Rudolfo sees Quincy out in Quincy's yard with some contractors, and he *suspects* Quincy is going to remove the tree (which is on Rudolfo's property) to build a swimming pool. If Rudolfo goes to court to seek an injunction preventing the removal of the tree, the court is going to require some proof of *propensity*, which in this case means proof that Quincy is really going to remove the tree. It might be, however, that Quincy is not considering removing the tree, or it might be that Quincy did not plan to remove the tree without first obtaining Rudolfo's permission.[5]

---

5. Occasionally, courts will mislabel this propensity concern as one about irreparable injury. *See* Dobbs § 2.5(1) ("'[I]rreparable harm' may be a short (and misleading) way of saying that, if the plaintiff seeks a preventive injunction to forestall harm, the threat of harm must be real.").

Why shouldn't a court simply issue the injunction so that Rudolfo can be sure that Quincy would think twice before removing the tree? (Quincy, remember, would be thinking twice because of the possibility that he would be held in contempt for violating a court order.) The power of a court order is not used lightly, and there is a danger that if injunctions were easily obtained, Rudolfo would be coming to court all the time seeking them. This could both put an administrative burden on the courts (and an unnecessary one at that, if there is no danger that Quincy or one of Rudolfo's other neighbors is going to do anything to harm him) and potentially give Rudolfo an unfair advantage in disputes with his neighbors. The fear of mistakenly being held in contempt by the courts might chill Quincy and others from exercising their legitimate property rights.

Propensity problems generally come in two varieties before the court: *ripeness* and *mootness*.[6] The revised Quincy-Rudolfo hypothetical is a good example of a ripeness problem: there is insufficient evidence that defendant will engage in the prohibited conduct to justify issuing an injunction. That's not to say it makes bad litigation sense for Rudolfo to *seek* such an injunction. To support Quincy's ripeness argument, if Quincy's lawyer provides an affidavit from Quincy swearing under oath that he's not going to touch Rudolfo's tree without permission, this will serve Rudolfo's interests. Even though that promise is not as good as a court order backed by the power of contempt, if Quincy later removes the tree after signing such an affidavit, a court will likely be unsympathetic to Quincy when Rudolfo later sues for damages (and possibly punitive damages, too).

Mootness claims arise when a defendant has engaged in certain injurious conduct in the past but has since ceased and stated that she won't engage in the conduct anymore. Courts in such circumstances will need to make a *credibility determination* as to whether the defendant is likely to engage in the prohibited conduct again. If the defendant is likely to do so, the propensity requirement is met because there is a realistic threat of further violation.

---

6. You may already be familiar with the concepts of mootness and ripeness from either a constitutional law or federal courts course. Federal courts, under Article III of the United States Constitution, are empowered to hear only "cases or controversies." Thus, if a case is not ripe or is moot, a federal court is without the power to hear it. Do not, however, equate the concepts of ripeness and mootness for *constitutional purposes* with ripeness and mootness for purposes of meeting the *propensity test* for the granting of an injunction. A case can be ripe enough to meet the constitutional requirement, yet a court could still deny an injunction for lack of propensity. *See, e.g., United States v. W.T. Grant Co.*, 345 U.S. 629, 635 (1953). In that case, the Supreme Court held that the plaintiffs met the constitutional standard because a controversy continued to exist in that the defendant could return to his old ways. But it upheld a district court decision to deny an injunction on mootness grounds. "The necessary determination is that there exists some cognizable danger of recurrent violation, something more than the mere possibility which serves to keep the case alive." That standard may be hard to apply in practice, but it does demonstrate the difference between the constitutional and non-constitutional mootness and ripeness questions.

But if the defendant has already engaged in harmful conduct, why not issue an injunction related to the prior conduct? The answer is that an injunction must be geared toward *future conduct* or toward the *future bad effects* of past conduct. As for past conduct that has already caused harm, the courts will have to deal with this using damages or some other backward-looking remedy, not through an injunction.

Suppose, for example, that Quincy was in the process of removing *four trees* from Rudolfo's property in order to put in a swimming pool. Rudolfo goes to court after three of the four trees have been removed. Suppose further that the removal of one of those trees has caused Rudolfo's garage to collapse, and the foundation of his house is threatened as well unless the ground on Quincy's property is shored up.

Rudolfo should be able to:

- Get damages for the loss of the three trees and the collapse of his garage (and potentially punitive damages, depending upon the state's law related to punitive damages).
- Obtain a preventive injunction barring the removal of the fourth tree (this is an injunction *preventing future harm*).
- Possibly obtain a reparative injunction requiring Quincy to shore up the area near the removed tree that is threatening the foundation of Rudolfo's house (this is an injunction preventing *future bad effects* of past harm).

Note that in this list of remedies, there is nothing that an injunction can do to deal with the loss of the three trees or the collapse of the garage. Remember, injunctions are aimed at the future, *not* the past.

Example 3

The city of Pacificana has a long history of official and unofficial discrimination against African-Americans. It conducts a local election in which the city does nothing to prevent the Ku Klux Klan from intimidating African-American voters and keeping them from the polls. The undisputed evidence shows that because there are more white than black voters and because blacks and whites vote for different candidates in the election, the election results would not have changed even if there had been no intimidation. The court determines that the city violated the Fourteenth and Fifteenth Amendment rights of African-American voters in the city.

Should African-American voters be entitled to an injunction ordering the holding of a new election? To what other relief, if any, should they be entitled?

Explanation

This example is loosely based on *Bell v. Southwell*, 376 F.2d 659 (5th Cir. 1967). At first glance, it might appear that an injunction would be useless to the plaintiffs. The harm has already occurred (like the removed trees in the revised Quincy-Rudolfo hypothetical), and rerunning the election would not make any difference to the outcome. Given what social scientists call "racially polarized voting," we can predict the same winner and loser even if there had been no voter intimidation.

But that misses the larger symbolic value of voting. African-American voters, and all other voters in the district, would be living in a city where the officials serving out their terms were elected in unconstitutional, racially discriminatory elections. That is the future negative effect of the past harm, and a reparative injunction can prevent this future bad effect through a new election (even if that means that the election *results* are the same).

Those plaintiffs who were denied the right to vote on account of race might also seek an action for damages to compensate them for this past dignitary harm. A new election minimizes *additional harm*, but it does not eliminate the dignitary harm that has *already taken place* on Election Day. As for how such harm should be calculated, consider the material in Part I of this book.

Example 4

Building on the facts of Example 3, before the next election, African-American plaintiffs seek a court order requiring the city of Pacificana to take steps to ensure that no voters are intimidated when they seek to exercise their constitutional right to vote free of racial discrimination. The city argues that no injunction is necessary because the question is now moot. How should the court rule?

Explanation

While it is true that the issue of voter intimidation is now moot for purposes of the *last* election, the question before the court now is whether the city is currently taking adequate steps to prevent a recurrence of the unconstitutional failure of the city to protect African-American voters from voter intimidation in the *next election*. In ruling on the request, the court is going to have to consider the likelihood that private actors would attempt to intimidate black voters again and the extent of the plans the city has undertaken to prevent such action from taking place in the future. The court's decision on whether to issue an injunction may turn at least in part on a *credibility determination* by the court on the intent of city officials. Are city officials vigilantly protecting voters' constitutional rights? If the court has doubts about the city's credibility, it would likely issue the injunction to prevent future harm that would come from *new* intimidation at the *next* election.

7.3.2 The Proper Scope of Injunctive Relief

Suppose Quincy makes it crystal clear to Rudolfo that he is going to remove the tree on Rudolfo's property to build a swimming pool on his own property. In such circumstances, Rudolfo will not have a problem proving propensity. Assuming he can meet the other requirements for an injunction (discussed below), the battle between the parties may shift from *whether the court should grant an injunction* to *the scope* of the injunction.

Consider these two alternative injunctions, both of which would prevent Quincy from removing the tree (and subject him to contempt for failing to do so):

Injunction A

The court hereby orders and decrees that Quincy shall not remove the old oak tree currently on the property line between Quincy's house, located at 123 Main Street, and Rudolfo's house, located at 125 Main Street.

Injunction B

The court hereby orders and decrees that Quincy shall not remove any tree currently on the property of Quincy or property line between Quincy's house, located at 123 Main Street, and Rudolfo's house, located at 125 Main Street. Furthermore, Quincy shall not construct a swimming pool on his property or make any other improvements on his property without obtaining the consent of Rudolfo or an order of this court. Furthermore, Quincy will take no steps to harm any trees located on the property of Quincy or on the property line between Quincy's house and Rudolfo's house, and will actively take steps to maintain the health of all trees on the property and the property line at all times.

Quincy, of course, would prefer Injunction A, and Rudolfo would prefer Injunction B. To decide which the court should choose, we first have to ask what the court is trying to accomplish when it issues an injunction. If the court is aiming for the rightful position standard, arguably Injunction A is better than Injunction B, which appears to put Rudolfo in a *better* position than he would have been in had Quincy not threatened to take down the tree. (Do you see why? For one thing, Rudolfo would have the benefit of a court order preventing Quincy from making *any* improvements on his property without Rudolfo's permission or a court order.)

On the other hand, some of the measures contained in Injunction B could be defended on rightful position grounds. One could say that the requirement that Quincy take no steps to harm trees on his property could protect Rudolfo's rightful position (i.e., the right to be on his property without any interference with his trees by Quincy). Some people refer to such measures as *prophylactic* injunctions because they *protect* the rightful position.

The choice between Injunction A and Injunction B is in some sense a choice between who should bear the risk of problems with the court's order. Injunction A puts that risk on Rudolfo because it offers very little by way of prophylaxis; there may be ways that Quincy could get what he wants without violating the court's order, such as by not watering the tree until it dies. Injunction B puts the risk on Quincy by barring him from engaging in a whole host of otherwise legal activities such as cutting down trees wholly on his property or making improvements unrelated to the disputed swimming pool project.

Some courts might choose Injunction B not to protect Rudolfo's place in the rightful position, but to serve an ill-defined desire to "do justice." Recall the origin of the equity courts: these began to give pleas to the king for a just result unattainable in the law courts. Some judges today still probably view their equity power more broadly than simply as a power to ensure that plaintiff stays in the rightful position. *See* LAYCOCK p. 307 ("At its extremes, [this] tradition says that once there is a violation that brings a case into the equity court, the chancellor has a roving commission to do good."). Furthermore, "[s]uch talk [about the flexibility of equity and the discretion of trial judges in equity cases] led to the famous complaint that relying on the chancellor's conscience as a measure of justice is like relying on the chancellor's foot as the measure of length." Id. at 308.

As we will see in the next chapter, as a matter of *constitutional law*, the Supreme Court has signaled that in institutional litigation (so-called "structural injunctions"), courts must aim for the rightful position standard and not give remedies less well connected (or completely unconnected) to the harm that could occur to the plaintiff. In certain circumstances, however, it may be hard to tell the difference between an Injunction B that is aiming at the rightful position (but providing a bit of extra protection for the plaintiff—the prophylactic injunction) and a broader injunction dressed up to look like a prophylactic injunction.

Example 5

Consider again the example of the voting discrimination in Pacificana (Examples 3 and 4). How would you draft a preventive injunction applicable to the next election? What prophylactic measures might you consider to keep the plaintiffs in the rightful position?

Explanation

This is a really difficult one to answer. It is not an easy exercise to actually draft an injunction. You want an order that would require the police department, with a history of discrimination, to protect its African-American residents from discrimination by third parties. You'll need to ask yourself the question about how specific the injunction should be. If you make it too general, it will be useless to coerce compliance through the contempt power. Imagine, for example, an injunction that says: "The police department of the City of Pacificana shall take all reasonable steps to prevent intimidation of voters on election day." If voters are still intimidated, how would these voters prove that the police department failed to take "all reasonable steps"?

On the other hand, getting into specifics could require some micro-managing of the police department beyond the expertise of the court. Imagine, for example, an injunction that provides in relevant part: "The police department of the City of Pacificana shall take all reasonable steps to prevent intimidation of voters on election day, including but not limited to the stationing of two police officers at every polling place for the duration of Election Day." The city may not have enough police officers to do so, and it is not clear that this is the best use of resources. (For example, if there is racial segregation in the city as well, it might make more sense to post the police officers in African-American neighborhoods only.)

The court also may be tempted to go beyond the rightful position standard in the name of a prophylactic measure. Consider, for example, part of an injunction requiring the city to "require all poll workers to attend racial sensitivity training before Election Day." Such training may be a very good thing, but it is not necessarily well connected to a problem of outside agitators (the KKK) disrupting polling place activities. That kind of problem requires a response by law enforcement, not sensitivity training. Yet there is going to be a temptation for some judges, while they are already writing an injunction, to put some other provisions into the injunction as well (just as judges or juries might be tempted to give plaintiffs more damages than they have proven for various reasons).

Example 6

How would you draft an injunction to ensure Pnina's performance of the Oscar-Pnina widget contract?

Explanation

The order might be as simple as requiring Pnina to deliver the widget by a set date. But depending upon the complexity of the project and the willingness (and need) of the court to remain involved to ensure Pnina's performance, a court might order Pnina to make certain amounts of progress by set dates, and to file reports with the court informing the court of such progress. Alternatively, the court might approve of some mechanism that would allow Oscar to check on Pnina's progress and bring matters to the court's attention as necessary.

7.4 THE IRREPARABLE INJURY REQUIREMENT

In most of the examples in this chapter so far, plaintiffs seeking injunctions should have little trouble with the irreparable injury requirement. Consider Oscar, who cannot get the custom-made widget that Pnina has begun manufacturing but has not completed. Or consider Rudolfo, who is going to lose the shade provided by a mature tree that Quincy is about to cut down. Or consider the African-American voters of the City of Pacificana, who stand to lose the constitutional right to vote because the city won't protect them against threats of violence and intimidation by the KKK.

These are *easy* cases under the irreparable injury rule. *In each case, damages are not going to be as good a remedy as injunctive relief.* Money is a poor substitute for the widget that runs the factory, the irreplaceable shade tree or the precious right to vote. Money provides *some* compensation, as it is obviously better than nothing, but money is not as good as getting the specific relief requested in the injunction.

For this reason, courts traditionally have found the irreparable injury rule met when the loss is something not easily replaceable. This instinct along with the overstated idea that each parcel of land is unique (and not replaceable by another[7]) explains the common law's allowance of specific performance for contracts involving the sale of land. The concept of irreplaceablity appears as well in Article 2 of the U.C.C.'s insistence that specific performance be available when the goods are unique, and in § 2-716's comment noting that specific performance is also appropriate when the non-breaching buyer cannot easily go out and cover through a substitute purchase. The more difficult it is to find a substitute product, the more clear it is that the contract is one that involves a unique good (which may make us

---

7. The idea might apply when one thinks of a family home or estate, but it is not true of fungible real estate, especially real estate that is purchased for its investment value. For an investor, Lot 233 may be no more or less desirable than Lot 422.

question whether the U.C.C.'s test for specific performance really applies outside the concept of unique goods).

But suppose cover *was* easy for Oscar. The widget is not custom-made, and he could easily get the widget elsewhere. The U.C.C. standard suggests that Oscar *cannot* get an order of specific performance. Instead, he is expected to cover and then sue Pnina for *damages* (or, if he fails to cover, then as we saw in Chapter 6, principles of mitigation treat him as though he covered). The common law standard appears to be the same, though Oscar could perhaps argue that damages are inadequate because he has to go through the hassle of making another purchase that might not be as good.

But think about this rule for a moment. Oscar and Pnina have entered into a contract, and midway through performance Pnina has announced that she plans to breach the contract. In most cases, Oscar is not going to *want* Pnina's performance and he would be happy to get damages; he may never want to conduct business with (or even see) Pnina again. By the time contract disputes end up in litigation, there is usually a great deal of acrimony between the two parties. If Oscar is nonetheless *asking* for specific performance, it must be because there is something particularly valuable to him about Pnina's performance such that he is willing to continue doing business with her (after all, if she fails to make the widget well, there is the risk of further litigation between two parties already angry with one another, and why risk that?).

What this analysis suggests is that when a non-breaching party to a contract *asks* a court to grant specific performance, that action itself is usually good evidence that the irreparable injury rule has been met; that is, if the non-breaching party is trying to force the breaching party to continue the contractual relationship, it is because damages are not as good a remedy as injunctive relief.

Speaking more generally, outside the context of specific performance, it will also often be the case that when faced with a defendant's propensity to commit a violation, a plaintiff seeking injunctive relief can quite easily show that a legal remedy would be inadequate. Consider even the extreme case in which Rudolfo couldn't care less about the tree on his property. It is difficult to imagine a court today holding that Quincy has the right to go onto Rudolfo's property, cut down one of Rudolfo's trees against his will, and simply pay Rudolfo for damages later. Such a rule seems to be an affront to our current notions about property rights and the ability to exclude outsiders from protected areas. A damages award intrinsically, then, is not as good as an injunction even when the party seeking the injunction has no reason to seek it other than as a vindication of his rights.

In some circumstances, however, courts may use the irreparable injury rule as a reason for denying an injunction even when damages would not be as good a remedy. The next section offers a number of policy reasons why courts might decide to bar an injunction even when plaintiff can prove propensity and irreparable injury.

Example 7

Toyota of Pacificana enters into a contract with Ursula to sell Ursula a ruby red Toyota Camry. It is a limited edition color, but otherwise, it is the same as other Camrys. The contract price is $20,000, which is the going market price. After the parties enter into a binding contract, but before the car is delivered, Victor offers to buy the car from the dealership for $28,000. Toyota of Pacificana tells Ursula it is going to breach the contract and sell the car to Victor. Toyota of Pacificana checks its computer database, and finds that there are no other ruby red Camrys available in the area. They offer to sell her a blue, white, or black Camry for $19,000, which is $1,000 below the market price. If Ursula goes to court seeking an order of specific performance, will the court grant it to her? What if the evidence shows that if the court grants her specific performance, she is going to turn around and sell the car to Victor for a quick $8,000 profit?

Explanation

This is a contract for the sale of a moveable good, meaning it is governed by Article 2 of the U.C.C. Recall that under § 2-716, a court will grant specific performance when a good is unique or in other proper circumstances, such as when a plaintiff cannot cover. The application of this rule to these facts depends on whether the "limited edition ruby red" color makes this good unique. Arguably it does, or Victor would not have come in to pay such a premium for the car, and Ursula would have settled for a Camry in another color at a discount. The court should grant specific performance.

It should not matter that Ursula might turn around and sell the car to Victor for an $8,000 profit. After all, a buyer's right to specific performance does not require that the buyer demonstrate some *sentimental* or *personal* value in the unique property. It might be unique *because* it yields a higher market price. Because the parties entered into a binding contract for a unique good, it looks like the U.C.C. will let Ursula get the car and capture any profits from Victor should she choose to sell it.

7.5 DOES *EBAY* SET A NEW STANDARD FOR GRANTING INJUNCTIONS IN FEDERAL COURT?

As noted in section 7.2 above, plaintiffs seeking injunctions typically must show irreparable injury and propensity in order to obtain an injunction, subject to certain policy concerns (discussed below in section 7.6). However, in a 2006 case, *eBay Inc. v. MercExchange, L.L.C.*, 547 U.S. 388

(2006), the Supreme Court added confusion to the standard for the issuance of injunctions, at least in federal courts.

In *eBay*, the Court rejected a rule adopted by the United States Court of Appeals for the Federal Circuit holding that a patent holder whose patent had been infringed in most cases had the right to an injunction against the infringer. Uncontroversially, the Supreme Court rejected such a *per se* rule. But controversially, the Court set out the standard for determining whether an injunction should issue:

> According to well-established principles of equity, a plaintiff seeking a permanent injunction must satisfy a four-factor test before a court may grant such relief. A plaintiff must demonstrate: (1) that it has suffered an irreparable injury; (2) that remedies available at law, such as monetary damages, are inadequate to compensate for that injury; (3) that, considering the balance of hardships between the plaintiff and defendant, a remedy in equity is warranted; and (4) that the public interest would not be disserved by a permanent injunction.

Although the Supreme Court referred to these as "well-established principles of equity," in fact, "Remedies specialists had never heard of the four-point test. . . . [T]he Court appears to vindicate a 'traditional' stand for a final injunction that never existed, except perhaps for a preliminary injunction." Doug Rendleman, *The Trial Judge's Equitable Discretion Following* eBay v. MercExchange, 27 REV. LITIG. 63, 76 n.71 (2007). Professor Laycock believes this new *eBay* case "has potential for enormous mischief." LAYCOCK p. 426.

Despite these academic criticisms, the Supreme Court recently reaffirmed this new *eBay* standard in *Monsanto Co. v. Geerston Seed Farms*, 130 S. Ct. 2743, 2757 (2010). Perhaps a new article on the subject by Professors Gergen, Golden, and Smith in the *Columbia Law Review* criticizing the Court for its perhaps unwitting *eBay* standard will get the Court's attention. Mark P. Gergen, John M. Golden & Henry E. Smith, *The Supreme Court's Accidental Revolution? The Test for Permanent Injunctions*, 112 COLUM. L. REV. 203 (2012).

One specific problem with the "*eBay*" test is that there does not appear to be a difference between the first and second prongs, a point that should be clear if you've read section 7.2 above. Indeed, on remand from the Supreme Court, the trial court said as much: "The irreparable harm inquiry and remedy at law inquiry are essentially two sides of the same coin; however, the court will address them separately in order to conform with the four-factor test as outlined by the Supreme Court." *MercExchange, L.L.C. v. eBay Inc.*, 500 F. Supp. 2d 556, 569 (E.D. Va. 2007).

Another problem with the *eBay* standard is the treatment of the balance of hardships and the public interest standard. Balance of hardships is a standard usually applied in *preliminary injunction* cases, as we shall see in Chapter 9. To the extent that the defendant argues that hardship on defendant or the public interest weighs against granting the injunction, these have typically been *affirmative defenses* raised by the defendant (see Rendleman, *supra*, at 82-88), and not factors to be *disproved* by the plaintiff. It is also not clear after *Monsanto* if "benefits to the public interest cannot count in favor of issuing the injunction, but that harm to the public interest is an absolute reason not to issue it." DOUGLAS LAYCOCK, MODERN AMERICAN REMEDIES — 2012 TEACHER'S UPDATE 35.

Example 8

The Pacifica Preservation Society (PPS) seeks a permanent injunction barring Big Developer Co. (BDC) from removing a historic oak tree from property that BDC recently bought. BDC wants to remove the tree to make way for a $10 million development project. PPS argues that the tree is protected by a state law preserving old trees. Assume that PPS can prove that the tree is protected by the statute. Neither PPS nor BDC puts on any evidence as to the hardship an injunction barring the removal of the tree would cause to BDC. Nor does either side put on any evidence of whether removing or preserving the tree would be in the public interest. How should a court rule on PPS's request for an injunction, assuming the court applies the *eBay* standard for the granting of permanent injunctions?

Explanation

Though it is not clear how the court should rule in this case, PPS has done itself no favors by failing to put in evidence regarding the balance of the hardships to the parties and the public interest. Under the *eBay* standard, the *plaintiff* bears the burden of bringing in evidence on these questions (though traditionally these were generally considered affirmative defenses to be raised and proved by defendants). There's still a chance that the court will grant the injunction, if there is enough evidence of irreparable injury/no adequate remedy at law (a single factor, but one that the Supreme Court lists as two factors in *eBay*). Even though irreparable injury should be easy to prove (after all, how can damages replace an historic tree?), proof of such injury might not be enough for the granting of an injunction in this case under the *eBay* standard.

7.6 OTHER POLICY REASONS FOR COURTS TO DENY INJUNCTIONS

The preceding section demonstrated that when a plaintiff who faces a defendant likely to violate plaintiff's rights asks for an injunction rather than settling for damages, it is usually for a good reason: damages just won't be as good as the specific relief offered by equity and backed by the power of contempt.

But courts sometimes hide behind the language of the irreparable injury rule to deny an injunction on policy grounds. More forthrightly, courts sometimes will deny an injunction expressly on policy grounds, even acknowledging that plaintiffs have proven irreparable injury and propensity.

Professor Laycock, in his book *The Death of the Irreparable Injury Rule*, offers some wonderful examples of courts misusing the irreparable injury rule to reach a result that many of us would agree with on policy grounds. *See* Laycock, The Death of the Irreparable Injury Rule, at 60-192. Most notable is his discussion of *Van Wagner Advertising v. S & M Enterprises*, 492 N.E.2d 756 (N.Y. 1986).[8]

In *Van Wagner*, the owner of a building near Manhattan's midtown tunnel leased to Van Wagner Advertising space to erect a billboard on the building's eastern wall. The space faced an exit to the tunnel (a prime billboard spot, no doubt). The lease period was three years with an option to renew for seven additional years. Van Wagner erected a billboard and subleased it to another party for three years. Near the beginning of the lease period, the building's owner sold to a new owner and purported to cancel the lease with Van Wagner. The new owner wanted to tear down the building (including the billboard) and some adjacent property it had purchased in order to build a new major residential-commercial development on the block, a major construction project.

By the time the case got to New York's highest court, the Court of Appeals, the main question was not about whether the building's owner had breached the contract (it did), but whether Van Wagner was entitled to specific performance. Under the rules we have already seen, this appears to be an easy case for the court to grant the injunction:

1. *Propensity:* The building's owner had already breached the contract and was going to tear down the building. There was no question that the owner posed more than a mere threat to violate Van Wagner's rights.

2. *Irreparable injury:* It does not look like damages would be as good a remedy for Van Wagner as the injunction. Remember that some courts treated contracts involving real estate as prime candidates for specific performance under the idea that each piece of land is unique. While that notion might not be true uniformly, this seems to be a particularly strong case: how much is the advertising seen by thousands of people each day stuck in traffic while trying to emerge from Manhattan's midtown tunnel worth? On top of that, remember that Van Wagner had subleased to another party, who is

---

8. Even though this is an interesting example for students of Remedies, it is not as interesting as the party name S & M *Enterprises* might lead you to think.

now going to be able to sue Van Wagner for breaching that lease. On top of that, what is the value of the seven-year option on the property? All of these factors are reasons for concluding that Van Wagner could meet the irreparable injury requirement.

But that's not what the New York court held. It first stated that the rule about specific performance being available as a matter of course in real estate contracts did not apply to the *leasing* but to the *sale* of property. It also noted that "at some level all property may be interchangeable with money" — a view the court conceded undermined the basis for ever finding irreparable injury. It then concluded that there was no irreparable injury because the trial court correctly determined "that the value of the 'unique qualities' of the demised space could be fixed with reasonable certainty and without imposing an unacceptably high risk of undercompensating the injured tenant."

Laycock (DEATH OF THE IRREPARABLE INJURY RULE, at 162) points out the inconsistency of this analysis with the usual understanding of the irreparable injury rule:

> These damages are imperfect at best, and may be seriously defective. Van Wagner lost any chance to charge a higher rent for years four through ten, and the court made no effort to compensate that loss. More important is the sublessee, the advertiser who bargained for three years of exposure to the tunnel exit. His damages seem entirely unmeasurable. Either he loses his expectancy entirely, receiving no compensation other than release of his obligation to pay rent, or Van Wagner is liable for the speculative value of the advertiser's lost expectancy. Van Wagner got no compensation for that liability, and the court did not venture an opinion on how to measure the advertiser's damages.

That's not to say that the court got the *result* wrong in this case. Indeed, the court's result was likely correct on an alternative ground cited by the trial court: there was so much *hardship on the defendant* that Van Wagner should be denied the right to an injunction. The court wrote: "It is well settled that the imposition of an equitable remedy must not itself work an inequity, and that specific performance should not be an undue hardship." What hardship? If Van Wagner gets its injunction, it can hold up a major redevelopment of a block of midtown Manhattan.[9] So the court likely reached the right result,

---

9. An economist might respond that it is very unlikely that Van Wagner, if given the right to specific performance, would actually hold up such a major development. Instead, the building's owner would likely pay Van Wagner some generous amount (more than the amount a court would award in damages to Van Wagner) to give up the property right to keep the billboard up. For a discussion of the economic analysis, and the likelihood of such bargaining, see this chapter's Example 1 and its explanation.

but it (unnecessarily, given the alternative ground for decision) mangled the irreparable injury rule along the way.

Hardship to the defendant is one policy reason for denying an injunction to a plaintiff who can prove irreparable injury and propensity. It is not, however, necessarily an easy argument to make. Courts do *not* simply balance the hardship to the plaintiff and the hardship to the defendant in deciding whether or not the plaintiff is entitled to an injunction.[10]

Even in cases when the defendant is an intentional wrongdoer, courts will often refuse "in equity" to consider such a hardship argument. (Ask yourself if the building owner is a wrongdoer here. As discussed in Chapter 4, at least some courts do not consider breaching parties to a contract to be wrongdoers, at least in most circumstances.) In some cases in which there is disproportionate harm to the defendant compared to the gain to the plaintiff in granting an injunction, however, a court may deny the grant of an injunction on grounds of preventing hardship.

There are other policy reasons as well why courts might deny injunctions to plaintiffs who otherwise meet the requirements for an injunction. Consider the right to a jury trial, which, as noted above, is guaranteed in federal courts by the Seventh Amendment and in many state constitutions. Considering our Oscar-Pnina widget breach of contract example again, if Oscar asks for a suit for damages, most state constitutions would grant Oscar the right to a jury trial. But if Oscar asks for specific performance, in many states he would have no right to a jury trial because he is seeking an equitable remedy.[11]

Oscar is in a good position: he can choose damages over specific performance if the right to a jury trial is important enough to him. But note that if Oscar chooses specific performance, that also deprives the defendant, Pnina, of the right to a jury trial. A court therefore might deny Oscar's claim for specific performance *because it deprives the defendant of the right to trial by jury.*

Many defendants may be just as happy with a bench trial (that is, a trial before a judge and not a jury). In my review of the cases involving equitable relief with requests by *defendants* for a jury trial, I found a number of cases in which a large corporate lender sought to foreclose on the property of a poor defendant or failing small business. You can see why in such circumstances *defendants* might want the right to a jury trial.

In many jurisdictions, a complaint like Pnina's for a jury trial would fall on deaf ears. *See National City Bank v. Abdalla,* 722 N.E.2d 130, 134 (Ohio App. 1999) (rejecting argument of defendant in foreclosure action to a jury trial: "Neither party may assert the right to a jury trial in an equitable action.").

---

10. Under the new *eBay* standard, as discussed in section 7.5 above, the plaintiff may bear the burden of coming forward with evidence as to the balance of the hardships.

11. In some states, statutes provide for the right to a jury trial for at least some equitable claims. *See Smith County Educ. Ass'n v. Anderson,* 676 S.W.2d 328, 337 (Tenn. 1984).

The rule from the Ohio case makes some sense; it would be a pretty harsh result for plaintiffs seeking injunctions if their rights to equitable relief could be quashed by a defendant's simple demand for a jury trial. Concerned with defendants' right to a jury trial, however, some jurisdictions have reached a compromise position. In North Dakota, for example, "one against whom an action is brought may not be deprived of the right to a jury trial unless the party seeking to avoid a jury trial clearly and unambiguously shows that he is seeking an equitable remedy and that he is clearly entitled to it if he proves the facts as alleged in his complaint." *Gen. Elec. Credit Union v. Richman*, 338 N.W.2d 814, 818 (1983).[12]

Freedom of speech as guaranteed by the First Amendment can also be the basis for denying an injunction to plaintiffs otherwise entitled to them. Consider the facts of *Animal Rights Foundation of Florida v. Siegel*, 867 So. 2d 451 (Fla. App. 2004). David Siegel sold timeshare condominiums in Florida. To draw customers, he hired "Tiger's Eye Productions" for twice-weekly animal shows. The Animal Rights Foundation of Florida began a letter writing campaign and picketing in front of Siegel's residence and business location, claiming he was promoting cruelty to animals through the shows. He sued for libel and slander.

The trial court initially denied a request for a preliminary injunction, but when the protests continued, the court granted it. (The fact that it was a preliminary injunction rather than a permanent injunction is irrelevant for our purposes. Assume that a court has determined that the animal rights group in fact engaged in libel and slander.) The injunction in pertinent part provided:

> That defendants Heather Lischin and the Animal Rights Foundation of Florida, and their servants, employees, agents and any person or entity acting on their own behalf or at their request, and any person in active concert or participation with them (hereinafter "Defendants") are forthwith and immediately enjoined from tortiously interfering with Plaintiffs' advantageous business relationships by directly or indirectly publishing verbally, or in writing the following statements:
>
>> "David Siegel abuses animals"
>> "David Siegel condones animal abuse"
>> "Now featuring at Westgate Animal abuse"
>> "David Siegel supports animal abuse"
>> "Westgate supports animal abuse"
>> "Westgate supports cat beater"
>> "David Siegel supports cruelty to animals"

---

12. For additional complications since *Richman* involving the North Dakota right to a jury trial in equitable cases, *see* Edward E. Erickson, *The Right to a Jury Trial in Equitable Cases*, 69 N.D. L. Rev. 559 (1993).

"Westgate supports cruelty to animals"
"Now featuring at Westgate animal abuse" and
"Westgate refuses to stop sponsoring animal cruelty," to:

(1) Plaintiffs' actual or prospective customers and their guests at the entrance to, or within any of Plaintiffs' timeshare in Florida. "Customers" shall mean all persons who have been invited by Plaintiffs, either directly or indirectly, to purchase or lease a timeshare unit at any of Westgate Resorts, Ltd's resorts. "Guests" shall mean all persons who have been invited by customers of Westgate Resorts, Ltd. "Invited" means those persons who have come to any of Westgate Resorts, Ltd's resorts as a result of any advertising, marketing or promotional activities by Westgate Resorts, Ltd.
(2) David Siegel's neighbors at the entrance to, or within, the subdivision wherein the Home is located.[13]

By a 2-1 vote, the Florida appellate court held that the injunction was an unconstitutional prior restraint on speech and therefore had to be reversed. The court also reversed other parts of the injunction limiting the number of protesters and the protesters' use of megaphones. The dissenting judge held that part of the injunction was constitutional because there was good evidence that some of the statements were libelous (defendants admitted that there was no evidence Siegel himself or his company Westgate were "abusing animals") and the defendants' conduct was harassing Siegel.

A First Amendment defense to injunctive relief did not leave Siegel without a remedy. If he could prove defamation, he would be allowed to recover damages. But damages in a defamation case, even "presumed damages" for loss to reputation (see Chapter 3.4), are rarely going to be as good for a defendant as an injunction: there is no way to know how many of Siegel's potential customers were scared away by the claims of the animal rights activists, or how many of those customers otherwise would have made a sale had they not been deterred by the statements. Plaintiff is left with a remedy, but likely a remedy that is not nearly as good as an injunction.

---

13. As a matter of drafting and the scope of the injunction, how would you grade this injunction? Consider whether it would be a violation of the injunction for defendants to hire an airplane to fly over Siegel's business location and residence with a large photograph of a tortured animal accompanied by a brightly colored sign reading: "David Siegel and Westgate want animals to DIE, DIE, DIE!!!!" If it would not be a violation, how could you rewrite the injunction to more effectively cover such conduct? You should see the trade-off between being specific and being general. By being specific, the defendant is less able to claim that his conduct did not violate the injunction. But by being specific, the plaintiff opens up "loopholes" that violate the spirit but not the letter of the injunction. Courts generally won't hold a person in contempt for violating the spirit of the injunction. The best way to deal with this problem (though it is an imperfect way) is to provide examples and add some general language such as "or similar language disparaging Siegel's treatment of animals."

Personal service contracts are another policy area where courts sometimes refuse to issue injunctions. Consider *Beverly Glen Music v. Warner Communications, Inc.*, 224 Cal. Rptr. 260, 260 (App. 1986):

> In 1982, plaintiff Beverly Glen Music, Inc. signed to EXA contract a then-unknown singer, Anita Baker. Ms. Baker recorded an album for Beverly Glen which was moderately successful, grossing over one million dollars. In 1984, however, Ms. Baker was offered a considerably better deal by defendant Warner Communications. As she was having some difficulties with Beverly Glen, she accepted Warner's offer and notified plaintiff that she was no longer willing to perform under the contract. Beverly Glen then sued Ms. Baker. . . .

The California appellate court noted that the universal rule that contracts to render personal services cannot be specifically enforced. "To do so runs afoul of the Thirteenth Amendment's prohibition on involuntary servitude." Thus, Beverly Glen could not get an injunction ordering Anita Baker to record the album for them.

A common way around the prohibition, however, is for the non-breaching party to seek an injunction barring the defendant from rendering personal services for someone else. "The net effect is to pressure the defendant to return voluntarily to his employer by denying him the means of earning a living. Indeed, this is its only purpose, for, unless the defendant relents and honors the contract, the plaintiff gains nothing from having brought the injunction."[14]

The court in *Beverly Glen* held that a California statute prohibited enforcing the "negative" contract against Baker,[15] but other courts have upheld such contracts. *See Nassau Sports v. Peters*, 352 F. Supp. 870 (E.D.N.Y. 1972) (upholding an injunction barring a professional hockey player signed with National Hockey League team from playing for a team in the rival World Hockey Association league). Still, it is difficult to find many modern cases analyzing the use of these negative injunctions, which suggests that plaintiffs may not be seeking them all that often. One reason is that such negative injunctions are unnecessary given that prohibitions on working for competitors are now

---

14. The leading case supporting the use of "negative" injunctions in personal service contracts is *Lumley v. Wagner*, 42 Eng. Rep. 687 (1852), involving breach of an opera singer's contract to sing at an opera house.

15. For a similar case on statutory grounds out of Montana, see *Reier Broadcasting Co. v. Kramer*, 72 P.3d 944 (Mont. 2003). The California statute, Cal. Civ. Code § 3423(e), has since been amended to allow courts to grant such negative injunctions only for "a contract in writing for the rendition of personal services from one to another where the promised service is of a special, unique, unusual, extraordinary, or intellectual character, which gives it peculiar value, the loss of which cannot be reasonably or adequately compensated in damages in an action at law, and where the compensation for the personal services" meets one of two complex formulas for the amount of compensation in the statute. It is unclear from the face of the statute why the California legislature wrote in these complex formulas. Perhaps there was pressure from some industry to include or exclude certain classes of contracting parties.

commonly contained in covenants not to compete, and litigation today centers on whether such covenants are enforceable or against public policy.

Burden on the court is a final policy reason why courts may decline injunctive relief. In this regard, consider *Diaz v. Kay-Dix Ranch*, 88 Cal. Rptr. 443 (App. 1970). A group of legal California farm workers concerned about competition from illegal workers from Mexico sought an injunction against three private ranches "requiring defendants to make some reasonable inquiry into the citizenship or immigration status of employment applicants as a preliminary to hiring." Among the reasons the appellate court had for sustaining the trial court's denial of an injunction was the burden on the courts:

> If defendants are to be enjoined, other California farm operators may be similarly enjoined. A network of these injunctions may cover growers in rural counties. A single superior court may be called upon to issue dozens of these injunctions. As this court envisions these injunctions in practical operation, farm operators or their foremen will put each new worker through a relatively simple interrogation and request for documentation. . . . The farm operator or foreman will be called upon to determine the status, legal or illegal, of each new worker. . . . Injunction violations would subject employers to judgments of contempt, punishable by fine or jail. . . . Eligible workers or other observers would report seeming violations, contempt citations would issue and judicial hearings held. At peak employment seasons the superior courts in rural counties would sit in judgment over charges of contempt and over the form and adequacy of investigations. Multiple injunctions covering a wide segment of California agriculture would have the cumulative effect of a statutory regulation, administered by the superior courts through the medium of contempt hearings. The injunctive relief sought by plaintiffs would subject farm operators to burdensome, if bearable, regulation, and the courts to burdensome, if bearable, enforcement responsibilities.

The court concluded that "[w]eighed alone on any scale of human values, the farmworkers' need is vastly more acute than the prospective predicament of injunction-saddled employers. [In addition], the comparative efficacy of federal action, tips the scales against injunctive relief."

Note the judgment the court made about the system of injunctions that give courts "burdensome, if bearable, enforcement responsibilities." Just how burdensome does an injunction have to be before it is too burdensome? There is likely no single answer to that question. The answer, however, turns not only on how burdensome an injunction might be on the courts, but also on how important the social policy is that the injunction seeks to further. On this point, think of injunctions aimed at desegregating public schools in the South. As we will see in the next chapter, these injunctions were terribly burdensome on the courts, with some lasting for decades and requiring that courts get into the micromanagement of school policy. Yet many would claim that the heavy burden of the injunctions on the courts was but a small price to pay given the value of desegregation.

In sum, courts sometimes deny injunctions to plaintiffs who can prove irreparable injury and propensity for policy reasons. Here is a non-exhaustive list of policy reasons discussed in this section:

- Undue hardship to the defendant
- Preserving defendant's right to a jury trial
- First Amendment concerns
- Concerns about restraining labor/involuntary servitude
- Burden on the court

As in *Van Wagner*, be wary of courts that find that a plaintiff cannot meet the irreparable injury requirement for the issuance of injunctions. Courts sometimes care more about an unstated policy reason for denying the injunction than the now-dead hand of the Chancellor that seems to be denying the plaintiff the specific relief that aims most directly — or at least more directly than damages — at the rightful position. Litigants should not be afraid to confront *both* irreparable injury and policy arguments directly.

Example 9

Same facts as in the Siegel animal rights case, but assume that the evidence conclusively shows that the animal rights activists have no assets. This means that if a jury awards Siegel damages, he would not be able to collect them. How, if at all, does this change the analysis of whether the court should grant the injunction prohibiting the activists' speech?

Explanation

The fact that the defendants have no assets is another factor (on top of others) showing that Siegel faces irreparable injury: damages are not going to be adequate to put the plaintiff in the rightful position. Whether that should trump the First Amendment right to speak is a difficult question. On the one hand, if the defendants have no assets, Siegel is going to be left with no remedy at all: the First Amendment precludes an injunction that keeps him in the rightful position and any damages awarded cannot be collected. On the other hand, making the inability to collect damages the dispositive factor in deciding this case has uncomfortable ramifications. Discussing a similar claim arising in *Willing v. Mazzocone*, 393 A.2d 1155 (1978), Laycock (The Death of the Irreparable Injury Rule, at 164) writes: "The court correctly saw that it could not enjoin indigent speakers if it would not enjoin wealthy speakers: 'conditioning the right of free speech upon the monetary wealth of an individual' would be intolerable."

Example 10

A client comes to you complaining about the conditions in which client's brother lives in state prison (the brother is in prison for life, without the possibility of parole). The client believes, and you agree upon diligent investigation, that the conditions violate numerous provisions of the U.S. Constitution, including the Eighth Amendment prohibition against "cruel and unusual punishment." Should you sue for damages, an injunction, both, or neither?

Explanation

As a first thought, you might consider damages for past harm and injunctive relief aimed at improving conditions in the future. But bringing either kind of claim carries serious complications. First, the Supreme Court has read the Eleventh Amendment of the U.S. Constitution to bar suits for damages against the state, allowing only injunctive relief (a sort of reverse "irreparable injury" rule). *Edelman v. Jordan*, 415 U.S. 651, 677 (1974). Individual state officers who have violated the brother's constitutional rights might be subject to damages claims under 42 U.S.C. § 1983 (most commonly known as a "section 1983" lawsuit).

Injunctive relief against the prison system is possible, and, as we will see in the next chapter, prisoners in the past have brought significant class actions in federal court to reform prisons. Such suits, however, are now limited by the Prison Litigation Reform Act (PLRA), which narrowly sets forth the kind of prospective relief that may be available. *See* 18 U.S.C. § 3626. The PLRA also requires that a complaining prisoner exhaust administrative remedies before suing in court, 42 U.S.C. § 1997e(a), a provision the Supreme Court recently construed against prisoners in *Woodford v. Ngo*, 548 U.S. 81 (2006). The next chapter considers in more depth how the PLRA limits prospective relief.

The more general point: if you are going to sue a government defendant for either damages or an injunction, you had better carefully check both the constitutional and statutory limits on such suits.

Example 11

The Wilkinsons lived in the Vista subdivision, where all the homes had to abide by the covenants contained in the deed of sale. Among the covenants was a prohibition on placing "manufactured homes" on the land, except for homes that (1) complied with federal and state requirements for safe homes and that (2) met all the regulations and standards of the New Mexico Construction Industries Division (CID). The Wilkinsons gave their property to their daughter, Jane Brown, who wanted to put a manufactured home on the land. Brown knew about the covenant. She contacted one company, Preferred, whose products complied with the covenant's requirements, but that company had a nine-month waiting list for a home. She then bought her home from another manufacturer that complied with federal and state requirements, but that failed to meet a few relatively minor standards of the New Mexico CID. The homeowners association immediately objected. Smith did not remove the home, and the association sued. The trial court found that the differences between a Preferred home and the one purchased by Brown to be inconsequential. It would cost $25,000 to $30,000 to remove the home. The entire home's purchase price was $60,000.

Assume there is no question that Brown's home violated the covenant and the only question is one of remedy. Should the court grant the association's request for an injunction to remove the home or should the association receive only damages?

Explanation

There is no question about *propensity* here. Brown had already brought the home onto the land in violation of the subdivision's restrictive covenant. Nor does there seem to be much of a question about irreparable injury. Presumably, these restrictions are in the covenant for either aesthetic or safety reasons. Either way, it will be hard to measure the losses to the association and other owners stemming from Brown's failure to abide by the restrictive covenant.

There are three policy reasons, however, why a court might wish to deny the injunction. The first is the burden to the defendant. The cost to remove the home is very high, especially when considered in relation to the cost of the unit itself. Hardship to the defendant is a tough claim to make here, even to a court acting in equity that has some discretion in granting a remedy. Brown knew of the restrictive covenant, and she even took steps to comply. Because she did not want to wait, however, she willfully violated the covenant. A court probably would be unsympathetic to her plight. (However, compare her plight to that of the defendant in *Van Wagner*. Is her behavior any worse than that of the seller who breached the lease for the billboard?)

Second, a court may think that the covenant itself is unfair, at least as applied to an owner who wishes to bring onto the land a manufactured home that comes close to complying with the standards of the association. To the extent that a court that sits in equity wishes to "do equity" (that is, to do what is fair), there is an argument to deny the injunction.

Finally, this might be a case in which the *defendant*, rather than the *plaintiffs*, wants the right to a jury trial. The defendant might reason that jurors are likely to be sympathetic with a homeowner fighting an association that appears to be enforcing its rules in a very strict manner. Sometimes those on such an association go on power trips, enforcing rules for their own sake rather than out of any logic.

The facts of this hypothetical are based on *Aragon v. Brown*, 78 P.3d 913 (N.M. 2003). In the actual case, the trial court denied the injunction on grounds that the covenant was "not reasonable, and should not, in equity, be enforced." A divided New Mexico Supreme Court reversed, finding that the provision was not against public policy, and that "a general inquiry into whether restrictive covenants running with the land are reasonable is not a proper inquiry in considering whether to grant an injunction to enforce such covenants."

The dissent thought the trial court was right to deny the injunction: "The Association failed to demonstrate to the trial court any real, much less legitimate, purpose served by excluding homes that are the functional equivalent of homes that are allowed."

The majority opinion did not discuss the right to a jury trial, nor was it moved by the amount that it would cost Brown to comply with the injunction.

Advanced Topics in Injunctions

Chapter 7 set forth the basic rules for the issuance of injunctions: injunctions are forward-looking court orders aimed either at preventing future harm (the *preventive* injunction) or at preventing the future bad effects of past harm (the *reparative* injunction). A plaintiff requesting an injunction must prove both that the defendant has engaged in — or at least made a realistic threat of engaging in — prohibited conduct (*propensity*), and that a legal remedy such as damages is not as good for the plaintiff as an injunction (*irreparable injury*). Even then, courts sometimes deny injunctions on various *policy grounds*. Courts typically tailor an injunction toward the goal of keeping the plaintiff in the rightful position (*the rightful position standard*), but courts sometimes go further and issue injunctions that protect the rightful position through broader steps (the *prophylactic* injunction). In some circumstances, courts granting injunctions view their role more broadly, and grant broad injunctions in the name of equity (evoking the image of the original Chancellor's discretion).

In this chapter, we consider three advanced topics in the law of remedies: (1) the proper scope of injunctive relief in public institutional litigation (structural injunctions) and the related question of consent decrees, (2) the standards for modifying already existing injunctions, and (3) the rights and obligations of third parties in relation to injunctive relief. Chapter 9 looks at *preliminary* injunctive relief, including preliminary injunctions, temporary restraining orders, and injunction bonds. Chapter 10 examines the *contempt power*, which courts use to enforce injunctions.

8.1 STRUCTURAL INJUNCTIONS

8.1.1 Structural Injunctions, the Rightful Position, and the Roving Commission to Do Good

As we saw in the preceding chapter, plaintiffs may seek injunctions in both private law and public law litigation. When Oscar asks a court to order Pnina to specifically perform the contract by requiring her to produce the promised widget, Oscar seeks an injunction that serves only his *private* aims. But when the voters of the City of Pacificana seek an injunction requiring the police to provide protection against KKK intimidation when they go to vote at the polls, the injunction is a form of *public law* litigation that benefits more than a private party.

Beginning with *Brown v. Board of Education* (Brown II), 349 U.S. 294 (1955), civil rights activists have used injunctive relief as a major public law tool for facilitating social change on a large scale. *Brown II* required courts to desegregate Southern schools using injunctive relief: "[T]he *Brown II* Court granted district courts the authority not only to overhaul every aspect of educational administration, but also to revise 'local laws and regulations which may be necessary in solving the foregoing problems.'" Marshall Miller, Note, *Police Brutality*, 17 YALE L. & POL'Y REV. 149, 194 (1998) (quoting Brown II).

Desegregating a school system takes time, and it requires a more complicated series of injunctions than a simple order such as that requiring Pnina to deliver the widget to Oscar by June 1. Professor Owen Fiss coined the term "structural injunction" to connote the series of injunctions necessary to restructure government institutions in civil rights litigation. As Fiss explains:

> The civil rights injunction takes many forms, but none as significant as the structural injunction: the formal medium through which the judiciary seeks to reorganize ongoing bureaucratic organizations so as to bring them into conformity with the Constitution. The structural injunction represents the most distinctive contribution to our remedial jurisprudence drawn from the civil rights experience, and though the structural injunction has been used in all manner of cases — housing, mental health, and prisons — its origins in civil rights litigation are never forgotten. The structural injunction received its most authoritative formulation in civil rights cases, specifically those involving school desegregation, and has been legitimated in terms of those cases.

Owen Fiss, *The Allure of Individualism*, 78 IOWA L. REV. 965 (1993).

Structural injunctions blossomed in the Warren Court era as scholars looked to courts to solve social problems, particularly problems of racial discrimination.[1] There were many success stories from such litigation, but the litigation also enmeshed federal courts in the micromanagement of government institutions — sometimes with mixed results.

Federal district courts have held on to some of these cases for years, with many litigants graduating (or even dying) before the cases reached a conclusion. Especially in the earlier years, some of these injunctions restructured government institutions in ways not tied to the rightful position standard (closer to the Chancellor's "roving commission to do good," discussed in Chapter 7), a role defended by some scholars and, in more recent years, rejected by the Supreme Court. As Fiss explains, "[t]he fate of the structural injunction has . . . been tied to that of the civil rights movement. The remedy grew in power and scope over a twenty-year period, beginning in 1954 and continuing until 1974. Ever since, it has been under attack." Id. at 965.

Swann v. Charlotte-Mecklenberg Board of Education, 402 U.S. 1 (1971), is a good example of the Supreme Court's treatment of structural injunctions in the pre-1974 period. In that case, the district court enacted a far-reaching mandatory busing plan to end school desegregation that was upheld by the Supreme Court. Arguably, the plan went much further than the rightful position because the plan integrated schools much more than they would have been had there been state-mandated school desegregation: even without *de jure* (formal, government-mandated) segregation, many Southern schools would have remained segregated because of *de facto* voluntary segregation in housing. The remedy of forced busing upheld by the Supreme Court in *Swann* put the plaintiffs in a *better* position than if there had been no state discrimination. This is not to say the structural injunction remedy was unjustified (a judgment call you can make yourself); it is to say only that the structural injunction was not tightly tied to the rightful position standard.

Milliken v. Bradley, 418 U.S. 717 (1974), marked the beginning of the change in the Supreme Court's attitude toward structural injunction remedies. There, the Court rejected a remedy to end school segregation in Detroit — which would have included busing children from Detroit and neighboring suburbs — that had not been found to violate the Constitution. The Court held that an *interdistrict* (i.e., between districts) remedy was not appropriate when there was proof only of an *intradistrict* (i.e., within one district) violation.

In more recent years, the *Milliken* line of cases has won out at the Supreme Court. Consider litigation over desegregation of the Kansas City, Missouri, public schools. Eighteen years (!) after the litigation began, the

---

1. In addition to Fiss's work, *see especially* Owen Fiss, Injunctions (1972); and Owen Fiss, The Civil Rights Injunction (1978). Abram Chayes wrote a leading defense of the courts' role in promoting social change through structural injunctions. See Abram Chayes, *The Role of the Judge in Public Law Litigation*, 89 Harv. L. Rev. 1281 (1976).

Supreme Court for the third (!) time considered a remedial aspect of the trial court's decision. This trip to the Court resulted in the Supreme Court's rejecting the district court's most recent remedial order, which, among other things, required a tax increase to fund massive spending to improve the school system. *Missouri v. Jenkins* (*Jenkins III*), 515 U.S. 70 (1995).[2]

The district court ordered major improvements to the school system to make the system more attractive to white students who had left the district for private schools (the goal of "desegregative attractiveness"). One of the court orders required spending at an annual cost of over $200 million, including financing for

> high schools in which every classroom will have air conditioning, an alarm system, and 15 microcomputers; a 2,000-square-foot planetarium; green houses and vivariums; a 25-acre farm with an air-conditioned meeting room for 104 people; a Model United Nations wired for language translation; broadcast capable radio and television studios with an editing and animation lab; a temperature controlled art gallery; movie editing and screening rooms; a 3,500 square foot dust-free diesel mechanics room; 1,875-square-foot elementary school animal rooms for use in a zoo project; swimming pools; and numerous other facilities.

By a 5-4 vote, the Supreme Court rejected the remedy adopted by the district court. The majority saw the remedy as not appropriately tied to the scope of the constitutional violation and therefore not tied to the rightful position. ("[T]he nature of the remedy . . . is to be determined by the nature and scope of the constitutional violation.") The constitutional violation was *state-mandated segregation* in the public schools, not the *private* decisions of white students (and their families) to leave the public school system once the courts ordered the schools' desegregation.[3]

The relevant question for the majority appeared to be: what position would students in the Kansas City school system have been in had the government not intentionally segregated students on the basis of race? The majority believed that these students likely would *not* have been in a racially integrated and well-funded public school system, and therefore the district court could not order such a remedy. In other words, for the majority, it was *court-ordered desegregation* rather than segregation that led to the white flight, and therefore the court could not impose a magnet-like

---

2. *Missouri v. Jenkins* (*Jenkins I*), 491 U.S. 294 (1989), considered attorney's fees. *Missouri v. Jenkins* (*Jenkins II*), 495 U.S. 33 (1990), considered whether court-ordered tax increases could be used to pay for the desegregation remedy.

3. The majority also held that to the extent to which the district court was seeking to attract students from *outside* the boundaries of the school system, it was improperly imposing an *interdistrict* remedy for an *intradistrict* problem, in violation of *Milliken v. Bradley*. We return to this issue in section 8.3 below.

remedy (i.e., very attractive public school programs) to attract back the white students.

The dissenters disagreed on this point, believing that it was ultimately the costs of *paying for desegregation* that led to the white flight:

> Property-tax paying parents of white children, seeing the handwriting on the wall in 1985, could well have decided that the inevitable cost of clean-up would produce an intolerable tax rate and could have moved to escape it. The District Court's remedial orders had not yet been put in place. Was the white flight caused by segregation or desegregation? The distinction has no significance.

Jenkins III (Souter, J., dissenting).

Regardless of whether the majority or the dissent had the better argument in *Jenkins III*, Supreme Court majorities in recent years have made it abundantly clear that courts should target remedies toward the rightful position. For example, in *Lewis v. Casey*, 518 U.S. 343 (1996), a prison reform case, the district court found that one prisoner had been injured by the failure of the prison library "to provide special services that [the prisoner] would have needed, in light of his illiteracy, to avoid dismissal of his case." Yet the district court ordered a variety of systemwide changes to the state's prison libraries, including the addition of "special services for non-English speakers, prisoners in lockdown, and the inmate population at large." The Supreme Court held that proof of two instances of inadequate library assistance "were a patently inadequate basis for a conclusion of a system-wide violation and imposition of systemwide relief."

While most of these recent Supreme Court structural injunction cases arose when lower courts gave plaintiffs *more* than the rightful position, the Supreme Court has affirmed that the same principle applies when courts give *less* than the rightful position. In *United States v. Virginia*, 518 U.S. 515 (1996), for example, the United States Court of Appeals for the Fourth Circuit had determined that the state-run Virginia Military Institute (VMI) unconstitutionally discriminated against women through its male-only admissions policy. But the lower court also had suggested that Virginia could solve the constitutional problem by opening a "parallel" "Virginia Women's Institute for Leadership" (VWIL).

The Supreme Court rejected this proposed solution, because the lower court "did not inquire whether the proposed remedy . . . placed the women denied the VMI advantage in 'the position they would have occupied in the absence of [discrimination].'" The Supreme Court rejected the remedy on grounds that the proposed women's program "was different in kind from VMI and unequal in tangible and intangible facilities." There was no way that the new VWIL, for example, could replicate the advantages that came from being a VMI alumnus — part of the "old boy" network.

In his dissenting opinion, Chief Justice Rehnquist agreed that VMI's gender admission policy was unconstitutional, but he argued that the remedy could include the creation of a separate women's school. He further wrote that the state need not create a "VMI clone for women"; it would be enough for the schools to be of the "same overall caliber." He concluded: "[One institution] could be strong in computer science; the other could be strong in liberal arts."

Despite these signals from the Supreme Court, the tradition of broad structural injunctions continues to have support among legal scholars,[4] and lower court judges involved in institutional litigation sometimes continue to "do equity" in structural injunction cases, going beyond the rightful position standard. Today, however, a judge doing that runs a higher risk of reversal by the Supreme Court, and may be more likely to write a broad remedy in the language of the "rightful position," defending broader remedies as "prophylactic measures" aimed at achieving that rightful position.

The Supreme Court's most recent word on structural injunctions was perhaps more forgiving of a strict "rightful position" standard. In *Brown v. Plata*, 131 S. Ct. 1910 (2011), the Court in a 5-4 vote upheld a three-judge court order in long-running California prison litigation to release California prisoners to alleviate prison overcrowding. The constitutional violations stemmed from serious deficiencies in the prison health care system. Justice Kennedy wrote the opinion joined by the Court's four liberal Justices. The dissenters did not believe that the remedy matched the wrong, and argued that releasing prisoners early would harm the public interest.[5]

Example 1

You are a federal district judge and you have just determined that a state-run mental hospital has been violating the constitutional rights of its patients through inadequate care. How would you begin the process of using a structural injunction to remedy the constitutional violation? Once the injunction is put in place, how would you monitor whether or not there has been compliance with your orders?

---

4. Some legal scholars agree with Owen Fiss's 1979 argument against the rightful position standard in structural injunction cases: "The object of the structural remedy is not to eliminate a 'violation' in the sense implied by the tailoring principle, but rather to remove the threat posed by the organization to the constitutional values. The concept 'violation' can be used to describe the object of the remedy only if it is understood in a prospective, dynamic, and systemic sense." Owen Fiss, *Foreword — The Forms of Justice*, 97 HARV. L. REV. 1, 47-48 (1979). Legal scholars who oppose Fiss's view fear giving judges such open-ended powers to craft remedies not tailored to the extent of the wrong committed by the defendant.

5. Justice Scalia, in his typical bombastic fashion, began his dissent by stating, "Today the Court affirms what is perhaps the most radical injunction issued by a court in our Nation's history."

Explanation

As a federal district judge, you likely would come in knowing very little about the running of a hospital. Courts sometimes appoint "special masters" to assist in evaluating problems and crafting solutions. In extreme cases, courts have actually appointed experts to temporarily run a hospital. Much of how well the remedy works to cure constitutional violations is going to depend upon the lawyers in the case. Competent plaintiffs' lawyers are usually essential to effective implementation of a structural injunction. In addition, the cooperation or recalcitrance of defendants may dictate the speed with which structural injunctions are implemented. Government lawyers can take steps that can slow down or sabotage the process of reform.

Monitoring compliance with ongoing structural injunctions is also a challenge for courts. At a minimum, courts in such cases often require the parties to file periodic reports and hold hearings to evaluate progress that is made. When there are problems with implementing the orders of the court, the court will often modify its order to better effectuate its remedies. Again, competent plaintiffs' counsel plays a key role in the successful implementation of a structural injunction.

Example 2

If you were a Justice of the U.S. Supreme Court reviewing the remedy imposed by the district court in *Jenkins* III, would you support it, or oppose it? Explain the reasons for your answer.

Explanation

Obviously, there is no right or wrong answer to this "thought" question. Rather, the question is aimed at getting you to think about whether you believe courts deciding public law litigation that restructures government institutions should aim their remedies at the rightful position standard or should have broader "equitable" power to improve the institutions and society. The risk of sticking with the rightful position is that courts may end up giving plaintiffs an incomplete remedy — one that, because of the limited power of the courts to enact social change and fully prevent the future bad effects of past harm, gives plaintiffs less than the rightful position. We call this a problem of "underremediation." The risk of going beyond the rightful position is that the courts give remedies completely untethered to the wrong committed by the defendants, thereby burdening the defendants (and, potentially, third parties, as we shall see) with obligations to solve problems not directly traceable to defendants' wrongs. We call this a problem of "overremediation."

Unsurprisingly, the willingness to bear these risks has some correlation to political preferences. Liberals are willing to give more than the rightful position to avoid underremediation, and conservatives are willing to risk underremediation so as not to place unfair burden on state defendants to solve social wrongs. Consider that the liberals on the Supreme Court were the dissenters in *Jenkins III* and that some of the conservatives on the Court dissented in the *VMI* case. (Justice Thomas, whose son was attending VMI, did not participate in the case.)

8.1.2 Consent Decrees

Some public law litigation over restructuring government institutions ends not with an adversarial trial and judgment, but with settlement of the case. In public law litigation, settlements tend to be embodied in *consent decrees*, which are court orders crafted by the parties that, like regular injunctions, are backed up by the power of contempt.

Why a consent decree rather than a simple private settlement agreement? A settlement agreement is a contract, and is not backed up by the power of contempt. Breach of a settlement agreement will ordinarily require a new lawsuit. In contrast, entry of a consent decree keeps the federal court's involvement in the case, and ensures that the court monitors the progress of the parties.

A good recent example is the consent decree that the Los Angeles Police Department entered into in 2000 following a U.S. Department of Justice investigation alleging that the LAPD violated the constitutional rights of L.A. residents. The decree was to last for five years, but at the end of the five-year period some of its central requirements (including the creation of a computer database to track police officers' disciplinary records) had not yet been implemented, leading to calls for the consent decree to be extended for at least another two years.[6] The fact that the requirements of the consent decree had not all been implemented in a five-year period demonstrates how difficult it is to get institutional change.

Consent decrees can be valuable tools for settling (and enforcing) government institutional litigation, but they raise two sets of concerns.

First, consent decrees can be used to bind successive government administrations to policies they may not agree with. *See* Michael W. McConnell, *Why Hold Elections? Using Consent Decrees to Insulate Policies from Political Change,*

---

6. Erwin Chemerinsky et al., *The LAPD Still Needs Policing,* L.A. Times, May 3, 2006.

1995 U. Chi. Legal F. 295. In the LAPD case, for example, the United States Department of Justice, which agreed to the consent decree, was headed by Democrats under Bill Clinton, who wanted a strong remedy. In 2006, however, when the consent decree was due to expire, the Department of Justice, this time headed by Republicans under George W. Bush, did not want the decree extended. The court did so anyway.[7]

Second, a consent decree can be the product of collusion from the start, because (outside of the prison context, as we will soon see), there is no requirement that a consent decree be limited to a remedy that keeps the plaintiffs in the rightful position. Imagine you are the head of the Kansas City Municipal School District involved in the *Missouri v. Jenkins* litigation. How hard would you fight against a court order that would raise property taxes in order to fund vast new programs for your district and to fund raises for your teachers? The trial court orders in effect achieved for the poor and over-extended public school system in Kansas City something that was likely impossible to achieve politically: a massive infusion of public funds to build up the school system.

Because of this danger of collusion, it is often left to other parts of the government (the state government in the *Jenkins* litigation) or other private parties to argue against the entry of consent decrees that can serve to benefit both plaintiffs and the (nominal) defendants.

When parties agree to a consent decree and no one objects, courts are not called upon to ensure that the agreements do more than keep the plaintiffs in the rightful position. After all, a defendant can settle an automobile accident by offering plaintiff more money than the plaintiff demands. But the public interest is at stake in structural injunction litigation, so overremediation can have consequences for others (such as the taxpayers who would foot the bill for the school system fix in Kansas City).

Example 3

You are a lawyer for the Pacifica Police Department, which has been sued for violating the constitutional rights of the citizens of Pacifica by using excessive force and making many false arrests. Your case has been set before a very liberal federal district court judge, who has made it clear that the court is very likely to find that the department indeed has violated the rights of Pacifica residents. Your client wants the courts to impose as little reform as possible. Do you favor (1) taking the case to trial, (2) consenting to the entry of a consent decree settling the case, or (3) making a settlement agreement with the plaintiffs?

---

7. Jim Newton, *LAPD "Warrior Cops" Test City's Will*, L.A. Times, July 16, 2006.

Explanation

This is a difficult question to answer in the abstract, because it requires you to compare the deal you could likely get from the plaintiffs with the likely remedies that the court would impose on you if the case goes to trial. What the plaintiffs might be willing to settle for will be influenced by plaintiffs' lawyer's own view of what the trial court is likely to impose as a remedy.

The one easy part of the question is the choice between a settlement agreement and a consent decree. Your client would much prefer a settlement agreement over the consent decree. If the plaintiff later believes your client violated a settlement agreement, the plaintiff would likely have to bring a new suit (alleging a breach of that contract), and could not rely on the power of contempt. The federal district court judge's hands will be kept in the matter for the duration of the consent decree.

8.1.3 How Congress May Limit Remedies: The Prison Litigation Reform Act Example

Though structural injunction litigation began in the school desegregation context, a large number of suits through the years have involved prisoners protesting prison conditions. *Lewis v. Casey*, the library assistance case described above, represents one of the less consequential of these claims. A case of much more consequence was *Hutto v. Finney*, 437 U.S. 678 (1978), involving the deplorable conditions in Arkansas prisons. To give but one of the disturbing examples mentioned in the case, prisoners in "punitive isolation" at one of the state's prisons faced the following conditions:

> An average of 4, and sometimes as many as 10 or 11, prisoners were crowded into windowless 8' × 10' cells containing no furniture other than a source of water and a toilet that could be flushed from outside the cell. At night the prisoners were given mattresses to spread on the floor. Although some prisoners suffered from infectious diseases such as hepatitis and venereal disease, mattresses were removed and jumbled together each morning, then returned to the cells at random in the evening. Prisoners in isolation received fewer than 1,000 calories a day; their meals consisted primarily of 4-inch squares of "grue," a substance created by mashing meat, potatoes, oleo, syrup, vegetables, eggs and seasoning into a paste and baking the mixture in a pan.

The Supreme Court upheld a part of the district court's order limiting prisoners to no more than 30 days' punishment in punitive isolation. The majority held that "[t]he vandalized cells and atmosphere of violence were attributable, in part, to overcrowding and to deep-seated enmities growing out of months of constant daily friction. The 30-day limit will help correct these conditions."

Then-Justice (later Chief Justice) Rehnquist, in dissent, stated that "[n]o person of ordinary feeling could fail to be moved by the Court's recitation of the conditions formerly prevailing in the Arkansas prison system," but he disagreed with the remedy: "[T]he district Court's order limiting the maximum period of punitive isolation to 30 days in no way relates to any condition found offensive to the Constitution."

In *Hutto*, the Supreme Court majority viewed the limit on time in punitive isolation as a prophylactic one to guard the rightful position; the dissent saw the link between wrong and remedy as too attenuated to justify the remedy — it saw the majority as simply imposing its vision of justice. Was Justice Rehnquist right? And if he was, does that mean that the majority reached the wrong result? The latter question is one each of us has to decide for himself or herself.

Prison litigation, both major and minor, continued to be a major factor in the late twentieth century,[8] and it provides a very good case study of the kinds of limits Congress might impose on court remedies in the institutional litigation context.

In 1996, Congress eventually stepped in with the Prison Litigation Reform Act[9] (PLRA) to limit prison-related litigation. The act imposes many barriers to prison litigation, including a requirement that a complaining prisoner exhaust administrative remedies before suing in court, 42 U.S.C. § 1997e(a), a provision the Supreme Court recently construed against prisoners in *Woodford v. Ngo*, 548 U.S. 81 (2006).

The most important limits on remedies appear in 18 U.S.C. § 3626, entitled "Appropriate Remedies with Respect to Prison Conditions." Part (a)(1)(A) appears to enshrine a narrow rightful position standard to be applied to prison condition litigation:

> Prospective relief in any civil action with respect to prison conditions shall extend no further than necessary to correct the violation of the Federal right of a particular plaintiff or plaintiffs. The court shall not grant or approve any prospective relief unless the court finds that such relief is narrowly drawn, extends

---

8. "By 1984 (the first year for which data are accessible), 24% of the nation's 903 state prisons (including at least one in each of forty-three states and the District of Columbia) reported to the federal Bureau of Justice Statistics that they were operating under a court order. In 1983 (the first year these data exist for jails), 15% of the nation's 3,338 jails (including at least one in all but two of the forty-five states that had jails, and the District of Columbia) reported court orders. Litigants had been particularly active — or particularly successful — in large facilities: the prisons under court order housed 42% of the nation's state prisoners, and the jails under court order housed 44% of the nation's jail inmates, and for both jails and state prisons, about half of the nation's largest facilities were under court order." Margo Schlanger, *Beyond the Hero Judge: Institutional Reform Litigation as Litigation*, 97 Mich. L. Rev. 1995, 2004 (1999) (book review).

9. Prison Litigation Reform Act, Pub. L. No. 104-134, 110 Stat. 1321 (1996).

> no further than necessary to correct the violation of the Federal right, and is the least intrusive means necessary to correct the violation of the Federal right. The court shall give substantial weight to any adverse impact on public safety or the operation of a criminal justice system caused by the relief.

This provision would appear to make it more desirable for lawyers representing prisoners to enter into consent decrees, which could give more than the constitutional floor allowed under § 3626(a)(1)(A). But § 3626(c) appears to foreclose that option: "In any civil action with respect to prison conditions, the court shall not enter or approve a consent decree unless it complies with the limitations on relief set forth in subsection (a)." In other words, just like court orders issued at the end of a trial, consent decrees may not offer more than the constitutional floor. The PLRA, however, allows the parties to enter into settlement agreements that are not consent decrees (and therefore lack the court supervision and court's power of contempt). The Act also changes the rules for the modifications of injunctions, the topic of the next part of this chapter.

The PLRA appears aimed at limiting both the amount of prison condition litigation and the extent of the remedies ordered or approved by the federal courts. But has it had that effect? Professor Schlanger concludes:

> By drastically widening the escape route for correctional jurisdictions seeking to terminate court orders, interposing a difficult administrative exhaustion hurdle for maintenance of a court-order lawsuit, and squeezing the funding for the advocates who seek court orders, the PLRA has contributed to a major decline in the regulation of prisons and jails by court order. Nonetheless, even after the PLRA, court-order incidence remains quite high in the final correctional censuses. There is increasing variation among states, and in a few states, jails and prisons continue to experience a great deal of injunctive regulation.

Margo Schlanger, *Civil Rights Injunctions over Time: A Case Study of Jail and Prison Court Orders*, 81 N.Y.U. L. REV. 550, 602 (2006).

The effect of the PLRA is important beyond the prison context: "This point is especially relevant now, as Congress considers the Federal Consent Decree Fairness Act proposed to implement restrictions similar to the PLRA's in other topical areas of governmental injunctive litigation." *Id.* at 557.

Example 4

If you were a member of Congress, would you support the Federal Consent Decree Fairness Act or similar legislation which would bar federal courts from, among other things, enforcing consent decrees that do more than give plaintiffs the constitutional floor? Why, or why not?

Explanation

Your answer to this question will likely mirror your response to Example 2. Both questions are aimed at making you consider to what extent federal court judges should be trusted with institutional reform litigation in the face of proven constitutional violations by state actors. Limits such as the PLRA and the proposed new federal legislation show a Congress that is skeptical that courts are going to be willing to stick with a narrow reading of the rightful position standard in crafting injunctions or in approving consent decrees. Professor Schlanger's research suggests that legislation like this could have the effect of limiting the amount of successful litigation. Are you willing to risk underremediation in the name of preventing over-remediation? Again, this question likely correlates with your political views about how much the government can be trusted to solve social problems.

Example 5

Returning to the situation in Example 1, you are a federal judge overseeing litigation regarding constitutional violations at a state-run mental health facility. The parties have reached an agreement that would vastly improve the conditions of the hospital, including the building of private rooms for most of the facility's patients. You do not believe that this remedy is constitutionally required to cure the constitutional violations by the health facility. Are you permitted to approve the consent decree? Should you do so?

Explanation

The Prison Litigation Reform Act does not apply outside the context of prison condition litigation—thus it does not pose any barrier to your approval of the consent decree. Normally, if both parties agree to a remedy (and there are no intervening parties who object), the court is bound to approve the consent decree. Judges tend to like settlement of litigation (if for no other reason than that it clears the docket for other cases), and in the absence of any indication that the settlement is against the public interest, most courts would likely sign the consent decree even if it gave a better remedy than the judge would have given at the end of the litigation. But the Supreme Court has recently said that there must be a connection between the consent decree and the "federal interests" plaintiffs sought to protect by bringing suit in the first place. Moreover, the consent decree must "further the objectives of the law upon which the complaint is based." *Frew v. Hawkins*, 540 U.S. 431, 437 (2004). So an appellate court could well reverse a consent decree that is completely untethered to the federal wrong alleged in the case.

8.2 MODIFYING EXISTING INJUNCTIONS

Not only in cases involving structural injunctions, but especially in those cases, because they can go on for many years, courts are often asked to modify or extend injunctions in the face of new or changed circumstances. Courts also may do so, as in the case of the LAPD consent decree described above, because the defendant has failed to comply with the court's original order. Oftentimes, a defendant's failure to comply won't lead to a finding of contempt (because the plaintiffs won't be able to prove a willful disobedience of the court's order); instead, the court will issue a new set of orders with which the defendant will need to comply.

The leading case on modifying injunctions (and consent decrees) in federal court is a pre-PLRA prison conditions case, *Rufo v. Inmates of Suffolk County Jail*, 502 U.S. 367 (1992). *Rufo* changed prior law by making it easier for parties to seek modification, such as when a party wishes to reopen a case that had gone to final judgment. (The proper procedure is for the party to make a motion for modification under Federal Rule of Civil Procedure 60(b).)

Rufo provides a non-exhaustive list of grounds for modifying an injunction or consent decree:

- "When changed factual conditions have made compliance with the decree substantially more onerous."
- "When a decree proves to be unworkable because of unforeseen obstacles."
- "When enforcement of the decree without modification would be detrimental to the public interest."
- "When the statutory or decisional law has changed to make legal what the decree was designed to prevent."
- "If the parties had based their agreement on a misunderstanding of the governing law."

The Supreme Court reaffirmed the "flexible standard" of *Rufo* in *Frew v. Hawkins*, 540 U.S. 431 (2004), explaining that when state defendants are involved, "principles of federalism require that state officials with front-line responsibility for administering the program be given latitude and substantial discretion." Moreover, "[t]he federal court must exercise its equitable powers to ensure that when the objects of the decree have been attained, responsibility for discharging the State's obligations is returned promptly to the State and its officials. . . . If the State establishes reason to modify the decree, the court should make the necessary changes; where it has not done so, however, the decree should be enforced according to its terms."

The Court made that point even more emphatically in *Horne v. Flores*, 557 U.S. 443 (2009). At issue was a federal district court's refusal to modify an injunction in a class action case involving Arizona's noncompliance with a federal statute requiring the state to take "appropriate actions to overcome language barriers in schools." The five conservative Justices on the Court criticized both the district court and the Ninth Circuit for their failure to apply the flexibility of *Rufo* when the state asked for an injunction against it to be modified. The *Horne* opinion includes a lengthy discussion of the propriety of modifying injunctions in what it termed "institutional reform litigation," stressing a point raised earlier in this chapter — the danger of collusion and of locking in reforms that bind successor elected officials: "Injunctions of this sort bind state and local officials to the policy preferences of their predecessors and may thereby 'improperly deprive future officials of their designated legislative and executive powers.'" *Id.* (quoting *Frew*).

According to the dissenting Justices in *Horne*, the majority opinion changes the *Rufo* standard for "institutional reform litigation" (though the majority and dissent cannot agree on what the term actually means): "The Court adds that in an 'institutional reform litigation case,' a court must also take account of the need not to maintain decrees in effect for too long a time, the need to take account of 'sensitive federalism concerns,' and the need to take care lest 'consent decrees' reflect collusion between private plaintiffs and state defendants at the expense of the legislative process." *Id.* (Breyer, J., dissenting). Justice Breyer questioned "whether the Court has set forth a correct and workable method for analyzing a Rule 60(b)(5) motion." *Id.* Laycock concludes that "the tone is very different even from *Rufo*; the Court seems to be pressing for easy and early modification in institutional reform cases." LAYCOCK p. 354.

The PLRA has its own provision on consent decrees in prison condition litigation, allowing the state to reopen any existing prison condition injunction or consent decree where the injunction or decree gave prison plaintiffs more than the constitutional minimum requirements. Under the PLRA, the defendant or intervenor "shall be entitled to the immediate termination of any prospective relief if the relief was approved or granted in the absence of a finding by the court that the relief was narrowly drawn, extends no further than necessary to correct the violation of the Federal right, and is the least intrusive means necessary to correct the violation of the federal right." 18 U.S.C. § 3626(b)(2). But the injunction does not terminate if the court finds that it now meets these requirements.

Example 6

While a United States Supreme Court case is pending over whether the double bunking of inmates violates the Eighth Amendment's prohibition on cruel and unusual punishment, the state of Pacifica and inmates at the Pacifica state prison enter into a consent decree to settle the inmates' suit over prison conditions. Among the terms of the decree is a prohibition on double bunking.

    a. Before the PLRA, could a trial court approve such a consent decree?
    b. After the PLRA, could a trial court approve such a consent decree?

Explanation

(a) The court may approve the consent decree. Before the PLRA, there was no requirement that consent decrees provide no more than the constitutional floor. The applicable federal right is uncertain, so even under the *Frew* standard there seems little question that a district court could justify its order as protecting of the federal rights at issue in the lawsuit.

(b) The PLRA would not necessarily bar a district court's agreeing to this aspect of the consent decree. If the question is uncertain and before the Supreme Court, then arguably a consent decree prohibiting double bunking goes no further than what federal law requires.

Example 7

Same facts as Example 6. Assume the trial court signs off on the consent decree, which is entered into before Congress passes the PLRA. After final judgment, the Supreme Court determines that double bunking does not violate the Eighth Amendment. The state moves to modify the consent decree to allow it to double-bunk prisoners.

    a. Before the PLRA, how should the district court rule?
    b. After the PLRA, how should the district court rule?

Explanation

(a) These are the facts of the *Rufo* case, and in the actual case the Supreme Court allowed modification. The Supreme Court in *Rufo* said that the change in law alone could not provide the basis for reopening the consent decree, and there was no requirement that the consent decree meet the constitutional minimum. However, the Court said that if the sheriff could establish "that the parties to the consent decree believed that single celling of pretrial detainees was mandated by the Constitution, this misunderstanding of the law could form a basis for modification." It appears that there was no "misunderstanding," only uncertainty over what the Supreme Court ultimately would hold.

Should the resolution of that uncertainty allow the parties to undo a bargain they struck when things were uncertain? If so, the incentive to settle cases will be lowered. To see why, consider this: Plaintiffs want a settlement package that includes X, Y, and Z. Defendants are willing to offer X and Y, but not Z. Plaintiffs agree to the bargain rather than litigating; plaintiffs' expectation is that the court will award X + Z, but not Y, and plaintiffs prefer X + Y over X + Z. The parties settle for X + Y. The Supreme Court later decides that Y is not required by federal law. The district court then modifies the injunction, removing the Y requirement, leaving plaintiff with only X. Plaintiffs would have been better off litigating, which would have left them with X + Z rather than now being left with only X.

(b) Under the PLRA, even if the parties entered into a binding settlement agreement enforced by the court through the consent decree, the state may move for immediate termination on grounds that the constitutional minimum has changed and the consent decree gives more than the constitutional minimum. Defendants from *Rufo* took just such an approach to modify the consent decree after Congress passed the PLRA. *See Inmates of Suffolk County Jail v. Rouse*, 129 F.3d 649 (1st Cir. 1997). As this example shows, there is less and less incentive for plaintiffs to settle these cases, because defendants can reopen them if and when courts further constrict the rights of prisoners to certain minimal prison conditions.

Example 8

As part of a final judgment brought by residents of a state-run mental health facility, the trial court orders the construction of a new hospital within five years, at an expected cost of $20 million. Two years later, before construction is to begin, the state seeks to modify the injunction on grounds that current construction costs would double the cost of the project to $40 million. The ballooning cost is partly the result of inflation, and partly the result of an unexpected housing boom that has raised the labor costs for construction. Should the court modify its order?

Explanation

The state will argue that factual conditions have changed to make compliance with the court's order substantially more onerous (double the price) because of a rise in construction costs that was not actually foreseen by the parties. The plaintiffs will likely argue that some inflation costs could have been foreseen, and mere additional expense should not be a basis for modifying the court's judgment. Under *Frew* and *Horne*, the court is going to have to give considerable deference to the state's call for modification.

To a great extent, the question will likely turn on the alternatives posed by the state. The court is not going to order modification if the state cannot come up with another plan that remedies the constitutional problems. In other words, it is not enough to show that a remedy is more expensive if in fact that remedy is still needed to vindicate a constitutional right. If, for example, the state can demonstrate that it could solve the constitutional problems much more cheaply through remodeling the existing facility rather than building a new facility, the court is likely to take very seriously a request for modification.

8.3 INJUNCTIONS AND THIRD PARTIES

In a typical private law adjudication, an injunction does not have much effect on third parties. For example, when the court orders specific performance against Pnina requiring her to produce the widget for Oscar, the order likely will have little to no impact on third parties (by third parties I mean individuals who are not parties to the lawsuit). In public interest litigation, by contrast, thousands of non-parties may be affected.

In the *Swann* case, for example, the court ordered a busing remedy that affected many students who were not parties to the litigation but who were made part of the remedy. Since *Swann*, the Supreme Court has grappled with the extent to which an injunction may *burden* third parties. In the *Milliken* case, for example, as noted above, the Court rejected an *interdistrict* remedy to solve school segregation problems in the single district of Detroit.

Somewhat contrary to *Milliken*, in *Hills v. Gautreaux*, 425 U.S. 284 (1976), the Supreme Court held that third parties could be *substantially burdened* in the pursuit of federal remedies. There, the Court upheld the ability of the United States Department of Housing and Urban Development to take remedial action outside the city limits of Chicago to remedy problems with race discrimination in a Chicago Housing Authority program. The remedy consisted in part of providing vouchers to poor Chicago residents to pay for housing in Chicago suburbs. "An order directed solely to HUD would not force unwilling localities to apply for assistance under these programs but would merely reinforce the regulations guiding HUD's determination of which of the locally authorized projects to assist with federal funds." The localities faced a large burden because as a result of the court's order to HUD, they were going to be faced with an influx of new poor residents who were likely going to need significant social services.

It is unclear whether *Gautreaux* remains good law following *Jenkins III*. Recall that one of the reasons the Supreme Court in *Jenkins III* rejected the proposed remedy for the Kansas City school district was its effect on neighboring school districts. But, as in *Gautreaux*, the effect was only indirect: the magnet programs of the Kansas City school districts were meant to attract "white flight" students from the suburbs.

The *Jenkins III* majority held that this remedy aimed at "desegregative attractiveness" placed too high a burden on the suburban school districts, which would lose students. The dissenters accused the majority of silently overruling *Gautreaux*. At this point, the extent to which third parties may be burdened in structural injunction litigation is somewhat unclear, but the Court today is obviously more concerned about protecting values of federalism (states' rights) than it has been in the past. If *Gautreaux* arose today, it is not clear that a Supreme Court majority would decide it the same way.

Though the precise extent to which injunctions may burden third parties remains unclear, clearer are the rules relating to *direct orders* to third parties. Those orders must be "minor and ancillary." Thus, even the filing of quarterly reports by a non-wrongdoing party might be too excessive. *See General Building Contractors Association v. Pennsylvania*, 458 U.S. 375 (1982); *see also Baltimore Neighborhoods Inc. v. LOB, Inc.*, 92 F. Supp. 2d 456, 472 (D. Md. 2000) (condominium association could be ordered to provide access to buildings to allow for retrofitting to comply with Americans with Disabilities Act and Fair Housing Act; court characterizes order as "minor" and "ancillary").

Although direct orders sound more onerous than indirect burdens, the distinction would probably be lost on most third parties. Consider a student who wants to remain at a nearby school: that student would find it much less burdensome to fill out occasional paperwork than to attend a different school under a busing plan.

Example 9

A federal district court issues an order requiring the forced integration of schools in the city of Pacificana, against the objections of the white residents of the city, including the police chief. Can the district court order the Pacificana police department to assist in integrating the schools?

Explanation

Certainly if the police department is part of the city, and the city has been adjudicated a constitutional wrongdoer, then a court may order the police department to carry out the mandates to effectuate the trial court's order.

The more difficult question arises when the police department is not an adjudicated wrongdoer, but is instead, like the suburban school districts in *Jenkins III*, a burdened innocent third party. LAYCOCK (p. 365 n.7) notes the debate among commentators on this issue. Some take the position that the police could not be ordered to provide assistance to the court absent some adjudication of wrongdoing. But Laycock also cites *In re Boung Jae Jang v. Brown*, 560 N.Y.S.2d 307 (App. 1990), holding that the trial court had inherent authority to enforce its order and that the police had a duty to enforce the law when ordered to do so by the court.

The court suggested that its rule might not extend to parties besides the police department, especially parties over whom the court had not exercised its jurisdiction: "We decline to hold that the Police Department's duty to enforce the law is contingent upon its being formally joined as a party to each and every proceeding in which it may ultimately be required to engage in some type of law enforcement activity."

What is interesting about the case is that it is not just one about burdens: the court actually *ordered* the police to keep demonstrators at least 50 feet from the entrance to a store. Why is this not more than a minor and ancillary order barred by the *General Building Contractors Association* case? Perhaps the answer is that the police are going to be treated differently in terms of direct orders as well.

Preliminary Injunctions and Other Preliminary Relief

9.1 INTRODUCTION TO PRELIMINARY RELIEF

All of the remedies considered so far in this book are those that come at final judgment, after a trial or dispositive motion (such as a summary judgment motion) leads the court to enter a judgment in favor of one of the parties.[1] Sometimes, however, a party wants relief before final judgment. Consider the following three scenarios:

- You represent the Pacifica Preservation Society, and you've just received a tip that tomorrow morning at 8 a.m. a wrecking ball is going to knock down the Oldtime Hotel, which you believe is a historic landmark protected against destruction by state law. You want to get an injunction barring the destruction of the hotel.
- William is severely injured in an automobile accident with Xandra. He can no longer work and has used up his savings. He sues Xandra for negligence, but in the meantime he has no money to live on.
- Yvette and Zane are business partners. Yvette believes that Zane, because of a recent severe psychological disorder, is causing the business to suffer serious financial losses. Yvette wants to dissolve the partnership and salvage at least her share of the partnership's assets.

---

1. The last chapter considered "consent decrees," which are settlement agreements by the parties signed by the district court and enforceable through the court's contempt power. These consent decrees are embodied in a final judgment.

In each of these cases, waiting for final judgment (which could literally be *years after* the time of the filing of the complaint) may cause the decision to come too late: the Oldtime Hotel might be destroyed, William may have to declare bankruptcy or even end up living on the street, and Zane could squander the partnership's assets.

What the plaintiffs in these cases really want is *preliminary relief*: some court order *before* final judgment that can aid the plaintiff. The problem is, however, that before final judgment the court does not know if, in fact, plaintiff is entitled to the relief sought. What if Pacifica law does not really protect the hotel as a historical landmark, or if a jury finds the accident was William's fault rather than Xandra's, or if Zane is sane? At the very least, any court granting preliminary relief is going to have to consider *the risk of error* that accompanies the granting of preliminary relief.

In this chapter, we consider the rules related to the most common type of preliminary relief sought, the preliminary injunction, and how the courts deal with the risk of error. In Chapter 17.2, we consider receiverships and freeze devices that can save Yvette from insane Zane. But before we go on, it is worth noting that in most jurisdictions the law generally will not allow William to seek "preliminary damages" in his suit against Xandra. That is, the law has no form of preliminary relief for the payment of damages.

Why is William treated worse than the historical society or Yvette? The answer again appears to be historical:

> The rule against preliminary damage awards is usually said to be absolute or nearly so. This rule is sometimes explained as a corollary of the irreparable injury rule: if plaintiff seeks only money, damages after final judgment will be an adequate remedy. That will sometimes be true, but not if plaintiff suffers severe financial hardships in the meantime. In fact, the rule seems to be an unjustified artifact of the law-equity distinction.

LAYCOCK, THE DEATH OF THE IRREPARABLE INJURY RULE 112 (1991).[2]

Besides history, there are two practical reasons why courts may not have developed the practice of allowing the preliminary recovery of damages. First, preliminary relief requests burden the courts by requiring that cases go through two iterations (first for preliminary relief and then for final judgment), running the risk of error the first time through. It may be worth the double gearing up of the court machinery in cases of truly irreplaceable losses (we cannot "un-demolish" the historic building), but it is not worth the effort for a fungible good such as money.[3] Perhaps too the "financial

---

2. Professor Laycock notes an exception to this rule for "cases enjoining the termination of a series of periodic payments." *Id.*

3. Fungible goods are those which are easily exchangeable and identical in quality. Thus, if you have a $100 bill and I have two $50 bills, they are fungible. I am indifferent between possessing my $100 worth of currency and yours.

hardship" cases such as William's are likely to be rare. Even in tort cases involving serious injury, plaintiffs often can obtain medical care either through their health insurance company or through the state. The plaintiff awaiting final judgment often can borrow money in the interim, sometimes against his future recovery if he has a good case, albeit at a high rate of interest if the plaintiff presents a financial risk to the lender.[4]

Second, it would be harder for courts to correct errors in the granting of "preliminary damages" compared to correcting erroneously issued injunctions or receivership orders. If the court gives William money from Xandra preliminarily pending final judgment, and it ultimately determines that Xandra is not liable, William may have used up (or hidden) the money he now needs to pay back to Xandra. In contrast, there are steps such as injunction bonds (see section 9.3 below) that courts can use to protect defendants against erroneously issued preliminary injunctions. Perhaps courts should consider allowing preliminary damages in cases in which a plaintiff could post a bond (similar to appeal bonds posted by defendants to avoid paying judgments during an appeal). But if a plaintiff could afford such a bond, she likely would not need the preliminary relief!

In sum, in most cases the social costs of awarding preliminary damages appear to exceed the benefits of doing so, except perhaps in the case where the failure to do so causes financial hardship. In the latter class of cases, a plaintiff is most likely to spend the money from the defendant and will be unable to repay it in the event the court determines at final judgment that the defendant in fact does not owe plaintiff any damages.

The remainder of this chapter considers three issues related to preliminary injunctive relief. We begin with the standards courts use when issuing preliminary injunctions. Next, we turn to injunction bonds. We conclude with a look at temporary restraining orders, including issues related to notice.

Example 1

Before reading the rest of this chapter, test your intuition. Considering the case of *Pacifica Preservation Society v. Oldtime Hotel, Inc.*, what factors should the court consider in deciding whether or not to grant preliminary relief preventing the Oldtime Hotel from being wrecked pending final judgment?

---

4. As noted in Chapter 4.3, when a defendant fails to pay money when due, the non-breaching party cannot recover consequential damages other than interest on the money owed. So if William becomes homeless while waiting for final judgment and has his teeth knocked out in a street fight, Xandra won't have to pay for William's teeth repair. Instead, if William wins, at final judgment William may recover only the general damages he is owed (the unpaid money) plus interest at the prevailing legal rate. If William is a high credit risk and can borrow money only at a very high rate of interest, he will not be able to recover at that higher rate.

Explanation

Chapter 7 explained that when a court considers granting a *permanent* injunction, it must consider matters related to *propensity* (the likelihood that the defendant will engage in prohibited conduct), *irreparable injury* (the inability of the court to fully remedy plaintiff's injury through damages or another legal remedy), and *policy considerations* (such as the burden on the court).

These factors are important in the preliminary injunction phase as well, but they must be considered in the context of the *preliminary* nature of the relief sought. As you think about the criteria that courts should use in evaluating a request for *preliminary* relief, they probably fall into these three categories:

a. Likelihood of plaintiff's success on the merits (which will include an evaluation of the propensity, irreparable injury, and policy considerations to be decided more fully in the trial on the merits)
b. Risk of error (what would happen to the defendant or plaintiff if the court should err in its preliminary evaluation)
c. The public interest

If you came up with these criteria on your own, congratulations! These are the three basic criteria the courts consider in deciding whether grant preliminary relief. If you did not come up with these factors, don't worry. The next section discusses these criteria in detail.

Example 2

Considering again *Pacifica Preservation Society v. Oldtime Hotel, Inc.* (from Example 1), suppose you find out that the Acme Wrecking Company is the company that will be using the wrecking ball to bring down the hotel tomorrow morning. Can the court order Acme not to bring down the building? (Note: this problem requires familiarity with the material in the previous chapter.)

Explanation

This question is meant to make you consider the material covered at the end of the last chapter, on injunctions and third parties. If Acme is a non-party, the rule from *General Building Contractors* says that Acme cannot be asked to do more than comply with a "minor and ancillary" order. Whatever else that means, it is probably not too much of a burden on Acme to refrain from knocking down the hotel pending a further order of the court. But there may be a way to avoid litigating this "third party" issue. If it is possible to join Acme as a wrongdoer, then it will be no problem having the court issue an order enjoining Acme from demolishing the hotel pending further proceedings in the court.

9.2 PRELIMINARY INJUNCTIONS (AND STAYS)

Back on the record in the case of *Pacifica Preservation Society v. Oldtime Hotel, Inc.*, you are now before Judge Unfriendly trying to get a preliminary injunction preventing the destruction of the Oldtime Hotel pending a final judgment. What are you going to have to show?

Before we turn to what you will need to show to get *preliminary* relief, it is useful to begin by thinking about what you would have to show if you were seeking a *permanent* injunction enjoining the destruction of the hotel on grounds that Pacifica's historic preservation law prevents its destruction. In seeking permanent relief, you would have to show:

1. *Propensity.* You need to show that there is a realistic threat of harm. This factor really breaks down into two parts. First, you have to show that the Oldtime Hotel is actually protected from destruction by the state law. Second, assuming that it is protected, you have to show that the defendant is likely to destroy the hotel.

   Note that the kinds of proof you would need for these two issues are very different. For example, it might be that there is no dispute that the defendant intends to tear down the hotel. The only question is one of statutory interpretation: does the state law protect the Old-time Hotel?[5] On the other hand, if the dispute turns on credibility, the judge might need to hear from witnesses before determining whether or not the defendant intends to tear down the building.

2. *Irreparable injury.* Thinking about this issue for purposes of a final judgment, there seems little question that the historic society (assuming it has standing — a question for a Federal Courts course) faces irreparable injury. Damages would not be as good as a preserved building: one cannot use money to build a "new" building of historic significance. As we shall see, the irreparable injury question is somewhat more complicated when it comes to requests for preliminary relief.

3. *Other policy considerations.* Issues such as the burden on the court or First Amendment concerns may arise in some cases.

---

5. If that's the heart of the case, and it presents a purely legal question, it is not uncommon for a court to combine a hearing on the preliminary injunction with a hearing on the merits and simply issue a final judgment. See FED. R. CIV. P. 65(a)(2).

How do things differ when a plaintiff is seeking a preliminary injunction rather than a permanent injunction? First, because the request is preliminary, plaintiff need not prove his case with as much evidence as will be needed for a final judgment: "The purpose of a preliminary injunction is merely to preserve the relative positions of the parties until a trial on the merits can be held. Given this limited purpose, and given the haste that is often necessary if those positions are to be preserved, a preliminary injunction is customarily granted on the basis of procedures that are less formal and evidence that is less complete than in a trial on the merits. A party thus is not required to prove his case in full at a preliminary-injunction hearing." *University of Texas v. Camenisch*, 451 U.S. 390, 395 (1981).

As with the case of permanent injunctions issued after final judgment, the court considering a request for a preliminary injunction is going to be concerned about propensity, irreparable injury, and other policy considerations.[6] But the test is somewhat different in the case of a preliminary injunction because the court has not yet adjudicated the defendant a wrongdoer, and there is a risk that the court could err in granting or denying a request for a preliminary injunction.

In general, the court is going to be most concerned about the plaintiff's likelihood of success on the merits (which takes a preliminary look at the issues of propensity, irreparable injury, and policy considerations at issue in the permanent injunction stage), the risk of error, and the public interest. Although there are many verbal formulations, the Supreme Court recently set forth the standard in this way: "A plaintiff seeking a preliminary injunction must establish that he is likely to succeed on the merits, that he is likely to suffer irreparable harm in the absence of preliminary relief, that the balance of equities tips in his favor, and that an injunction is in the public interest." *Winter v. National Resources Defense Council, Inc.*, 555 U.S. 7, 20 (2008).[7] Also, as we shall see, in many courts' plaintiffs will have a much easier time seeking a preliminary injunction that *preserves (or at least appears to preserve) the status quo* than one that seeks to *change the status quo.*

---

6. You may recall that in the *Animal Rights Foundation of Florida v. Siegel* case, discussed in Chapter 7, the court held that an injunction barring animal rights protesters from carrying signs in front of defendant's business and residence violated the First Amendment. That case involved a preliminary, not a final, injunction. The court there barred the preliminary injunction on policy grounds.

7. There remains controversy over whether the plaintiff must prove *all* the elements in each case seeking a preliminary injunction, or whether a "sliding scale" approach applies. Justice Ginsburg, in her dissent in the *Winter* case, wrote that historically, "courts have evaluated claims for equitable relief on a 'sliding scale,' sometimes awarding relief based on a lower likelihood of harm when the likelihood of success is very high. This Court has never rejected that formulation, and I do not believe it does so today." *Id.* at 392 (citation omitted). Lower courts have retained a sliding scale on the understanding that under *Winter* the party seeking the preliminary injunction must make at least some showing on each of the elements. *See Alliance for the Wild Rockies v. Cottrell*, 632 F.3d 1127 (9th Cir. 2011).

Courts and others sometimes refer to the balancing process that the court undergoes in deciding on a motion for a preliminary injunction as a *balancing of the hardships*. This balancing is different from the balancing that courts sometimes undertake at final injunction. Recall from Chapter 7 that when the defendant who has been found liable faces a very serious hardship from an injunction, and that hardship greatly outweighs the benefits of the injunction to the plaintiff, courts will sometimes deny an injunction (think of *Van Wagner* and the billboard). Typically, however, proof that an adjudicated wrongdoer will endure some hardship will not be enough to defeat a successful plaintiff's request for a *permanent injunction*.[8]

But because of the risk of error in the *preliminary injunction* stage — the defendant has not yet been adjudicated a wrongdoer — courts must more carefully balance hardships to *each side*. Importantly, in thinking about the hardships to each side for purposes of the risk of error analysis, we are concerned *only* with the irreparable harm that can occur between the time the plaintiff seeks the preliminary injunction and final judgment — we are not concerned with irreparable harm that would occur only *after* final judgment.

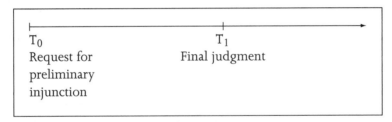

Figure 9.1

Thus, looking at Figure 9.1, plaintiff makes a request for a preliminary injunction at time T_0, and a final judgment will be issued at time T_1. For a preliminary injunction, we are concerned only about irreparable harm faced by plaintiff or defendant in the T_0-T_1 time period. At the preliminary injunction stage, courts should not consider irreparable harm occurring at or after time T_1. For a permanent injunction issued at final judgment, courts are concerned about irreparable injury from time T_1 into the future.

Consider these rules for granting preliminary injunctions in the context of *Pacifica Preservation Society v. Oldtime Hotel, Inc.* If the court fails to issue the preliminary injunction and it erred in doing so (because at final judgment the court decides that the Oldtime Hotel is protected by the state's historic preservation laws), the plaintiff is going to suffer a great deal of irreparable

---

8. As noted in Chapter 7.5, the *eBay* case may be imposing a new test for *permanent* injunctions, including new requirements for plaintiffs to come forward with evidence regarding the "balance of the hardships."

harm. The building will be destroyed, and there will be no way to resurrect it as a historic building.

On the other hand, if the court grants the preliminary injunction and it erred in doing so (because at final judgment the court decides that the Oldtime Hotel is *not* protected by the state's historic preservation laws), the defendant is going to suffer some harm (perhaps irreparable harm). Imagine, for example, that the defendant planned on building a new development on the property, and this delay will cost the defendant a great deal of money (perhaps even exposing the defendant to liability to Acme Wrecking Company and other contractors for breach of contract) as well as inconvenience. It is possible the whole project could fall apart.

In thinking about the harm faced by each party, we might agree that the harm facing the plaintiffs is greater than the harm facing the defendant because the building is irreplaceable but money is not. But that's too simplistic an analysis. First, your answer might change if the defendant faces *millions of dollars* in losses if the project is delayed. It is going to be very hard to *value* the loss of a historic building, but at some point a court may decide that the harm to the defendant for delaying the project is just too high (though if the society could pay for the million dollars of harm should it turn out on final judgment the preliminary injunction should not have been issued, perhaps the court should not take it into account in looking at *irreparable* loss).

Moreover, an analysis that just compares the harm to each party if the court guesses wrong ignores the likelihood of success on the merits. A court should be more willing to grant an injunction if a plaintiff has a 95% chance of ultimately winning the case than if she has only a 5% chance.

So let's say that if the preliminary injunction is erroneously denied, plaintiff would suffer the loss of the building, which we will value at $1 million, and defendant would suffer $50,000 in delay costs if the preliminary injunction is erroneously granted. Suppose further that if the court took a peek at the merits, it would estimate that plaintiff's chances of succeeding on the merits — in this case, proving that the state law in fact prevents the destruction of the hotel — is 10%. The fact that the chances of plaintiff's success are relatively low must be factored into the court's balancing.

Judge Posner has presented an algebraic way to factor in both likelihood of success on the merits and the harm to each party that comes from an erroneously granted injunction:

> Grant [the preliminary injunction] but only if $P(H_p) > (1 - P)H_d$, where P is the probability that the plaintiff will prevail in the full trial on the merits (and therefore $(1 - P)$ is the probability that the defendant will prevail), H_p is the irreparable harm that the plaintiff will suffer unless a preliminary injunction is granted to maintain the status quo pending the trial, and H_d is the irreparable harm the defendant will suffer if the preliminary injunction is granted.

RICHARD A. POSNER, ECONOMIC ANALYSIS OF LAW 595 (7th ed. 2007).[9] In other words, under the Posner formula a court calculates the *expected loss* each side would face if the court erred, by multiplying likelihood of each party's success by the extent of loss the party would face if the court guessed wrong at the preliminary injunction stage.

Applying this formula to the *Oldtime Hotel* example above yields the conclusion that the court should grant the preliminary injunction:

> P, the probability of plaintiff's success on the merits, is .10 (10%).
>
> H_p, the irreparable harm that plaintiff will suffer if the preliminary injunction is denied, is $1 million.
>
> $1 - P$, the probability of defendant's success on the merits, is .90 (90%).
>
> H_d, the irreparable harm that the defendant will suffer, is at most[10] $50,000.

Multiplying, $P(H_p) = .10 \times \$1,000,000$, or $100,000, which is greater than $(1 - P)H_d = .90 \times \$50,000$, or $45,000. Because $100,000 > $45,000, the preliminary injunction should be granted.

As you can see, this formula is very sensitive to the numbers that are put into it. For example, if the court valued the harm to the plaintiff at $400,000 (rather than $1 million), or the harm to the defendant at $150,000 (rather than $50,000), the court would conclude that the injunction should not be issued.

This formula is helpful in getting courts and parties focused on the right factors, but its importance could be exaggerated. Indeed, the formula gives a false aura of scientific exactness to the process of a court's balancing the hardships, which often will be more of a gestalt, seat-of-the-pants analysis than a hard calculation. (*See American Hospital Supply Corp. v. Hospital Products, Ltd.*, 780 F.2d 589, 609 (7th Cir. 1986) (dissenting opinion stating, in a case where Judge Posner set forth the mathematical test in a majority opinion, that the traditional test for preliminary injunctive relief "may not exhibit the 'precision' the majority seems to demand, but such 'precision' is antithetical to the underlying principles of injunctive relief. Equity, as the majority concedes, involves the assessment of factors that cannot be quantified.").)

In the real world, courts will often find it impossible to come up with numbers to plug into the formula, especially because in many cases we are dealing with harm that is "irreparable" *because* it is so hard to value. Think of the loss of a historic landmark like the Oldtime Hotel. How is a court to put a

---

9. To take into account the public interest, its value (represented by some dollar amount) could be added to either side of the equation as appropriate.

10. I say "at most" because arguably this $50,000 is not *irreparable* harm and there is no irreparable harm at all. If there is no irreparable harm at all, then under Judge Posner's formula the injunction should be granted because defendant's side of the equation equals zero: $.90 \times 0 = 0$.

price on the value of its preservation to the society or to the public? Or suppose a delay would cost the defendant a partner in a new development project. How is the court to value that lost benefit? Finally, how is the court to assess the likelihood of success on the merits other than by reaching a preliminary decision on the merits and self-assessing the likelihood the judge will change his or her mind after a fuller exploration of the merits?

On this last point, it is worth considering Judge Posner's analysis of the stay order issued by the Supreme Court in *Bush v. Gore*. A *stay* is an order by an appellate court suspending the implementation of a lower court order or judgment. The standards for granting a stay are very much like those governing the issuance of a preliminary injunction because a stay too is a preliminary order in effect only until the higher court decides the merits of the appeal. *See Rostker v. Goldberg*, 448 U.S. 1306, 1308 (1980) (Brennan, J., in chambers).[11]

Arguably the most famous stay order in American history was issued in the midst of the dispute over the 2000 presidential election in Florida. The winner of the electoral votes in Florida would become the next president (thanks to the workings of the Electoral College), and Democrat Al Gore and Republican George W. Bush were battling in court over the recounting of ballots, with Bush leading by 537 votes out of about 6 million cast.[12] On Friday, September 8, 2000, the Florida Supreme Court ordered a counting of all "undervoted" ballots across the state of Florida. *Gore v. Harris*, 772 So. 2d 1243 (Fla. 2000). The next day, the U.S. Supreme Court stayed that order, *Bush v. Gore*, 531 U.S. 1046 (2000), and the Court, after briefing and oral argument in the course of two days, reversed the Florida Supreme Court, ending the recount and leading to the election of George W. Bush. *Bush v. Gore*, 531 U.S. 98 (2000).

In a later-published analysis, Judge Posner (who was not a judge in any of the proceedings) agreed that the harm to Al Gore in granting the stay of the recount was much greater than the harm to George W. Bush in rejecting the stay. The period of time within which to certify the presidential electors for Florida was fast approaching, and the decision to stay the counting meant that the counting likely could never be completed and Gore never would have the possibility of taking the lead in the recount. Bush, in contrast, risked a hard-to-value "cloud" over the legitimacy of his election should the Florida courts declare Gore the winner, and be reversed later by the U.S. Supreme Court.

---

11. When a party seeks to stay enforcement of a money judgment (such as a judgment for damages) pending appeal, it is often necessary to obtain an *appeal bond* guaranteeing payment to the plaintiff. *See, e.g.*, CAL. CODE CIV. PROC. § 917.1 (setting forth rules and amounts of appellate "undertakings" to stay money judgment on appeal). The text refers to stay orders not involving money judgments.

12. For more detail about the Florida controversy, *see* RICHARD L. HASEN, THE SUPREME COURT AND ELECTION LAW: JUDGING EQUALITY FROM BAKER V. CARR TO BUSH V. GORE 41-46 (2003).

Despite the much greater harm facing Gore (let's value it at $1 million, compared to $100 for Bush[13]), Judge Posner concluded that the court was right to grant the stay, because Gore's chances of success were zero. *See* RICHARD A. POSNER, BREAKING THE DEADLOCK: THE 2000 ELECTION, THE CONSTITUTION, AND THE COURTS 164-165 (2001). In other words, Judge Posner concluded that *by the time the Supreme Court agreed to grant the stay,* a majority of Justices had made a conclusive determination that Gore was going to lose on the merits: $1 million times zero is still zero, and Bush's expected losses, while low — in this case $100 (1 × $100) — exceeded zero.

We might think of Judge Posner's position as a hyperlegal realist position, but look at how sensitive it is to his estimation. If, at the time the Court decided on the stay, Gore had just a 1% chance of changing one Justice's mind following briefing and oral argument (the Supreme Court was 5-4 on the stay and in the final case on the remedy), Posner's formula tells us that the Supreme Court should have denied the stay.[14]

Finally, an important note about the status quo and about mandatory and prohibitory injunctions. In the *University of Texas* case, the Supreme Court wrote about the purpose of the preliminary injunction as being "merely to preserve the relative positions of the parties until a trial on the merits can be held." The idea that preliminary injunctions should generally preserve the status quo is one that many courts and lawyers adhere to. But in some cases plaintiffs want affirmative relief (a court order to defendant to do something) rather than just preservation of the status quo.

Judge McConnell offered a defense of preserving the status quo in *O Centro Espirita Beneficiente Uniao Do Vegetal v. Ashcroft,* 389 F.3d 973, 1015 (10th Cir. 2004) (McConnell, J., concurring): "It is one thing for a court to preserve its power to grant effectual relief by preventing parties from making unilateral and irremediable changes during the course of litigation, and quite another for a court to force the parties to make significant alterations in their practices before there has been time for a trial on the merits."[15]

---

13. These numbers are, of course, arbitrary, but they are useful in the sense that it demonstrates that the harm to Gore in halting the recount (losing the presidency) was arguably much higher (in this numerical example, 10,000 times greater) than the harm to Bush in allowing the recount to go forward.

14. One percent of $1,000,000 is $10,000 ($H_d$), which greatly exceeds the expected loss for Bush of $99 (.99 × $100) ($H_p$).

15. What is the "status quo"? It is "the last uncontested status that preceded the parties' controversy." *Department of Parks and Recreation v. Bazaar Del Mundo,* 448 F.3d 1118, 1124 (9th Cir. 2006). But it may not always be easy to recognize the status quo. Commenting on Judge McConnell's opinion in *O Centro,* Judge Posner wrote: "Now it may be that [the considerations raised by Judge McConnell] are better invoked on a case-by-case basis than made the basis of a rule that depends on a judge's ability to determine what state of affairs should be viewed as the status quo." *Chicago United Industries Ltd. v. City of Chicago,* 445 F.3d 940, 946 (7th Cir. 2006).

Most courts also hold that plaintiffs must meet a higher standard when seeking a *mandatory injunction*, or ordering a defendant to do something and thereby changing the status quo, as opposed to a *prohibitory injunction*, or ordering a defendant to refrain from doing something. In addition, there's a connection between this point and the status quo point: in most cases, a prohibitory injunction is most likely to preserve the status quo and a mandatory injunction is most likely to change the status quo.[16]

Cases indeed say that plaintiffs face a higher burden when requesting a mandatory preliminary injunction, *see, e.g., Louis Vuitton Malletier v. Dooney & Bourke, Inc.*, 454 F.3d 108 (2d Cir. 2006), but courts do grant mandatory preliminary injunctions in appropriate cases, even if it means making a change in the status quo. Even Judge McConnell noted: "In recent decades, most courts — and all federal courts of appeal — have come to recognize that there are cases in which preservation of the status quo may so clearly inflict irreparable harm on the movant, with so little probability of being upheld on the merits, that a preliminary injunction may be appropriate even though it requires a departure from the status quo." *O Centro*, 389 F.3d at 1013 (McConnell, J., concurring).

To avoid issuing a "disfavored" mandatory injunction, a court will sometimes use language to cast a mandatory injunction in a prohibitory way. For example, in *Bingham v. Oregon School Activities Association*, 24 F. Supp. 2d 1110 (D. Or. 1998), a trial court held that, under the Americans with Disabilities Act, a high school had to let a student play on a sports team despite state eligibility rules that appeared to exclude him. But rather than order the school in a preliminary injunction to allow the student to play, the court characterized its order as prohibitory: "Relief can be afforded by an order prohibiting defendant from imposing any sanctions against [plaintiff], plaintiff's coach, or the athletic programs in which plaintiff participates pursuant to this court's ruling."[17] *Id.* at 1115. Semantics aside, it seems pretty clear that this was an affirmative order to include plaintiff in the sports program.

---

16. This is not inevitably so, however, when the status quo is one of action. For example, a city clerk routinely considers parade permit requests promptly and issues the permits when the group requesting one meets all of the city's requirements. However, the clerk refuses to promptly consider a parade permit request submitted by a politically unpopular group. The group might seek a preliminary injunction that would require the clerk to consider the permit request promptly. That would be a mandatory injunction (it requires the clerk to do something), but arguably it *preserves* the status quo of the clerk routinely considering parade permit requests promptly.

17. To its credit, the court added: "At any rate, even pursuant to the higher standards [for mandatory injunctive relief], I find that plaintiff is entitled to preliminary injunctive relief." *Id.* at 1115.

Example 3

Another election law example: In 2003, enough California voters signed petitions to trigger the "recall" election of Governor Gray Davis, the first such election in California history. A number of lawsuits were filed challenging different aspects of the recall election. One of the suits argued that, following *Bush v. Gore*, it would violate the Equal Protection Clause of the U.S. Constitution to conduct a statewide recall election under which voters in some counties used antiquated punch card voting machines (the same machines that became so notorious in the 2000 Florida controversy) while other voters used much more reliable voting machinery. With the recall scheduled for October 2003, the ACLU moved for a preliminary injunction in August, two months before the election, asking for the election to be delayed until California election officials could replace the punch cards (which would have been in March 2004, when the state, pursuant to an earlier consent decree, was scheduled to discontinue using punch card voting machines). The trial judge denied the request for a preliminary injunction, holding, among other things, that plaintiffs were not likely to succeed on the merits because they misread the requirements of the Supreme Court's holding in *Bush v. Gore*. There was also a dispute over how many votes would be lost by the use of punch card voting machines. The district court took two weeks to deny the motion, and the ACLU appealed to the Ninth Circuit. A Ninth Circuit panel heard argument at the beginning of September, about a month before the election. By that time, the campaigns (both for and against the recall, and for replacement candidates, should the recall succeed) were well underway.

What factors should the Ninth Circuit consider in deciding whether or not to grant the injunction? How should it decide the case?

Explanation

It is very common for election-related disputes, because of their time sensitivity, to be decided on a motion for a preliminary injunction followed by interlocutory appeal on an expedited basis to an appellate court. The first question faced by any appellate court is the standard for review. It is often said that an appellate court reviews a trial court's decision on a preliminary injunction under a rather deferential "abuse of discretion" standard. But that is a bit misleading in the election context, because many of these cases are decided on pure issues of law, and appellate courts have held that a trial court abuses its discretion when it decides an issue on an improper legal basis: appellate courts generally do not defer to trial courts' interpretation of applicable law, and therefore in many of these cases the review can be broad and not deferential to the lower court.

In considering whether or not to grant the preliminary injunction, the first question was the likelihood of success on the merits. When the Ninth

Circuit first heard the case, a three-judge panel concluded plaintiffs were likely to succeed on the merits: the use of these unreliable punch card machines in only some California counties violated voters' equal protection rights under *Bush v. Gore*. *Southwest Voter Registration Education Project v. Shelley*, 344 F.3d 882 (9th Cir. 2003). The panel that made that decision included some of the more liberal Ninth Circuit judges, who for various reasons likely favored this reading of *Bush v. Gore* and the prospect of slowing down the recall election. And in doing so, the Ninth Circuit reversed a much more conservative federal district court judge who denied the injunction.

The case was immediately taken en banc, and an 11-judge panel (with many more conservatives than liberals) disagreed with the original appellate court's reading of *Bush v. Gore*, though it did not officially reject that reading. *Southwest Voter Registration Education Project v. Shelley*, 344 F.3d 914 (9th Cir. 2003) (en banc) ("We have not previously had occasion to consider the precise equal protection claim raised here. That a panel of this court unanimously concluded the claim had merit provides evidence that the argument is one over which reasonable jurists may differ.").[18]

The court, however, held the first Ninth Circuit panel erred in granting the injunction because it did not sufficiently consider the public interest:

> If the recall election scheduled for October 7, 2003, is enjoined, it is certain that the state of California and its citizens will suffer material hardship by virtue of the enormous resources already invested in reliance on the election's proceeding on the announced date. Time and money have been spent to prepare voter information pamphlets and sample ballots, mail absentee ballots, and hire and train poll workers. Public officials have been forced to divert their attention from their official duties in order to campaign. Candidates have crafted their message to the voters in light of the originally-announced schedule and calibrated their message to the political and social environment of the time. They have raised funds under current campaign contribution laws and expended them in reliance on the election's taking place on October 7. Potential voters have given their attention to the candidates' messages and prepared themselves to vote. Hundreds of thousands of absentee voters have already cast their votes in similar reliance upon the election going forward on the timetable announced by the state. These investments of time, money, and the exercise of citizenship rights cannot be returned. If the election is postponed, citizens who have already cast a vote will effectively be told that the vote does not count and that they must vote again. In short, the status quo that existed at the time the election was set cannot be restored because this election has already begun.

---

18. The court then said the district court judge did not abuse his discretion in finding no *Bush v. Gore* violation (an odd ruling, because this was a legal question and the district court's legal opinion was not entitled to any deference), but that plaintiffs had a stronger case on the merits on a claim under the federal Voting Rights Act.

Id. at 919. The public's interest was a weighty one to be sure, but the public's interest cut both ways in this case. What about the harm to voters who would be voting on voting machines that (the ACLU alleged) were much less likely to count a valid vote? The Ninth Circuit en banc court held: "We must of course also look to the interests represented by the plaintiffs, who are legitimately concerned that use of the punch-card system will deny the right to vote to some voters who must use that system. At this time, it is merely a speculative possibility, however, that any such denial will influence the result of the election." Id. at 919-920.

That analysis had it wrong because there was no easy post-election remedy. The harm was really irreparable. Indeed, statistics after the election showed that more than 5% of ballots cast in Los Angeles County (a punch card county) did not include a valid vote on the recall, compared to only 0.74% of ballots in Alameda County (using electronic voting machines). Had the election been close, there would have been no way to figure out how to count votes that were not properly recorded on the punch cards. Would the Ninth Circuit have voided the election and ordered a new one, an even more intrusive remedy than the delay ordered by the first, three-judge panel? Fortunately for the people of California, the recall election was not close, so the Ninth Circuit did not have to consider a possible post-election remedy for punch card problems.

This recent real-world example should show you how limited the Posner formula is in answering the question whether a court should issue a preliminary injunction, and how fluid the balancing must be. Indeed, the balancing equation changed over time. The public's investment in the recall election was relatively minimal on August 7, when the ACLU filed its initial case in the federal district court, but by mid-September, when the Ninth Circuit heard the recall case (for the second time), those public interests were great. Not only were there public interest concerns on both sides; there was considerable uncertainty as to both the facts (how unreliable *are* punch card machines compared to other voting devices?) and the law (what does the Equal Protection Clause require when it comes to voting?). Moreover, all of this occurred in a highly charged political atmosphere, where the political leanings of the judges at least appeared to have some correlation with their views on the propriety of preliminary injunctive relief.

Example 4

You represent Oscar in his long-running dispute (after all, it has been going on since Chapter 7) with Pnina over Pnina's failure to produce the widget she promised that is needed to run Oscar's factory. Pnina argues that Oscar breached the contract first by failing to pay the promised price and by failing to give Pnina the specifications to make the widget. Oscar's factory is closed, and he wants you to obtain a preliminary injunction requiring Pnina to continue working on the widget. What kind of evidence will you need to bring in to support your client's motion for preliminary relief?

Explanation

This is a nuts-and-bolts type of question involving a dispute — unlike the dispute in Example 3 — that has little or nothing to do with the public interest (unless Oscar's factory is producing something that the public needs and cannot get elsewhere). You want to marshal evidence showing that Oscar is likely to succeed on the merits and that the irreparable harm he faces in the T_0-T_1 period will greatly exceed Pnina's harm.

In terms of likelihood on the merits, of course, you will want to have a copy of the contract itself, plus any other documentary evidence such as receipts, bank statements, letters, and e-mails. It also would be useful to have an affidavit from Oscar and any other material that can prove that Oscar is likely to succeed in proving that Pnina, rather than Oscar, breached the contract.

It will also be necessary to get evidence supporting the irreparable harm claim; perhaps you can find a factory engineer or other employee who can sign an affidavit about how crucial the widget is for the operation of the factory. Someone else might need to write an affidavit about the lack of availability of the widget elsewhere on the market. Finally, any evidence showing that continued work on the widget pending final judgment will not create any irreparable harm for Pnina would be useful (though you may not be in possession of any such information).

One argument that Pnina might make against Oscar is that the court should impose a higher standard because he is seeking a *mandatory injunction*, ordering Pnina to produce the widget, rather than a *prohibitory injunction*, ordering Pnina to refrain from doing something. (It seems a stretch for Oscar to argue for a prohibitory injunction on grounds that the court would be preventing Pnina from not continuing work on the widget.) Still, if Oscar has a strong showing of success in his favor and a balance of the hardship strongly favoring him, why should the court deny preliminary relief simply because the relief he requests is affirmative relief?

Finally, in thinking about how to present Oscar's case to the court, it is useful to draft a proposed order for the court to sign. It should be carefully drafted and tailored to the rightful position standard. It should be easy to enforce through the power of contempt if necessary, and not full of unclear language. If you are in federal court, the order must comply with FED. R. CIV. P. 65(d):

> Every order granting an injunction and every restraining order shall set forth the reasons for its issuance; shall be specific in terms; shall describe in reasonable detail, and not by reference to the complaint or other document,

the act or acts sought to be restrained; and is binding only upon the parties to the action, their officers, agents, servants, employees, and attorneys, and upon those persons in active concert or participation with them who receive actual notice of the order by personal service or otherwise.

Take a few minutes and try to write out the court order. It is not as easy as you might think.

9.3 INJUNCTION BONDS, WITH A NOTE ON *NE EXEAT*

As we saw in section 9.2, much of what drives preliminary injunction analysis is uncertainty and the risk of error. The balancing test for preliminary injunctions is one way that courts deal with the risk. The injunction bond is another means of doing so. Under Federal Rule of Civil Procedure 65(c), "No restraining order or preliminary injunction shall issue except upon the giving of security by the applicant, in such sum as the court deems proper, for the payment of such costs and damages as may be incurred or suffered by any party who is found to have been wrongfully enjoined or restrained."

The injunction bond works to reduce the risk of uncertainty by shifting some of that risk to the plaintiff. The bond requires the plaintiff to pay the defendant for damages that accrue during the period between the granting of the preliminary injunction and final judgment if the court determines at final judgment that injunctive relief is not warranted.

To see how the injunction bond changes plaintiffs' incentives and thereby reduces the risks of uncertainty, let's return to the case of *Pacifica Preservation Society v. Oldtime Hotel*. Suppose that the Society values the preservation of the hotel at $100,000. Stopping the hotel demolition project from the point of preliminary injunction to final judgment is going to cost the defendant $400,000 in costs for delay.

Without the injunction bond, the plaintiff would not take the defendant's costs into account in deciding whether to seek a preliminary injunction. (The court presumably would do so in balancing the equities.) Suppose, however, that the court requires the Society to purchase an injunction bond worth $400,000. The Society will go to a bonding company that likely will require the Society to sign over property worth $400,000 to the bonding company, plus pay some additional premium for the service in writing the bond (we'll set the premium amount here at $20,000), an amount which will not be refunded whether or not the Society succeeds at final judgment.

Would the Society agree to purchase the injunction bond, or would it forgo the preliminary injunction? The answer may well depend upon the

Society's assessment of its likelihood of succeeding on the merits. If the Society believes it has a 10% chance of succeeding at final judgment, its expected loss on the bond is .90 (the defendant's chance of success) multiplied by the $400,000 value of the bond, or $360,000, plus the $20,000 premium, for a total of $380,000. The Society would not seek the preliminary injunction, because the $380,000 cost greatly exceeds the $100,000 value of preserving the hotel.

In contrast, if the Society believes it has a 95% chance of success on the merits, it could well decide to go forward in seeking the injunction even if it has to purchase the bond. Under these circumstances, its expected loss is .05 (the defendant's chance of success) multiplied by the $400,000 value of the bond, or $20,000, plus the $20,000 premium, for a total cost of $40,000. The Society could decide to seek the preliminary injunction, because the $40,000 cost is less than the $100,000 value of preserving the hotel.[19]

Injunction bonds benefit defendants, and smart defense counsel will do what they can to get bonds to fully cover the losses their clients would suffer if the court erroneously grants the plaintiff's request for a preliminary injunction. Injunction bonds also are likely to discourage plaintiffs from seeking preliminary injunctions, especially in cases where the plaintiff's case appears weak or where the defendant's damages during the T_0-T_1 period (see Figure 9.1) are expected to be large.

The main social problem with injunction bonds is that they can discourage public interest litigation, or even private litigation where poor plaintiffs face defendants who would suffer substantial losses upon the granting of a preliminary injunction.

For example, suppose that the Society has very few assets, but it values the Oldtime Hotel at $1 million. Under these circumstances, it could well want to seek an injunction even under the conditions described above, where the society has only a 10% chance of success. But the society may not have the money to pay for the bond. Indeed, even if the Society is confident (95%) that it is going to win, it still may have trouble pledging adequate security for the bond.

For this reason, courts sometimes waive the requirement of a bond.[20] The First Circuit, for example, set forth a two-part test:

> First, at least in noncommercial cases, the court should consider the possible loss to the enjoined party together with the hardship that a bond requirement would impose on the applicant. Applicants in commercial cases — merchants, manufacturers, and others — can be assumed capable of bearing most bond

---

19. This example assumes that the Society is neutral about risk. If the society is risk-averse, it might be less willing to seek an injunction if required to post an injunction bond.

20. Consider whether such discretion is consistent with the language of FED. R. CIV. P. 65(c), requiring a bond "in such sum as the court deems proper." To argue that it is consistent, one would have to take the position that zero could be a proper sum.

requirements, so hardship to them is less of a factor. Second, in order not to restrict a federal right unduly, the impact that a bond requirement would have on enforcement of the right should also be considered. One measure of the impact lies in a comparison of the positions of the applicant and the enjoined party. A bond requirement would have a greater adverse effect where the applicant is an individual and the enjoined party an institution that otherwise has some control over the applicant than where both parties are individuals or institutions.

Crowley v. Local No. 82, Furniture & Piano Moving, 679 F.2d 978, 1000 (1st Cir. 1982), *rev'd on other grounds,* 467 U.S. 526 (1984). Is it fair to cut more slack for a plaintiff in a noncommercial case than in a case involving a small business seeking an injunction against a much larger corporation?

Once the bond is in place, most courts take the view that trial courts do not have the discretion to decide whether or not to allow successful defendants to recover damages up to the amount of the bond. *Coyne-Delany Co. v. Capital Development Board,* 717 F.2d 385 (7th Cir. 1983). But in such circumstances the plaintiff cannot be liable to the defendant for damages in excess of the bond, even if the defendant proves damages exceeding that amount. At some state courts, however, damages for a wrongfully issued preliminary injunction can exceed the amount of the bond when the plaintiff sought the preliminary injunction in bad faith. *See Ex parte Waterjet Systems Inc.,* 758 So. 2d 505, 513 (Ala. 1999).

Note that to the extent defendant's harm can be protected with an injunction bond, it looks less "irreparable" in the balancing of the hardships that courts undertake in deciding whether or not to issue the preliminary injunction.

A final note on preliminary relief and bonds: In rare circumstances, courts will issue a preliminary injunction *barring a person from leaving a jurisdiction* pending some further action. Such injunctions traditionally required the plaintiff to seek a writ called *ne exeat* (Latin for "let him not go out"). One way of helping to enforce such an order is requiring the defendant to post a *ne exeat* bond, which is forfeited if the defendant leaves the jurisdiction.

The federal government sometimes seeks *ne exeat* writs and bonds when a defendant owes taxes and appears to be preparing to leave the country. More commonly today, *ne exeat* orders relate to custody proceedings. Consider the case of *Faris v. Jernigan,* 939 So. 2d 835 (Miss. App. 2006). Husband and Wife got a divorce and had a bitter custody dispute, which included allegations of sexual abuse of the couple's child that were raised by the mother but rejected by the court. The court had originally awarded custody of Child to Wife, but the court awarded custody to Husband after finding that Wife had made material misrepresentations to the court about Husband's treatment of Child.

Wife moved out of state, and the court required Wife to post a $5,000 *ne exeat* bond in order to be able to have Child visit Wife overnight out of state.

Wife posted the bond and then failed to return the child. The court held Wife in criminal contempt and ordered the bond forfeited. Wife returned Child, surrendered to authorities, and spent 13 months in jail for her willful contempt of court. After release, the court allowed Wife increasingly less restrictive and more frequent visits. Wife again requested that Child visit her out of state, and the court agreed to allow such visits, but only upon the posting of a new *ne exeat* bond in the amount of $40,000 (plus the payment of Husband's $40,000 in attorney's fees in the contempt and custody actions).

The appellate court upheld the $40,000 *ne exeat* bond requirement against Wife's claim that the amount was too high: "the amount of the bond was proper in light of [Wife's] past willingness to forfeit a $5,000 *ne exeat* bond, and related actions which resulted in [Husband] incurring more than $75,000 in attorneys' fees and other associated expenses."

Example 5

Alice, on behalf of a nonprofit neighborhood association, obtained a preliminary injunction in federal court barring the construction of Betty's new commercial development on grounds that the development would constitute a nuisance. Betty maintains that the property is not a nuisance. The nuisance question is a factual one that ultimately will require the court to consider the testimony of witnesses.

   a. Is the court required to make Alice post an injunction bond?
   b. If the court fails to require the bond, may Betty obtain damages caused by the delay, if the federal court on final judgment determines that Betty's project is not a nuisance?

Explanation

(a) Some courts reading Rule 65(c) would say that an injunction bond in some amount is required. Other courts, following the *Crowley* test or a similar test, could decide that the hardship on Alice is too great, and the public interest is served by no bond, or a bond in a very small amount. Likely a court will want to know more about the financial positions of the parties before deciding whether or not to waive a bond requirement. Ask yourself whether you would waive the bond requirement if you were the judge and you had the power to do so. If your answer is yes, should it matter if Alice's chances of success on the merits are only 10%? If your answer is no, should it matter if Alice's chances of success on the merits are as high as 90%?

(b) If there is no bond, generally speaking, there will be no liability for the costs of delay. *See Manta Management Corp. v. City of San Bernardino*, 44 Cal. Rptr. 3d 35, 41 (App. 2006) (nonpublished) ("Under most circumstances, if a preliminary injunction is dissolved as having been improperly granted, the formerly enjoined party may recover damages only by proceeding against the injunction bond or surety. If no bond was required as a condition of issuance of the preliminary injunction, or if the amount of the bond was insufficient to compensate the enjoined party, the party may recover his damages only if he can prevail in an independent action for malicious prosecution, i.e., by showing that the injunction was obtained maliciously and without probable cause. This is true both under California's statutory scheme relating to injunctions and under federal law.").

The *Manta* case presents an interesting variation on these facts. Defendant operated a business, and converted that business into an "adult cabaret" featuring nude dancing. The City of San Bernardino claimed that the adult cabaret violated applicable zoning laws, and it sought an injunction preventing the business from operating. The defendant claimed the zoning law violated the First Amendment and could not be enforced.

The court granted the preliminary injunction, and the city was not required to post an injunction bond because state law provided that preliminary injunctions obtained by municipalities were exempt from the bond requirement. The appellate court later held that the preliminary injunction was improperly granted because the zoning law violated the First Amendment.

The defendant then sued the city for lost profits during the time his business was closed. The appellate court held that the defendant could in fact obtain damages even though there was no injunction bond, despite the usual rule limiting defendants to recovery under the bond. It analogized the "malicious prosecution" exception described above to the city's violation of the defendant's constitutional rights. In both cases, the court said, the tortious action justified allowing the wrongfully enjoined defendant to recover damages that exceeded the amount (if any) of the injunction bond.

Example 6

Same facts as in Example 5, but assume that the court requires Alice and her association to post a $50,000 bond. The court later rules for Betty at final judgment and she seeks to recover damages for delay of the project. How much can Betty recover if she can prove that she suffered (a) $20,000 in damages? (b) $60,000 in damages?

To what extent can Alice defend against Betty's claim for payment on the bond on the basis that she honestly and reasonably believed she had a good case against Betty?

Explanation

(a) Betty can recover the full $20,000 under the bond, provided she can prove her damages with reasonable certainty. *Nintendo of America, Inc. v. Lewis Galoob Toys*, 16 F.3d 1032, 1038 (9th Cir. 1994).[21]

(b) Betty can recover only up to the $50,000 amount of the bond, unless perhaps she can prove in a separate malicious prosecution action that Alice had no reasonable basis for bringing her suit or that Alice sought the injunction in bad faith. See the explanation to Example 5(b).

Whether Betty seeks $20,000 or the full $50,000 amount of the bond, it is no defense to payment on the bond that Alice prosecuted the case in good faith. Betty is entitled to recover the damages she can prove with reasonable certainty up to the amount of the bond.

9.4 TEMPORARY RESTRAINING ORDERS

If you were really the lawyer representing the Pacifica Preservation Society seeking to prevent the wrecking ball from knocking down the Oldtime Hotel tomorrow morning, you would need to move faster than the wheels of justice usually turn to obtain a preliminary injunction. In some places, it might take months to get a preliminary injunction motion heard and an injunction issued by a court.

The fastest type of relief available is a *temporary restraining order*, or TRO. The standard for issuing a TRO is basically the same as the standard for issuing a preliminary injunction, *Bieros v. Nicola*, 857 F. Supp. 445, 446 (E.D. Pa. 1994), but because of exigent circumstances and the usual short duration of the TRO, the court will issue one on less of a showing than is required for a preliminary injunction. In other words, if you are waking up a judge in the middle of the night for an emergency order, you are typically asking the judge to issue a TRO, not a preliminary injunction.

There are a few salient differences between a preliminary injunction and a TRO.

1. *Notice.* Fed. R. Civ. P. 65(a)(1) provides that a court cannot issue a preliminary injunction without first giving notice to the adverse party. In contrast, Fed. R. Civ. P. 65(b) provides:

> The court may issue a temporary restraining order without written or oral notice to the adverse party or its attorney only if:
> (A) specific facts in an affidavit or a verified complaint clearly show that immediate and irreparable injury, loss, or damage will result to the movant before the adverse party can be heard in opposition; and

---

21. For more on the reasonable certainty requirement, see Chapter 6.1.

(B) the movant's attorney certifies in writing any efforts made to give notice and the reasons why it should not be required.

Courts generally require the party seeking the TRO to provide some kind of informal notice to the adverse party as a matter of constitutional imperative,[22] at least when it is possible to do so, absent some compelling justification for not giving notice.

2. *Appealability.* Preliminary injunction orders are appealable in federal courts under 28 U.S.C. § 1292(a)(1). In contrast, orders granting or denying TROs are typically not appealable. *See* 11 WRIGHT, MILLER & KANE, FEDERAL PRACTICE AND PROCEDURE § 2947 (2006). However, a court's refusal to modify a temporary restraining order might be appealable as an interlocutory order under 28 U.S.C. § 1292(b), which grants discretion to courts of appeal to review otherwise non-appealable orders when the district court is "of the opinion that such order involves a controlling question of law as to which there is substantial ground for difference of opinion and that an immediate appeal from the order may materially advance the ultimate termination of the litigation." Moreover, as we will see, TROs lasting more than 28 days may be appealable.

3. *Duration.* A preliminary injunction may remain in effect pending a final judgment in the case. In contrast, a TRO issued without notice "expires at the time after entry — not to exceed 14 days — that the court sets, unless before that time the court, for good cause, extends it for a like period or the adverse party consents to a longer extension. The reasons for an extension must be entered in the record." Fed. R. Civ. P. 65(b). Thus, TROs *without notice* can last no more than 28 days total.

The rules do not provide how long a TRO *with notice* may last. What becomes of a TRO issued with or without notice that lasts for more than 28 days? Does it dissolve on its own, or morph into a preliminary injunction?[23] The text of Rule 65 is not clear, and the precedents are somewhat unclear as well, though courts seem to be following the morphing rationale. *See* LAYCOCK p. 66. Judge Posner, writing for a Seventh Circuit panel, recently held that if a TRO is "kept in force by the district court for more than 20 days without the consent of the parties, the order is deemed a preliminary injunction and so is appealable, since otherwise a district court could by the simple expedient of extending the TRO circumvent . . . the right of appeal." *Chicago*

---

22. On this point, see *Carroll v. President of Princess Anne*, 393 U.S. 175 (1968). *Carroll* discussed the issue in the context of a First Amendment case, but such notice (in normal circumstances and where possible) seems required by the Due Process Clause.

23. As we will see in Chapter 10, the decision has real consequences for a litigant who decides to violate a temporary restraining order that has been in effect for more than 28 days (or 14 days if not renewed). If the TRO remains in effect, violating it can result in a finding of contempt. But if the order is not in effect, there is no possibility of a contempt holding.

United Industries Ltd. v. City of Chicago, 445 F.3d 940, 943 (7th Cir. 2006).[24] It would probably make sense for the drafters of the Federal Rules of Civil Procedure to clarify this rather fundamental question.

Example 7

You are the lawyer for the Pacifica Preservation Society, and you are earnestly preparing your motion for a TRO to prevent the destruction of the Oldtime Hotel tomorrow morning at 8 a.m. You honestly believe that if you give notice to the lawyers for the Oldtime Hotel, their clients would bring in the wrecking ball earlier than the hearing on the TRO, thereby avoiding violating any court order but altering the status quo. Can you seek a TRO without notice? What should be in the papers supporting your request for a TRO?

Explanation

The rule itself does not require notice, only an explanation for why notice may not have been given. An affidavit from you stating your belief that actions would be taken before the TRO could be issued if you gave notice would likely be sufficient. If you are not giving notice to the other side, you should ask the court to issue an order of short duration, to be followed up by a second hearing, with notice, that would allow the court to hear from both sides of the controversy (without the risk of the wrecking ball mooting a later court order) before extending or modifying the TRO.[25]

There are probably not many real-world situations where an adverse party would go ahead and change the status quo after receiving notice of a hearing

---

24. The court ruled that this treatment of TROs lasting more than 20 (now 28) days applied to TROs issued with or without notice. Applying the rule only to TROs issued without notice "would enable a district court to issue a preliminary injunction of indefinite duration without any possibility of the defendant's appealing, simply by calling the injunction a temporary restraining order and being careful to notify the defendant in advance of issuing it. Moreover, a TRO issued after notice, especially if there is a hearing, is procedurally as well as functionally even more like a preliminary injunction than a TRO issued without notice and hearing, so it would be a considerable paradox if only the latter type of TRO were appealable after 20 [now 28] days." *Id.* at 946.

25. Rule 65(b) provides in pertinent part: "If the order is issued without notice, the motion for a preliminary injunction must be set for hearing at the earliest possible time, taking precedence over all other matters except hearings on older matters of the same character. At the hearing, the party who obtained the order must proceed with the motion; if the party does not, the court must dissolve the order . . . on 2 days' notice to the party who obtained the order without notice — or on shorter notice set by the court — the adverse party may appear and move to dissolve or modify the order. The court must then hear and decide the motion as promptly as justice requires. . . . On 2 days' notice to the party who obtained the order without notice — or on shorter notice set by the court — the adverse party may appear and move to dissolve or modify the order. The court must then hear and decide the motion as promptly as justice requires."

aimed at preserving that status quo. (The most common such case is a temporary restraining order in a domestic violence situation, where it might put the plaintiff's life or well-being at risk to give notice in advance of a hearing that the plaintiff is seeking a "stay away" order.) Even though a party changing the status quo before the court issues the TRO technically would not be in contempt (see the next chapter), doing so is not likely to endear the party to the judge who will be handling any future litigation arising out of the controversy.

If you are going to literally wake up a judge in the middle of the night to get a TRO, it had better be important. Most matters can wait until the next business day, and a lawyer who uses extraordinary procedures to obtain relief that could be obtained in the normal course of business runs the risk of alienating the judges who are going to be deciding that case and others the lawyer might bring later.

What should the TRO request look like, whether on an examination or in real life? Be organized and comply with local court rules. Especially when courts must make decisions on an expedited basis, the clearer you can make the issues for the court, the better. Make it clear:

- Who are the parties in the lawsuit?
- What is the legal issue?
- Why is immediate preliminary relief required? (Include a discussion of immediate and irreparable harm facing the party seeking the relief.)
- Why is plaintiff likely to prevail on the merits?

Remember, a court cannot issue a TRO without notice unless it "clearly appears from specific facts shown by affidavit or by the verified complaint that immediate and irreparable injury, loss, or damage will result to the applicant before the adverse party or that party's attorney can be heard in opposition." Fed. R. Civ. P. 65(b). Include necessary affidavits, copies of relevant statutes, regulations, contracts, or other relevant documents. You will also want to carefully prepare a proposed court order for the judge to sign.

Enforcing the Injunction: The Power of Contempt

10

10.1 INTRODUCTION TO THE CONTEMPT POWER

One of the great benefits plaintiffs get from injunctions (including preliminary injunctions and temporary restraining orders — and this same benefit applies to other equitable relief) is that the court's order is backed up by the *contempt power.* When we speak of the power of contempt, however, we are really talking about three separate powers used by courts (though courts in some jurisdictions do not possess the third power):

1. *Civil coercive contempt.* This is the power of the court to impose fines payable to the state, or jail time, *to coerce the defendant's compliance* with the court's order.

Example: In Oscar's suit against Pnina for specific performance of their contract for the widget, the court (in a final judgment) orders Pnina to turn over the widget to Oscar by January 1. Pnina fails to do so. The judge threatens Pnina with fines of $1,000 per day until she does so. Pnina turns over the widget after five days, and must pay a $5,000 contempt fine for disobedience of the court's order.

2. *Criminal contempt.* This is the power of the court to *punish a defendant's willful failure to comply* with the court's order.

Example: In the same Oscar-Pnina suit, the judge orders Pnina to turn over the widget by January 1. Pnina deliberately refuses to do so, though she has the widget hidden at her factory. The judge finds beyond a reasonable doubt that Pnina willfully disobeyed the court's order and fines her $20,000.

3. *Civil compensatory contempt.* This is the power of the court to *award damages to the plaintiff* for defendant's failure to comply with the court's order.

Example: In the same Oscar-Pnina suit, the judge orders Pnina to deliver the widget to Oscar by January 1. Pnina does not do so until January 10. Oscar proves that he has suffered $40,000 in damages because of the delay in complying with the court's order. The court will order Pnina to pay Oscar $40,000.

We will consider each of these contempt powers in turn, and then examine two additional issues. First, we consider the "collateral bar rule," which prevents defendants from defending themselves against a *criminal* contempt charge on grounds that the court's injunction was unlawful or incorrect. Second, we consider whether third parties may be held in contempt for violating court orders.

Although the three contempt powers appear to be distinct from one another, sometimes courts have trouble identifying which category a type of contempt citation fits into, or label an order as "contempt" when it doesn't squarely fit into any of the three categories. In addition, as we shall see, when civil coercive contempt payments are high enough, courts sometimes require the additional criminal procedure protections required for criminal contempt.

Example 1

While driving a Ford pickup truck, Mark was involved in a rollover accident. Mark then brought a products liability damages action against Ford Motor Company. A federal district court imposed sanctions after determining that Ford's lawyer, Lawrence, violated two pretrial orders prohibiting Ford from introducing evidence that Mark had been drinking before the accident and had not been wearing his seat belt at the time of the accident. The district court ordered Ford and Lawrence to pay sanctions to Mark and to the district court, intended to reimburse Mark for unnecessary expenses and attorney's fees, and to reimburse the district court for the costs of empaneling the jury. The court also found Lawrence in contempt of court for deliberately violating the pretrial order relating to alcohol use and revoked his *pro hac vice* status (which allowed him to appear in court in a state in which he was not a member of the bar) and permanently barred Lawrence from appearing *pro hac vice* in the Missoula Division of the United States District Court for the District of Montana.

What kind of contempt order did the court impose?

Explanation

This example is based upon *Lasar v. Ford Motor Co.*, 399 F.3d 1101 (9th Cir. 2005), and it is a useful example for you to test your own instincts before we get into more of the details about the rules courts use to differentiate among the different types of contempt. To analyze this case, note that the order can be broken down into three parts:

a. *Money to compensate Mark for his attorney's fees and costs.* This looks like civil compensatory contempt, because it is intended to compensate Mark for Lawrence's (and therefore Ford's) violation of a court order.

b. *Money to compensate the court for its time.* It is hard to see that this is compensatory contempt because it is aimed at compensating the court, not the plaintiff, and the money will be going to the government. However, the court stated a purpose to compensate, not punish, so it does not look like the court was requiring proof of deliberate intent. Nor is there any way defendants could have avoided the fine, meaning it does not look like civil coercive contempt. In the actual case, the Ninth Circuit concluded that this was a kind of civil contempt, and the greater protections of criminal procedure did not apply. The money was going to the government, true, but it was going there to compensate the court for its wasted time. The court's result makes some sense, but that result is not an obvious one given the various definitions of contempt.

c. *Revocation of pro hac vice status.* This looks punitive: the court is punishing the defendant for disobeying the court's orders. In the actual case, the Ninth Circuit agreed this was criminal contempt, but the court said that the punishment was relatively minor and therefore the defendants did not get the full panoply of criminal procedure protections: "So long as the [trial] court did not impose serious criminal penalties, due process did not require the district court to conduct a full-blown trial." *Id.* at 1112. The court did hold that the sanction of a *lifetime ban* was improper in this case, because the court did not give notice before imposing the penalty that it was considering such a ban. It therefore did not reach the question whether a full-blown trial would have been required to impose a lifetime ban—assuming adequate notice of the potential punishment was made in advance.

The lesson here: though we will examine the "three" categories of contempt orders, it is sometimes difficult to tell which kind of contempt a court was imposing on a defendant. Because the protections for the defendant differ depending upon the type of contempt found by the court, it is necessary to impose some rules for categorization. The material in the rest of the chapter helps in that process, but difficult cases remain.

10.2 CIVIL COERCIVE CONTEMPT

Civil coercive contempt is the type of contempt often presented in the movies, usually featuring the obstinate journalist who goes to jail rather than reveal the name of a protected source. In recent years, there have been a number of real-world examples along these lines, with the most famous case being that of Judith Miller, then a reporter for the *New York Times*.

Miller had learned the name of a CIA operative from someone in the Bush administration, and she was subpoenaed by a U.S. attorney investigating the leak of the name to testify before a grand jury about who leaked the information. Miller refused to testify, and she remained in jail for 85 days. She then agreed to testify, after receiving a personal assurance from her source, I. Lewis Libby, who was then serving as Vice President Dick Cheney's chief of staff, that Miller was free to do so. Once she testified, a federal judge lifted the contempt order and Miller was freed. *See* David Johnston, *Contempt Finding Is Lifted in Case of Times Reporter*, N.Y. TIMES, Oct. 13, 2005.

Libby then resigned after he was charged with perjury and obstruction of justice for lying to the grand jury about whether he had revealed the name of the CIA operative to Miller and to other journalists. *See* Neil A. Lewis, *Court Turns Aside Libby's Request for Many Documents*, N.Y. TIMES, June 3, 2006. He was convicted on four counts, and President Bush commuted his sentence.

Journalists, of course, are only the most prominent among those who might be fined or imprisoned by a court using *civil coercive contempt*. Depending upon your politics, you might find Miller to be a heroine or a villain, but there are others held in contempt who are likely to seem villainous to most of us: think of organized crime members who won't testify against co-conspirators upon a grant of immunity, or a parent in a custody dispute who has illegally kidnapped a child and taken that child to an undisclosed location. In such circumstances, many of us would be sympathetic to court efforts to use the contempt power to coerce the release of important information.

Here are a few notable features about coercive contempt:

- It is meant to be coercive, not punitive, though it certainly is going to feel like punishment to someone sitting in jail for refusing to comply with a court order.
- The contemnor (the term we use for the person who has been found in contempt) has "the keys to the jailhouse door in his pocket." The contempt lasts for an indefinite duration. What made Miller's jail time 85 days rather than 82, 92, or 0 days was Miller's decision to testify.[1]

---

1. In certain jurisdictions, including at the federal level, contempt for refusing to testify must end when the 18-month term of the grand jury expires, 28 U.S.C. § 1826, though contempt could begin again with a newly empaneled grand jury. *See also Matter of State Grand Jury Investigation*

- Sometimes jail is not a practical means of coercion, because the defendant must be free in order to do certain things. For instance, if Pnina is refusing to manufacture the widget, and her presence is necessary for its manufacture, her imprisonment for contempt hardly seems a productive way to coerce compliance. In such a case, the use of fines may be a more productive means to coerce Pnina's compliance. Jail time might work if Pnina has manufactured the widget, but has hidden it and refuses to turn it over to Oscar.

Two main legal issues may arise in the context of civil coercive contempt. The first arises when the defendant is unable or has proven unwilling to comply with the court's order. The second concerns civil coercive cases in which courts require protections usually afforded only in criminal proceedings.

Imprisonment Without Coercion. In some circumstances, coercive contempt has lost (or never had) the power to coerce the contemnor and must be halted as improper punishment. *Acceturo, supra,* 576 A.2d at 903. This standard creates a difficult situation for the court, because defendants always have an incentive to lie and say that imprisonment has lost its coercive power. A hearing on the matter gives contemnors a chance to convince the court to lift the contempt order because further incarceration will prove futile.

The question becomes one of credibility. "Since a prediction is involved and since that prediction concerns such uncertain matters as the likely effect of continued confinement upon a particular individual, we think a district judge has virtually unreviewable discretion both as to the procedure he will use to reach his conclusion, and as to the merits of his conclusion." *Simkin v. United States,* 715 F.2d 34, 38 (2d Cir. 1983). Other courts require that there be some hearing at which a judge determines credibility.

An interesting case study is *Catena v. Seidl,* 343 A.2d 744 (N.J. 1975). Gerardo Catena refused to testify regarding organized crime activities despite being granted immunity from prosecution for his testimony. Catena had been held for nearly 5 years. He was 73 years old and in ill health, and he moved for release on grounds that coercive contempt had failed and confinement had become punitive.

At first the trial court summarily decided that Catena had to remain imprisoned until he agreed to testify. The New Jersey Supreme Court,

---

re *Acceturo v. Zelinski,* 576 A.2d 900, 904 (N.J. Super. 1990) ("We have no doubt that as a matter of due process, [a hearing on whether contempt is still coercive] should without question be provided no later than the expiration of 18 months of incarceration, as that is the maximum sentence which a court may impose for criminal contempt. . . .").

however, then required a hearing on Catena's motion for release to determine "whether or not there was a substantial likelihood that continued commitment of Catena would accomplish the purpose of the order upon which the commitment was based." Id. at 746.

On remand, "[t]he trial court noted Catena's age (73 years old), state of health and confinement since March 1970. It reviewed the reason given by Catena for remaining silent (essentially Catena testified that he believed he had a right of privacy which could not be taken away from him), and while it did not believe him in that regard, concluded that no matter what Catena's real reason was, he had demonstrated such total obstinacy that the trial court was satisfied that he would never answer any questions." Id. at 746-747. The New Jersey Supreme Court upheld the trial court's judgment to release Catena, deferring to that court's credibility determination.

The dissent contended that the majority was rewarding an organized crime Code of Silence, and believed that Catena's consistent legal efforts to win release — along with the absence of any psychiatric testimony — meant Catena had not met his burden of proving he was no longer subject to coercion through continued incarceration.

Of course, Catena's case gives hope to others being held in contempt that by holding out long enough, the courts might eventually grant their release. It appears that Catena lived a long life after release, quietly retiring to Boca Raton, Florida, and dying of natural causes at age 98.[2] But waiting for the court is a big gamble for many contemnors, and it could be years before a court would seriously entertain the argument for release. Indeed, some judges may agree with the view of the dissent here: the more often the contemnor brings legal proceedings to win release, the more it shows that the contemnor cares about the incarceration and could be motivated to comply with the court's order to win release from prison.

Criminal-like Protections in Civil Contempt Proceedings. In cases of criminal contempt, a full array of procedural protections apply; when the fine is large enough or the jail time long enough, for example, the defendant gets the right to a jury trial. These protections generally do not apply in the context of civil coercive contempt, but the Supreme Court held that sometimes they do. In International Union, United Mine Workers v. Bagwell, 512 U.S. 821 (1994), a union involved in a labor dispute faced an order from the court to stop certain activities. The court held a hearing, determined that the union had violated its injunction 72 times, and fined it for the violations. It then announced a set of future fines of up to $100,000 per violent breach of the injunction. The trial court later held a contempt hearing where the court required proof beyond a reasonable doubt but it did not give a jury

---

2. Thanks to Loyola Law School librarian Lisa Schultz for tracking down what appears to be Catena's death record.

trial, holding the union liable for $64 million in fines, with part payable to the companies and part payable to the state. Though the union and companies settled, the state still wanted its $52 million.

The Supreme Court held that the procedure the court used to assess the contempt fines violated due process, because the union was not given full criminal protections. In a confusing opinion that never fully explained the factors the Court used to reach its result — though the Court placed emphasis on the "complex fact finding" involved and the large amount of the fines — it characterized the fines as "criminal" and therefore improperly imposed by the court without adequate criminal procedure protections. (A simpler standard, proposed by Justice Ginsburg in her concurrence, would have found the fines criminal because they were paid to the state, and not to the plaintiff.)

The Supreme Court's *Bagwell* decision means that in certain cases involving civil contempt, courts are going to have to give criminal procedure protections to defendants. But which cases? The United States Court of Appeals for the Tenth Circuit gave its answer to that question in F.T.C. v. *Kuykendall*, 371 F.3d 745 (10th Cir. 2004) (en banc). The en banc court rejected the idea that "high-end" civil contempt awards or complex facts triggered additional criminal procedure protections for defendants charged with civil contempt. The case itself involved civil *compensatory* contempt, not civil *coercive* contempt, but its language applies to both types of contempt. Stating that the main question after *Bagwell* was "whether the contempt of which the defendants were accused is criminal or civil in nature" (how helpful is that?), the court declined to set forth a general explanation of *Bagwell*'s test. Instead, the Tenth Circuit announced a bright-line rule that "where the sanctions sought in contempt proceedings are solely to be used to compensate injured consumers, the proceedings are civil in nature." Id. at 752. And in the civil contempt hearing, "because this case was one for civil, compensatory sanctions, the burden of proof is clear and convincing evidence as to liability and preponderance of the evidence as to damages. We affirm the district court's resolution of evidentiary issues." Id. at 767.

After *Bagwell* and *Kuykendall*, many open questions remain about which "civil" contempt proceedings are really "criminal" and which protections apply in such cases.

Example 2

Carrie and Donald are divorced, and have a child, Emily. The court had awarded custody of Emily to Carrie; Donald had weekend visitation rights. The divorce was very bitter. At the end of one weekend, Donald did not show up to return Emily to Carrie. The court orders Donald to disclose the location of Emily. Donald later states that he does not know where Emily is, though airline records show he visited Canada over the weekend when Emily went missing. May the court use civil coercive contempt to get Donald to reveal Emily's location?

Explanation

The court must first make a credibility determination that Donald in fact knows Emily's location and is lying about not knowing it. If the court makes such a determination, it certainly can try to use civil coercive contempt to get Donald to reveal the location. Whether or not he can be coerced is unclear.

Sometimes a contemnor's cooperation is not required. If there is information about where Emily is located outside the United States, an international convention to which the United States is a signatory and federal law provide for the return of children improperly taken across international boundaries. *See* Scott M. Smith, *Construction and Application of International Child Abduction Remedies Act* (42 U.S.C. §§ 11601 *et seq.*), 125 A.L.R. Fed. 217 (1995).

What if Donald honestly does not know where Emily is? In that case, of course, he would be *unable* (rather than *unwilling*) to comply with the court's order. If Donald does not know Emily's location, he cannot legally be held by the court. The question is whether Donald can convince the court of that fact. The example shows that in these circumstances, we place a great deal of confidence in the trial court's ability to make a credibility determination — staking a defendant's personal freedom on it.

Example 3

Jake operated an "adult" business featuring nude dancing. The City of Coates passed a zoning ordinance barring its operation. Jake filed a declaratory judgment action (see Chapter 16) asking the court for a declaration that the zoning ordinance violated the First Amendment. The City counterclaimed, requesting an injunction barring Jake from operating the business in violation of zoning laws. The court held the ordinance was constitutional and issued the injunction barring Jake from operating a "sexually oriented business" in violation of the zoning ordinance, and requiring that Jake pay $1,000 per day for violating the injunction going forward. Jake closed his nude dancing business and reopened it a few days later with "lap dancers" who were fully clothed. Jake operated the business for 68 days, and the court at a contempt hearing fined him $68,000. Assume the court found that this conduct violated the terms of the injunction. Is this fine civil coercive contempt or criminal contempt (in which case Jake was entitled to criminal procedure protections, including the right to a jury trial)?

Explanation

This example is based upon *Jake's, Ltd. v. City of Coates*, 356 F.3d 896 (8th Cir. 2004). Though the fine was intended to coerce Jake's compliance — making it appear to be *civil* coercive contempt — the Eighth Circuit read *Bagwell* as requiring the court to give Jake's additional criminal procedure protections, including the right to a jury trial. "First, the injunction was complex, in that it enjoined Jake's from conducting any type of sexually-oriented business prohibited by the ordinances, not just the live nude dancing that Jake's had admitted was a sexually-oriented business in raising its First Amendment challenge." *Id.* at 902-903. Second, "the $68,000 fine imposed by the second contempt order was far different from this type of coercive remedy. The fine was substantial, it was payable into court, rather than to compensate the City, and it was 'determinate and unconditional,' that is, not capable of being purged."[3] *Id.* at 903.

Though the court was purportedly applying the two factors of *Bagwell*, the second part of its analysis is odd. After all, isn't what the court says about the fines applicable to any fines imposed to coerce compliance, when looked at after the fact?

It is unclear whether this case, and *Kuykendall*, ultimately will require all coercive contempt fines paid to the court to be governed by criminal procedure protections.

10.3 CRIMINAL CONTEMPT

Criminal contempt punishes the contemnor for past actions. This, too, is the stuff of the movies. Think of the classic movie "My Cousin Vinny" and the judge holding Vinny in contempt for being disrespectful to the judge:

> **Judge Haller**: I don't like your attitude.
> **Vinny**: So what else is new?
> **Judge Haller**: I'm holding you in contempt of court.
> **Vinny** [to Bill]: Now there's a f***ing surprise.
> **Judge Haller**: What did you say? What did you just say?
> **Vinny**: Huh? What did I say?[4]

---

3. The court suggested that Jake's may have had a good argument that the injunction was unconstitutionally vague, an argument that Jake's did not raise below and the court therefore did not address. It also suggested the injunction violated Fed. R. Civ. P. 65's prohibition on incorporating other documents — in this case, the zoning ordinance.
4. MY COUSIN VINNY (20th Century–Fox 1992).

Not much process is due when a court punishes for such "petty contempt": when committed in the presence of the court, it can be punished summarily. As the Supreme Court explained in *Bagwell*, "The necessity justification for the contempt authority is at its pinnacle, of course, where contumacious conduct threatens a court's immediate ability to conduct its proceedings, such as where a witness refuses to testify, or a party disrupts the court. . . . Thus, petty, direct contempts in the presence of the court traditionally have been subject to summary adjudication, 'to maintain order in the courtroom and the integrity of the trial process' in the face of an 'actual obstruction of justice.' . . . In light of the court's substantial interest in rapidly coercing compliance and restoring order, and because the contempt's occurrence before the court reduces the need for extensive fact-finding and the likelihood of an erroneous deprivation, summary proceedings have been tolerated."

When the court uses contempt to punish a defendant for alleged violations outside the court's presence,[5] criminal procedure protections are required. *See* Dobbs § 2.8(4). Often, an independent prosecutor will be appointed to prosecute the case, where the prosecution will have to prove *beyond a reasonable doubt* that the defendant *willfully violated* the court's order.[6]

In cases involving jail time of over six months, or large enough fines, defendants accused of criminal contempt have the right to a trial by jury. How large does the fine have to be? In footnote 5 of *Bagwell*, the Court wrote that a jury trial was required for "serious criminal contempt fines." It noted that it had held in an earlier case that no jury trial was necessary in a case imposing a $10,000 fine on a union, and that a federal statute defining "petty offenses" required a jury trial for amounts over $5,000. The precise amount triggering the right to a jury trial remains uncertain.

Civil coercive contempt and criminal contempt are not mutually exclusive. A contemnor such as Gerardo Catena who is released from civil coercive contempt after a finding that imprisonment was no longer coercive could later face *criminal contempt* as punishment for willfully violating the court's order. Laycock provides a real-world example of a court following civil coercive contempt with criminal contempt: "Susan McDougal, the much publicized defiant witness who refused to testify in Kenneth Starr's

---

5. *Bagwell* requires additional procedure even for some petty contempts: "If a court delays punishing a direct contempt until the completion of trial, for example, due process requires that the contemnor's rights to notice and a hearing be respected."

6. Dobbs explains: "In criminal as distinct from civil cases, the burden of proof is on the prosecution to show beyond a reasonable doubt that the defendant was guilty. Guilt requires an intent to violate the order and an ability to comply, so the prosecution must also show that the defendant had the ability to comply and that he wilfully violated the decree." Dobbs, § 2.8(4), pp. 204-205.

investigation of President Clinton, served the full 18 months in coercive contempt. Then she was charged with criminal contempt and obstruction of justice; the jury acquitted on obstruction and hung on contempt." LAYCOCK p. 782.

Example 4

After a hearing on the merits in the Oscar-Pnina dispute, the court determines that Pnina breached the contract, that Oscar is suffering irreparable injury by Pnina's failure to deliver the widget, and that Oscar is therefore entitled to an order of specific performance. The trial court orders Pnina to produce the widget for Oscar no later than January 1. Pnina does not produce the widget. On January 10, the court holds another hearing, and threatens Pnina with fines of $100 for the first day she is late after January 10 in producing the widget for Oscar, with fines doubling each day thereafter, until she produces the widget. Suppose Pnina comes to court on January 15, having not produced the widget. The judge fines her $3,100 for the first five days ($100 + $200 + $400 + $800 + $1,600). He then gives her five more days to produce the widget. He tells her that if she does not, the court will impose an additional fine, this time a punishment for noncompliance. On January 20, Pnina comes back to court. She tells the judge she is trying to produce the widget as fast as she can, but she does not have it ready yet. The court then finds beyond a reasonable doubt that Pnina failed to produce the widget as she promised in the contract, and fines her an additional $7,000. How may Pnina defend herself against the second fine? Does she have a defense to imposition of the first fine? If the fines are upheld and she later produces the widget, does she get her money back?

Explanation

Pnina probably has some good arguments against imposition of the second fine. This fine ($7,000) looks to be punitive (though certainly it was aimed in part at coercing Pnina's compliance). If the fine is criminal, it is necessary to find beyond a reasonable doubt that Pnina willfully disobeyed the court's order. Note, however, that the court did not make such a finding. Instead, the finding was only that Pnina had disobeyed the court's order beyond a reasonable doubt. Without willfulness, Pnina cannot face a criminal punishment. Moreover, because of the size of the fine involved, she could be entitled to a jury trial if the court determines that a "serious" fine is involved. A $7,000 fine against an individual may or may not be a large enough criminal fine to trigger the right to a jury trial.

The first fine ($3,100) looks like an amount intended to coerce performance rather than to punish. A court would likely conclude it is coercive, not punitive, and therefore criminal procedures likely would not apply. The standard is not proof beyond a reasonable doubt, but is instead a lower, "clear and convincing evidence" standard.

But if Pnina can prove that she was *unable* to comply with the court's order (because she was trying to produce the widget but simply could not do so), the coercive fine appears improper. This will require a credibility determination by the court. However, if Pnina inadvertently violated the injunction — imagine that she negligently failed to have the widget, which had been completed, delivered on time — she could be liable for civil contempt, which does not require willfulness.

Pnina cannot get her money back if she eventually complies with the court's order. But note that the payment of a civil coercive contempt fine after compliance is no longer motivating future compliance. On the back end, the civil coercive contempt fine looks as much like punishment as a criminal contempt fine imposed by the court.

Example 5

Judy, a newspaper reporter, refuses to reveal to the federal grand jury the "source" who leaked confidential information to her. She is jailed for civil coercive contempt until such time as she reveals the source. She tells the judge she will never reveal the source, and demands a jury trial on grounds that she is going to remain in jail for more than 6 months. (Recall that in federal court, the coercive contempt for failing to testify before a grand jury can last for only 18 months.) Does she get the right to a jury trial?

Explanation

Judy does not get the right to a jury trial. Remember that this is coercive contempt aimed at getting Judy to comply with the court order to testify; it is not about punishing her. Judy "holds the keys to the jailhouse door" in her pocket, meaning she can be out in less than 6 months if she agrees to testify.

This again points out some of the ironies of distinguishing among the types of contempt. Judy may spend up to 18 months in jail, without getting all of the criminal protections such as the right to a jury trial. But someone who faces only 6 months in jail for *criminal* contempt gets full criminal procedures, including the right to a jury trial. For Judy to be in jail for 18 months will feel like punishment even if the court's purpose is to coerce her testimony.

10.4 CIVIL COMPENSATORY CONTEMPT

"Compensatory contempt is a money reward for the plaintiff when the defendant has injured the plaintiff by violating the injunction." Doug Rendleman, *Compensatory Contempt: Plaintiff's Remedy When a Defendant Has Violated an Injunction*, 1980 U. Ill. L. F. 971. In this way, compensatory contempt is more like damages than like an injunction. As Rendleman explains, "Courts utilize compensatory contempt to restore the plaintiff as nearly as possible to the original position." *Id.* at 972. If that sounds familiar, it is because it mirrors the purpose of compensatory damages discussed in Part I of this book. The difference is that compensatory contempt looks at a more limited time frame, awarding only the measurable damages occurring between the time the court enters the injunction and the time the defendant complies with the injunction.

Thus, if Pnina fails to comply with the specific performance order and her delay in complying with the injunction costs Oscar $40,000 in lost profits, compensatory contempt allows Oscar to recover those lost profits. Unlike the other forms of contempt, the money here goes to the plaintiff, not to the court. It is also retrospective, based upon damages for the finite period between the time of the injunction and the contempt finding. It does not apply to damages incurred prior to the issuance of the injunction.

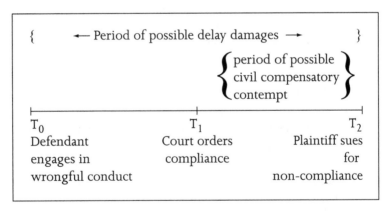

Figure 10.1

Figure 10.1 contrasts civil compensatory contempt with delay damages. At T_0, the defendant engages in the wrongful conduct. In our current example, this is the time when Pnina fails to deliver the widget at the time promised. At time T_1, the court issues an order of specific performance requiring the defendant to comply. In this case, the court orders Pnina to deliver the widget. At time T_2, plaintiff sues for non-compliance. In jurisdictions allowing for civil compensatory contempt, Oscar can seek damages that accrued during the T_1-T_2 period (but he cannot seek damages for the T_0-T_1 period).

In jurisdictions in which civil compensatory contempt is unavailable, Oscar can seek delay damages for the T_0-T_2 period.[7] From the entire period of T_0 to T_2, Oscar has suffered additional damages because of Pnina's delay in complying.

Rendleman has noted the "irony" of civil compensatory contempt: the court has awarded an injunction because, under the irreparable injury rule, it has determined that damages are not an adequate remedy for the plaintiff. Yet the injunction did not work to keep the plaintiff in the rightful position, and so damages are awarded for that purpose.

The way of resolving the irony is recognizing that the monetary award through civil compensatory contempt is a second-best solution. The plaintiff's first choice is compliance with the injunction. Plaintiff's second choice is this set of damages.

Finally, awarding such damages does not mean that the injunction issued was not necessary. To see this point, let's say that when Pnina fails to deliver the widget as promised (a widget that was not available from another seller for some time), Oscar had to close his factory, sustaining $30,000 in losses. At that point, the court could issue a judgment holding Pnina liable for $30,000 in damages for the delay and ordering Pnina to turn the widget over to Oscar immediately. When Pnina has not done so a week later, Oscar suffers another $40,000 in damages. The civil compensatory contempt remedy allows Oscar to recover those damages. But that still does not put Oscar in the rightful position. Pnina must turn over the widget, or Oscar will continue to pile on damages. Thus, the injunction, which ultimately forces Pnina to turn over the widget, working with delay damages and civil compensatory contempt, keeps Oscar in the rightful position.

Although civil compensatory contempt is no different in concept from delay damages (just measured in a narrower time period after the court issues the injunction), there is no right to a jury trial to recover these damages; instead they are proven before a judge, in some jurisdictions using a "clear and convincing evidence" standard. Id. at 978. Because civil compensatory contempt would deprive defendants of a jury trial to seek damages, some jurisdictions do not allow plaintiffs to seek such damages through contempt, and instead require a separate action for further delay damages. Id. at 983-984.

Plaintiff does get one advantage in some jurisdictions by using the contempt route to collect these damages: the court can use coercive techniques such as threats of imprisonment or additional fines to require

---

7. As a matter of civil procedure, a request for delay damages may need to accompany the demand for specific performance; res judicata principles may preclude a later demand for such damages. See Mycogen Corp. v. Monsanto Co., 51 P.3d 297 (Cal. 2002).

compliance with the order. In contrast, as we shall see in Chapter 17, ordinary money judgments generally are not collectible through a court order.[8]

Example 6

A slight variation on the Oscar-Pnina example: Pnina fails to deliver the widget as promised (a widget that would not be available to Oscar from another seller for some time), causing Oscar to close his factory and sustain $30,000 in losses. His lawyer brings suit, asking only for an injunction ordering Pnina to turn over the widget. After trial, the court orders Pnina to turn over the widget, and Pnina does so immediately. Can Oscar recover the $30,000 as civil compensatory contempt?

Explanation

No. Oscar cannot recover these damages because Oscar did not sustain them as a result of Pnina violating the injunction. These were damages from the delay in performance that occurred *before* the issuance of the injunction. Pnina turned over the widget immediately after it issued, so there are *no* damages that Oscar may recover through civil coercive contempt.

Oscar should be entitled to the $30,000 in delay damages (to bring him back to the rightful position, along with the injunction), but not through a contempt proceeding. In many jurisdictions, however, Oscar's request for delay damages needs to be brought as part of his underlying suit for breach of contract against Pnina. Under civil procedure principles of *res judicata*, an action for delay damages must accompany a request for specific performance. A lawyer who fails to sue for delay damages along with a request for specific performance could be committing malpractice.

Example 7

You are Oscar's lawyer. In addition to the losses in Example 6, Oscar has suffered $40,000 in delay damages because of Pnina's failure to comply with the injunction. In your jurisdiction, you have a choice between bringing an ancillary action for civil compensatory contempt to collect these damages or initiating a separate damages proceeding. Which do you prefer?

---

8. Some courts allow plaintiffs to recover defendants' gains — a restitutionary measure, not a compensatory measure — through civil compensatory contempt.

Explanation

The answer to this question will turn on any salient differences between the two procedures in the jurisdiction. For example, if you believe Oscar would benefit from a jury trial and a lower "preponderance of the evidence" standard, you might be better off with a separate damages action. On the other hand, if you believe the additional money would be difficult to collect through usual damage collection measures, you could well prefer the contempt route. Another factor to consider is any state law or contractual provision in the Oscar-Pnina contract governing the availability of attorney's fees.

10.5 THE COLLATERAL BAR RULE (MORE ON CRIMINAL CONTEMPT)

Recall Example 3, in which Jake seeks a declaratory judgment that the city's zoning law prohibiting his operation of an "adult" business is unconstitutional. If Jake violates the city's zoning law and the law is in fact struck down as unconstitutional, Jake cannot be lawfully prosecuted for violating the zoning law. Indeed, if Jake were criminally prosecuted for violating the zoning, he could defend himself against that criminal prosecution by raising the unconstitutionality of the law as a defense.[9]

In contrast, imagine that the trial court declares the zoning law *constitutional*, and it issues an injunction barring Jake from operating his business in violation of the injunction. Jake appeals the trial court's issuance of the injunction to the appellate court. If he disobeys the trial court's order while the appeal is pending, thereby violating the injunction, he can be found liable and punished for *criminal contempt*. Suppose the appellate court later holds that the trial court erred, and in fact the injunction violated the Constitution. Can Jake defend himself in the criminal contempt prosecution by raising the unconstitutionality of the injunction as a defense?

The answer is no, and the doctrine used to explain this concept is the *collateral bar rule*: "One who disobeys an injunctive order that is later reversed on appeal for error may be held in criminal contempt for the disobedience in spite of the reversal." DOBBS, § 2.8(6), p. 213. It is called the *collateral* bar rule because the rule prevents a litigant from attacking the validity of an

---

9. Though Jake could go to state or federal court seeking a declaratory judgment that the city's zoning law is unconstitutional, federal courts will not entertain such suits once the state has begun a criminal prosecution. *See Younger v. Harris*, 401 U.S. 37 (1971). More on this issue in Chapter 16.3.

injunction in the collateral matter of a defense to a criminal prosecution. The appropriate course of action suggested by the collateral bar rule is a *direct appeal* of the order granting the injunction. Jake should have waited for the outcome of the appeal.

Note the contrast between the first and second of these scenarios. In the first scenario, Jake's claim of unconstitutionality trumps a legislatively enacted law. In the second, Jake's claim of unconstitutionality *does not trump* a court-issued injunction. Why the difference?

The Supreme Court explained and defended the collateral bar rule in *Walker v. City of Birmingham*, 388 U.S. 307 (1967), a case arising out of a civil rights march (including Dr. Martin Luther King, Jr.) planned for Good Friday in Birmingham, Alabama. A state court issued an *ex parte* order (an order without giving notice to the protesters of the right to be heard in opposition) barring the demonstration, but the marchers marched anyway. When they were later put on trial for criminal contempt, the marchers raised the unconstitutionality of the court's order. The courts held that the collateral bar rule prevented raising the defense.

The Supreme Court justified the rule as one that preserved the power of the courts and indeed civilization itself:

> The rule of law that Alabama followed in this case reflects a belief that in the fair administration of justice no man can be judge in his own case, however exalted his station, however righteous his motives, and irrespective of his race, color, politics, or religion. This Court cannot hold that the petitioners were constitutionally free to ignore all the procedures of the law and carry their battle to the streets. One may sympathize with the petitioners' impatient commitment to their cause. But respect for judicial process is a small price to pay for the civilizing hand of law, which alone can give abiding meaning to constitutional freedom.

Id. at 320-321. The Court suggested the more appropriate procedure would have been for the protesters to obey the injunction and seek immediate appellate relief in the Alabama courts. Indeed, the court suggested that if such a claim had been met with "delay or frustration," the protesters perhaps could have violated the injunction without facing criminal penalties.

The Supreme Court in dicta also mentioned two other possible exceptions to the collateral bar rule beyond "delay or frustration" in attacking the underlying injunction:

- *Court lacks jurisdiction over controversy.* If a court lacks jurisdiction over a controversy, the collateral bar rule does not apply. But a court has jurisdiction to check its own jurisdiction, and an order issued while the court is determining its own jurisdiction is valid.

- Injunction is transparently invalid or has only a "frivolous pretense to validity." When a court issues an order that is obviously invalid, it may be ignored. In theory, but not in practice, this may be a large loophole. The order issued in *Walker* looked to be blatantly unconstitutional (the *Walker* Court itself noted that "[t]he breadth and vagueness of the injunction itself would also unquestionably be subject to substantial constitutional question"). But the Court did not apply the "transparently invalid" exception to the injunction in *Walker*. If it did not apply there, it is not clear when it would apply.

Some have criticized the collateral bar rule and its exceptions as being inconsistent in preserving the integrity of the courts and not sufficiently protective of other constitutional values.[10] Why, for example, should the collateral bar rule apply when the court issues an unconstitutional (but not transparently invalid) order but not apply when the court is without jurisdiction to issue its order? Is jurisdiction more important than preserving the First Amendment?

Example 8

In the Oscar-Pnina case, a court orders Pnina to produce the widget for Oscar by January 1. Pnina does not do so, and on January 15 the court determines that Pnina's delay in complying with the court's order has cost Oscar $10,000 in additional damages. The court awards Oscar $10,000 in civil compensatory contempt. Pnina does not pay, arguing that the court was wrong in the first place in ordering specific performance. An appellate court then reverses in the underlying case, holding that Oscar, not Pnina, breached the contract, and that therefore Pnina does not have to produce the widget. Can Oscar still collect the $10,000 under the collateral bar rule?

Explanation

No. The collateral bar rule applies only to criminal contempt, and Oscar's award comes from civil compensatory contempt. The purpose of the rule is to protect the integrity of the courts, and allowing Oscar to recover would be giving a private plaintiff the benefit of an erroneously issued injunction rather than protecting that integrity.

---

10. For an early critical view, see Doug Rendleman, *More on Void Orders*, 7 GA. L. REV. 246 (1973).

Example 9

BigCorp sues MegaCorp in federal court for an injunction blocking MegaCorp from selling its handheld "Blueberry" PDA, which BigCorp alleges violates certain patents that it holds. MegaCorp makes a special appearance in court arguing that the court never acquired personal jurisdiction over the company. The court issues a temporary restraining order enjoining MegaCorp from selling the "Blueberry" while the court examines the jurisdictional question. MegaCorp violates the order by selling the "Blueberry," and is charged with criminal contempt. The court then holds that indeed it has no personal jurisdiction over MegaCorp and dismisses Big-Corp's suit. Can MegaCorp defend itself at the criminal contempt trial on grounds that the trial court lacked personal jurisdiction over it?

Explanation

No. As noted, a court always has jurisdiction to determine jurisdiction. MegaCorp had to obey the trial court's order or seek an emergency ruling from the appellate courts on the jurisdictional question, perhaps through appeal of a motion to dissolve the TRO.

Example 10

A group of medical facilities and doctors who provide reproductive health care services commenced suit on March 22, 2012, against 68 defendants, including Gerald and Michael, for various state and federal charges related to blocking access to abortion clinics. The plaintiffs sought a TRO and preliminary injunction to establish limited buffer zones around abortion facilities to prevent the defendants from engaging in illegal activities designed to disrupt access to those abortion facilities. On April 15, the trial court issued a TRO against the 68 defendants barring them from being present within a "buffer zone" around certain reproductive health clinics. At an April 29 status conference, the court, over the objection of the defendants, extended the TRO pending a trial on a preliminary injunction. On May 18, Gerald and Michael protested within one of the "buffer zones" around a protected clinic. They believed the TRO was unconstitutionally vague and a violation of their First Amendment rights. If Gerald and Michael are charged with criminal contempt for violating the TRO, do they have any defense?

Explanation

This example is based upon In re Criminal Contempt Proceedings Against Gerald Crawford and Michael Warren, 329 F.3d 131 (2d Cir. 2003). The collateral bar rule appears to bar Gerald and Michael's defense. A TRO is a kind of injunction. Parties must obey it in the same way that they would have to obey a preliminary or permanent injunction. It is no defense that Gerald and Michael believe the TRO violates their constitutional rights. Unless the order is "transparently invalid" or issued with only a "frivolous pretense of validity" (which did not apply to the apparently invalid order in Walker), litigants must obey it. Nor is there a question about the court's jurisdiction over Gerald and Michael. Finally, nothing indicates that they were met by "delay and frustration" in getting a ruling on the merits dissolving the TRO. The strongest argument Gerald and Michael could make against contempt is that the TRO dissolved after (at most) 28 days under Fed. R. Civ. P. 65, meaning they were not violating any order at the time they acted. Though there is a Supreme Court case that supports this view, Granny Goose Foods, Inc. v. Brotherhood of Teamsters and Auto Truck Drivers Local No. 70, 415 U.S. 423, 442-443 (1974) (suggesting that TROs of undisclosed duration dissolve after the 28-day [then a 20-day] period), most courts now appear to follow the Supreme Court's view in Sampson v. Murray, 415 U.S. 61 (1974), that TROs lasting more than 20 days [now 28 days] morph into appealable preliminary injunctions. In the actual case that this example illustrates, it was significant to the Second Circuit that in Sampson and in the case before it, but not in Granny Goose Foods, the defendants had notice that the TRO was being extended and had the opportunity to move to dissolve the TRO. In the actual case, the Second Circuit held it was proper to try Gerald and Michael for violating the TRO. (For more on these issues involving TROs, see Chapter 9.4.)

10.6 CONTEMPT AND THIRD PARTIES

We have already seen in Chapter 8.3 that courts may direct only "minor and ancillary" orders against third parties (that is, non-parties to the lawsuit or parties to the lawsuit who have not been adjudicated as wrongdoers).[11] But can a third party be held in contempt for violating a minor and ancillary order? Fed. R. Civ. P. 65(d)(2) provides that injunctions may be binding only on people with actual notice of the court's order[12] who are either parties, parties' officers, agents, servants, employees, attorneys, or persons who are

---

11. Third parties may be burdened by injunctions somewhat more substantially, as Chapter 8.3 discussed.

12. Notice of the order here is in contrast to notice of the hearing at which the court issues the order. We consider the latter point below.

in active concert or participation with parties or their agents. Thus, at least some third parties may be held in contempt for violating a court order.

Even without the express statutory provision, notice seems required as a matter of constitutional due process; otherwise someone could be charged with contempt for violating an order she knew nothing about. Second, notice is required as an element of proof of the criminal contempt: one cannot be held criminally liable for contempt without proof of a willful violation of a court's order; one cannot willfully disobey an order one knows nothing about.

A somewhat more difficult question is whether a court may hold a third party in contempt for violating a court order if that person was not an officer, agent, employee, or attorney of a party, or in active concert or participation with a party. The leading case in the affirmative is *United States v. Hall*, 472 F.2d 261 (5th Cir. 1972). In *Hall*, a federal district court enjoined everyone from entering the grounds of a certain high school except for limited purposes listed in the order. This order was part of a larger desegregation suit. Eric Hall was not a party to the lawsuit but he was served with the court order, and charged with criminal contempt when he entered the school grounds apparently to "prevent the normal operation of [the school] through student boycotts and other activities." Id. at 263.

The Fifth Circuit held that Hall could be charged with contempt even though he did not meet any of the criteria of Fed. R. Civ. P. 65(d). The *Hall* court held that the court had an inherent power to issue the order against Hall, because his activities "imperiled the court's fundamental power to make a binding adjudication between the parties properly before it." Id. at 265. The court also supported its ruling by noting the power of courts to issue in rem injunctions: "Federal courts have issued injunctions binding on all persons, regardless of notice, who come into contact with property which is the subject of a judicial decree." Id. at 265-266. In rem jurisdiction is not mentioned in Rule 65, but it existed before Rule 65 and the *Hall* court held that courts retained the inherent power to issue such injunctions.

The Fifth Circuit sidestepped a due process argument raised by Hall. As we saw in Chapter 9.4, constitutional due process requires that notice of the hearing at which a TRO is to be issued be given to the adverse party, absent some good excuse for not giving notice. Though Hall had notice of the court's order after it issued and before he violated it, he was not given notice of the court's hearing at which the order was issued (nor was there any reason offered why Hall was not given notice so as to satisfy Rule 65(b)). The court held that the order was properly classified as a TRO without notice because it was violated within four days of its issuance.[13] That may well be true, but it

---

13. As we saw in the last chapter, Rule 65(b) limits the length of TROs issued without notice to 10 days, though such an order may be extended for an additional 10 days in appropriate circumstances.

did not answer the constitutional objection to binding Hall to the order without giving him a chance to be heard before the order issued.

Hall's reach is unclear. Some courts have expressed skepticism about holding third parties not named in Rule 65(d) in criminal contempt for violating court orders. *See, e.g., Planned Parenthood Golden Gate v. Garibaldi*, 132 Cal. Rptr. 2d 46 (App. 2003); *Doctor's Associates, Inc. v. Reinert & Duree, P.C.*, 191 F.3d 297 (2d Cir. 1999). But *Hall* continues to be cited by courts for the principle that in certain cases third parties may be held in contempt for violating court orders.

Example 11

Same facts as in the *Hall* case, but imagine that Hall's friend, Oates, was neither named in the trial court's order nor served with a copy of it. Oates heard about the order of the district court (which prohibited everyone from entering school grounds except for limited, enumerated purposes) from Hall. Oates too went onto campus to arrange student protests and was charged with criminal contempt for violating the court's order. Can Oates be held liable for criminal contempt?

Explanation

Oates may raise two arguments against holding him in contempt. First, he may argue that the court must single him out for treatment by either giving him notice of the hearing, listing him as bound in the order, or personally serving him with the order. That line of argument divided a panel of the Second Circuit in *U.S. v. Paccione*, 964 F.2d 1269 (2d Cir. 1992). A majority held that a third party could be held liable for criminal contempt so long as he had actual notice of the order; it was not necessary that the third party be listed on the order or served with it. A dissenting judge disagreed, holding that at the very least the order by its terms had to apply to non-parties or that the non-party had to be acting in concert with defendants in the lawsuit. In the Hall and Oates example, it is possible that they were acting in active concert. If the court has authority to bind Hall, even if he is a third party, perhaps it could bind Oates as well, though that appears to be beyond what the text of Rule 65 allows.

The other argument Oates may raise is that he needed to receive some kind of official notice of the court's order, rather than informally hearing about it from his friend, Hall. That argument is likely to fail. Fed. R. Civ. P. 65(d)(2) provides for actual notice "by personal service *or otherwise*" (emphasis added).

Example 12

Nina, Pnina's sister, learns that Pnina has been ordered to turn over the widget to Oscar immediately. Nina knows Pnina does not want to do so. Without talking to Pnina about it but knowing her sister would likely approve, Nina sneaks into Pnina's factory and hides the widget. She won't tell Pnina where it is, and Pnina honestly tells the judge that she does not know where the widget is, and therefore she cannot turn it over. Can Nina be held for criminal contempt?

Explanation

The order is binding on Pnina, as well as upon her agents and those in active concert or participation with Pnina who have actual notice of the court's order. In this case, Nina has actual notice of the court's order: she knows that the court has ordered Pnina to turn over the widget. The case turns on whether the court could call Nina an "agent" or someone working in "active concert" with Pnina. In this case, it appears that Nina was working independently of Pnina to save Pnina from complying with the court's order. But the court may not believe it; it may be tempting to ask your sibling to help you out of a jam, and that's just what it looks like here (even if that is not in fact what happened). Even if Nina is working independently, perhaps the court, following *Hall*, could also order Nina to turn over the widget in order to effectuate its judgment and hold Nina in contempt if she fails to do so.

In any case, even if the court could not punish Nina criminally for contempt, it arguably could require Nina to appear in court to reveal the location of the widget. That appears to be a "minor and ancillary" order to a third party. Nina, of course, would have to receive notice of both the hearing and the order. If at that point Nina refuses to comply, she could be held in civil coercive contempt until she agreed to reveal the location of the widget. Recall that Gerardo Catena was a witness who was held in contempt for five years for refusing to testify with his grant of immunity.

PART III

Restitution

No Gain, No Pain: Restitution and the Unjust Enrichment Principle

11.1 INTRODUCTION TO RESTITUTION

In a classic *Saturday Night Live* television commercial parody, a husband and wife argue over whether a new product, "Shimmer," is a floor wax or a dessert topping. Announcer Chevy Chase proclaims that it is *both*, spraying some on the wife's mop and some on the husband's butterscotch pudding, to which the couple proclaim: "Tastes terrific . . . and just look at that shine!"

Restitution is a lot like "Shimmer"—not because it is the "greatest shine you've ever tasted"—but because it has two different functions. Restitution functions as both a *substantive area* of the law (much like torts and contracts) in cases in which a plaintiff would have no other remedy, and as an alternative *remedy* for certain tort and contract breaches. In this way, it is unlike any of the other remedies we consider in this book. And it is what makes the material tricky for students. *See* RESTATEMENT OF THE LAW THIRD: RESTITUTION AND UNJUST ENRICHMENT ("RTR"), ch. 7, Introductory Note ("The awkwardness of using the word 'restitution' to identify both a claim based on unjust enrichment and the corresponding remedy means that this simple division of the overall subject matter is not always apparent from its terminology.").

What do I mean by cases in which a plaintiff would have no other remedy? Consider this true example. A friend of mine—a law professor—went to close a bank account that held $1,250. When the bank gave her the check for the balance of her account, a bank employee made an error (most likely hitting the "00" rather than the "0" key), and the check arrived for $125,000. My friend naturally returned the check (wouldn't you?), asking for the bank to cut a new check in the proper amount. But suppose she had not returned the $125,000 check, and had instead cashed it and put the $125,000 in her safe. The bank could not sue my friend for breach of contract (there was no contractual obligation to return mistakenly paid monies) or for tort (her actions may not meet the substantive test for conversion or any other tort). Restitution provides the *substantive basis* for the bank's suit to seek return of the excess paid ($125,000 paid less the $1,250 it actually owed). To allow my friend to keep the extra $123,750 would *unjustly enrich* her at the expense of the bank.

This bank check example shows how restitution can provide a cause of action when there is no other as a means of preventing unjust enrichment. Additionally, restitution can also provide a basis for a remedy measured by defendant's gain in a torts or contracts suit *when damages are also available as an alternative.* Suppose Anita steals Brianna's digital camera, worth $200. Anita sells it to a pawnshop for $150, and she bets the money at the racetrack. Anita wins at the track, and the $150 is now worth $1,000. When Brianna sues Anita for the tort of conversion (the appropriate tort for this kind of theft), she would ask for damages of around $200.[1]

The law, however, would allow Brianna the alternative restitutionary remedy measured by Anita's gains: $1,000. Naturally, Brianna would prefer this remedy to a claim for damages. As we will see in Chapter 13, the law will allow Brianna to trace "her" property, from the camera to the cash from the pawnshop to the winning tickets at the race track to the cash Anita got from the track in exchange for her winning tickets.

If you learn nothing else from this part of the book, you should know the following two basic points about restitution:

- Restitution is about *unjust enrichment.* Generally speaking, there will be no recovery in restitution absent proof that a defendant has been unjustly enriched. We will need to consider both what it means for a defendant to be *enriched* and when the law terms such enrichment *unjust.*

- As a matter of remedy, restitution gives plaintiff an award based on *defendant's gains* rather than plaintiff's losses. When defendant has no gains, restitution is an inappropriate remedy. When defendant has gains, there may be alternative ways of calculating and awarding the gains that sometimes will be subject to dispute between the parties. Whether a plaintiff may recover a defendant's gains gets complicated when defendant has other creditors and defendant is bankrupt.

---

1. Part I of this book explains the complications involved in computing Brianna's damages.

Restitution is like "Shimmer" in another way. Just like the husband and wife who cannot agree on what Shimmer is and how it should be used, there is a great deal of fundamental disagreement over precisely what restitution is and how it works. For example, among Remedies scholars, there is a debate over whether suits brought to recover defendants' gains in torts or contracts cases are properly considered suits brought under the substantive law of restitution or, rather, are suits in torts or contracts in which restitution is one of a number of possible remedies. *See* James S. Rogers, *Restitution for Wrongs and the Restatement (Third) of the Law of Restitution*, WAKE FOREST L.R. 55 (2007). This debate is not about substance; for example, the two sides would agree that Brianna can recover $1,000 from Anita as a restitutionary recovery. But there is a practical significance to naming the cause of action: depending upon how one answers the question in the jurisdiction, the case either would be pled as an action for conversion, where the plaintiff "waives the tort and sues in *assumpsit*,"[2] or it would be pled as an action under the substantive law of restitution. The characterization could affect the applicable statute of limitations period as well.

There are also debates over other fundamental questions in the field, such as whether the contractual remedies of rescission and reformation are properly considered part of the law of restitution, whether there can ever be a restitutionary remedy without defendant's unjust enrichment, and even over what the field should be named.[3] There's also criminal "restitution," but that is a form of compensation awarded in criminal proceedings that we will ignore in this book. *See* RTR § 1, cmt. *e*.

Part of the reason for the confusion and disagreement is that restitution as a field did not exist historically as a unified substantive body of law (like torts and contracts) or remedy (like damages and injunctions). Instead, courts of law and equity developed a number of doctrines and remedies we would now consider "restitution" across a broad array of categories. You may recall one of these concepts, *quantum meruit*, from your Contracts class. This doctrine allowed those workers who provided labor under an unenforceable contract to recover the reasonable value of their services.

Because these doctrines developed in both law courts and equity courts before the merger of law and equity, some restitutionary remedies are legal while some are equitable. This distinction will matter in a subset of restitution cases, especially when it comes to "tracing" remedies in Chapter 13. In some cases, a plaintiff will seek *specific* restitution in terms of the return of the very thing that was taken from him or her. In other circumstances, the

---

2. This is simply arcane language pointing to the old writ for a restitutionary recovery stating that plaintiff wants to recover defendant's gains, not plaintiff's losses.

3. For some criticism on some of the basic points at issue, *see* Peter B.H. Birks, *A Letter to America: The New Restatement of Restitution*, 3 GLOBAL JURIST FRONTIERS (ISSUE 2) (2003), http://www.bepress.com/gj/frontiers/vol3/iss2/art2.

result of a restitution claim might be a money judgment. Finally, in some circumstances, defendant gets a legal interest in some kind of property.

The modern field of restitution traces its evolution to the first Restatement of Restitution, published in 1937 by the American Law Institute. The second Restatement of Restitution project began in the 1980s, but it was never completed. Drafting of the Third Restatement of Restitution and Unjust Enrichment has just been completed, and it is likely to be influential in how courts approach the topic. This chapter uses as illustrations a number of examples from the new Third Restatement. The examples are useful even if your professor does not cover the Third Restatement. I've put some details about the Third Restatement's treatment of issues into footnotes, which you might wish to skim or to ignore if your professor does not cover the Third Restatement.

The remainder of this chapter focuses on the substantive law of restitution. When is a defendant unjustly enriched so as to allow for a restitutionary remedy? Why is it that the law sometimes allows a plaintiff to recover more than her losses in apparent violation of the rightful position principle first set forth in Chapter 1? Finally, in which torts and contracts cases is it most advantageous for plaintiffs to pursue a restitutionary recovery rather than recover compensatory damages?

Chapters 12 and 13 focus on measuring the extent of defendants' gains in an unjust enrichment action. Chapter 12 considers fundamental issues of measuring gain — such as from whose perspective do we measure defendants' gains? Consider, for example, whether in a *quantum meruit* claim we use the reasonable value of plaintiff's services or the value added to defendant's property. What if the defendant mixes a misappropriated item of plaintiff's with his own to produce something of value? Should there be an apportionment of profits? If so, how should the apportionment be done?

Chapter 13 turns to constructive trusts, equitable liens, and other restitutionary remedies aimed at getting defendants' gains into the hands of plaintiffs. How can equitable restitutionary remedies help plaintiffs to capture gains and to gain a preference when the defendant is bankrupt? This chapter includes materials on "tracing" defendants' gains. Finally, Chapter 14 considers the contractual remedies of rescission and reformation, which, as noted above, are viewed by some scholars as part of the law of restitution.

Example 1

Same facts as in our Anita-Brianna hypothetical, but this time assume that Anita took the $150 and lost all but $50 at the track. Would Brianna prefer a compensatory damages remedy or a restitutionary remedy?

Explanation

Okay, the field of restitution is hard, so I thought I would start out with an easy question. Of course, Brianna would prefer the damages remedy because under these facts, the gains to the defendant are smaller than the losses to the plaintiff. But the example is meant to hammer home a basic idea early on: where restitution is potentially available as a remedy, plaintiffs will prefer it to damages only when the amount of defendant's gain exceeds plaintiff's loss.

Example 2

Same facts as in our law professor–bank hypothetical, but this time, assume that the law professor took all the funds and put the funds in a safe. That safe, along with all of the law professor's other worldly possessions, are destroyed in a fire. Would the bank prefer a damages remedy or a restitutionary remedy?

Explanation

Trick question. Recall that in the bank hypothetical, there is no tort or contract cause of action that the bank could use to recover any damages. The only choice is a restitutionary remedy. The fact that all of the law professor's property is destroyed means that it is going to be very difficult for the bank to collect anything in restitution from the law professor. Still, the bank should at least be able to get a money judgment for $123,750, collectible from the law professor should she have any assets.

Example 3

Carmen steals $1,000 out of Diego's wallet. Carmen has held on to the cash. Does Diego prefer a remedy of tort damages for conversion, or a restitutionary remedy?

Explanation

In these circumstances, Diego is likely indifferent between a damages remedy and a restitutionary remedy because defendant's gains are equal to plaintiff's losses. In particular jurisdictions, there may be reasons to prefer one remedy over another. For example, punitive damages generally may not be awarded unless there is also an award of compensatory damages. (See Chapter 15.) In some jurisdictions, punitive damages are not available for a restitutionary claim. So if Diego has a strong punitive damages claim, he would likely prefer the remedy of damages in those jurisdictions. In addition, there may be different statutes of limitation applicable to the claims. Depending on the timing of the suit, Diego may prefer one cause of action over the other if one of the claims is time-barred.

Example 4

Test your intuition on "unjust" enrichment: Ella goes into sudden cardiac arrest while dining at a restaurant. She is unconscious and alone.

(a) Dr. Felice, a prominent cardiac surgeon, is at the next table. Dr. Felice performs CPR, saving Ella's life. Dr. Felice later sends Ella a bill for $1,000. Should Dr. Felice be able to recover the $1,000, or anything, in restitution?

(b) Same facts as (a), but Felice is not a doctor. She is instead an accountant who took a CPR class a few years back. Should Felice be able to recover the $1,000, or anything, in restitution?

Explanation

The law provides a "right answer" to these questions (as we will see in the next section) in that, generally speaking, the doctor but not the accountant would get to recover for the "reasonable value" of professional emergency services rendered. It is, however, more important for you now to focus on what you think is right. Would it be "unjust" for Ella not to pay anything to Felice the doctor? Should it matter that she is a doctor and not an accountant? If money should be paid in restitution, how should it be valued? Based on Dr. Felice's usual charges? The usual charges in the area? The value to Ella of having her life saved?

Note that we cannot get around these questions through contract law. Because Ella was unconscious, she could not have reasonably assented to assistance from Dr. Felice (nor was there anyone there, such as a spouse, who could consent on her behalf). You might be tempted to say (if you remember something from your Contracts class) the law should treat Ella and Felice *as though* they had a contract. We might call it a *quasi-contract*. Congratulations if you remembered this terminology — but it doesn't solve the problem of defining "unjust" enrichment. "Quasi-contract" is just another term for a restitutionary claim. If the law concludes that Ella should be treated *as though* she had a contract with Felice, it is because of a judgment that it would be unjust enrichment for Ella not to pay anything to Felice. More on these issues in the coming chapters.

11.2 THE MEANING OF "UNJUST ENRICHMENT": WHEN IS RESTITUTION AVAILABLE?

11.2.1 Introduction

Not every wrong by a defendant involves a gain to the defendant. Consider, for example, when Gwen accidentally runs over Horatio's foot with her Maserati, causing Horatio to suffer $10,000 in damages. Gwen's conduct might be sufficiently wrongful to qualify as negligence for purposes of tort law, but Horatio would not consider trying to recover in restitution from Gwen, for the simple reason that Gwen has had no gain from their interaction. No enrichment, no valid claim in restitution.

Similarly, not every gain to a defendant involves unjust conduct. Ivan is drowning in the water and Jane throws him a life preserver, saving Ivan's life. Ivan has gained a great deal, but if Jane sues Ivan for compensation based upon Ivan's gain, Jane's going to lose. As we will see, the law generally provides that good Samaritans do not get compensation for coming to the assistance of a stranger. No *unjust* enrichment, no valid claim in restitution.

The Gwen-Horatio hypothetical is an easier one to understand because it is usually not a problem to ascertain whether or not a defendant has been enriched. In the Ivan-Jane hypothetical, in contrast, courts are going to need to make a *judgment* about when a defendant's enrichment at plaintiff's expense is unjust. That judgment about justice is at the heart of the substantive law of restitution.

This section explores some of the basics of that substantive law. Courses in Remedies vary in their coverage of the substantive law of restitution, with some focusing only on the restitutionary remedies described and analyzed in Chapters 12-14. But this section should be useful even in those courses emphasizing only the remedial aspects of restitution because the available remedies sometimes turn upon understanding the nature of the injustice forming the basis for plaintiff's restitutionary claim.

Putting aside some detail, the next few subsections explain the major types of cases in which courts will find *unjust enrichment* allowing the plaintiffs to recover in restitution.

11.2.2 Benefits Conferred by Mistake

Claims for a restitutionary remedy often result from a mistaken payment or benefit conferred by the plaintiff to the defendant. The bank–law professor hypothetical fits into this category: the law professor had no rightful claim to the money (at least that in excess of the $1,250 owed by the bank), and it would be an easy call for the courts to decide that the law professor would have to return the bank's money.

We would not want to allow *all* mistaken transactions to result in a claim for restitution. The Restatement offers the following simple example of a mistake that would not allow a restitutionary claim: "Believing that her nephew would make good use of it, Donor makes him a gift of Blackacre. Nephew mismanages the property, causing Donor intense regret." RTR § 5, cmt. *b*, illus. 7. The Restatement, consistent with the approach of the courts, would deny Donor the right to undo the transaction under some restitutionary theory.

In deciding which mistakes should provide the basis for a restitutionary claim, the Restatement takes the position that the person transferring the property must make a mistake of fact or law that caused the transfer to take place, and that the transferor does not bear the risk of the mistake. RTR § 5. It is this last term — who bears the risk of the mistake — that allows for applications of principles of justice.

Why does the law professor have to return the money but the nephew gets to keep Blackacre? The doctrinal answer is that the bank did not bear the risk of the mistake while the donor/aunt did bear the risk. That, of course, simply postpones the question of injustice to the risk bearing question.[4]

In making the determination of who bears the risk of the mistake, part of the answer depends upon the transferor's *fault* in making the mistake. But it is more complicated than that. The bank was somewhat at fault in giving the law professor too much money. But carelessness, as in the bank–law professor hypothetical, isn't enough to defeat the bank's claim for restitution. In contrast, Donor's *conscious bad judgment* in making the gift of Blackacre is enough to defeat the restitutionary claim.

The issue may turn upon the *relative* culpability of the parties. If Chauncey the gardener comes to mow Peter's lawn but mistakenly mows Paul's lawn, a court decision whether to allow Chauncey's claim against Paul for restitution (based on the value of the mowing services) could turn on whether Paul knew Chauncey was making a mistake and stood by without letting Chauncey know of the mistake. If Paul knew, restitution for the reasonable

---

4. The Restatement takes the position that this risk could be allocated by an agreement of the parties (express or implied), or to the transferor when the transferor acts "in conscious ignorance of the relevant circumstances." RTR § 5, cmt. *b*(2). Presumably the donor/aunt assumed the risk of the mistake, because she transferred Blackacre without adequately assuring herself that nephew would manage it well.

value of the mowing services could well be available; if Paul did not, a court is more likely to say Chauncey is out of luck.

Assessing relative culpability of the parties appears to matter most in mistake cases involving improvement of real estate. Consider this hypothetical: Ken and Liam are neighbors in a rural area. Making a negligent mistake about their property line, Ken builds a barn on Liam's land — intending to put it on his own land. The barn cost $10,000 to build, and it has increased the value of Liam's property by at least that amount, if not more.

As in the bank–law professor hypothetical, the plaintiff (Ken) has mistakenly conferred a benefit on the defendant (Liam). If it is unjust for the law professor to keep the cash, it seems unjust for Liam to keep the barn. The real estate context, however, creates two problems that do not exist in the law professor–bank hypothetical: problems of *valuation* and problems of *liquidity*.[5]

As to valuation, there may be a gap between objective and subjective valuation. If Ken mistakenly puts a barn on Liam's property, it might increase the property value, but it may have no immediate subjective value to Liam, who has no intention to use the barn or to sell the property in the foreseeable future. As to illiquidity, it could be that the barn adds $20,000 in value to the property, but if Liam has no assets besides the house, it would be quite harsh to force the owner to move to pay for the barn he never wanted.

Because of these problems common to the real estate context, in mistaken improvement cases, the courts may fashion remedies to ensure fairness. For example, a court could delay Ken's compensation for the barn, requiring payment for it only when Liam sells the house.[6]

---

5. As the Restatement explains:

> Valuation is a problem because there is no necessary correlation between the objectively measurable value of an improvement to property and the value actually realized by the owner, which may be limited by subjective factors. Even if the value of an improvement can be stipulated, its relative illiquidity — by comparison to monetary benefits — means that an award of restitution may require the payment of money the owner does not have or would not have chosen to spend.

RTR § 10, cmt. *a*.

6. The Restatement provides that a person who improves the real or personal property of another by mistake may obtain restitution "as necessary to prevent unjust enrichment. A remedy for mistaken improvement that subjects the owner to a forced exchange will be qualified or limited to avoid undue prejudice to the owner." RTR § 10.

As with the "risk of loss" question discussed above, the Restatement test gives courts a great deal of discretion. In this case, courts may look at relative culpability and other factors in deciding whether restitution is "necessary" to prevent "unjust" enrichment. In this context, the Restatement takes the position that good faith, notice, and negligence of the parties are relevant in determining "what constitutes undue prejudice to the owner and substantial justice to the parties." RTR § 10, cmt. *e*. Section 10 also gives courts the ability to fashion a remedy, such as barring plaintiff from forcing the sale of property.

Example 5

Adam's life is insured with Beta Company for $5,000. Carrie is the named beneficiary. The body of a shipwreck victim is identified as that of Adam. Neither Beta Company nor Carrie questions the accuracy of the identification. On receipt of formal proof of Adam's death, Beta Company pays Carrie $5,000. Adam is later discovered alive. May Beta obtain restitution from Carrie for the $5,000 payment?

Explanation

This example appears in RTR § 5, cmt. a, illus. 1. Courts could well reach different conclusions in this case, depending upon how the court decides who should "bear the risk of the mistake" or whose conduct is more culpable. The court also might be swayed by liquidity concerns. At this point, does Carrie still have the money to pay back the insurance company?

For what it's worth, the Restatement takes the position in Illustration 5 that this kind of error results from the kind of mistake that allows for restitution, and we can see that it is much like the payment by the bank to the law professor. Yet this stands in contrast to Illustration 4 in the same Restatement section, involving a similar payment after Adam disappears without explanation. Illustration 4 assumes that the insurer "decides to pay the claim in view of (i) the perceived likelihood that A[dam] is in fact dead, and (ii) the small amount of the policy as compared to the anticipated cost of further investigation and litigation." As in Illustration 5, the insurer pays, and then Adam turns up alive. The Restatement takes the position that in Illustration 7 the insurer acted "in conscious ignorance of the relevant circumstances" and therefore assumed the risk of mistake, thereby taking away the insurer's claim to restitution. It is not clear why the Restatement treats the two cases differently, and the contrast illustrates how courts may well treat similar kinds of cases in very different ways.

Example 6

Maria contracts with Nancy to build a shed on what Maria believes to be Nancy's property. Maria builds the shed at a cost of $5,000, and Nancy has not paid. In fact, Otto is the real owner of the property, and he did not give Nancy permission to have the shed constructed. Otto evicts Nancy, tears down the shed, and sells the land to Penelope. The land contract price was unaffected by the razed shed. May Maria recover the $5,000, or perhaps some other amount, in restitution from Otto?

Explanation

This example too is based upon an illustration in the Restatement, and the answer is no under both the common law and the Restatement. RTR § 10, cmt. g, illus. 17. Remember one of our earliest rules: no restitution without enrichment. In this case, Otto was not enriched by Maria's actions. Otto did not receive any additional funds from Penelope in the sale of the property because of Maria's actions. Maria might have a contractual claim or a claim in restitution against Nancy, but not against Otto.

If Otto had not razed the shed and in fact received additional consideration from Penelope because of the shed, it appears that Maria in this case would be able to get restitution from Otto for the value added by the shed. If Otto had neither razed the shed nor sold his property, the court would have had to decide whether Otto in fact gained by the presence of the shed. If he did receive a benefit, the court would then have to decide both how to value that benefit and whether Otto should be forced to make a payment now. It could be that Maria would get an interest that would allow her to receive the proceeds only upon the eventual sale of Otto's property.

11.2.3 Benefits Conferred by Transferor with Defective Consent or Authority

The preceding section discussed mistaken transfers and the possibility of a restitutionary remedy. The remedies we focused on there concerned monetary damages or the transfer of property. In certain cases of mistakes involving *contracts*, a mistake may provide the basis for the contract's rescission (or cancellation). For example, if Uncle intends to convey to Niece a life estate in Whiteacre but he mistakenly conveys a fee simple, a court may allow the restitutionary remedy of canceling the action.

We'll discuss rescission of contracts in more detail in Chapter 14. For now, though, it is worth looking at the kinds of defective consent or authority that may provide grounds for rescission. These include claims of fraud, innocent material misrepresentation, duress, undue influence, and incapacity.

First, consider fraud. For example, suppose Niece tells Uncle he is signing a promissory note guaranteeing a loan to Niece to pay for schooling expenses. Uncle is in fact signing away his fee interest in Whiteacre. A court will rescind the transaction upon discovery of the fraud, returning Whiteacre to Uncle. If Niece has already sold Whiteacre, Uncle will be able to use restitution to get the proceeds from the sale from Niece. Alternatively, under some circumstances, he might be able to get Whiteacre back from the new purchaser. RTR § 13.

Some courts will even allow restitution in cases of *innocent material misrepresentations*. *Id.* So if Niece honestly believes (and tells Uncle) that Uncle's loan guarantee "isn't binding" on Uncle, the contract might be rescinded because of this innocent, though material (important), misstatement of fact.

Alternatively, suppose Niece tells Uncle he must sign over his property interest in Whiteacre or she will break Uncle's legs. A court will rescind the transaction upon proof that Uncle made the promise under *duress*. RTR § 14. Similarly, if Niece takes care of Uncle and uses *undue influence* to get him to sign over his property interest in Whiteacre, a court could rescind the transaction. RTR § 15.[7]

Finally, if Niece secures Uncle's signature transferring Whiteacre to her at a time when Uncle is mentally incompetent, the court will rescind the transaction on grounds of *incapacity* unless the transferor has regained legal capacity before the transfer and ratified the transaction. RTR § 16(1).[8]

Example 7

Quincy and Rita are brother and sister, the sole, equal heirs of their mother's estate. Sonia, a friend of Quincy and Rita's late mother, tells Quincy that his mother had very little personal property. Quincy then disclaims any interest in his mother's personal property in favor of his sister. It turns out that — unbeknownst to Sonia, Quincy, or Rita — Quincy and Rita's mother had a safe deposit box filled with diamonds worth millions of dollars. Sonia finds the key, retrieves the diamonds, and sells them for $2 million. Can Quincy recover half the value of the diamonds from Sonia?

Explanation

The case does not appear to involve either intentional fraud or misrepresentation. Whether we consider this a mistake case or an innocent material misrepresentation case (by Sonia), the result is the same: a court is likely to allow Quincy to recover in restitution. RTR § 13 covers both fraud and innocent material misrepresentations. *See* RTR § 13, cmt. *c*, illus. 3. The best argument for Sonia is that this should be treated as a mistake case, and that Quincy disclaimed his interest in conscious disregard of his rights (see Example and Explanation 5), and he should therefore be allocated the risk of his mistake.

---

7. The Restatement defines "undue influence" as "excessive and unfair persuasion" between parties in a "confidential relation" or "relation of dominance on one side and subservience on the other" and in which "the free will of the transferor is overcome by the will of the person exerting undue influence." RTR § 15(1).

8. Minors too can rescind their transactions, and a transfer by a municipal corporation acting wholly beyond its powers is void. RTR § 16(2)(a); RTR § 16 (2)(c).

11.2.4 Benefits Conferred Intentionally in Emergency, by Officious Intermeddlers, and by Contract

The first two types of cases in which courts allow restitution involve transfers occurring by mistake or through some lack of full consent or authority. We now turn to cases where the transferor intends to transfer a benefit and then later asks for compensation in restitution for the benefit conferred.

We certainly would not want a rule that lets anyone confer a "benefit" without your consent and then charge you for it. Just think of someone who mails you return address labels and then asks for payment. We call people who try to throw benefits at you in exchange for compensation "officious intermeddlers." The rationale for denying restitution to such persons is simple: if I want to buy return address labels, I can enter into a voluntary transaction. Otherwise, we would always have to be on our guard to prevent benefits from being forced upon us.

That said, there are situations where someone intentionally (and with full capacity and authority) confers benefits on another and is able to recover restitution for the benefits conferred. Think back to the Ella-Felice hypothetical in this chapter's Example 4. Ella goes into sudden cardiac arrest while dining at a restaurant. She is unconscious and alone. Dr. Felice, a prominent cardiac surgeon, is at the next table. Dr. Felice performs CPR, saving Ella's life. Dr. Felice later sends Ella a bill for $1,000.

A professional who confers benefits in an emergency is eligible for compensation through restitution. *Cotnam v. Wisdom*, 104 S.W. 164 (Ark. 1907); RTR § 20. Unlike the officious intermeddler who bypasses a voluntary transaction by foisting benefits on you, the professional acting in an emergency cannot negotiate with the person in need of emergency assistance. If there were a possibility of bargaining, the bargain would be so one-sided and unfair as to be voidable under duress or other principles of contract law.

Though professionals may be able to obtain the reasonable value of their services in restitution, nonprofessionals cannot get the same benefit. It is not that nonprofessionals are all "officious intermeddlers"; any one of us would be grateful if a stranger gave us life-saving CPR when we needed it. Instead, the law presumes that benefits conferred by Good Samaritans are conferred gratuitously (that is, as a gift), and therefore there is no expectation or requirement of restitution.[9]

---

9. The Restatement goes so far as to say that the Good Samaritan rescuer should not receive restitution even if the rescuer suffers "crippling injuries" as a result of the rescue, unless the rescued party has made a promise to pay the rescuer. (Such a promise, as you may remember from your first-year Contracts class, would be voidable because it is made under duress.) RTR § 20, cmt. *a*, illus. 7. The Restatement's explanation for denying restitution to Good Samaritans is unpersuasive. *See* RTR § 20, cmt. *b*. The Restatement writes that "[s]ervices of physicians, hospitals, and ambulance drivers are readily valued, while emergency rescue by a

Though the officious intermeddler is denied recovery, not all self-interested transactions are considered "intermeddling." For example, restitution might be allowed when one spares a neighbor an expense by taking an action to preserve one's own property. For example, Uri owns an easement consisting of a road over Victor's adjoining property. The road is used by Uri 60% of the time and Victor 40% of the time. Both Uri and Victor have a legal right to make necessary repairs to the road. If Uri makes the repairs he will have an action in restitution against Victor for 40% of the reasonable cost of the repairs. See RTR § 26, cmt. b, illus. 12.[10]

A more common example of this type of claim arises in the case of unmarried cohabitants. Wilma and Xavier lived together like a married couple. Wilma owns some land and Xavier contributes some of his funds for the building of a house upon the land. The house is for both of their benefits. When the couple splits, Xavier may be entitled to restitution for the value he contributed to the house on Wilma's land, at least if a court does not view the payments as a gift to Wilma. See RTR § 28.

People often confer benefits on another and raise a claim in restitution in one of three contractual settings.

First, *restitution may be available when the contract is unenforceable.* For example, imagine if Yolanda and Zena make an oral contract for the sale of Yolanda's land to Zena. Zena makes improvements on the property, and Yolanda then successfully claims the contract is unenforceable because it fails to satisfy the statute of frauds. In many jurisdictions, despite the statute of frauds, Zena may assert a restitutionary claim for the value of the improvements.

Restitution also might be available when a contract fails for: indefiniteness or lack of formality, RTR § 31; illegality, RTR § 32; incapacity of recipient, RTR § 33; or mistake or supervening change of circumstances, RTR § 34.

Second, *restitution may be an alternative measure of recovery by a non-breaching party for breach of an enforceable contract.* Suppose Alexa signs a contract to work for Betty for $30,000 for one year, payable in equal monthly installments. After six months, Betty breaches the enforceable contract by wrongfully terminating Alexa, having paid Alexa only $15,000. Both parties know that the first six months of the contract is the "hard season" in Alexa's line of work, and the reasonable value of Alexa's services during that period was $3,500 per month. See RTR § 38, cmt. c, illus. 12.

Alexa might choose to sue for damages. As Part I of this book shows, Alexa would be able to recover damages for the breach for the remaining

---

bystander is literally priceless." It is difficult to see why the law should assign something that is so highly valued (such as CPR) a value of zero. The Restatement seems to suggest that allowing recovery would somehow deter altruistic rescue, a point I have refuted. See Richard L. Hasen, *The Efficient Duty to Rescue*, 15 INT'L REV. L. & ECON. 141 (1995).

10. Indemnity and equitable subrogation fit into this category as well. These claims are discussed in detail in Chapter 13.

portion of the contract, plus incidental and consequential damages (such as the cost to find another job), but she must *mitigate* by trying to find reasonable alternative employment. Suppose she easily finds another job that pays the same salary. In that case, she might have no damages.

As an alternative, Alexa should be able to raise a restitutionary claim based on the reasonable value of what she provided to Betty during those six months. Recall she was paid $2,500 per month for work that was worth $3,500 per month, a difference of $1,000 per month. She should be able to obtain restitution for the $6,000 worth of value she gave Betty during those first six months.[11]

As we will see in section 11.4, restitution as an alternative basis of recovery for breach of contract is especially attractive in the case of "losing" contracts, but in some jurisdictions it is subject to an important limit: the restitutionary measure cannot exceed the amount of compensatory damages for breach of contract. Consider the following example.

> A promises B to build a barn for $60,000. A is wrongfully discharged after completing part of the work and receiving $20,000 in progress payments. The court finds that the cost reasonably incurred by A in partial performance has been $30,000, and that the reasonable cost of completion (by A or anyone else) will be $45,000. From these facts the court determines that A has performed 40 percent of the work covered by the contract; the price of this work at the contract rate is $24,000. A's claim to restitutionary damages is limited to $4000 (representing the ratable portion of the contract price less $20,000 already paid).

RTR § 38, cmt. c, illus. 11.

The first thing to note about this example is that it was a losing contract. If A had completed the contract, A would have spent $75,000 (the $30,000 already incurred plus an additional $45,000 in performance) to complete the performance. But A would have received only $60,000 for the project, with a projected loss of $15,000. Damages therefore do not look like an attractive option for A. Restitution looks more promising: A conferred a benefit on B worth $30,000 and received only $20,000, leading to a potential restitutionary recovery of $10,000. But some courts (and the Restatement) cap restitution at the amount of contract damages, meaning restitutionary recovery would be reduced to $4,000 (the pro rata portion of the contract was $24,000, less the $20,000 that had already been paid).

---

11. The Restatement adopts the terminology of referring to this restitutionary recovery as "performance based" damages." *See* RTR § 38, cmt. a (explaining relationship between damages and restitution claim). I prefer to call the $6,000 a recovery "in restitution" as an alternative to contract damages. This terminology makes it easier to separate the concept of restitution from the concept of compensatory damages. The Restatement also allows the recovery of "incidental or consequential loss" on top of the recovery in restitution. RTR § 38.

This raises the question why Alexa was able to recover more than the $15,000 contract price given that she had worked for half the time of the contract and received half the contract price. Shouldn't the $15,000 have capped the recovery? The answer is no, because the value of Alexa's performance during the first six months (the "hard season") was more than half the value of the contract.

Consider a harder variation on the Alexa-Betty contract (which you might want to skip if your instructor does not cover Restatement § 39, on "opportunistic breach" of contract). One clause of the contract provides that if Alexa's work for Betty increases Betty's overall profits by $1,000,000, Alexa would be entitled to a $100,000 bonus provided that she was not fired for good cause during the one-year term of the contract. Alexa in fact increased Betty's profits by over $1,000,000, but Betty dismisses Alexa to avoid paying the money (claiming, without merit, that she has good cause to fire Alexa). Alexa should have a good claim for the $100,000 in damages—but might she try to go after Betty's $1,000,000 in profits?

Ordinarily, the answer would be no, but the Restatement includes a new section that might allow Alexa to recover those profits. Breaching parties who engage in "opportunistic breach" may have to pay their profits in restitution. RTR § 39. The section is quite complex, but it is likely to be very influential in the future in defining the kinds of cases in which restitution will be denied to breaching parties.

Someone like Alexa would have to prove all of the following:

- The breaching party's breach was material (that is, sufficiently important to the contracting parties).
- The breaching party's breach was opportunistic in that it was deliberate and profitable (meaning that the gains are greater than the breaching party would have received from performance of the contract).
- Damages would afford inadequate protection to the non-breaching party's contractual entitlement.

The Restatement says that such cases will be "infrequently available" because "a breach of contract that satisfies the cumulative tests of § 39 is rare." RTR § 39, cmt. a. It looks like Alexa's claim would fail because a contract remedy that would award Alexa the $100,000 bonus would be sufficient.

So if Alexa could not recover all of Betty's gains in such circumstances, precisely when would § 39 apply? The Restatement offers the example of a landlord who leases Blackacre to a tenant. Tenant subleases the property without the landlord's consent in violation of the contract. Landlord learns of the sublease after its term has expired. The Restatement takes the position that the landlord can recover the profits Tenant earned on the sublease even though Landlord could prove no damages. RTR § 39, cmt. *e*, illus. 8.

Third, *restitution may be available to a breaching party of an enforceable contract to obtain benefits provided to the non-breaching party.* Imagine that A had promised to build the barn for B at a cost of $60,000, and that B had not yet paid anything to A for the performance. After A had completed 40% of the construction at a cost of $30,000, A breached the contract, refusing to do any more work. B hired another contractor to complete the performance for $45,000, the reasonable value of the services. A and B sue each other.

B makes a claim for breach of contract, claiming as damages the extra amount she had to pay for performance (plus any costs associated with finding a new contractor). There was 60% of the contract left to be performed, and the pro rata cost to B under the contract was $36,000 (60% of the $60,000 contract price). B had to pay $45,000 for that performance, leaving her with damages of $9,000.

A, however, has conferred the benefit of a 40% completed barn on B without receiving any payment. It would be unjust for B to be able to keep this value without paying anything, even though A breached the contract. A court would likely allow A to recover the reasonable value in restitution (perhaps the $30,000), but *capped* at the contract price (in this case, as in a previous A-B example, at $24,000, for 40% of the $60,000 contract price). In the end, a court would likely order B to pay A $15,000 in restitution, which represents the (capped) restitutionary value of what A conferred on B, $24,000, less the $9,000 in damages that A owes B for the breach of contract.

Some jurisdictions would not allow A to recover anything for breach of this contract, at least if A's breach was "willful." This standard is difficult to apply, and seems to be in tension with the "efficient breach" concept discussed in Chapter 4.2.[12]

Example 8

Shana finds a boat floating near her lake house. She repairs the boat and stores it until its rightful owner comes to claim it. Two years later, Tammy discovers that Shana has been holding her boat and retakes it, refusing to pay for its repair or storage. Does Shana have a right to restitution? Should it matter whether she expected compensation from the boat's owner?

---

12. The Restatement does not embrace the "willfulness" exception as a whole, but does note that in certain circumstances, such as those involving fraud or inequitable conduct, a breaching party may be denied the opportunity for restitution. RTR § 36, cmt. *b*.

Explanation

The facts do not tell us whether or not Shana is a professional in handling boats — which could be required by some courts in order to allow her recovery; otherwise courts could adopt the presumption applied in other "Good Samaritan" situations that Shana intended to offer her services as a gift to the boat owner. The Restatement provides that when someone comes to the protection of another's property (unlike when rendering emergency aid to a person), restitution is available if "the circumstances justify the claimant's decision to intervene without request" and "it is reasonable to assume the owner would wish the action performed." RTR § 21. This is a very reasonable rule, and perhaps the Restatement should have extended it to cases involving the rendering of emergency aid to a person by a Good Samaritan.

Example 9

"Mother tells Son that if he will construct an addition to her house, she will allow him to live in it and convey the property to him before her death. Son makes the requested improvements at a cost of $35,000, increasing the value of the property by a like amount. Repudiating her promise to Son, Mother sells the house to Daughter for one dollar. Daughter evicts son from the premises. Mother's promise to convey to Son is unenforceable." RTR § 27, cmt. *e*, illus. 12. Does Son have a claim in restitution against Daughter?

Explanation

Yes. Son conferred the benefit to benefit both himself and his mother. Now Daughter has benefited through the increased value of the property, and it would be unjust to allow her to keep this benefit. Because the benefit is attached to the land and raises questions of valuation and liquidity, a court might not give Son the right to an immediate money judgment. Instead, Son may end up with an equitable lien (discussed in Chapter 13) against Daughter's interest in the property.

Example 10

Carol signs a written contract to buy a used car from Dino for a purchase price of $5,000. The fair market value of the car is $4,000. Carol pays $5,000, and promptly crashes the car, destroying it. Carol is 16, and the law in Carol's state allows minors to rescind contracts for sale, receiving back the purchase price. Can Dino recover anything in restitution?

Explanation

Yes. Restitution often is available when a contract is unenforceable, including for reasons of incapacity. In this case, Dino would bring a claim for the reasonable value of the car, $4,000, not the contract price. Had the car not been destroyed, the restitutionary remedy of rescission would have required Carol to return the car. She can't do so in this case because the car has been destroyed. If Dino brings his counterclaim at the time Carol asks for rescission, the court is likely to offset the $5,000 Dino must pay Carol (refund of the purchase price) against the reasonable value of what Dino provided Carol (a car worth $4,000). The end result would be that Dino would pay Carol $1,000 and keep $4,000 as restitution.

11.2.5 Benefits Obtained Through Tortious or Otherwise Wrongful Conduct

The final common type of case in which plaintiffs claim restitutionary remedies arises from a defendant's tortious (or otherwise wrongful) conduct. Recall the example from the beginning of the chapter: Anita steals Brianna's digital camera, worth $200. She sells it to a pawnshop for $150 and bets the money at the racetrack. Anita does well at the track, and the $150 is now worth $1,000.

Brianna has a cause of action in tort for conversion. She can sue Anita for conversion, and recover her tort damages of about $200, or Brianna could decide to pursue a restitutionary remedy based on Anita's larger gains. Each jurisdiction has its own rules regulating how and when Brianna must decide whether to seek tort damages or to go for restitution.[13]

The Restatement lists the most common types of tort cases in which plaintiffs may seek a restitutionary remedy: (1) cases involving trespass, conversion, and comparable wrongs, RTR § 40, (2) misappropriation of financial assets, RTR § 41, (3) interference with intellectual property and similar rights, RTR § 42, and (4) breach of fiduciary duties or confidential relations, RTR § 43. The Restatement also includes a catch-all provision for other wrongs. RTR § 44.

Suppose that Shrek has gone onto Fiona's land to cut down some trees. He hauls off the trees and converts them to timber, yielding a nice profit. Under substantive tort law, Shrek committed a tort when he entered Fiona's land. His state of mind is irrelevant; if Fiona wants damages for the reasonable value of her trees, she can get it.

---

13. Recall that the language some jurisdictions use to describe this election of restitution: Brianna would "waive the tort" and sue in assumpsit. This is misleading because Brianna must prove the conversion by Anita: she's not waiving the tort at all. Instead, Brianna is electing to sue to recover Anita's gain rather than Brianna's loss.

But if Fiona prefers a restitutionary recovery based upon the profits that Shrek received, Shrek's state of mind may be relevant. Consider these alternatives: (1) Shrek entered the land, innocently and reasonably believing that it was his own land (and his own timber), not Fiona's. (2) Shrek negligently thought the land (and timber) was his. (3) Shrek knew it was Fiona's land (and Fiona's timber), and he consciously chose to steal her timber.

Most courts (as well as the Restatement) would likely agree that in all three scenarios, Fiona would have the option of suing for damages or recovering Shrek's profits under a restitutionary recovery. But the measure of restitutionary recovery will differ depending upon Shrek's culpability. If Shrek acted innocently or negligently (the first two scenarios), Fiona is entitled only to the direct benefits received by Shrek (which in appropriate cases could be the reasonable rental or license value). In contrast, if he acted as a "conscious wrongdoer," Shrek "will be required to disgorge all gains (including consequential gains) derived from the wrongful transaction." RTR § 40 cmt. *b.*

To make this a bit more concrete, let's apply some numbers to these concepts. Suppose that the market value of the unfinished trees taken from Fiona's land is $1,000. Shrek invests another $500 to process the trees into lumber, yielding lumber with a market value of $2,100. If Shrek is a conscious wrongdoer, he could have to pay the entire $2,100 gain to Fiona. In contrast, if Shrek was an innocent or negligent trespasser, a court could well give him a $500 credit for his costs in processing the lumber. He might even get credit for one-third of the $600 profit because he added one-third of the inputs ($500 processing cost divided by $1,500 in inputs to production) to produce the finished lumber. That one-third figure here is $200, meaning that Fiona might be able to obtain in restitution:

$2,100   (Shrek's profit)
− $ 500   (cost to Shrek for processing)
− $ 200   (portion of profits attributable to Shrek's inputs)
= $1,400[14]

Either way, you can see that Fiona would prefer the restitutionary remedy. Damages get her only $1,000; restitution gets her either $2,000 or some lower amount of at least $1,400 depending upon the apportionment rules in the jurisdiction. There is one caveat to this point: if Shrek has acted as a conscious wrongdoer, his conduct might make him liable for punitive damages (discussed in Chapter 15). Punitive damages would be available if Fiona received compensatory damages; some jurisdictions would not allow punitive damages to be coupled with a claim in restitution.

---

14. We will look further at these issues of accounting and apportionment in the next chapter.

In making the election, Fiona (and her lawyers) will have to decide which looks like a more lucrative recovery for her.

Example 11

Kaavya writes her first novel. It sells well, earning her $100,000 in profits. Megan discovers that a number of the passages in the book have been copied from Megan's earlier novels. When confronted with the copied passages, Kaavya claims that the copying was innocent and done without the conscious intent to do so. She says she is a great fan of Megan's works and must have inadvertently copied the material. Is Megan entitled to Kaavya's profits, looking at the common law (and not the Copyright Act)?

Explanation

This hypothetical is based on a controversy surrounding the work of Kaavya Viswanathan. *See* Mokoto Rich & Dinitia Smith, *Publisher Decides to Recall Novel by Harvard Student*, N.Y. TIMES, Apr. 28, 2006. This is a case involving misappropriation of intellectual property, and because it is a copyright claim, in real life it is going to be governed by copyright law. Copyright law is strange in that it allows for the recovery of both actual damages and the profits of the infringer in some circumstances. *See* 17 U.S.C. § 504(b); RTR § 42, cmt. d (noting the potential for a double recovery if a plaintiff whose written work has been misappropriated could recover both damages and restitution).

But the question asked you to consider this case only as a matter of the common law rules. Under the common law, the amount of restitution available to Megan could well depend upon whether Kaavya was a conscious wrongdoer. If she really innocently copied the passages as claimed, the profits might be the value of a license to use the copyrighted material. Expert testimony on the cost of obtaining such a license appears necessary. To the extent it was conscious stealing of intellectual property, however, Kaavya might have to give up her entire $100,000 profit.

11.3 WHY ALLOW FOR THE RECOVERY OF DEFENDANT'S GAINS IN CASES OF UNJUST ENRICHMENT?

What explains why the law allows some plaintiffs to recover in restitution? There is no single answer because, as we saw in section 11.2, restitution is available for a variety of different claims.

In those cases involving mistaken payments and improvements, the rationale for restitution appears be to approximate the *rightful position standard*: the position the plaintiff would have been in but for the wrong.[15] Restitution can serve in some cases to put plaintiff back in the position she would have been in before the plaintiff conferred a benefit on defendant.

Figure 11.1 illustrates this idea in connection with the law professor–bank hypothetical from the beginning of the chapter:

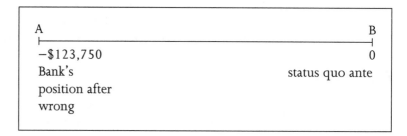

Figure 11.1

Recall that the bank owed the law professor $1,250, but paid the law professor $125,000 instead. Return of the excess $123,750 is necessary to put the parties back to the status quo ante position.

It is important to note that the analysis in Figure 11.1 *assumes* that there has been a wrong. That, of course, is what the substantive law of restitution needs to determine. Recall the Ella-Felice example, where Felice performs CPR on Ella, saving her life. If Felice is a doctor, the law allows her to recover the reasonable value of her services in restitution. We can conceive of that payment as moving Felice from position A (where she has conferred a benefit on Ella that has a reasonable value) back to B, the status quo ante. But recall that if Felice is a nonprofessional who gives CPR, she gets nothing *even though she still has conferred a benefit on Ella that has the same reasonable value.* So we must invoke the substantive law of restitution before we can use the rightful position standard as a justification for a payment for benefits conferred.

Though the rightful position standard can explain *some* restitution cases, it cannot explain *all* of them. Think again about Brianna, whose digital camera with a $200 value was stolen by Anita. Anita pawns the camera for $150, bets that money at a racetrack, and ends up with $1,000. Because

---

15. The rightful position standard is discussed in the introduction and in Parts I and II as the main organizing principle for both compensatory damages and injunctions.

Anita is a conscious wrongdoer, Brianna has a strong claim to recover the full $1,000 in restitution.

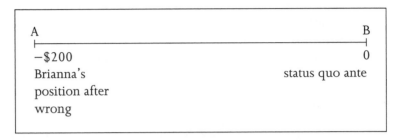

Figure 11.2

For those of you who have already reviewed Part I of this book, you know that, putting aside some complications, Brianna's tort damages would be (B − A) or $200. See Figure 11.2. If the jury could award Brianna an amount equal to Anita's gains of $1,000, she is placed in a *better position* than she would have been in had there been no wrong. The first $200 of that $1,000 award would bring Brianna back to B, the status quo ante. The next $800 makes her better off than if there had been no wrong.

The $800 gain to Brianna cannot be explained as an attempt to put Brianna in the rightful position. Instead, the restitutionary measure may be justified for two reasons: deterrence and punishment. We don't want conscious wrongdoers like Anita going around and taking things without permission. When these wrongdoers "bypass the market," they interfere with property rights in a way that offends both principles of justice (because people should not take what belongs to someone else) and principles of economics (because there would be a great deal of societal loss if we had to invest resources into protecting what we have rather than into new, productive activity). The potential for disgorgement of defendants' gains can deter wrongful activity and punish wrongdoers (serving a similar function to punitive damages that are potentially available only when a plaintiff seeks compensatory damages, not restitution).

This idea that restitution can serve deterrent and punitive functions is underlined by the fact that there are different measures of restitution in the case of conscious wrongdoers compared to innocent or negligent ones. When Shrek innocently converts Fiona's timber, the measure of restitution is one that comes closer to the rightful position standard: Fiona gets the value of her timber and a reasonable share of Shrek's profits. In contrast, when Shrek intentionally converts the timber, he must disgorge *all* of his profits, even if he added substantial value to the timber before it was sold. In that case, restitution looks more like a deterrent and punishment.

Example 12

The rightful position standard arguably justifies allowing restitution for someone who confers a benefit in the course of performing under an unenforceable contract. What is the justification for allowing (a) non-breaching parties to recover restitution rather than contract damages in some cases, and (b) breaching parties to recover in restitution under certain circumstances?

Explanation

(a) The ability of non-breaching parties to choose restitution can be justified under the rightful position standard to the extent the non-breaching party would have difficulty proving contract damages, and the gains to the defendant and losses to the plaintiff are substantially equivalent. See RTR § 38, cmts. a, b. To the extent that a non-breaching party can capture a breaching party's gains even when they exceed the value of the contract, restitution appears to serve a deterrent and punitive function.

(b) As far as breaching parties seeking restitution goes, the rationale appears to be to restore the breaching party to the rightful position, after the plaintiff has been put in that position. If anything, the rule giving the breaching party the right to restitution might create situations of underdeterrence.

11.4 MORE ON LOSING CONTRACTS: SHOULD THE CONTRACT PRICE BE THE CAP?

Recall the example discussed in section 11.2.4:

> A promises B to build a barn for $60,000. A is wrongfully discharged after completing part of the work and receiving $20,000 in progress payments. The court finds that the cost reasonably incurred by A in partial performance has been $30,000, and that the reasonable cost of completion (by A or anyone else) will be $45,000. From these facts the court determines that A has performed 40 percent of the work covered by the contract: the price of this work at the contract rate is $24,000. A's claim to restitutionary damages is limited to $4,000 (representing the ratable portion of the contract price less $20,000 already paid).

As the example explains, the Restatement of Restitution takes the position that a non-breaching party's recovery in restitution should be capped by the amount of contract damages. That puts the Restatement position at odds with that taken by the Restatement of Contracts. RESTATEMENT (SECOND) OF CONTRACTS § 373, cmt. d (1981). Under the alternative position, non-breaching plaintiffs in losing contracts are not limited by the contract price, and person A in the last illustration may recover the $30,000 benefit conferred on the breaching party. The rule of some jurisdictions allowing a non-breaching party to recover restitution exceeding the contract price is subject to an important limit: restitution is not available when the non-breaching party has *completed performance*. RTR § 38, cmt. d.

Courts are split on their approaches to whether restitutionary measures should be capped by the amount of contract damages in the case of losing contracts. *See* RICHARD A. LORD, 24 WILLISTON ON CONTRACTS § 64:2 nn.52-55 (4th ed. 2006).

Which rule is better? In other words, *should* non-breaching parties to losing contracts be limited in restitution to the contract price? Again, it depends upon the reason that these parties are entitled to restitution. From the perspective of the rightful position, allowing the non-breaching party to recover in restitution an amount exceeding the contract price puts the party in a *better position* than had there been no contract. In our hypothetical, A is better off with B's breach than had B performed: A may recover $30,000, more than if there would have been no breach. In this way, the cap could be justified as keeping contracting parties in the rightful position. On the other hand, from the perspective of deterrence and punishment, it may be better to have no cap. But that might upset the expectations of contracting parties.

Example 13

Gerry is a contractor who has substantially completed a major remodel of Harry's kitchen. The contract price is $40,000, and Harry paid half in advance. Harry tells Gerry that he won't pay the $20,000 remaining because he believes Gerry's work is shoddy. In fact, Gerry's work has been perfect and it is Harry who has breached the contract under applicable contract law. Gerry has spent $50,000 so far on remodeling, which is the reasonable value of the contracting work, and needs to put in about another $500 to complete the project. What, if anything, can Gerry recover in restitution?

Explanation

Gerry is a party to a losing contract. He agreed to remodel Harry's kitchen for a contract price of $40,000, and complete performance is going to cost $50,500. For those of you who have completed Part I, you know that Gerry's contract damages would be $20,000, the remainder of the contract price, which Harry has not paid. Gerry, however, would like to recover $30,000 in restitution, the difference between the reasonable value of what he has provided ($50,000) and what he has received ($20,000).

In some jurisdictions following the Restatement, Gerry's restitutionary recovery would be capped at $20,000, the amount of contract damages.

In other jurisdictions, restitution may exceed the contract price, meaning Gerry has a chance to recover the $30,000. Harry, however, would argue that restitution should not be available because Gerry has completed performance, leaving Gerry only with contract damages. There are just a few odds and ends to fix up (worth $500): is Gerry's performance really completed? In a jurisdiction without a cap, but with the rule barring restitution when there is completed performance, the court will have to decide whether or not Gerry's performance was really complete. Such a ruling could in fact turn on the relative culpability of the parties, especially the reason why Harry breached, though a court might not discuss culpability as the legal basis for the ruling.

Unjust Enrichment: Measuring Ill-Gotten Gains and Apportioning Profits

12.1 MEASURING ILL-GOTTEN GAINS

The previous chapter explained the circumstances under which a plaintiff may recover a defendant's gain through restitution. It dealt with the "unjust" aspect of the "unjust enrichment" principle. This chapter and the next explore the meaning of "enrichment": specifically, how courts identify and measure the defendant's gains. As we shall see, in some circumstances, the extent of the defendant's "injustice" (or culpability) sometimes can affect how courts measure "enrichment."

Consider the following scenarios in which a plaintiff might seek a restitutionary remedy, some of which are drawn from the discussion in the preceding chapter. Ask yourself how courts should measure the defendant's gain, if any:

- Gwen accidentally runs over Horatio's foot with her Maserati, causing Horatio to suffer $10,000 in damages.
- The bank, owing the law professor $1,250 from a bank account, mistakenly pays the professor $125,000.
- Dr. Felice, a cardiac surgeon, performs emergency CPR on an unconscious Ella, saving Ella's life. Dr. Felice normally charges $5,000 for a consultation. A reasonable fee for a professional performing CPR is $700. Ella's life is insured for $3 million.
- Anita steals Brianna's digital camera, worth $200. She sells it to a pawnshop for $150 and bets the money at the racetrack. Anita does well at the track, and the $150 is now worth $1,000. Anita is bankrupt.

- Shrek enters onto Fiona's land, taking timber with a market value of $1,000. Shrek invests another $500 to process the trees into lumber, which he sells on the market for $2,100.

By the time you are done with this chapter and the next, you should be comfortable answering the question of how courts are likely to measure the defendant's gain in these and other scenarios. For now, notice the following kinds of questions that these hypotheticals raise about restitutionary remedies: Do we measure value based upon the market? Should we measure the value of the gain to the defendant or the plaintiff's cost of providing the gain? If a defendant takes a misappropriated item and mixes it with his own labor or materials, does the defendant have to give up all of his gains, or just a portion? If a portion, which portion? If a defendant sells or exchanges a misappropriated item for something else, can the plaintiff get that new item? Should it matter if the defendant is bankrupt and there are other creditors who want the new item? These questions form the core of issues surrounding restitutionary measures of recovery.

We begin with two basic principles for measuring defendants' gains. The first principle, noted in the last chapter, is that *restitution is not available when a defendant has no gains.* Horatio may be able to sue Gwen successfully for negligence for running over his foot, but the remedy will be the remedy of tort damages, not restitution.

Second, *the measurement issue is easy when the transfer from plaintiff to defendant involves cash or another easily valued item,* at least when the defendant is not bankrupt and the defendant has not traded the cash for a different item. *See* RTR §49(2) ("Enrichment from a money payment is measured by the amount of the payment or the resulting increase in the defendant's net assets, whichever is less."). Consider again the law professor–bank hypothetical: here, it is hard to argue for any measure of gain besides the difference between the amount paid to the law professor ($125,000) and the amount the professor was owed ($1,250), a total of $123,750.

In a case such as the law professor–bank hypothetical, the restitutionary award usually would be *embodied in a money judgment, enforceable in the same way as a money judgment for damages.*[1] If the law professor is insolvent, or if the money has been used to purchase another asset, the bank would likely prefer an equitable restitutionary remedy, such as a constructive trust or an equitable lien. These additional restitutionary remedies are discussed in the next chapter.

Measurement problems arise when (1) the transfer from plaintiff to defendant does not involve an easily quantifiable gain (think Dr. Felice–Ella) or (2) the defendant has mixed the item misappropriated from plaintiff with other items to produce an integrated product that yields profits to the

---

1. Chapter 17.1 discusses the rules for enforcement of money judgments.

defendant (think Shrek-Fiona). We'll deal with that first kind of problem now, and with the second problem in the next part of this chapter.

Consider Dr. Felice and Ella. Suppose the reasonable market value of a doctor's services is $700. Dr. Felice, however, is a famous (and expensive) cardiac surgeon who charges $5,000 for a consultation. These measurements reflect the market cost of the services. From the defendant's perspective, the gain is much more. Consider the immense benefit to Ella, whose life is saved. Though measuring the value of her life is fraught with difficulties (see the discussion in Chapter 4 on the problem in the context of tort damages), one piece of evidence of the value of Ella's life is her life insurance, which is set at $3 million.

Generally speaking, Dr. Felice is entitled to recover only the reasonable value of defendant's services, measured by a competitive market and not the idiosyncrasies of the plaintiff or defendant. The leading case on point is *Cotnam v. Wisdom*, 104 S.W. 164 (Ark. 1907). A doctor came to the aid of a person thrown from a streetcar. The doctor rendered emergency aid, but the person died. The doctor sued to recover from the estate. The Arkansas Supreme Court held that the doctor could successfully state a cause of action in *quasi-contract*.[2]

As to the *amount* of recovery, the court rejected the idea that the plaintiff could introduce evidence that the person aided by the doctor was wealthy despite the fact that the evidence showed that doctors at the time set their fees in part based upon a patient's ability to pay:

> In order to admit such testimony, it must be assumed that the surgeon and patient each had in contemplation that the means of the patient would be one factor in determining the amount of the charge for the services rendered. While the law may admit such evidence as throwing light upon the contract and indicating what was really in contemplation when it was made, yet a different question is presented when there is no contract to be ascertained or construed, but a mere fiction of law creating a contract where none existed in order that there might be a remedy for a right. *This fiction merely requires a reasonable compensation*

---

2. *Quasi-contract* is another term for restitution that uses the fiction that the parties had a contract. Sometimes this will be referred to as a contract "implied in law." Don't be confused by the contractual terminology. There could be no valid contract between the parties, as one of the parties was unconscious. Under either the old, subjective "meeting of the minds" test or the modern, objective theory of contract, there is no way that any court would say that the parties entered into a voluntary transaction that formed the basis for a valid contract. Instead, the court allows recovery through the fiction of an "implied" or "quasi" contract to allow the suit in restitution.

Here is how the Arkansas Supreme Court explained *quasi-contract* in *Cotnam*: "A contract implied by law . . . rests upon no evidence. It has no actual existence. It is simply a mythical creation of the law. The law says it shall be taken that there was a promise, when in point of fact, there was none. Of course this is not good logic, for the obvious and sufficient reason that it is not true. It is a legal fiction, resting wholly for its support on a plain legal obligation, and a plain legal right. If it were true, it would not be a fiction."

for the services rendered. The services are the same be the patient prince or pauper, and for them the surgeon is entitled to fair compensation for his time, service, and skill. It was therefore error to admit this evidence, and to instruct the jury in the second instruction that in determining what was a reasonable charge they could consider the "ability to pay of the person operated upon." (Emphasis added.)

Cotnam certainly is authority for the principle that courts should use the reasonable value of the plaintiff's services rather than the benefit to the defendant in assessing the amount of restitution. See also LAYCOCK p. 633 ("The benefit in these cases is measured by the market value of the treatment, whether or not successful, and not by the value of the life saved or the pain and suffering avoided."). But Cotnam does not directly say the reasonable value should either be set at the $700 reasonable market value for a medical professional's giving of CPR or the $5,000 typical fee of the doctor. The better argument is that the $700 fee is more appropriate because the $5,000 typical fee is likely imposed for rendering more complex diagnosis and treatment by the cardiac surgeon than for rendering services roughly equivalent to giving CPR. Indeed, if a lawyer who earns $500 an hour gives up her time to give Ella CPR, the lawyer gets nothing because it is presumed that good Samaritans render services gratuitously (without expectation of payment); the lawyer does not get her usual hourly rate.

In a situation such as that involving an unconscious patient, the law's measure of recovery is a moderate one. It is a measure that makes sense if you think about the kind of transaction the parties likely would have entered into had they been able to freely bargain (but for prohibitive transaction costs). In a free market, the patient would have expected to pay for the reasonable value of a doctor's services. Though Dr. Felice, the cardiac surgeon, might not have been interested in work that would pay her only $700 instead of her $5,000 fee, she would reasonably understand that if she agreed to do work worth $700, a patient would likely pay her only that amount.

The unconscious patient such as Ella who receives gains is innocent; there was nothing wrongful about her conduct (except perhaps her unwillingness to pay the doctor after she rendered CPR). When the defendant is more culpable, however, courts allow plaintiffs more generous measures of a defendant's gains. Consider Shrek again. Recall that he enters onto Fiona's land, taking timber with a market value of $1,000. He invests another $500 to process the trees into lumber, which he sells on the market for $2,100. As noted in the last chapter, the Third Restatement of Restitution and Unjust Enrichment takes the position that if the defendant is a conscious wrongdoer — here, if Shrek knew the trees belonged to Fiona and he took them anyway — he could have to give up all of his profits, even those that are attributable to the $500 worth of processing that he put into the lumber.[3] Shrek, the conscious wrongdoer, has enrichment measured in a pro-plaintiff manner because he has engaged in especially unjust behavior.[4]

The famous case of *Olwell v. Nye & Nissen Co.*, 173 P.2d 652 (Wash. 1946) is another example of a court using a tough — indeed punitive — measure of defendant's gains in a case of a defendant deliberately bypassing the market. In *Olwell*, plaintiff sold his interest in an egg packing business, but not an egg washing machine, to defendant. The plaintiff's machine was stored next to defendant's leased property, but not on the defendant's property. The defendant's treasurer, without seeking permission of the plaintiff, had the egg washing machine taken out of storage; apparently the defendant needed the machine because of a labor shortage during World War II. Defendant used the machine for about three years before the plaintiff learned of its use. When plaintiff found out, plaintiff offered to sell defendant the machine for $600; defendant countered with a $50 counteroffer, which plaintiff rejected. Plaintiff then sued for conversion, "waived the tort," and sued in assumpsit for restitution. The court awarded plaintiff a money judgment in the amount of $10 per week for the period of 156 weeks, or $1,560, representing the labor cost saved by defendant each week. The appellate court upheld this measure of restitution.

In understanding the case, it is important to begin with what is *not* at issue. First, there is no question that the plaintiff, who owned the egg washing machine, was wronged. Defendant took and used plaintiff's property without permission. Nor does there seem any doubt that under substantive principles of restitution, the plaintiff could elect to receive a restitutionary remedy based upon defendant's gain rather than the plaintiff's loss. The question is how to *measure* the defendant's gain. Here, there are at least three options:

1. *The reasonable value of the machine.* The plaintiff offered to sell the machine for $600, which is pretty good evidence of (the upper value) of the machine.

2. *The reasonable rental value.* The Defendant argued for the reasonable rental value of the machine, which was probably somewhere at or below the $600 figure for owning the machine. (If the amount were

---

3. In the next section, we'll talk about how to apportion those profits in the event that a court believes they should be apportioned.

4. As a "conscious wrongdoer," Shrek "will be stripped of gains from unauthorized interference with another's property." RTR § 40 cmt. b. "However, courts are sometimes visibly reluctant to measure the unjust enrichment of a conscious trespasser by the full cost of making alternative arrangements, or by the full extent of consequential gains that an intentional trespass may have facilitated. Even against a conscious wrongdoer, restitution may be limited to avoid a liability for gains that are unduly remote (§ 51(5)(a)) or disproportionate to the loss on which liability is based (§ 58(3)(c))." Id.

higher to rent the machine for three years, a rational buyer would choose to buy the machine rather than rent it.)

3. *The profits defendant received from using the machine.* In this case, the court determined that the defendant saved $10 per week by not having to pay workers to wash the eggs in a less labor-efficient way, leading to savings of over $1,500.

The award of $1,500 gives a generous benefit to plaintiff, but at a high cost to defendant. The court in *Olwell* appeared to justify this measure by pointing to the defendant's "consciously tortious" actions, and so it might be that the higher measure is necessary to punish the defendant for willfully bypassing what could have been a voluntary market transaction, and to deter similar actions by others in the future. The Third Restatement endorses the principle that the measure of unjust enrichment depends in part on culpability. RTR § 40, cmt. *b*.[5]

If you don't see the deterrence point, ask yourself this question: if the measure of restitution was the reasonable rental value that plaintiff would have charged defendant, what incentive would an unscrupulous defendant have to negotiate for the rental of the egg washing machine? If defendant is caught, the defendant pays what it should have paid in a fair transaction. If defendant is not caught, the defendant pays nothing.[6]

To understand how the measure of market gain might fluctuate depending upon the defendant's culpability, consider whether the court would have upheld the $1,560 award if the defendant's treasurer, who ordered the machine taken out of storage, did not know (and perhaps reasonably

---

5. The Restatement provides that innocent recipients of enrichment generally pay "by the standard that yields the smallest liability in restitution" for unrequested benefits, but "[u]njust enrichment from requested benefits is measured by their reasonable value to the recipient. Reasonable value is normally the lesser of market value and a price the recipient has expressed a willingness to pay." RTR § 50. For those enriched by misconduct, unjust enrichment is "not less than their market value." RTR § 51. For "conscious wrongdoers," "the unjust enrichment . . . is the net profit attributable to the underlying wrong. The object of restitution in such cases is to eliminate profit from wrongdoing while avoiding, so far as possible, the imposition of a penalty." Id. Finally, the Restatement offers a third, middle category of recipients of enrichment who are not wrongdoers, but who are enriched for other reasons, such as their own negligence. These recipients in appropriate cases may be liable for greater liability in restitution than innocent wrongdoers. RTR § 52 (They "may be subject to a greater liability in restitution than an innocent recipient of the same benefits, in order that the defendant rather than the claimant bear the costs of the transaction.").

6. This analysis suggests that if society wishes to deter those who infringe in the market, the measure of the gains should be substantial. Consider this example. Suppose that the reasonable rental value in *Olwell* is $600 and the profits to defendant are $1,560. Defendant knows that there is only a 25% chance the plaintiff will sue the defendant for conversion and recover in restitution for $1,560. That means the expected loss to the defendant of breaking the law is $390 (25% chance of paying $1,560), compared to a sure payment of $600 for the honest rental of the machine. An unscrupulous, risk-neutral defendant would still decide to bypass the market and take the chance on being caught.

could not have known) that the machine belonged to the plaintiff. It seems more likely the court would have chosen a lower rental or sale value.

There is one important caveat to the principles set forth in this chapter. To the extent that a defendant misappropriates intellectual property (for example, infringes on copyrighted material or a patent), the measure of recovery is dictated primarily by federal statutory law and not general restitutionary principles. Infringers of patents, for example, are liable only for damages (and may be penalized up to three times the amount of damages). 35 U.S.C. § 284 (2000). But an alternative restitutionary measure is not allowed. See RTR § 42, cmt. c ("The Patent Act of 1946 has been interpreted (though only since 1964) to foreclose a claim by the patentee to disgorgement of the infringer's profits. Were it not for this statutory bar, the rule of this section would authorize such a claim against a conscious infringer — as did previous versions of the Patent Act, and as did the current version as previously interpreted.").

Copyright law provides another interesting remedy. 17 U.S.C. § 504(b) (2004) allows recovery of a plaintiff's "actual damages" along with "profits of the infringer that are attributable to the infringement and are not taken into account in computing actual damages."[7] The draft Restatement notes the risk of "double counting" from this formula that could lead to "a recovery exceeding both the claimant's loss and the infringer's profits." It calls such an outcome "strictly anomalous in restitution terms." RTR § 42, cmt. d.

State statutes in appropriate circumstances also may alter or augment the common law for particular types of claims. It is always worth checking relevant state statutes.

Example 1

Andy's tire blows out while he's driving on State Route 5 in a remote area during a cold winter. There is no cell phone reception. He has no spare tire and does not know how to change a spare tire. After three hours with no one on the road, he spots Betty, a retired accountant who is driving down the road. He's very happy because if Betty had not come by, he would have suffered from hypothermia or worse. He stops Betty's car and asks her for help. Betty says: "I'm no good Samaritan, but I've got a tire that would fit on your car. I'll sell you the tire and put it on for $1,000." (A towing company would have charged Andy $150 for the service call and $100 for the tire.) Andy reluctantly agrees, promising to send Betty a check for $1,000 when he gets back home. Betty puts the tire on Andy's car, and Andy safely goes on his way. Andy does not send Betty the check. Betty sues Andy for breach of contract or, in the event the contract is unenforceable, for restitution.

---

7. Section 504(c) gives plaintiff an alternative to elect "statutory damages," which may be more advantageous for plaintiffs in certain circumstances.

Assume a court would hold the contract void on grounds of duress. To what amount, if any, is Betty entitled in restitution?

Explanation

Assuming the contract is void for duress, Betty should be able to recover the reasonable value of what she provided Andy, at least as to the tire. Betty will *not* be able to obtain the value to Andy of being saved from hypothermia, or worse. The best evidence of the tire's value is the $100 that a towing company would have charged Andy, though Betty could have other evidence. The $1,000 bargain was struck during conditions of bilateral monopoly (where there is only one buyer and one seller, meaning an efficient price won't emerge through competition) and duress, and is likely not good evidence of the value of the transaction.

Under the substantive law of restitution, there's a question of whether Betty is entitled to recover anything in restitution for the value of her services in putting on the tire (as opposed to the value of the tire itself). Betty is not a professional, and the presumption is that non-professionals who render emergency services do so gratuitously. In this case, Betty can likely overcome that presumption because she told Andy up front that she was "no Good Samaritan" and would not help him except for a fee. For this reason, a court could well allow Betty to recover the $150 reasonable value of the services provided. This is analogous to the "necessity" issue discussed in the next example. It seems only fair that a person who has benefited in times of emergency pay the reasonable costs of rescue after the emergency is over.

Example 2

The S.S. Minnow was out at sea for a three-hour tour. The weather started getting rough; the tiny ship was tossed. Thanks to the courage of the fearless Skipper and his first mate, Gilligan, the ship was brought safely into Davy Jones's dock as the storm was raging. Though Jones protested, Skipper and Gilligan kept the ship tied to the dock, to prevent the loss of life and property damage that would have resulted had the S.S. Minnow remained at sea. The dock suffered $500 in damages. Had the ship not remained at the dock, it is likely that there would have been $50,000 in personal injury and property damage. A reasonable fee to dock the boat under normal circumstances would have been $50.

Tort law provides that under conditions of "necessity," a person may use another's private property even without permission. *See Ploof v. Putnam*, 71 A. 188 (Vt. 1908). But the plaintiff whose property has been damaged should be able to recover damages or restitution. If plaintiff Jones seeks restitution, how should it be measured?

Explanation

Arguably, the amount of restitution should be $50, the normal dock fee that Jones would have charged in normal conditions. If Jones could show that he charged additional docking fees during inclement weather — perhaps to compensate for the increased risk of dock damage during such conditions — he perhaps could be entitled to those additional fees as well. If all Jones could get in restitution is $50 (or a bit more if additional fees are allowed), he could well prefer to sue for damages, possibly recovering the $500 worth of damage to the dock.

Wait a minute, you might say. In *Olwell*, the defendant chose not to enter into a voluntary transaction, and consciously chose to bypass the market. The penalty was that the defendant had to give up all those consequential gains, the labor savings equal to $1,560. Why doesn't that same reasoning apply here? Skipper and Gilligan docked the ship against the owner's wishes, again bypassing the market. Maybe they should have to pay the consequential gains of $50,000.

That reasoning is likely flawed, because Skipper and Gilligan did not bypass the market in the way that the defendant did in *Olwell*. In *Olwell*, there was presumably a functioning market for egg washing machines. The plaintiff could have rented his egg washing machine to defendant or refused to do so; the defendant could have agreed to rent the machine from plaintiff or refused to do so. There was no emergency.

In contrast, in the emergency S.S. Minnow hypothetical, there was no possibility of free bargaining. It is true that Skipper tried to get permission from Jones, who refused, but this was under the conditions of a non-working market. Again we have a bilateral monopoly: there is only one buyer (Skipper and Gilligan) and only one seller (Jones). In such circumstances, parties are not expected to bargain to efficient results. It is just like a bargain struck under duress, which a court would void had they entered into a one-sided bargain under these conditions.

The lack of a well-functioning market means that the court would likely excuse defendants' bypassing of the market. Moreover, Skipper and Gilligan are not "conscious wrongdoers" in the way the *Olwell* defendant was; in other words, a court would likely say that the S.S. Minnow "needed" the dock more than the *Olwell* defendant "needed" the egg washing machine.

12.2 APPORTIONING PROFITS

In cases where a misappropriated item has been mixed with other items to create a benefit for the misappropriator, courts have to determine a method for calculating the appropriate amount of profits to award to the plaintiff whose item has been misappropriated. To get a handle on these issues of *apportioning profits*, let's take a look at my favorite case to teach in all of Remedies, *Gaste v. Kaiserman*, 863 F.2d 1061 (2d Cir. 1988).

Gaste involves an awful musical hit from the 1970s called "Feelings."[8] Here's a sample of the song's lyrics:

Feelings, wo-o-o feelings
wo-o-o, feel you again in my arms.

Though "Feelings" was a hit in the 1970s, it turns out that the song's author, Morris Albert, wrote the lyrics but stole the melody from a 1956 French song, "Pour Toi," written by a Frenchman named Louis Gaste. Gaste sued Albert (whose real last name was Kaiserman) as well as Albert's publisher, Fermata, for copyright infringement. The jury determined that Albert had indeed misappropriated the music from Gaste. Gaste did not claim credit for the words.

From the perspective of a Remedies course, the interesting question is what a court should do once it has been determined that a misappropriated item was mixed with other items to produce something profiting defendant. Here we have a typical example of a mixture of an appropriated item (in this case, the infringed melody — a protected intellectual property right) with non-appropriated inputs (most importantly, in this case, the words to the song, "Feelings"). Individuals were buying the "package" of words and melody together, and Albert and Fermata had expenses associated with selling the package. The question becomes how these costs and revenues should be disentangled.

Let me assign some (fictional) numbers to this case to illustrate the choices facing the court. Assume the following numbers:

$300,000	Gross receipts from the sale of the song "Feelings" for the year in question
$50,000	Fermata's variable costs for creating the song and marketing it (these are costs that Fermata would not have incurred had the song "Feelings" not been sold)
$500,000	Fermata's fixed costs for overhead during the relevant period (Fermata marketed 100 songs for the relevant period; revenues from "Feelings" made up 25% of its total revenue)

---

8. My Remedies students are subjected to my singing of the song a cappella to introduce this case. It is an experience they will never forget (even with years of therapy). I thought of posting an MP3 version of my singing the song for readers of this book, but I worry that I'd be sued for copyright infringement and negligent infliction of emotional distress!

| $60,000 | Royalties for Feelings paid by Fermata to Albert, who spent 50 hours writing, working on, and recording the song |
| $10,000, plus 10% of Albert's profits | A reasonable royalty that the parties would have negotiated but for Albert's stealing of the music from Gaste |

The reasonable royalty figure ($10,000 plus 10% of Albert's profits) might be a reasonable approximation of Gaste's damages. This is the loss that Gaste incurred but for Albert's misappropriation of his music. Under the principles of Part I of this book, awarding this royalty figure arguably puts Gaste back into the rightful position — the position Gaste would have been in but for Albert's wrong.

Let's turn to the "infringer's profits," however, which copyright law says that Gaste is entitled to as well (from both Albert and Fermata). The amount due to Gaste is not immediately obvious, which is why a court will order an *accounting for profits* to determine the appropriate amount of profits payable to plaintiffs in restitution cases like this one.

Turning first to Fermata, it seems pretty clear that $300,000 does not represent Fermata's *profits*. This number instead represents the *income* that Fermata has received from sales of the song "Feelings." To get to Fermata's profits, we need to subtract the $50,000 in variable costs Fermata had in marketing and selling the song, and the $60,000 it paid Albert in royalties. That brings us from $300,000 down to $190,000.

Fermata also has an argument that a portion of its $500,000 in "fixed costs" (utility bills, rent, salaries), which it has to pay regardless of the sales of "Feelings," should be deducted. A stingy allocation might give Fermata just $5,000 for this overhead, because "Feelings" was just 1 of 100 songs (or 1% of the $500,000 costs). A more generous measure would allocate a whopping $125,000 for this overhead because "Feelings'" sales made up 25% of the revenues for the company (and 25% of $500,000 is $125,000).

The courts vary in how they treat the question of subtracting out portions of overhead. The Second Circuit has said that infringers must demonstrate a "direct and valid nexus between each claimed overhead expense category and the production of" the infringing product. Then the infringer must propose a "fair and acceptable allocation formula." *Hamil America, Inc. v. GFI*, 193 F.3d 92 (2d Cir. 1999). The Ninth Circuit has suggested that willful infringers cannot deduct any fixed costs for overhead. *Frank Music Corp. v. Metro-Goldwyn-Mayer, Inc.*, 772 F.2d 505 (9th Cir. 1985). A good rule of thumb in those jurisdictions which allow deductions for fixed costs is that the more culpable the infringer, the likelier the court is going to be stingy about deducting expenses for overhead.

The Restatement rejects what it terms "punitive accounting" that would "disallow a provable deduction, logically relevant to a determination of the net profit attributable to the infringement" in the case of conscious wrong-doers. RTR § 42, cmt. i. It recognizes, however, that the infringer "bears the burden of proof and the risk of uncertainty," and that "a court may properly adjust the stringency of the defendant's evidentiary burden in response to the character of the defendant's wrongdoing." Id. It further provides that when it comes to conscious wrongdoers, "the court may apply such tests of causation and remoteness, may make such apportionments, may recognize such credits or deductions, and may assign such evidentiary burdens, as reason and fairness dictate, consistent with the object of restitution as spec-ified in subsection (4)." RTR § 51(5).

Suppose the court determines that Fermata was not a conscious wrong-doer (Fermata did not know that Albert had stolen the music for the song from Gaste), and the court allows the deduction of $125,000 in fixed costs,[9] bringing the total profits down to $65,000:

$300,000   (receipts)
− $ 50,000   (variable costs)
− $ 60,000   (royalty payments)
− $125,000   (portion of fixed costs)
= $ 65,000

Some courts might allow Gaste to recover this full $65,000 amount from Fermata. See, e.g., Maier Brewing Co. v. Fleischmann Distilling Corp., 390 F.2d 117 (9th Cir. 1968) (awarding all profits from infringing product to plaintiff without apportioning portion of profits due to infringement).

Other courts, however, would say that it is appropriate to apportion the $65,000 in profits to account for the fact the success of the song was attributable in part to the (misappropriated) melody of "Feelings" and in part to the (non-appropriated) words. In the actual Gaste case, the jury was asked to come up with such an apportionment, and it determined that 80% of the song's value came from the music and only 20% from the words.

Indeed, my favorite fact from Gaste is the following: "[Albert's expert] testified that he 'loved' the song 'Feelings' and that he believed the title and lyrics were 'far better' than the music itself. Nonetheless, he was unable to recall the words to the song on the stand and yet was able to sing the opening tune." (Talk about not adequately preparing an expert witness!)

Under this 80/20 allocation, Gaste would be entitled to $52,000 from Fermata, representing 80% of its $65,000 profits. (The entitlement would

---

9. In the actual Gaste case, the court rejected Fermata's argument that it should get to deduct 90% of its overhead because "Feelings" contributed to 90% of Fermata's profits.

obviously be higher if a court allowed a smaller — or no — deduction to Fermata for the portion of its fixed costs.)

So to summarize our first-cut analysis on how to account for — and apportion — profits in cases of misappropriated items, follow these steps:

1. Identify revenues from misappropriated/mixed item;
   then
2. Deduct variable costs;
   then
3. Deduct appropriate portion of fixed costs if allowed by court (evidentiary burden and method of allocation may depend upon culpability of infringer);
   and finally,
4. Apportion profits attributable to misappropriated item in mixed item cases using some reasonable method of apportionment, except that some courts will refuse to apportion and will award all profits to the plaintiff.

When it comes to Albert (as opposed to Fermata), the analysis has a few more twists. Recall in our example we said that Albert earned $60,000 in royalties from Fermata for the sale of the song "Feelings." Like Fermata, Albert wants to be able to deduct his expenses, and like Fermata, Albert wants to have as much of the allocation as possible for the song's profits attributable to anything besides the misappropriated item.

Some courts will put two roadblocks in Albert's path. First, they won't allow Albert to deduct the value of his own labor. Even if Albert spent 50 hours writing the song (and suppose we could place an hourly value on that 50 hours), some courts hold that a wrongdoer cannot deduct the cost of his own labor; he can only deduct things he has *bought and paid for*. *See* LAYCOCK pp. 670-71. In addition, some courts reason that in performing the allocation of profits for the infringing and non-infringing portions of the work, the infringer could not get credit for the extent of profits attributable to the infringer's general reputation. *See Sheldon v. Metro-Goldwyn Pictures Corp.*, 309 U.S. 390, 408 (1940) (affirming the trial court's ruling that infringing defendants "could not count the effect of 'their standing and reputation in the industry'" in apportioning profits.).

In the actual *Gaste* case, the court said there was no percentage of profits attributable to Albert's reputation because he was unknown. But the court referred to a similar dispute involving one of the Beatles, George Harrison. Harrison had written a song called "My Sweet Lord," which infringed on the music from an earlier hit, "She's So Fine." The court in *ABKCO Music, Inc. v. Harrisongs Music, Ltd.*, 508 F. Supp. 798 (S.D.N.Y. 1981), found that 75% of the song's profitability came from the value of the lyrics of "My Sweet Lord" and George Harrison's general reputation.[10]

Suppose that of that 75%, a jury would determine that 40% of the value came from the lyrics and 35% from Harrison's general reputation — some people would just buy whatever song Harrison recorded. In some jurisdictions, then, Harrison, as a wrongdoer, could not get the allocation for the 35% of the profits attributable to his reputation; that percentage of the profits would go to the plaintiff, whose song was infringed. Note that in *ABKCO* itself, the court gave the infringer credit for profits attributable to Harrison's own reputation.

Adding in these complications, we now have a more complete picture of the means of apportioning profits in these mixed misappropriation cases:

---

1. Identify revenues from misappropriated/mixed item;
   then
2. Deduct variable costs, but (*in some courts*) *not costs associated with the infringer's own labor;*
   then
3. Deduct appropriate portion of fixed costs, if allowed by court (evidentiary burden and method of allocation may depend upon culpability of infringer);
   and finally,
4. Apportion profits attributable to misappropriated item in mixed item cases using some reasonable method of apportionment, except that some courts will refuse to apportion, awarding *all* profits to the plaintiff; *some courts that will allocate do not give the infringer any credit for profits attributable to the infringer's reputation.*

To bring this back to the apportionment in *Gaste*, in some courts Albert would have very little by way of deductions from his $60,000 in profits. He would have to point to any variable costs associated with producing the song "Feelings," along with a portion of his fixed costs if allowed by the court. Then the court would award a percentage based upon the jury's allocation of the profitability of the songs, in some places, not taking into account any profit as a result of Albert's reputation. It could be that Albert would have to pay 80% of the full $60,000, or $48,000, to Gaste. Even worse for Albert: a court could refuse to apportion, awarding Gaste $60,000.

---

10. Unlike *Sheldon*, the *ABKCO* court did not seem to have a problem with counting the value of Harrison's reputation, though it noted that had the court found that Harrison deliberately plagiarized the music, it would have awarded *all* of the profits of "My Sweet Lord" to the plaintiffs.

Example 3

Shrek enters onto Fiona's land, taking timber with a market value of $1,000. Shrek invests another $500 to process the trees into lumber, which he sells on the market for $2,100. How much should a court award Fiona in restitution?

Explanation

This is a mixed misappropriation example, just like the *Gaste* case discussed in the text. Here, Shrek has mixed Fiona's misappropriated lumber with his $500 investment to yield the finished lumber. Let's work our way through the four steps.

1. **Identify revenues from misappropriated/mixed item.**

In this case, it is easy to identify the revenues. Shrek sold the finished lumber for $2,100.

2. **Deduct variable costs, but (in some courts) not costs associated with the infringer's own labor.**

The facts tell us that Shrek invested $500 to finish the lumber. To the extent these represent variable costs that Shrek "bought and paid for," a court is likely to deduct the full $500, bringing the amount down to $1,600. If this $500 includes the value of Shrek's own labor, that is likely to be excluded (at least if Shrek is a willful infringer) on grounds that courts don't want to give infringers credit for the time they spend misappropriating items from others or using misappropriated items for their own profits.

3. **Deduct appropriate portion of fixed costs, if allowed by court (evidentiary burden and method of allocation may depend upon culpability of infringer).**

Shrek will have the burden of proving any of his fixed costs. The facts don't tell us about any fixed costs. We are still at $1,600.

4. **Apportion profits attributable to misappropriated item in mixed item cases using some reasonable method of apportionment. However, some courts will refuse to apportion, awarding *all* profits to the plaintiff; some courts that will allocate do not give the infringer any credit for profits attributable to the infringer's reputation.**

It seems unlikely that the price of the finished lumber was in any way enhanced by Shrek's reputation. If Shrek was a conscious wrongdoer (i.e., he entered Fiona's land with the intent to steal her lumber), a court might award Fiona the full $1,600. If Shrek was not a conscious wrongdoer (and even if he was one, in certain courts), the court might allow an allocation between Shrek and Fiona's contribution to the profit. Fiona's contribution was worth $1,000, or two-thirds of the total value of the inputs. Shrek's contribution was $500, or one-third of the total value of the inputs. A court might award Fiona two-thirds of $1,600, or $1,067. A somewhat more generous approach would be to award Fiona the $1,000 value of her stolen timber, along with two-thirds of the $600 in real profits on the transaction (remember, there was a $2,100 sale price after Fiona's forced contribution of $1,000 worth of timber and Shrek's $500 in expenses). That allocation would give Fiona $1,400 and leave Shrek (after taking his $500 expense into account) with $200.

Whether Fiona could get $1,600, $1,067, or $1,400, the choice of restitution appears to make sense for Fiona, who could get only $1,000 if she chose damages rather than restitution. The only benefit to Fiona of seeking damages is if she could get punitive damages as an additional remedy, a remedy which, as noted in the last chapter, is not available in some jurisdictions to a plaintiff who elects restitution over punitive damages.

One other point on choice of remedies questions here: state statutes might provide for more generous damages remedies, such as a trebling of actual damages in stolen lumber cases. Fiona's lawyer will need to determine if statutory law displaces the common law.

Example 4

Producer negotiates with Writer to buy the movie rights to Writer's fictionalized novel about George Washington's life. The two parties were close to a deal for the rights at $50,000, but the deal fell apart. Producer made a movie about George Washington anyway, using a script written by someone else. Unbeknownst to anyone but Producer, Producer inserted a few pages of dialogue into the script lifted directly from Writer's novel. The movie was a great success. The lead role of George Washington was played by Movie Star, an actor who recently starred in a string of hit movies. Producer made $10 million in royalties from Studio, devoting two years of his time exclusively to the production of the movie, and spending $200,000 for assistants and office space. Writer seeks restitution from Producer (in addition to any actual damages allowed under the Copyright Act). How much, if any, of the $10 million in profits should Writer receive? What else would you need to know to answer this question fully?

Explanation

These facts are based roughly on the *Sheldon* case discussed above, 309 U.S. 390 (1940). Beyond the Copyright Act damages (which could be close to $50,000 if the evidence of that negotiation shows the reasonable royalty figure), Writer is going to want as much of the $10 million in restitution as possible. Consider again our four-step process.

1. **Identify revenues from misappropriated/mixed item.**

In this case, Producer's revenues from the film are $10 million.

2. **Deduct variable costs, but (in some courts) not costs associated with the infringer's own labor.**

From that $10 million, Producer should be able to subtract a good portion, if not all, of the $200,000 in assistant cost and office space. Ordinarily speaking, these are fixed costs (so we could discuss them under Step 3 next). But the facts tell us that Producer worked *exclusively* on the George Washington movie for two years, so it could be that *all* of his costs are attributable to the movie.

Producer cannot subtract the value of his own labor, which in this case is worth a significant amount of money. After all, he used his labor to produce a very valuable product, one that earned him a $10 million royalty.

3. **Deduct an appropriate portion of fixed costs, if allowed by court (evidentiary burden and method of allocation may depend upon culpability of infringer).**

See the discussion under Step 2 above. Best-case scenario for Producer is a deduction of $200,000 for his costs during the production of the movie.

4. **Apportion profits attributable to misappropriated item in mixed item cases using some reasonable method of apportionment. However, some courts will refuse to apportion, awarding *all* profits to the plaintiff; some courts that will allocate do not give the infringer any credit for profits attributable to the infringer's reputation.**

Here is where Producer may stand to lose most of that $9.8 million (or worse, all of the profits in courts (such as *ABKCO*) that allow no deductions for willful infringers).

A jury is going to have to decide what portion of Producer's hefty profit is attributable to the stolen lines from the novel and what portion is attributable to everything else (besides the profits attributable to the reputation of

Producer, if applicable). Likely the few lines of dialogue contributed only a negligible amount to the profit of the movie. People likely went to this movie because they like Movie Star, they like movies about historical figures, or for numerous other reasons. Realistically speaking, it is likely that the profits of the movie would have been the same had Producer not stolen the dialogue from Writer. (In this way, this case is fundamentally different from *Gaste* or the Shrek-Fiona hypothetical, both cases in which the misappropriated item added a great deal of value to the mixed product, creating its profitability).

> *Sheldon* demonstrates that especially in cases of willful infringements, courts may be lax in apportioning for the benefit of plaintiffs. A holding that the stolen lines were worth 5% of the movie's profitability would give Writer in this case $490,000 in profits, but it is likely based on a gross overestimate about the importance of those stolen lines. Still, when it comes to deliberate infringers, evidentiary doubts are going to go against the infringer.

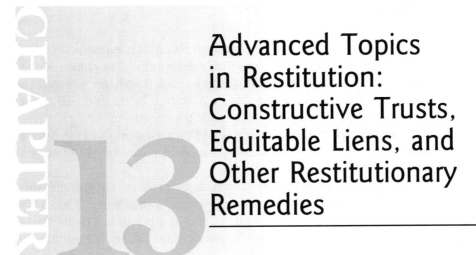

Advanced Topics in Restitution: Constructive Trusts, Equitable Liens, and Other Restitutionary Remedies

13.1 CONSTRUCTIVE TRUSTS

13.1.1 Constructive Trusts: The Basics

The previous chapter described how plaintiffs who seek a restitutionary remedy may measure (and then collect) defendants' gains. In all but the simplest real-world cases, the measurement process requires courts to disentangle defendants' finances. How much revenue did plaintiffs' misappropriated item produce? Did defendant add something to the misappropriated item to produce value? If so, how much credit should defendant get for defendant's contribution? Courts will order an accounting for profits to determine the relevant dollar figures.

After the court conducts an accounting for profits and reaches a final dollar total, the amount may be embodied in a money judgment, collectible under the rules described in Chapter 17. If defendant is solvent and has assets that are easy to find and not protected by law, a money judgment will be an adequate way to ensure that plaintiff can collect defendant's gains. If defendant is bankrupt, however, a money judgment would be an inadequate remedy: plaintiff would have to stand in line with other creditors of the defendant, and might only receive a small portion of the judgment as defendant's assets are divided up among the creditors. So if Mr. Gaste (from Chapter 12) has obtained a six-figure money judgment from Fermata, but Fermata is insolvent, a money judgment won't be worth much to Mr. Gaste.

Additionally, if the defendant has taken plaintiff's misappropriated item and used it to purchase other assets that have appreciated in value, a money judgment may not fully capture that appreciation. Recall, for example, the case of Anita from the preceding chapter. Anita stole Brianna's digital camera and sold it to a pawnshop for $150. Anita then bet the money at the racetrack. She did well at the track, and the $150 is now worth $1,000. Brianna would prefer the $1,000 in track winnings over the camera's $200 value or the pawnshop value of $150.

A money judgment may also not be a good remedy for plaintiff when defendant has transferred plaintiff's property to a third party. If Anita, for example, has given Brianna's digital camera as a gift to her friend David, Anita may wish to go after David for return of the camera (rather than sue Anita for damages).

The *equitable* restitutionary remedy of a *constructive trust* can be more beneficial to a plaintiff than a simple money judgment in at least three situations:

1. Defendant is bankrupt, and plaintiff can trace his or her property to an identifiable asset.
2. Defendant has purchased an identifiable asset with plaintiff's property, and this asset has appreciated in value.
3. Defendant has transferred plaintiff's property to a third person, and plaintiff wants the third person to return the item.

A word about equitable remedies before explaining what a constructive trust is: Part II of this book discussed equitable remedies in great detail (but some of you may be reading this part of the book before Part II). The most important equitable remedy is the injunction, but it is not the only one. To recap from Part II (or remind readers who have forgotten), an equitable remedy is one that was traditionally available in England in the courts of equity, and it requires the plaintiff to show that a traditional legal remedy — such as damages — is "inadequate" (the "irreparable injury rule"). (The new Restatement, however, takes the position that proof of irreparable injury should not be required to get any restitutionary remedy. RTR § 4(2).) Equitable remedies are backed by the court's contempt power, meaning that the court can coerce a reluctant defendant to comply and can punish willful disobedience of the court's order.

A constructive trust is an equitable restitutionary remedy that in some circumstances (1) gives plaintiff seeking restitution a preference in bankruptcy, (2) allows plaintiffs to "trace" defendant's gains from plaintiff's misappropriated item into an item purchased by defendant that has appreciated in value, or (3) allows plaintiffs to "trace" plaintiff's item from defendant to a third person. There is a technical requirement (owing to the remedy's equitable origins) that plaintiffs seeking constructive trusts demonstrate irreparable injury, but many courts ignore this requirement.

A constructive trust is not a real trust: instead, the law engages in the fiction that the defendant was holding the plaintiff's property in trust, and that transactions with the plaintiff's property were transactions defendant entered into with the intent to benefit the plaintiff. The constructive trust is a fiction because the defendant need not have had the intent to hold the property for the benefit of the plaintiff: rather, the law treats the defendant *as if* he or she had this intent.[1] *See Wadlington v. Edwards*, 92 So. 2d 629, 631 (Fla. 1957) ("[A] constructive trust is a relationship adjudicated to exist by a court of equity based on particular factual situations created by one or the other of the parties. The element of intent or agreement either oral or written to create the trust relationship is totally lacking. The trust is 'constructed' by equity to prevent an unjust enrichment of one person at the expense of another as the result of fraud, undue influence, abuse of confidence or mistake in the transaction that originates the problem.").

Thus, when Anita steals Brianna's camera, hocks it at the pawnshop, and bets the money at the track, you can be sure that Anita is not doing all these things to benefit Brianna as Brianna's "trustee." But if the court imposes a constructive trust, Brianna can recover the entire $1,000 winnings at the track (assuming she can identify those funds — more about this point coming up) under the constructive trust fiction: it is *as though* Anita was holding the property in trust for Brianna.

A court acting in equity has discretion to impose a constructive trust or not depending upon whether justice requires doing so.[2] As the quotation from the *Wadlington* case shows, some courts will impose a constructive trust not only in cases of fraud or theft, but also in cases of mistake, such as when the bank mistakenly overpaid the professor upon closing her bank account.

In some other states, and everywhere in the bankruptcy context, however, courts will not impose a constructive trust for mere mistakes. The plaintiff must prove fraud, theft, or similarly bad conduct and be able to identify specific assets. *In re North American Coin & Currency, Ltd.*, 767 F.2d 1573 (9th Cir. 1985).

Why these limits? The issue in bankruptcy is not just about the fairness of dividing goods or money between the plaintiff and the defendant; third parties are involved as well. Consider, for example, Anita's other creditors, such as her landlord, the bank holding her car loan, and other people Anita has wronged. Bankruptcy law sets up a system of priorities to determine which classes of creditors get to collect money first and how much each

---

1. The constructive trust is no more of a real trust than a quasi-contract (or "contract implied in law") is a real contact. See Chapter 11 for more on quasi-contract claims.
2. The Restatement generally follows the common law tracing rules, RTR § 59(2), but it does not allow plaintiffs to trace into the gains of *innocent* recipients of unjust enrichment. *Id.*, § 59(3). It includes detailed rules on priority of competing claims, beginning with § 60. See especially §§ 66-67, on bona fide purchasers.

creditor obtains. Those at the bottom of the list often will get nothing. The constructive trust, using the fiction that the money is really the "plaintiff's money," in effect gives the plaintiff a preference in bankruptcy over other creditors who would have priority to collect from defendant's assets.

One way of limiting the plaintiff's preference in bankruptcy obtained through a constructive trust is to grant the preference to plaintiff only to the extent of plaintiff's losses. For example, recall that Brianna lost a camera worth $200. A court could well say that in the bankruptcy context, Anita held in constructive trust $200 of the $1,000 track winnings for Brianna, allowing Brianna to use the constructive trust to recover through a preference only to the extent of her losses. Without the constructive trust giving Brianna a preference in bankruptcy, Brianna might get a judgment for $200 but no realistic possibility of collecting that amount. Instead Brianna would stand in line with other creditors to receive only a small portion of her $200 loss (or nothing at all). With the constructive trust, Brianna gets priority against other creditors over $200 of Anita's winnings (but not the full $1,000).

Recall that in bankruptcy, the plaintiff must not only show fraud, theft, or similar wrongdoing; the plaintiff must also point to identifiable assets. Indeed, this identification requirement is a prerequisite to court imposition of a constructive trust in or out of bankruptcy. RTR § 55 cmt. a ("A transaction in which the defendant (i) has been unjustly enriched (ii) by acquiring legal title to specifically identifiable property (iii) at the expense of the claimant or in violation of the claimant's rights is one in which — by the traditional formula — the defendant's title to the property is subject to the claimant's equitable interest.").[3]

To understand the identification requirement, consider three variations on the Anita-Brianna hypothetical. Anita steals the camera and hocks it at the pawnshop for $150. After that, one of the following three scenarios occurs:

1. Anita takes the $150 and bets it at the track. She loses all the money.
2. Anita takes the $150 and deposits it into her bank account, which had a balance of $500. She later withdraws $150 and bets it at the track, winning $1,000.

---

3. The Restatement offers the example of a son who works in his father's business for a nominal salary, upon an oral promise that at the father's 75th birthday, the son will receive a 50% share of the business. The father repudiates the promise, which is unenforceable under the Statute of Frauds. Though the son has a claim in restitution, and possibly a claim for an equitable lien (discussed below), he cannot get a constructive trust "because the transaction by which Father was unjustly enriched was not the source of Father's title to identifiable property." Id., illus. 14 & 15.

3. Anita takes the $150 and deposits it into one of her bank accounts, which had a balance of $500. She then withdraws $150 from a different bank account and bets it at the track, winning $1,000.

In hypotheticals 1 and 3, Brianna will not be able to use the constructive trust remedy, whether or not Anita is in bankruptcy. The problem for Brianna is that she cannot point to an *identifiable asset* of hers that Anita used to realize a gain.

In hypothetical 1, there simply was no gain, and therefore no assets to trace. Brianna's best bet is to seek damages for the $200 loss of her camera, and hope that the damages (or at least part of them) will be collectible from Anita in bankruptcy.

In hypothetical 3, there was a gain, but it is not traceable to Brianna's loss. Figure 13.1 contrasts the original hypothetical with hypothetical 3, showing traceability only in the original hypothetical. In the original hypothetical, we can say that the digital camera was Brianna's. Anita turned that camera into $150 cash at the pawnshop, which she later converted to winning racetrack tickets and finally to cash. In hypothetical 3, in contrast, Anita turned Brianna's camera into $150 cash at the pawnshop, and that money then stayed in bank account 1. The track winnings came from separate money in bank account 2. Because Brianna cannot trace her assets to the track winnings in hypothetical 3, she cannot trace to Anita's gains in a constructive trust either to realize a greater gain or, in the case of bankruptcy, to gain a preference in bankruptcy.

> *Original hypothetical*
>
> Digital camera → $150 from pawnshop → racetrack tickets → $1,000 track winnings
>
> *Hypothetical 3*
>
> Digital camera → $150 from pawnshop → bank account 1
> Bank account 2 → racetrack tickets → $1,000 track winnings

Figure 13.1

Note the odd happenstance of hypothetical 3. Anita could just as easily have taken the $150 she bet at the track from bank account 1 rather than bank account 2. If she would have done so, then Brianna would have been able to trace to the track winnings. See Figure 13.2.

Hypothetical 3: *Variation with money taken from same bank*

Digital camera ➝ $150 from pawnshop ➝
bank account 1 ➝ racetrack tickets ➝
$1,000 track winnings

Figure 13.2

If you reexamine the three hypotheticals, you will notice that this last variation is actually hypothetical 2. Courts facing a situation like hypothetical 2 will allow Brianna to trace the digital camera to the pawnshop money to the bank account to the track winnings — either to allow Brianna to capture Anita's gain at the track or, if Anita is bankrupt, to give Brianna a preference in bankruptcy.

Consider, however, for a while longer the tracing illustrated in Figure 13.2. It does not seem farfetched to say either that Anita transformed Brianna's camera into $150 or to say that the $150 Anita took from the bank was transformed into winning tickets that allowed her to receive $1,000. But in the middle of that transaction was the bank deposit. Let's suppose the pawnbroker gave Anita a $100 bill and a $50 bill. When Anita brought those bills to the bank and "deposited them" in her account, the bank did not keep the two particular bills for Anita. Instead, the bank simply noted on Anita's account a credit in the amount of $150, payable on demand to Anita either in new bills or in some other financial instrument such as a check. It took the $100 and $50 bills and used them for other bank purposes, such as giving the bills to another bank customer.

When Anita withdrew $150 in cash, did the money really come "from" Brianna's camera, or was it from Anita's own $500 funds or from somewhere else? Despite the reality that the $150 deposited into the bank account is gone, courts routinely will treat plaintiff's money that goes into a bank account (or similar financial account) as traceable to plaintiff (at plaintiff's option) when it is removed — at least when it is advantageous for plaintiff to so treat the money (it would not be advantageous if, for example, Anita lost all of her bets with that $150). In the next subpart of this chapter, I address the details on fictions related to tracing — particularly when the defendant has commingled her assets with plaintiff's assets. The bottom line here is that courts will engage in a fiction that monies deposited in a bank account remain identifiable for tracing purposes, even though the actual dollars are exchanged for a bank's promise to pay the depositor later when depositor demands the money.

Finally, a constructive trust is useful when plaintiff's asset (or something the defendant converted the asset into) has fallen into the hands of third parties. The example again is David, who obtains Brianna's stolen digital camera as a gift from Anita. So long as David is not a bona fide purchaser — that is, someone who paid fair market value for the item without actual or constructive ("reasonably should have known") knowledge that the seller did not possess good title to the item (see RTR §§ 66, 67) — Brianna will be in a position to ask for return of the item as a form of specific restitution (or replevin, see section 13.3.1 below) under the fiction that David was holding the camera for Brianna in a constructive trust. *See* RTR § 58(2). Brianna can trace even further. For example, if David took the gift camera from Anita, sold it for $150 at the pawnshop and went to the track, winning $1,000 with the money, Brianna should be able to get a constructive trust over that $1,000, though it again would be limited to $200 if David were insolvent. If David, unaware of the theft, adversely changed his position after receiving the camera, the Restatement gives room for courts to limit Brianna's remedies. RTR § 65.

Example 1

Defendants sold rare coins over the Internet. The business was not doing very well. It looked as though the business might fail. Defendants took all the orders that arrived during the week of January 1 and put the payments for those orders in a special bank account. Defendants knew there was a risk that they could not fulfill the orders and wanted to protect their newest customers. Defendants did not fill the orders, and a week later, Defendants went bankrupt. Rather than receive only pennies on the dollar in the bankruptcy court, a group of plaintiffs whose orders arrived during the week of January 1 asked the court to grant them a constructive trust over the assets in that bank account. Should the court grant the constructive trust remedy, giving the January 1 plaintiffs a preference in bankruptcy?

Explanation

This hypothetical is based on *North American Coin*, a case cited earlier in the chapter. In that case, state law provided that plaintiffs in the position of the January 1 plaintiffs should be entitled to a constructive trust. That, of course, stretches the identifiability requirement somewhat. We already engage in the fiction that when a defendant deposits plaintiff's money in an account, that money remains identifiable in that account. Here, we have a commingling of a number of plaintiffs' assets, and so a court granting a constructive trust to the class engages in the fiction that the bank is holding this set of plaintiffs' funds separately for each plaintiff.

There is a further problem here, however, concerning the application of the constructive trust in the bankruptcy context. Though the assets are (arguably) identifiable, a court will not impose a constructive trust in bankruptcy in the absence of fraud, theft, or similar bad conduct. In this case, defendants were not guilty of fraud. (It is not fraud to continue to solicit orders for your company even if the company faces a risk of bankruptcy.) Were this not a bankruptcy case, some courts in equity might have imposed a constructive trust.

This example is good for thinking about whether the fraud and identifiability requirements are sensible criteria for determining when certain plaintiffs should obtain a benefit in bankruptcy. Let's analyze the fraud requirement first. Imagine that, in the coin case, Defendants were committing fraud on all of their clients. They promised to send them rare gold coins but they were sending counterfeits. Someone at the company, however, segregated the money coming in the week of January 1 out of fear that the company was going to go under soon.

If a court would grant the January 1 plaintiffs a preference in bankruptcy under these conditions, it would mean that those plaintiffs who were lucky enough to be defrauded last would have a preference over those customers of Defendants who were defrauded earlier. It is not clear why these later-defrauded plaintiffs should get such a preference from the court.

Now vary the hypothetical a bit. Suppose only the January 1 plaintiffs were victims of fraud by Defendants. (For all pre–January 1 orders, Defendants had every intention of filling the orders; for the January 1 plaintiffs, Defendants knew the company was going to go bankrupt, and they committed fraud by soliciting sales they knew they could not fulfill.) Defendants took the money from all plaintiffs and deposited it into an account with money from all sources, including pre–January 1 order payments. Under these circumstances, plaintiffs can prove the requisite fraud, but they cannot identify their assets — because their money went into a larger bank account with income from a variety of sources. It is not clear why this fact, either, should be dispositive in the decision whether or not to grant plaintiffs a preference in bankruptcy.

Example 2

Back to our Anita-Brianna hypothetical, with a new twist. This time, after Anita steals the camera, she sells it to the pawnshop for $200, its fair market value. The owner of the pawnshop is a bona fide purchaser and later sells the camera to another person (who cannot be located) for $225. Anita deposits the $200 into her bank account. Anita is not bankrupt; indeed, she has many assets. Should the court impose a constructive trust on the $200 in Anita's bank account?

Explanation

At first glance, this looks like a no-brainer. Brianna's asset is still identifiable: Anita transformed the camera into $200 that is now in Anita's bank account. Moreover, Anita's conduct in stealing the camera likely would be sufficiently bad to convince most courts that a constructive trust is warranted in the court's discretion.

The complication here is that a constructive trust is an *equitable* remedy, and at least formally, courts are not supposed to grant an equitable remedy unless the plaintiff can demonstrate that there is no adequate remedy at law. (Much more about this "irreparable injury" requirement can be found in Part II of the book.) Here, Anita could argue that damages are just as good a remedy as a constructive trust because Anita is not bankrupt, and therefore Brianna will be able to collect her money with a money judgment. The measure of Brianna's loss is the same as the measure of Anita's gain: $200.

Anita might prefer that Brianna seek a legal remedy so that she can have a jury trial—not available when a plaintiff seeks equitable relief—and because court enforcement of legal remedies is not backed by the court's power of contempt. Still, it appears that many courts do not take the irreparable injury requirement seriously in the context of equitable restitutionary remedies such as constructive trusts. In some courts, however, it will be necessary to show that damages are not as good a remedy as the constructive trust remedy would be.

13.1.2 Advanced Tracing Problems

We have now seen the constructive trust concept applied to allow for tracing into defendant's assets or even into the hands of third parties who are not bona fide purchasers. In this section, we consider some additional complications that arise in tracing, particularly when there has been a mingling of plaintiff's assets and defendant's (or a third party's) assets.

Let's begin with a straightforward example to illustrate the problem, continuing with variations on our Anita-Brianna hypothetical. Again Anita steals Brianna's camera and sells it to the pawnshop for $150. Anita takes the $150 and deposits it into her bank account, which had a balance of $150, so the new balance is now $300. Anita withdraws the full $300, bets $150 on red at the roulette wheel, and loses it all. She then bets $150 on the horses, winning $1,000. See Figure 13.3.

Digital camera ⟶ $150 from pawnshop ⟶
bank account (prior $150 balance, new $300 total)
⟶ $150 ⟶ roulette wheel ⟶ 0
⟶ $150 ⟶ racetrack ⟶ $1,000

Figure 13.3 Anita's Commingled Funds

A look at Figure 13.3 reveals the problem. Anita would want to argue that she spent Brianna's $150 on the roulette wheel (the bad investment) and Anita's own $150 at the racetrack (the good investment that yielded a $1,000 payoff). If that were the case, Brianna's attempt to trace would fail because the assets from the camera fell to zero. Brianna, in contrast, would want to argue that Anita's money went to the bad investment and Brianna's to the track winnings. Maybe the fairest thing to do would be to say that $75 of Brianna's money and $75 of Anita's money went into the good investment, meaning Brianna would be able to trace to $1,000.

Fortunately for those who like simplicity, the law lets the plaintiff engage in whatever fictions yield the best result for her, *determined with perfect hindsight*. This is a key point, but it is rather counter-intuitive: when a plaintiff uses a constructive trust for tracing in the case of commingled assets, the plaintiff gets to use two fictions to identify the most advantageous means of tracing (LAYCOCK pp. 714-715):

1. The wrongdoer spends his own money first on *bad* investments.
2. The wrongdoer spends plaintiff's money first on *good* investments.

In the case illustrated in Figure 13.3, Brianna gets to use the fiction that Anita spent Anita's money first on bad investments, and spent Brianna's money first on good investments. The question is *not* one of Anita's intent. Her intent is irrelevant.

The fictions have their limits however. Consider this further variation on the Anita-Brianna hypothetical. Again Anita steals Brianna's camera and sells it to the pawnshop for $150. Anita takes the $150 and deposits it into her bank account, which had a balance of $0. Anita withdraws the $150 and bets the $150 on red at the roulette wheel and loses it all. Anita then deposits $150 of her own money in her account, then withdraws it and bets $150 on the horses, winning $1,000. See Figure 13.4.

Digital camera —→ $150 from pawnshop —→
bank account (prior $0 balance, new $150) —→
$150 —→ roulette wheel —→ 0
Anita's own $150 —→ bank account —→
$150 —→ racetrack —→ $1,000

Figure 13.4 Anita's Non-commingled Funds

A court will not allow Brianna to trace in this situation because her asset went down to zero: it went from the camera to the pawnshop to the bank account to the cash to the loss at the roulette wheel. The winnings at the track indisputably came from money that was not Brianna's. "Once plaintiffs trace their money into a commingled account, anything that was possible is presumed in their favor, however unlikely, but the impossible is not presumed." LAYCOCK p. 715. In other words, the plaintiff can never trace more than that which originated from the *lowest intermediate balance* in the bank account.

While there is some logic to the rule that prevents tracing where chronology makes it impossible to do so, it does show the limits of the fictions and the serendipity of tracing. Comparing Figures 13.3 and 13.4, Anita committed exactly the same wrong and had exactly the same gains and losses with exactly the same bets. The only difference between the two examples is that in Figure 13.4, Brianna was unlucky that Anita did not commingle her own $150 in her bank account before Anita withdrew the money for the two investments.

The fictions themselves are not difficult to apply with enough practice. The key is to work backward, keeping some kind of ledger as to which funds and assets should be attributable to plaintiff and which to defendant.

Consider the following example. Larry takes care of his old aunt Gertrude's finances. Unbeknownst to Gertrude, Larry cashes a $100,000 certificate of deposit belonging to Gertrude and deposits it in his own account, which had a balance of $50,000 in it. Larry takes $75,000 out of his account and buys 7,500 shares of Loserco stock. He takes another $25,000 out of his account and buys 2,500 shares of Winnerco stock. He then takes $40,000 from his bank account, losing it in Las Vegas. Gertrude discovers the fraud and sues for restitution. At this point, Loserco stock had fallen to $30,000 and Winnerco stock had gone up to $100,000. Larry is not bankrupt. How can Gertrude trace most advantageously in this case?

Let's begin by making a ledger showing Larry's bank account and transactions:

Bank account total	Action/explanation
$50,000	Larry's initial balance
$150,000	Addition of Gertrude's $100,000
$75,000	Withdrawal of $75,000 to buy Loserco stock
$50,000	Withdrawal of $25,000 to buy Winnerco stock
$10,000	Withdrawal of $40,000 for Vegas losses

Looking at this with hindsight (as Gertrude's lawyer can and should do), one thing that's for sure is that Gertrude wants to use the fiction that she bought the Winnerco stock for $25,000 that went up to $100,000. After tracing $25,000 to the Winnerco Stock, Gertrude has $75,000 more of her money to allocate. She could simply use the fiction that she spent this $75,000 on Loserco stock. That would mean the total value of her recovery would be the Winnerco and Loserco stock, currently worth a total of $130,000.

That's not bad for Gertrude, because she would be getting $30,000 more than the return of her $100,000 loss. But there's something she can do that's even more advantageous. The Loserco stock has declined in value by more than half (it was bought for $75,000 and has fallen to $30,000). But there is $10,000 in the account that has not declined in value at all. Gertrude can therefore do the following:

1. Allocate $25,000 of her funds for the purchase of Winnerco stock.
2. Allocate $10,000 of her funds to remain in the bank account.
3. Allocate the remaining amount of the funds ($65,000) to buy Loserco stock.

If Gertrude takes these steps, she maximizes her recovery:

1. Her purchase of Winnerco stock is now worth $100,000.
2. Her $10,000 bank account allocation is still worth $10,000.
3. Her purchase of $65,000/$75,000 worth of the Loserco stock means that she now has stock worth $26,000. (This is a 65/75, or 13/15, interest in stock worth a total of $30,000.)

$100,000 + 10,000 + 26,000 = $136,000, which is better than if Gertrude had taken all of the Loserco stock.

The lesson: from the plaintiff's perspective in tracing, watch the bottom line, looking for the most advantageous way to allocate money used by defendant. Work backward and look at options to maximize plaintiff's recovery.

Example 3

Same facts as in the Larry-Gertrude example just given, but assume that Larry's bank account started with nothing, and that Larry deposited his own $50,000 in the account after he purchased the Loserco stock. How, if at all, does that change Gertrude's tracing options?

Explanation

Let's begin by making a ledger so we can keep these transactions straight:

Bank account total	Action/explanation
$0	Larry's initial balance
$100,000	Addition of Gertrude's $100,000
$25,000	Withdrawal of $75,000 to buy Loserco stock
$75,000	Addition of Larry's $50,000
$50,000	Withdrawal of $25,000 to buy Winnerco stock
$10,000	Withdrawal of $40,000 for Vegas losses

As this sequence indicates, Gertrude has no choice but to allocate to herself the purchase of the Loserco stock for $75,000. Larry *had no money of his own in the account at the time*, so a court will not allocate any Loserco stock to him. This is an application of the lowest intermediate balance rule. This leaves Gertrude with $25,000 remaining to allocate. She could allocate some or all of it for the purchase of the Winnerco stock. One possibility is that she allocates all of it to the Winnerco stock. Another possibility is that she allocates $15,000 to the Winnerco stock and $10,000 to the money remaining in the bank account. The former allocation is more advantageous for Gertrude. If she buys all the Winnerco stock, she gets stock now worth $100,000. If she allocates only $15,000, she gets $15,000/$25,000 (3/5) of the stock now worth $100,000, for $60,000. This $60,000 plus the $10,000 in the bank account gives Gertrude a total of $70,000.

Gertrude's best allocation under these facts is to take all the Loserco stock, now worth $30,000, plus all the Winnerco stock, now worth $100,000, for a total of $130,000. The example shows that Gertrude gets $6,000 less than she would have gotten in the original hypothetical because of the timing of Larry's $50,000 deposit into his own account.

Example 4

Hilda steals Ike's car and sells it for $25,000 cash to a buyer, who has disappeared with the car. Hilda gives $10,000 of the cash to her boyfriend, Jake. Jake deposits the money into his bank account, which had a balance of $1,000. Jake then withdraws $100 from his account and uses it to buy groceries and a lottery ticket. The lottery ticket is a winner, and Jake wins $1,000,000. Meanwhile, Hilda takes the $15,000 remaining and goes on a shopping spree, buying a plasma television set and nice new furniture. What, if anything, can Ike recover from Hilda and/or Jake?

Explanation

Let's consider tracing to Jake first. Jake received the $10,000 as a gift, so Ike can trace his assets to Jake. (In the common legal jargon, we would call Jake a gratuitous donee, rather than a bona fide purchaser for value.) Let's begin again with a ledger:

Bank account total	Action/explanation
$1,000	Jake's initial balance
$11,000	Jake's balance after the addition of Ike's $10,000
$10,900	Jake's balance after the $100 withdrawal

To maximize Ike's recovery, he should trace $9,999 of his $10,000 into Jake's bank account. He would argue that one of his dollars was part of the $100 withdrawn by Jake and used to purchase the lottery ticket worth $1,000,000. This gives him a restitutionary recovery from Jake of $1,009,999.

Hilda has taken Ike's $15,000 and converted it into specific household goods. Ike may recover these goods — in addition to his recovery from Jake — in restitution.

Example 5

Same facts as in Example 4, except Hilda has sold her car to Karen, who buys it knowing that it is stolen. Also, Jake did not win the lottery. How does this change Ike's options?

Explanation

Like Jake in the preceding example, Karen is not a bona fide purchaser for value. For this reason, Ike can trace to get back the car itself from Karen. He does not have to do so, however. He could instead choose to trace the funds that Hilda gave to Jake (there's still Ike's $10,000 in Jake's account) and to the household goods Hilda has purchased. The choice is Ike's. The significant point is that Ike must *choose*. He can't trace to both the car and the proceeds of the car: to do so would violate the fiction that one is tracing the assets.

In this case, it is not clear that one choice is better than the other for Ike. It depends on the values as discovered by Ike's lawyer. If, however, Jake had won the lottery, it would certainly make sense to trace the money and not the car.

13.2 EQUITABLE LIENS

An *equitable lien* is another restitutionary remedy that can give plaintiffs seeking restitution an advantage in certain situations. Like a constructive trust, an equitable lien is an *equitable* remedy that is subject to the requirements and benefits of equitable relief discussed earlier.

Before describing how an *equitable* lien works, it is important first to understand how a *lien* works. "A lien is a charge against property that makes the property stand as security for a debt owed. A creditor who has a lien upon property of the debtor is entitled at a proper time to have the property sold and the proceeds used for payment of the debt. The lien creditor thus stands in a better position than a general, unsecured creditor of the same debtor, because he has a priority: the property subject to his lien is in effect set aside for the satisfaction of his claim first." DOBBS § 4.3(3), at 600. So, for example, my car loan with my bank is subject to a lien. If I don't pay my debt, the bank can repossess my car and get priority over the car even if I am in bankruptcy and have other creditors. This repossession occurs instead of the bankruptcy trustee's selling the car, putting the proceeds into the rest of the pot of my money, and paying off creditors in the order set by bankruptcy law. Similarly, if I don't pay my home mortgage, the holder of the mortgage can force a sale of my house ("foreclosure"), using the proceeds first to pay the debt I owe, then turning the rest of the money over to me (or to other creditors who may have a secured interest in the house).

An equitable lien "is a money judgment secured by a lien on specific property." LAYCOCK p. 729. It creates a real lien on property that (in most circumstances) can be subject to foreclosure. The lien that is created is real, but it is not created through any agreement of the parties (as when the bank and I agreed on the conditions of my car loan); instead, it is created by the court to prevent unjust enrichment. DOBBS § 4.3, pp. 600-601.

For example, suppose that Mona owns land adjacent to Ned's land. Mona builds a shed on Ned's land, mistakenly believing that it is on Mona's land. Ned realizes that Mona is making this mistake as she builds the shed, and he does nothing to correct the error. Under the substantive law of restitution (as described in Chapter 11), Ned has been unjustly enriched. If Mona can move the shed off Ned's property, a court will allow Mona access to remove it. But if it cannot be removed, an equitable lien may be an appropriate remedy. Suppose the shed has increased the value of Ned's land by $20,000. A court can award Mona a money judgment in the amount of $20,000, backed up by the equitable lien. If Ned does not pay up, Mona can foreclose on Ned's land, keep the first $20,000 of the proceeds for herself, and give the rest of the money to Ned.

As the Mona-Ned example shows, an equitable lien can be a powerful remedy. There is the danger that in some cases, however, it is too powerful a remedy. Suppose, for example, that Ned is poor and old, and cannot afford to pay Mona the $20,000. A foreclosure would force him out of his modest house. For this reason, a court in equity might award Mona the equitable lien, but not allow her to foreclose on the property until Ned transfers ownership of his property to someone else or dies. RTR § 10, cmt. g, illus. 19. Whether a court would delay the possibility of foreclosure is a question of fairness the court would address; Ned's case for a delay in foreclosure would be even stronger if he did not learn of Mona's mistake until after she built the shed.

The Mona-Ned hypothetical illustrates the flexibility that courts can employ in difficult cases such as those involving mistaken improvements to land.[4]

---

4. The RTR's general position on remedies in mistaken improver cases states, "A remedy for mistaken improvement that subjects the owner to a forced exchange will be qualified or limited to avoid undue prejudice to the owner." RTR § 10.

The Restatement notes the range of options for courts in mistaken improver cases:

The remedy for a given instance of mistaken improvement will be fashioned by the court in the interest of substantial justice. Possible remedies available for use in an appropriate case include:

(1) an order permitting the improver to remove all or part of the improvement, on condition that the owner be indemnified against damage to the property;

(2) a money judgment for the increased value of the property resulting from the improvement, or for the cost of the improvement to the improver, whichever is less, payable on such terms as the court may specify;

(3) an equitable lien securing the improver's allowable money claim, subject to such limitations (concerning the time of foreclosure and otherwise) as the court may specify;

(4) an order allowing the improver to remain in temporary possession of the improvements, subject to appropriate limitations regarding the extent and nature of such possession, on payment to owner of the value thereof;

(5) an order giving the owner an option either (i) to pay the improver for the increased value of the property attributable to the improvement or for the cost of the improvement, whichever is less, or (ii) to sell the improved property to the improver at its unimproved value;

Delaying the timing for foreclosure can sometimes work to ensure a fair remedy in appropriate cases.

An equitable lien is typically used in real property disputes (though it is not limited to such applications), and when it is, the dispute must be connected to the real property. When Anita steals Brianna's camera worth $200, for example, Brianna may be entitled to restitution for any gains Anita receives from the theft. But Brianna cannot get an equitable lien for the value of these gains over Anita's home. *The wrong must be connected to the property itself. See* RTR § 56(1)(b).

In some circumstances, it might appear that either a constructive trust or an equitable lien would be an appropriate restitutionary remedy. Suppose, for example, that Olivia is Pauline's lawyer. Olivia is holding Pauline's money in a client trust account to pay future legal bills. Olivia steals $20,000 of Pauline's money from the account and uses the money to remodel her kitchen. One possible remedy for Olivia's tort is that the court will impose an equitable lien in the amount of $20,000, forcing Olivia to either pay up or face Pauline's foreclosure. An alternative remedy a court might impose is a constructive trust made up of an interest in Olivia's house equal to the $20,000 increased value. For example, a court could award a constructive trust over 5% of Olivia's $400,000 home.

Which remedy should Pauline prefer? The answer may depend upon whether the property is increasing or decreasing in value. An equitable lien defines the remedy in set dollar amounts (here $20,000), a good choice for *declining assets*. A constructive trust defines the remedy as a percentage interest in the property (here 5% of Olivia's home), a good choice for *assets appreciating in value*.

Thus, if Olivia's house decreases in value from the time of the wrong (value of $400,000) to the time of trial (value of $300,000), an equitable lien preserves Pauline's right to $20,000. Conversely, if Olivia's house increases in value from the time of the wrong (value of $400,000) to the time of trial (value of $500,000), a constructive trust gives Pauline a chance to share in that appreciation. Rather than getting only $20,000 (5% of the

---

(6) an order giving the owner an option either (i) to pay the improver for the increased value of the property attributable to the improvement or for the cost of the improvement, whichever is less, or (ii) to exchange the improved property for a specified tract, substantially equivalent to the improved property in its unimproved state; and

(7) an order directing that the improved property be sold, as on partition, the improver to receive the increased amount of the net proceeds attributable to the improvement or the cost of the improvement, whichever is less.

RTR § 10, cmt. g; *see also* RTR § 56(2) ("An equitable lien secures the obligation of the defendant to pay the claimant the amount of the defendant's unjust enrichment as separately determined. Foreclosure of an equitable lien is subject to such conditions as the court may direct.").

$400,000 value), Pauline will be able to get $25,000 (5% of the new $500,000 value).

Note that not all courts will allow Pauline to obtain a constructive trust in these circumstances. Dobbs takes the view that "if the defendant merely uses plaintiff's money to add a house on a lot he already owns, it is clear that plaintiff has no claim to a constructive trust on the house and lot because his money did not go into the lot. He is entitled instead to an equitable lien on the house and lot for the amount of money embezzled from him." DOBBS § 4.3(3), p. 602. Whether courts allow constructive trusts, equitable liens, or a choice between the two in appropriate cases depends upon each state's case law as well as the judge's views of the equities of the particular case. The Restatement's position is that anyone who meets the requirements for a constructive trust may, at her option, choose an equitable lien instead. RTR § 56(3).

Example 6

"A dies, leaving a tract of unimproved land by will to B. B sells the land to C, a bona fide purchaser, who clears the land and builds a house which he occupies. The will is found to be invalid, with the result that the title to the land passes to D, A's heir. D intends to sell the property as soon as title can be cleared." RTR § 10, cmt. g, illus. 14. (a) Can C get an equitable lien over the value of the improvements he made to D's property? (b) What if D did not intend to sell the property but instead intended to build a house and live there?

Explanation

(a) The Restatement says that D should be given an election between paying C the portion of the sale attributable to C's improvements or selling to C at the property's unimproved value. To secure C's right to one of the remedies, the court should grant C an equitable lien on the property until D decides.

(b) The Restatement illustration does not pose (or answer) the second question, but it is considerably harder as a matter of justice. In the original example, the tract of land had value to D only for its sale value. Under the alternative scenario, D intends to use the land to build a home; perhaps the land has sentimental value to D that exceeds the market value. Perhaps D does not have the funds to pay C for the extensive improvements C has made to the property; D perhaps planned to build a more modest home. The Restatement gives courts the power to be flexible with remedies in the interest of justice. In this case, a court likely would have a difficult time deciding whether to give C the right to foreclose on an equitable lien for the value of the improvements he made to the property.

Example 7

Quentin steals $1,000 from Rana, his employer. Quentin uses the $1,000 to buy a gold necklace for his girlfriend, Samantha. Can Rana get an equitable lien against the necklace?

Explanation

An equitable lien does not appear to be the appropriate remedy in this case. Although the necklace is property, it is not real property, and some courts will limit the remedy to real property claims. Further, recall that the equitable lien would give Rana the right to a money judgment secured by the property. Though that's a possible remedy, the more straightforward thing for Rana to do is to use the constructive trust remedy to gain the necklace itself, which Rana could then sell or keep. A constructive trust would be especially attractive if the necklace appreciated in value between the time of the wrong and the time of judgment.

Example 8

Shrek steals lumber from Fiona's property and uses it to build a house on his land. The lot alone was worth $50,000; the lot and house together are worth $150,000. The market value of the lumber that Shrek stole from Fiona's property and used to build his house is $10,000. The other building materials cost Shrek $40,000. Is Fiona entitled to an equitable lien? If so, for how much? If Fiona is entitled to an equitable lien, would she prefer a constructive trust (if allowed by a court) over that remedy?

Explanation

Fiona should be entitled to an equitable lien. Shrek has stolen her lumber, giving Fiona a right either to damages or to restitution. An equitable lien appears to be an appropriate remedy here, given that Shrek has used Fiona's property to add value to his home.

The amount of the equitable lien presents an interesting question. At the very least, Fiona should be entitled to an equitable lien for the fair market value of the lumber, or $10,000. She might, however, also claim a higher amount based upon her share of the appreciation under an apportionment of profits. As explained in the previous chapter, when a defendant mixes a misappropriated item with other items the defendant bought and paid for to produce something of value, courts will sometimes allow an apportionment of profits between plaintiff and defendant based upon each of their contributions. Here, Shrek combined his $50,000 in land with Fiona's $10,000 worth of lumber and with $40,000 in additional materials, to equal $100,000 in total costs to produce the house and land worth $150,000. Of the $100,000 in costs, Fiona's lumber represented 10% ($10,000/$100,000). Arguably, she should be entitled to 10% of the $50,000 profit, or an additional $5,000, meaning that Fiona should get an equitable lien of $15,000. Some courts could give Fiona an even greater recovery, allowing her the full $50,000 profit in addition to the $10,000 value of lumber because Shrek was a conscious wrongdoer. Whatever the value — $10,000, $15,000, or $60,000 — the money judgment against Shrek will be backed up by the equitable lien, giving Fiona the ability to force the sale of the house if Shrek does not pay.

A court may give Fiona the option of a constructive trust instead. (Not all courts would do so in these circumstances.) Recall that a constructive trust is expressed not as a dollar amount (the way an equitable lien is), but rather as an interest in property. Fiona could argue that her $10,000 contribution toward the total $100,000 cost entitles her to a 10% interest in Shrek's home and land. With the house now worth $150,000, her interest would be worth $15,000. If the house is appreciating in value, a constructive trust could be a good choice — though if a court would give Fiona an equitable lien in the amount of $60,000, that might be a better choice.

13.3 OTHER RESTITUTIONARY REMEDIES

13.3.1 Replevin and Ejectment

Most of the restitutionary remedies we have considered are *substitutionary remedies*. As defined in Chapter 1, substitutionary remedies are those in which the court awards plaintiff a sum of money rather than the very thing that was lost or has the potential to be lost. Considering Example 8 above, Fiona's equitable lien (or possible constructive trust) is substitutionary in that she gets a sum of money representing Shrek's gain at her expense; she does not get her lumber back.

The other type of remedy discussed in Chapter 1 was *specific relief*. Specific relief gives the plaintiff the very thing that was lost or has the potential to be lost. The remedy of specific performance in contract, for example, gives plaintiff the performance that defendant promised to deliver under the contract.

Replevin is an example of specific restitution for the return of plaintiff's personal property. It is a *legal remedy*, meaning there is no requirement to prove irreparable injury.[5] It requires defendant to return to the plaintiff the very thing that was lost and pay any additional damages for loss of use during the time that plaintiff was deprived of possession. Until recent times, courts did not consider replevin as a restitutionary remedy; historically in England, it was a writ that was distinct from the writs used to obtain forms of restitution. LAYCOCK p. 754. Today, however, a number of scholars (with courts likely to follow) consider replevin restitutionary because the remedy takes away defendant's gain: defendant gives up plaintiff's property (which defendant presumably kept because it had some value). The Restatement seems to allow for this remedy, referring to it generally as a type of "specific restitution" rather than "replevin." See RTR § 4, cmt. e.

Replevin has a compensatory aspect as well. Plaintiff gets back the thing that was lost, which serves as compensation for plaintiff's loss. Plaintiff can recover additional compensation in damages for the value of the loss of use of the item during the time defendant possessed it. In rare circumstances, courts have also allowed a plaintiff to recover damages for any loss in value of the item caused by defendant's mishandling of plaintiff's property. Welch v. Kosasky, 509 N.E.2d 919 (Mass. App. Ct. 1987); LAYCOCK pp. 754-756.

In Welch, defendant stole plaintiff's property that at the time of the theft was worth $7,500. By the time plaintiff recovered the property 13 years later, it would have appreciated in value to $25,000, but it did not because defendant damaged it, making it worth only $3,000. In addition to the return of the property, plaintiff was awarded $10,000 for the loss of use of the property for 13 years and $22,000 for the diminution in value of the property.[6]

Replevin is not always available as a remedy. Consider Shrek's theft of Fiona's lumber in Example 8. Shrek has used the lumber in construction, and it cannot be removed in any useful way from the finished home. But when the personal property is still available, whether in the hands of defendants or in the hands of third parties who are not bona fide purchasers, replevin can

---

5. See Chapter 7.2, comparing the legal remedy of replevin with the equitable remedy of injunction for the return of personal property. Some courts also recognize a cause of action for "equitable replevin." See Desiderio v. D'Ambrosio, 463 A.2d 986, 988 n.3 (N.J. Super. 1983) ("An equitable replevin, as distinct from a legal replevin, is an action for return of an item which has a special value apart from its intrinsic value and for which, therefore, there can be no measure of money damages."). In those jurisdictions recognizing the cause of action, equitable replevin, as an equitable remedy, presumably is subject to the same irreparable injury rule as an injunction.

6. The court also allowed plaintiff to recover consequential damages of $5,000, representing costs to find and recover the property that had fallen into the hands of third parties.

Not all courts would grant plaintiff the right to recover these additional damages for the diminution in value of the property. Some courts would give plaintiff the choice between (1) replevin plus damages for loss of use and (2) damages for conversion (damages through an action for theft of personal property traditionally called "trover"), which would be measured at the time of loss, plus interest since the time of loss. Though the interest on the $7,500 would be considerable for a 13-year loss, an award of market value plus interest likely would yield a smaller recovery for plaintiff than the remedy the court allowed in Welch.

be an attractive option. It is especially attractive for certain personal property, such as property with sentimental value to the plaintiff, where plaintiff's subjective valuation exceeds the market valuation of the property.

Ejectment is a form of specific restitution for *real property*, paralleling replevin's remedy for personal property. Thus, if Shrek had come onto Fiona's land as a trespasser and hoped to gain title by adverse possession, ejectment was the common law writ Fiona would have used to force Shrek to leave her property.

Ejectment has been replaced by statutory remedies in a number of states; a common type of claim (brought under these statutory successors to the writ of ejectment) involves landlords and tenants who have not paid their rent. Ejectment was not used as a remedy in cases involving genuine disputes about the title of property. These disputes were more commonly resolved through an action to quiet title, similar to a declaratory judgment action, discussed in Chapter 16.

Example 9

Sandy and Tom were law school classmates. Sandy stole Tom's state-of-the-art laptop computer. At the time it was stolen, the laptop was worth $2,000. Tom promptly went to the store and bought an identical laptop as a replacement for the same $2,000 price. Three years later at a graduation party, Tom noticed his computer in Sandy's house. Sandy refuses to give it back but offers to pay Tom $400, the reasonable value of a three-year-old laptop (which was no longer state-of-the-art) given falling prices for laptops and advances in technology.

Is Tom entitled to replevin? If so, to what else should he be entitled? Should Tom prefer a damages remedy to replevin? Why or why not?

Explanation

Tom is definitely entitled to replevin if he wants it. Replevin is a legal remedy, not an equitable one. Tom does not have to prove irreparable injury as he would if he wanted to obtain an injunction. He does not have to accept Sandy's $400 offer.

If Tom opts for replevin, a court will award Tom possession of the laptop. (He'll have to send the sheriffs to seize it; if he wants a court order requiring Sandy to turn over the laptop, he will need to get an injunction or other equitable remedy backed by the power of contempt.) In addition to the return of the laptop, Tom should be entitled to damages for loss of use. Because Tom went out and covered by buying a substitute item, a court may find that Tom suffered no damages for the loss of use. (This is unlike personal, sentimental property for which there is no substitute. In that case, there are real damages for loss of use, though they are difficult to measure for reasons explained in Part I of this book.) For this reason, Tom may use replevin to get his three-year-old laptop and nothing else.

Tom likely would prefer a damages remedy for Sandy's conversion of the laptop, which would be measured by the market value of the laptop at the time of theft plus interest. (See Part I of this book.) Because the laptop is an item that has depreciated in value, Tom would be better off with a remedy measuring value at the time of the loss (when the value was higher).

The damages remedy also does a better job of putting Tom back into the rightful position. Recall that Tom immediately went out after the theft and bought a replacement computer for $2,000. An award of $2,000 plus interest from the time of the theft appears likely to put the plaintiff in the position he would have been in but for the theft.

Example 10

Albert steals the melody from Gaste's hit song in France to write the hit song "Feelings." Albert uses the proceeds to buy a plasma television set and a piece of land, Blackacre. Can Gaste use replevin to obtain the television set? Can he use ejectment to obtain Blackacre? Alternatively, can Gaste use any other restitutionary remedies to obtain the television and/or Blackacre?

Explanation

Gaste cannot use replevin to obtain the television and he cannot use ejectment to obtain the land. Replevin is a remedy for the return of *plaintiff's personal property*. In this case, the television was never Gaste's property. It might have been bought with proceeds from Albert's misuse of Gaste's music, but that does not give Gaste a right to replevin. A parallel analysis applies to Gaste's use of ejectment: because Blackacre is not *real property to which Gaste holds title*, ejectment is not available. The point of this part of the question is to make you realize that you should not use replevin or ejectment simply because you see that there has been unjust enrichment and defendant is holding personal or real property.

It is still possible that Gaste could end up with the television set and/or Blackacre. First, if Gaste seeks restitution through a money judgment (such as after a successful claim for quasi-contract or accounting for profits), he might be able to force a sale of the television or Blackacre to collect his winnings. The details on collection appear in Chapter 17.

In addition, Gaste may attempt an accounting for profits and tracing into a constructive trust to obtain an interest in either the real or personal property. If Albert, for example, took his royalty check for "Feelings" and used it in a traceable way to buy the television set or Blackacre, Gaste may be able to get a constructive trust over all or a partial interest in the items. This is a restitutionary recovery, but it is not recovery through replevin or ejectment.

13.3.2 Subrogation, Contribution, and Indemnity

The final set of restitutionary remedies we consider in this chapter are subrogation, contribution, and indemnity. We begin with subrogation.

Subrogation is a remedy that prevents a defendant from being unjustly enriched when the plaintiff pays a sum to a third party to settle a liability or debt owed to that third party by the defendant. Subrogation can arise through a contractual agreement, in which case it is termed *conventional subrogation*, or it can arise in the absence of agreement through court creation, termed *equitable (or legal) subrogation*.

Consider this example of conventional subrogation: Ursula negligently causes an automobile accident, injuring Vicki. Vicki has health insurance with Worldwide Insurance. Worldwide pays all of Vicki's health bills. Vicki does not sue Ursula for her personal injury damages, because Vicki's contract with Worldwide has a "subrogation clause" stating that any monies Vicki receives from third parties to compensate for personal injuries must be paid over to Worldwide to compensate for the expenses Worldwide incurs in providing health care to Vicki for her personal injuries.[7] Subrogation gives Worldwide the right to "step into Vicki's shoes" and recover from Ursula the medical expenses incurred by Worldwide in bringing Vicki back to the rightful position. *See* RTR § 57 cmt. f ("Subrogation . . . yields a claim against the recipient that is strictly derivative.").

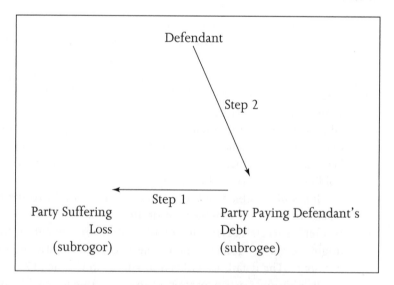

Figure 13.5 Flow of Payments in Subrogation

---

7. Without such a subrogation clause, Vicki would be able to receive both the health care from Worldwide *and* tort damages from Ursula under the collateral source rule. The collateral source rule is an exception to the rule barring plaintiff from recovering compensatory damages that exceed plaintiff's losses. See Chapter 4.

Figure 13.5 illustrates the concept of subrogation. Subrogation involves a triangle consisting of the party that caused the loss (the defendant), the party that suffered the loss (the subrogor), and the party paying the defendant's debt to the subrogor (the subrogee). In the absence of a subrogee, the defendant would be responsible to pay damages directly to the party suffering loss. Once the subrogee has paid the party suffering loss (the subrogor), the defendant no longer has an obligation to pay the subrogor (because the subrogor has already received satisfaction for her losses). After the subrogee pays the subrogor (see Step 1 in Figure 13.5), defendant would be unjustly enriched if defendant did not have to pay the subrogee. Under subrogation, defendant pays the subrogee (see Step 2 in Figure 13.5).

Equitable (or legal) subrogation[8] works similarly to conventional subrogation, in that a subrogee pays a debt that defendant owes to the subrogor and then demands payment from the defendant, who caused the loss to the subrogor. For example, Distributor is a widget distributor for a number of manufacturers, including Manufacturerco. Distributor delivers widgets from Manufacturerco to Customerco, one of Distributor's best customers. The widgets are defective. Though Distributor has no liability for the defective widgets to Customerco, Distributor buys replacement widgets for Customerco as an accommodation to keep the customer happy. Distributor then turns around and sues Manufacturerco for the cost of the replacement widgets.

You should see that this subrogation suit parallels the earlier, conventional subrogation hypothetical. In Step 1, Distributor makes Customerco whole, thereby relieving Manufacturerco of the obligation to do so. In Step 2, Distributor sues Manufacturerco to obtain the costs it expended in making Customerco whole.

There is an important limitation on equitable (or legal) subrogation: the subrogee cannot be a "volunteer." The non-volunteer requirement echoes the rules discussed in Chapter 11 depriving "officious intermeddlers" of the right to restitution.

What does it mean to be a "volunteer," a status precluding the right to subrogation? A volunteer makes the payment even though it has no business reason to do so. Subrogees, in contrast, pay the subrogor for rational business reasons. The subrogee need not have a *legal obligation* to pay the subrogor; it is enough that it is in the subrogee's business interests to do so. *See Am. Nat'l Bank & Trust Co. of Chicago v. Weyerhaeuser Co.*, 692 F.2d 455, 463 (7th Cir. 1982) ("[T]he *potential* for legal liability *to the subrogor*, as well as the disruption of normal relations and the frustration of reasonable expectations can, in many cases, supply sufficient compulsion to support subrogation."). So

---

8. Though some courts refer to this type of subrogation as "legal subrogation," it is in fact an equitable remedy and subject to the rules discussed earlier in this chapter and in Part II for equitable remedies.

Distributor gets to recover in subrogation because it acted to placate and maintain its normal relationship with its long-time customer, Customerco.

Whether a subrogee seeks conventional or equitable subrogation, the subrogee's rights are no broader than the rights of the subrogor. This principle is sometimes expressed as the subrogee "stepping into the shoes" of the subrogor. So, for example, if Vicki could not recover from Ursula because a jury would determine that Ursula's conduct was not negligent, Worldwide Insurance would not be able to recover from Ursula through subrogation after paying Vicki's medical expenses. Similarly, if Customerco's claims against Manufacturerco would be barred because of the statute of limitations, Distributor's claims would be similarly barred.

The tort doctrines of *contribution* and *equitable indemnity* work in a way that is similar to subrogation, but involve joint tortfeasors. So imagine that Allie and Betty both drive negligently, causing injury to Curt. Curt sues Allie only, and obtains a complete recovery from Allie.[9] Under the state's applicable tort doctrine, Allie may have a right to sue Betty to obtain *all* of the money she paid Curt (under traditional principles of equitable indemnity), a *pro rata share* of the money she paid Curt (under traditional principles of contribution), or a *share based on a percentage of the defendant's relative share of responsibility or fault* of the money she paid Curt (under modern principles of comparative equitable indemnity). *See Am. Motorcycle Ass'n v. Super. Ct. of Los Angeles County,* 578 P.2d 899 (Cal. 1978).

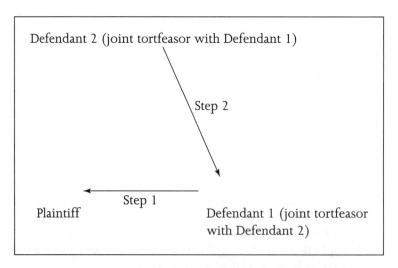

Figure 13.6 Flow of Payments in Contribution/Equitable Indemnity/ Partial Equitable Indemnity

---

9. Under the traditional tort principle of joint and several liability, a plaintiff injured by multiple defendants has the right to collect all or part of his damages from any or all plaintiffs. Though many states have modified this principle, these modifications are not important for the remedies issues discussed in the text.

Figure 13.6 illustrates the concepts of contribution and indemnity. Like subrogation, contribution and indemnity involve a three-party triangle. Here, there are two defendants, Defendant 1 and Defendant 2, who jointly caused injury to plaintiff. Under principles of joint and several liability, either defendant could be required to pay the total amount of plaintiff's loss. If Defendant 1 pays the entire amount of plaintiff's loss, Defendant 2 could be unjustly enriched if he too caused injury to plaintiff but did not have to pay. Under joint and several liability, however, Defendant 2 has to pay nothing on account of Defendant 1's payment. Once Defendant 1 satisfies the judgment to the plaintiff in Step 1, contribution or indemnity works in Step 2 to require Defendant 2 to partially or completely reimburse (the amount depending upon the state's applicable tort law doctrine) Defendant 1 for Defendant 1's payment to plaintiff.

When is subrogation appropriate, and when is contribution or indemnity appropriate? According to the Restatement, contribution or indemnity is appropriate when there are joint tortfeasors, and subrogation is appropriate when there are no joint tortfeasors. See RTR §§ 23, 24. Neither Worldwide Insurance and Ursula nor Distributor and Manufacturerco were joint tortfeasors; in these cases, subrogation was the appropriate remedy. If Distributor and Manufacturerco were in fact jointly liable for Customerco's losses, it would appear that contribution or indemnity would have been the appropriate remedy under the Restatement.

Example 11

Nephew buys a used car from Ripoff Motors for $5,000 "as is," with no warranties. The car is a lemon, and its fair market value is only $2,000. Aunt feels sorry for Nephew, and agrees to take the lemon from Nephew and to buy him a good used car for $5,000. After she buys Nephew the replacement car and takes title to the lemon, she sues Ripoff Motors, claiming subrogation. Will Aunt's subrogation claim succeed?

Explanation

Aunt's claim against Ripoff Motors will not succeed. There are two problems with this claim. First, it appears that Aunt is a volunteer. She acted out of the goodness of her heart; she did not act out of any business reason, as in the Distributor-Customerco hypothetical.[10]

Even if we disregard the volunteer problem, Aunt's claim appears likely to fail, as she has "stepped into the shoes" of Nephew in asserting a claim

---

10. As an aside, we might ask why the law bars volunteers from pursuing these kinds of claims. If Nephew, after all, had a valid claim, Ripoff Motors would have been unjustly enriched if it were lucky enough to have Aunt pay the claim. If the idea is that courts are trying to prevent volunteers from reviving stale claims, it is difficult to see the gain to the volunteer: at best, the volunteer recovers no more than the amount volunteer paid to the subrogor.

against Ripoff Motors. Nephew bought the car "as is," with no warranties. Unless there is some basis for Nephew to somehow bring a damages claim or void the contract (such as under the doctrine of unconscionability), it looks like Nephew's claim against Ripoff would fail. If Nephew's claim would fail, then the claim of Aunt, as subrogee, will fail as well.

Example 12

Patient sues Doctor and Nurse for medical malpractice in connection with a colonoscopy done negligently, leading to Patient's infection and hospitalization. The jury determines that Patient incurred $10,000 in medical expenses and suffered $20,000 of emotional distress damages. It also determines that both Doctor and Nurse were negligent, Doctor being 60% at fault and Nurse being 40% at fault. Patient's hospitalization was covered by insurance and paid for by Insurco. The Patient-Insurco contract contained no subrogation clause. Patient collects $30,000 from Doctor. The state uses comparative equitable indemnity for joint tortfeasors. (a) What, if anything, can Doctor recover from Nurse? (b) What, if anything, can Insurco recover from Patient?

Explanation

(a) Doctor and Nurse are joint tortfeasors in a state that has adopted comparative equitable indemnity. Doctor has fully satisfied the judgment to Patient in the amount of $30,000. The jury found Nurse 40% at fault, and therefore Doctor can recover 40% of the $30,000 judgment, or $12,000, from Nurse through a comparative equitable indemnity action.

(b) At issue here is the $10,000 in medical expenses; the $20,000 in emotional distress damages is not at issue. Ordinarily, a plaintiff cannot obtain a double recovery, as appears to occur here: plaintiff's $10,000 in medical bills are picked up by Insurco, and Patient recovers another $10,000 in damages from Doctor and Nurse. But the collateral source rule allows plaintiff to recover both amounts, and some insurance companies do not seek subrogation in such circumstances. In this case, the contract contains no subrogation clause; for this reason, conventional subrogation will not be available. However, there may be a claim for equitable (or legal) subrogation here, with a twist. Instead of going after Doctor and Nurse, Insurco goes after Patient to prevent Patient's unjust enrichment. Some courts may allow the case to go forward on this basis. But Insurco should be smart if it wants to pursue such remedies in the future by including a subrogation clause in the contract. A court may find that the failure to do so should bar Insurco's right to seek equitable subrogation.

CHAPTER 14

Rescission and Reformation

14.1 INTRODUCTION: ARE RESCISSION AND REFORMATION RESTITUTIONARY REMEDIES?

This chapter, the last of Part III, addresses two additional remedies that arise out of contract disputes: rescission and reformation. *Rescission*, generally speaking, is a remedy giving a plaintiff the right to cancel a contract, and it is often followed by a restitution, whereby each side returns the consideration it has received under the contract. *Reformation* is a judicial rewriting of the parties' contract.

Some remedies scholars view these remedies as falling in the "restitution" category because they can be used to prevent unjust enrichment. *See, e.g.*, RTR § 1, cmt. c; LAYCOCK p. 694 (calling rescission "the quintessential restitutionary remedy"). *But see* DOBBS § 4.3(6), pp. 614-616 (calling rescission "less a remedy and more a matter of the conceptual apparatus that leads to the remedy . . ." and stating that "rescission is not the restitution that follows and it is the restitution that follows that is remedially important."); LAYCOCK p. 615 (noting disagreement with other scholars' treatment of reformation as restitutionary, and calling the remedy "declaratory"[1]).

---

1. Chapter 16 covers declaratory remedies. Laycock calls reformation declaratory "because it can be brought to resolve the potential claims created by the mistaken writing before those claims give rise to any other justiciable dispute." *Id.*

What is the connection between these remedies and restitution? Consider these examples: (1) Child sells Dealer a baseball card worth $1,000 for $20. Rescission by Child prevents Dealer's unjust enrichment. (2) Smith signs a contract to buy Blackacre from the seller, Jones. Both parties believe that the contract contains a clause giving Jones the right to remain on Blackacre for one year after the sale, and the negotiations over the purchase price made it clear that Jones agreed to a lower purchase price in order to have the right to stay for a year incorporated into the contract. The contract as written mistakenly does not provide Jones with the right to remain. If Smith seeks to force Jones to leave before one year, a court would likely reform (rewrite) the contract to give Jones the right to remain. By reforming the contract, the court prevents Smith's unjust enrichment; the bargain gave Jones the right to be on the land for a year, yet the contract as written did not accurately summarize the bargain.

Though it may be appropriate to classify these remedies as restitutionary because they often prevent unjust enrichment, rescission and reformation can occur even when there is no unjust enrichment. Thus, when Child sells baseball card to Dealer for a fair $1,000 price, Child still has the right to rescind under substantive contract law, which makes contracts with minors voidable at the minor's option. Rescission would not prevent unjust enrichment in that case. Similarly, if a court reforms the Jones-Smith contract to specify that the land contract covers a certain 500 acres of Jones' land rather than an equivalent other 500 acres of Jones' land, the correction of the error might not prevent any unjust enrichment; it would just ensure that the contract accurately reflected the parties' deal.

The remaining sections of this chapter consider the contours of rescission claims, the contours of reformation claims, and a small group of cases in which a plaintiff may have a choice between rescission and reformation. For most students, the question of how to classify these remedies is unimportant; most students will care about this categorization only if their instructors care about such issues.

Example 1

Dealer sells Child a baseball card for $20 that Dealer falsely and intentionally misrepresents as worth $300. The card in fact is worthless. Child pays $20 and is in possession of the baseball card. You are Child's lawyer. Assume the law allows Child to seek rescission of the contract. How would the court grant rescission? Is it restitutionary? Is rescission a good remedy for Child? What other remedies might you as Child's lawyer want to consider to maximize Child's recovery?

Explanation

The court would rescind the contract by declaring it void, and then order the parties to each return the consideration received to the other. Under this order, Child gives the baseball card back to Dealer and Dealer gives the $20 back to the Child. Dealer would be unjustly enriched in the absence of rescission (or some other remedy); Dealer would be receiving $20 for a baseball card worth nothing.

While rescission is a better remedy for Child than no remedy at all, it may not be the best remedy. Child, for example, might seek to affirm the contract (that is, not void the contract but enforce it) and sue for damages for breach of contract. Dealer promised a card worth $300 and delivered a worthless card. In some jurisdictions, this contractual fraud claim would allow Child to receive the difference between what was promised (a card worth $300) and what was received (a card worth nothing), for damages of $300. See Chapter 5.2.

14.2 THE REMEDY OF RESCISSION

Rescission is a remedy for canceling the contract (a process sometimes termed "avoidance" or "termination"[2]). When a court grants rescission, it requires an undoing of the contract to the extent possible, a step necessary to prevent unjust enrichment. Undoing can sometimes be complicated, and the longer a party waits to claim rescission, the harder the undoing might be.

We now consider five major points about rescission.

1. *Contract necessary.* First and foremost, for rescission to be available, the parties must have entered into a *contract*; it is insufficient that there be only unjust enrichment. When Albert steals Gaste's music to write the song "Feelings" (see Chapter 12), for example, Gaste has a valid claim in restitution for Albert's profits. But he could *not* seek rescission, because there is no contract to be canceled or undone.

2. *Rescission available for void or voidable contracts.* Second, rescission is available when contract law provides that a contract is void or voidable. Chapter 11.2, discussing the various grounds for restitution, raised a number of circumstances in which rescission is available for void or voidable contracts. A void contract is one that courts will not enforce (such as a contract to engage in illegal activity); a voidable contract is one that may be terminated at the

---

2. Dobbs draws some minor distinctions among these terms, DOBBS § 4.3(6), but many lawyers will use these terms interchangeably.

option of one party, but may be enforced at that party's election. Here are some circumstances involving void or voidable contracts in which rescission appears to be an appropriate remedy:

- Uncle intended to sell Niece his inexpensive but reliable old watch for a fair price. In fact, neither Uncle nor Niece knew that the watch was a very valuable antique. Some courts would allow this *mutual mistake of fact* to render the contract voidable, allowing for rescission and restitution. Rescission also might be available in some cases of *unilateral mistake of fact*, where the non-mistaken party did not rely on the mistake at all. *See* LAYCOCK p. 695.
- Niece tells Uncle he is signing a promissory note guaranteeing a loan to Niece to pay for schooling expenses. Uncle is, in fact, signing away his fee interest in Whiteacre. This *fraudulent conduct* renders the contract voidable, allowing for rescission and restitution.
- Niece tells Uncle he must sign over his property interest in Whiteacre or she will break Uncle's legs. This *promise under duress* renders the contract voidable, allowing for rescission and restitution.
- Niece takes care of Uncle and uses "undue influence" to get him to sign over his property interest in Whiteacre. This *undue influence* renders the contract voidable, allowing for rescission and restitution.
- Niece secures Uncle's signature transferring Whiteacre to her at a time when Uncle is mentally incompetent. Unless Uncle ratifies the sale at a time when he is judged competent, his *lack of capacity* renders the contract voidable, allowing for rescission and restitution. The Child-Dealer hypothetical falls into this same category.
- Yolanda and Zena make an oral contract for the sale of Yolanda's land to Zena. Zena makes improvements on the property, and Yolanda then successfully claims the contract is unenforceable because it fails to satisfy the statute of frauds. The *failure to comply with the statute of frauds* renders the contract voidable, allowing for rescission and restitution.

3. *Rescission sometimes available for breach of enforceable contract, when there has been a substantial breach of contract.* Courts will sometimes allow the non-breaching party to an enforceable contract to cancel it when the breaching party has committed a substantial (as opposed to minor) breach of contract. In O.C.T. *Equipment, Inc. v. Shepherd Mach. Co.*, 95 P.3d 197 (Okla. Civ. App. 2004), for example, Buyer paid $42,000 to seller for delivery of a farming tractor. The tractor arrived without antifreeze in it, and because the delivery person drove the tractor without antifreeze (before the risk of loss passed to the buyer), the engine burned up and was ruined. The court held that

under Oklahoma's version of U.C.C. § 2-711(1),[3] Buyer had the right to reject the goods, cancel (rescind) the contract, and receive back its $42,000 purchase price.

4. *Undoing of contracts can be complicated.* As noted, once a court cancels a contract, it has to undo any performance that has already taken place. Sometimes such undoing is straightforward. In the Child-Dealer example, Child returns the card and Dealer returns the money. But other situations are much more complicated. In the Yolanda-Zena hypothetical, suppose that Zena made $10,000 worth of improvements to the land over the course of a month before Yolanda brings suit to void the contract on statute of frauds grounds. To undo the contract, it is inadequate for Yolanda to return the consideration Zena paid for the contract and cancel the deed to Zena. In order to *put the parties in the same position they would have been in had there been no contract,* a court would likely order Yolanda to pay Zena for the value of the improvements and require Zena to pay Yolanda a reasonable rent for the one month Zena was in possession.

The court is going to have to figure out how to value the improvements and the rent. On top of that, complications may arise if one of the parties does not have the money to pay the other. If Yolanda, for example, cannot afford to pay Zena for the improvements, a court may grant Zena a money judgment for the amount of improvements (offset by the value of the rent Zena paid Yolanda), backed up by an equitable lien (see Chapter 13.2). In the interest of justice, a court might delay Zena's ability to foreclose on the property through the equitable lien to satisfy the judgment.

There's a certain unfairness in Yolanda's waiting a month (until after Zena has invested significant costs in reliance) before seeking to rescind the land contract. Some courts will say that, as a matter of substantive contract law, contracts voidable under the statute of frauds become enforceable once a party has relied on the contract. *See* Restatement (Second) of Contracts § 139(1) (1981). Even in those jurisdictions rejecting reliance as a means of overcoming a statute of frauds objection, a court could hold that Yolanda's claim should be barred because she waited too long to sue, prejudicing Zena. This is a defense referred to as *laches,* discussed in Chapter 18. *See also* RTR § 70(2).

---

3. This section provides:

> (1) Where the seller fails to make delivery or repudiates or the buyer rightfully rejects or justifiably revokes acceptance then with respect to any goods involved, and with respect to the whole if the breach goes to the whole contract (Section 2-612), *the buyer may cancel* and whether or not he has done so may in addition to recovering so much of the price as has been paid
>
> (a) "cover" and have damages under the next section as to all the goods affected whether or not they have been identified to the contract; or
>
> (b) recover damages for nondelivery as provided in this article (Section 2-713).

U.C.C. § 2-711(1) (emphasis added).

5. *Plaintiffs sometimes have the choice between (a) voiding a contract and suing for rescission and (b) standing on the contract and suing for compensatory damages.* When a contract is void — as opposed to merely voidable — rescission may be one of the only remedies available to a plaintiff. In contrast, when the contract is merely *voidable*, the law gives the plaintiff an option between voiding the contract and suing for rescission or standing on the contract and suing for compensatory damages.

Which choice the plaintiff should make depends upon the facts of the particular case. Consider one of my favorite contracts cases, *Stambovsky v. Ackley*, 572 N.Y.S.2d 672 (N.Y. App. Div. 1991). Buyer contracted to buy a house from Seller. Seller failed to disclose that the house had a reputation for being haunted. The fact that the house had this reputation had a negative impact on its market value. The *Stambovsky* court held that Buyer could rescind the contract, receiving back its contract price (though Buyer would need to pay a reasonable rent for the period of time Buyer remained in the house).

This failure to disclose a material fact provided a basis for rescission. Though New York (like many other states) held that mere non-disclosure ordinarily would not provide the basis for rescission, "[w]here a condition which has been created by the seller materially impairs the value of the contract and is peculiarly within the knowledge of the seller or unlikely to be discovered by a prudent purchaser exercising due care with respect to the subject transaction, nondisclosure constitutes a basis for rescission as a matter of equity." *Id.* at 676.

New York law did not give Buyer the option to sue for damages arising out of a nondisclosure, *id.* at 675, but other states might give Buyer the option to do so. And in cases of affirmative fraud by Seller, even New York courts should give Buyer the option of rescission or standing on the contract and suing for damages.

Assuming the jurisdiction gave plaintiff a choice of remedy, which remedy is better for Buyer? Imagine that the purchase price of the house was $200,000. The house's "haunted" reputation "greatly impair[ed] both the value of the property and its potential for resale." *Id.* at 674. Suppose the fair market value of the house with the haunted reputation was only $150,000. Buyer discovers the reputation the day escrow closes on the house.

If Buyer asks for rescission, Buyer gets back the $200,000 consideration and Seller keeps the house. Buyer could then turn around and buy another house worth $200,000. Alternatively, Buyer could keep the house, really worth $150,000, and get $50,000 in damages. From here, Buyer could either keep the house and the damages or sell the house for $150,000 and use the proceeds plus the damages to buy another house worth $200,000.

Framed this way, the rescission and damages options look equivalent: both put Buyer back in the rightful position of having a house (or the equivalent in house and money); both put Buyer in the same position as if there had been no wrong. But there may be reasons why Buyer would prefer rescission over damages:

- Buyer may have lost confidence in Seller, questioning what else might be wrong in the house and thus preferring the chance to "start over."
- Buyer may not trust the court to accurately estimate the difference between the purchase price and the house's true market value.
- The market may have changed during the period between the close of the deal and the trial, and plaintiff might want to use rescission to get out of a bad bargain.

The last point is worth emphasizing. Suppose, for example, that the purchase price of the house was $200,000 but market values have dropped in the interim by $25,000. Rescission gives Buyer back the purchase price of $200,000, allowing Buyer to buy a new house equivalent to the old one (without the bad reputation) for only $175,000, saving $25,000. In contrast, if Buyer sues for damages, the damages would be measured at the time of the wrong, meaning Buyer would get only $50,000, not $75,000, in damages.

This point can be generalized: when it comes to losing contracts, rescission presents an enticing opportunity. Rather than have to stick to the bad deal and take damages (if there are any), plaintiff can undo the deal and cut her losses.[4] Consider this powerful example: an insurance company that insured a man's life under non-smoking rates gets to rescind the contract (returning premiums paid and interest) after the man dies and an investigation revealed the man lied about being a non-smoker. The insurance company did not have to pay substantial benefits under the contract. *See* Laycock p. 695 (citing *Mut. Benefit Life Ins. Co. v. JMR Elecs. Corp.*, 848 F.2d 30 (2d Cir. 1988)). Note that U.C.C. § 2-711(1) (quoted in footnote 3 of this chapter, and applicable to contracts for the sale of goods) gives plaintiff the right both to rescind a contract *and* to obtain damages for the cost of cover when appropriate. Thus, using the tractor example, Buyer gets back its $42,000 purchase price and returns the tractor to Seller. If Buyer's reasonable substitute price for a similar tractor is $45,000, Buyer is entitled to receive the $3,000 in damages as well as the right to rescission.

---

4. The Restatement hedges a bit on the propriety of such a move: "The fact that rescission permits the claimant to escape from an unfavorable bargain does not by itself make rescission inequitable, but rescission will be denied it if its effect could be the unjust enrichment of the claimant at the expense of the other party. The potential for unjust enrichment is obvious when one party seeks rescission to pursue opportunistic gain, or as a means of speculating at the other's expense." RTR § 54, cmt. f.

Example 2

Seller promises to sell Buyer 50 tons of carrots for $20/ton. Buyer sends $1,000 to Seller, but Seller fails to deliver the carrots. At this time, the price of carrots had fallen to $15/ton. What is the best remedy for Buyer?

Explanation

Buyer will want to rescind the contract and receive back his $1,000 payment. With the price falling to $15/ton, Buyer will be able to get the 50 tons of carrots for $750, saving $250. This was a lucky break for Buyer, because Seller breached what would have been a losing contract for Buyer. This is a sale of goods contract governed by U.C.C. § 2-711. In addition to rescinding the contract, Buyer would have the right to damages under § 2-711, but Buyer has suffered no damages because he can cover for less than the contract price. For more on this damages point, see Chapter 4.

Example 3

Owner makes a contract with Contractor to remodel Owner's kitchen for $40,000. The contract specifies that Contractor will use "Cohoe" brand copper pipes in the remodel. Contractor inadvertently uses "Reading" brand copper pipes instead. The quality of the pipes is identical. Owner would like to rescind the contract because Owner believes the fair market value of the remodel is $30,000. Will a court allow Owner to rescind the contract and pay Contractor in restitution?

Explanation

The facts of this hypothetical are loosely based upon *Jacob & Youngs, Inc. v. Kent*, 129 N.E. 889 (N.Y. 1921). It appears that Owner would like to use a minor breach of contract by Contractor in order to get out of a bad contract, paying a lower price than the contract price. A court is unlikely to allow Owner to rescind the contract on the basis of a minor breach; under substantive contract law, as the *Jacob & Youngs* case establishes, the inconsequential breach here does not count as a "substantial breach" that courts would require for rescission.

Example 4

Alberto is on a small pleasure boat (worth $50,000) that is sinking during a storm. Bill is on a larger pleasure boat that is passing by. Alberto asks Bill for his help. Bill agrees to tow Alberto and his boat to safety, but only if Alberto agrees to let Bill keep the boat. Alberto, fearing for his life, reluctantly agrees. Bill tows the boat to shore, saving Alberto's life but keeping the boat. Alberto sues to rescind the contract. What result? Explain.

Explanation

A court is likely to void this contract on grounds of duress because Alberto entered into it without free choice. Rescission would allow Alberto to receive his boat back. That might leave Alberto unjustly enriched, however: Bill rescued him without receiving any compensation. The fact that Bill demanded compensation should serve to refute the presumption that Bill was rendering his services gratuitously. (See Chapter 11.) A court will need to determine the reasonable value of Bill's services, perhaps considering the amount that a professional rescuer would have charged under the circumstances.

Example 5

Carmen sells his home to Deborah for $250,000. Before the sale, Deborah asked about termite damage. Carmen lied, saying there was no damage. In fact, there was damage that Carmen took active steps to hide and that will cost $20,000 to repair. Deborah discovers the damage shortly after she moves in. The house is appreciating in value, and is now worth $300,000 (once the termite damage is repaired). Should Deborah rescind the contract? Why or why not?

Explanation

Rescission is certainly a possibility: Deborah would receive back her $250,000 purchase price, and Carmen would get back the deed to the home (plus a reasonable rental value for the period of time that Deborah lived in the house). Deborah could then go out and buy a new house without the damage. The problem with this remedy for Deborah is that prices are appreciating, and a new home of similar quality will cost her more, perhaps $300,000.

A more desirable alternative, if it is available, is for Deborah to affirm the contract and sue for the $20,000 in damages. If Carmen pays for that repair, Deborah gets to keep the house for the $250,000 contract price (which turns out to be a good deal given the home's appreciation), paying nothing for the termite repair.

14.3 THE REFORMATION REMEDY

Reformation is an equitable remedy that gives courts the power to rewrite a contract of the parties.[5] "When parties come to an agreement, but by fraud or mistake write it down in some fashion that does not truly reflect their contract, equity will reform the writing to make it reflect the parties' true intention." DOBBS, §4.3(7), p. 617.

To take a typical example, A and B sign a land contract that they both believe covers a sale of the property at 123 Elm Street. In fact, because of a typographical error that no one notices, the contract describes property at 124 Elm Street. The parties may simply agree to rewrite their contract to correct the error. In the event there is a disagreement (for example, if A owned both 123 Elm Street and 124 Elm Street, and B prefers buying 124 over 123), the reformation matter may end up in court. Assuming the party seeking reformation can prove that the parties' intent was not accurately reflected in the written contract, a court will order the contract reformed so that it covers the correct property.

Note that the mistake in the A-B contract is one that goes to *the content of the writing.* If the parties make a mistake as to the contract's *substance,* reformation will not be available. If, for example, A believes the contract is for the sale of 123 Elm Street and B believes the contract is for the sale of 124 Elm Street, reformation is obviously not an appropriate remedy: to see why, ask yourself how the court would rewrite the contract (not for 123.5 Elm Street!). Rescission may be a more appropriate option in such circumstances.

Fraud as to the content of the writing — leading to the other party's unilateral mistake — can also be a basis for reformation of a contract. Thus, if A and B agree to the sale of 123 Elm Street, but B, desiring 124 Elm Street (which A also owns), has the contract written to state the contract as covering 124 Elm Street, a court will allow the contract to be rewritten for the sale of 123 Elm Street.[6]

Reformation may be accompanied by a plea for another remedy, such as damages for breach of contract. Thus, suppose Eddy is renting a retail site

---

5. Despite reformation's status as an equitable remedy, Laycock reports that "[t]here does not seem to be any ripeness or irreparable injury requirement for reformation, although not many cases are filed in which these issues could plausibly be raised." LAYCOCK p. 615.

6. If it seems odd to you that the court will rewrite a contract when there has been no "meeting of the minds" regarding the sale of 123 Elm Street, remember that under modern substantive contract law, it is not the parties' subjective desires that count. In this case, both A and B outwardly indicated their intent to enter into a contract for the sale of 123 Elm Street. Under the objective theory of contract, that should be sufficient to allow such a sale to go through. If you don't like that theory, it is also possible to see the reformation remedy as a kind of punishment for B's fraud. If B pretended to be interested in buying 123 Elm Street (when B secretly desired 124 Elm Street), reformation would make B stick with the deal to which B pretended to agree.

from Francesca for one year. Their lease contract was supposed to include a provision requiring Francesca to have the windows washed twice per week. Because of a typographical error, the contract states the requirement that the windows are to be washed twice per *year*. Francesca refuses to wash the windows for four months, so Eddy has them washed twice per week at a cost of $300 per week. Eddy may go to court to have the contract reformed to reflect the "twice per week" agreement. He may then seek damages for breach of contract, based upon Francesca's failure to wash the windows twice weekly as promised by the reformed contract. If the $300 per week was a reasonable cost for the service, a court is likely to award the value of those expenses to Eddy. Additionally, if Eddy is convinced that Francesca will not wash the windows twice a week for the remaining portion of the contract, he might seek an order of *specific performance* requiring that she do so.[7]

Example 6

Restaurant enters into an insurance contract with Insurer covering certain liability related to the operation of the restaurant. Restaurant accurately told Insurer that it served alcohol, but Insurer erroneously classified Restaurant as not serving alcohol. Had Insurer known that Restaurant served alcohol, it would have included a provision in the insurance contract excluding liability for alcohol-related incidents. After the insurance policy drafted by Insurer arrived at Restaurant, Restaurant's manager noticed that the policy incorrectly described Restaurant as not serving alcohol. Restaurant sent Insurer a letter pointing out the error, but Insurer did nothing about it. A few months later, while the policy was in effect, one patron stabbed another patron in Restaurant's parking lot in an alcohol-related incident. May Insurer, in order to avoid paying damages arising out of the stabbing, bring suit to reform the contract to correctly classify Restaurant as an establishment that serves alcohol and to exclude liability for alcohol-related incidents? Can Insurer alternatively seek rescission of the contract on the grounds of mutual mistake?

Explanation

This example is based loosely on *Alea London Ltd. v. Bono-Soltysiak Enter.*, 186 S.W.3d 403 (Mo. Ct. App. 2006). This case involves no mistake as to the writing or as to fraud related to the writing. The court is likely to reject reformation for this reason. It is also likely to reject rescission, as the case involves neither a mutual mistake of fact nor a unilateral mistake of fact accompanied by fraud. As the Missouri court wrote in rejecting the claim: "[Insurer] adduced absolutely no evidence, let alone clear and convincing

---

7. Specific performance is a kind of injunction requiring that a party perform as promised in a contract. For more on specific performance, see the discussion in Chapter 7.

evidence, that [Restaurant] acted in bad faith, committed fraud or deceived [Insurer]. Moreover [Restaurant] did nothing to hinder [Insurer] in the discovery of its error. It is well settled that '[e]quity will not relieve against mistake when the complaining party had within his reach the true state of facts, and, without being induced by the other party, neglected to avail himself of his opportunities of information.' " *Id.* at 416 (citation omitted).

Note that because reformation is an equitable remedy, a court may be especially disinclined to grant reformation given these facts. Not only was this a unilateral mistake for which the party seeking reformation was totally responsible; the other party told the mistaken party of the mistake, and the mistaken party did nothing to correct it until the positions of the parties had changed dramatically with the stabbing. See also Chapter 18, discussing the equitable defenses of *waiver*, *estoppel*, and *laches*, which could come into play here to bar the reformation claim based on the delay even if there *were* initially a mutual mistake.

14.4 THE CHOICE BETWEEN RESCISSION AND REFORMATION

In rare circumstances, a party may have the choice between rescission and reformation. Consider the case of *Hand v. Dayton-Hudson*, 775 F.2d 757 (6th Cir. 1985). Hand worked as an attorney for Dayton-Hudson Corporation. The company decided to lay off Hand. He was offered $38,000 in exchange for his agreement to release all claims he might have against the company. After initially refusing the offer, Hand took the proposed contract offering the $38,000 and copied it using the same typewriter,[8] so that it appeared to be the company's offer. He secretly changed the language of the release to exclude claims for age discrimination (leaving him the right to sue for age discrimination). Both parties then signed the contract, but Dayton-Hudson did not know Hand had altered it. Hand then turned around and sued Dayton-Hudson for age discrimination.

The *Hand* case nicely illustrates the choice that Dayton-Hudson faced. As should be clear from the previous two sections, Hand's conduct entitled the company to seek either rescission of the contract or reformation. Rescission was appropriate because the parties had a voidable contract as a result of Hand's fraud; the company could rescind the contract if it chose to do so. Alternatively, *Hand* is a classic case of unilateral mistake in the writing

---

8. Some of you may be old enough to remember what a typewriter is. Hand's fraud would likely be much easier today with computer-based word processing.

procured by fraud. Reformation is appropriate to make the contract reflect a full release in exchange for the $38,000 payment.

In this circumstance, reformation was a much better option for the company than rescission. (Before reading on, see if you can answer why.) As Laycock explains, "Reformation leaves the release in effect as reformed. Hand gets to keep the $38,000; Dayton-Hudson is still released; Hand cannot sue for breach of contract or age discrimination. . . . Rescission would reverse the transaction. Dayton-Hudson would get its $38,000 back, Hand would get the release back, and Hand could sue for breach of contract and age discrimination." LAYCOCK p. 613.

Though *Hand* is a unilateral mistake with fraud case, *mutual mistake as to a writing* also could provide a choice between rescission and reformation in appropriate cases. If Hand and Dayton-Hudson both thought, for example, that they were signing a release that excluded age discrimination claims, but the contract was drafted without the exclusion, Hand might either seek to reform the contract to put back in the exclusion or seek to rescind the contract on grounds of mutual mistake. However, if the court finds that it was clear what both parties thought they were contracting for, the court could deny rescission and grant only reformation.

Example 7

If you were Hand in the mutual mistake variation described immediately above (as opposed to the actual fraud case), would you prefer the remedy of reformation or rescission?

Explanation

The answer to this question will depend upon the facts of the case. If Hand believes he has viable claims besides age discrimination, he might ask a court to rescind the contract, allowing him to sue for various claims beyond age discrimination. In doing so, he would need to return the $38,000 he received as consideration for giving up these claims. In contrast, if Hand believes his only viable claim is one for age discrimination, he is better off asking for reformation so that he can have both the payment and the right to sue for age discrimination.

Again, a court might not be willing to give Hand the choice of remedies in such circumstances. But if the court gives the choice, it is important for Hand (and for Hand's lawyer) to carefully consider the costs and benefits of the various choices.

Example 8

In another variation on the Hand–Dayton-Hudson hypothetical, the parties sign a contract paying Hand $38,000 and releasing Dayton-Hudson from all of Hand's claims against it *except* for age discrimination claims. Dayton-Hudson claims that Hand committed fraud by altering the contract. Hand says that the parties agreed to include the age discrimination exclusion as a condition for him to sign the contract. Is Dayton-Hudson entitled to reformation to exclude the release from the age discrimination claim? Is it entitled to rescind the contract?

Explanation

The answer will depend upon what the judge as fact finder believes about the case. (Because these are equitable remedies, they will be tried before a judge, not a jury.) Reformation usually requires that the party seeking reformation prove by clear and convincing evidence what the parties intended the written contract to say. If Dayton-Hudson can prove that this was a case of fraud under the strict evidentiary standards, it will be entitled to reformation. The same goes for rescission. The issue may come down to a swearing contest between the parties, and the right of Dayton-Hudson to any remedy is going to depend upon what it can prove to the court. (In the actual *Hand* case, attorney Hand admitted to altering the document without informing Dayton-Hudson!)

PART IV

Other Important Remedies Concepts

Dishing It Out: Punitive Damages and Their Constitutional Limits

15.1 INTRODUCTION TO PUNITIVE DAMAGES

In Part I, especially Chapter 3, we considered the rightful position standard and tort damages. Tort damages are *compensatory*; they aim to put the plaintiff back in the "rightful position," the position that plaintiff would have been in but for the defendant's wrong. Consider Figure 15.1.

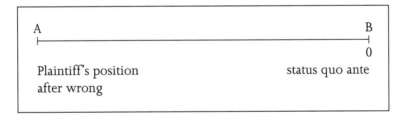

Figure 15.1

At least in theory, an award of damages equal to (B − A) puts the plaintiff back in the position she would have been in but for the wrong. For example, if Adam steals Beverly's new iPod valued at $300, Beverly is at −$300 after the theft (putting aside some additional damages for the delay and for the costs of obtaining the new iPod, which we will ignore for the rest of this discussion). As Figure 15.2 shows, Beverly started at B (or 0, the status quo ante) before the theft. The theft moved Beverly to A, at −$300. Compensatory tort damages would be (B − A), or (0 − (−300)), or $300, an award which will, at least in theory, put Beverly in the same position as if there had not been a theft. In this way, Beverly has been *compensated* for the loss of her iPod.

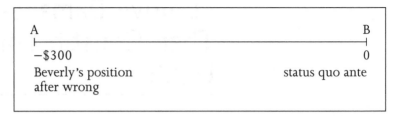

Figure 15.2 Adam and Beverly

Economists have long noted that compensatory damages may serve a *deterrent* function as well. The fact that Adam would have to pay Beverly for the cost of the iPod may make him less likely to steal it, and Adam's payment may make others think twice before engaging in the same tortious activity.

But compensatory damages may not be enough to deter Adam and others who otherwise might have no moral qualms about taking someone else's property. Adam might not be found, and if he is found, Beverly may have difficulty proving one or more elements of her tort case against Adam. Indeed, given that only $300 is at stake, Beverly would have a tough time finding a lawyer who would take her case; would you put in many hours of your time to get a 25% contingent recovery on a $300 claim?

Punitive damages may serve that deterrent function. Punitive damages are damages awarded *in addition to* compensatory damages that are aimed at *punishing and making an example* out of the defendant.

Imagine if, in addition to the $300 that Beverly could receive in compensatory damages, a jury has the discretion to award her another $3,000 in punitive damages. The possibility of that larger punitive damage award could deter Adam and those like him. Suppose Adam thinks there is only a 20% chance he would be located, served, and successfully sued for damages. If he thinks he would pay $300 if Beverly finds him and successfully sues him, his expected loss is 20% of $300, or $60. But if he expects to pay $3,300 if a judgment is issued against him ($300 in compensatory damages and $3,000 in punitive damages), his expected loss is 20% of $3,300, or $660. There will be some thieves, perhaps including Adam, who would be deterred by a $660 expected loss but not a $60 expected loss. After all, even if the iPod is not worth $300 to Adam, it is likely worth more than $60 but less than $660.

The possibility of punitive damages also may make the case more appealing to lawyers who would work for a contingency fee: better to have 25% of $3,300 than 25% of $300. Punitive damages therefore make some suits economically viable for plaintiffs when they otherwise would not be viable.

Punitive damages are sometimes referred to as *exemplary* damages because they make an example out of the defendant. This name stresses a *corrective justice* feature of these damages unconnected with the economic deterrence argument. A $3,300 damage judgment is going to hurt Adam a lot more than a $300 award, and the fact that a jury has awarded a large punitive award tells the community that Adam has done something worthy of their condemnation.

With all of these pluses for punitive damages, perhaps they should be available in every case as a way of making up for the fact that a number of lawsuits that should be successful are not successful because of procedural barriers or other problems.[1] But this would create some problems. Consider the case of Carla, who is engaged in the abnormally dangerous activity of dynamite blasting. Carla uses all reasonable care to avoid causing any damage while demolishing a building, but flying debris still busts the window on David's car. Blasting is a strict liability tort offense, so Carla will be paying even though she is not at fault. *See* RESTATEMENT (THIRD) OF TORTS— LIABILITY FOR PHYSICAL AND EMOTIONAL HARM § 20.

Economic theory suggests we might want to allow punitive damages against Carla for the same reason as we might want them available for Beverly's suit against Adam: to create additional incentives for people like Carla not to injure others. But Carla likely is already using a high level of care to avoid paying damages in a strict liability system. Creating additional incentives for Carla to take care might lead to *overdeterrence*: she might become too careful, and not engage in the risky but useful activity of blasting.

In addition, there are justice problems with holding Carla liable for punitive damages. If she has done nothing wrong, corrective justice might still support requiring her to *compensate* David.[2] But even if the law says Carla should compensate David, why should we also make an example out of Carla and punish her? And if we are going to punish her, is it right to do so through the *civil justice* (as opposed to the criminal justice) system? In the civil justice system, we generally require proof by only a preponderance of the evidence (just more likely than not), and not proof beyond a reasonable doubt. Think if you were in Carla's place, acting as carefully as you could while engaging in a dangerous but useful activity. The threat of punitive damages, imposed under a preponderance standard, just might drive you out of business.

---

1. Economists would think of punitive damages simply as serving as a "multiplier" of the compensatory damages. These damages would be calibrated somehow to make up for the underdeterrence caused by failures of the tort system to make every defendant pay who should pay under the applicable legal rule.
2. Corrective justice theorists have long debated whether a rule of negligence or a rule of strict liability is the appropriate one for unintended conduct that causes injury to persons. For an introduction, *see* RICHARD A. EPSTEIN, CASES AND MATERIALS ON TORTS 159-161 (9th ed. 2008). But this debate concerns the question of compensation, not punishment.

Just as compensatory damages may serve a *deterrent* purpose, punitive damages serve a *compensatory* purpose because plaintiff gets to collect the punitive damages as well. But they can *overcompensate*. Even in the Adam-Beverly hypothetical, there is the windfall feature of punitive damages that some people find troubling. Consider Figure 15.3.

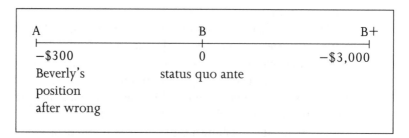

Figure 15.3 The Windfall Aspect of Punitive Damages in the Adam-Beverly Hypothetical

When Adam steals Beverly's iPod, she moves from B, the status quo ante, to A, −$300. Putting aside search and other incidental costs, a compensatory award of $300 moves her back to B, the rightful position in a typical tort damages suit. But with the addition of punitive damages, she ends up at B+, a gain of $3,000. If the first $300 of the award truly compensated her, Beverly *is now better off* than had there been no theft; a $3,300 award makes her $3,000 richer than she would have been had there been no theft. This is why punitive damages are so appealing to plaintiffs (and plaintiffs' lawyers).

Recognizing both the potential benefits of punitive damages as well as the concerns raised in the last few paragraph, courts (and legislatures) have created special rules for punitive damages:

- *Conduct.* The conduct that merits the award of punitive damages must be quite bad. Though states use different language to express this idea (such as "malice" (Tex. Civil Prac. & Remedies Code § 41.001(7)) or acting with an "evil mind" (Linthicum v. Nationwide Life Ins. Co., 723 P.2d 675, 679 (Ariz. 1986)), one general point is that the conduct must be *worse than negligence*.[3] Defendant's intent to injure is an easy case for imposition of punitive damages, but such an intent is not required; in some states recklessness as to injury may be enough. In determining

---

3. How much worse? It depends upon the jurisdiction. Certainly all states allow punitive damages when a defendant has been proven to have an intent to harm a plaintiff. The harder cases are when the defendant acts with something like recklessness, ignoring a substantial probability of serious harm to others.

if the conduct merits the award of punitive damages, you should not focus on the name of the cause of action, but rather on the nature of the conduct. For example, the fact that the tort raised against Carla for blasting is a strict liability tort does not prevent an award of punitive damages against her if, for example, she acted recklessly by not taking any steps to minimize injury from blasting.

- *Burden of proof.* Many states raise the burden of proof for a plaintiff to be eligible to collect punitive damages. Rather than proving the requisite bad conduct by a preponderance of the evidence, a plaintiff might have to prove it by a higher standard, such as California's "clear and convincing evidence" standard (a standard greater than the preponderance standard but less than the criminal standard of proof beyond a reasonable doubt). *See* CAL. CIV. CODE § 3294.

- *Need for award of compensatory damages.* Many states require that a jury must first find plaintiff entitled to *compensatory damages* before the jury may award punitive damages. Nominal damages may qualify in some jurisdictions, as noted in Chapter 2.4,[4] and plaintiffs sometimes seek nominal damages precisely because they want to use such damages as a hook to get punitive damages. Most states do not award punitive damages in equity cases; a few states will allow plaintiff to couple a punitive damages claim with equitable relief,[5] such as when an injunction prevents a defendant from engaging in a bad act. In at least some jurisdictions, a plaintiff cannot couple a restitutionary remedy with a claim for punitive damages. *See, e.g., Merritt v. Craig*, 746 A.2d 923, 931 (Md. App. 2000) (plaintiff cannot couple rescission claim with claim for punitive damages); *Hong v. Kong*, 683 P.2d 833, 841 (Haw. App. 1984) (punitive damages not awardable in an action for restitution); *but see Thomas Auto Co., Inc. v. Craft*, 763 S.W.2d 651, 654 (Ark. 1989) ("We can think of no reason why punitive damages should not accompany a restitutionary award if there is proof of the elements of deceit as a basis of revocation of acceptance or extrajudicial rescission.").

- *More state-specific rules.* Some states have statutes that limit the ability to sue certain defendants for punitive damages without a preliminary showing of wrongdoing. Some states require that some of the punitive award go to the state rather than to the plaintiff. And states are

---

4. *See* Richard C. Tinney, *Sufficiency of Showing of Actual Damages to Support Award of Punitive Damages — Modern Cases*, 40 A.L.R 4th 11 §§ 6-9 (1985 & 2012 Supp.) (collecting cases on both sides of issue); *but see* N.J. STAT. ANN. 2A:15-5.13(c) (nominal damages cannot support the award of punitive damages).

5. Chapter 7 discusses the distinction between legal and equitable remedies in some detail. See also Chapter 13's discussion of how some restitutionary remedies are legal and some are equitable.

split over whether an employer may be *vicariously liable* for punitive damages based on the actions of its employees.[6] In some states, vicarious liability is available as a matter of course. In other states, for the employer to be liable the employee must have exercised managerial discretion, or approved or participated in the tort of the employee. *See* RESTATEMENT (SECOND) OF TORTS § 909 (1979).

- *Punitive damages in contract actions.* As we will see in the next section of this chapter, courts make it very difficult to recover punitive damages in *contract* actions.
- *Constitutionality of high damage awards.* Finally, as we will see in the last section of this chapter, many courts impose limits on and strict judicial review of the *amount* of punitive damages. In recent years, the United States Supreme Court has imposed limits on the amount of punitive damages under the Due Process Clause of the Fourteenth Amendment to the United States Constitution.

Example 1

Ellen is driving down the street, paying more attention to her cell phone conversation than to the road conditions. Because of her carelessness, she strikes Frank, who is crossing the street, causing him serious personal injuries. A jury finds that Ellen was negligent and caused Frank economic and noneconomic losses of $10,000. May the jury also award Frank punitive damages?

Explanation

Probably not. The answer will depend upon each state's standard for the award of punitive damages, but this looks like a garden-variety negligence case, for which punitive damages will *not* be available. Her conduct would have to be worse than carelessness.

---

6. Under *vicarious liability*, one person is strictly liable for the tort of another. Most states hold employers strictly liable for the torts of their employees, requiring the employer to pay damages to a person injured by an employee. The doctrine applied in the tort context is sometimes referred to by the Latin term *respondeat superior*.

Example 2

After Ellen hit Frank and gave information to the police, she got back into her car and resumed driving. Again she picked up her cell phone, and she became so engrossed in a conversation that she did not notice the large flashing sign stating that she was entering a school zone and that children were present. As she tried to hold the cell phone with one hand and roll down her car window with the other, she ran over Gina, Harry, and Ivan, three schoolchildren who were on the sidewalk waiting for the school bus to take them home. A jury finds that Ellen was negligent and caused the children each $25,000 in economic and noneconomic losses. May the jury also award the children punitive damages? If Ellen was driving in the course and scope of her employment, may her employer be vicariously liable for any punitive damages?

Explanation

Ellen likely will be liable for punitive damages. Again, the answer will depend upon each state's standard for the award of punitive damages and the jury's assessment of blameworthiness, but this case looks like Ellen engaged in worse conduct than in Example 1. Although she did not have an intent to injure, a jury could well conclude that Ellen acted with substantial disregard of the high probability of causing injury to others, a form of reckless conduct. She had just been in an accident after using her cell phone while driving, yet she continued the practice. She ignored the flashing warning lights and took both hands off the steering wheel simultaneously for non-emergency reasons. She was so inattentive that she let her car go onto the sidewalk in a school zone. Although Ellen did not have an intent to injure, this kind of bad conduct is likely to merit an award of punitive damages in most states.

Note that the cause of action here is negligence, but the cause of action alone does not dictate whether or not punitive damages are available. Focus on the conduct, not the name of the tort.

Jurisdictions are split over whether Ellen's employer may be vicariously liable for Ellen's tort. In some states, it depends upon whether the bad conduct meriting punitive damages was an exercise of managerial discretion. In this case, her driving habits were not a managerial decision, so in those jurisdictions Ellen's employer would not be vicariously liable for punitive damages. Some states require that the employer actually approve of or participate in the tort of the employee. Under these facts (without more) there would be no punitive damages available against Ellen's employer unless the state automatically held an employer vicariously liable for the employee's torts.

Example 3

Suppose in Example 2 the jury agreed that it was more likely than not that Ellen engaged in bad conduct required for the award of punitive damages in the state, but they do not agree that she engaged in such conduct beyond a reasonable doubt. May the jury award punitive damages?

Explanation

You would need more information to answer the question. First, you would need to know the burden of proof in the jurisdiction for proving the conduct relevant for an award of punitive damages. Suppose the standard is one of "clear and convincing evidence." Even knowing the standard, you would need more information. Because the "clear and convincing" standard falls somewhere between the preponderance standard and the reasonable doubt standard, we do not know how the jury would conclude under the correct standard: was there in fact clear and convincing evidence that she engaged in the bad conduct?

Example 4

Jared spits in Ken's face, deliberately, with no one else present, to express his disgust at the style of shoes that Ken is wearing. In his tort suit, Ken successfully proves the elements of an offensive battery, but he suffers no damages. The jury awards Ken $1 in nominal damages and finds by clear and convincing evidence (the right state standard) that Jared engaged in his actions with malicious intent, meeting the state's punitive damages standard. May the jury award punitive damages?

Explanation

Yes, if (as in many states) nominal damages count as compensatory damages. As we saw in Chapter 2.4, nominal damages serve a *declaratory* rather than a compensatory function: they tell the world the respective rights of plaintiff and defendant rather than compensating the plaintiff. Nonetheless, many courts will allow an award of punitive damages to piggyback on a nominal damages award. Without this rule, many dignitary harms that do not cause actual damage could be difficult to deter.

Example 5

Anita steals Brianna's digital camera worth $200, hocks the camera at a pawnshop for $150, and bets the $150 at the racetrack, winning $1,000. Brianna brings suit in restitution, and the court awards a constructive trust over the $1,000 winnings. (A constructive trust is an equitable restitutionary remedy discussed in detail in Chapter 13.) (a) May the court also award punitive damages? (b) Should the court be allowed to award punitive damages? (Note this second part asks for your opinion; there is no "correct" answer.)

Explanation

(a) The court probably cannot also award punitive damages. Generally speaking, punitive damages are not available when a plaintiff seeks an equitable remedy rather than a remedy at law. In this case, the constructive trust is an equitable remedy. There is also a split of authority on whether punitive damages are available when the plaintiff gets a restitutionary remedy.

(b) The normative question whether the law should allow punitive damages is an interesting one. The purpose of the constructive trust is to take away the defendant's ill-gotten gains. In this hypothetical, Anita never would have been able to get the $1,000 winnings if she did not steal Brianna's digital camera. This "disgorgement principle," which is central to certain restitutionary claims, has a punitive element to it. Certainly it would feel more like punishment for Anita to pay $1,000 as part of a restitutionary remedy than $200 (or so) in damages. But should Anita be on the hook for additional punitive damages?

Consider this first from the perspective of justice. On the one hand, perhaps the disgorgement of profits punishes Anita enough. On the other hand, if Anita's conduct is particularly bad (and we would all agree that theft is bad conduct), perhaps a jury should decide whether Anita should have to pay more than the $1,000. After all, think of Anita's position before and after the wrong: if a court forced Anita to pay the $1,000 gain back and nothing else, Anita would be left in the same position as if she had not engaged in the wrong. In other words, disgorgement puts Anita financially in no worse a position than had she not stolen Brianna's camera. See Figure 15.4. Anita steals the camera and bets the money, leaving her at C, up $1,000. The restitution measure forces her to pay this money back, moving her to down to B, the status quo ante. In other words, she is no worse off than had she not engaged in the theft. It would take additional punitive damages to move Anita into negative territory.

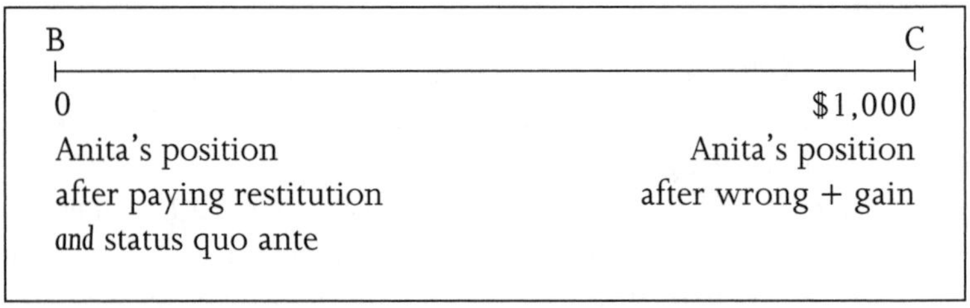

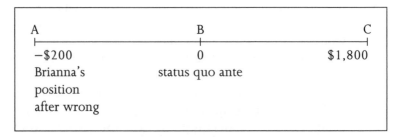

Figure 15.4 Wrongdoer's Position After Disgorgement in
Anita-Brianna Hypothetical

Of course, allowing Brianna to recover *both* Anita's gains through the constructive trust *and* punitive damages gives Brianna something of a double windfall. Brianna ultimately would be in a much better position than she would have been in had she not suffered the $200 loss of her camera. To illustrate, suppose the court awards Brianna $1,000 in restitution and another $1,000 in punitive damages. As shown in Figure 15.5, after the wrong Brianna is at A, −$200. An award of $2,000 moves her to C: the first $200 compensates Brianna for the wrong, and the remaining $1,800 counts as gain. Is that fair to Anita and Brianna? Perhaps it is. given the wrongful nature of Anita's conduct.

Figure 15.5 The Windfall Aspect of Punitive Damages and Restitution
in Anita-Brianna Hypothetical

As for economic arguments, the same arguments for punitive damages in the context of compensatory damages might apply here as well. That is, a court might want to allow punitive damages to make up for the under-deterrence that comes from imperfections in the tort system. If there is only a 10% chance that Anita is going to have to pay the $1,000 in restitution, the expected loss is $100, and the camera is worth at least $150 to her (the value she can obtain from the pawnshop). Adding the possibility of punitive damages could cure the problem of underdeterrence.

15.2 PUNITIVE DAMAGES AND CONTRACT

It is sometimes said that punitive damages are not available in a claim arising out of a contract, but this is an oversimplification. Consider these three scenarios:

> *Scenario 1:* Lawrence, a professional photographer, promises to take pictures at Marvin and Naomi's wedding for a price of $2,000. Lawrence fails to show up as promised because he was home drunk, and Marvin and Naomi are left without any professional photographs of their wedding. They sue Lawrence for breach of contract and also want punitive damages.
>
> *Scenario 2:* Ophelia promises to deliver widgets to Polonius for $15 per widget. Ophelia breaches, selling the widgets instead to another buyer, who pays $18 per widget. Polonius sues for breach of contract and punitive damages.
>
> *Scenario 3:* Dr. Quinn negligently treats Roger for an ailment. Roger sues Dr. Quinn for breach of contract, alleging and proving that Dr. Quinn breached an implied term of their contract for medical care to use reasonable care. Roger also asks for punitive damages.

A court would likely hold that punitive damages would not be available in either *Scenario 1* or *Scenario 2* because punitive damages are generally unavailable for breach of contract. A court could treat plaintiffs in *Scenario 1* more generously than plaintiff in *Scenario 2* by allowing the recovery of *emotional distress damages*. Usually emotional distress damages are not recoverable in breach of contract actions either, but courts occasionally allow such damages when such losses are particularly foreseeable. *Compare Lewis v. Holmes*, 34 So. 66 (La. 1903) (allowing emotional distress damages for failure to deliver promised wedding dress), *with Carpel v. Saget Studios, Inc.*, 326 F. Supp. 1331 (D. Pa. 1971) (barring emotional distress damages for photographer's breach of promise to take wedding pictures). To the extent that emotional distress damages *are* available in *Scenario 1*, they can increase the amount of the plaintiffs' damages award in the way that punitive damages do, potentially creating greater deterrence for defendants like Lawrence. Unlike punitive damages, however, emotional distress damages, at least in theory, are designed to serve a compensatory function.

Scenario 3 is a different story. A court is quite likely to allow Roger to recover punitive damages for Dr. Quinn's conduct. Doctrinally, the reason Roger gets to recover punitive damages (while Marvin, Naomi, and Polonius do not) is that Dr. Quinn did more than breach a contract; she has also *committed an independent tort*, the tort of negligence. But this doctrinal answer is an unsatisfying one. It does not explain *why* breach of the medical contract is

347

a tort, while breach of the widget contract or the photography contract is not.

There seems widespread consensus that certain breaches of contract also constitute an independent tort, allowing for the award of punitive damages. *This is essentially a policy determination that courts make in each jurisdiction.* Besides the medical malpractice context already discussed, one of the most important areas where breaches of contract are also torts is in the insurance context. When an insurer denies an insured's claim in "bad faith," many states will treat that as a tort, allowing not only for the award of emotional distress and other tort damages, but also the possibility of punitive damages.

For example, consider the facts of *State Farm v. Campbell*, 538 U.S. 408 (2003), a very important case for the constitutional questions we consider in the next section. In *Campbell*, two drivers sued a third driver, Campbell, for negligent driving leading to personal injuries and wrongful death. Campbell had an insurance policy with State Farm. The two drivers offered to settle for Campbell's policy limits — $25,000 each. State Farm's own investigation showed that Campbell was completely at fault.

Under applicable insurance law, State Farm had the obligation not to put its interest over that of the insured. The only reasonable conclusion on the facts as read most favorably to the plaintiff is that State Farm should have settled this case for the policy limits. With liability clear for its insured and the injured parties ready to settle for the policy limits (having sustained serious injuries), the insurer's job was to settle. If the case were not settled, then Campbell would have been on the hook personally for any of the damages over the limit. Rather than settle, State Farm fought the claims. It put false facts in the file (for example, falsely alleging that one of the other drivers had a pregnant girlfriend), and there was evidence that its handling of the case was part of a nationwide practice of rejecting good offers to settle.

The tort case against Campbell went to trial. The jury found Campbell 100% liable, and ordered damages in the amount of $185,000. State Farm refused to pay the extra $135,000 and told Campbell to start putting his assets up for sale. Eventually, State Farm agreed to pay the entire damages award, but by then Campbell had sued State Farm for bad faith (fraud) and intentional infliction of emotional distress.[7] In Campbell's bad faith claim against State Farm, the jury found Campbell suffered $2.6 million in compensatory damages (primarily for emotional distress, an amount the trial court reduced to $1 million) and an additional $145 million in punitive damages, an amount the United States Supreme Court later reduced for reasons discussed in the next section.

It is easy to see why on policy grounds courts would decide that breaches of an insurance contract like the one in *Campbell* should constitute

---

7. To settle his claim with the other two drivers, he assigned 90% of his bad faith claim against State Farm to the other two drivers.

a tort. The possibility of tort damages can serve to deter bad behavior such as that of State Farm in contracts where consumers are trying to buy peace of mind and reduce risk through the purchase of insurance.

But not all breaches of insurance contracts create an independent tort and the possibility of punitive damages. For example, suppose in the *Campbell* case that State Farm refused to pay because it had a reasonable argument that the policy did not cover these kinds of accidents. Suppose further that a court later determines that State Farm's argument about what the policy covered, though reasonable, was wrong. Then State Farm's failure to pay would constitute a breach of contract, but not a tort (and, for this reason, not a kind of action allowing Campbell to recover punitive damages for the failure to pay).

In the end, the question of what kind of breach of contract also counts as an independent tort (allowing for punitive damages) comes down to a balancing of policy considerations. On the one hand, courts may want to deter certain bad conduct, especially in cases involving vulnerable plaintiffs. On the other hand, allowing punitive damages routinely in contract cases would upset parties' expectations. Parties would be wary of entering into a contract if they did not know what their total exposure was for breach of that contract. Indeed, for those who subscribe to the theory of "efficient breach" described in Chapter 4, allowing for punitive damages would upset the theory of efficient breach.

To understand why punitive damages in a typical contract case would upset the theory of efficient breach, consider *Scenario 2* above. The theory of efficient breach says that Ophelia *should* breach the contract for the sale of widgets at $15 per widget and pay Polonius compensatory damages when Ophelia would make a profit in doing so *after compensating Polonius for his damages.*[8] Doing so moves the widgets to the highest-valued user, and does not make Polonius worse off (assuming he is actually compensated for his loss). But punitive damages upset this calculation. Both the possibility that Ophelia might have to pay punitive damages for breach and the amount of such damages, if awarded, are highly uncertain. The uncertainty alone may deter the efficient breach. More significantly, if the punitive damages amount to an additional $3 per widget, these damages might deter Ophelia's breach of contract even if it would have been efficient for her to have breached.

---

8. For example, suppose that the fair market value of the widgets is $16 per widget, but Ophelia could sell them to another buyer (who perhaps has a special need for the widgets) at $18 per widget. The Ophelia-Polonius contract was for $15 per widget, so (we know from Chapter 4 that) an award of $1 per widget (plus incidental and consequential damages, less expenses saved) would compensate Polonius. Ophelia could breach the contract, compensate Polonius for the loss, and still pocket an extra $2 per widget by selling to the user who values the goods more highly.

In striking this balance, courts have generally rejected arguments to create independent torts (allowing for punitive damages) out of typical breach of contract cases. For a time, some jurisdictions (including California) allowed punitive damages when a party to a contract in bad faith denied the contract's existence. But courts have pulled back from recognizing this tort. *See Freeman & Mills, Inc. v. Belcher Oil Co.*, 900 P.2d 669 (Cal. 1995).

Still there is a temptation in certain contract cases to continue to find the independent tort so as to allow for punitive damages. California Supreme Court Justice Mosk, concurring and dissenting in the *Freeman & Mills* case, listed three categories of contract breaches for which tort damages (including punitive damages) should be awarded:

(1) Breach accompanied by a traditional common law tort, such as fraud or conversion;

(2) Tortious means used by one contracting party to coerce or deceive another party into forgoing its contractual rights; and

(3) The case where one party breaches the contract intending or knowing that such a breach will cause severe, unmitigable harm in the form of mental anguish, personal hardship, or substantial consequential damages.

Of Justice Mosk's three proposed categories, the third is the most controversial. It suggests that in a number of consumer *and* business contracts, where one contracting party uses sharp practices along with breaching the contract, punitive damages should be available. Many courts would likely reject such an extension on grounds that it would interfere with contractual expectations. (Query whether Justice Mosk's third proposed category would apply to Lawrence, the drunk photographer in *Scenario 1*.)

Example 6

Sally is a dog sitter. She agrees to come twice a day for one week to Tabitha's house to walk, feed, and take care of Tabitha's dog while Tabitha is on vacation. In exchange Tabitha agrees to pay Sally $200. Sally is lazy, and she neglects to visit Tabitha's dog for two days. During that time, Tabitha's dog became quite ill and died. When Tabitha confronted Sally about her conduct, Sally lied and said she had in fact shown up twice a day to feed the dog. Tabitha's security camera tapes conclusively proved otherwise at trial. Expert testimony established that if Sally had performed as promised and obtained prompt veterinary attention, Tabitha's dog would have survived. In Tabitha's suit against Sally, may Tabitha recover punitive damages? If so, does it matter that Sally lied about her conduct?

Explanation

Tabitha certainly has a strong case for breach of contract. Sally promised to show up twice a day to walk, feed, and take care of Tabitha's dog during the week Tabitha was on vacation. Sally indisputably failed to do so. In addition to return of the contract price, Tabitha may be able to get consequential damages given how foreseeable they were. (See Chapter 4.)

The question of punitive damages, however, turns upon whether there is an independent tort. Arguably, Sally committed the independent tort of fraud when she lied about whether or not she performed under the contract. It is not clear that lying about performance itself should be enough to turn the breach of contract into a tort. Compare the majority and dissenting opinions in *Robinson Helicopter Co., Inc. v. Dana Corp.*, 102 P.3d 268 (Cal. 2004).

Without the lie, there's still a potential argument to treat this like a tort, to the extent a court accepts Justice Mosk's third category of contract breaches where punitive damages should be available: situation in which one party breaches the contract intending or knowing that such a breach will cause severe, unmitigable harm in the form of mental anguish, personal hardship, or substantial consequential damages.

If you were the judge deciding this case, would you allow the jury to consider the award of punitive damages? If so, to what degree is your answer driven by your view of the relationship between people and their pets? To test that sentiment, imagine that Sally had promised instead to simply house-sit for Tabitha (with no pets involved), and because of Sally's failure to check on the house as promised, she did not catch in time a leak in the laundry room which caused serious property damage to Tabitha's house. Sally then lied about her performance. If you would award lower (or no) punitive damages in this situation, but would in the former situation, your views are probably being driven in part by the pet factor.

Example 7

Universal Insurance Company receives a claim from its insured, Vicki, related to an automobile injury caused by Vicki that seriously injured Walter. Walter is prepared to settle the case with Vicki for $100,000, Vicki's policy limits. Universal employees perform an investigation to determine whether or not Vicki was negligent in causing the accident. But the employees themselves were negligent in the investigation. Because of their carelessness, they overlook evidence that makes it very clear that Vicki was negligent in causing Walter's injuries. Universal refuses to settle and the case goes to trial, leading to a jury verdict in Walter's favor of $250,000. Because Vicki's policy limits were $100,000, Vicki is personally liable for the additional $150,000.

Vicki then sues Universal for breach of contract in handling the claim, alleging that Universal breached the contract and acted in bad faith when they negligently evaluated her claim. Assume that a jury would agree that this conduct constituted a breach of the contract and would conclude that to compensate Vicki, Universal must compensate Vicki for the additional $150,000 she paid out to Walter. May Vicki also recover *punitive* damages in her suit against Universal?

Explanation

Vicki likely will not be able to recover punitive damages in this case. Recall that the conduct which allows for the award of punitive damages must be worse than negligence. In this case, it does not appear that Universal's conduct was anything worse than negligent. So even if Universal's negligent claims handling constituted both a breach of the insurance contract and a tort, it likely is not bad enough conduct to merit the imposition of punitive damages.

15.3 CONSTITUTIONAL LIMITS ON THE *AMOUNT* OF PUNITIVE DAMAGES

Thus far, this chapter has focused on the question *whether* or not punitive damages would be available in particular lawsuits and the standards for courts and juries to determine their appropriateness. Though this is an important question in the law of punitive damages, equally important is the question of how juries determine (and courts review) the *amount* of punitive damages if such damages are to be awarded. Consider the rules from New Jersey on the amount of punitive damages:

> If the trier of fact determines that punitive damages should be awarded, the trier of fact shall then determine the amount of those damages. In making that determination, the trier of fact shall consider all relevant evidence, including, but not limited to, the following:
> (1) All relevant evidence relating to the factors [used to determine whether punitive damages are to be awarded];[9]

---

9. The factors include the following:

(1) The likelihood, at the relevant time, that serious harm would arise from the defendant's conduct;
(2) The defendant's awareness o[r] reckless disregard of the likelihood that the serious harm at issue would arise from the defendant's conduct;
(3) The conduct of the defendant upon learning that its initial conduct would likely cause harm; and
(4) The duration of the conduct or any concealment of it by the defendant.

N.J. Stat. Ann. § 2A:15-5.12b.

(2) The profitability of the misconduct to the defendant;
(3) When the misconduct was terminated; and
(4) The financial condition of the defendant.

N.J. STAT. ANN. § 2A:15-5.12c.

When faced with instructions such as these, a jury could well choose a very high amount for the punitive damages. This is true in part because a jury considering the "financial condition of the defendant" is going to pick a large amount to punish a wealthy defendant. After all, a $100,000 punitive damage award would feel different to you compared to how it would feel to a very wealthy person such as Bill Gates. Moreover, the awards are going to be high because of the very conduct involved. "The purposes of the award — the deterrence of egregious misconduct and the punishment of the offender — when mixed with a finding that the defendant is malicious, can readily inflame an otherwise-dispassionate jury." Lockley v. State of New Jersey Dep't of Corrections, 828 A.2d 869, 878 (N.J. 2003).

For these reasons and others (notably a push by business entities for "tort reform" to reduce their potential liability), many states either cap the amount of damages or provide for courts to lower the amount of damages in certain circumstances. In New Jersey, for example, the maximum amount of punitive damages that may be assessed against a defendant is "five times the liability of that defendant for compensatory damages or $350,000, whichever is greater." N.J. STAT. ANN. § 2A:15-5.14b. According to one count, "five states either prohibit punitive damages or severely restrict their use. Statutory caps in at least in some form exist in half the states. Limits tied to the amount of actual or economic damages exist in 14 states." Joseph Sanders, Punitive Damages in Consumer Actions, 8 J. TEX. CONSUMER L. 22 (2004) (footnotes omitted).

Some states, however, provided no meaningful review of punitive damage awards. In Honda Motor Co. v. Oberg, 512 U.S. 415 (1994), the U.S. Supreme Court held that some kind of review of the amount of a punitive damage award was necessary to comply with the U.S. Constitution.

You might reasonably ask what the U.S. Constitution has to do with state awards of punitive damages. This is a fair question, and one that turns out to be quite controversial. For those of you who have not yet taken a Constitutional Law course, you should know that the U.S. Constitution provides in the Fourteenth Amendment that no state may deprive any person of life, liberty, or property "without due process of law." The meaning of this "Due Process Clause" consumes quite a bit of time in the typical Constitutional Law course, and one of the major questions is whether the clause guarantees only fair procedures (so-called "procedural due process") or also fair outcomes (so-called "substantive due process").

The U.S. Supreme Court began its examination of the constitutionality of large punitive damage awards in 1989, when it rejected the idea that the Constitution's Eighth Amendment, prohibiting excessive fines, served as a limit on punitive damages awards. *Browning-Ferris Industries of Vermont, Inc. v. Kelco Disposal Inc.*, 492 U.S. 257 (1989). But two years later, in *Pacific Mutual Life Insurance Co. v. Haslip*, 499 U.S. 1 (1991), the Court first suggested that a high punitive damages award could violate substantive due process; the Court talked about punitive damages that "run wild" and said that an award of punitive damages that was four times the amount of compensatory damages was "close to the line" of constitutional excessiveness. The Court next refused to overturn a punitive damages award with a 500:1 ratio of punitive to compensatory damages (*TXO Production Corp. v. Alliance Resources Corp.*, 509 U.S. 443 (1993)), leading some to wonder whether the Court was serious about reining in the amount of large punitive damages awards.

The breakthrough for defendants came in the 1996 case *BMW v. Gore*, 517 U.S. 559 (1996). If you were on the Supreme Court and looking for a case to rein in punitive damages, this case was a good one because it featured a relatively unsympathetic plaintiff and a relatively non-culpable defendant, and involved a very large damages award for little injury.

In *BMW*, Dr. Gore purchased a $40,000 BMW sports sedan in Alabama. After driving it for nine months, he took it to "Slick Finish" to make the car look "snazzier." Mr. Slick (I'm not making this up) informed Gore that his car had been repainted by the dealership before Gore purchased it. It turns out that the car had suffered some damage from acid rain before it arrived at the dealership. BMW's policy was to repaint new cars with minor damage, without disclosing the practice. In Alabama, the non-disclosure counted as a fraud, though in other states it did not.

The jury determined that Gore's compensatory damages were $4,000, based upon expert testimony that the repainting reduced the value of the car by about 10%. It then assessed $4 million (!) in punitive damages, finding the non-disclosure policy to be "gross, oppressive or malicious fraud." The Alabama Supreme Court reduced the award to $2 million, on grounds that acts that occurred in other jurisdictions should not be the basis for punishment. BMW further appealed to the U.S. Supreme Court, which struck down the award on substantive due process grounds.

The *BMW v. Gore* opinion was quite tentative, suggesting three "guideposts" for courts to consider in determining whether the amount of punitive damages was constitutionally excessive:

1. *The degree of reprehensibility of the conduct.* The more reprehensible the conduct, the higher the punitive award should be.
2. *The ratio of punitive damages to actual damages.* The higher the ratio, the more constitutionally suspect the punitive award.
3. *Sanctions for comparable misconduct.* If civil or criminal penalties for similar conduct are low, then a punitive award should be low as well,

because those penalties signal that the state does not consider the conduct to be highly blameworthy.

The first factor, of course, seems relevant in any discussion of the proper amount of punitive damages: certainly BMW should not be punished as harshly as someone who intentionally causes physical injury to another person. The ratio factor is somewhat less defensible; the Court did not explain why ratio should matter so much, and it issued some caveats related to the use of the ratio. First, the comparison is between punitive damages and the amount of actual *and potential* damages that a defendant could have caused had he not been stopped from acting. Moreover, the Court suggested there was no "simple mathematical formula" to determine the constitutionality of a punitive damage award. (Keep this language in mind.) The Court gave the example of "a particularly egregious act [that] has resulted in only a small amount of economic damages," which would justify a high ratio. It also noted that a higher ratio "may be justified in cases where the injury is hard to detect or the monetary value of noneconomic harm might have been difficult to determine."

The last factor, sanctions for comparable misconduct, sends a somewhat perverse message. Punitive damages may be *most useful* when the state does not have other civil or criminal sanctions in place to deter bad conduct.

Four Justices (Chief Justice Rehnquist, the liberal Justice Ginsburg, and the conservative Justices Thomas and Scalia) dissented, stating that the amount of punitive damages should be determined by state law, and not federalized in this way.

After *BMW v. Gore*, courts began to review awards of punitive damages for constitutional excessiveness. In states without great limits on punitive awards, the case had the potential for greater impact than in those states that already conducted some kind of excessiveness review. But because *BMW* imposed a squishy multifactor "guideposts" test, it did not appear likely to lead to great changes in the law. But then along came the *State Farm v. Campbell* case, described in the last section. Laycock rightly says that *Campbell* put "the *BMW* guideposts on steroids." LAYCOCK p. 239.

You've already read the *Campbell* case's facts. Here is how the Supreme Court in *Campbell* changed the *BMW* guideposts related to constitutional review of the amount of the awards in striking down the $145 million punitive award.

1. *The Court has limited what evidence may be considered for purposes of judging reprehensibility.* The majority said that State Farm's conduct "merits no praise," quite an understatement if one accepts the plaintiff's view of the conduct (as the Court ordinarily does on appeal). More importantly, the Court said that in judging reprehensibility for purposes of determining the amount of punitive damages, a

jury may consider only similar conduct that has a *close nexus* to the kind of bad conduct at issue in the case itself. So defendants will be able to exclude much evidence of a pattern of similar bad conduct.

2. *The Court has begun using mathematical formulas to limit the ratio of punitive and compensatory damages.* Though the *Campbell* Court said that there are "no rigid benchmarks," it suggested that it would be the rare case where damages could exceed a 9:1 ratio of punitive damages to actual and potential compensatory damages: "Single-digit multipliers are more likely to comport with due process, while still achieving the State's goals of deterrence and retribution, than awards with ratios in the range of 500 to 1 or, in this case, 145 to 1." Indeed, in cases like this one, with "substantial" compensatory awards (recall the $1 million in damages plaintiff was awarded for emotional distress), "then a lesser ratio, perhaps only equal to compensatory damages, can reach the outermost limit of the due process guarantee."

3. *The wealth of the defendant cannot be used as a reason to increase the award of punitive damages.* This is perhaps the biggest and most important change coming from *Campbell*. "The wealth of a defendant cannot justify an otherwise unconstitutional punitive damage award." While absence of wealth might be a reason to *lower* the amount of damages, the presence of wealth cannot be a reason to *raise* the amount.

Arguably, the third factor is the most indefensible part of the *Campbell* test. Note the New Jersey factors for the award of punitive damages listed earlier in this section. Of course, the New Jersey courts (like the courts in many other states) consider the wealth of the defendant to be a relevant factor in assessing the amount of the award, for the reasons discussed above in relation to wealthy people such as Bill Gates: it take a lot more money to deter a rich person (or corporate management) than a poor person. How this factor is supposed to square with the deterrent purpose of punitive damages is yet to be explained.

On remand in *Campbell* the Utah Supreme Court reduced the punitive award to $9 million. *State Farm Mutual Insurance Co. v. Campbell*, 98 P.3d 409 (2004). Not coincidentally, that created a 9:1 ratio between punitive damages and compensatory damages. The U.S. Supreme Court declined to hear the case a second time.

Campbell is not the last word from the Supreme Court on policing the amount of punitive damages. A more recent Supreme Court case has created added confusion about constitutional standards. In *Philip Morris USA v. Williams*, 549 U.S. 346 (2007), the Court held on a 5-4 vote that a jury cannot consider the defendant's similar conduct toward other in-state residents for purposes of punishing the defendant through punitive damages. But the Court added that a jury *could* consider that similar conduct for purposes of determining reprehensibility (which in turn is a factor to consider when juries determine the amount of punitive damages). The dissenters thought this distinction "elus[ive]" (Justice Stevens) and the opinion's logic "inexplicable" (Justice Ginsburg).

Philip Morris was followed by yet another Supreme Court punitive damages case. In Exxon Shipping Co. v. Baker, 554 U.S. 471 (2008), the Court reviewed a $2.5 billion punitive damages award (on top of $500 million in compensatory damages) arising out of the infamous Exxon Valdez oil spill. Sitting as a common law court (and therefore not making a constitutional pronouncement) considering the propriety of a punitive damages award under federal admiralty law, the Supreme Court held that the punitive award had to be limited to a 1:1 ratio of punitive to compensatory damages. The opinion is likely to be influential, though its reach is far from clear; technically speaking, this was the Supreme Court deciding a case in admiralty, and its ruling is not binding on state courts reviewing the amount of punitive damages under state law.

The Court in Exxon Shipping Co. limited the scope of its holding, explaining that the 1:1 ratio applies to "this particular type of case." Id. at 511. It is not clear if cases involving wrongs motivated by the hope of financial gain, or those leading to more serious personal injuries, would be subject to a different ratio. Despite the limiting language, the fact that the Supreme Court of the United States put its stamp of approval on a 1:1 ratio in such a high-profile case could well lead state courts to follow Exxon Shipping Co. in review of punitive damages award amounts under state law.

In the meantime, four Justices have left the Court since BMW and Campbell, and it is unclear where the new Justices stand on the question of constitutional analysis of punitive damages. Of the six Justices in the majority in Campbell, only Justices Kennedy and Breyer remain, while the three dissenters (Ginsburg, Scalia, and Thomas) are still on the Court. It is possible that the Court could reverse this entire line of cases should someone seek to have them overturned.

But one scholar suggests "that the Court is almost certainly entering an extended silent phase in its punitive damages jurisprudence and will not be reviewing any more punitive damages awards in the foreseeable future." Jim Gash, The End of An Era: The Supreme Court (Finally) Butts Out of Punitive Damages for Good, 65 FLA. L. REV. 525, 527 (2011). Professor Gash notes that the Supreme Court declined to hear Philip Morris's second cert. petition (raising a substantive due process claim) after the Oregon Supreme Court upheld the $79.5 million punitive damages award on remand. Whether this means that substantive due process claims are "dead" as Professor Gash claims or that the Court majority was just not ready to wade into these waters again at this time remains to be seen. See id. at 580-583.

Example 8

Defendant ran a hotel that was infested with bedbugs. Though hotel guests complained about the bedbugs, the hotel did nothing serious to correct the problem and misrepresented its rooms as clean. Bedbug bites are uncomfortable and unsightly, though not life-threatening. A group of hotel guests sue the hotel in tort for fraud and other torts. A jury awards $5,000 in compensatory damages and $186,000 in punitive damages. The defendant is quite wealthy. May the *amount* of the punitive award stand?

Explanation

This hypothetical is based upon *Mathias v. Accor Economy Lodging, Inc.*, 347 F.3d 672 (7th Cir. 2003). In an opinion written by the influential Judge Richard A. Posner, the court upheld the punitive award against a challenge that it was unconstitutionally high. The ratio of the award was quite high, 37.2:1, but the court held it did not violate the rules of *Campbell*, arguing it fit into an exception for cases involving egregious facts but low compensatory damages: "The defendant's behavior was outrageous but the compensable harm done was slight and at the same time difficult to quantify because a large element of it was emotional. And the defendant may well have profited from its misconduct because by concealing the infestation it was able to keep renting rooms."

Perhaps most interesting about *Mathias* is what Judge Posner said about the defendant wealth issue:

> Finally, if the total stakes in the case were capped at $50,000 . . . , the plaintiffs might well have had difficulty financing this lawsuit. It is here that the defendant's aggregate net worth of $1.6 billion becomes relevant. A defendant's wealth is not a sufficient basis for awarding punitive damages. *Campbell*; BMW (concurring opinion); *Zazu Designs v. L'Oreal, S.A.*, 979 F.2d 499, 508-09 (7th Cir. 1992). That would be discriminatory and would violate the rule of law . . . by making punishment depend on status rather than conduct. Where wealth in the sense of resources enters is in enabling the defendant to mount an extremely aggressive defense against suits such as this and by doing so to make litigating against it very costly, which in turn may make it difficult for the plaintiffs to find a lawyer willing to handle their case, involving as it does only modest stakes, for the usual 33-40 percent contingent fee.
>
> In other words, the defendant is investing in developing a reputation intended to deter plaintiffs. It is difficult otherwise to explain the great stubbornness with which it has defended this case, making a host of frivolous evidentiary arguments despite the very modest stakes even when the punitive damages awarded by the jury are included.

One of my former students has written a law review note arguing, I think correctly, that *Mathias* is in fact inconsistent with *Campbell* in considering the wealth of the defendant. It seems that Judge Posner is trying to get defendant's wealth information into the case through the back door. My student further argues that *Mathias* is right and that *Campbell* is wrong on the role of the wealth of the defendant in punitive damages cases. Leila C. Orr, Note, *Making a Case for Wealth-Calibrated Punitive Damages*, 37 LOY. L.A. L. REV. 1739 (2004).

Following *Campbell*'s pronouncement about the role of wealth in assessing the amount of punitive damages, it is not clear that jury instructions such as those used in New Jersey (allowing the jury to consider the wealth of the defendant) remain constitutional.

Example 9

Acting with malicious intent, X shoots Y, causing Y to become permanently disabled and in constant pain. X is convicted criminally for attempted murder, receiving a 25-years-to-life sentence, and then Y sues X in tort for a number of torts, including battery. A jury determines that Y suffered $1 million in compensatory damages for past and future medical care, past and future lost wages, and emotional distress. It then awards an additional $2 million in punitive damages. X has very few assets. May the *amount* of the punitive award stand?

Explanation

Certainly X's conduct is reprehensible; indeed, it is probably among the most reprehensible conduct juries likely would see in a punitive damages case. The ratio here is 2:1, which is relatively low. Recall that in *Campbell*, the Court discussed how, in cases involving "substantial" compensatory damages, a ratio of 1:1 might be the most appropriate. Still, it is difficult to imagine a court reducing the punitive damages on this basis in this case; unlike the $1 million award in *Campbell*, which was exclusively for emotional distress damages, here the $1 million award is compensating in great part for medical expenses and lost wages — which a court may see as serving a greater compensatory purpose. In addition, criminal sanctions are severe; X has received a serious criminal sentence.

Even though all three of the *BMW/Campbell* guideposts support upholding the amount of punitive damages in this case, it is still possible a court would reduce the award because of the defendant's *lack of wealth*. Courts sometimes say that a punitive award cannot bankrupt or destroy the defendant, and someone with few assets facing a $2 million punitive award (on top of a $1 million compensatory award) would indeed face the possibility of bankruptcy.

The Supreme Court's opinion in *Campbell* does not say it is improper to *reduce* a large award to take into account defendant's lack of wealth. It says only that it is improper to *increase* a punitive award to take into account defendant's great wealth. Still, with such an unsympathetic defendant, it would not be surprising for a court to uphold this award, leading to X's bankruptcy.

Declaratory Judgments and Related Remedies

16.1 INTRODUCTION: WHY DECLARATORY JUDGMENTS?

Federal law gives federal courts the power in most cases to "declare the rights and other legal relations of any interested party seeking such declaration, whether or not further relief is or could be sought." 28 U.S.C. § 2201. An earlier uniform act that served as a model for federal law, the Uniform Declaratory Judgments Act (1922), adopted by many states, gives state courts the power to grant similar relief.

When would a party want a declaratory judgment from a court, as opposed to seeking another kind of remedy? Consider the following scenarios, and ask yourself whether a declaration of the parties' respective rights is the best solution, or a different remedy might be better:

- Zelda and Alex are neighbors. Alex wants to build a shed on his land, but Zelda objects because she believes that Alex's plans would go over the property line, putting part of the shed on her property.
- Barbara owns a patent on an espresso maker. She has been threatening to sue Carrie, the manufacturer of a different espresso maker, for patent infringement unless Carrie pays a royalty. Carrie does not believe her patent is infringing.
- Marchers wish to stage a protest in the city square, protesting the city's treatment of the homeless. City leaders tell Marchers that if they

march, they would be violating a city ordinance prohibiting any public assembly without the posting of a $100,000 bond for any damage that may be caused. Marchers believe the city law is unconstitutional under the First Amendment.

In each of these cases, a declaratory judgment may be the best, or one of the best, remedies. In the first example, Alex might not want to build his shed while there is a dispute over the boundary line; a court might force Alex later to pay damages for trespass, or even possibly to remove the structure after it has been built. A declaration of rights would save Alex money and both parties possible further inconvenience.

From Zelda's perspective, a declaration would be useful as well to determine the parties' respective rights. Assuming Zelda believes that her neighbor Alex is likely to abide by a court's determination of the boundary line, a declaration may be all that Zelda needs and may be cheaper than obtaining other remedies, such as an injunction. In contrast, if there's a chance that Alex might build anyway, despite a declaration of rights, Zelda might prefer an injunction barring Alex from building over the (now determined) property line. (See Part II of this book for more on the rules related to injunctions.) As we shall see, it is procedurally easier to get a declaratory judgment compared to an injunction.

The contrast between injunctions and declaratory judgments reveals an important fact about declaratory judgments: they are *implicitly coercive*. When a court declares the parties' respective rights, a violation of those rights is not the same as violating a court injunction. In other words, a party who ignores a declaratory judgment cannot be held in contempt of court (the way a party can be for violating a court injunction). But once a court has declared the parties' respective rights, a court will be quite receptive to the option of later issuing an injunction, should it be necessary in case one of the parties fails to respect those rights. Knowing this, most parties will simply obey declaratory judgments *as if* they were coercive.

The Zelda-Alex hypothetical demonstrates that declaratory judgments are useful because they *reduce uncertainty* and can be *implicitly coercive*, like injunctions. The reduction of uncertainty is especially useful in two contexts.

First, *declaratory judgments can be used to eliminate frivolous threats of litigation*. In the patent context, Barbara may have a "scarecrow patent," one that is used to intimidate others to pay royalties for a patent that may be invalid or not infringing. The declaratory judgment ends Barbara's ability to threaten Carrie with a patent infringement suit. In this regard, consider *Cardinal Chemical Co. v. Morton International, Inc.*, 508 U.S. 83 (1993), a case that shows the true economic value of declaratory judgments in appropriate cases.

Morton International sued Cardinal Chemical Co. for patent infringement related to some chemical compounds. Cardinal denied infringement and filed a counterclaim for declaratory relief, asking the court to declare Morton's patents invalid. A trial court had determined that Cardinal had not infringed on Morton's copyright and issued a declaration that Morton's patent was invalid. The United States Court of Appeals for the Federal Circuit (which handles such patent disputes) affirmed the holding on patent infringement, but vacated the declaration on grounds that the question was moot. Indeed, the Federal Circuit had a per se rule dismissing all declaratory judgment requests as moot upon a finding of no infringement. The Supreme Court reversed the Federal Circuit on the declaratory judgment point, noting that the circuit's rule denied patentees meaningful appellate review. Moreover, the Supreme Court said, the Federal Circuit's refusal to issue declaratory judgments in these circumstances "prolongs the life of invalid patents [and] encourages endless litigation (or at least uncertainty) over the validity of outstanding patents."

Second, *declaratory judgments can serve to vindicate important constitutional rights.* In some circumstances, a group might decide to schedule a march (or engage in other political activities) precisely to test a law that the group believes is unconstitutional. This is a variation on eliminating uncertainty in the very important context of protecting the right to free speech and assembly (along with other constitutional rights).

Though declaratory judgments can serve useful social purposes, they can be abused as well. A party might try to use a declaratory judgment for tactical reasons, such as forum shopping. *See* Laycock pp. 586-587. For this reason, courts have wide discretion whether or not to entertain declaratory judgment suits.

For example, consider a recent case between Xoxide, Inc. and Ford Motor Company. *Xoxide, Inc. v. Ford Motor Co.,* 448 F. Supp. 2d 1188 (C.D. Cal. 2006). Xoxide operated a business that manufactured accessories for Ford Mustangs, advertising its accessories on a website. Ford sent a letter to Xoxide claiming that some of the company's activities violated Ford's trademarks.[1] The parties exchanged more letters, but reached no resolution. Xoxide, anticipating trademark infringement litigation brought by Ford in Michigan, filed a declaratory judgment action in federal district court in California seeking a declaration that Xoxide was *not* infringing on Ford's

---

1. "Ford specifically alleged that Xoxide: (1) had allegedly "misappropriated the world-famous trademark Mustang® in the internet domain name MustangTuning.com" in violation of the Anticybersquatting Consumer Protection Act ('ACPA'); (2) misappropriated the Mustang trademark in its business name, MustangTuning; (3) wrongfully incorporated Ford's Mustang trademark or a variation thereof into Xoxide's vanity phone number, 1-888-STANG-GT; and (4) was 'manufacturing, marketing, advertising, and/or distributing wheels bearing a confusingly similar variation of Ford's registered' trademarks."

trademarks.[2] The court, citing a rule against anticipatory suits and forum shopping, refused to allow Xoxide's suit to go forward. Xoxide had to settle Ford's claims or defend itself in a Michigan suit.

Declaratory judgments do present some risk to parties in terms of issue preclusion and claim preclusion (collateral estoppel and res judicata). As to issue preclusion (collateral estoppel), suppose Zelda asks for and obtains declaratory relief with regard to the boundary between her land and Alex's land. Alex ignores the declaration and builds over his property line and onto Zelda's land. Zelda sues for a court order requiring Alex to remove his new construction. In that later suit, Alex cannot litigate the boundary line question again. So long as Alex had a fair opportunity to make his case in the declaratory judgment action, that issue is now closed.

As to claim preclusion (res judicata), a party is certainly allowed to couple a claim for declaratory relief with a claim for additional relief, such as an injunction or damages for past conduct. See 28 U.S.C. § 2201 (a party may obtain declaratory relief "whether or not further relief is or could be sought"). Moreover, a party can ask for additional relief in an action after first requesting declaratory relief. See 28 U.S.C. § 2202 ("Further necessary or proper relief based on a declaratory judgment or decree may be granted, after reasonable notice and hearing, against any adverse party whose rights have been determined by such judgment.").

Here's the tricky part. If a plaintiff *couples* declaratory relief with a request for *any other relief* (such as an injunction or damages), the plaintiff is barred from asking for additional relief in a later case. This may seem like an arcane point (and it is), but the point was worth a quarter of a billion dollars in a California Supreme Court case, *Mycogen v. Monsanto Co.*, 51 P.3d 297 (Cal. 2002).[3] Two parties to a complex license agreement disputed if and how it applied. The licensee successfully sought a declaration that the licensor had an obligation to license its technology to the licensee; it also asked for an order of specific performance requiring the licensor to do so. In subsequent litigation, the licensee sought damages for the licensor's delay in licensing the technology. A lower court allowed the delay damages case to go forward, leading to a $175 million judgment (plus interest).

The California Supreme Court held that the later case should not have gone forward,[4] citing the reasons given by a federal district court in

---

2. Why would Xoxide prefer a California court over a Michigan court? One possibility is Xoxide's fear that a Michigan court would be too sympathetic to Ford, a powerful corporation in Michigan. In addition, Xoxide's lawyers are likely based in California, and they would be more familiar with California judges and procedure. It is also cheaper to engage in litigation locally than halfway across the country.

3. Disclosure: I consulted for one of the parties in this case.

4. In other words, the licensee should have sought the delay damages in the same suit as that for specific performance and a declaratory judgment. Such damages would not have given the licensee a double recovery. The specific performance prevented future harm from the failure

Christe v. City of Steamboat Springs, 122 F. Supp. 2d 1183, 1189 (D. Colo. 2000):

> First, to allow the exception to extend beyond purely declaratory relief would run counter to the purpose of declaratory actions, which is "to provide a remedy that is simpler and less harsh than coercive relief." [Citation.] Perhaps more importantly, to permit some but not other coercive actions to accompany a request for declaratory relief would open the door to uncertainty and potential claim splitting. The Court sees no justification, for example, for applying ordinary claim preclusion rules to cases where the plaintiff seeks declaratory and damage relief, but a different set of rules to cases where the plaintiff seeks declaratory and injunctive relief. Moreover, if courts were to apply a more lenient set of rules to the latter situation, this would encourage parties to split their causes of action to gain a second bite at the apple if not successful in the first lawsuit. To avoid uncertainty, application of preclusion rules must be clear. Once a party seeks and obtains coercive relief, the basis for applying the declaratory judgment exception evaporates, and ordinary rules of claim preclusion must apply.

Bottom line: either bring suit *solely* for pure declaratory relief or, if you couple declaratory relief with requests for other forms of relief, make sure that you've asked for *everything* you'll ever want to ask for from this defendant for this series of transactions.

Example 1

Darcy and Eunice got into a traffic collision in Texas in which Eunice sustained serious personal injuries. Eunice is a resident of Arkansas; Darcy is a resident of Texas. Anticipating that Eunice would file a suit for negligence in Arkansas, Darcy filed suit against Eunice first, asking for a declaration from a Texas court that Darcy was not driving negligently. Should the Texas court hear the declaratory judgment suit?

Explanation

The Texas court is likely to decline to hear Darcy's declaratory judgment suit. Like the Ford Mustang case described above, this looks like an anticipatory suit and forum shopping. Darcy presumably expects to get a more favorable reception from courts in her own state, which is likely why she is engaging in this forum shopping. Laycock reports that "[t]here is an

---

to perform under the contract. The delay damages compensated for the *past harm* caused by the failure to comply with the contract. For more on specific performance, see Chapter 8.

especially strong presumption that personal injury plaintiffs are entitled to choose their forum." LAYCOCK p. 587.

Example 2

Same facts as in Example 1. Only this time, Eunice files the suit first. Her lawyer files suit asking only for a declaration that Darcy was negligent. The lawyer figures that if the court finds Darcy was negligent, he can later sue for damages. In the meantime, seeking only a declaratory judgment can save some time and money. Did Eunice's lawyer make a wise choice?

Explanation

No. There is no good reason for Eunice's lawyer to seek a declaratory judgment in this case. There is no benefit to reducing uncertainty so as to avoid any future litigation: Eunice has been injured, and if Darcy has been negligent in causing Eunice's injuries, Darcy is going to have to pay damages. Such a piecemeal approach to litigation serves no useful purpose. Besides the delay, such a tactic could work against Eunice's interests. Declaratory judgments are determined by *courts*, not juries. Having a court make a determination of negligence would end up depriving Eunice of the chance to have her case heard by a jury, and a jury could well be more sympathetic (and generous, when it comes to damages) than the trial judge. If Eunice's lawyer files a suit only for a declaratory judgment Eunice could have a strong cause of action — against her own lawyer for attorney malpractice!

Example 3

Variation on the Zelda-Alex hypothetical: Alex begins building his shed on what Zelda believes is Zelda's land. Zelda seeks a declaratory judgment that Alex is building on her land. She asks for no other relief. The court issues the declaration that Alex is building on Zelda's land. Alex refuses to remove the shed. (a) Can Zelda go back to court to have Alex held in contempt of court? (b) Does claim preclusion or issue preclusion prevent Zelda from obtaining an injunction ordering Alex to remove the property and pay damages for the past trespass?

Explanation

(a) Alex cannot be held in contempt of court. The declaration addressed only the parties' rights; it did not impose any obligation upon Alex to remove his structure or to compensate Zelda. Subject to a few exceptions not applicable here (see Chapter 10), a party cannot be held in contempt absent a valid injunction which the party disobeys. Zelda can go back to court and ask for an injunction, and Alex could be held in contempt *at that point* if he fails to abide by the court's order.

(b) Because Zelda brought a suit for *pure* declaratory relief (i.e., a request for a declaratory judgment with no other relief requested), Zelda may bring a follow-up lawsuit asking for an injunction, damages, or both. (Thus, this situation is unlike *Mycogen v. Monsanto*.) The question of where the parties' property line is, however, has already been settled in the declaratory judgment action. Both parties should be precluded from re-litigating that issue.

16.2 RIPENESS REQUIREMENTS FOR DECLARATORY JUDGMENTS

Declaratory judgments are different from some other kinds of remedies in that a plaintiff usually seeks the remedy *before* there has been an injury. This feature of declaratory judgments makes them like injunctions, and raises the same problem that the remedy may be brought *before* there is an actual, live controversy between the parties. As we saw in Chapter 7, the "propensity" requirement a plaintiff must meet to get injunctive relief deals with this problem in the context of injunctions. (Plaintiffs seeking injunctions also must prove "irreparable injury," something not required when plaintiffs seek declaratory judgments.)

In the context of declaratory relief, courts impose a "ripeness" requirement on declaratory judgment actions. If a court holds a case is "unripe," it will not consider a claim for declaratory relief. This section considers how much of a controversy there must be before a claim is considered ripe enough for courts to consider it.

In the federal courts, ripeness has a *constitutional* dimension. Article III of the United States Constitution grants federal courts jurisdiction only to hear "cases" or "controversies." In *Nashville, Chattanooga & St. Louis Railway v. Wallace*, 288 U.S. 249 (1933), the United States Supreme Court held it had Article III jurisdiction to hear an appeal of a declaratory judgment action brought in a Tennessee state court. The Supreme Court held a declaratory judgment case may be heard under Article III "so long as the case retains the essentials of an adversary proceeding, involving a real, not a hypothetical controversy, which is finally determined by the judgment below."

When federal courts consider ripeness questions in declaratory judgment cases, they may use a "refined" ripeness test, considering "(1) the adversity of the parties' interests[,] (2) the conclusiveness of the judgment, and (3) the utility of the judgment." *Pic-A-State Pa., Inc. v. Reno*, 76 F.3d 1294 (3rd Cir. 1996). A recent case applying this test is *Khodara Environmental, Inc. v. Blakey*, 376 F.3d 187 (3d Cir. 2004). In *Khodara Environmental*, a landfill developer brought a declaratory judgment action against the Federal Aviation Administration (FAA), seeking a declaration that a new federal law regulating the building of landfills near airports did not bar its proposed construction of a landfill.[5] The developer claimed that its development — optimistically named the "Happy Landing Landfill"[6] — fell under a "grandfather clause" to the new law because it had already begun construction of the landfill. The FAA argued that the developer's request for a declaratory judgment was unripe, because the developer had not shown it would be able to obtain the state permits to complete construction of the landfill.

The Third Circuit, in an opinion by then-Judge (and now Supreme Court Justice) Alito, held the declaratory judgment suit was ripe. Applying the *Pic-A-State Pa.* test, the court noted that the parties were clearly adverse to one another, the judgment would conclusively establish whether or not the Happy Landing Landfill fell into the statute's grandfather clause, and, most important, a judgment would put the developer "in a position to know whether it should undertake the expensive project of redesigning the site plan and trying once again to obtain state permits."

Although state courts are not limited in their jurisdiction by Article III of the United States Constitution, some also impose ripeness requirements on declaratory judgment claims. (Other state courts are more willing to issue purely advisory opinions.) A recent example out of Texas is instructive. In *Save Our Springs Alliance v. City of Austin*, 149 S.W.3d 674 (Tex. App. 2004, no pet.), an environmental group sought a declaration that the City of Austin's approval of a land use project violated a city ordinance.[7] The court held the claim was unripe because the City had not yet approved the project; it had only been approved by a land use committee, and not the agency with the final power to approve the project. It was possible that the city would never approve the project. If it ever did, the dismissal of the original suit without prejudice would allow a new suit to be filed once there was a riper controversy.

The court opinion gave some reasons in favor of the ripeness doctrine. "The doctrine has a pragmatic, prudential aspect that is directed toward

---

5. The presence of birds near landfills and the birds' potential interference with the safe operation of aircraft is what made this a matter for the FAA.
6. Again, I'm not making this up. Truth is often funnier than fiction, particularly in this book.
7. The group also sought an injunction barring development of different property in the same area that had already been approved by the city. The court held that this claim was moot for reasons that do not concern us here.

'[conserving] judicial time and resources for real and current controversies, rather than abstract, hypothetical, or remote disputes.' [Citation.] Moreover, avoiding premature litigation prevents courts from entangling themselves in abstract disagreements, while allowing other branches of government and governmental agencies to perform their functions unimpeded."

Example 4

Professors F and G have a heated argument over an arcane but important point of state insurance law. The disagreement is so intense that the two of them refuse to speak to each other or work together on faculty committees. They agree to jointly petition the state supreme court to resolve the issue "once and for all" through a declaratory judgment. They prepare and file briefs with the court presenting well-researched and written arguments on the two sides of this issue. Should the court agree to the request for a declaratory judgment?

Explanation

Laycock posits that "courts shouldn't grant declaratory judgments to resolve law professors' hypotheticals." LAYCOCK p. 576. The *Save Our Springs Alliance* case provides some rationales for the ripeness doctrine, and they seem to apply here: it would be a waste of judicial resources for courts to be decide hypothetical questions where there is nothing of substance at stake. Though the question posits that the law professors care passionately about the question and have prepared good briefs on the topic, that's not the kind of "real controversy" that courts care about. If the question presented in the petition is really an important one about state insurance law, it will eventually arise in a real controversy, where someone's property interests (at the least) are at stake. Putting aside bad feelings between two law professors, there's no good reason to gear up the machinery of the state supreme court to involve itself in a case like this, and it is difficult to imagine any court that would do so — even in jurisdictions where courts issue advisory opinions. These professors would be better off designing a "moot court question" judged by state supreme court justices to get some feedback on their dispute.

Example 5

Same facts as in the original Zelda-Alex hypothetical about building the shed, except Alex files papers with the court saying he has no intention of building the shed, either on his property or across the property line. Zelda counters by showing pictures she took of Alex outside near her property with a surveyor. Should the court issue a declaratory judgment regarding the property boundary between the two parties?

Explanation

This case comes down to a credibility issue for the court. If the court believes there is a live controversy between the parties, then the court is likely to decide the matter through a declaratory judgment. If the court does not believe that a dispute is likely to arise, then the court will not decide the case.

If a court declines to hear a declaratory judgment motion, then the case is dismissed without prejudice. This dismissal would allow Zelda to file a later suit (perhaps for an injunction and/or for damages) in the event that Alex actually begins construction of the shed on what Zelda believes to be her land. Of course, in this variation on the hypothetical, Alex has represented to the court that he has no intention of building a shed either on his land or on Zelda's land. If Alex actually builds such a shed and then faces new litigation from Zelda (especially before the same judge), a court is likely to be very unfavorable to Alex's position in this case.

16.3 DECLARATORY JUDGMENTS AND FEDERALISM

Consider again the example of Marchers and the city from earlier in this chapter. Marchers believe that the city's bond requirement unconstitutionally burdens their First Amendment rights to free speech and assembly. City officials believe the law is constitutional, and plan to arrest Marchers if they in fact march.

Marchers have a few options (besides complying with the law by posting a bond). First, they could decide to break the law and, if arrested for violating it, defend themselves on the ground that the law is unconstitutional. Such prosecution would take place in state court. If the suit is successful, the prosecution will be dismissed. If it is unsuccessful, Marchers can be punished under criminal law. This strategy therefore is risky unless Marchers are quite confident that the courts will strike down the law as unconstitutional.

Second, Marchers could seek an injunction from a court barring the city from enforcing its law against Marchers. Provided Marchers can prove irreparable injury and propensity (see Chapter 7), the court will consider whether to bar enforcement of the law. This suit could be brought in either federal or state court; both courts have the power to enjoin enforcement of a law that violates the U.S. Constitution. In Ex parte Young, 209 U.S. 123 (1908), the Supreme Court approved of an injunction to eliminate the tough choice to obey an arguably unconstitutional law or violate it and risk prosecution.

Third, Marchers could seek a declaration from a court that the city's law is unconstitutional, at least as applied to Marchers. Marchers would need to show that the claim was ripe, as noted in the previous section of this chapter. The declaration would not hold the power of contempt, but the city would be expected not to prosecute Marchers following a declaration that the bond provision is unconstitutional; if the city did prosecute, the issue of the provision's unconstitutionality should be collaterally estopped in any future criminal prosecution, thereby barring that prosecution. This suit could be brought in either federal or state court; assuming state law allows for declaratory judgments, both courts have the power to declare a law in violation of the U.S. Constitution. *See Steffel v. Thompson*, 415 U.S. 452 (1974).

To this point, everything should seem pretty straightforward. The complication arises if Marchers violate the law, get prosecuted in state court for violating the city provision, and *then* go to *federal court* seeking a *declaration* that the city provision is unconstitutional. Once a state prosecution is pending, a federal court will abstain from hearing the case requesting a declaration that the city provision is unconstitutional; nor will a federal court issue an injunction barring state prosecution. *Younger v. Harris*, 401 U.S. 37 (1971); *Samuels v. Mackell*, 401 U.S. 66 (1971). Federal courts abstain out of federalism concerns; it would be a big deal for federal courts to interfere with ongoing state criminal law prosecutions.

Here are three important details about these issues. First, given that both federal and state courts have the power to declare laws in violation of the U.S. Constitution, it may not be clear what is at stake; after all, Marchers can simply defend themselves in the state court prosecution on grounds that the law is unconstitutional. The answer is that historically — though perhaps no longer true today — many litigants (particularly those involved in civil rights struggles) saw federal courts as more protective of federal constitutional rights than state courts.

Second, timing is everything in these cases, and the rules are complicated. Once state prosecutors take formal steps to begin criminal prosecution (such as filing an indictment), *Younger* abstention applies. However, even if a would-be criminal defendant files a declaratory relief action in federal court *first*, *Younger* abstention still applies if the state commences a prosecution "before any proceeding of substance on the merits" takes place in the federal court. *Hicks v. Miranda*, 422 U.S. 332, 349 (1975). The *Hicks* rule bars criminal defendants who go to federal court too late as plaintiffs seeking a declaratory judgment. Of course, the would-be criminal defendant cannot file the suit too early either, or else the suit may not be ripe. *See* LAYCOCK pp. 595-596.

Third, assuming no state prosecution has commenced, there still must be a *ripe controversy* for a federal court to declare a state or local law unconstitutional. *See Steffel* ("[R]egardless of whether injunctive relief may be appropriate, federal declaratory relief is not precluded when no state prosecution is pending and a federal plaintiff demonstrates a genuine threat of enforcement of a disputed state criminal statute, whether an attack is made on the constitutionality of the statute on its face or as applied."). In *Steffel*, the lower court had held that injunctive relief was inappropriate because the plaintiff could not show irreparable injury.[8] *Steffel* then firmly established the right to a declaration of unconstitutionality even absent proof of irreparable injury, so long as the case was ripe.

Example 6

A city passes an ordinance barring topless dancing. The three clubs in the city that produced topless dancing shows ceased the practice and went to federal court seeking a declaration that the ordinance was unconstitutional and an injunction barring its enforcement. One of the three clubs then began featuring topless dancing again. Before the federal court considered the request for a declaratory judgment and injunction on the merits, the state commenced prosecution of the club that resumed the topless dancing. (a) Should the state be held in contempt for prosecuting the club that began the topless dancing again? (b) Does the federal court have the power to declare the law unconstitutional and enjoin its enforcement?

Explanation

(a) The state cannot be held in contempt for prosecuting the club. Although the three clubs filed a complaint seeking a declaratory judgment and an injunction, the court had not yet granted these requests. Indeed, it had not done anything on the merits in the case. Without an injunction issued, a federal court would not hold the state in contempt for commencing prosecution of the clubs for violating the ordinance.

(b) The facts of this problem are based upon *Doran v. Salem Inn, Inc.*, 422 U.S. 922 (1975). To begin with, the three plaintiff clubs in the federal suit are not in the same situation. The two clubs that ceased their activities and did not restart the topless dancing should be entitled to declaratory relief under *Steffel* and, if they can prove irreparable injury, to an injunction in the event the federal court determines that the ordinance is unconstitutional. However, the third club, which continued the topless dancing, cannot get the benefit of declaratory relief or injunction. The state began its prosecution of the third club before there had been any proceeding of substance on the merits, meaning the state prosecution was commenced first for purposes of *Younger* abstention. (See *Hicks*.)

This ruling creates an anomaly: three similarly situated defendants are going to be treated differently even though all three were at one point engaging in activities violating the local ordinance, which may be

---

8. The plaintiff in *Steffel* abandoned his request for injunctive relief in the Supreme Court. The Court therefore did not rule on whether the lower court was right in concluding that plaintiff could not prove irreparable injury.

unconstitutional. In *Doran*, the Supreme Court recognized the anomaly but held that "each of the three [clubs] should be placed in the position required by our cases as if that [club] stood alone."

Example 7

The state of Pacifica has a long-standing statute on the books declaring the practice of homosexual sodomy illegal. Harry, a gay rights activist, thinks the law is unconstitutional under the U.S. Supreme Court's opinion in *Lawrence v. Texas*, 539 U.S. 558 (2003). (a) No one has been prosecuted under this statute for 80 years. May a federal court declare it unconstitutional? (b) Harry calls a press conference covered by the local television news in which he announces that next week he plans to invite police to his home to arrest him for engaging in activity that violates the statute. He then goes to federal court seeking a declaration that the statute is unconstitutional. May the federal court declare it unconstitutional?

Explanation

(a) Even though this law appears to violate the applicable Supreme Court precedent of *Lawrence*, it is possible the court would refuse to declare the law unconstitutional on grounds that the case is not ripe. The state has not prosecuted anyone for violating the statute for 80 years, and absent evidence of a new prosecution, it may not be worth gearing up the judicial machinery if only to make a symbolic point. On the other hand, the law remains on the books, and we do not know how many people might be deterred from engaging in likely legal conduct because of this statute. To the extent that Harry can demonstrate that the law would chill him (or others, who might be joined as plaintiffs), there is a chance the court would agree to decide the declaratory judgment case.

(b) Harry's conduct here seems aimed at creating a "test case" to avoid the possibility that the challenge to the law will be declared unripe. The federal court might well intervene, particularly if Pacifica officials give some indication they actually intend to arrest Harry for violating the law. On the other hand, if this law is unquestionably unconstitutional under *Lawrence*, perhaps the federal court will decide it is better to let the unconstitutionality of the statute be determined in state court as part of Harry's defense should he be prosecuted for violating the statute.

Arguably, Harry does not like either of these scenarios; he would prefer that any negative publicity generated by his opposition to the statute will cause the legislature to repeal it, as the statute appears to be unconstitutional. Legislative action would remove any of the reasons for either a declaratory judgment or a prosecution.

16.4 OTHER DECLARATORY REMEDIES

Though declaratory judgments are a relatively new judicial remedy (having found acceptance in many courts only within the last 100 years), courts have for a much longer time given other remedies that serve a similar declaratory purpose.

We have already seen two of these remedies earlier in this book. First, in Part I we considered *nominal damages*. To illustrate the declaratory nature of this remedy, let's return to our Zelda-Alex hypothetical. Suppose that Alex is out surveying the land where he intends to build his new shed. In doing so, he crosses what Zelda believes to be the line dividing their properties. Zelda could, at least in theory, sue Alex for trespass. (The tort does not require knowledge that defendant is on plaintiff's land, just an intent to enter that land.) Zelda suffered no damages by Alex's trifling trespass. But a jury determination that Alex indeed trespassed and must pay $1 to Zelda in nominal damages could serve a function similar to a declaratory judgment in having a court determine the boundary line between the parties.

Today, with declaratory judgments easier to get, it is less likely that a party would need to use nominal damages to achieve the declaratory result.

Second, the contract remedy of reformation is declaratory, at least in form. As we saw in Chapter 14, reformation is a court rewriting of the parties' contract, especially in cases where the writing does not conform to the parties' outward manifestations of the intentions they held when entering into the contract. Reformation may be considered declaratory because the court declares what the parties' contract now contains. But reformation is more than a declaration of the parties' rights: it imposes new obligations on the parties to a contract. Indeed, as noted in Chapter 14, some scholars consider reformation to be more restitutionary rather than declaratory, because it puts the parties in the position they would have been in had there been no error in the recording of their intentions in the written contract.

Besides nominal damages and reformation, a traditional declaratory remedy predating many courts' adoption of a Declaratory Judgment Act is the equitable *bill to remove cloud on title* (also referred to in some jurisdictions as a bill to quiet title or a bill to determine adverse claims). This declaratory-type remedy was (and in some states remains) useful in dealing with disputes over ownership of real property, particularly if those disputes concern the validity of any document related to title.[9] In some states this equitable remedy has been replaced with a statutory one, and today in many

---

9. As early as 1936 some courts were allowing the remedy to be used to resolve disputes involving personal property as well. *See Right to Quiet Title or Remove Cloud on Title to Personal Property by Suit in Equity or under Declaratory Judgment Act*, 105 A.L.R. 291 (1936).

jurisdictions a declaratory judgment action can serve the same purpose as a bill to remove cloud on title.

The rules on when to use this remedy for property disputes have varied from state to state. One question concerns the overlap of the remedy with the remedy of *ejectment*. Laycock reports that, in some states, "[i]f defendant is in possession, the action is still called ejectment, or analogized to ejectment, and either party can demand a jury; if not, the action is analogized to removing a cloud on title and is said to be equitable." LAYCOCK p. 607. When an action is equitable, it is decided by a court rather than a jury.

The rules for what to call your cause of action can be a malpractice trap in certain states. Especially if you are handling a land dispute in a different state from the one you ordinarily practice in, it is prudent to consult local sources to determine the proper form for your action. And you should always consider whether to couple your request for relief under a traditional form of remedy with a request for a declaratory judgment.

As to the labels used for remedies to declare rights in property disputes, consider a recent Indiana case, *Wetherald v. Jackson*, 855 N.E.2d 624 (Ind. App. 2006). The Jacksons and Strahls had adjoining lots on lakefront property. The Jacksons used their lot on Sundays for recreational purposes. The lot had a boat dock. "There was also a sandy beach area which the Jacksons believed was situated on their lot. On the side of the beach area nearest to Lot 66, a wooden board jutted out into the water. James Strahl told the Jacksons that the board was the boundary line between the two properties." In fact, the property was on Strahl's side of the line.

The Jacksons replaced the dock and built a deck and gazebo. The Strahls sold their property to Wetherald, who then installed a jet ski dock near the Jacksons' beach area. The Jacksons objected, claiming the dock was on their side of the property line, and asked Wetherald to remove it. Wetherald filed a complaint to quiet title alleging that the Jacksons had no legitimate claim to the transfer area and that they were interfering with his use of the property. In response, the Jacksons filed a counterclaim for declaratory judgment of adverse possession.

Note that Wetherald filed the complaint as an action to "quiet title" because he alleged he was the rightful owner of the property as recorded by the deeds to the properties. In response, the Jacksons sought a declaratory judgment that they had acquired the disputed property through adverse possession. (It does not appear that a claim for adverse possession could be resolved through a quiet title action in the jurisdiction.) The claims were tried before a trial court, which determined that the Jacksons had acquired the property through adverse possession. Though this procedure for resolving this garden-variety property dispute appears correct under Indiana law, the proper procedure in other jurisdictions may differ and will require some research.

Example 8

Wife dies as the separate owner of some real property. Wife's siblings claim that the property belongs to them, not to Husband. Husband brings a declaratory judgment action asking the court to declare that Wife's siblings have no interest in the real property. Should the court consider Husband's claim in a declaratory judgment action?

Explanation

It would appear that this dispute would be a fine candidate for a declaratory judgment action, so long as the claim was ripe. If Husband can present evidence that there is a genuine dispute over the ownership of the land between him and Wife's siblings, a declaratory judgment action can remove uncertainty and allow all parties to move forward knowing their rights.

But appearances can be deceiving. As noted in the text, the rule here about the proper form of action to bring in land disputes is quite jurisdiction-specific. In *Porter v. Houghton*, 542 S.E.2d 491 (Ga. 2001), the Georgia Supreme Court held that a declaratory judgment action was *not* the proper method for resolving this controversy, because "a party must establish that it is necessary to relieve himself of the risk of taking some future action that, without direction, would jeopardize his interests." (It is not clear why he could not make this showing if he planned to use or dispose of Wife's real property and Wife's siblings would oppose such action.) The court held that, under Georgia law, the statutory action to quiet title would be appropriate. GA. CODE. ANN. § 23-3-60. According to the *Porter* court, the purpose of that statute is for "readily and conclusively establishing that certain named persons are the owners of all the interests in land defined by a decree entered in such proceeding." Again, beware of the malpractice trap.

Help! I Need Somebody: Ancillary Remedies

17

17.1 COLLECTING MONEY JUDGMENTS

Ancillary remedies are helping remedies — that is, they are remedies that help other remedies work properly. We have already considered the most important ancillary remedy in Chapter 10: contempt. The contempt power gives injunctions their bite. When a party fails to follow an injunction, the contempt power allows for coercion, punishment, and, in some cases, compensation.

Unfortunately for prevailing plaintiffs in suits seeking a legal remedy such as compensatory damages, the contempt power is generally unavailable, except in some family law cases, as discussed below. The practical effect of this distinction is enormous. In some cases a damages judgment isn't worth anything because it is uncollectible.

Consider perhaps the most famous damages judgment in recent years: the O.J. Simpson civil case. As you probably know, the former football star was acquitted in a criminal trial of killing his ex-wife, Nicole Brown Simpson, and her friend, Ron Goldman. Families of the victims then sued Simpson in civil court for the tort of wrongful death. The jury concluded that Simpson was liable for their deaths in the amount of $8.5 million in compensatory damages and $25 million in punitive damages.[1]

---

1. You might wonder why the first trial did not have an issue-preclusive effect in the second trial; that is, if jurors in the first trial found Simpson not guilty of murder, how could a second jury find him liable for Brown Simpson and Goldman's deaths? The answer turns on the different evidentiary standards in the case. Jurors in the first trial considered whether Simpson

377

Simpson refused to pay the judgment voluntarily, as happens with a number of defendants (called "judgment debtors," after judgment against them) who are found liable for damages. In cases where defendants do not voluntarily pay, plaintiffs (called "judgment creditors," after judgment in their favor) have three ways to try to collect. First, a judgment creditor may place *a judgment lien on the judgment debtor's non-exempt real property*. Second, the judgment creditor may *execute on the judgment debtor's non-exempt personal property*. Third, a judgment creditor may *garnish the judgment debtor's wages or bank accounts*.

Judgment Lien.   If the judgment debtor owns real property, the judgment creditor may file a lien on that property, eventually forcing a sale to pay for at least some of the judgment. The judgment creditor, however, does not take before other lenders with priority, such as the bank that holds a secured mortgage on the property. For example, suppose Simpson owned some real property as an investment worth $300,000 and subject to a $200,000 mortgage. The judgment creditors could force the sale of the house, with the first $200,000 going to pay the mortgage holder and the rest of the money going toward paying the judgment.

The possibility of a judgment lien is subject to a very large exception, however. States have instituted so-called "homestead exemptions," which prevent a creditor's executing on a judgment debtor's home, or at least protect *a portion* of that home's value; as a result, if judgment creditors do force a sale, a judgment debtor will have a way to find other living accommodations through the proceeds from the value protected by the homestead exemption. In some circumstances, the exemption prevents the judgment lien altogether. For example, during the Simpson controversy, O.J. Simpson moved to Florida and purchased an expensive home in which to live. Florida has an unlimited homestead exemption, meaning that Simpson's home could not have been sold to satisfy the judgment.[2]

Execution.   The first step that the judgment creditors in the Simpson case tried to take after judgment was "execution": having sheriffs seize some of

---

was guilty of murder *beyond a reasonable doubt* (the applicable criminal standard). But in the civil trial, for purposes of liability and compensatory damages, the jurors used the easier-to-meet *preponderance of the evidence* standard in determining that Simpson was responsible for the murders. Regarding the punitive damages, the jurors used a *clear and convincing evidence* standard in judging whether Simpson acted with fraud, oppression, or malice. *See* Cal. Civ. Code § 3294. The *clear and convincing evidence* standard is harder to meet than the *preponderance of the evidence* standard, but still weaker than the criminal standard. Accordingly, the jurors' conclusion in the first trial under the very difficult criminal standard did not preclude the possibility they would have found Simpson liable (and worthy of punishment) under the civil court standards. As a result, the criminal trial did not have a preclusive effect on the civil claim.

2. Under the Bankruptcy Abuse Prevention and Consumer Protection Act of 2005, under certain circumstances a person in bankruptcy may not protect more than $146,450 in a home's value from creditors even if state law, like Florida's, allows for an unlimited homestead exemption. Pub. L. No. 109-06 (codified as amended in 11 U.S.C. § 522(p)(1)).

Simpson's personal property and then sell it to satisfy the judgment. Judgment creditors face two major hurdles when they execute on a judgment debtor's property. First, they have to find the property. If the defendant has been successful in hiding his assets during trial, a plaintiff will have little to go after once there is a judgment.[3] The sheriff will not conduct an investigation to find the property; instead, the judgment creditor needs to tell the sheriff where and when to go to collect the property. More importantly, not all assets can be seized. We have already considered the homestead exemption. State law and federal law provide exemptions from execution on other property as well. For example, federal law prevents execution on money in certain pension funds. Thus, creditors could not touch Simpson's $25,000-per-month draw from his $4 million pension. Anne McDermott, *The O.J. Simpson Case +5 Years: Where Are They Now?*, CNN, June 11, 1999. Despite the huge judgment, Simpson said in an interview with *People* magazine that "a lot of guys would like to be in my position, raising my kids and playing golf." *Id.*

Exemptions from execution have left the judgment creditors in the Simpson case with few options. In 1997, Simpson's lawyers were fighting attempts by the judgment creditors to seize his $40,000 Ford Expedition and a baby grand piano Simpson claimed was a gift to his mother. *Simpson's Vehicle, Piano Focus of Court Battle*, CNN, Aug. 7, 1997, http://www.cnn.com/US/9708/07/simpson.hearing/index.html. Twelve years later, the battles continued. In 2009, the original award had doubled with interest, with most of it still uncollected. Harriet Ryan, *Agent Hems on Simpson Clothes*, L.A. Times, June 19, 2009, http://articles.latimes.com/2009/jun/12/local/me-oj-suit12.

Garnishment. "Garnishment is an independent action against a third party who owes money to the judgment debtor. The most common garnishees are banks and employers." Laycock p. 839. Thus, if Simpson had a regular job or money in bank accounts that could be located, the judgment creditors could go to the employer or bank and have at least some of that money diverted to them. State law can limit the amount that may be garnished from wages, and on top of any state limits, federal law limits the percentage of a worker's wages that can be garnished, again to prevent the judgment creditor from being able to force the judgment debtor onto the street. *See* 15 U.S.C. § 1673. Outside the family law context, where percentages are higher, garnishment is limited to 25% of the worker's take-home pay, or 30 times the minimum wage, whichever is less.

In 2006, Simpson agreed to write a book called "If I Did It," in which he said how he would have committed the murders if he were the killer.

---

3. If a plaintiff suspects that a defendant is hiding assets to avoid paying a judgment, a plaintiff might seek a pre-judgment freeze order, the topic of the next section of this chapter.

The publisher of the book, Judith Regan, called it a confession. Amidst the controversy, the book deal was canceled and Regan was fired. Before the deal was canceled, Regan claimed that Simpson himself would not receive the reported $3.5 million advance; the money would go through a third party to his children. *Raw Data: Judith Regan Statement: "Why I Did It,"* FOXNews, Nov. 17, 2006, http://www.foxnews.com/story/0,2933,230280,00.html. Depending upon state law, such an attempt to avoid creditors through a third party would fail, and the advance would be obtainable through execution (once Simpson received it) or through a garnishment order to the publisher. (The book was eventually published for the benefit of the judgment creditors.)

Because of the possibility of execution or garnishment, wealthy judgment debtors with easily seized assets will tend to pay to avoid execution. Consider one case involving this author and a major national company. Plaintiffs obtained a multimillion-dollar punitive damages verdict against the company, and the company filed a petition in the U.S. Supreme Court to reverse the judgment. A petition for certiorari to the Supreme Court does not stay execution of a judgment automatically; the company moved for a stay with a Supreme Court Justice, and plaintiffs voluntarily agreed not to execute until the Supreme Court had ruled. When the Justice denied the stay, the company (as was its right) filed a stay petition with another Justice. At that point, the plaintiffs told the company that it would not wait any longer. If the second stay was denied, the sheriff would be at one of the company's offices seizing office equipment. The company quickly had the checks cut to the plaintiff to avoid this result. (The second Supreme Court Justice quickly denied the stay, and the full Court later declined to hear this case.)

The nitty-gritty details on how to accomplish execution or garnishment differ from state to state and are not covered here. There are some general rules, however, on execution, as summarized by Professor Moringiello:

> In most states, if the property is real estate, a judgment creates a lien on the property when it is docketed or recorded in the records specified in the applicable statute. The resulting lien is known as a "judgment lien." . . .
>
> If a judgment creditor cannot perfect a lien against the debtor's property by recording a document, the judgment creditor must seize or otherwise gain control over the property in order to obtain and perfect the lien. A judgment creditor has no right to use self-help to seize a debtor's property to satisfy the judgment, but instead must enlist the help of the sheriff. After winning a judgment, a creditor has the right to a writ of execution, originally known and still known in some places as a writ of fieri facias. . . .
>
> The creditor must deliver the writ to a sheriff and it is the sheriff's job to execute the writ. The sheriff does so by way of a levy. When the property is easily movable, to "levy" means to take actual physical possession of the property. At common law, a sheriff could execute the writ of fieri facias only by

physical seizure of tangible property. When the property cannot be moved easily, constructive possession can result in a levy. Whether the seizure is actual or constructive, notice is key. So long as the owner of the property and third parties have notice that the property is levied upon and will be sold, the levy is effective.

Juliet M. Moringiello, *Seizing Domain Names to Enforce Judgments: Looking Back to Look to the Future*, 72 U. CINN. L. REV. 95, 130-131 (2003) (footnotes omitted). Professor Moringiello notes that these rules have not traditionally applied to intangible property rights, such as intellectual property.

One complication with levying on goods is that other creditors may have an interest in the same good. In such circumstances, state statutes will set the order of priority. This priority often depends upon who filed first, but not always. For example, secured creditors who properly noticed their security interest in property have a right in property that is superior to that of the judgment creditor.

Regarding the nitty-gritty of garnishment, let's begin with a hypothetical and some terminology. Eric runs over Frannie, injuring her. Frannie obtains a judgment against Eric for $20,000, and Eric refuses to pay. Eric is employed by G-Corp. Frannie can go to G-Corp and get an order of garnishment requiring G-Corp to pay a portion of Eric's wages directly to Frannie (subject to state and federal limits on the amount of garnishment). In this situation, Eric is the defendant and judgment debtor. Frannie is the plaintiff, judgment creditor, and garnishor. G-Corp is the garnishee. See Figure 17.1.

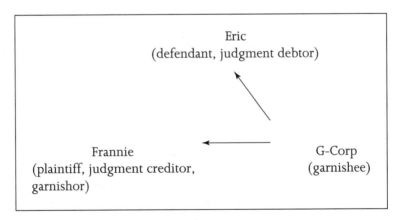

Figure 17.1. The Three-Sided Relationship in Garnishment

In Figure 17.1, garnishment causes G-Corp (the garnishee) to divert some of the wages it would be paying to Eric over to Frannie (the garnishor). Though this looks like it poses no big deal to the garnishee (beside the accounting hassle of writing two checks), garnishment imposes a risk on the garnishee. If G-Corp, the garnishee, makes a mistake and pays all the money to Eric rather than to Frannie, a court is going to require G-Corp to pay Frannie as well. *See Lakeshore Bank & Trust Co. v. United Farm Bureau Mut. Ins. Co., Inc.*, 474 N.E.2d 1024, 1027 (Ind. App. 1985) ("It is said that by commencement of the proceedings and service of the summons the creditor acquires an equitable lien on the credit or funds due to the debtor. . . . Thus, if the garnishee transfers the funds to the debtor after the equitable lien attaches, he will still be liable to the creditor in the garnishment proceedings and is treated as still having the funds in his possession. The court may order the garnishee to make payment a second time, this time to the creditor.").

The rules on execution and garnishment show that successful plaintiffs often have to jump through a lot of hoops to become successful judgment creditors. To put it another way, for plaintiffs (and the lawyers who work for them, often for a percentage of the recovery — see section 17.3), getting a judgment is not much good if the defendant is likely to be "judgment proof" — i.e., without the ability to pay a money judgment. That factor must be considered when one is deciding who to sue and how much effort to expend on such suits. It is what motivates plaintiffs in civil lawsuits to join "deep pocket" defendants with other defendants, when possible.

We could instead have a system that allows money judgments to be backed by the power of contempt. With a few exceptions that appear not to be used routinely, coercive collection of money judgments is not available outside the family law context. It is routinely available in child support situations and, less typically, in spousal support (alimony) contexts. *See In re McCarty*, 98 P. 540 (Cal. 1908) (allowing use of contempt power for failure to pay alimony).

So if Henrietta fails to pay her child support obligations to support her son Isaiah, a court can order her to pay or risk jail time if she does not. Some judgment debtors owing child support are certainly motivated to pay by that kind of coercion, which accompanies the contempt power. But this kind of coercion raises new problems, primarily questions over a judgment debtor's inability to comply.

As Chapter 10 explains in detail, a court may not use contempt if it has no ability to coerce a party into complying with a court order. Thus, if Henrietta is homeless and destitute, with no possibility of paying her child support obligations for the foreseeable future, a court cannot use the contempt power: such a power would cease to be coercive and it would only be punitive. This rule means that courts must inquire into the *ability* of judgment debtors to pay, and that raises additional questions as to how much money is necessary to support oneself.

Suppose, for example, that Henrietta lives in an apartment in a nice, but not the nicest, part of town, paying $1,500 per month rent. Should a court say she could afford to pay at least $500 more a month in child support, upon proof that in less nice parts of town, Henrietta should be able to rent a somewhat dilapidated apartment for $1,000 per month?

And what if Henrietta was capable of holding a job she could use to pay child support but refused to work? The California Supreme Court held that a judgment debtor owing back child support could be held in contempt for failing to find and keep a job. *See Moss v. Superior Court*, 950 P.2d 59 (Cal. 1998).

Given the importance of child support, perhaps society has made the best choice by allowing the contempt power to be used in that context but not in the general context of judgments. From the position of judgment creditors, however, perhaps the child support example shows that it is possible to have a workable system for coercing the payment of money. Certainly O.J. Simpson has some earning capacity, and his choice not to use it to pay his debts is one that society may think Simpson should not have the freedom to make. Would you support the extension of the contempt power to the collection of ordinary judgments? From the point of view of the additional burden on the courts, would such a change be worth the administrative hassle in the general case?

Example 1

Umbro International, a company that sells popular soccer clothing and other merchandise in England and elsewhere, sued 3263851 Canada, Inc. for its use of the web domain name "umbro.com." Umbro obtained a declaratory judgment that Umbro had the right to use the "umbro.com" domain name, an injunction barring 3263851 Canada, Inc. from use of the name, and a $24,000 judgment. 3263851 Canada, Inc. did not have easily seized assets, but it did own the rights to 38 other web domain names. Umbro brought a garnishment action against Network Solutions, Inc., which held the domain names for 3263851 Canada. Umbro wanted to auction off the right to these domain names (some of which are valuable) to satisfy its judgment. Should the court allow Umbro to do so?

Explanation

The Virginia Supreme Court said that Umbro could not force Network Solutions to give Umbro the power to sell these domain names. *Network Solutions, Inc. v. Umbro Int'l, Inc.*, 529 S.E.2d 80, 87-88 (Va. 2000). The court construed Virginia statutes as not applying to these new technologies. Professor Moringiello, in the article cited earlier in this chapter, argued that the Virginia Supreme Court got it wrong:

Many garnishment and execution statutes have not been amended in decades and state legislatures could not have anticipated the new types of property that technology would create. It is unquestioned that a domain name registrant can receive the benefits of a domain name. The name leads people to his business and when the registrant no longer wants the name, he is entitled to the potentially enormous proceeds of its sale. The holder of a domain name should also be forced to bear the corresponding burdens of holding valuable rights. Allowing creditors to enforce money judgments by seizing and selling domain names would force domain name registrants to bear those burdens.

Moringiello, *supra*, at 149-150.

Example 2

Back to the Eric-Frannie hypothetical. Eric refuses to pay Frannie, and Frannie discovers that Eric has a bank account with $10,000 in it at Happy Bank. Frannie properly files a demand for garnishment of this bank account with Happy Bank. Before Happy Bank makes a notation in its computer system, Eric walks into a bank branch and removes his $10,000, closing the account. Is Happy Bank liable to Frannie?

Explanation

Yes. Once Happy Bank received notice of the garnishment, it was the bank's responsibility to direct payment to Frannie, not Eric. The bank can try to go after Eric in restitution for return of the money, but whether it is successful in doing so or not does not affect Frannie's ability to obtain the $10,000 from the bank.

Example 3

Here's another variation on the Eric-Frannie hypothetical. After Frannie files a garnishment order against Eric requiring his employer to turn over 25% of his wages to Frannie, Eric quits his job and moves back in with his parents. Eric tells Frannie: "I'd rather not work than work for you!" Can Frannie get an order requiring Eric to go back to work to pay off the judgment?

Explanation

In most jurisdictions, the answer is no. Outside the context of family law cases, a court will not use the power of contempt to force Eric to work to pay off his debt. Some judgment debtors hope that if they stall long enough, the judgment creditor will go away (and some will do so). But the O.J. Simpson case shows that this is not always the case. Indeed, sometimes it is not even about the money. The father of the deceased Ron Goldman in the O.J. Simpson case promised to give up his right to Simpson's assets if Simpson gave a full written confession to the crime. In the Simpson case, as in others, the judgment may be about much more than money, or about issues besides money. But when it is primarily about money, as in the Eric-Frannie case, coercive contempt is not an option.

17.2 PRE-JUDGMENT FREEZE ORDERS, ATTACHMENTS, AND RECEIVERSHIPS

In the first section of this chapter, we saw just how difficult it is for judgment creditors to collect from judgment debtors who are unwilling, or unable, to pay after judgment. Defendants in civil cases will often be tempted to try to hide or transfer their assets before judgment, in an effort to prevent the judgment creditors from collecting. Under applicable state laws, a defendant may not hide assets or transfer them in an attempt to defraud creditors or prevent enforcement of a valid judgment. But what can a plaintiff do to prevent such conduct?

When fraudulent transfers are discovered after a judgment, a court can reverse the transaction and order the asset sold to pay the creditors. Thus, if a court believed O.J. Simpson had not really made a gift of the baby grand piano to his mother before judgment, but did so to protect his assets, the court could have ordered the gift returned and sold to pay the judgment creditors.

But sometimes plaintiffs want to take steps *before* judgment to prevent defendants from hiding and dissipating assets in anticipation of a verdict against them. Plaintiffs have three potential tools to help them before judgment.

1. *Freeze orders.* A freeze order is a kind of preliminary injunction that prevents a defendant from transferring specific assets pending judgment. Chapter 9 details the requirements for a preliminary injunction; to understand how freeze orders work, one must first understand the workings of preliminary injunctions. In brief, a plaintiff seeking a freeze order must show a likelihood of success on the merits of the underlying suit, as well as the irreparable harm that would come from denial of the order.

In deciding on whether or not to grant the freeze order, the court must balance the harm to the plaintiff if the court errs in failing to grant the freeze order against the harm to the defendant if the court errs in granting the freeze order. A court may require the plaintiff to post a bond to cover costs associated with an erroneously granted freeze order.

Consider the facts of In re Estate of Ramlose, 801 N.E.2d 76 (Ill. App. 2003). Mr. Haneberg was a trustee of the Ramlose Trust. The trust's beneficiary, Alexander Ramlose, filed a suit for breach of fiduciary duty against Haneberg, alleging that he was diverting funds from the trust for personal use. Eventually, the Public Guardian successfully petitioned to represent Ramlose's interests, on grounds that Ramlose, who was 95 years old, was suffering from dementia. The Public Guardian alleged that Haneberg transferred over $700,000 from the Ramlose Trust to the Haneberg Trust soon after Ramlose was diagnosed with dementia. Haneberg resisted discovery requests, eventually being held in contempt for failing to appear, and in the course of the litigation, Ramlose died, with the Public Guardian then representing the estate.

The Public Guardian, fearing that Haneberg would dissipate assets during trial, asked the trial court for a freeze order over certain bank accounts and real property owned by Haneberg. The court, without holding an evidentiary hearing, issued an order as follows: "All of the assets and accounts, whether involving real or personal property of Elmer Haneberg, including all such assets and accounts held individually or jointly with any person or held in a trust wherein he is named as a trustee for any family member, including himself, his wife, *** his mother, *** and his children *** or any trust in which Elmer Haneberg has any beneficial interest are hereby frozen and may not be accessed for any reason without further order of Court."

The appellate court reversed the order to give Haneberg a chance for a hearing on whether or not the order was appropriate. The appellate court further noted that the freeze order went too far in covering more of Haneberg's property than requested by the Public Guardian, including freezing sale of a Park City, Utah, time-share. Finally, the appellate court saw a potential due process problem: "no nexus was ever established between the Ramlose Trust funds and Haneberg's bank accounts, assets and real estate properties and those of his family, who are not and have never been parties to these proceedings." The lesson from this case is that even when a defendant appears to be engaging in bad conduct, it is important to carefully craft a freeze order that complies with due process and delineates both the property to be frozen and the reasons for it to be frozen.

2. *Attachments.* An attachment "generally refers to a preliminary garnishment or seizure before judgment." LAYCOCK p. 865. It is a more extreme order than a simple freeze order, which prevents a defendant from dissipating assets pending judgment; it puts the defendant's assets into the hands of the plaintiff before there has been a final judgment on the merits.

States differ on the standard for obtaining an attachment. In New York, for example, a plaintiff must show that the defendant has an "intent to defraud his creditors or frustrate the enforcement of a judgment that might be rendered in plaintiff's favor" and that the defendant has "assigned, disposed of, encumbered or secreted property, or removed it from the state or is about to do these acts." N.Y. C.P.L.R. § 6201(3). In Connecticut, in contrast, it is enough to show "that there is probable cause that a judgment in the amount of the prejudgment remedy sought, or in an amount greater than the amount of the prejudgment remedy sought, taking into account any known defenses, counterclaims or set-offs, will be rendered in the matter in favor of the plaintiff." CONN. GEN. STAT. ANN. § 52-278c(a)(2). The defendant has the right to a hearing to contest the attachment. *Id.* at § 52-278c(g).[4]

Consider a recent Connecticut case illustrating how the Connecticut scheme works, again from the "truth is stranger than fiction" department. Two neighbors, the A Family and the B Family, had an ongoing series of disputes. When the A Family put two homes it owned up for sale, the B Family

> caused several inoperable Jeep vehicles and a trailer to be placed on their property. The Jeeps looked like they had come from a junkyard. The trailer parked on the street right next to [one of the for-sale properties and] had bumper stickers that stated, "Bambi makes cute sandwiches," and, "I'd Rather Be Loading My Muzzle." [The A family] erected a six foot high fence between their property and that of the defendants, and [the B family] thereafter constructed a ten foot high structure that consisted of two wooden posts with several rusty cylinders hanging on a wire between the posts. The [B Family] also put up "No Trespassing" signs on their property and targets in their windows.

See Kinsale, L.L.C. v. Tombari, 897 A.2d 646, 647 (Conn. App. 2006) (internal quotations omitted).

The A Family sued for nuisance and raised a separate libel claim. On the nuisance point, the A family argued that the sale of their property was decreased by $250,000 because of the junk in the B Family's yard (which the B Family defended as art protected by the First Amendment). The A Family also asked for an attachment for $250,000, arguing that it would obtain that much money in its suit on the merits. The trial court granted an attachment in the amount of $100,000, finding that the A Family was likely to prevail on its nuisance claim and to prove

---

4. The Connecticut legislature added this right to a hearing after lawsuits successfully arguing that granting the plaintiff the right to an attachment in the absence of a hearing violated due process rights guaranteed by the U.S. Constitution. *See Kinsale*, 897 A.2d at 651 (dissenting opinion).

$100,000 in damages. A Connecticut appellate court, over a dissent, upheld the attachment, holding that the trial court's factual findings were not clearly erroneous.

What is to stop the A Family from now dissipating the $100,000, making it unavailable, if after a trial on the merits the court finds for the B Family? CONN. GEN. STAT. ANN. § 52-278d(d) provides in pertinent part that "the defendant may request that the plaintiff post a bond, with surety, in an amount determined by the court to be sufficient to reasonably protect the defendant's interest in the property that is subject to the prejudgment remedy against damages that may be caused by the prejudgment remedy." In deciding on whether a bond is appropriate and, if so, the right amount, "the court shall consider the nature of the property subject to the prejudgment remedy, the methods of retention or storage of the property[,] and the potential harm to the defendant's interest in the property that the prejudgment remedy might cause." Id. at § 52-278d(e). The court can also waive the bond requirement for indigent plaintiffs. Id. at § 52-278d(f).

3. *Receiverships.* A receivership is a kind of preliminary injunction like an attachment, but one that allows a neutral third party to run an ongoing business, or take steps to wind it down, during a dispute involving the business. Thus, if shareholders or business partners end up in litigation, a neutral third party might be required to run the business during litigation to prevent fraud or mismanagement.

The Texas statute sets out many of the reasons why a court might want to grant a receivership, as well as the standards for determining whether the court should create one:

> A receiver may be appointed for the assets and business of a corporation . . . whenever circumstances exist deemed by the court to require the appointment of a receiver to conserve the assets and business of the corporation and to avoid damage to [the] parties at interest, but only if all other requirements of law are complied with and if all other remedies available either at law or in equity, including the appointment of a receiver for specific assets of the corporation, are determined by the court to be inadequate, and only in the following instances:
>
> (1) In an action by a shareholder when it is established:
>
> (a) That the corporation is insolvent or in imminent danger of insolvency; or
>
> (b) That the directors are deadlocked in the management of the corporate affairs and the shareholders are unable to break the deadlock, and that irreparable injury to the corporation is being suffered or is threatened by reason thereof; or
>
> (c) That the acts of the directors or those in control of the corporation are illegal, oppressive or fraudulent; or
>
> (d) That the corporate assets are being misapplied or wasted; or
>
> (e) That the shareholders are deadlocked in voting power, and have failed, for a period which includes at least two consecutive annual

meeting dates, to elect successors to directors whose terms have expired or would have expired upon the election and qualification of their successors.

(2) In an action by a creditor when it is established:

(a) That the corporation is insolvent and the claim of the creditor has been reduced to judgment and an execution thereon returned unsatisfied; or

(b) That the corporation is insolvent and the corporation has admitted in writing that the claim of the creditor is due and owing.

(3) In any other actions where receivers have heretofore been appointed by the usages of the court of equity.

TEX. CIV. CODE ANN. § 1396-7.05(A).

Despite the seemingly broad language of the Texas statute, it is not as inclusive as it may appear. For example, in *Humble Exploration Co., Inc. v. Fairway Land Co.*, 641 S.W.2d 934 (Tex. App. 1982), a group of oil well owners sued an oil well operator, claiming that the operator was not conducting business in a "good and workmanlike manner." The owners sought to have the operator put in receivership pending resolution of the claims brought by the owners against it.

The trial court had granted a receivership but the appellate court reversed, relying on language in an earlier version of § 7.05. The oil well owners were not shareholders of the operator's corporation; they were not creditors who had a judgment reduced to writing or an admission of debt by the operator; and, over a dissent, the majority concluded that a receivership was not consistent "with the usages of the court of equity":

> We hold that mere proof of a need to conserve specific corporate assets (the applicant's proof here) does not justify a receiver of the entire corporation, its assets and its business, as a "usage of equity." To conserve specific assets by a receivership of the whole corporation would, in fact, defeat equity.

Humble, 641 S.W.2d at 939.

Example 4

Greta is injured seriously when Horace punches her in the face in a barroom fight, causing serious damage to her nose that will require corrective surgery. Greta is poor and has no health insurance. She sustains $25,000 in damages, and is facing possible bankruptcy before her tort case for battery against Horace will be going to trial. Horace will be claiming self-defense as an affirmative defense at trial. Horace is quite wealthy and has a number of easily found assets that could be used to satisfy any judgment that Greta might receive. Might Greta use a freeze order, attachment, or receivership to obtain money from Horace before trial?

Explanation

A freeze order does not appear to be an appropriate remedy in this case. There are no specific assets Greta can point to that Horace is planning on dissipating before trial. Indeed, the fact that he has many assets that could be found after judgment suggests any freeze order would be unnecessary to satisfy the judgment. In any case, a freeze order does not put any money into Greta's hands before judgment.

Attachment is a better possibility here, depending on the jurisdiction. In a jurisdiction like New York, attachment would be difficult to obtain absent proof of some kind of attempt at fraud or waste of Horace's assets. Greta would have an easier time in a jurisdiction like Connecticut, if she can prove she is more likely than not to succeed at trial. The decision by the court would require taking a peek at the merits to see if Greta's claim of battery is likely to succeed in the face of Horace's claim of self-defense. This kind of swearing contest might not be easily resolvable before trial.

In the event that a court would grant an attachment, Horace might demand a bond. If the court gives Greta her $25,000 and she uses it to pay medical bills, it would not be available to pay Horace back in the event Horace prevails in the actual trial. Under Connecticut law, a court would have discretion to waive the bond requirement because of Greta's indigence.

Finally, a receivership is not an appropriate remedy here. There is no business that Horace is running in which Greta has some interest, nor is there fear of Horace hiding or dissipating any business assets.

17.3 ATTORNEY'S FEES AND LITIGATION EXPENSES

Lawyers, like law students, need to eat, and — aside from some pro bono assignments — few attorneys work for free. In addition to legal fees, litigation brings additional expenses: court costs, expert witness fees, and other expenses. Under the *American rule*, in the absence of a provision in a contract or as provided by statute, each side to a lawsuit bears its own attorney's fees.[5] (The contrasting rule used in England, the unsurprisingly named *English rule*, has the loser pay the winner's attorney's fees.)

The fact that a plaintiff must bear her own attorney's fees affects the rightful position standard. Recall an example from Chapter 2: Alex carelessly burns down Barbara's house, causing Barbara $100,000 in damages. As illustrated in Figure 17.2, we would calculate Barbara's damages as (B − A), or $100,000.

---

5. Attorney's fees also may be available as a penalty for bad faith litigation, as a sanction for contempt of court, in family law cases, when a private plaintiff sues as a private attorney general, and in common fund cases such as class action suits. *See* LAYCOCK pp. 883-884.

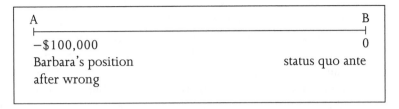

Figure 17.2

As Chapter 2 noted, calculating $100,000 as the amount to put Barbara in the rightful position masks a number of complications, and we now focus on one of them: attorney's fees. Suppose Carla is Barbara's attorney. The Barbara-Carla contract might require Barbara to pay Carla by the hour, or it might have some other financial arrangement, such as a *contingency fee*. With a contingency fee, Barbara would pay nothing to Carla if the suit is unsuccessful, but Carla would receive a *percentage of the recovery* in the event that the suit is successful.

Suppose that Carla successfully obtained a $100,000 verdict for Barbara against Alex, and was able to collect from Alex. Suppose Carla's fee, whether by the hour or through a contingency fee, is $25,000. In that case, Barbara is not really brought back to the rightful position by the $100,000 verdict. (See Figure 17.3.) Barbara instead is brought to B−, equal to −$25,000. In other words, Barbara has $25,000 less wealth than she would had there been no wrong, leaving her short of the rightful position.

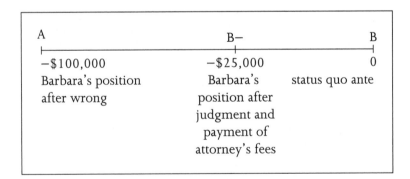

Figure 17.3

Society can deal with the undercompensation of plaintiffs caused by the American rule in a few ways. One way is to switch to the English rule. It is not clear, however, that switching to the English rule would result in a net gain for plaintiffs. For plaintiffs with strong suits, the English rule looks like a good idea. But for plaintiffs with suits that may be harder to prove, the English rule can be a deterrent. A contingency fee allows the plaintiff to shift the risk of paying *her own* attorney's fees to the plaintiff's attorney, but it does nothing to shift the risk of having to pay the *defense* attorney's fees.[6]

A second way to deal with the undercompensation problem is to allow only *one-way fee shifting*, in which the plaintiff gets attorney's fees if she wins, but does not pay defendant's attorney's fees if she loses. That system, of course is a great benefit to plaintiffs (and a burden on defendants). Such fee shifting has been adopted in particular areas by statute, as we'll see, but it is not the general rule.

Third, rules like the collateral source rule and the possibility of punitive damages in particular cases could increase the return to plaintiffs, thereby making up for some of the compensation that is lost through the payment of attorney's fees. These rules work in a haphazard way to solve the general problem, however.

Finally, juries — which likely will contain jurors who understand the American rule — might *overcompensate* plaintiffs so that plaintiffs are really put in the rightful position *after* plaintiff's attorney is paid.

Recall the earlier statement of the American rule: *in the absence of a provision in a contract or as provided by statute*, each side to a lawsuit bears its own attorney's fees. Consider first the *contractual* exception to the American rule. It is very common that parties to a contract will include a contractual provision providing that if a dispute arises between the parties over the contract, the losing party shall pay the winner's attorney's fees.

If you were a clever lawyer, you might try to draft a one-way fee shifting provision in the contract. If my client is sued and wins, the other contracting party pays his attorney's fees. But if my client loses, each party bears his or her own attorney's fees. That drafting may be too clever by half. Under California law, for example, courts construe such one-sided provisions to apply *reciprocally* to both sides of the contract. Cal. Civ. Code § 1717(a).

Attorney's fees may also be provided by *statute*. Laycock reports that "[m]ore than 200 federal statutes and 4,000 state statutes authorize awards of attorney's fees." Laycock p. 882. For example, under the Copyright Act, the prevailing party — plaintiff or defendant — is entitled to reasonable attorney's fees. 17 U.S.C. § 505.

Some statutory attorney's fees provisions expressly impose one-way fee shifting. *See, e.g.*, 15 U.S.C. § 1640(a)(3) (allowing prevailing plaintiffs suing for federal truth-in-lending violations to recover reasonable attorney's fees). Sometimes the courts read *facially evenhanded* attorney's fees provisions as applying in ways that primarily help plaintiffs. Certainly one of the most important attorney's fees provisions on the federal level,

---

6. Some proof that the English rule is not necessarily a good thing for plaintiffs is that change to the English rule has been advocated by defense-oriented "tort reform" groups.

42 U.S.C. § 1988(b), allows prevailing plaintiffs who succeed in civil rights litigation to recover attorney's fees in most cases in which plaintiff prevails. However, a prevailing defendant may recover fees under the statute from the plaintiff only if the plaintiff brought the suit frivolously or with intent to harass the defendant. *See Hensley v. Eckerhart*, 461 U.S. 424, 429 n.2 (1983).

Once a court determines that a party is entitled to reasonable attorney's fees for whatever reason,[7] it must determine what a reasonable fee is.[8] Typically, the party entitled to fees will put in a request for fees, itemizing the attorney expenses. The losing party will then argue that the fees are excessive, and the court, sometimes going line by line over the attorney's bills, will decide on what would be a reasonable fee.

Courts sometimes use the "lodestar" method to calculate reasonable attorney's fees: "the number of hours reasonably expended on the litigation multiplied by a reasonable hourly rate" *Id.* at 433; see also *City of Riverside v. Rivera*, 477 U.S. 561, 568 (1986). As explained in *Rivera*, though the lodestar is the starting point in calculating reasonable fees, it is not the whole story. In enacting the Civil Rights Attorney's Fees Awards Act of 1976, 42 U.S.C. § 1988, Congress did not define the method for calculating reasonable attorney's fees. But House and Senate reports accompanying the legislation endorsed a 12-factor test set forth in *Johnson v. Georgia Highway Express, Inc.*, 488 F.2d 714 (5th Cir. 1974). These factors are (1) the time and labor required, (2) the novelty and difficulty of the questions, (3) the skill requisite to perform the legal service properly, (4) the preclusion of employment by the attorney due to acceptance of the case, (5) the customary fee, (6) whether the fee is fixed or contingent, (7) time limitations imposed by the client or the circumstances, (8) the amount involved and the results obtained, (9) the experience, reputation, and ability of the attorneys; (10) the "undesirability" of the case, (11) the nature and length of the professional relationship with the client, and (12) awards in similar cases. *Id.* at 717-719.

In civil rights litigation, where a court awards only nominal damages, the reasonable fee is often zero. *See Farrar v. Hobby*, 506 U.S. 103, 115 (1992). Even though the precedent created by such cases may be valuable, a lawyer who wants to recover fees should therefore seek more than nominal damages; for example, the lawyer might want to seek an injunction barring defendants from engaging in certain proscribed conduct in the future. The lawyer can then point the court to the injunction as a benefit of the

---

7. First the court will have to determine who the "prevailing party" is, which is sometimes difficult to do when a plaintiff has received some of the relief requested, but not most of it.
8. The timing for filing a fee application is a malpractice trap. Check the rules carefully, and know that a pending motion for attorney's fees, at least on the federal level, does not delay the time to file an appeal from the underlying judgment.

litigation that should entitle the lawyer to higher attorney's fees. Even without the injunction, some courts will still grant fees, relying on Justice O'Connor's concurring opinion in *Farrar* noting that fees might be permissible if the litigation, in addition to earning plaintiff nominal damages, "also accomplished some public goal other than occupying the time and energy of counsel, court, and client." *Id.* at 122.

One of the most contentious areas for dispute over reasonable attorney's fees has been class action lawsuits, particularly those involving cases in which the plaintiffs each receive awards with small value — sometimes including nothing more than a coupon for a discount on a future purchase from the wrongdoer! In some of these cases, each plaintiff has little at stake, and therefore little reason to police the plaintiff class attorneys for self-dealing. In such cases, the plaintiffs' attorneys may have economic interests that line up with the defendants' interests; for example, attorneys might be willing to settle each plaintiff's claim for less than the claims are worth (such as a coupon instead of a small monetary award) in exchange for defendant agreeing to an acceptable amount of attorney's fees.

The details of attorney's fees issues in class actions are better left for a treatise on class actions or advanced civil procedure. Suffice it to say here that there has been a great deal of both litigation and legislation to deal with these problems. Some courts have tried to resort to "reverse auctions," whereby plaintiffs' attorneys bid against each other for the right to represent the plaintiffs' class for the lowest fee. There has also been much debate over whether these lawyers' fees should be calculated on an hourly rate or as a percentage of the total recovery.

Congress also made some changes in this area in the Class Action Fairness Act of 2005. Pub. L. No. 109-2, 119 Stat. 4 (codified as amended at 28 U.S.C. §§ 1711 *et seq.*). For example, to stop the coupon abuse, § 1712(a) of the Act provides:

> If a proposed settlement in a class action provides for a recovery of coupons to a class member, the portion of any attorney's fee award to class counsel that is attributable to the award of the coupons shall be based on the value to class members of the coupons that are redeemed.

For a detailed analysis of the Act, *see Class Action Fairness Act of 2005, With Commentary and Analysis by Georgene M. Vairo of the Moore's Federal Practice Board of Editors, in* MOORE'S FEDERAL PRACTICE (Daniel R. Coquillette et al. eds., 2005).

Finally, a word about litigation costs, such as court reporter costs. These costs are generally recoverable by the prevailing party in both state and federal court. But, absent special mention in a statute, costs generally do not include expert witness fees, which can be quite expensive in complex cases involving such witnesses.

Example 5

If you were drafting a contract for a client, would you want to include an attorney's fees provision? What are the costs and benefits of its inclusion?

Explanation

There is, of course, no right or wrong answer to the first part of this question. As a matter of practice, most commercial contracts do include such provisions. Especially in consumer contracts, the provisions might discourage litigation brought by consumers against the companies whose lawyers draft the contracts. Besides discouraging litigation, these clauses reduce some uncertainty about the cost of contracting.

It is also possible that attorney's fees provisions increase the chance of settlement of disputes by raising the costs to both sides of failing to settle in the face of a possible losing case. Thus, if there is a contract dispute worth $100,000 and each side expects to incur $25,000 in attorney's fees in litigation, the parties deciding whether or not to settle or litigate will consider the fact that the costs of litigating are increased by an additional $25,000 when the contract contains an attorney's fees provision, making settlement more attractive.[9]

The major downside of including such an agreement is that your client might be on the wrong end of litigation, losing in court and now saddled with additional attorney's fees. A party believing that there is a fair chance that she will lose in court (whether rightfully so or not) in the event of a contract dispute would likely not be enthusiastic about an attorney's fee provision. But parties tend to overestimate their chances of winning in the event of a dispute, so it is hard to imagine a large number of contracting parties deciding to exclude the attorney's fee provision on this basis.

Example 6

Jarius Piphus was a freshman at Chicago Vocational High School. During school hours, the school principal saw Piphus and another student standing outdoors on school property passing back and forth what the principal described as an irregularly shaped cigarette. The principal approached the students unnoticed and smelled what he believed was the strong odor of burning mari[j]uana.

---

9. Unsurprisingly, there is a rich literature in the law and economics field on how attorney's fees provisions affect settlement. For an introduction to the issue in the context of principal-agent problems, see Geoffrey P. Miller, *Some Agency Problems in Settlement*, 16 J. LEGAL STUD. 189 (1987).

395

He also saw Piphus try to pass a packet of cigarette papers to the other student. When the students became aware of the principal's presence, they threw the cigarette into a nearby hedge. The principal took the students to the school's disciplinary office and directed the assistant principal to impose the "usual" 20-day suspension for violation of the school rule against the use of drugs. The students protested that they had not been smoking mari[j]uana, but to no avail. Piphus was allowed to remain at school, although not in class, for the remainder of the school day while the assistant principal tried, without success, to reach his mother.

The above quotation comes from *Carey v. Piphus*, 435 U.S. 247, 248-249 (1978). In *Piphus*, the student sued under § 1983, alleging that his right to procedural due process was violated because he was not given a hearing where he could have defended himself. The Court held that the failure to hold a hearing was a due process violation, but absent proof of emotional distress damages stemming from the failure to grant a hearing, Piphus could receive only nominal damages. The case did establish that the failure to provide a hearing in this school context constituted a denial of due process.

If Piphus's lawyer sought attorney's fees under 42 U.S.C. § 1988, could he get them? What could his lawyer have done to maximize the chances of recovery?

Explanation

Generally speaking, the reasonable attorney's fee in a case resulting in only nominal damages for plaintiff is zero. However, if Piphus's lawyer could show some other public purpose for the litigation, attorney's fees might be available. It would strengthen the case if Piphus's lawyer could couple the nominal damages claim with another remedy, such as an injunction barring future school suspensions without a hearing, that accomplishes such a public purpose.

Remedial Defenses

CHAPTER 18

18.1 PLAINTIFF'S BAD CONDUCT: UNCONSCIONABILITY, UNCLEAN HANDS, AND *IN PARI DELICTO*

In a typical civil suit, for the plaintiff to win, she will have to prove a prima facie case by a preponderance of the evidence. If plaintiff succeeds in proving all the elements, plaintiff wins, unless the defendant can prove an affirmative defense by a preponderance of the evidence. For example, in a typical tort suit for battery, the plaintiff will have to prove that the defendant engaged in a nonconsensual, intentional touching, as well as proving the elements of actual cause, proximate cause, and damages. *See* RESTATEMENT (SECOND) OF TORTS §§ 13, 18. The defendant wins if the plaintiff cannot prove one of these elements — for example, if the jury believes that it is more likely than not that plaintiff consented to the touching, or if the defendant can prove an affirmative defense, such as self-defense. *Id.* at § 63.

Typically, defenses taught in first-year law courses are substantive: defendant wins by presenting a substantive defense (e.g., "I wasn't the person who touched the plaintiff" or "I win because it was self-defense"). But there are other defenses that do not depend upon substantive law, and typically these defenses are available in a variety of substantive law areas — from battery, to breach of contract, to a property dispute.[1] Many of these defenses were developed in the equity courts before the merger of the courts of law and equity,[2] and some remain available only when the plaintiff seeks equitable relief. This chapter examines these remedies — typically, but not exclusively, equitable remedies — available across a variety of civil cases. We begin with a cluster of defenses concerning plaintiff's bad conduct.

1. *Unconscionability.* Consider the case of *Campbell Soup Company v. Wentz*, 172 F.2d 80 (2d Cir. 1948). Campbell's entered into a contract with the Wentzes, who were farmers in Pennsylvania, for delivery "by the Wentzes to Campbell of all the Chantenay red cored carrots to be grown on fifteen acres of the Wentz farm during the 1947 season" at a price of $23-$30 per ton, depending upon the time of delivery. This kind of carrot had special commercial value to Campbell's: "Its blunt shape makes it easier to handle in processing. And its color and texture differ from other varieties. The color is brighter than other carrots. . . . It also appeared that [Campbell's] uses these Chantenay carrots diced in some of [its soups] and that the appearance is uniform."

The contract contained a number of provisions that were especially beneficial to Campbell's. The court singled out one provision that was so one-sided that the court described the provision as "a good joke [carried] too far . . .":

> . . . Campbell is excused from accepting carrots under certain circumstances. But even under such circumstances the grower, while he cannot say Campbell is liable for failure to take the carrots, is not permitted to sell them elsewhere unless Campbell agrees. . . . What the grower may do with his product under the circumstances set out is not clear. He has covenanted not to store it anywhere except on his own farm and also not to sell to anybody else. . . .

Id. at 83. The Wentzes breached the contract to Campbell's at a time when Chantenay carrots were in short supply and the market price of the carrots had skyrocketed to $90 per ton. The Wentzes sold 62 tons of carrots to a neighboring farmer, who turned around and sold 58 tons of them on the open market, half of them to Campbell's.

Viewing the original deal between Campbell's and the Wentzes as unconscionably one-sided, the court refused to order specific performance (an injunction ordering the Wentzes to deliver the carrots as promised).[3] The court decided that "a party who has offered and succeeded in getting an

---

1. Of the defenses discussed in this chapter, unconscionability is a defense that arises only in the context of contract disputes. The defenses considered in the remainder of this chapter apply in a variety of contexts.
2. See Part II, especially Chapter 7, for background on the courts of law and equity.
3. The Wentzes had sold their carrots, but presumably, under the contract, they would have had to go out on the open market and buy carrots at the new market price to supply to Campbell's.

agreement as tough as this one is, should not come to a chancellor and ask court help in the enforcement of its terms. That equity does not enforce unconscionable bargains is too well established to require elaborate citation." *Id.*

Wentz is an illustration of the principle that courts may refuse to grant specific performance or other equitable remedies in the face of an unconscionable contract. The ruling would not prevent Campbell's from suing the Wentzes for contract damages, which in this case would have been quite large,[4] except for the fact that the contract contained a liquidated damages clause providing the meager remedy of $50 *per acre* of crops planted.[5]

It is not clear what benefit the classic rule had for defendants who entered into unconscionable contracts with plaintiffs. If the Wentzes were not protected by the liquidated damages clause, they would have had to fork over as much in damages as they would have lost had they had to sell the carrots to Campbell's at the contract price. Probably for this reason, some modern courts, including those following the U.C.C. for sales contracts, now allow unconscionability to be a defense for both equitable relief *and* legal relief. *See* U.C.C. § 2-302. Indeed, the U.C.C. gives courts great flexibility in crafting an appropriate legal remedy in the face of an unconscionable contract. Section 2-302 gives the court the power in essence to *rewrite* the parties' contract to avoid an unconscionable result, allowing the court to split the difference between the parties in appropriate cases. The fact that unconscionability has become more generally available as a defense does *not* mean, however, that it has become a cause of action: someone cannot sue another for "unconscionability."

The *Wentz* court determined that the contract at issue was so one-sided as to be unconscionable, barring an equitable remedy by the contract's drafter. This decision appears to be one based upon the *substantive unfairness* of the contract. You may recall from your Contracts class that some courts are skeptical of substantive unconscionability claims, believing that if two parties freely enter into a contract knowing its terms, courts should enforce the contract even if it appears one-sided. But even in those skeptical jurisdictions, defects in the bargaining process, such as onerous terms being written in dense language or buried in the fine print, can lead to successful defenses of *procedural unconscionability*. Some courts say that procedural and substantive unconscionability should be considered together; the more of

---

4. Using the rules for U.C.C. buyers' damages set forth in Chapter 4.5, it appears that if Campbell's is entitled to damages, such damages would be measured by the difference between the market price and the contract price at the time of breach (which is a difference of $60-$67 per ton multiplied by the number of tons produced by the Wentzes), plus any incidental and consequential damages in making the cover purchase, less expenses saved. These would be considerable damages, especially for 1949.

5. Why would Campbell's have included such a meager liquidated damages figure? Perhaps Campbell's figured that it was the party more likely to breach, and it was trying to keep its exposure for damages low.

one type of unconscionability that is present, the less the defendant needs to show the other type.

Unconscionability and related doctrines have been very important for consumer laws, which are often enforced by private lawyers bringing class actions against companies allegedly engaging in bad practices. The U.S. Supreme Court dealt a major blow to consumer class actions in a recent case, *AT&T Mobility LLC v. Concepcion*, 131 S. Ct. 1740 (2011). California law barred companies like the wireless mobile company AT&T from blocking class actions against it in arbitration agreements signed by consumers. California recognized that such class actions are often the only way to make such litigation economically feasible. The U.S. Supreme Court, however, held that California's rule was preempted by the Federal Arbitration Act. Thus, states cannot prevent companies from requiring arbitration of disputes and banning the use of class actions to resolve them.

2. *Unclean hands. Unclean hands* is an equitable defense in which the defendant claims that plaintiff's bad conduct should bar plaintiff from obtaining equitable relief such as an injunction. Many courts require that defendant demonstrate not only that the plaintiff's conduct is inequitable, but also that "the conduct relates to the subject matter of its claims." *See Fuddruckers, Inc. v. Doc's B.R. Others, Inc.*, 826 F.2d 837, 847 (9th Cir. 1987). How bad does the conduct have to be? "Almost any kind of conduct the chancellor may consider to be unethical or improper might suffice to bar the plaintiff's claim, even if the conduct is not actually illegal." DOBBS § 2.4(2).

What better case to discuss "unclean hands" than one involving Häagen-Dazs ice cream bars? In *Häagen-Dazs, Inc. v. Frusen Glädje Ltd.*, 493 F. Supp. 73 (S.D.N.Y. 1980), the Häagen-Dazs ice cream company found itself it in a sticky situation. (Groan!) It brought a claim against an ice cream competitor for unfair competition under the Lanham Act. Among the claims made by Häagen-Dazs was that the competitor Frusen Glädje sought to confuse customers into thinking its ice cream was related to the Häagen-Dazs line by:

> (i) the phraseology used in reciting the ingredients of the product in issue; (ii) a recitation of the artificial ingredients not contained in the product; (iii) the manner in which the product is to be eaten in order to enhance its flavor; (iv) a two-word germanic-sounding name having an umlaut (ä) over the letter "a" and, (v) a map of Scandinavia.

Id. at 74. Nevertheless, the district court refused to grant a preliminary injunction against the competitor. It gave three reasons. First, Häagen-Dazs failed to demonstrate that the competitor's marketing would confuse members of the public. Second, there was no proof of irreparable harm. Finally, the court held that Häagen-Dazs itself had unclean hands.

I turn finally to consider plaintiff's allegations that defendants' container is intended to deceive the public into believing that their product is made and/or sold in Sweden. In particular, plaintiff charges:

> defendants claim their ice cream is manufactured "under the authority" of a Swedish corporation, although Frusen Glädje is produced in Pennsylvania by an American company and is not sold in Sweden at all; defendants fail to reveal the actual manufacturer, packer or distributor, all of which are American companies, which violates the applicable statutory labelling requirements; defendants also employ three lines of Swedish language on their container to add to the false impression that their product is sold or made in Sweden; and the English translation appearing beneath the Swedish language states that the recipe for Frusen Glädje comes "From Old Sweden," whereas, in fact, the recipe is American.

> Although defendants dispute the accuracy of these charges, even if true[,] they simply do not advance plaintiff's case at all. On the contrary, since plaintiff itself has attempted to package its product in such a way as to give the impression that it is of Scandinavian origin, although it too is, in fact, of domestic origin, [plaintiff] is guilty of the same deceptive trade practices of which it accuses defendants. In short, since plaintiff's hands are similarly unclean, they may not secure equitable relief simply because defendants' hands may be a shade or two less clean.

Id. at 75-76. The unclean hands rule no doubt has some appeal. After all, why should a court, especially one that is charged with "doing justice" like an equity court, be in the business of helping a wrongdoer? The classic case illustrating this principle is one involving a group of robbers who have a dispute over how to divide up their loot and want the court to help — a remedy the court declines to impose. *Highwayman's Case*, 9 L.Q.R. 197 (1893). But there are at least three important criticisms raised against the unclean hands doctrine:

- First, because it is not clear exactly what conduct is bad enough for the doctrine to apply, it could be used unfairly by judges, turning the right to sue into a mere privilege. DOBBS § 2.4(2).
- Second, if plaintiff has been guilty of bad conduct in relation to the subject matter of the lawsuit, it is not clear why that conduct should bar only equitable relief and not a claim for legal relief, such as damages, as well. *See* LAYCOCK p. 938 ("Is there any reason to deny injunctive relief for plaintiff misconduct that would not be sufficient to deny damages or rescission?").
- Third, if plaintiff has engaged in bad conduct, but defendant has engaged in worse conduct, unclean hands does not (at least in theory) allow for courts to balance the equities between the two parties. That can be unfair to plaintiffs, and can hurt the public when the plaintiff's suit cannot stop the defendant's bad conduct. But *see* LAYCOCK p. 940 (stating

that courts in "most unclean hands cases" engage in balancing and citing some cases where courts engage in balancing, such as illegal gambling cases involving defendants who cheated at gambling).

The third (failure to balance) argument may not be as serious as first appears. In some cases, a court can engage in de facto balancing by determining that the plaintiff has not engaged in bad conduct (when in fact the plaintiff has engaged in such conduct, but it is not nearly as bad as defendant's conduct) or that the conduct does not relate sufficiently to the defendant's wrong. Thus, the first criticism of the doctrine, that the term "unclean hands" is not easily defined, may help deal with the third criticism about the lack of balancing under the doctrine.

3. *In pari delicto.* The defense of *in pari delicto* (literally "in equal fault") "is rooted in the common law notion that a plaintiff's recovery may be barred by his own wrongful conduct." *Pinter v. Dahl,* 486 U.S. 622, 632 (1988). This definition makes *in pari delicto* sound like unclean hands, and the two are often raised at the same time. However, there are two major differences between the two defenses:

- First, *in pari delicto* can apply to bar suits in equity *or law,* while unclean hands (at least traditionally) applies only to suits in equity.
- Second, *in pari delicto* requires balancing. A defendant *must* prove that plaintiff's conduct was *at least as bad as defendant's conduct* for the *in pari delicto* defense to apply.

As with the common understanding of unclean hands, the *in pari delicto* defense requires that the wrongful conduct of the plaintiff and defendant arise from the same bad act.

Consider the case of *Parente v. Pirozzoli,* 866 A.2d 629 (Conn. App. Ct. 2005). Defendant approached Plaintiff about the opportunity to run a restaurant Defendant owned. Plaintiff agreed to do so, but because Plaintiff was a convicted felon, he could not obtain a liquor license. Defendant agreed to become a partner with Plaintiff and to keep all the business records in Defendant's name in order to get the license. After a while, Defendant forced Plaintiff out of the business, and Plaintiff sued for breach of contract, recovering $138,000 in damages.

The Connecticut appellate court reversed. The contract between Plaintiff and Defendant was an illegal one, because the parties hid the true identity of one of the partners in order to obtain a liquor license. Plaintiff therefore could not get damages. The court acknowledged that its ruling would give Defendant a windfall, but noted:

. . . in the case of a contract whose inherent purpose is to violate the law, if both parties [thereto] are in pari delicto, the law will leave them where it finds them. Knowing that they will receive no help from the courts and must trust completely to each other's good faith, the parties are less likely to enter an illegal arrangement in the first place.

Id. at 639 (internal quotations and citations omitted).

Example 1

A made a deal to sell Blackacre to B for $100,000. A then refused to deliver the deed to Blackacre. B brought an action for specific performance. A raised the defense of unclean hands, pointing to B's conviction 10 years earlier for attempted armed robbery. (a) Should the court deny B the right to specific performance on grounds of unclean hands? (b) If B instead seeks damages, should the court deny the right to damages on grounds of either unclean hands or in *pari delicto*?

Explanation

(a) No. *See Morey v. Sings*, 570 N.Y.S.2d 864, 872-873 (N.Y. App. Div. 1991). There seems to be no question that attempted armed robbery is bad conduct and that the plaintiff is seeking equitable relief (specific performance). Nonetheless, there is absolutely no connection between B's prior wrong and this contract. To allow A to raise an unclean hands defense would mean that anyone convicted of a crime, such as attempted armed robbery, would never be able to use the courts to obtain equitable relief, a result that most people would probably think is an unfair kind of punishment.

(b) No. Besides the reasons for denying unclean hands listed in the answer to part (a) of this question, traditionally unclean hands has been available as a defense only when the defendant sought *equitable relief*. If B is seeking damages, this is a form of legal relief, not equitable relief, and therefore unclean hands is not available as a remedy. In *pari delicto* also should be unavailable. Although B's conduct in life might be worse than A's (we have no evidence A has engaged in violent crime like B has), the comparison involves conduct in *relation to the transaction at issue in the case*. Because the armed robbery is unconnected to the real estate sale, in *pari delicto* should not bar a suit for damages for breach of the land contract.

Example 2

Wisconsin Auto Loans (WAL) entered into an agreement with Jones for an auto loan. Jones borrowed $900 toward the purchase of an automobile, signing a standard form contract prepared by WAL. The contract contained many terms in fine print, including a number establishing finance charges and fees that were not readily understandable to the average consumer.

The contract also contained an arbitration clause requiring that disputes over the contract be subject to binding arbitration, except for any claims by WAL against a borrower to enforce the lender agreement. Jones defaulted on his auto loan and WAL brought an action for replevin (see Chapters 7.2 and 13.3.1) to force Jones to return the car. Jones brought counterclaims for himself and a class of other WAL borrowers, alleging that the contract transaction violated various state consumer protection laws. In response, WAL moved for the court to dismiss the counterclaims and issue an order to compel Jones to arbitrate those claims pursuant to the contract. How should the court rule on that motion in the face of Jones' claim that the clause is unconscionable? If the court agrees the clause is unconscionable, what is the remedy?

Explanation

The Wisconsin Supreme Court faced these facts in *Wisconsin Auto Title Loans, Inc. v. Jones*, 714 N.W.2d 155 (Wis. 2006). The court held that the arbitration provision was unconscionable and, thus, unenforceable. It therefore denied the company's motion to compel arbitration of the counterclaims. The majority found both procedural and substantive unconscionability in the contract, particularly the arbitration clause. On the substantive unconscionability point, the majority wrote:

> The exception to the arbitration provision is far too broad and one-sided, granting Wisconsin Auto Title Loans a choice of forum — arbitration or the circuit court — for its claims, while permitting the borrower to raise claims only before an arbitrator. The doctrine of substantive unconscionability limits the extent to which a stronger party to a contract may impose arbitration on the weaker party without accepting the arbitration forum for itself.

Id. at 173.

Once the court found the clause unconscionable, it had the option under modern views of unconscionability doctrine to enforce the contract without the objectionable clause. In the context of this case, this meant that the arbitration clause was unenforceable, and the court could consider WAL's claim for replevin as well as the defendant's counterclaims.

The dissenting judge would have upheld the arbitration provision. The judge agreed that the clause was substantively unconscionable as a matter of law, but held that there was no evidence of procedural unconscionability as well. The dissenting judge said that both kinds of unconscionability were required in Wisconsin before a court could decline to enforce a contractual provision on unconscionability grounds. *Id.*

18.2 ESTOPPEL AND WAIVER

If you've already read Chapter 16, you will remember the series of hypotheticals involving two neighbors with a property dispute. Alex is building a shed near the property line with his neighbor Zelda. Zelda believes the shed is over the property line and either brings a declaratory judgment action, to have the court determine the property line, or seeks an injunction barring Alex from building the shed on grounds that part of the structure extends onto Zelda's land. Chapter 16 considered the merits of these alternative approaches for Zelda.

But suppose we add the following facts. Before Alex undertakes the building of his shed, he asks Zelda where the property line is. Zelda tells him where she believes the property line is, and it turns out that she gives him wrong information: she erroneously indicates that a portion of her land belongs to Alex. Alex then builds about half of the shed before Zelda seeks the declaratory judgment or injunction.

You can easily see why these additional facts could change the entire course of the case. Though Zelda could well meet the elements of her prima facie case showing that Alex is trespassing on her land, Alex has a good affirmative defense: *Alex relied on a statement of Zelda's to his detriment, causing him damage.* This indeed is the essence of the defense of *equitable estoppel.*

Note the three requirements for estoppel: (1) a misstatement or action by plaintiff, (2) reliance by the defendant, and (3) injury to the defendant. So if Zelda gave Alex the wrong information about the property line, but she then corrected it before Alex incurred any costs in building over the property line, estoppel would not defeat Zelda's claim.

Though estoppel is an equitable doctrine, it can be used to defeat a claim for either equitable relief or legal relief. Thus, if Alex completed building the shed and Zelda sued later for damages, then her misstatement, Alex's reliance, and his subsequent injury should bar Zelda's case.

Equitable estoppel is an interesting doctrine in that it can be used as an affirmative defense by a defendant against a plaintiff, as in the Zelda-Alex hypothetical, or *as a way of defeating an affirmative defense* by a plaintiff against a defendant. This is a tricky point to understand, so consider this example: Montel and Norine get into an automobile accident in which Montel sustains serious personal injuries. Montel wants to sue Norine for negligence. Norine is a lawyer, and Norine tells Montel that he should not rush to sue because Montel has five years to sue under the applicable statute of limitations (statutes of limitation are considered in the next section of this chapter). In fact, the statute of limitations in the jurisdiction is only two years. Montel waits until nearly five years to sue. Watch what happens next:

1. Montel sues Norine for negligence.
2. Norine raises the statute of limitations as an affirmative defense.
3. Montel *defeats* Norine's affirmative defense by raising equitable estoppel.

Norine made a misstatement about the applicable statute of limitations period, Montel relied on it by suing later, and he suffered injury (because his suit would be barred). As you can see, in the Montel-Norine hypothetical the plaintiff uses estoppel to defeat the defendant's affirmative defense.

Closely related to the doctrine of equitable estoppel is the doctrine of *waiver*. Waiver is the *intentional relinquishment of a known right*. To begin with some easy examples, if Zelda signed a quitclaim deed covering the land where Alex was building his shed, or if Montel signed a release of liability stating that he would not sue Norine for any damages resulting from their automobile accident, the court is likely to accept an affirmative defense of waiver by Alex or Norine to defeat any claims against them. It is likely that Zelda or Montel would not sign such documents, absent some compensation in settlement of their claims. But once that sign-off does occur, a court is likely to use waiver to say that the sign-off ends the matter, unless there is some evidence that Zelda or Montel did not intentionally relinquish their rights to sue through these documents.

Note one important difference between waiver and estoppel: for waiver, the plaintiff need not prove reliance. Laycock finds it puzzling that reliance is unnecessary for waiver defenses but required for estoppel; he suggests the answer might be that in cases of waiver, reliance is usually easy to find. Thus, the waiver doctrine avoids "litigation over attenuated reliance questions." LAYCOCK p. 954.

How does a party show that the other party intentionally relinquished a known right? When that relinquishment is express, as in the quitclaim deed or release of liability described above, proof may be rather easy. In contrast, sometimes a party will claim an *implied* waiver based upon conduct, and courts may require proof of an implied waiver by *clear and convincing evidence*.

For example, consider *Baumann v. Capozio*, 611 S.E.2d 597 (Va. 2005). Tyler was injured in a fight with Allen when Tyler was 17 years old. Tyler's parents initially brought suit against Allen on Tyler's behalf in tort. In response to an interrogatory, Tyler's parents listed about $20,000 in medical expenses incurred to take care of Tyler's injuries. When Tyler turned 18, he took control of the litigation and settled the case against Allen for $75,000. Under Virginia law involving injury to minors, the child has one cause of action for his pain and suffering, for any permanent injury, and for impairment of earning capacity after attaining majority. The parents have a separate cause of action for loss of services during minority and necessary expenses incurred for treating the minor. Tyler's parents then sought to recover their medical expenses in a separate suit; Allen argued that the parents impliedly waived that suit by listing their medical expenses in the interrogatory and having the son settle his suit afterward.

The trial court held that the parents impliedly waived their right to seek medical expenses in a second suit, but the Virginia Supreme Court, applying a clear and convincing evidence standard to implied waiver claims, reversed:

> Even though Tyler[']s mother signed an interrogatory in her capacity as next friend that identified medical bills as damages that Tyler's parents had incurred while he was an infant, the parents lost control of that litigation when their son reached the age of majority and signed a release that resulted in the settlement of that lawsuit. Plaintiffs in this appeal were not parties to the release, and they had not filed a lawsuit in their own name to recover damages that they had incurred. We hold that [Allen] failed to prove by clear and convincing evidence that the plaintiffs impliedly waived their right to recover any medical expenses that they incurred for the treatment of their son proximately caused by [Allen's] alleged tortious conduct.

Id. at 600.

It is common for parties to raise waiver and estoppel as alternative claims in a single pleading. The more proof there is of the intentional relinquishment of a right, the stronger the waiver claim will be. The more reliance that a party can show, the stronger the case for estoppel. But the claims are not completely interchangeable. In *Baumann*, there was no misstatement that Allen could point to by Tyler's parents that could meet the first element of equitable estoppel.

One final point: generally speaking, one may not raise an estoppel argument against the government. For example, Smith calls the Social Security office and receives incorrect advice on how to apply for benefits. As a result of the incorrect advice, Smith files the wrong papers and loses the ability to receive certain benefits. The Supreme Court has held that in a suit to recover such benefits, the government cannot be estopped from denying the benefits on grounds of erroneous advice. *Schweiker v. Hansen*, 450 U.S. 785 (1981). Though this rule certainly seems unfair to plaintiffs who innocently rely on erroneous government advice, some have defended it on grounds that it protects against "misconduct by the executive" or permitting "the executive to effectively override legislation." LAYCOCK p. 948. It is also possible that allowing estoppel claims against the government would cause the government to give less advice. *Id.*[6]

---

6. In contrast to estoppel, it is easier to raise waiver arguments against the government, at least if the official who waived the government's rights had the authority to do so.

Example 3

Jane Doe brings a tort action against the Archdiocese of Cincinnati alleging that when she was a teenager, she became pregnant following an alleged sexual relationship with a priest. The Archdiocese raises the affirmative defense of the statute of limitations because it has been many years since the event took place. Doe responds by arguing equitable estoppel, stating that Archdiocese employees told her that her pregnancy was solely her fault; that a teacher at her Catholic school pressured her to give the child up for adoption and remain silent about the priest's identity; and that the teacher told her that her child would not be baptized and, therefore, not cleansed of original sin if she did not consent. How should the court rule on Doe's attempt to use equitable estoppel to defeat the limitations period?

Explanation

This hypothetical is based upon *Doe v. Archdiocese of Cincinnati*, 855 N.E.2d 894 (Ohio Ct. App. 2006). This case is difficult because, unlike the Montel-Norine hypothetical, which involved a misstatement about the limitations period itself, this case involves alleged statements of opinion, particularly religious opinion, about the effect of revealing the priest's actions. The court nonetheless allowed the issue of estoppel to be presented to a jury:

> Doe's complaint asserts that the statements made to her by various representatives of the Archdiocese were "made with the sole purpose and intent to coerce Ms. Doe to forgo the best legal interests of her and of her child." It further alleges that the conduct of, and the actions taken by, the Archdiocese "were calculated to, and resulted in, Ms. Doe's relinquishment of her parental rights and the forbearance from any legal action." After reviewing Doe's complaint, we conclude that these statements adequately allege that the Archdiocese's conduct was motivated by a desire to prevent Doe from bringing suit. Again, we emphasize that we pass no judgment as to whether the Archdiocese was actually motivated by such a desire; rather, our conclusion is based on the well-pleaded allegations in Doe's complaint.

Id. at 899 (footnotes omitted).

Example 4

From the "truth is stranger than fiction" department: Crystal Lovely contracted with Dr. Percy, a plastic surgeon, for breast augmentation surgery. Lovely claims that Percy orally promised the surgery would increase her breast size to at least a "34C." Dr. Percy denied making such a promise. Dr. Percy performed the surgery, but Lovely alleges her breast size after surgery was a smaller, "34B" size. She sued the doctor for breaching his promise regarding breast size and for other causes of action. The jurisdiction's statute of frauds provides in pertinent part that "[n]o action shall be brought to charge a person licensed by [the code] to practice medicine or surgery . . . in this state, upon any promise or agreement relating to a medical prognosis unless the promise or agreement is in writing and signed by the party to be charged therewith." Statute of frauds is to be pled in the state as an affirmative defense, but Dr. Percy failed to plead it. Can Lovely use waiver or estoppel to block Dr. Percy's affirmative defense? *Lovely v. Percy*, 826 N.E.2d 909 (Ohio Ct. App. 2005).

Explanation

The *Lovely* court held that the doctor waived the defense by not listing it as an affirmative defense in the answer to the complaint. It looks like poor lawyering on both sides of the case; the court raised the issue *sua sponte* and noted: "We mention this issue only because it does make available to physicians a legal defense against claims of oral promises concerning outcomes should a physician desire to avail himself or herself of the defense."

Estoppel would not work as a defense here because Dr. Percy made no statement to Lovely such as one that he would not rely upon a statute of frauds defense in the suit (nor was there any proof of reliance by Lovely on such a statement).

18.3 LACHES AND STATUTES OF LIMITATION

Laches. Laches is an affirmative defense that applies only when the plaintiff seeks an equitable remedy. The defendant must show that *the plaintiff unreasonably delayed bringing suit against the defendant and that the defendant suffered prejudice because of the unreasonable delay.*

The first part of the defense requires not only delay in suing, but *unreasonable* delay in suing. Consider in this regard the facts of *Emery v. Smith*, 603 S.E.2d 598 (S.C. Ct. App. 2004). Husband and Wife get a divorce, and as part of the divorce decree, Husband promises Wife 25% of his retirement benefits when he retires from the military. He also agrees, among other provisions, to provide "any and all information necessary" for Wife to get the 25% share of the benefits.

Husband retires from the military and does not tell Wife for 10 years. When Wife discovers that Husband had retired, she sues for an order requiring Husband to pay her share of the benefits, and Husband asserts laches as an affirmative defense. There is no question that Wife delayed for a long period before asking for the court order to the pension. But the reason she delayed is that she did not know that Husband had retired. The trial court and appellate court rejected the laches argument:

> [Wife]'s ten-year delay in enforcing her rights came as a result of [Husband]'s own failure to comport with the court decree. [Husband] admitted that he did not inform his ex-wife of his retirement, and the family court found credible [Wife's] testimony that she did not know [Husband] had retired. Thus, it was [Husband] who acted unreasonably by failing to honor his duty to [Wife].

Id. at 604. The court further held that Husband was barred from asserting laches because of his own "unclean hands."

In addition to showing *unreasonable* delay, a defendant asserting laches must show reliance. On this point, consider *National Association for the Advancement of Colored People v. N.A.A.C.P. Legal Defense & Education Fund*, 753 F.2d 131 (D.C. Cir. 1985). The NAACP and the NAACP Legal Defense and Education Fund (LDF) were once affiliated, with the LDF group created for tax purposes. The NAACP granted permission to the LDF to use "NAACP" as part of its name. Eventually the groups split and tension arose between them, with NAACP withdrawing permission to use its name and threatening litigation to get the LDF to change its name.

Though the NAACP *threatened* litigation, it has never brought litigation in the 13 years since the threat. In the meantime, the LDF has continued to build name recognition and goodwill using the NAACP name. For this reason, the court accepted the laches claim of the LDF, barring the NAACP from suing the LDF for infringement.

Note that because a laches claim may be brought only to defeat a plaintiff's claim for *equitable relief*, laches-like conduct in a suit in which plaintiff seeks *damages or other legal relief* must be recast as some kind of estoppel or waiver. Thus, in the *NAACP* case, if the NAACP sought some kind of damages from the LDF, the LDF would need to argue either (1) estoppel — with the act being the failure to sue after threatening to do so — reliance, and injury, or (2) waiver — that the NAACP's failure to sue after asserting a right to do so 13 years earlier constituted the intentional relinquishment of a known right. This analysis should show you that plaintiff's conduct can sometimes be recast to fit into more than one of these remedial defenses. But it is a bit tricky here because it requires a finding of estoppel or waiver primarily by a party's *failure to act*.

Statutes of Limitation. Statutes of limitation are also about time limits, but they differ in substantial ways from laches. Whereas the defense of laches applies only in cases where plaintiff seeks equitable relief, statutes of limitation bar suits brought for either legal relief or equitable relief.[7] In addition, while the doctrine of laches is flexible and depends upon a case-by-case analysis, the time limits for statutes of limitation are set by statute, and are usually inflexible.

To use an easy illustration first, let's return to the Zelda-Alex hypothetical. Let's suppose that Alex builds over his property line and Zelda considers a suit for trespass. The jurisdiction will have a set of statutes imposing time limitations for different causes of action. Suppose the statute of limitations for trespass in the jurisdiction is two years from the date of injury. Generally speaking, if Zelda does not sue within two years from the date when Alex trespassed on her property, her claim will be barred by the statute of limitations.

Now on to some complications:

- As we have already noted, in some circumstances a defendant may be *estopped* from asserting the statute of limitations, such as when the defendant gives the plaintiff false information about the length of the limitations period.
- One particular circumstance of estoppel occurs when defendant *fraudulently conceals* the existence of a cause of action. Suppose Doctor operates on plaintiff while plaintiff is unconscious. Doctor commits malpractice, injuring plaintiff during surgery. When plaintiff complains of symptoms caused by Doctor's malpractice, Doctor falsely claims the symptoms are a normal side effect of surgery. In such circumstances, courts are likely to hold that the statute of limitations is "tolled" (that is, suspended) by Doctor's fraudulent concealment, until such time as the plaintiff discovers, or reasonably should have discovered, that Doctor concealed the cause of plaintiff's injury.
- In a certain class of cases — those involving injuries with long latency periods, such as an individual who contracts cancer from prolonged exposure to chemicals at a nearby factory — the statute of limitations presents a major obstacle to a successful suit. In some jurisdictions, the statute begins to "accrue" (that is, run) when the plaintiff suffers injury, regardless of whether plaintiff knows she's been injured or who caused the injury. Thus, in some circumstances, a plaintiff's recovery could be barred before the plaintiff even knew about it.

To illustrate this last point, consider the time line in Figure 18.1. Suppose that plaintiff is exposed to defendant's chemicals from 1990 through

---

7. The only exception to this rule is suits for causes of action where the only kind of relief a plaintiff may seek is equitable relief. "Breach of trust was the most important example, but most states now apply statutes of limitations to claims for breach of trust." LAYCOCK p. 963. In suits such as those historically for breach of trust, the only time limit would be set by a laches defense, not a statute of limitations.

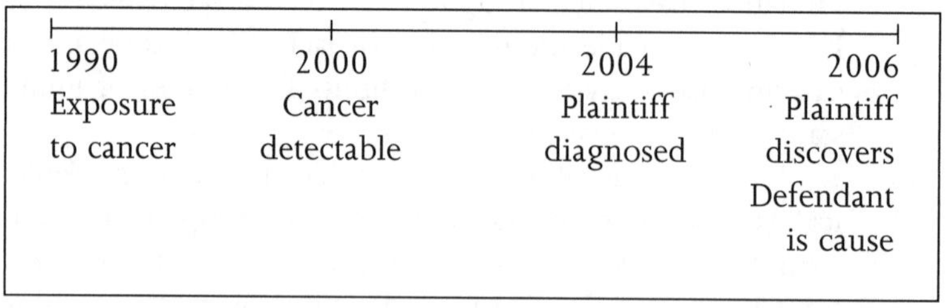

1990	2000	2004	2006
Exposure	Cancer	Plaintiff	Plaintiff
to cancer	detectable	diagnosed	discovers
			Defendant
			is cause

Figure 18.1

2000. By 2000, plaintiff has cancer that is detectable, but it is not detected. In 2004 plaintiff detects the cancer, and in 2006 plaintiff learns that defendant is responsible for the cancer through the factory pollution. The applicable statute of limitations is one year.

In some jurisdictions, plaintiff's cause of action would begin running in 2000, at the time plaintiff's injury *could have been discovered*, even if the injury was not actually discovered until 2004 and the cause of injury discovered until 2006. In that circumstance plaintiff's action would be time-barred because it was not filed within one year of 2000, or 2001. The statute of limitations will be measured to the day. So if the court determines that the cause of action accrued on May 5, 2000, the action would be barred if not brought by May 5, 2001. Therefore, a suit brought on May 6, 2001, or later would be time-barred.

In other jurisdictions, the cause of action would accrue at the time plaintiff *actually discovered the injury*, in this case 2004. Plaintiff would have only until 2005 to sue, which means that the suit would again be too late under these facts.

Some jurisdictions have a *discovery rule*, which either delays accrual or tolls the statute of limitation (functionally the same thing) until such time as plaintiff discovers, or reasonably could have discovered (with due diligence), both her injury and that the defendant is a cause of the injury. In those jurisdictions with the discovery rule, it is unnecessary for a plaintiff to prove fraudulent concealment; any reasonable basis for not discovering the injury or the cause of plaintiff's injury is enough. In the present example the one-year period would run from 2006.

There's one final complication for us to consider regarding statutes of limitation. How should courts deal with statutes of limitation in cases of *continuing violations*? Consider again the *NAACP* case. If the LDF indeed was infringing on the NAACP name, it was doing so continuously. Assuming the NAACP sued for damages (making laches an unavailable defense) and assuming no other defenses such as estoppel applied, how should the statute of limitations deal with this kind of continuous conduct?

The majority approach appears to be, for cases of continuous violations, to award damages for the period of injury that accrues during the limitations

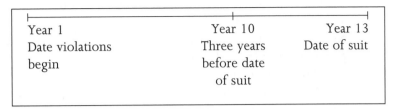

Figure 18.2

period. Thus, consider Figure 18.2. Assume a 3-year statute of limitations. The LDF has been infringing for 13 years, and has continued to infringe during the entire 13-year period. But the NAACP is able to get damages only for the final 3-year period (from year 10 to year 13), looking at the date of the suit and counting back from the limitations period.

Note that it is not enough that *harm* continues into the future. Take the Montel-Norine case again, where Norine injures Montel in an automobile accident. Assume a 3-year statute of limitations. Suppose the injury occurs in year 1 and Montel continues to suffer harm from the accident through year 13. He cannot sue in year 13 to recover damages he sustained from year 10 to year 13. The statute of limitations would completely bar the suit in year 13 because there must be *continuing violations* that *cause harm* during the period of limitations.

In the last few years, the issues of continuing violations and statutes of limitation have gained some national prominence thanks to a Supreme Court case and subsequent federal legislation. In *Ledbetter v. Goodyear Tire & Rubber Co.*, 550 U.S. 618 (2007), Lilly Ledbetter, who worked as a production supervisor at a Goodyear plant, sued her employer for sex discrimination under Title VII of the Civil Rights Act of 1964. Among her claims was an argument that she was paid less than male workers doing similar jobs. Title VII imposed a short, 180-day limitation period to sue, and there was no dispute that the decision to pay her less because of her gender had been made years before. Goodyear took the position that because Ledbetter filed her claim more than 180 days after it made its discriminatory pay decision, her claim was time-barred. Ledbetter argued that her claim was not barred, because each paycheck, including her recent ones, reflected the past discrimination: she received raises based upon an earlier discriminatory pay scale.

By a 5-4 vote, the Supreme Court sided with Goodyear. The Court rejected both a discovery rule and a continuing violation argument raised by Ledbetter. In dissent, Justice Ginsburg wrote that under the majority's decision, "Any annual pay decision not contested immediately (within 180 days) . . . becomes grandfathered, a *fait accompli* beyond the province of Title VII ever to repair." She urged Congress to rewrite the statute.

Congress did revisit the question, and the first bill Barack Obama signed as President was the Lilly Ledbetter Fair Pay Act of 2009, Public Law No. 111-2, 123 Stat. 5 (2009). The Act explicitly rejected the *Ledbetter* interpretation and provided that for discrimination claims under Title VII, the Age Discrimination in Employment Act, the Americans with Disabilities Act, and the Rehabilitation Act, a cause of action for pay discrimination occurs, among other times, "when an individual is affected by application of a discriminatory compensation decision or other practice, including each time wages, benefits, or other compensation is paid, resulting in whole or in part from such a decision or other practice." *Id.*, § 3. Whether this Act will affect how the Court interprets other statute of limitations questions is uncertain. *See* LAYCOCK 971 ("It remains to be seen whether this Act leaves *Ledbetter*'s reasoning on the books to influence limitations analysis in other cases of continuing violations that can be characterized as flowing from some time-barred past decision.").

Example 5

Jerry is running against Chuck for state attorney general. Jerry is the Democrats' nominee; Chuck is the Republican nominee. About two weeks before the election, supporters of Chuck file a lawsuit claiming that Jerry is ineligible to run for the office of attorney general. State law requires that candidates for the office be admitted to the state bar for the five years immediately preceding the election. Jerry had been admitted to the bar for many decades, but he was on "inactive" status while he served as mayor of one of the state's cities. Should the suit be dismissed on laches grounds?

Explanation

This question is based upon the facts surrounding the 2006 race in California between Democrat Jerry Brown and Republican Chuck Poochigian. My view, which I've set out most fully in Richard L. Hasen, *Beyond the Margin of Litigation: Reforming U.S. Election Administration to Avoid Electoral Meltdown*, 62 WASH. & LEE L. REV. 937 (2005), is that courts should aggressively use laches to prevent election lawsuits (which have increased by 250% since the 2000 Florida election fiasco) that easily could have been brought at an earlier date.

Think about this from the perspective of the election system. Suppose that opponents of Brown knew for a long time about the bar membership issue. Without an aggressive application of laches, you would be giving these opponents an option: if Brown does poorly in the polls before the election, don't sue and let your favored candidate win. On the other hand, if Brown does well, bring suit at the last minute so that the other side won't have time to come up with a viable replacement candidate. This shows the prejudice that could be caused by unreasonable delay. Strong application of laches in the election system helps to ensure that candidates, parties, and other agents don't try to manipulate election outcomes through the court system.

Example 6

From *Burns v. McClinton*, 143 P.3d 630, 631, 135 Wa. App. 285, 290 (Wash. Ct. App. 2006):

> For many years Dennis Burns, a wealthy inventor and investor, used the professional accounting services of David McClinton. Burns gave McClinton carte blanche over his personal finances in 1995. They orally agreed to an indefinite retainer agreement pegging McClinton's monthly fee at $1,500. Burns fired McClinton in 2001 after discovering that McClinton had long been paying himself at the rate of $2,500 per month, as well as additional sums for special projects.

Burns had not agreed to the fee increase. Burns sued McClinton in 2003 for breach of an oral contract, whose applicable statute of limitations is three years. Should the statute of limitations bar any or all of Burns' claims?

Explanation

It appears that Burns could, at most, get damages for the period going back three years from the date of suit. This is a case with a continuing violation, in which the defendant is committing the wrong each month by taking out the money.

If the jurisdiction has a discovery rule, Burns might try to argue that the statute of limitations should have been tolled, and he should be able to recover damages during the entire period, because he did not discover the breach of contract before 2001. But the question is not only what the plaintiff *actually discovered*, but what he *reasonably could have discovered with due diligence*. In the actual case, the court said there was nothing that would have prevented Burns from looking at the books to discover the defendant's breach of contract. Indeed, the fact that the defendant did not conceal the payments prevents any claim of fraudulent concealment from tolling the statute of limitations.

The *Burns* court did note an exception for the case of attorney malpractice claims in which an attorney's *continuous representation of a client* tolls the statute of limitations. The doctrine is meant to prevent disruption of the attorney-client relationship that could result if the client always had to be looking over the shoulder of the attorney. But the court held that this exception did not apply to the accountant's breach of contract in this case, even if it might apply to certain accountant malpractice cases:

> The wrong occurred during the general course of an ongoing professional relationship, not in continued representation with respect to a particular undertaking or specific transaction in which McClinton had committed a professional error. Burns did not have to choose between engaging in speculative litigation and waiting to see if things might turn out all right after all in some specific matter. . . .

Burns, 143 P.3d at 636, 135 Wash. App. at 299.

Putting It All Together: Taking a Remedies Exam

19.1 HOW TO PREPARE FOR A REMEDIES EXAM

If you have worked your way diligently through the chapters of this book, including the Examples and Explanations, you are well on your way toward mastering the basic concepts across the variety of issues discussed in most Remedies courses. This body of knowledge is *necessary* to do well on Remedies exams, but it is not going to be *sufficient* in many courses. This final chapter is aimed at giving you practice with the two other components you will need for success: *issue spotting* and *comparing remedies*.

Issue spotting is important for successfully answering many essay questions. It is also a valuable real-life lawyering skill. In earlier chapters, you did not have to guess what issue would be tested in the Examples; the Examples are designed to test the ideas in the immediately preceding text. But in many essays, as in real life, Remedies questions don't come in nicely labeled packages. Instead, you will see a fact pattern and you will need to decide which issues are viable enough to be worth considering.

Comparing remedies is another skill valuable for both essays and real life. For example, a client could come into your office complaining about some kind of misappropriation tort, and you might be able to draft a beautiful complaint for damages and recover those damages. But you would be committing malpractice if you did not consider the possibility of a restitutionary alternative based upon defendant's gains. On Remedies exams, as in real life, think of the various remedies in this book as a toolbox, or a menu, or whatever metaphor works to help you remember that you may have *choices* about how to proceed, and existing law makes some choices better (more lucrative, more appropriate, or more in line with your client's goals) than others.

Unfortunately, learning how to spot issues and compare remedies is harder than learning the black letter law and its exceptions. The learning comes not from memorization but from sustained practice of the skill. The essay questions in the rest of this chapter will give you that opportunity to practice, though the best set of practice questions are your own professor's old exams. (We professors tend to recycle ideas, so past exams are often a good predictor of future exam style and coverage.) Some professors emphasize issue spotting and comparing remedies skills; other professors expect more in-depth treatment of easily identified issues.

The following are real essay questions I have included on past examinations, along with my answer keys. Of course, I have no guarantee that your instructor will give questions or answers that are similar to mine, but I hope these will help you nonetheless.

When writing a good Remedies essay examination answer, make sure you:

- *Write clearly and understandably*, underlining or otherwise emphasizing key terms;
- Look at the *call of the question* to figure out what the professor wants you to do;
- *Consider the range of potential options* for the plaintiff in choosing a remedy;
- *Evaluate the strength of plaintiff's arguments for each remedy* and in light of defendant's (likely) counterarguments;
- When appropriate, *reach conclusions* about the call of the question; you might need to explain
  - what is *plaintiff's best remedy* and why,
  - how much could plaintiff *recover*,
  - what are the *best counterarguments* or *defenses* a defendant may raise, and/or
  - whether a particular remedies claim is likely to be *successful* and why.

Of the above elements, it is most important that you be sure that you are answering the question the professor wants you to answer. Again, look at the call of the question.

Finally, be organized and logical in your answer. Make it easy for the professor to follow your argument and reasoning. While you may be fatigued when completing your exam, keep in mind that your professor will probably be fatigued when reading your exam. Make it easy for the professor to give you points.

19.2 SAMPLE REMEDIES ESSAY EXAMINATION QUESTIONS AND ANSWER KEYS

Each of these is a 60-minute question. If your professor gives a closed-book examination, answer these with a closed book. If it is an open-book examination, feel free to use whatever materials the teacher will allow you to consult.

Many of these questions are based on some real-world cases, but I have altered the facts to make them better for testing certain concepts. Nothing in these questions should be taken as reflecting any real-world events; they are for pedagogical purposes only.

Here are the instructions I give my students on typical Remedies exams:

Subparts within questions are not equally weighted. Be sure to follow any special instructions and to answer only the questions asked. Do not identify yourself on your examination by name or in any other way that sacrifices anonymity until after you have received your grade in this course.

Use the parties' initials; don't write out their names. Don't write on the backs of the pages.

Assume each question takes place in the state of Pacifica, a state in the United States that applies the common law and its own statutes.

Please note that I do not intend to call for any detailed discussions of the underlying *substantive* law involved in any of these questions, except as you deem necessary for a complete analysis of the *remedial* aspects of the questions.

If you feel any additional facts are required, indicate what facts, explain why they are important, and make reasonable assumptions. I will not respond to questions about ambiguities during the exam. Good luck!

The answer keys below are *not* what I expect student answers to look like. Instead, they are my guide to grading the exam, noting the key points and the areas requiring more extensive discussion.

Examples

1. In the Bag. BagCo manufactures a heavy-duty polyethylene bag known as the "Model Oscar." The bag design is protected by various patents and trademarks. The Model Oscar incorporates a heavy-duty handle with a snap-style closure across the top of the bag, and the bag is typically resold at retail as a durable shopping bag.

FunCo runs a major amusement park, and it was interested in purchasing 300,000 Model Oscar bags for resale at its park. Each bag would feature a picture of "Ricky the Rat," the FunCo mascot.

BagCo and FunCo signed a contract for the purchase of the 300,000 bags at the price of $1 per bag, provided that BagCo produced a bag "to the satisfaction of FunCo" using artwork provided by FunCo. Among the other provisions of the contract were the following:

1. BagCo shall provide a prototype bag using FunCo's artwork for FunCo's approval within one month of the signing of the contract.

2. All designs which may be submitted in whatever form to FunCo, or copies or derivatives of such designs, remain the exclusive property of BagCo. It is prohibited to reproduce, use, or remit to third parties such designs, artwork, etc., without BagCo's express written consent.

3. In the event of a dispute arising out of this contract leading to a court determination that either BagCo or FunCo breached the contract, damages shall be set at 10 cents per bag.

Two weeks after the parties signed the contract, BagCo produced a prototype "Ricky the Rat" Model Oscar bag for FunCo's approval. The head of FunCo's marketing department, Jane, sent an email message to Mike, the FunCo employee working on the BagCo contract: "These bags look perfect, but the price is way too high. See if you can find an overseas supplier who could make these bags cheaper."

Mike sent the BagCo prototype bag to CheapCo, along with a copy of the BagCo-FunCo contract. CheapCo promised to manufacture 300,000 bags for 50 cents per bag. It promised FunCo that the bags would be "identical in quality and appearance" to the BagCo prototype. FunCo paid $150,000 to CheapCo to deliver the bags. It cost CheapCo $50,000 to make the 300,000 bags.

Mike sent a note to BagCo reading: "Sorry, but we don't like the quality of the bags. Accordingly, since you have not made bags to our satisfaction, we are under no obligation to buy any bags from you. We have no binding contract." FunCo had not sent BagCo any money.

BagCo executives had been counting on the money from FunCo, and they missed a mortgage payment to the bank, costing them a late fee of $10,000. They had no other work at the moment, despite looking hard for new projects. BagCo executives had expected to make a profit of 40 cents per bag, and they were disappointed. The president of the company sent back a note to Mike reading: "We really tried hard, and we are sorry that the bags disappointed you. Maybe next time."

Despite the email, BagCo executives later decided to sue FunCo over the dispute. In discovery, BagCo executives learned from the email that the bags actually were satisfactory to FunCo.

The bags from CheapCo arrived at FunCo's amusement park. They were inferior in terms of both the quality and strength of the bag and the artwork. FunCo will not sell the lousy bags to its customers; they are a total loss.

Assume that FunCo breached its contract with BagCo and that CheapCo breached its contract with FunCo.

    A. What remedy or remedies, if any, may BagCo pursue against FunCo and/or CheapCo? Explain and be specific. Do *not* discuss ancillary remedies and do *not* discuss any federal statutory remedies (for example, under patent or trademark law).

    B. What remedy or remedies, if any, may FunCo pursue against CheapCo? Explain and be specific. Do *not* discuss ancillary remedies.

2. **Occupy Pacificana!** The "Occupy Pacificana" movement was very active in Pacificana City. The movement protested against what its supporters saw as too much influence of corporate wealth over the political process and unacceptably high rates of unemployment. About 100 Occupy Pacificana supporters had been camped at a Pacificana park across from City Hall for the last month, many sleeping at the park in tents. The group has no official leaders or official membership. Although the overnight protesters violated a city ordinance banning sleeping in city parks or remaining in a city park after sunset, the police had not moved to evict the protesters.

Pacificana City officials were worried about sanitation and health in the park, as well as occasional violence perpetrated against others who had come to visit the park. Pacificana City's mayor, Mayor McCheese, also was "tired of all the bellyaching" by the Occupy Movement. He told his aides: "I can hardly concentrate on improving my putting game in my office with this racket across the street!"

City attorneys went to Pacifica state judge Jones and sought a temporary restraining order requiring members of Occupy Pacificana to exit the park and to be there only during the park's normal hours of sunrise to sunset. When city attorneys appeared before Judge Jones at an *ex parte* hearing, Judge Jones asked where the attorney for the Occupy Pacificana movement was. The city attorney said: "The group has no official leaders. We did not know whom to serve regarding this hearing, so we served no one."

Judge Jones then issued the following order. "It is hereby ordered that all members of 'Occupy Pacificana' and their agents and those acting in concert with them shall immediately leave Pacificana Park to allow for park cleaning. Following that, no one may enter the park for any reason without the permission of city police for a period of 20 days following the issuance of this order. Following the 20-day period, everyone must obey the 'sunrise to sundown' time restrictions on entering the park. Anyone violating this order shall be subject to imprisonment, fines, or both under the contempt power of this Court. It is so ordered."

Police went to Pacificana Park and used bullhorns to repeatedly read Judge Jones's orders to the crowd in the park. The police posted prominent signs stating that no one may enter the park for any reason for the next 20 days.

A. Amy is one of the people who had camped out in the park during the Occupy Pacificana protest. She refused to leave the park after hearing the judge's order over the bullhorn. Police forcibly removed her from the park and she was charged with criminal contempt. What result? Explain.

B. Three days after Judge Jones issued her order, members of the Social Freedom Party, which has no official ties to the Occupy Pacificana movement, held a silent vigil in Pacificana Park running from 5 p.m. to midnight. They held signs reading, "Mayor McCheese is a Capitalist Tool." Police removed Gayle, a member of the Social Freedom Party, from the protest and charged her with violating the city ordinance and with contempt of Judge Jones' order. She was released on bail, and at the bail hearing Judge Jones told her: "Stay out of Pacificana Park or I will fine you $1,000." Fifteen days after Judge Jones issued her original order, Gayle attended another protest in the park and was charged again with violating the ordinance and with civil and criminal contempt. May Gayle raise the First Amendment as a defense against any of these charges? Explain. (Do not evaluate the merits of the First Amendment argument.) What other arguments may Gayle raise against any of the contempt charges, and how likely is each argument to succeed?

C. Tom, who is a homeless 40-year-old man and has been unemployed for many years, was asleep on a park bench in Pacificana Park 25 days after Judge Jones issued her order. At midnight, police entered the park and told Tom he had to leave or he would be violating a city ordinance and thus be in contempt of court. Tom, who had been drinking heavily, arose very slowly in an attempt to get up. Police officers, who felt Tom was not moving quickly enough to satisfy their desire to go on break, sprayed pepper spray in Tom's eyes. Tom, reacting to the pain of the pepper spray, fell off the park bench and injured his spinal cord. He will never be able to walk again. Tom sued the police department for damages in tort. If Tom proves the police acted tortiously and the police can raise no defenses successfully, to what damages, if any, will Tom be entitled? Explain. What remedial defenses, if any, may the police department raise against Tom? Explain. Do not discuss substantive tort defenses, such as comparative negligence.

3. Fit-for-Life. The Fit-for-Life Corporation sells a number of dietary supplements, including Fit-for-Life 356, a supplement containing the drugs ephedra and caffeine, that the corporation promotes to reduce weight as well as to increase physical strength and endurance. Fit-for-Life 356 is the most widely sold supplement containing ephedra in the state of Pacifica.

In the five years that Fit-for-Life 356 has been on the market, the corporation has received 13,000 health-related complaints about the product from across the United States. Most complaints involved stomach ailments such as nausea or diarrhea, though there were more than 80 reports of heart attacks, strokes, and other serious ailments occurring after someone had used the product for an extended period. The product does appear to be effective in promoting weight loss in some users. The product package says that Fit-for-Life 356 is "safe and effective when used as directed."

Scientists have begun studying the safety of products containing ephedra. The Food and Drug Administration (FDA) has received 1,200 reports of serious reactions to ephedra. A recent preliminary FDA review of some 16,000 adverse event reports revealed two deaths, four heart attacks, nine strokes, one seizure, and five psychiatric cases involving ephedra in which the records appeared thorough and no other contributing factors were identified. The FDA called such cases "sentinel events," because they may indicate a safety problem but do not prove that ephedra caused the adverse event. On January 1, 2003, the FDA issued a press release on the potential problems with products containing ephedra. The ephedra issue has since received extensive media coverage.

Two recent studies of ephedra's safety were published too late to be included in the FDA's review, and each raises further concerns about ephedra. One study found that although ephedra products make up less than 1% of all dietary supplement sales, these products account for 64% of adverse events associated with dietary supplements. Another study concluded that the statistical rate of strokes among ephedra users was significantly higher than among non-users. Additional research continues.

The Fit-for-Life website links to the FDA report. In response to proposed legislation to ban the sale of products containing ephedra, the website contains the following statement: "In Fit-for-Life's opinion, there is no scientific basis for a ban, and we believe that our ephedra products are safe and effective when taken as directed on our product label." At this point, no federal or state laws or regulations prohibit or even regulate the sale of products containing ephedra.

A. Assume the following for purposes of this subpart only. You have just been retained as class counsel for Pacifica consumers who have used or currently use Fit-for-Life 356 and have suffered, or may suffer, strokes or heart attacks. You believe that a fact finder could well determine that Fit-for-Life violated applicable Pacifica tort law in selling Fit-for-Life 356. The issue will turn on questions of actual causation. Can you get preliminary relief (1) enjoining the sale of

Fit-for-Life 356? (2) enjoining Fit-for-Life from selling any of its products in Pacifica? Explain.

B. Assume the following for purposes of *this subpart only*. Percy took Fit-for-Life 356 every day over a period beginning Jan. 1, 1999, and ending Jan. 1, 2000, when Percy had a stroke. Percy sues Fit-for-Life on Feb. 1, 2003, for damages under Pacifica's applicable tort law, claiming the product caused Percy's injury. The statute of limitations for a tort suit in Pacifica is two years from the date of injury. Fit-for-Life argues that Percy's suit is time-barred. Evaluate the arguments both sides may make on the timeliness of Percy's filing.

C. Assume the following for purposes of *this subpart only*. Jane, a Pacifica resident, used Fit-for-Life 356 and then suffered a debilitating stroke. After Jane filed her tort suit, Fit-for-Life removed Fit-for-Life 356 from the Pacifica market, but it is still sold in other states. Jane was a 50-year-old unemployed janitor at the time of her stroke. The jury holds Fit-for-Life liable for negligence under Pacifica law, and awards Jane $10 million in compensatory damages, including $2 million for future lost wages, $3 million for past and future medical expenses, and $5 million for pain and suffering. The jury also awards Jane $60 million in punitive damages, which happens to equal the national profits of Fit-for-Life in the five years since it started selling Fit-for-Life 356. On appeal, Fit-for-Life attacks the damages awards but does not contest liability for negligence. What result? Explain.

4. Robert vs. Therese. In early 1989, Robert explained to his sister Therese that he was suffering from financial and emotional difficulties relating to his job and a failed marriage. He was unable to make the mortgage payments on his home, and he was concerned that he would lose it through foreclosure. He had investigated selling the house, but he had no equity in the house, which meant that a sale would not generate sufficient proceeds to cover closing costs. He asked his sister if he could transfer the house to her, which would require her to assume the mortgage.

Therese agreed, even though the house was located in southern Pacifica, and she lived in the far north end of the state. Robert transferred the house (in which his ex-wife had no interest) to Therese. As part of the transaction, Therese assumed a $49,500 debt, which was secured by a mortgage on the property. Also, she was required to pay an assumption fee on the loan and to obtain hazard insurance for the house.

In 1990, the siblings executed a lease which provided that Robert was to pay $500 in monthly rent and was to provide an additional $200 per month in maintenance and services on the house. Robert has taken the position that the lease was not binding on either party, but was executed for the sole purpose of enabling Therese to obtain a loan. Therese, on the other hand, takes the position that she and Robert had a binding lease agreement.

From 1989 until 1997, Robert exercised control over the house. Therese executed a power of attorney giving him the authority to manage the property, make deposits into the rental account, and otherwise maintain and care for the property. Robert lived in the house, performed necessary maintenance and services on the house, and paid rent about half the time.

After Robert transferred the house to his sister, he applied for public assistance. In his initial and subsequent applications for public assistance, Robert represented that he rented the house from Therese — failing to disclose that he often did not pay rent on the home.

The siblings agree that Robert transferred the house to Therese with the understanding that he could repurchase it. What they disagree about is the timing. Therese stated that Robert told her that the arrangement "would just be for a little while" until he could get his affairs in order. She further stated her belief that if Robert was unable to take back his house, it would belong to her, meaning that she could sell it to a third party and retain the proceeds. Robert disputes this characterization.

Therese began talking to her brother about taking the house back shortly after its initial transfer. However, Robert was never able to put his affairs in order so that he could accomplish the task. Finally, in 1993, she told her brother that he must either repurchase the house or the house would be sold to a third party. Robert continued living in the house, and continued paying rent about half the time, for four more years.

In October 1997, Therese sent Robert a letter informing him that his power of attorney was revoked. She further informed him that she was putting the house on the market. Robert moved out. Soon thereafter, Therese sold the house for $80,000, generating net proceeds of $30,000. She took half the proceeds and spent it on a trip around the world. She used the other half to pay off a car loan.

A. What remedy or remedies may Robert and Therese pursue against one another? What else might you need to know about the substantive law before you could fully answer this question? (Do not go on to analyze the substantive law questions in any depth.) Do not discuss preliminary or ancillary remedies. Assume the parties' claims are not barred by the statute of limitations.

B. Assume the following for purposes of this subpart only: During the course of the lawsuit, the trial judge orders Therese to turn over all records showing how much rent Robert paid to Therese from 1989 through 1997. Therese claims that her accountant, Juan, keeps all of her business records, and Juan has told Therese that the relevant information is lost. Juan has not testified in court and is not a party to the lawsuit.

The trial judge disbelieves Therese and then summarily issues the following order: "Therese and Juan are each fined $100,000 for willfully disobeying my court order. In addition, Therese and Juan each shall pay a $1,000 fine per day until the material is turned over." Therese and Juan each challenge the trial judge's order. What result? Explain.

5. FruityIce. The FruityIce Corporation manufactures frozen desserts sold in supermarkets. Its most popular dessert is a chocolate-covered dessert "pop" in strawberry and banana flavors. The pops have become very successful, in large part because FruityIce advertises the pops as "low fat." The dessert box's "Nutrition Facts" label lists the pops as having only 2 grams of fat per pop. It is a violation of federal statutes to knowingly or unknowingly provide inaccurate information in the "Nutrition Facts" box on a product.

Since its inception in 1998, FruityIce has made profits of $1 million per year, half of that from the sale of its chocolate-covered dessert pops in strawberry and banana flavors, and half from the sale of other products.

You are a plaintiff's lawyer. Bob comes into your office with the following story. Bob is very overweight and has been attending Weight Crushers, a diet support group. Bob tells you that at a number of support group meetings beginning in 1998, fellow support group members talked positively about these FruityIce pops. Bob reported that people at the meetings would say things like, "The pops really fill you up, and they are very low fat."

Bob has been eating a box of six pops each day, thinking he was getting only 12 grams of fat. But Bob has been gaining rather than losing weight. So he had the pops tested by a lab.

It turns out that each pop contains 10 grams of fat per serving, well exceeding the fat content classified as "low fat" under federal regulations. At this point, it is unclear why the labeling is incorrect: it may have been an honest mistake in calculating the fat content; it may be affirmative fraud to induce people concerned about fat content to buy the pops.

Assume any lawsuit you might bring would be timely.

A. What remedy or remedies might you pursue on Bob's behalf, and how likely are you to be successful pursuing each remedy? Do not discuss ancillary remedies or remedial defenses.
B. Assume the following facts for purposes of this subpart only. You bring suit on Bob's behalf. After you file suit, FruityIce changes the "Nutrition Facts" box on its pops so as to provide correct information. At the trial on the merits, the judge is outraged by the facts of the case. She enters the following order: "FruityIce is hereby enjoined from selling frozen dessert products in the United States for a period

of three years." FruityIce appeals the issuance of the injunction and continues to sell products after judgment, but while the appeal is pending. The trial judge holds a hearing and summarily fines FruityIce "$1 million for contempt." How successful may FruityIce be (1) in its appeal of the injunction and (2) in overturning the contempt fine? Explain.

6. Greg vs. Phyllis. In 1990, Greg went to work as the only associate in a law firm owned by Phyllis. Greg had an "at will" employment contract with Phyllis, meaning that either Greg or Phyllis could terminate the agreement at any time for any reason. Greg never signed a covenant not to compete or any other documents governing the employment relationship. Phyllis promised to pay Greg an annual salary of $60,000 per year for as long as the employment relationship existed. (In law firms similar to Phyllis's, attorneys who work by the hour generally receive $100 per hour from their employers.) All revenue the firm received for work done by Greg and Phyllis went into Phyllis's business account.

Phyllis's law firm handled primarily personal injury cases, almost always on a contingency fee. In 2000, Greg decided he would open up his own firm to handle personal injury cases. He told Phyllis of his decision; Phyllis responded, "Good luck. You've helped me for many years, and I won't do anything to prevent you from getting rich like me."

At the time Greg left the firm, he had put in 100 hours on the "Smith" personal injury case, and 50 hours on the "Jones" personal injury case. Phyllis had put in no time on these cases. Both cases were pending at the time Greg left.

After Greg left, Smith and Jones each decided to terminate their retainer agreements with Phyllis (as is their absolute right under the law) and to retain Greg to handle their cases. Smith and Jones told Phyllis of their decisions. Greg did nothing improper to solicit Smith and Jones, and the action did not constitute a tort or breach of the at-will contract between Greg and Phyllis.

Greg put an additional 100 hours into the Smith case and an additional 25 hours into the Jones case. Thereafter, Greg settled the Smith case for $300,000, taking his one-third contingency fee of $100,000 to buy Blackacre for his nephew, John. However, Blackacre may turn out to be a bad investment, because a new sewage treatment plant likely will be built nearby.

Greg won a $225,000 verdict in the Jones case, pocketing a $75,000 contingency fee. Greg kept that money in an account for one year, then took that $75,000 to Las Vegas and bet it all on roulette. He walked away with $75. He put that $75 back in an account with $50,000 that he had obtained from work unconnected with his immediately prior employment.

Phyllis decides to sue, and she files her suit two years after Greg left the firm, within the applicable limitations period. *Assume that the Model Rules of Professional Conduct provide no guidance on how to resolve this case.*

What remedy or remedies may Phyllis pursue against Greg and/or John, and how likely is Phyllis to prevail in obtaining these remedies, taking into account both remedial requirements and remedial defenses that may be raised? Explain. Do not discuss preliminary or ancillary remedies.

7. Victor's Secret. Victoria's Secret, Inc., is the owner of the "Victoria's Secret" trademark, which has been registered in the United States Patent and Trademark Office since 1981. Victoria's Secret sells a complete line of women's lingerie, as well as other clothing and accessories.

Victoria's Secret operates over 750 stores and distributes 400 million copies of the Victoria's Secret catalog each year, including 39,000 in Pacific Heights, Pacifica. Victoria's Secret products are also sold over the Internet. Victoria's Secret has two stores in Oceanville, Pacifica, within 60 miles of Pacific Heights. In 1998, Victoria's Secret spent over $55 million dollars on advertising its products. According to a recent survey, Victoria's Secret is rated as the ninth most famous brand in the apparel industry.

In February 1998, Victor Moseley opened "Victor's Secret," a store in a strip mall in Pacific Heights selling a wide variety of items, including men's and women's lingerie, adult videos, and other adult-oriented products. Although Victoria's Secret sells women's lingerie, it does not sell men's lingerie or adult products.

Attorneys for Victoria's Secret sent Moseley a letter in February 2001, two years after learning of the existence of Moseley's store, demanding that Moseley change the name of his store to a name unrelated to the Victoria's Secret mark. Moseley subsequently changed the name of the store to "Victor's Little Secret."

In 1998, Moseley's store made profits of $50,000. In 1999, the number reached $100,000. Since 2000, the store has averaged $250,000 per year in profits.

In March 2001, Victoria's Secret sued Moseley under a Pacifica statute regulating use of trademarks. Under the statute, Victoria's Secret must prove that Moseley's use of the "Victor's Secret" name "dilutes" the quality of the Victoria's Secret mark. *Assume that Victoria's Secret can prove such dilution.*

The Pacifica statute allows plaintiffs to obtain any remedy that otherwise would be available and appropriate under the common law. It imposes a one-year statute of limitations.

What remedy or remedies may Victoria's Secret pursue against Moseley, and how likely is Victoria's Secret to prevail in obtaining these remedies, taking into account both remedial requirements and remedial defenses Moseley may raise? Explain. Do not discuss preliminary or ancillary remedies.

Explanations

1. In the Bag

A. BagCo v. FunCo: Remedies (CheapCo discussed in Section B)

1. Compensatory Damages **(0-15 points)**

[Preliminarily, let me note that while this contract is governed by Article 2 of the U.C.C. (because these bags are moveable goods), I told you that you were not responsible for the U.C.C. damages formulas. The analysis of the issues in this problem does not differ whether one uses those formulas or the general rules we learned in class.]

The facts tell us that F breached the contract with B (it did so by not acting in good faith under the "satisfaction" clause of the contract). One remedy which F might seek is expectation damages, which ordinarily would be the difference between what was promised and what was received. However, this contract contains a "liquidated damages" provision, and if that provision is enforceable, damages would be limited to the liquidated damages of $30,000 (300,000 bags @ 10 cents/bag).

It is not clear that the provision is enforceable and is not an unenforceable penalty. For such a provision to be enforceable, (1) it would have to be difficult to measure actual damages and (2) the liquidated damages figure must be a reasonable approximation of actual damages. It does not appear that it would be difficult to measure damages: this is a typical business dispute about which it would probably not be difficult to gather relevant information on costs of producing the bags and other particulars. More importantly, it does not appear that the 10 cents/bag figure is a good way of figuring loss. It applies to breach by either party, and the amounts appear to be tied to how much either party would actually suffer in the event of a breach (we know, for example, that B expected to make 40 cents per bag). If the court strikes the liquidated damages provision, then the regular expectation measure would apply.

Under the usual expectation damages, B would be entitled to the difference between what was promised and what was received, less any expenses saved in mitigation. We know what was promised ($300,000 contract price) and nothing was received. While we don't know the expenses B saved by not having to make the bags, we do know that B expected profits of 40 cents per bag, leading to damages of $120,000. While it might be possible to get incidental or consequential damages (we are not told of any limitation on such damages in the contract), the only ones listed are the $10,000 cost of missing the mortgage payment to the bank. In the first place, for contract damages, consequential damages must be foreseeable (*Hadley*). Arguably, these are not (no indication of any communication of the payment to the buyer). Further, under the *Meinrath* rule, consequential damages for failure to pay money are limited to interest at the legal rate. Thus, the $10K is not recoverable.

Credit is also given in this section for any discussion of whether the email from B to F promising to try harder next time creates an estoppel or waiver from suit. (It likely does not because it is not an unequivocal statement not to sue, and there is no evidence of prejudice.)

2. Punitive Damages **(0–8 points)**

It is possible that B will also be able to get punitive damages in this case. Ordinarily punitive damages are not available for breach of contract. But they are available when the breach of contract also includes an independent tort. Here, there are two theories, one weak and one stronger. The weak theory is that F committed the *Seaman's* tort, by denying in bad faith the existence of a contract. ("We have no binding contract.") The reason this is weak is that most, if not all, courts to consider this possible tort have rejected it. The stronger theory is that the breach was accompanied by fraud: F lied about whether or not the bags were satisfactory in order to avoid its contractual obligations. This could provide a basis for an independent tort, as well as fraudulent conduct, which, as in California (we don't know Pacifica's precise law), would serve as a basis for punitive damages.

3. Specific Performance **(0–5 points)**

Specific performance is a theoretical alternative to damages in this case, but because the breaching party failed to pay money, an order of specific performance would have F paying the contract price and getting the bags from B — putting B in no better a position and costing F more money for performance it doesn't want. You also receive points here for any discussion of an injunction barring C from using B's intellectual property in its products.

4. Restitution **(0–6 points)**

One other possible option for B to pursue is to go after F (or perhaps C; see below) in restitution. The restitutionary claim would be based upon F taking B's intellectual property (in the form of the bag prototype) in violation of the B-F contract and using that prototype to produce a cheaper version of the bag. Had the F-C contract actually produced a successful set of bags, then perhaps B could get both F and C's profits on the contract. (C knew full well about the theft of the intellectual property, as it was supplied with a copy of the B-F contract barring the use of the prototype.) But the contract failed. So although both F and C arguably were wrongdoers, it is hard to see where the profits would come from. (If F is successful in suing C, perhaps B can get some of those funds.) If you discussed apportionment correctly, you get some credit here.

Note that there do not appear to be any other claims that B could bring against C aside from the injunction and restitition. C did not breach a contract with B, though perhaps there could be some tort for interfering with an existing contract (not covered in this text).

B. FunCo v. Cheapco: Remedies

1. Compensatory Damages/Defenses **(0-10 points)**

Here, C breached the contract by not providing the goods as promised to F. The goods arrived, but they are worthless and not in conformance with the contract ("a total loss"). The amount of damages to which the buyer F here would be entitled is equal to the difference between what was promised and what was received, which in this case is the cost difference of substitute performance. Here, F contracted to get $300,000 worth of performance (the cost for B to produce bags, though perhaps it is a bit lower) for $150,000. So it needs $150,000 to make up the difference. Plus it already paid $150,000 for the worthless bags. $150K − (−$150K) = $300,000 in damages. (The first $150K refunds the purchase price, and the second $150K represents the difference in value.) F would also be allowed to get any incidental/consequential damages, such as the cost of contracting performance.

C, however, may raise the defense of *in pari delicto*, claiming that F was just as much at fault in this contract as C was. Both of them conspired to steal the intellectual property of B for use in this contract. (*Unclean hands* would not be available as a defense in seeking a legal remedy.) Although it does seem that F is just as much at fault in using B's intellectual property, it is not clear that this wrong is closely enough connected to the contract to deprive C of a remedy.

2. Specific Performance **(0-5 points)**

Alternatively, F could ask for C to perform as promised under the contract, by producing higher-quality bags. First, it is not clear that F would want that (given the earlier shoddy work) or that C is even capable of providing it. Would damages not be as good? In this case, they might be better, by allowing F to get performance from B directly. If F seeks specific performance, the court might have to address an unclean hands defense (see above).

3. Rescission **(0-5 points)**

Since C did not fully perform under the contract (its bad performance does not count), F could seek to undo the contract, getting a return of its purchase price. This would seem a weaker remedy than damages, and it is not clear why F would pursue it. (There do not appear to be any other gains to serve as the basis for a restitutionary claim.)

2. Occupy Pacificana!

A. Amy in Criminal Contempt (0-12 points)

It appears A willfully disobeyed a court order, which she heard over the bullhorn. If a fact finder/jury believes beyond a reasonable doubt that A willfully violated the order, she will be in contempt of court.

Under the *collateral bar rule*, she would not be able to attack the validity of the injunction (including on First Amendment grounds) as a defense to a prosecution for criminal contempt. She would have had to raise the issue before violating the court order in a direct attack on the order.

A may make a few arguments as to why she cannot be bound by the order. First, she may argue that neither she nor Occupy Pacificana (OP) representatives were given notice of the court's hearing before the order was imposed. We are in state court, so Fed. R. Civ. P. 65 does not apply. Under the Supreme Court's decision in the *Princess Anne* case, it violates the Due Process Clause of the Fourteenth Amendment for a state to subject someone to a TRO without giving the person an opportunity to be heard. This may be subject to an exception when the person to serve cannot be found (or giving notice would allow the person to cause irreparable harm before notice can issue). In this case, the city attorneys explained that because the group was amorphous, they did not know whom to serve. This seems like a stronger case than the facts of the *Princess Anne* case (where the leaders were easy to find), but not a very strong case, as they might have been able to serve all at the park or somehow get a representative to serve. If this was a due process violation, and the court had no jurisdiction over A, then the contempt charge likely would not stand.

A could also argue that she cannot be bound because the court has no jurisdiction over her, because she is not a "member" of OP, or an "agent" or someone "acting in concert" with the group. But the facts tell us that she is "one of the people who camped out in the park during the Occupy Pacificana protest." So it would be hard for her to argue that she is not acting in concert with this group.

Finally, A might try to claim some of the possible exceptions to the collateral bar rule mentioned in the *Walker* case. But aside from the jurisdiction issue (discussed above), none of these exceptions seem to apply. For example, the order does not appear to be transparently invalid (there was a public health and safety reason to clear the park, even if the order raised First Amendment concerns), and there were no attempts to appeal that were frustrated by state courts.

B. Claims Against G

1. First Amendment Defense Against the Charges **(0-6 points)**

The collateral bar rule applies only to criminal contempt proceedings. It does not apply to any criminal proceeding for violating a city ordinance (as opposed to a court order), and it does not apply to any proceedings for civil contempt. So G can raise a First Amendment defense for being charged (1) with violating the Pacificana ordinance and (2) in the civil contempt proceedings.

As to the criminal proceedings, the collateral bar rule will bar that defense. (As to the second criminal contempt charge, she could have raised the First Amendment issue at the bail hearing.)

2. Other Arguments G May Raise Against Contempt Charges **(0-10)**

As to the first criminal contempt charge, G has a strong argument that she cannot be bound by the order because she was not given notice of it as well as an opportunity to be heard. Note that the part of the order she violated was not the order to vacate the park (applicable only to OP and its agents and those acting in concert; see the *Planned Parenthood* case); instead, it was the order to the entire world, stating that "no one may enter the park for any reason without the permission of city police for period of 20 days following the issuance of the order." As noted above, on due process grounds generally people need an opportunity to be heard before an order can be made against them, and G had no opportunity to be heard before the order was imposed (nor did anyone acting in concert with her). Accordingly, the court never acquired jurisdiction over her.

However, the city is likely to point to the 5th Circuit's *Hall* case and argue either that the court had in rem jurisdiction over the park itself or that the order was needed to effectuate the court's judgment to keep the park open. How the *Hall* case gets resolved may depend in part upon what the state's statute governing TROs looks like, and how it compares to Rule 65 (which contains neither of these exceptions but which the court in *Hall* said existed in the common law before Rule 65 and survived Rule 65). Under either of these theories, G could be bound and held in criminal contempt.

One other possibility: if Pacificana's statute provides (like Rule 65) that TROs issued without notice expire after 14 days (unless renewed for a like period), then the order could be a nullity.

As to the second criminal contempt charge, the judge specifically ordered G to stay out of the park. She had a chance to be heard at the bail hearing, and to appeal that order if she did not like it. There seems little chance she could find some way of attacking the second criminal contempt charge collaterally.

There's no problem with G collaterally attacking the charge of civil coercive contempt and its penalty, in this case likely a fine for $1,000 for entering the park. If, for example, it violates the First Amendment, she would be able to raise that as a defense to the contempt charge. Aside from that, she will not have much of a defense as this looks like willful conduct.

C. T's Claims Against the City

1. T's Damages **(0-10 points)**

If T can prove the police acted tortiously and the police have no defenses, then he can get the following damages: (1) costs of past and expected future medical and health care, which are likely to be substantial given his permanent paralysis (with future damages reduced to present value) and (2) pain and suffering, although those costs will be difficult to measure given that we have no market to compare to (and these will include the current pain and suffering as well as the pain from the pepper spray). T likely will not get any past or expected future lost wages, as he has "been unemployed for many years" and he will have difficulty proving future lost wages with reasonable certainty.

T also may be able to recover *punitive damages*, in addition to the tort damages meant to compensate him for past (and likely future) harm. We do not know the precise language of Pacifica's statute, but if it is typical and anything like California's, the conduct here might constitute implied malice or oppression. The police decided to evict T from the park using pepper spray because T "was not moving quickly enough to satisfy their desire to go on break." This sounds like conduct showing a conscious disregard for the safety of others. The amount would be one appropriate to punish and deter, but the amount must comply with state standards as well as U.S. constitutional standards in cases such as *Campbell v. State Farm*.

2. The City's Possible Defense **(0-5 points)**

T was violating the city's ordinance when he was in the park, and he was also violating the court's order to stay out of the park between sundown and sunrise (if that order remained in effect 25 days after the order; see above). The city may point to T's violation of (at least) the ordinance as a basis for claiming the *in pari delicto* defense (unclean hands would not be available in an action for damages). It is hard to imagine a court saying that a person sleeping in the park was at least as blameworthy as the police who tortiously used pepper spray on a sleeping person they needed to evict from the park.

None of the other defenses (unconscionability, estoppel, waiver, laches) would seem to apply.

3. **Fit-for-Life**

A.1. Preliminary Relief to Enjoin Only the Sale of Product 356 **(0-10 points)**

The two kinds of preliminary relief the consumers may try to get are a *temporary restraining order* and a *preliminary injunction*. To get any injunctive relief, the plaintiff must prove *propensity*, that there is a substantial threat of a violation; and *irreparable injury*, that damages at law are not as complete, practical, and efficient as injunctive relief.

Because the relief is preliminary, however, there is an additional showing required here. Although there are many verbal formulations of the test, there are two central questions: (1) the plaintiff's *likelihood of success on the merits*, and (2) whether the *balance of the equities* favors plaintiff. This latter requirement takes into account that plaintiff suffers if the court fails to give preliminary relief when it should, and that defendant suffers if the court grants the preliminary relief when it shouldn't — in light of what comes out at trial. We look only at the period between the time the preliminary relief is requested and the time of final judgment. The courts also consider (3) the *public interest*, in appropriate cases.

In terms of *propensity*, there is no question that F is going to continue to sell the product. However, it is not clear that this is going to be a violation. It depends on whether the product violates the substantive law. On that point, we do not know yet whether there is a substantive violation.

In terms of the usual *irreparable injury* requirement, the threat here is that 356 causes a variety of serious physical ailments, including strokes and heart attacks. Certainly a court would say that damages after the fact would not be so great.

The most vigorous dispute in seeking preliminary relief would turn on likelihood of success on the merits, balancing the hardships, and the public interest. It is very difficult to measure the *likelihood of success on the merits*. There's lots of evidence here showing some kind of link between people who used the product and serious ailments, but nothing has been definitively established yet. The court will need to take a sneak peak at the evidence and make an evaluation.

Balancing the hardships is also difficult. On the one hand, serious injury could occur to class members using 356 in the interim period. On the other hand, this looks like a major portion of F's business, and preliminary relief could lead to the business's closing. To the extent that the court views this as a public health issue, the public interest might favor granting the injunction.

If the court agrees to a preliminary injunction, it might require the plaintiffs to post an injunction bond in case the court turns out to have issued the relief in error. This could be in a very high amount, depending on the losses that F might suffer because of the granting of the injunction.

A.2. Preliminary Relief to Enjoin the Sale of All of F's Products **(0-3 points)**

It seems much less likely that the court would grant preliminary relief to prevent the sale of all of F's products. An injunction must be proper in *scope* and limited to the extent to which it has been shown that the defendant committed a violation. Absent any evidence that F's other products create any dangers, a court order would likely be limited to F's products containing ephedra or to 356 itself.

B. Timeliness Issue **(0-10 points)**

Is P's claim time-barred? The relevant Pacifica statute runs to two years from the date of injury. Injury probably occurred on January 1, 2000, when P suffered a stroke. It might be possible to argue that the injury occurred earlier, some time in 1999, when the ephedra did appreciable harm to the body, but that would depend upon what scientific evidence might show. Two years from January 1, 2000, is January 1, 2002. Because P did not sue until February 1, 2003, the claim appears to be time-barred unless P can make a good argument for *delayed accrual or tolling.*

This is not a case of a *continuing violation.* At the latest, the violation ended for P on January 1, 2000, when P stopped taking the ephedra. We do not know if Pacifica has a *discovery rule.* If Pacifica has such a rule, then the question would be whether the case was tolled until P reasonably discovered both her injury and the cause of injury. Here, P discovered the injury on January 1, 2000. The open question is when P discovered the cause of the injury. On these facts, P may argue that the statute of limitations was tolled until January 1, 2003, when the FDA issued its press release challenging the safety of ephedra. We are told that there were extensive media reports, but we do not know precisely when they began. This issue may turn out to be dispositive.

If the jurisdiction does not have a discovery rule, P may still win by claiming *fraudulent concealment.* P would have to prove everything proven for the discovery rule, plus that F had superior information about 356's safety (likely true here) and that F made affirmative misrepresentations relied upon by P (F is not a fiduciary, so there is no duty to disclose). Here, the website indicated as late as 2003 that F believed the product was "safe and effective." This may be enough. To show reliance, we would need some evidence that P relied upon the promises of safety included on the box or in advertisements.

Laches is another possible way to raise a problem with delay, but here P is seeking *legal relief* of damages, not equitable relief; thus, laches is not available.

Estoppel, because of delay, seems a stretch. Where is the prejudice to F?

C. Damages Issues

1. Challenge to Compensatory Damage Awards **(0-10 points)**

F can raise challenges to all three elements of J's compensatory damages award.

First, on the $2 million for *lost wages*, F may have a good argument that the damages are excessive given J's work history. It is hard to believe that a 50-year-old, unemployed janitor has $2 million in lost future wages as reduced to present value — to take into account that the money will be paid now and will earn interest to compensate for a loss in the future. Even putting present value aside and assuming another 20 years of work, J's lost wages award represents an average of $100,000 per year — well above the average annual salary of virtually any janitor in America. The court might remit such an award to a reasonable amount, or it might order a new trial on this damages issue.

Second, the $3 million for *past and future medical expenses* is much more difficult to judge. The facts tell us that J had a "debilitating stroke." We need to know more about how much it costs to care for her now, and what medical economists predict for the future in light of her prognosis. Any amount will have to be reduced to present value.

Third, the $5 million for *pain and suffering* is also going to be difficult to evaluate. Unlike lost wages or medical care, there is no functioning market in pain and suffering. When a court reviews these awards, it sometimes takes into account awards in like cases. While there is serious harm here, how is the court to draw the line? One might discuss how a court *should* evaluate whether such a figure is an appropriate measure of compensation, and how a plaintiff's lawyer might use a per diem argument to package such a large award in smaller chunks.

2. Challenges to the Punitive Damage Award

a. Challenges on Level of Conduct **(0-5 points)**

The first challenge F might bring to the punitive award is to argue that its conduct is not sufficiently reprehensible to merit the award of punitive damages. We know that F is not contesting the finding of negligence; but in no state is negligence enough for punitive damages. The question is what conduct the Pacifica statute uses to determine if punitive damages are available. If Pacifica's punitive standard is like the California standard, the question will be whether J can prove by clear and convincing evidence that F acted with fraud, oppression, or malice, express or implied. On these facts, one could argue that F consciously disregarded a high probability of harm to others. Evaluating whether the punitive damages standard would be met would require reviewing the testimony about what F's managerial personnel knew and when they knew it.

You need to also address the impermissibility of punishing F's conduct in other states, as well as the limited nature of the role of F's conduct directed toward others in Pacifica in determining whether the punitive award is appropriate.

b. Challenges to the Amount of the Award **(0-10 points)**

We do not know if there is any particular state statute that governs the review of the amount of punitive damages. In California, we would look at reprehensibility (again, we need to know more about how bad this conduct is), ratio (is a 6:1 ratio too much?), the wealth of the defendant (we don't know much, but do know that it had average profits of $12 million per year for the last five years), and sanctions for comparable conduct (a reason to go higher to compensate for failure of other means).

Under the *BMW/State Farm v. Campbell* factors, the U.S. Constitution's Due Process Clause provides some "guideposts" on whether the punitive damages amount is excessive.

First, *reprehensibility*: how bad is this conduct? The conduct here is potentially worse than the repainting in *BMW* or the bad claims handling in *Campbell* because this case involves human health. But it may be that F was only negligent. So it is difficult to determine how reprehensible the conduct is. The jury is not supposed to consider conduct outside of Pacifica (such as continuing to sell the product) unless it can demonstrate some kind of causal nexus (such as that the product is dangerous and F continues to market it).

Second, *ratio*: a ratio of 6:1 may be too high. The *Campbell* court suggested that a 1:1 ratio might be appropriate in cases, like this one, where there are significant compensatory damages. J might argue for a higher ratio, looking at potential harm that could be stopped by the suit (strokes that won't happen in Pacifica), thus helping the overall public health. The *wealth* of F cannot be considered as a reason to uphold an otherwise unconstitutionally high award (though its lack of wealth could be a reason to lower the award). What else is necessary for deterrence (note tension with the recent Posner opinion)?

Third, *sanctions for comparable conduct*: the higher these sanctions are, whatever their nature, the higher the amount that the courts will accept.

One should draw whatever conclusion one can about what the court will do with the $60 million punitive damages award.

4. Robert vs. Therese

A.1.a. Contract Damages (0-7 points)

R may attempt to recover *contract damages* for breach of the agreement to reconvey the house to him. R would claim that T breached the promise by selling the house to someone else. We would need to know more about substantive contract law to know whether the contract is enforceable (for example, is it barred by the Statute of Frauds?) and what the terms (for example, the terms of the repurchase) would be. Would R simply assume the mortgage and pay T the amounts she had paid in the interim? Would he have to compensate her for the appreciation in value of the house? We would need to know such information to measure the contract damages as the difference between what was promised and what was received. It will be difficult to value the promised position.

Note: Specific performance is no longer possible, as T no longer owns the house, and there does not appear to be a way to go after the bona fide purchaser (BFP).

A.1.b. Restitution (0-10 points)

Rather than pursuing contract damages, which present the problems of valuation described above, R might instead seek to recover restitution for the gains that T received in selling the house. Restitution requires a showing of unjust enrichment. This can possibly be shown by the breach of contract. Alternatively, even if the contract were unenforceable, R might argue, under the substantive law of restitution, that it would be unjust for T to keep the gains from the house, because T had promised to reconvey the house to R at the appropriate time.

If the court allows restitution, the question will center on the proper *amount* of restitution. The question is: how much did T gain? R might argue that he is entitled to the $30,000 gain on the sale of the house, which shows how much T was enriched by not selling the house at its initial value back to R. The court might not agree that this measure is appropriate, given that T had made mortgage payments over the years and did not always receive rent to make up for it. Thus, it may be that T's gain overall (when she was not living in the house and R was) was lower than the $30,000 figure. Indeed, if courts take *relative culpability* into account, the court may choose a lower number. The transaction started out with T doing a favor for R so that R could avoid foreclosure, and for many years T let R live at the house even when he did not pay rent.

If the court allows some measure of restitution, the court would likely use something like an *accounting for profits* or *quasi-contract* theory to measure the value. This would lead to a money judgment that R could seek to enforce against T. Alternatively, R might try to seek a *constructive trust* over at least the $15,000 that he can still identify; this sum paid off the car loan and so the value can be traced to the car. The other $15,000 was dissipated, and therefore R cannot trace to it.

Note that even though this is a case involving a contract, *rescission* does not appear possible. Rescission would have each party return the consideration received from the other. Here, the property has been sold, presumably to a BFP, and therefore the contract cannot be undone.

A.1.c. Remedial Defenses **(0-10 points)**

T may be able to raise a number of remedial defenses.

First, to the extent that R is seeking any *equitable relief* (such as the constructive trust), T may argue *laches*. There was unreasonable delay in R seeking to get the house back. It had been eight years, after numerous warnings that he must leave. T could then argue prejudice in being forced to turn over money after she had already dissipated half of it. R may counter the *laches* argument by claiming that T *waived* it. She threatened to get rid of the house by 1993, and did not do so for four more years. So she could be said to have intentionally relinquished her known right to sell to another.

Second, in opposing R's request for *legal relief* (such as damages and any legal forms of restitutionary relief), T may seek to recast her delay argument as an *estoppel argument* (as we talked about in connection with the *NAACP* case). With the failure to repurchase the house when he said he would do so a little while later, R's words or acts are arguably inconsistent with a right he later asserted. T detrimentally relied by selling to someone else, and she would be hurt now if she had to pay back the money. T may similarly argue *waiver* in that R intentionally relinquished his known right to buy back the house.

Finally, T may raise *unclean hands* or *in pari delicto*. R apparently lied when he applied for public assistance while he was paying rent (something he did only half the time). A court may find such conduct sufficiently blameworthy as to deny any *equitable relief* (though it is not clear that this conduct is sufficiently connected to the wrong). Although some courts won't balance under unclean hands, if a court does engage in balancing, it might look at R's conduct in possibly signing a false lease agreement in order to secure a loan. For *legal relief*, T may raise *in pari delicto*, and she will have to show that R's conduct is at least as bad as T's.

A.2.a. Damages or Restitution for Unpaid Rent **(0-7 points)**

T may seek to recover damages or restitution for the *unpaid rent*. The facts tell us that he paid rent about half the time. To the extent that there is an enforceable rental agreement (contract law will tell us that), or under the property principles of lessor-lessee, R breached the lease-contract when he failed to pay. Even if there is no enforceable lease-contract, for R to live in the house without paying anything probably would constitute *unjust enrichment* entitling T to the *reasonable rental value* of the property in restitution. (A counterargument is that this was a gift in a family relationship for which T should not expect consideration.) If restitution applies, we would measure the lost rent with the contract price (plus interest at the prevailing legal rate), and we would need more facts to know the reasonable rental value. How the court sets that amount may, again, depend upon the culpability of the parties.

A.2.b. Remedial Defenses **(0-5 points)**

R may not make a *laches* argument, as it appears any remedy here would be legal, not equitable. R's strongest defense is *waiver*: T knew she had a right to collect rent, never insisted on it, and let T live there for years paying the rent only half the time. Implicitly, then, T thereby intentionally relinquished her known right to rent. The same argument could be recast as an *estoppel argument*: T's act was not collecting the rent consistently, R detrimentally relied by continuing to live there, and R would suffer damage now if he had to pay all that rent back. Particularly given the family relationship, R may even have thought his no-rent residence was a gift. The same *unclean hands* and *in pari delicto* arguments enunciated above could also apply here.

B.1. The Trial Judge's Contempt Order Against Therese **(0-7 points)**

The trial judge appears to have issued an order that imposes a *criminal contempt* citation (for willful past violations) as well as threatening a *civil coercive contempt* citation (to get T to comply with the court's order).

In challenging the criminal contempt, T may argue that the judge failed to provide sufficient criminal procedure protections, given that the facts tell us that the judge summarily issued the order. The rights implicated include the right against self-incrimination, potentially the right to counsel, and given the high amount of the fine, the right to a jury trial. T may argue that there must be proof of a willful violation, and that willfulness needs to be proven beyond a reasonable doubt.

There is not much that T can do about the civil coercive contempt except convince the court that she is unable to comply. To the extent that the fine becomes large, she might be entitled to criminal procedure protections under *Bagwell*.

B.2. The Trial Judge's Contempt Order Against Juan **(0-7 points)**

J can raise all the arguments that T can raise for both kinds of contempt. He can also argue that he cannot be held in criminal contempt because he received no notice of the hearing at which to make his case. Under *Princess Anne* (*but see Hall*), he should have had a right to notice of the hearing. It is also not clear whether the court had jurisdiction over him, as he had never been in court. As to holding him in contempt, we do not need to use the *Hall* exceptions for *in rem* proceedings or to effectuate the judgment of the court, since J appears to be an agent of T under Fed. R. Civ. P. 65.

J may also argue that, as a non-party, he cannot be ordered to do anything more than "minor and ancillary" actions under the *General Service Contractors* case. But here he is being asked to turn over records, and that looks about as minor as you can get.

5. *FruityIce*

A. Remedy or Remedies

1. Preliminary Relief **(0-10 points)**

You could move in court for a *temporary restraining order* or a *preliminary injunction* — pursuant to Fed. R. Civ. P. 65(d), if you are in federal court. One would likely seek preliminary relief to enjoin F from mislabeling the boxes of its pops pending a trial on the merits. (One might also ask for the mislabeled boxes to be pulled from the shelves and/or for F to alert the public about the past errors in labeling.)

A TRO is the fastest way to get relief. You could approach a judge even in the middle of the night for a TRO. However, this does not look like the kind of immediate relief case that would cry out for a TRO. If you seek a TRO under Rule 65 (and under the Constitution; *see Princess Anne*), you will have to either give notice to F or provide a reason why you couldn't/didn't give notice. However, no grounds for avoiding notice appear to be present here. If you go for the preliminary injunction, notice will be required, though the statute does not define the difference between a preliminary injunction and a TRO.

As a threshold matter, B will need to prove *propensity* and *irreparable injury*. *Propensity* means that there is a realistic threat that the defendant will engage in the prohibited conduct. Here, B has told us the results of the lab tests. There is no question that if the lab tests are reliable, F is committing prohibited conduct (it is a strict liability offense). But you will have to convince the judge that the tests are reliable. Right now, you just have B's word for it.

B will also need to show *irreparable injury* — that damages would not be as complete, practical, and efficient. Such an argument may not work in B's suit. If B tried to bring his suit as a class action for others, then damages would not be nearly as good (at least in part because a court may have a hard time valuing damages; see below). But B already knows the pops are mislabeled. So where's the harm to *him*?

Because this is a suit seeking *preliminary relief*, the court also will have to engage in balancing. Although we looked at a number of tests for balancing, the tests all look at the *probability of success on the merits and irreparable harm during the period until final judgment*. As for success on the merits, we are told of B's test, but again we don't know how reliable it is. The judge will need to determine reliability. The irreparable harm to B occurs if the goods continue to be mislabeled (maybe a stretch, for the reasons given above). The irreparable harm to F would come if the court forces the pops to be relabeled as containing 10 grams of fat when in fact they only contain 2 grams of fat. This could well hurt F's sales.

Note: You should give your opinion based upon the factors stated above regarding the likelihood that the court will grant such preliminary relief.

2. Compensatory Damages **(0-5 points)**

Moving on to the first of the permanent remedies, B could seek compensatory damages. Assuming he can prove the mislabeling, he is entitled to be put in the rightful position — i.e., the position he would have been in but for the wrong.

Where would B have been? He will argue that he would have eaten many fewer pops, and that he thus would have not gained as much weight and would have been healthier. Damages must be proven with reasonable certainty, and there are certainty problems here. (The problems do seem reasonably foreseeable, however — especially if the mislabeling was intentional.) Would he really have eaten healthier and not gained the weight? There's also a serious valuation problem here; how do we measure the cost of additional pounds to a person who is overweight? Could this be analogized to a dignitary harm? Given these factors, B may have a difficult time proving his damages. Getting some actual damages might be important as a hook for punitive damages. (See below.)

3. Injunction **(0-5 points)**

See the discussion of propensity and irreparable injury above — although with the permanent injunction, there would no question about whether F was engaging in prohibited conduct. The scope of the injunction would also be at issue here. The idea here would be to prevent future harm or future effects of past harm. Such prevention would be easier to argue if B brought this as a class action. Then an injunction would protect all those people who would otherwise buy the pops mistakenly believing they are low fat. (If you discussed declaratory judgments, you get points for that here as well.) Be sure to address the new standard.

4. Restitution **(0-5 points)**

Rather than attempt to recover his losses through damages, B might go after restitution, claiming that F was unjustly enriched by its conduct of mislabeling the items. This seems like a plausible claim. At least some of the people are buying the pops because the pops are advertised as low fat, with only 2 grams of fat per pop. Thus, F is enriched (getting money) and it is unjust (based upon the misstatement, which may be fraudulent). The issue would then become measuring the gains to F. Unless this is brought as a class action or other common fund claim, it is hard to see how B can claim half of the $1 million per year in profits for the pops. Perhaps he can claim all of the profits that F made from selling pops to B. But how many pops did B buy, and how much did F make on those sales to B? This may be a relatively low number. (Again, the class action may be the only way to make this worthwhile to bring as a suit, from a recovery perspective.)

5. Punitive Damages **(0-5 points)**

Punitive damages are aimed at punishing and deterring. At this point, we do not have enough evidence to evaluate a punitive damages claim. First, we don't know what the Pacifica statute says is the requisite bad conduct. Second, we don't know yet why F engaged in this conduct. If it was affirmative fraud intended to induce people to buy the pops, then punitive damages seem in order. If it was mere negligence, that likely won't be enough to warrant punitive damages. One issue will be the amount of damages. If it will be hard to prove much actual damage, then the ratio of punitive damages to actual damages may be high, raising a potential constitutional problem (though *BMW v. Gore* and later cases contain some language that might limit such an argument).

B. Appeal of the Injunction/Contempt Order

1. Appeal of the Injunction **(0-10 points)**

F has strong grounds for appeal. First, F can argue mootness: no injunction should issue at all, because it has voluntarily ceased engaging in the prohibited conduct (*W.T. Grant*). The relevant question will then be whether F is likely to start engaging in the conduct again. The key here is credibility. Nothing would prevent F from engaging in the conduct again — that is, from reprinting the boxes with the incorrect labels. So an injunction seems right; the case is probably not moot.

But a serious problem is the *scope* of the injunction. The court did not simply order F to use correct labeling. It told F that it could not sell its products in the United States for three years. This looks punitive.

It seems very tough to argue that this injunction is consistent with the rightful position, or that this injunction is a prophylactic measure aimed at protecting the rightful position. The injunction goes well beyond preventing future harm to B.

2. Contempt Order **(0-10 points)**

F arguably committed criminal contempt when it defied the judge's order not to sell products in the United States for three years. Criminal contempt requires a *willful violation*, and it does not seem plausible for F to argue that this was an accidental violation. This looks like criminal contempt, not an attempt to coerce F into complying (no ability to purge) or to compensate B. F may wish to argue that it did not need to obey the order, because it was a wrongful order. However, under the collateral bar rule, a court order, even if erroneous, must be complied with. This is not a case where the court lacked jurisdiction. F could argue that the order is so wrong as to be transparently invalid; but if that did not work in the *Walker* case, it is difficult to see how it would work in this case.

F has a stronger argument that the court failed to follow the procedural requirements for finding contempt. Whether we call it criminal or not, F should be entitled to the full panoply of criminal protections, including the right to a jury trial (given the high fine amount). Under *Bagwell*, full criminal procedures apply in cases where violations take place outside the presence of the court (which is the case here) and where a large penalty is involved (this is a $1 million penalty). The facts say that the court summarily fined F this amount. At the least, a jury should make these decisions and other criminal protections should apply.

6. Greg vs. Phyllis

A. No Cause of Action for Compensatory Damages, Injunction, or Punitive Damages **(0-5 points)**

P vs. G is one of those cases where the only viable cause of action is restitution. The facts tell us that there was an at-will contract and that G did not breach the contract and did not commit a tort when he took on the S or J work. Thus, there does not appear to be a breach of contract or tort entitling P to any damages. For similar reasons, there would be no injunction available. Correspondingly, there is no requisite bad conduct that would entitle P to punitive damages (and we would need at least nominal actual damages in order to get any punitive damages). Accordingly, nothing besides restitution has any reasonable chance of success. (You could consider a declaratory remedy, but that won't work because all the court could declare is a right to restitution. Thus, it would end up coupled with a restitutionary remedy anyway.)

B. Restitution Against G and Possibly Against the Nephew

1. Entitlement to Restitution **(0-5 points)**

P should be entitled to restitution under principles of unjust enrichment. Here, restitution is the substantive cause of action (as in the example of the professor and the check from the bank). G certainly was enriched: half the work (100 of 200 hours) that G put in on the Smith case and two-thirds of the work (50 of 75 hours) that G put in on the Jones case was performed while G *was an employee of P*. Under the former P-G arrangement, G got a set salary of $60,000 per year, and all the revenue received for G's work went into P's account. G thus earned the $175,000 in commissions with much of that work attributable to P's business. It would be unjust for G to keep all these funds when P did most of the work. If that does not seem clear to you, imagine that a totally new lawyer took over at this stage of the S or J cases; would it not be unjust for the new lawyer to keep all the fees?

2. Form of Restitution **(0-5 points)**

The facts do not tell us that G is bankrupt, and the fact that he had $50,000 in his business account suggests that he has some assets. P might bring a claim simply to get a money judgment in *quasi-contract* (or perhaps called just "restitution," "accounting for profits," or some similar term in the jurisdiction) in an amount equal to the enrichment of G that was attributable to P. Alternatively, P may wish to use the equitable restitutionary device of a *constructive trust* or an *equitable lien*. Such a device will allow for recovery of additional gains through the fiction of tracing (more about the tracing fiction below) and allow the asset to be followed into the hands of a third-party donee (more about that issue below). With the equitable restitutionary remedy, P will have the power to enforce the judgment, perhaps by forcing a sale. To get this remedy, at least in theory, G will have to prove *irreparable injury*. P may be able to do so by showing that it is a hassle to try to recover funds from G; success will depend upon whether the court will insist on proof of irreparable injury and, if so, on how much proof is required by the court.

3. Amount of Restitution (Aside from Tracing) **(0-10 points)**

Putting aside tracing for the moment, there may be a few ways to value G's unjust enrichment. One way may be simply allocating the percentage of time spent by each firm on the case. For the Smith case, that would be a 50/50 allocation, meaning that restitution should be in the amount of $50,000 (50% of the $100,000 contingency fee) from G to P. For the Jones case, that would be a 50/25 allocation (or the two-thirds attributable to P), meaning that restitution should be in the amount of $50,000 (two-thirds of the $75,000 contingency fee) to P from G. So P may simply seek a money judgment in the amount of $100,000 from G by way of aggregate time-share allocation.

An alternative way to measure restitution might be to use the average hourly rate paid to attorneys who work by the hour (i.e., $100 per hour). That would be $100 multiplied by 150 hours for both cases, which yields $15,000 total. This is a much stingier measure of restitution. The court could perhaps choose this measure if the relative culpability of the parties suggests that P should get a small recovery, but this seems unlikely.

Finally, G may make some arguments that the allocation on the basis of time percentage spent would be inappropriate because G did more important work on the cases during the time he handled the cases for his own firm. We would need more facts to evaluate such an approach. Again, it may depend upon the culpability of the parties. Neither party seems particularly culpable. Absent a compelling reason not to use such a measure, a court would likely use the allocation of percentage of time measure.

4. Tracing in the Smith Case: Blackacre/Nephew **(0-7 points)**

For purposes of a constructive trust (or equitable lien), the line for tracing is fairly straightforward. G took the $100,000 contingency fee and used it to purchase Blackacre for N. N looks like a gratuitous donee, rather than a good faith purchaser for value. We generally can trace to donees in such circumstances. Right now, P likely will be entitled to $50,000. She might try to get a constructive trust over half of Blackacre, or an equitable lien over 50% of Blackacre. Because the property looks like it will decline in value, the equitable lien, if a court agrees to give it, would be a better bet because it preserves the full $50,000, rather than giving away half of whatever Blackacre is worth at the time P enforces the judgment.

5. Tracing in the Jones Case: Bank Account **(0-5 points)**

G put the $75,000 contingency fee from the Jones case into the account and he withdrew the money a year later. If the problem ended at this point, P could trace to nothing in the account under the "lowest intermediate balance" rule. G took all the money out; and then, after losing most of it in Las Vegas, he put $75 back in the account, along with $50,000 attributable to G. Only the $75 is attributable to P, and that is all that she could trace to in that account.

C. Possible Defenses to Restitution Action

Even if restitution would otherwise be proper, G (and perhaps N) may raise a few defenses.

1. Laches **(0-5 points)**

Although the case was filed within the applicable limitations period (and therefore there is no statute of limitations issue), laches may be a partial defense for G. P must have *unreasonably delayed* in bringing suit and G must have suffered *prejudice* as a result. Here, we know that P waited two years before bringing suit. The facts do not tell us how much time elapsed between settlement of the S and J cases and P's bringing suit, and it may be that the delay for a typical business dispute like this one is not too long. G has a stronger argument on prejudice. He held that $75,000 in the account for an entire year before blowing it in Vegas. If he knew he would owe $50,000 on it, then he likely would not have indulged in the gambling. (Depending on the timing of the house purchase for N, G may make the same argument for the Smith contingency fees.)

Laches works for only equitable remedies; to the extent that P seeks a legal form of restitution, this argument would have to be recast as an estoppel argument (see below).

2. Estoppel **(0-8 points)**

G has two potential estoppel arguments. First, G may argue that P's statement that she won't "do anything to prevent [G] from getting rich like [P]" was an act or statement inconsistent with suing, that P reasonably relied upon that statement in taking the work from S and J, and that G thereby suffered prejudice by having to pay the amounts of restitution. This argument is rather weak. Specifically, the statement is ambiguous; it also seems unreasonable for G to rely upon such a flimsy statement as an agreement not to sue.

Second, G could also make a laches-like argument cast as estoppel as a way to get around the use of laches only for equitable remedies. The act or statement would be failure to sue, the reasonable reliance would be shown by G's spending the money in Las Vegas, and the prejudice would be the same as above. For the same reason that the laches argument is weak, this pseudo-estoppel argument would likely fail as well.

3. Waiver **(0-5 points)**

Waiver is the intentional relinquishment of a known right. Here, G would argue that the same statement referred to above, under laches, amounted to intentionally giving up the right to obtain any money from the S or J case. This also seems a stretch. At the time P made the statement, she did not know that S or J would be taking their business to G. So this does not look like a known right that is being intentionally relinquished. There is nothing in the equities here that militates in favor of accepting the waiver argument. This argument is also likely to fail.

7. Victor's Secret

VS can perhaps pursue an injunction, compensatory damages, restitution, and punitive damages (thought not necessarily all of them). M has a number of possibly meritorious defenses.

A. Injunction **(0-10 points)**

A permanent injunction would be aimed here at future conduct (or perhaps as a reparative injunction, to prevent future bad effects of past harm) to prevent further trademark dilution of the VS trademark. VS would like an injunction to prevent future dilution by M of its mark. To get an injunction, VS must prove both *propensity* and *irreparable injury*.

Propensity poses somewhat of a problem here. It is true that M has diluted VS's trademark in the past. But now M has changed the name of the store to "Victor's Little Secret." The facts do not tell us whether the new name would be considered dilution under the law as well. If it would not, then there's a chance of *mootness*. If the new name constitutes a dilution as well, it looks like M is continuing the unlawful conduct, and propensity is likely shown thereby.

Irreparable injury would be easier to prove. It is hard to put a value on the losses that come to VS from the dilution of the mark. Certainly there could be some losses by causing people to think less of the VS mark because M sells items that might impugn the reputation of VS. But it will be hard to put a dollar value on such losses for damages purposes. Because damages are not as complete, practical, and efficient as equitable remedies, irreparable injury is probably shown.

M could perhaps argue that the injunction should not issue because of the hardship on the defendant. For example, M could lose some of his business if he must change the name. This argument probably won't succeed for at least two reasons. First, the hardship on the defendant does not seem very great; he has already changed the name once. Second, if (and we don't know) M chose the name in order to take advantage of the VS mark, he might be considered a wrongdoer, who thus cannot raise this argument.

B. Defenses to Injunction

Even if the injunction is otherwise proper, M may raise a few defenses.

1. Statute of Limitations **(0-5 points)**

The applicable statute of limitations is one year. In this case, M started diluting the VS trademark in February 1998, but suit was not brought by VS until March 2001. It may be that the entire case is barred by the statute of limitations. However, VS could argue for a continuing violation, through the continuing dilution on the trademark (as in the *NAACP* case, each infringement is a new violation). Here, every day that

M is out there using the "Victor's Secret" name, he is further diluting the VS mark. Because M was diluting the mark within a year of the suit, the statute of limitations does not appear to be a problem. There could be a problem if the change to "Victor's Little Secret" means that the dilution has ended.

2. Laches (0-5 points)

Laches may be a stronger defense for M. VS must have *unreasonably delayed* and M must have suffered *prejudice* as a result. Here, we know that VS waited three years after learning of the infringement before bringing suit. There do not appear to be any excuses for the delay, such as settlement negotiations. This may well be too long to wait. M suffered prejudice (as in the *NAACP* case) because it continued to build up goodwill using the diluting name. Had VS brought suit earlier, M could have minimized the damage by choosing a new name in the early stages of promoting his new store. (This laches argument may also be cast as an estoppel argument, described below.)

C. Compensatory Damages (0-10 points)

In addition to an injunction to prevent future harm, VS may ask for compensatory damages *to compensate for past harm*. The goal of compensatory damages is to put the plaintiff back in the rightful position, the position that VS would have been in had M not diluted its trademark. That's very easy to state in theory, but it will be very difficult in fact to *prove* those damages. Damages to reputation are always difficult to prove (that's why in defamation cases court sometimes allow "presumed damages"). Perhaps through the use of focus groups or surveys, VS could try to prove its losses. But such proof may be very difficult to establish.

Even if VS can prove damages, under the *statute of limitations* those damages will be limited to the last year of loss for continuing violations. M could try to make a *laches-like* argument to prevent the suit for damages as well. Strictly speaking, laches does not apply to suits for damages (even though the *NAACP* court assumed it did). But the same argument could be recast as an *estoppel* argument: (1) VS, through its inaction over three years of knowing of the trademark dilution, did nothing about it, and it later took a position in the lawsuit that is inconsistent with its inaction; (2) M relied on the inaction by not changing the name (indeed, it is not clear that M was even aware of the VS trademark or of VS's potential infringement action); and (3) M suffers injury by paying damages in the lawsuit.

D. Restitution (0-10 points)

Instead of seeking compensatory damages, VS might try to get restitution (along with an injunction preventing future dilution of the trademark). A plaintiff can get restitution from a defendant when there is unjust enrichment. In this case, VS will argue that M was unjustly enriched because he used the VS trademark without permission. VS may make a claim for M's profits.

VS likely will not be able to get *all* of M's profits under restitution. An accounting for profits will show the amounts available; but because of the *statute of limitations* issue raised above, the profits would likely only be for the last year, or $250,000. M likely will argue that there should be an apportioning of profits, with some portion of the profits allocated to the value caused by the infringement and some portion to non-infringing activities. Not every court will so apportion. It may depend upon how bad M's conduct was: we don't know if he was a willful infringer.

The burden will be on M to prove the apportionment. In many (but not all) jurisdictions, M cannot attribute to himself any value that his own reputation brought to the store (there's no evidence in the facts on this point here). It is likely that most of the profits are attributable to factors other than use of the "Victor's Secret" name. A jury will make the determination.

Laches may apply if VS seeks an equitable form of restitution, such as a constructive trust. Otherwise, M may try to make an estoppel argument, as described above.

If the claim is successful, VS may try to get the profits delivered in the form of a *constructive trust* so that it is backed with the contempt power.

E. Punitive Damages (0-5 Points)

If VS succeeds in getting compensatory damages, it might seek punitive damages as well. Punitive damages will not be available with restitution, which itself may serve a punitive function. The purpose of punitive damages is to punish and deter. We don't know Pacifica's specific punitive damages statute, but the statute will prescribe the requisite bad conduct for punitive damages. We also don't know much about M's conduct, such as whether he was a willful infringer. If the jury finds M's conduct sufficiently bad, it may award punitive damages, but the amount will be reviewed, possibly under state law and definitely under federal constitutional requirements (*BMW v. Gore*) to make sure they are not excessive. In this case, the compensatory damages may be low because they are difficult to measure, so the "ratio" guidepost may be less important.

Table of Cases

Table of Cases

Table of Books and Articles Cited

Abel, Richard, General Damages Are Incoherent, Incalculable, Incommensurable, and Inegalitarian (But Otherwise a Great Idea), 55 DePaul L. Rev. 253 (2006),   40

Akerlof, George, The Market for Lemons, 84 Q.J. Econ. 488 (1970),   26

American Heritage Dictionary of the English Language (4th ed. 2000),   15

Atiyah, P.S., The Rise and Fall of Freedom of Contract (1979),   64

ATLA's Litigating Tort Cases,   50

Birks, Peter B.H., A Letter to America: The New Restatement of Restitution, 3 Global Jurist Frontiers (Issue 2) (2003), http://www.bepress.com/gj/frontiers/vol3/iss2/art2/,   251

Black's Law Dictionary (8th ed. 2004),   51

Calabresi, Guido & A. Douglas Melamed, Property Rules, Liability Rules and Inalienability: One View of the Cathedral, 85 Harv. L. Rev. 1089 (1972),   147

Chayes, Abram, The Role of the Judge in Public Law Litigation, 89 Harv. L. Rev. 1281 (1976),   179

Coase, Ronald H., The Problem of Social Cost, 3 J.L. & Econ. 1 (1960),   147

Dobbs, Dan B., The Law of Remedies: Damages, Equity, Restitution (1993),   *passim*

_____, The Law of Torts (2000),   51

Epstein, Richard A., Cases and Materials in Torts (9th ed. 2008),   46, 49, 51, 339

Erickson, Edward E., The Right to a Jury Trial in Equitable Cases, 69 N.D. L. Rev. 559 (1993),   168

Farnsworth, Ward, Do Parties to Nuisance Cases Bargain After Judgment? A Glimpse Inside the Cathedral, 66 U. Chi. L. Rev. 373 (1999),   147

Final Report of the Special Master of the September 11 Victim Compensation Fund of 2001,   137

Fiss, Owen, Foreword—The Forms of Justice, 97 Harv. L. Rev. 1 (1979),   182

_____, Injunctions (1972),   179

_____, The Allure of Individualism, 78 Iowa L. Rev. 965 (1993),   178

_____, The Civil Rights Injunction (1978),   179

Fried, Charles, Contract as Promise (1981),   63

Gash, Jim, The End of An Era: The Supreme Court (Finally) Butts Out of Punitive Damages for Good, 65 Fla. L. Rev. 525 (2011),   357

Gergen, Mark, John M. Golden & Henry E. Smith, The Supreme Court's Accidental Revolution? The Test for Permanent Injunctions, 112 Colum. L. Rev. 203 (2012),   163

Hasen, Richard L., Beyond the Margin of Litigation: Reforming U.S. Election Administration to Avoid Electoral Meltdown, 62 Wash. & Lee L. Rev. 937 (2005),   414

_____, The Efficient Duty to Rescue, 15 Int'l Rev. L. & Econ. 141 (1995),   262

_____, The Supreme Court and Election Law: Judging Equality from Baker v. Carr to Bush v. Gore (2003),   206

Table of Books and Articles Cited

Knoll, Michael S., and Jeffrey M. Colon, The Calculation of Prejudgment Interest (May 31, 2005), http://ssrn.com/abstract=732765/, 31

Langevoort, Donald C., Agency Law Inside the Corporation: Problems of Candor and Knowledge, 71 U. Cinn. L. Rev. 1187 (2003), 71

Laycock, Douglas, The Death of the Irreparable Injury Rule (1991), 150, 165, 166, 172, 198

_____, Modern American Remedies (4th ed. 2010), *passim*

_____, Modern American Remedies — 2012 Teacher's Update, 164

Lord, Richard A., Williston on Contracts (4th ed. 2006), 64, 273

Maitland, F.W., Equity (1969), 148

McConnell, Michael W., Why Hold Elections? Using Consent Decrees to Insulate Policies from Political Change, 1995 U. Chi. L. Forum 184

McCormick, Charles T., Handbook On The Law Of Damages (1935), 104

Miller, Geoffrey P., Some Agency Problems in Settlement, 16 J. Legal Stud. 189 (1987), 395

Miller, Marshall, Note, Police Brutality, 17 Yale L. & Pol'y Rev. 149 (1998), 178

Moore's Federal Practice, Class Action Fairness Act of 2005, With Commentary and Analysis by Georgene M. Vairo of the Moore's Federal Practice Board of Editors (Daniel R. Coquillette et al. eds., 2005), 394

Moringiello, Juliet M., Seizing Domain Names to Enforce Judgments: Looking Back to Look to the Future, 72 U. Cinn. L. Rev. (2003), 381, 384

Orr, Leila C., Note, Making a Case for Wealth-Calibrated Punitive Damages, 37 Loy. L.A. L. Rev. 1739 (2004), 359

Posner, Richard A., Breaking the Deadlock: The 2000 Election, the Constitution, and the Courts (2001), 207

_____, Economic Analysis of Law (7th ed. 2007), 19, 205

Pryor, Ellen Smith, The Tort Law Debate, Efficiency and the Kingdom of the Ill: A Critical Critique of the Insurance Theory of Compensation, 79 Va. L. Rev. 91 (1993), 41

Rasmussen, Robert K., The Uneasy Case Against the Uniform Commercial Code, 62 La. L. Rev. 1097 (2002), 81

Rendleman, Doug, Compensatory Contempt: Plaintiff's Remedy When a Defendant Has Violated an Injunction, 1980 U. Ill. L. Forum 971, 235

_____, More on Void Orders, 7 Ga. L. Rev. 246 (1973), 240

_____, The Trial Judge's Equitable Discretion Following eBay v. MercExchange, 27 Rev. Litig. 63 (2007), 163

Right to quiet title or remove cloud on title to personal property by suit in equity or under declaratory judgment act, 105 A.L.R. 291 (1936), 374

Rogers, James S., Restitution for Wrongs and the Restatement (Third) of the Law of Restitution, 42 Wake Forest L.R. 55 (2007), 251

Sanders, Joseph, Punitive Damages in Consumer Actions, 8 J. Tex. Consumer L. 22 (Fall 2004), 353

Schlanger, Margo, Beyond the Hero Judge: Institutional Reform Litigation as Litigation, 97 Mich. L. Rev. 1995 (1999), 187

_____, Civil Rights Injunctions Over Time: A Case Study of Jail and Prison Court Orders, 81 N.Y.U. L. Rev. 550 (2006), 188

Smith, Scott M., Construction and Application of International Child Abduction Remedies Act (42 U.S.C. § 11601 et seq.), 125 A.L.R. Fed. 217 (1995), 230

460

Table of Books and Articles Cited

Smyth, Todd R., Annotation, Parent's Right to Recover for Loss of Consortium in Connection with Injury to Child, 54 A.L.R. 4th 112 (1987 & Supp. 2005),   50

Symposium, Who Feels Their Pain?: The Challenge of Noneconomic Damages in Civil Litigation, 55 Depaul L. Rev. 249 (2006),   40

Tinney, Richard C., Sufficiency of Showing of Actual Damages to Support Award of Punitive Damages — Modern Cases, 40 A.L.R. 4th 11 (1985 & 2005 Supp.),   28, 341

Weinrib, Ernest J., Corrective Justice in a Nutshell, 52 U. Toronto L.J. 349 (2002),   16

Wright, Miller and Kane, Federal Practice and Procedure (2006),   219

Table of Statutes, Restatement Sections, and Uniform Commercial Code (UCC) Provisions

Index

Index